Lecture Notes in Artificial Intelligence 1484

Subseries of Lecture Notes in Computer Science
Edited by J. G. Carbonell and J. Siekmann

Lecture Notes in Computer Science
Edited by G. Goos, J. Hartmanis and J. van Leeuwen

W0245798

Springer-Verlag Berlin Heidelberg Gmbh

Helder Coelho (Ed.)

Progress in Artificial Intelligence – IBERAMIA 98

6th Ibero-American Conference on AI
Lisbon, Portugal, October 5-9, 1998
Proceedings

 Springer

Series Editors
Jaime G. Carbonell, Carnegie Mellon University, Pittsburgh, PA, USA
Jörg Siekmann, University of Saarland, Saarbrücken, Germany

Volume Editor

Helder Coelho
Dep. Informática, Fac. Ciências de Lisboa
Bloco C5, Piso 1, Campo Grande, 1700 Lisboa, Portugal
E-mail: hcoelho@di.fc.ul.pt

Cataloging-in-Publication Data applied for

Die Deutsche Bibliothek - CIP-Einheitsaufnahme

Progress in artificial intelligence : proceedings / IBERAMIA 98, 6th
Ibero-American Conference on AI, Lisbon, Portugal, October 5 - 9,
1998. Helder Coelho (ed.). - Berlin ; Heidelberg ; New York ;
Barcelona ; Budapest ; Hong Kong ; London ; Milan ; Paris ;
Singapore ; Tokyo : Springer, 1998
    (Lecture notes in computer science ; Vol. 1484 : Lecture notes in
    artificial intelligence)

CR Subject Classification (1991): I.2

ISBN 978-3-540-64992-2   ISBN 978-3-540-49795-0 (eBook)
DOI 10.1007/978-3-540-49795-0

© Springer-Verlag Berlin Heidelberg 1998
Originally published by Springer-Verlag Berlin Heidelberg New York in 1998.

Typesetting: Camera ready by author
SPIN 10638790   06/3142 – 5 4 3 2 1 0   Printed on acid-free paper

Preface

When in October 1996 in Cholula (Puebla, Mexico), I took charge of organizing the scientific program of the next Ibero-American Congress on Artificial Intelligence (IBERAMIA 98) I bet on a couple of ideas. First, I adopted the spirit of the Portuguese adventurers to get the Sixth Congress on a truly international track. In order to attain this aim I needed to convince everybody that the Ibero-American AI community had improved over the years and attained a very good level in what concerns individuals. Second, I brought my colleagues beside me so that we were able to collect sufficient excellent papers without destroying the pioneering spirit of those who first inaugurated the Congress. Getting together to find out what is in progress in the vast region in which Latin languages (Portuguese and Spanish) are spoken, attracting others to exchange ideas with us, and by doing this advancing AI in general, is a risky untertaking. This book is the result, and it sets a new standard to be discussed by all of us.

IBERAMIA was established in 1988 (Barcelona) by three Ibero-American AI Associations (AEPIA from Spain, SMIA from Mexico, and APPIA from Portugal), after a first meeting in Morelia (Mexico) in 1986 of SMIA and AEPIA. The event was organized every two years from then on in Morelia (1990), La Habana (1992), Caracas (1994), and Cholula (1996), taking Portuguese and Spanish as official languages and with the aim to promote and diffuse the research and development carried out in the countries associated with those two Latin languages and connected by strong historical links from the 16th century. Over the years, the Executive Committee of IBERAMIA was enlarged with the inclusion of AVINTA (Venezuela), SMC (Cuba) and SBC (Brazil).

The IBERAMIA 98 scientific program is structured along two main modules, the open discussion and the paper track. The first day of the conference (Tuesday, October 6, 1998) is organized with tutorials directed to informatics professionals, the formal opening, the IBERAMIA lecture delivered by a distinguished Ibero-American researcher, and the declaration of the José Negrete prize awarded by the Scientific Committee to the best paper submitted. The open discussion track (Wednesday, October 7) is composed of working sessions devoted to the most important areas of research in Ibero-American countries, the AI Education Symposium dedicated to confronting ideas about the best ways to teach AI, a session presenting the best M.Sc. and Ph.D. theses of the whole region, and a video conference panel to establish bridges between Europe and America (involving those unable to attend this panel). The paper track (Thursday and Friday, October 8–9) is composed of invited talks and paper presentations from all over the world on the full range of AI research and covering both theoretical and foundational issues, and applications as well.

We received more than 150 technical papers distributed along 21 countries and 14 areas (see below). From those 149 accepted for reviewing, 30 were written in Spanish and Portuguese, and were the only candidates to the open discussion track. All were rigorously reviewed by the program committee, and only 32 were accepted as full papers to be published by Springer (the paper track). This high rejection rate was a reflection of the care and thought that the program committee and area chairs put into the review and selection process in order to obtain a standard of quality for the first publication of IBERAMIA proceedings by Springer.

Countries	Submitted	Paper Track
Argentina	2	-
Austria	1	1
Brazil	14	4
Canada	1	-
Colombia	2	-
Cuba	1	-
Ecuador	1	-
France	12	2
Germany	1	-
Italy	1	-
Japan	2	1
Mexico	26	7
Netherlands	1	-
Paraguay	1	-
Portugal	16	3
Singapore	1	-
Spain	45	10
Tunisia	1	-
UK	9	2
USA	2	-
Venezuela	9	2
Total	**149**	**32**

Areas	Submitted	Paper Track
Case-Based Reasoning	5	-
Constraint Programming	5	1
Distributed AI	22	5
Genetic Algorithms	15	5
Intelligent Tutoring Systems	9	1
Knowledge Engineering	5	2
Knowledge Representation	12	-
Machine Learning	17	6
Natural Language Processing	18	1
Neural Nets	9	1
Planning	3	1
Reasoning	13	5
Robotics	6	-
Vision	10	4
Total	**149**	**32**

We have included five invited lectures by Héctor Geffner, James Allen, Cristiano Castelfranchi, Aaron Sloman, and Ricardo Baeza-Yates to ensure an adequate interaction between different fields, and also to assure a broadening of the thematic spectrum of the whole conference.

The Conference is accompanied by two workshops, the Second Ibero-American DAI and Multiagent Systems Workshop, to be held in Toledo, on October 2–3, 1998, and the First Ibero-American Causal Networks (From Inference to Data Mining), to be held in Lisbon, on October 3, 1998, and also by a set of four tutorials: Agent Programming by José M. Ramirez (Venezuela), Mining the World Wide Web by Tom Mitchell (USA), Intelligent Information Retrieval by Ricardo Baeza-Yates (Chile), and Arquitecturas Multiagentes y sus Aplicaciones, by Fernando de Arriaga (Spain), Ana Lilia Laureano Cruces (Mexico), and Mohamed El Alami (Spain). In the week before, September 28 – October 4, the AI Portuguese association (APPIA) organizes the Sixth International Summer School (EAIA-98) dedicated to Knowledge Discovery in Databases and Data Mining: Methods and Applications.

We would like to thank the following institutions that contributed (financially or otherwise) to the organization of this conference and to the editing of the proceedings: Fundação Calouste Gulbenkian, ESPRIT, IBM Portugal, Fundação para Ciência e a Tecnologia, Caixa Geral de Depósitos, Agência Abreu, Compulog-Net, União Latina, Eival, British Council, RDP–Rádio Difusão Portuguesa, SA, Câmara Municipal de Lisboa, FLAD–Fundação Luso-Americana para o Desenvolvimento, EDP–Electricidade de Portugal, Edições Colibri, Editorial Verbo and Esotérica.

Particular thanks are due to all those who helped us with the local organization, namely Gabriel Lopes, António Ribeiro, Berilhes Garcia, Gael Dias, Irene Rodrigues, João Balsa, Joaquim Ferreira da Silva, Nuno Marques, Paulo Quaresma, Sérgio Freitas, and Vitor Rocio. The final thanks go to Springer-Verlag for their help and assistance in producing this book.

Lisbon, June 1998   Helder Coelho
                                                            Program Chair
                                                            IBERAMIA 98

President and Local Chairman:
Gabriel Pereira Lopes (Portugal)
Departamento de Informática,
Faculdade de Ciências e Tecnologia,
Universidade Nova de Lisboa
Quinta da Torre
2825 Monte da Caparica, Portugal
Phone: (351 1) 294 85 36
Fax: (351 1) 294 85 41
gpl@di.fct.unl.pt

Program and Scientific Chairman:
Helder Coelho (Portugal)
Departamento de Informática,
Faculdade de Ciências,
Universidade de Lisboa
Bloco C5, Piso 1, Campo Grande
1700 Lisboa, Portugal
Phone: (351 1) 750 00 87
Fax: (351 1) 750 00 84
hcoelho@di.fc.ul.pt

Scientific Committee

Alexis Drogoul (France)
Alfred Kobsa (Germany)
Alvaro del Val (Spain)
Angel Puerta (Spain)
Anna Reali Costa (Brazil)
Antonio Sánchez (Mexico)
Carlos Bento (Portugal)
Carlos Pinto-Ferreira (Portugal)
Christian Lemaitre (Mexico)
Cristiano Castelfranchi (Italy)
Ernesto Costa (Portugal)
Felisa Verdejo (Spain)
Fernando Moura Pires (Portugal)
Francisco Cantú (Mexico)
Gabriel Pereira Lopes (Portugal)
Guillermo Simari (Argentina)
Héctor Geffner (Venezuela)
Jaime Simão Sichman (Brazil)
Javier Pinto (Chile)
John Self (United Kingdom)

Jorge Villalobos (Colombia)
José Cuena (Spain)
José Félix Costa (Portugal)
José Moreno (Venezuela)
José Ramírez (Venezuela)
Juan Carlos Santamaria (Venezuela)
Leopoldo Bertossi (Chile)
Luciano Garcia (Cuba)
Olga Padron (Cuba)
Pedro Barahona (Portugal)
Ramon López de Màntaras (Spain)
Raul Carnota (Argentina)
Rosa Viccari (Brazil)
Suresh Manandhar (United Kingdom)
Tarcisio Pequeno (Brazil)
Veronica Dahl (Canada)
Werner Nutt (Germany)
W. DePauli-Schimanovich (Austria)
Wilmer Pereira (Venezuela)

Area Chairs

Case-Based Reasoning and Planning (Carlos Bento)
Constraint Programming (Pedro Barahona)
Distributed Artificial Intelligence (Jaime Simão Sichman and Alexis Drogoul)
Genetic Algorithms (José Ali Moreno)
Intelligent Tutoring Systems (John Self)
Knowledge Engineering (Antonio Sánchez)
Knowledge Representation (Javier Pinto)
Machine Learning (Fernando Moura Pires)
Natural Language Understanding (Suresh Manandhar)
Neural Networks (José Ramírez)
Reasoning (Alvaro del Val)
Robotics (Jorge Villalobos)
Vision (Anna Reali Costa)

Reviewers

Agostinho Rosa
Alexis Drogoul
Alfred Kobsa
Alípio Jorge
Alma Barranco
Alvaro del Val
Amedeo Cesta
Amilcar Cardoso
Ana Fred
Ana Martins
Ana Paiva
Angel Puerta
Angelo Oddi
Anna Reali Costa
Antonio Sánchez
Arlindo Oliveira
Blai Bonet
Carlos Bento
Carlos Lourenço
Carlos Pinto-Ferreira
Christian Lemaitre
Cristiano Castelfranchi
Daya Gaur
Dimitar Kazakov
Edson Satoshi Gomi
Eduardo Ferme
Ernesto Costa
Eugénio Oliveira
Felisa Verdejo
Fernando Carvalho
Fernando Moura Pires
Flávio Correa da Silva
Flávio M. de Oliveira
Francisco Cantú
Gabor Loerincs
Gabriel Pereira Lopes
Gerardo Ayala
Graça Gaspar

Guillermo Simari
Héctor Geffner
Helder Araujo
Helder Coelho
Hercules Prado
Horacio Rodriguez
Irene Rodrigues
Isabel F. de Castro
Isabel Trancoso
Ivette Carolina Martínez
Jaime Simão Sichman
Javier Pinto
João Balsa
João Gama
João Neto
João Sequeira
John Self
Jorge Marques
Jorge Villalobos
José Abracos
José Cuena
José Félix Costa
José Luis Ferreira
José Maia Neves
José Moreno
José Ramírez
Juan Carlos Santamaria
Julio Gonzalo
Kinshuk
Leliane de Barros Nunes
Leopoldo Bertossi
Lucia Giraffa
Luciano Garcia
Luis Antunes
Luis Botelho
Luís Correia
Luis Moniz
Luis Otavio Alvares

Luis Torgo
Manuel Campagnolo
Manuel Filipe Santos
Marcelino Pequeno
Marcelo Ladeira
Mário Gaspar da Silva
Markus Specht
Markus Stumptner
Miguel Angel Oros
Milton Corrêa
Nuno Guimarães
Nuno Mamede
Nuno Marques
Nuria Castell
Olga Padron
Paulo Quaresma
Paulo Urbano
Pavel Brazdil
Pedro Barahona
Pedro Lima
Pere Garcia
Ramon L. de Màntaras
Raul Carnota
Raul Wazlawick
Ricardo Rodriguez
Rino Falcone
Rosa Viccari
Sandra Zabala
Stephen Watkinson
Suresh Manandhar
Suzanne Pinson
Tarcisio Pequeno
Tomaž Erjavec
Veronica Becher
Veronica Dahl
Werner Nutt
Werner Schimanovich
Wilmer Pereira

Table of Contents

Reasoning

Vision

Genetic Algorithms

Knowledge Engineering

Intelligent Tutoring Systems

Natural Language Processing

Neural Nets

Constraint Programming

Planning

Modelling Intelligent Behaviour: The Markov Decision Process Approach

Héctor Geffner

Depto de Computación
Universidad Simón Bolívar
Aptdo. 89000, Caracas, Venezuela
http://www.ldc.usb.ve/~hector

Abstract. The problem of selecting action in environments that are dynamic and not completely predictable or observable is a central problem in intelligent behavior. From an AI point of view, the problem is to design a mechanism that can select the best actions given information provided by sensors and a suitable model of the actions and goals. We call this the problem of *Planning* as it is a direct generalization of the problem considered in Planning research where feedback is absent and the effect of actions is assumed to be predictable. In this paper we present an approach to Planning that combines ideas and methods from Operations Research and Artificial Intelligence. Basically Planning problems are described in *high-level action languages* that are compiled into general mathematical models of sequential decisions known as *Markov Decision Processes* or *Partially Observable Markov Decision Processes*, which are then solved by suitable *Heuristic Search Algorithms.* The result are *controllers* that map sequences of observations into actions, and which, under certain conditions can be shown to be optimal. We show how this approach applies to a number of concrete problems and discuss its relation to work in Reinforcement Learning.

1 Introduction

The problem of selecting actions in environments that are dynamic and not completely predictable is a central problem in AI. Given a model of the actions and goals, the problem is to produce a *controller* that can map sequences of observations into suitable actions [27]. We call this the problem of *Planning* as it is a general version of problem traditionally considered in Planning research where feedback is absent and actions are assumed to be deterministic (e.g., [23, 27]). In this paper we will be concerned with this problem and show how it can be addressed by a suitable combination of *models, languages* and *algorithms.* Models will allow us to understand the problem, while languages and algorithms will allow us to represent and solve specific problem instances.

A simple planning problem is Levesque's Omelette Problem [20] that involves an agent that has a large supply of eggs and whose goal is to get three good eggs and no bad ones into one of two bowls. The eggs can be either good or bad,

Helder Coelho (Ed.): IBERAMIA'98, LNAI 1484, pp. 1–12, 1998.

and at any time the agen t can find out whether a bowl contains a bad egg by inspecting the bowl. A sensible plan for this problem is to follow a loop in which an egg is grabbed from the pile and brok en into a bowl. If the egg is good, it's passed to the other bowl, else it is discarded. The loop is con tinued until three eggs have been passed.

The Planning problem is ho w to model problems of this type and how to obtain the corresponding plans from a suitable description of the actions and goals. As this example illustrates, the *form* of plans is intimately related to the presence or absence of *feedback*. In general, the sequence of actions depends on the observations. W e refer to planning in the presence of observations as *closed-loop planning,* and planning in the absence of observations as *open-loop planning* [24, 13, 1]. Classical planning is open-loop planning, while con tingent and reactive planning are forms of closed-loop planning. While open-loop planning has been the focus of most researc h in AI Planning, closed-loop planning is normally regarded as superior as it is more robust. Closed-loop plans can reco ver from perturbations (e.g., a block falling off the gripper) and errors in the initial conditions or action models (e.g., lik e assuming that actions are deterministic when they are not), while open-loop plans cannot. Closed-loop planning, ho w ever, requires more sophisticated models, languages and algorithms. Models have to make precise what closed-loop plans are, languages ha ve to make room for both physical and information gathering actions, and algorithms ha ve to produce *functions* mapping observ ation sequences into actions.

In this paper w e present an approach to closed-loop planning that is based on these three elemen ts. First w e review SEARCH, MDP, and POMDP *models* for planning, then w e consider a suitable com bination of heuristic search and dynamic programming *algorithms* for solving these models, and finally, we consider high-level action *languages* for representing MDPs and POMDPs in a convenient w ay. We have actually implemen ted a shell that supports this approach, and given a high-level representation of actions and goals, produces the appropriate controllers [16]. W e report empirical results for a n um ber of problems, and discuss how this approach relates to current ideas in Reinforcemen t Learning [31].

2   Models

Three standard mathematical models of sequential decisions allow us to make precise what open and closed-loop plans are, and ho w they can be deriv ed from suitable descriptions of actions and goals. They are SEARCH models, Mark ov Decision Processes or MDPs, and Partially Observable Markov Decision Processes or POMDPs.

2.1   Search Models

SEARCH models [22] are the most basic action models in AI and are characterized by three assumptions: the initial state is completely known, actions are deterministic, and their effects are not observable. Formally a SEARCH problem is comprised of

- a state space S
- an initial state $s_0 \in S$
- actions $A(s) \subseteq A$ applicable in each state $s \in S$
- a transition function $f(s, a)$ for $s \in S$ and $a \in A(s)$
- action costs $c(a, s) > 0$
- a set $G \subseteq S$ of goal states

A *solution* of a SEARCH problem is a sequence of actions a_0, a_1, ..., a_n that generates a state trajectory s_0, $s_1 = f(s_0)$, ..., $s_{n+1} = f(s_i, a_i)$ such that each action a_i is applicable in s_i and s_{n+1} is a goal state, i.e., $a_i \in A(s_i)$ and $s_{n+1} \in G$. The solution is *optimal* when the total cost $\sum_{i=0}^{n} c(s_i, a_i)$ is minimized.

Classical planning, i.e., open-loop planning with complete knowledge of the initial situation and deterministic actions, is a SEARCH problem where states are represented by sets of atoms, action costs are all equal, and both the transition function f and the sets of executable actions $A(s)$ are defined in a high-level language such as Strips. The *computational* problem in classical planning has been approached by looking at planning as a nearly decomposable problem [33]. Recent work suggests other formulations and algorithms that may scale up better [3, 17], and in [5] we argue that SEARCH methods can scale up well too, provided a suitable heuristic function is obtained from the Strips representation of the problem (see also [21]).

2.2 MDPs

Markov Decision Processes (MDPs) [26, 2] differ from SEARCH models in two main respects: they accommodate *probabilistic actions*, and they assume that the effect of actions is *fully observable*. An MDP is thus given by:[1]

- a state space S
- actions $A(s) \subseteq A$ applicable in each state $s \in S$
- transition probabilities $P_a(s'|s)$ for $s \in A$ and $a \in A(s)$
- action costs $c(a, s) > 0$
- a set $G \subseteq S$ of goal states

The state s_{i+1} that results from a state s_i and an action a_i is *not predictable* but is *observable*, and hence provides feedback for selecting the next action a_{i+1}. As a result, a *solution* of an MDP is not an action sequence, but a function π mapping states s into applicable actions $a \in A(s)$. Such a function is called a *policy*. A policy π assigns a probability to every state trajectory $s_0, s_1, s_2, \ldots$ starting in a state s_0, that is given by the product of all transition probabilities $P_{a_i}(s_{i+1}|s_i)$

---

[1] We are considering a subclass of MDPs, the so-called *stochastic shortest-path* MDPs [2]. For general treatments, see [2] and [26]. For uses of MDPs in Planning and AI, see [30, 7, 1, 27].

where $a_i = \pi(s_i)$. We assume that actions in goal states have no costs and no effects (i.e., $c(a, s) = 0$ and $P_a(s|s) = 1$ if $s \in G$). The *expected cost* associated with a policy π starting in state s is the weighted average of the probability of such trajectories times their cost $\sum_{i=0}^{\infty} c(\pi(s_i), s_i)$. An *optimal solution* is a control policy π^* that has a minimum expected cost for all states $\in S$.

While Classical Planning can be formulated as a SEARCH problem, Closed-loop Planning with *complete information* can be formulated as an MDP [11, 1]. The desired closed-loop plans are the optimal policies π^*.

2.3 POMDPs

POMDPs generalize MDPs allowing the state to be *partially observable* [28, 8]. Information about the state comes from observations o whose probabilities $P_a(o|s)$ depend on the action a performed and the unobserved but true resulting state s. In addition, a prior probability distribution over the states encodes the prior belief about the initial state of the environment. A POMDP is thus characterized by:

- states $s \in S$
- actions $A(s) \subseteq A$ applicable in each state s
- costs $c(a, s) > 0$ of performing action a in s
- transition probabilities $P_a(s'|s)$ for $s \in S$ and $a \in A(s)$
- initial belief state b_0
- final belief states b_F
- observations o after action a with probabilities $P_a(o|s)$

Since feedback from the environment is only partial, the *solution* of a POMDP is not a function mapping states into actions, but a function mapping *belief states* into actions, where belief states b are probability distributions over the real states s of the environment. The effect of the actions on *belief states* is completely predictable. Indeed the belief state b_a that results from performing action a in the belief state b is:

$$b_a(s) = \sum_{s' \in S} P_a(s|s')b(s') \qquad (1)$$

while the belief state b_a^o that results from performing action a in b and then observing o is

$$b_a^o(s) = P_a(o|s)b_a(s)/b_a(o) \qquad (2)$$

where $b_a(o)$ is the probability of observing o after doing a in b given by

$$b_a(o) = \sum_{s \in S} P_a(o|s)b_a(s) \qquad (3)$$

Actions a thus transform a belief state b into a new belief b_a^o with probability $b_a(o)$. The planning task is to go from the initial belief state b_0 to a final belief state b_F at a minimum expected cost. This is nothing else but an MDP over *belief space,* where the real states s of the environment have been replaced by belief states b. The 'goal' belief states b_F can be defined in various ways; as the belief states in which we are certain to have reached a real goal state (i.e., $b(s) = 0$ for $s \notin G$), as the belief states in which we are pretty sure to have reached a goal state (i.e., $\sum_{s \in G} b(s) > 1 - \epsilon$), etc.

Closed-loop Planning with Incomplete Information is a POMDP problem whose solutions are the closed-loop policies mapping belief states into actions. In the AI literature, such policies are often represented by contingent plans, i.e., sequential plans extended with tests and branches [14, 10, 20].

3 Algorithms

We have seen that Planning problems can be formulated as either SEARCH, MDP, or POMDP problems according to the type of feedback (observations) available to the planner at run time. Techniques for solving SEARCH problems are reviewed in details in most AI texts; e.g., [27], and include algorithms such as A* and greedy search, all based on an heuristic function $h(s)$ that estimates the cost from any state s to a goal state. A* is guaranteed to find the optimal action sequence when the heuristic function is *admissible* (i.e., does not overestimate the true cost the goal), yet it may take exponential space. Greedy search, on the other hand, takes constant space but is not guaranteed to find optimal solutions, or any solutions at all. An heuristic search algorithm for classical planning problems was shown to be competitive with the state of the art planning algorithms such as GRAPHPLAN and SATPLAN in [6]. The algorithm is basically a version of A* with a limited buffer size, and uses an heuristic function extracted from the Strips encoding of the problem to guide the search.

While extensions of the heuristic search methods such as AO* [23, 25] could be used to solve problems with *probabilistic actions,* the standard approach to solve MDPs and POMDPs is by means of *dynamic programming* methods [26, 2]. The idea is to compute from any state s (or belief state b) the optimal expected cost $V(s)$ $(V(b))$ to the reach a goal and then use these values to select the optimal actions. These optimal expected costs $V(\cdot)$ obey the following fixed point equations in SEARCH, MDPs, and POMDPs models

$$\text{SEARCH: } V(s) = \min_{a \in A(s)} [c(a, s) + V(s_a)] \tag{4}$$

$$\text{MDP: } V(s) = \min_{a \in A(s)} [c(a, s) + \sum_{s'} P_a(s'|s) V(s')] \tag{5}$$

$$\text{POMDP: } V(b) = \min_{b \in A(b)} [c(a, b) + \sum_{o} b_a(o) V(b_a^o)] \tag{6}$$

Value iteration finds the solution to these equations by an iteration method in which initial estimates V_0 are plugged on the right hand side of the equations to yield new estimates V_1 on the left hand side, which are used again to get estimates V_2 and so on. Under suitable conditions it can be proved that the

6   Héctor Geffner

---

1 **Evaluate** each action a applicable in s as:

$$Q(a,s) = c(a,s) + \sum_{s' \in S} P_a(s'|s)V(s')$$

initializing $V(s')$ to $h(s')$ when needed
2 **Apply** action **a** with minimum $Q(\mathbf{a},s)$ value, breaking ties randomly
3 **Update** $V(s)$ to $Q(\mathbf{a},s)$
4 **Observe** resulting state s'
5 **Exit** if s' is a goal, else set s to s' and go to 1

Fig. 1. RTDP Loop

estimates V_i approach the optimal values when $i \to \infty$ [26, 2]. The operation that yields new estimates V_{i+1} in terms of old estimates V_i is called an *update*. Thus, each step of value iteration involves a parallel update of the estimates $V_i(s)$ for all $s \in S$.

Problems involving up to hundred of thousands of states can be solved by these methods in a reasonable amount time and memory. Yet larger problems are not uncommon in AI, and certainly arise in POMDPs where the set of belief states is continuous and infinite. The problem with methods such as value iteration is that they compute the optimal values of *all* (belief) states. In many problems, however, only the value of a small number of states matter. This occurs in particular in problems in which the initial state (or b) is known a priori. In such cases, most of the updates in value iteration are wasted on irrelevant states.

The idea of the so-called *Real Time Dynamic Programming* (RTDP) methods [1] is to allow the solution of much larger problems by focusing the updates on the states that are likely to be relevant. This is achieved by using the current estimates $V(s)$ (or $V(b)$ in POMDPs) to guide a greedy search while limiting the updates to the states that are visited. Interestingly, repeated trials of this greedy search algorithm with updates, eventually delivers an optimal policy *even if a large fraction of the states is never or seldom visited* [18, 1, 2]. For this reason RTDP algorithms can scale up to much larger problems provided good initial estimates are available.

The RTDP algorithm for SEARCH and MDPs is shown in Fig. 1. Note that RTDP is basically a *greedy* or *hill-climbing* algorithm that from any state s searches for a goal state using estimates $V(s)$ of the *expected cost* to reach the goal. The main difference with standard hill-climbing is that these estimates are updated dynamically. Initially $V(s)$ is set to $h(s)$, where h is a suitable *heuristic function*, and every time an action a from s is taken, $V(s)$ is updated to make it consistent with the estimates of its successor states (Step 3 in Fig. 1, Equation 5). The updates, guarantee that in any *single trial* the algorithm will eventually find the goal, and that after *repeated trials*, the cost estimates will eventually converge to their optimal values, provided that the heuristic function h used to initialize the estimates is admissible [1, 18].

In the implementation, the estimates $V(s)$ are stored in a hash table that initially contains an estimate $V(s_0)$ for s_0 only. Then when the value $V(s')$ of a state s' that is not in the table is needed, a new entry with $V(s')$ set to $h(s')$ is created.

RTDP is an 'anytime' algorithm for solving MDPs in the sense that after any number of steps and trials, the hash table along with the heuristic function determines a greedy control policy that eventually converges to the optimal policy when h is admissible. Since POMDPs correspond to MDPs over belief states, RTDP can be used to solve POMDPs as well by simply substituting the current state s in the RTDP loop in Fig. 1 by the current *belief state* b, and the observed state s' by the new belief state b_a^o (Equations 1–3), where o is the observation obtained. Problems of *open-loop* planning can be solved in a similar way, as they are a special case of problems of closed-loop planning with incomplete information in which there are *no* observations, and hence $b_a^o = b_a$. This includes, for example, the problems considered by the probabilistic planner BURIDAN [19].

4   Representation

SEARCH, MDP and POMDP models are useful for analysis but not for modeling. In AI it has been a standard practice to model planning problems by means of high-level languages such as Strips [15]. In recent years similar languages have been defined for modeling probabilistic actions [19, 12] and general POMDPs [16]. We illustrate the latter with a problem of planning with incomplete information due to Levesque [20]. It involves an agent that has a large supply of eggs and whose goal is to get three good eggs and no bad ones into one of two bowls. The eggs can be either good or bad, and at any time the agent can find out whether a bowl contains a bad egg by inspecting the bowl. In [16] this problem is encoded by expressions such as the ones in Fig. 2, which are automatically compiled into a POMDP, whose solution obtained by the RTDP algorithm provides the desired plan.

Such a language extends Strips in several ways: states are not associated with sets of atoms but with assignments to arbitrary fluents; probabilities, costs and primitive operations like '+' are included, and a special predicate **obs** is used to indicate observability. The fluents in this problem are the number of good eggs and bad eggs in each bowl ($ngood(a)$, $ngood(b)$, $nbad(a)$, $nbad(b)$), and the boolean variables *holding?* and *good?* that represent whether the agent is currently holding an egg and whether such an egg is good. The fluent *holding* is always observable, but the value of the expression $nbad(nbowl) > 0$) is only observable after doing the action *inspect*. For the formal syntax and semantics of this language, see [16].

Action: **grab-egg**()
Precond: ¬*holding*
Effects: *holding* := **true**
            good? := (**true** 0.5 ; **false** 0.5)

Action: **break-egg**(*bowl* : *BOWL*)
Precond: *holding* ∧ (*ngood*(*bowl*) + *nbad*(*bowl*)) < 4
Effects: *holding* := **false**
            good? → *ngood*(*bowl*) := *ngood*(*bowl*) + 1
            ¬*good*? → *nbad*(*bowl*) := *nbad*(*bowl*) + 1

Action: **pour**(*b1* : *BOWL*, *b2* : *BOWL*)
Precond: (*b1* ≠ *b2*) ∧ ¬*holding*
            ngood(*b1*) + *nbad*(*b1*) + *ngood*(*b2*) + *nbad*(*b2*) < 4
Effects: *ngood*(*b1*) := 0 , *nbad*(*b1*) := 0
            ngood(*b2*) := *ngood*(*b2*) + *ngood*(*b1*)
            nbad(*b2*) := *nbad*(*b2*) + *nbad*(*b1*)

Action: **clean**(bowl:BO WL)
Precond: ¬*holding*
Effects: *ngood*(*bowl*) := 0 , *nbad*(*bowl*) := 0

Action: **inspect**(*bowl* : *BOWL*)
Effect: **obs**(*nbad*(*bowl*) > 0)

Fig. 2. High-level encoding of Omelette Problem

5   Results

5.1   Classical Planning

Tables 3 and 4 show results comparing RTDP with two recent and powerful planners, GRAPHPLAN [3] and SATPLAN [17], over the suite of problems in [17]. These tables are from [6], except that the RTDP column shows the result of the algorithm with no look ahead[2]. The heuristic used is very informative but is *not* admissible [6]. For this reason the algorithm does not improve much after successive trials, and hence, only a single trial is considered.

As it can be seen from the tables, RTDP reaches the goal very fast (Fig. 1), but the length of plans is sometimes far from optimal (Fig. 2). One way to decrease the average length of plans is thus to run the algorithm several times keeping only the best run. Other methods are the addition of 'noise' in the selection of actions (see [6]), increased lookahead, and variations on the heuristic function. In principle RTDP can produce optimal plans, but cannot guarantee the optimality of the plans produced as planners such as GRAPHPLAN.

---

[2] The algorithm in [6] is referred to as ASP for Action Selection for Planning, and is presented as a variation of Korf's LRTA* [18], which is the deterministic version of RTDP.

Problem	GRAPHPLAN	SATPLAN	RTDP
rocket_ext.a	268	0.17	1.3
logistics.a	5,942	22	7
logistics.b	2,538	6	6
12 blocks	1,119	18	1
15 blocks	—	524	5
19 blocks	—	4,220	19

Fig. 3. Time performance in seconds of RTDP in comparison with GRAPHPLAN and SATPLAN

Problem	GRAPHPLAN	SATPLAN	RTDP
rocket_ext.a	34	34	35/28
logistics.a	54	54	64/57
logistics.b	47	47	58/48
12 blocks	9	9	16/12
15 blocks	—	14	24/19
19 blocks	—	18	32/25

Fig. 4. Quality performance. Averages and minimal plan lengths over 25 runs shown

5.2   Planning with Incomplete Information

Figures 5 displays the performance curve for the Omelette problem discussed above. The curve that is flat shows the average number of actions to solve the problem for the obvious plan in which an egg is grabbed and broken it into one of the two bowls, and after inspecting the bowl, it's either passed to the other bowl or discarded, until three eggs have been passed. The other curve shows the performance of the greedy controller produced by RTDP after different number of trials. The heuristic function used in this case is admissible and follows from assuming that the next state will be observable [9, 16]. The convergence takes more than 1000 trials, as the algorithm has to 'learn' the value of the action 'inspect', which as all information-gathering actions, appears useless to the heuristic. The time for 2000 trials in this problem is in the order of 192 seconds on an UltraSparc running at 143Mhz.

The second problem is originally from [10] where it is presented as a challenging problem for contingent planning. It deals with a robot that is inside a room where there is a table, two boxes, a pile of red things by the door, and a key that may be in either of the two boxes. The goal is to get one red thing outside the room. In order to get out of the room the key must be placed by the door. The robot cannot hold two things at the same type, and while it knows whether it's holding something or not, it does not know *what* it is holding. The resulting POMDP for this problem involves 480 states, 21 actions, and 6 observations (see [5] for a complete high-level description). An optimal plan for this problem is "go to the door, pickup a red thing, leave it on the table, then go for the key in one of the boxes and place it by the door; finally, go to the table, pick up what's

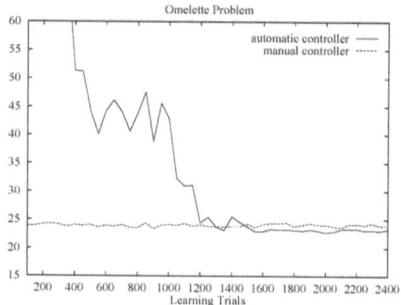

Fig. 5. Comparison of RTDP policy vs. handcrafted plan for the 'Omelette' problem

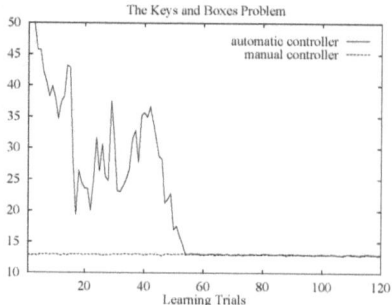

Fig. 6. Comparison of RTDP policy vs. handcrafted plan for 'Key and Boxes' problem

in there and go outside". Other plans are possible but most plans are no good as they leave the robot in a state of knowledge from whic h the goal can't be achieved. The a verage cost of this plan is shown by the flat curve in Fig. 6. The other curve shows the performance of the RTDP controller as a function of the num ber of trials. The average time to compute the first 60 trials is 561 seconds. No times for the solution are reported in [10].

6   Discussion

SEARCH, MDPs and POMDPs are key models for understanding v arious forms of open and closed-loop planning. Effective planning, how ever, also requires suitable languages and algorithms. F rom this perspectiv e, the planning languages are a convenient way for defining these models and rev ealing their structure so that it can be used by suitably defined heuristics. We have also considered a simple and general RTDP algorithm that can be used for open and closed-loop planning with either complete or incomplete information, and presented some empirical results.

MDP

models and RTDP algorithms are closely related to the models and algorithms used in Reinforcement Learning [29]. Indeed, reinforcement learning algorithms are currently understood as algorithms for solving MDPs by trial and error with no prior knowledge of cost and probabilities [32, 1]. The Q-learning algorithm in particular [32] is basically the model-free version of RTDP. For two recent books on MDPs and Reinforcement Learning; see [31] and [2].

Acknowledgement. My work on planning and MDPs has been in collaboration with Blai Bonet. Partial support is due to Conicit, Grant S1-96001365.

References

1. A. Barto, S. Bradtke, and S. Singh. Learning to act using real-time dynamic programming. *Artificial Intelligence*, 72:81–138, 1995.
2. D. Bertsekas and J. Tsitsiklis. *Neuro-Dynamic Programming*. Athena Scientific, 1996.
3. A. Blum and M. Furst. Fast planning through planning graph analysis. In *Proceedings of IJCAI-95*, Montreal, Canada, 1995.
4. B. Bonet and H. Geffner. Learning sorting and decision trees with POMDPs. To appear in *Proceedings ICML-98*, 1998.
5. B. Bonet and H. Geffner. Planning and control with incomplete information using POMDPs: Experimental results. Available at http://www.ldc.usb.ve/~hector, 1998.
6. B. Bonet, G. Loerincs, and H. Geffner. A robust and fast action selection mechanism for planning. In *Proceedings of AAAI-97*, pages 714–719. MIT Press, 1997.
7. C. Boutilier, T. Dean, and S. Hanks. Planning under uncertainty: structural assumptions and computational leverage. In *Proceedings of EWSP-95*, 1995.
8. A. Cassandra, L. Kaebling, and M. Littman. Acting optimally in partially observable stochastic domains. In *Proceedings AAAI94*, pages 1023–1028, 1994.
9. A. Cassandra, L. Kaebling, and M. Littman. Learning policies for partially observable environments: Scaling up. In *Proc. of the 12th Int. Conf. on Machine Learning*, 1995.
10. G. Collins and L. Pryor. Planning under uncertainty: Some key issues. In *Proceedings IJCAI95*, 1995.
11. T. Dean, L. Kaebling, J. Kirman, and A. Nicholson. Planning with deadlines in stochastic domains. In *Proceedings AAAI93*, pages 574–579. MIT Press, 1993.
12. T. Dean and K. Kanazawa. A model for reasoning about persistence and causation. *Computational Intelligence*, 5(3):142–150, 1989.
13. T. Dean and M. Wellman. *Planning and Control*. Morgan Kaufmann, 1991.
14. O. Etzioni, S. Hanks, D. Draper, N. Lesh, and M. Williamson. An approach to planning with incomplete information. In *Proceedings of the Third Int. Conference on Principles of Knowledge Representation and Reasoning*, pages 115–125. Morgan Kaufmann, 1992.
15. R. Fikes and N. Nilsson. STRIPS: A new approach to the application of theorem proving to problem solving. *Artificial Intelligence*, 1:27–120, 1971.
16. H. Geffner and B. Bonet. High-level plannnig and control with incomplete information using POMDP's. In *Proceedings AIPS-98 Workshop on Integrating Planning, Scheduling and Execution in Dynamic and Uncertain Environments*, 1998. Available at http://www.ldc.usb.ve/~hector.

17. H. Kautz and B. Selman. Pushing the en velope: Planning, propositional logic, and stochastic search. In *Proceedings of AAAI-96*, pages 1194–1201, Protland, Oregon, 1996. MIT Press.
18. R. Korf. Real-time heuristic searc h.*Artificial Intelligence*, 42:189–211, 1990.
19. N. Kushmeric k, S. Hanks, and D. W eld. An algorithm for probabilistic planning. *Artificial Intelligence*, 76:239–286, 1995.
20. H. Lev esque. What is planning in the presence of sensing. In *Proceedings AAAI-96*, pages 1139–1146, Portland, Oregon, 1996. MIT Press.
21. D. McDermott. A heuristic estimator for means-ends analysis in planning. In *Proc. Third Int. Conf. on AI Planning Systems (AIPS-96)*, 1996.
22. A. New ell and H. Simon.*Human Pr oblem Solving* Prentice–Hall, Englewood Cliffs, NJ, 1972.
23. N. Nilsson. *Principles of Artificial Intelligence*. Tioga, 1980.
24. L. Padulo and M. Arbib. *System Theory*. Hemisphere Publishing Co., 1974.
25. J. Pearl. *Heuristics*. Morgan Kaufmann, 1983.
26. M. Puterman. *Markov De cision Processes – Discrete Stochastic Dynamic Pr ogramming*. John Wiley and Sons, Inc., 1994.
27. S. Russell and P. Norvig. *Artificial Intelligence: A Mo dern Appvach*. Prentice Hall, 1994.
28. E. Sondik. *The Optimal Contr ol of Partially Observable Markov Pr ocesses* PhD thesis, Stanford University, 1971.
29. R. Sutton. Learning to predict b y the method of temporal differences. *Machine Learning*, 3:9–44, 1988.
30. R. Sutton. In tegrated architectures for learning, planning and reacting based on approximating dynamic programming. In *Proceedings of ML-90*, pages 216–224. Morgan Kaufmann, 1990.
31. R. Sutton and A. Barto. *Introduction to Reinforcement L earning* MIT Press, 1998.
32. C. J. C. H. Watkins. *Learning from Delayed Rewards*. PhD thesis, Cam bridge University, 1989.
33. D. W eld. An in troduction to least commitmen t planning*AI Magazine*, 1994.

Emergence and Cognition:
Towards a Synthetic Paradigm in AI and Cognitive Science[1]

Cristiano Castelfranchi

National Research Council - Institute of Psychology
Division of "Artificial Intelligence, Cognitive and Interaction Modelling"
cris@pscs2.irmkant.rm.cnr.it

1   Premise. At the frontier of a millennium: The challenge

Will the "representational paradigm" - that characterised Artificial Intelligence (AI) and Cognitive Science (CS) from their very birth - be eliminated in the 21st century? Will this paradigm be replaced by the new one based on dynamic systems, connectionism, situatedness, embodiedness, etc.? Will this be the end of the AI ambitious project? I do not think so. Challenges and attacks to AI and CS have been hard and radical in the last 15 years, however I believe that the next century will start with a renewed rush of AI and we will not assist to a paradigmatic revolution, with connectionism replacing cognitivism and symbolic models; emergentist, dynamic and evolutionary models eliminating reasoning on explicit representations and planning; neuroscience (plus phenomenology) eliminating cognitive processing; situatedness, reactivity, cultural constructivism eliminating general concepts, context independent abstractions, ideal-typical models. I claim that the major scientific challenge of the first part of the century will precisely be the construction of a new "synthetic" paradigm: a paradigm that puts together, in a principled and non-eclectic way, cognition and emergence, information processing and self-organisation, reactivity and intentionality, situatedness and planning, etc. [Cas98a].

AI is going out of a crisis: crisis of grants, of prestige, and of identity. This crisis was not only due - on my view- to exaggerated expectations and overselling of specific technologies (like expert systems) tout court identified with AI. It was due to the restriction of cultural interests and influence of the discipline, and of its ambitions; to the dominance either of the logicist approach (identifying logics and theory, logics and foundations) or of a mere technological/applicative view of AI (see the debate about the 'pure reason' [McD87] and 'rigor mortis'). New domains were growing as external and antagonistic to AI: neural nets, reactive systems, evolutionary computing, CSCW, cognitive modelling, etc. Hard attacks were made to the "classical" AI approach: situatedness [Suc87], anti-symbolism, reactivity [Bro89] [Agr89], dynamic systems, bounded and limited resources, uncertainty, and so on (on the challenges to AI and CS see also [Tha96]).

---

[1] This is a preliminary version. Some of the sub-sections (such as "How to (partially) reduce social power to individual power", in section 4; "Delegation" and "Conflict", in section 5) were omitted due to space limitations of the whole text.

Helder Coelho (Ed.): IBERAMIA'98, LNAI 1484, pp. 13–26, 1998.

However, by relaxing previous frameworks; by some contagion and hybridisation, by incorporating some of those criticisms; by re-absorbing as its own descendants neural nets, reactive systems, evolutionary computing, etc.; by developing important internal domains like machine learning and DAI-MAS; by important developments in logics and in languages; and finally with the new successful Agents framework, AI is now in a revival phase. It is trying to recover all the original challenges of the discipline, its strong scientific identity, its cultural role and influence. We may in fact say that there is already a neo-cognitivism and a new AI. In this new AI of the '90s systems and models are conceived for reasoning and acting in open unpredictable worlds, with limited and uncertain knowledge, in real time, with bounded (both cognitive and material) resources, interfering --either co-operatively or competitively-- with other systems. The new password is *interaction* [Bob91]: interaction with an evolving environment; among several, distributed and heterogeneous artificial systems in a network; with human users; among humans through computers.

1.1   The synthesis

Synthetic theories should explain the dynamic and emergent aspects of cognition and symbolic computation; how cognitive processing and individual intelligence emerge from sub-symbolic or sub-cognitive distributed computation, and causally feedbacks into it; how collective phenomena emerge from individual action and intelligence and causally shape back the individual mind. We need a principled theory which is able to reconcile cognition with emergence and with reactivity:

Reconciling "Reactivity" and "Cognition"

We shouldn't consider reactivity as alternative to reasoning or to mental states [Cas95]. A reactive agent is not necessarily an agent without mental states and reasoning. Reactivity is not equal to reflexes. Also cognitive and planning agents are and must be reactive (like in several BDI models). They are reactive not only in the sense that they can have some hybrid and compound architecture that includes both deliberated actions and reflexes or other forms of low level reactions (for example, [Kur97]), but because there is some form of high level *cognitive reactivity*: the agent reacts by changing its mind: plans, goals, intentions. Also Suchman's provocative claims against planning are clearly too extreme and false.

In general we have to bring all the anti-cognitivist claims, applied to sub-symbolic or insect-like systems, at the level of cognitive system [1].

---

[1] Cognitive agents are agents whose actions are internally regulated by goals (goal-directed) and whose goals, decisions, and plans are based on beliefs. Both goals and beliefs are cognitive representations that can be internally generated, manipulated, and subject to inferences and reasoning. Since a cognitive agent may have more than one goal active in the same situation, it must have some form of choice/decision, based on some "reason" i.e. on some belief and evaluation. Notice that I use "goal" as the general family term for all motivational representations: from desires to intentions, from objectives to motives, from needs to ambitions, etc. By "sub-cognitive" agents I mean agents whose behaviour is not regulated by an internal explicit representation of its purposes and by explicit beliefs. Sub-cognitive agents are for example simple neural-net agents, or mere reactive agents.

Reconciling "Emergence" and "Cognition"

Emergence and cognition are not incompatible: they are not two alternative approaches to intelligence and cooperation, two competing paradigms. They must be reconciled:

- first, considering **cognition itself as a level of emergence:** both as an emergence *from sub-symbolic to symbolic* (symbol grounding, emergent symbolic computation), and as a transition *from objective to subjective* representation (awareness) (see later for example on dependence and on conflicts) and from *implicit to explicit knowledge*;

- second, recognising the necessity for going **beyond cognition**, modelling emergent unaware, functional social phenomena (ex. unaware cooperation, non-orchestrated problem solving, and swarm intelligence) also *among cognitive and planning agents*. In fact, for a theory of cooperation and society among intelligent agents *mind is not enough* [Con96]. We have to explain how collective phenomena emerge from individual action and intelligence, and how a collaborative plan can be only partially represented in the minds of the participants, and some part represented in no mind at all [Hay67].

This is the most challenging problem of reconciliation between cognition and emergence: unaware *social functions* impinging on intentional actions. AI can significantly contribute to solve the main theoretical problem of all the social sciences [Hay67]: the problem of the micro-macro link, the problem of theoretically reconciling individual decisions and utility with the global, collective phenomena and interests. AI will contribute uniquely to solve this crucial problem, because it is able to formally model and to simulate at the same time the individual minds and behaviors, the emerging collective action, structure or effect, and their feedback to shape minds and reproduce themselves. Thus in the (formal and experimental) elaboration of this *synthetic paradigm* a major role will be played by AI, in particular by its agent-based and socially oriented approach to intelligence.

2   Neo-reductionism and the micro-macro integration of scientific theories

The real problem is the "integration" between different levels of description and/or explanation of reality; between different levels of granularity and complexity of systems. I claim that simple "compatibility" (non obvious contradiction) between principles and laws of one level and principles and laws of another level is only a minimal requirement. Much more is needed. We should systematically orchestrate one scientific layer (macro) with the other scientific layer, and one kind/level of explanation with a deeper level of explanation.

I adopt a "neo-reductionist" perspective (as Miguel Virasoro defines it [Vir96]). *Neo-reductionism* postulates that from the number and the interactions of the elements of a complex system some behaviours will emerge whose laws *can and must* be described at such superior layer. *Old reductionist* position claims that the emerging level has no autonomy of description, that you cannot formulate specific concepts and laws; you have just to explain it in terms of the underlying level: the only valid scientific position is to study the micro-units. By contrast, an *anti-reductionist* position will claim that the laws of the higher level of description (organisation) have nothing to do with the laws at the underlying level, and that there is no reason for searching a strong link between the two levels. The neo-reductionist position considers both approaches as necessary, by describing the laws typical of each level and investigating how from the basic level a complex behaviour can emerge and organise at the macro-level, and how it can possibly feedback into the micro-level (Virasoro does not take into account the feedback from macro to micro: he only considers the process of emergence -as typical of physics- while ignoring the process of "immergence" so relevant at the psychological and sociological levels).

I claim that the integration between different description layers requires at least three devices.

A) **Cross-layer Theories** - By 'Cross-layer Theories' I mean general models and laws valid at any or at least at several levels. The evolutionary framework for example can be successfully applied from molecules to species, cultures, organisations, ideas. Analogously, the system dynamics approach can be applied to weather, to atoms, to neurons, to animal populations, to market [Wei97].

B) **Bridge-Theories.** By 'Bridge-Theories' I mean theories that explicitly connect two levels of explanation, i.e. theories able to explain how a high level complex system works through (is implemented in) the micro-activities of its components; how complex phenomena emerge from simple behaviours; how the emerging global structure and behaviour feed-backs into and shapes the behaviours of its units.

C) **Layered Ontologies and Concepts**. General broad notions are needed -applicable at different levels - but also level-specific definitions of the same notion are needed. For example we cannot have two independent notions of action, or of communication, one for simple reactive agents (for ex. for insects), the other for intentional agents (for ex. for human kind). We have to characterise the general features of 'action' or of 'communication' and at the same time to have more specific notions for sub-cognitive and for cognitive agents.

I will give some examples of all these different integrating devices in modelling agents and MAS .

3   Cross-layer Theories

Also in AI some principles are valid at different levels of granularity and complexity, both at the micro and at the to macro level. For example general principles of coordination, or general principles of search, and so on. I will shortly illustrate only one very important structure emerging at any Multi-Agent level independently of the granularity and cognitive complexity of the agents: the interdependence objective structure.

3.1   An emergent social structure: The dependence network

The Dependence network [Cas92] [Con95] [Sic95] *determines* and *predicts* partnerships and coalitions formation, competition, cooperation, exchange, functional structure in organisations, rational and effective communication, and negotiation power. The dependence theory (and the related power theory - see 4.2) is a Cross-layer theory: it usefully applies to different level of agenthood and contributes to theoretically unify these levels.

4   Bridge-Theories: the *micro-implementation* and *counterparts* of macro behaviours and entities

Macro-level social phenomena are implemented through the (social) actions of the individual agents. In the case of cognitive agents, without an explicit theory of the agents' minds that founds agents' actions we cannot understand and explain several macro-level social phenomena (like team work, organizations), and in particular how they work.
Let's consider the individual counterparts of social norms, social power, organisational commitment and team-work.

4.1   The mental counterpart and cognitive implementation of social norms

Social norms are a multi-agent and multi-facets social object: in fact in order to work they should be represented in the minds of the involved agents, but these representations are not always the same: the agents play different *normative roles* and have different mental representations of the norms. Consider the *addressee* of the norm: it has to understand (believe) that there is a given expectation and prescription regarding its behaviour, and that it has to adopt this goal; but it has also to understand that this is not a personal or arbitrary request, but a 'group will', issued by some authority and in principle not aimed at personal interests. The addressee has also to believe that it is concerned by the norm and that a given act is an instance of the class of prescribed behaviours. The attitude and the normative mind of a "policeman", i.e. of an agent entitled to control norm obedience, is different. And also different is the mind of a neutral observer or of the "legislator" issuing the norm [Con95]. In other words, a norm N emerges *as a norm* only when it emerges as a norm *into the mind* of the involved agents; not only *through* their minds (like in approaches based on imitation or behavioural conformity, ex. [Bic90]). In other words, it works as an N only when the agents *recognise* it as an N, use it as an N, "conceive" it as an N [Con95] [Cas98b]. Norm emergence and formation implies "cognitive emergence" (hence cognitive agents): *a social N is really an N after its Cognitive Emergence (CE)* [2]. As long as the agents interpret the normative behaviour of the group merely as a

---

[2] When the micro-units of emerging dynamic processes are cognitive agents, a very important and unique phenomenon arises: the Cognitive Emergence (CE) [Con95] [Cas98b]. There is "cognitive emergence" *when agents become aware, through a given "conceptualisation", of a certain "objective" pre-cognitive (unknown and non deliberated) phenomenon* that is influencing their results and outcomes,

statistical "norm", and comply by imitation, the real normative character of N remains unacknowledged, and the efficacy of such "misunderstood N" is quite limited. Only when the normative (which implies "prescriptive") character of N becomes acknowledged by the agent the N starts to operate efficaciously as an N through the true normative behaviour of that agent. Thus *the effective "cognitive emergence" of N in the agent's mind is a precondition for its social emergence in the group, for its efficacy and complete functioning as a N.*

4.2   Grounding joint action in group-commitment, social commitment, and personal commitment

Many of the theories about joint or group action try to build it up on the basis of individual action: by directly reducing, for example, joint intention to individual intentions, joint plan to individual plans, group commitment (to a given joint intention and plan) to individual commitments to individual tasks. In [Cas97a] I claim that in this attempt the intermediate level between individual and collective action is bypassed; the real basis of all sociality (cooperation, competition, groups, organization, etc.) is missed: i.e. *the individual social action and mind. One cannot reduce or connect action at the collective level to action at the individual level without passing through the social character of the individual action.*

It is right that we cannot understand and explain collaboration [Gro95], cooperation [Tuo93] [Tuo88] [Con95], teamwork [Lev90] without explicitly modelling -among cognitive agents - the beliefs, the intentions, plans, commitments of the involved agents. However the attempt to connect collective intentions and plans to individual intentions has been too direct and simplistic, in that some mediating level and object has been ignored: in particular social intentions and social commitments.

How to reduce collective goals to individual goals

In my view the most important point is that in joint activity (be it cooperation or exchange):

•   the agents do not have only *beliefs* about the intentions of the other agents, but they have *positive expectations* about the actions (and then the *goals*) of their partners. Expectations imply beliefs + goals about the actions (the goals) of the other: each agent *delegates* the partner to do part of the joint plan. So the *social goal* that the other intends to do a given action and does it, is the first basic ingredient of collaboration.

On the other side:

•   each partner or member has to *adopt* (agree about) this delegation (task assignment), then she has the goal of doing her share not only because she shares a

---

and then, indirectly, their actions. CE is a feedback effect of the emergent phenomenon on its ground elements (the agents): the emergent phenomenon changes their representations in a special way: it is (partially) represented into their minds. The "cognitive emergence" (through experience and learning, or through communication) of such "objective" relations, strongly changes social situation: from known interference, relations of competition/aggression or exploitation can rise; from acknowledged dependence, relations of power, goals of influencing and asking, possible exchanges or cooperation, will rise.

common goal and/or a common plan, but also because she *adopts* the expectations of the other members and of the group (as a whole, as a collective-agent). She *adheres* to the explicit or implicit request of the group or of the partners.

In several approaches basically derived from Tuomela and Miller's theory of we-intentions [Tuo88] both the delegation goals, the expectations (not just beliefs) about the others' intentions, and the G-adoption among the members are not explicit.

Social Commitment

Social Commitment is exactly such a relation of complementary individual social goals that results from the merging of a strong delegation and the corresponding strong adoption: *reciprocal Social Commitments constitute the real structure of group and organizations.*

Also here, we need a notion of Commitment as a mediation between the individual and the collective one. There is a pre-social level of commitment: the **Internal Commitment** (I-Commitment) that corresponds to that defined by Cohen and Levesque (on the basis of Bratman's analysis) [Coh90]. It refers to *a relation between an agent and an action.* The agent has decided to do something, the agent is determined to execute a certain action (at the scheduled time), the goal (intention) is a persistent one.

A "social commitment" is not an individual Commitment shared by several agents. **Social Commitment** (S-Commitment) is a relational concept: *the Commitment of one agent to another* [Sin91] [Cas96]. It expresses a relation between at least two agents. More precisely, S-Commitment is a 4-argument relation: (S-COMM x y a z); where x is the committed agent; a is the action x is committed to do; y is the other agent whom x is committed to; z is a third agent before whom x is committed. Let us neglect the third agent (z), i. e. *the witness.* Here, I will focus on the relation between x and y.

We should also distinguish S-Commitment from **Collective Commitment** (C-Commitment) or Group Commitment. The latter is just *an Internal Commitment of a Collective agent* or Group to a collective action. In other terms, a set of agents is Internally Committed to a certain intention and (usually) there is mutual knowledge about that. It remains to be clarified which are the relationships between S-Commitment and C-Commitment.

x's I-Commitment on a is neither a necessary nor a sufficient condition for his S-Commitment on a. Just y's belief that x is I-Committed to a, is a necessary condition of x's S-Commitment. Anyway, postulating that our agents are always "honest" like in other models of Commitment, we may remark that *the S-Commitment of x to y to a implies an I-Commitment of x to a.*

Relationships between Social and Collective Commitment

In strictly "cooperative" groups (which in our sense are based on a Common Goal and Mutual Dependence), in team work, an S-Commitment of everybody to everybody arises: each one not only intends but *has to* do his own job. Given that the members form the group, we may say that *each member is S-Committed to the group* to do his share [Sin91].

So, the C-Commitment (defined as the I-Commitment of a collective agent) will imply (at least in the case of a fully cooperative group):
  - the S-Commitment of each member to the group: x is S-Committed not simply to another member y, *but* to the all set/group X he belongs to;
  - the S-Commitment of each member to each other; then also many Reciprocal Commitments;
  - the I-Commitment of each member to do his action.
Joint Intentions, team work, coalitions (and what I call C-Commitments) imply S-Commitments among the members and between the member and her group, and S-Commitment (usually) implies I-Commitment. This is the bridge-theory connecting joint activity and individual mind. Although, the S-Commitment is not completely "reducible" to the I-Commitment, because it is an intrinsically relational /social notion (among agents), and contains much more than the I-Commitment of the involved agents, the social level construct is clearly linked to the individual level construct. Notice also that the I-Commitment is a cross-layer notion.

5   Layered Ontologies and Concepts

Clearly we need the notions of communication, coordination, cooperation, social action, of conflict, deception, agenthood, etc. both for cognitive, intentional agents and for sub-cognitive, merely reactive agents.

5.1   Agent

The proliferating notion of "agent" - so crucial that it is transforming the whole AI and the notion of computing itself - waits for some "systematisation". However, my claim is that what is needed is *not* a unique definition, which will be either too generic or too specific to computer science and technical. I think that what is needed is a system and, more precisely, a hierarchy of well-orchestrated definitions.
The notion of agent (both the one we need, and the natural concept) is a layered one: there are broader notions (ex. any causal factor) and narrow notions (ex. intentional actors), but these notions are in a definable conceptual relation that can/should be made explicit. The problem is that there is not just one simple conceptual hierarchy. This is a heterarchical notion: a hierarchy with several independent roots. For ex. the dimension "delegated"/"non delegated" is very important for the notion of "agent" in economics and in some AI domain. Another very important hierarchy to be clarified is that relative to "software" agents: a piece of software; an 'object'; an agent: what the relationships? Also other notions from system and control theory seem important.

What is an agent? Elements for a definition
The weakest and more basic notion of "agent" is that of a causal entity able to produce some change, some effect on a world, in an environment. This is the very poor meaning of physical forces as agents, or of "atmospheric agents" and so on. This *capability to cause effects* holds (as a component of the notion of "action") in each of the more specific notions of agent. An agent can cause, can do something. More than this, when we conceive some causal force as "agent" we do not focus on the previous

possible causal chain; we focus on this cause as an initial *causa prima*, as independent if not autonomous. This notion of agent (relevant for example in semantics) is not sufficient either in AI or in Psychology. The notion starts to be interesting for Cognitive Science when the effects are no longer accidental or simply "efficient": when the causal behaviour is finalistic (teleonomic) and becomes a true "action". This is the case of Teleonomic or Goal-oriented agents.

Mere Goal-oriented Vs Goal-governed systems
There are two basic types of system with finalistic (teleonomic) behaviour: intentional (more generally: goal-governed) and functional (mere goal-oriented).
Goal oriented systems [McF83] are systems whose behaviour is finalistic, aimed at realising a given result which is not necessarily understood or explicitly represented (as an anticipatory representation) within the system itself. A typical sub-type of these systems are in fact *Mere-Goal-oriented systems* which are rule-based (production rules or classifiers) or reflex-, or releaser-, or association-based: they react to a given circumstance with a given behaviour (and they can possibly learn and adapt).
Goal-governed systems are anticipatory systems. I call goal-governed a system or behaviour that is controlled and regulated purposively by an internally represented goal, a "set-point" or "goal-state" (cf. [Ros68]). The simplest example is a boiler-thermostat system. A "goal-governed" system responds to external functions through its internal goals.
This is the basic notion of Agent of interest to AI: exploitable *goal-oriented processes*. This substantially converges with Franklin & Graesser' definition [Fra96]. It is crucial to stress that mere goal-oriented systems and goal-governed systems are mutually exclusive classes, but that goal-governed systems can be also goal-oriented. Goal-government can be incomplete. It implements and improves goal-orientation, but it does not (completely) replace the latter: it does not make the latter redundant (contrary to Elster's claim [Els82] that intentional behaviour excludes functional behaviour - see later). So we have causal entities, teleonomic causal entities, and, among the latter, mere goal-oriented and goal-governed agents including also intentional agents. However, this is only one hierarchy. Another very important one is that based on delegation: AI agents in fact frequently need to work autonomously but 'on behalf of' the user or of some other agent. So one should distinguish between non-delegated and delegated agents, and between different kind of delegation (see later) and different kinds of autonomy.
I propose to call *Agenthood* the capability to act; and to call *Agency* the capability to act under "delegation" of another agent. In this definition Agency presupposes Agenthood: only an agent in the full sense (goal-oriented) can be an agency, and necessarily it is delegated by (acts on behalf of) another agent.

5.2   Social Action

A SA is *an action that deals with another entity as an agent, i.e. as an active, autonomous, goal-oriented entity*
For *cognitive agents*, a SA is *an action that deals with another cognitive agent considered as a cognitive agent, whose behavior is regulated by beliefs and goals.*

[Cas97a]. In SA the agent takes an Intentional Stance towards the other agents: i.e. a representation of the other agent's mind in intentional terms [Den81].

An action related to another agent is not necessarily social. Also the opposite is true. A merely practical action, not directly involving other agents, may be or become social. The practical action of closing a door is social when we close the door to avoid that some agent enters or looks inside our room; the *same* action performed to block the wind (or rain or noise) is not social. *Not behavioral differences but goals distinguish social action from non social action.*

We may call "weak SA" the one based just on *social beliefs*: beliefs about other agents' minds or actions; and "strong SA" that which is also directed by *social goals*.

It is common agreement in AI that "social agents" are equivalent to "communicating agents". According to many students communication is a necessary feature of agenthood (in the AI sense) [Woo95] [Gen94] [Rus95]. Moreover, the advantages of communication are systematically mixed up with the advantages of coordination or of cooperation. Communication is an instrument for SA (of any kind: either cooperative or aggressive). Communication is also a kind of SA aimed at giving beliefs to the addressee. This is a true and typical Social Goal, since the intended result concerns a mental state of another agent. However, *communication is not a necessary component of social action and interaction.* To kill somebody is for sure a SA (although not very sociable!) but it neither is nor requires communication. Also pro-social actions do not necessarily require communication. In sum, neither agency nor sociality are grounded on communication, although, of course, communication is very important for social interaction.

Strong social action is characterised by social goals. A social goal is defined as a goal that is *directed toward* another agent, i.e. whose intended results include another agent as a cognitive agent: *a social goal is a goal about other agents' minds or actions* . Examples of typical social goals (strong SAs) are: changing the other's mind, communication, hostility (blocking the other's goal), strong delegation, adoption (favouring the other's goal). In this case, we not only have *Beliefs* about others' Beliefs or Goals (weak social action) but also *Goals* about the mind of the other: A wants that B believes something; A wants that B wants something. We cannot understand social interaction or collaboration or organisations without these *social goals*. Personal intentions of doing one's own tasks, plus beliefs (although mutual) about others' intentions (as used in the great majority of current AI models of collaboration) are not enough.

Action and social action are possible, of course, also at the reactive level, among sub-cognitive agents (like bees). A definition of SA, communication, adoption, aggression, etc. is possible also for non-cognitive agents. However, also at this level those notions must be goal-based. Thus, a theory of merely goal-oriented (not "goal-directed") systems and of *implicit goals* is needed. However, there are levels of sociality that cannot be attained reactively. Also at a sub-cognitive level, a SA is an action that deals with another entity *as an agent,* i.e. as an active, autonomous, goal-oriented entity. However the problem here is that there is not an agent's mind for considering the other agent 'as an agent'. Subjectively the first agent acts as towards a physical entity: it just reacts to stimuli or conditions. So, in which sense its action is social? in which sense it treats the other entity 'as an agent'? We cannot consider social any behaviour that simply *accidentally* affects another agent; teleonomy is needed: either the behaviour is intended (and this is not the case) or it is goal-oriented, functional to affecting another agent.

5.3   Communication

The same reasoning applies to communication (which in fact is a social action). As I said a definition of communication is possible also for non-cognitive agents. However, also at this level, that notion must be goal-based: either intentional or functional. We cannot consider as communication any information/sign arriving from A to B, unless it is aimed at informing B. For example, B can observe A - A not being aware of this - and can understand a lot of things about A, but A is not communicating with B or informing B about all those things.

6   Constructing a Bridge

It is necessary to discuss how we may advance towards a bridge between cognition and emergence, intention and function, autonomous goal-governed agents and goal-oriented social systems.

6.1   Emergent forms of cooperation among cognitive agents

Social cooperation does not necessarily need agents' understanding, agreement, contracts, rational planning, collective decisions [Mac,98]. There are forms of cooperation that are deliberated and contractual (like a company, a team, an organised strike), and other forms of cooperation that are emergent: non contractual and even unaware. Modelling those forms is very important. Our claim [Cas97b] [Cas92] is that it is important to model them not just among sub-cognitive (using learning or selection of simple rules) [Ste90] [Mat92], but also among cognitive and planning agents whose behaviour is regulated by anticipatory representations. In fact, also *these agents cannot understand, predict, and dominate all the global and compound effects of their actions at the collective level.* Some of these effects are self-reinforcing and self-organising.

•   For instance in the case of *hetero-directed or orchestrated cooperation*, only a boss' mind conceives and knows the plan, while the involved agents may even ignore the existence of a global plan and of the other participants.

•   This is also the case of *functional self-organising forms of social cooperation* (like the technical division of labour) where no mind at all conceives or knows the emerging plan and organisation. Each agent is simply interested in its own local goal, interest and plan; nobody directly takes care of the task distribution, of the global plan and equilibrium.

6.2   Social Functions and Cognition

Both objective structures and unplanned self-organising complex forms of social order and social functions emerge from the interactions of agents in a common world and from their individual mental states; both these structures and self-organising systems feedback into the agents behaviours through the agents' individual minds either by the agent's understanding the collective situation (cognitive emergence) or by constraining and conditioning agent goals and decisions. The aim of this section is to analyse the crucial relationship between social "functions" and cognition: cognitive agents' mental representations. I claim, in fact, that *without a theory of emerging functions among cognitive agents, social behavior cannot be fully explained* .

In my view, current approaches to cognitive agent architectures (in terms of Beliefs and Goals) allow for a solution of this problem; though perhaps we need some more treatment of emotions. One can explain quite precisely this relation between cognition and the emergence and reproduction of social functions. In particular, functions install and maintain themselves parasitarely to cognition. For a Social Norm to work as a social norm and be fully effective, agents should understand it as a social norm. However the effectiveness of a social function is independent of the agents' understanding of this function of their behavior. In fact:

a) the function can rise and maintain itself without the awareness of the agents;

b) if the agents intend the results of their behavior, these would no longer be "social functions" of their behavior but just "intentions" [Els82].

I accept Elster's crucial objection to classical functional notions, but I think that it is possible to reconcile intentional and functional behavior. With an evolutionary view of "functions" it is possible to argue that *intentional actions can acquire unintended functional effects*.

How to build unaware functions and cooperation on top of intentional actions and intended effects? How is it possible that positive results -thanks to their advantages- reinforce and reproduce the actions of intentional agents, and self-organise and reproduce themselves, without becoming simple intentions? [Els82]. This is the real theoretical challenge for reconciling emergence and cognition, intentional behavior and social functions, planning agents and unaware cooperation. We need more complex forms of reinforcement learning, not just based on classifiers, rules, associations, etc. but *operating on the cognitive representations governing the action, i.e. on beliefs and goals*.

Functions are just effects of the behavior of the agents, that go beyond the intended effects and succeed in reproducing themselves because they reinforce the beliefs and the goals of the agents that caused that behavior. Then:

- First, behavior is goal-directed and reasons-based; i.e. is intentional action. The agent bases its goal-adoption, its preferences and decisions, and its actions on its Beliefs (this is the definition of "cognitive agents").
- Second, there is some effect of those actions that is unknown or at least unintended by the agent.
- Third, there is circular causality: a feedback loop from those unintended effects to increment, reinforce the Beliefs or the Goals that generated those actions.

- Fourth, this "reinforcement" increases the probability that in similar circumstances (activating the same Beliefs and Goals) the agent will produce the same behavior, then "reproducing" those effects.
- Fifth, at this point such effects are no longer "accidental" or unimportant: although remaining unintended they are teleonomically produced [Con95, ch.8]: *that behavior exists (also) thanks to its unintended effects; it was selected by these effects, and it is functional to them.* Even if these effects could be negative for the goals or the interest of (some of) the involved agents, their behavior is "goal-oriented" to these effects.

7   Towards Social Computing?

I will conclude with the importance of the new "social" computational paradigm [Gas98], and with some doubts and questions about the 'invisible hand' and the 'emergent character' of computation in Agent Based Computing.

References

[Agr89] Agre, P.E. 1989. *The dynamic structure of everyday life.* Phd Thesis, Department of Electrical Engineering and Computer Science, Boston: MIT.

[Bic90] Bicchieri, C. 1990. Norms of cooperation. *Ethics,* 100, 838-861.

[Bob91] D. Bobrow. "Dimensions of Interaction", *AI Magazine,* 12, 3,64-80,1991.

[Bro89] Brooks, R.A. 1989. *A robot that walks. Emergent behaviours from a carefully evolved network.* Tech. Rep. Artificial Intelligence Laboratory. Cambridge, Mass.: MIT.

[Cas92] C. Castelfranchi., M. Miceli, A. Cesta. Dependence Relations among Autonomous Agents, in Y.Demazeau, E.Werner (Eds), Decentralized A.I.-3, Elsevier (North Holland), 1992.

[Cas95] C, Castelfranchi, Guaranties for Autonomy in Cognitive Agent Architecture. In [Woo95]

[Cas96] Castelfranchi, C., Commitment: from intentions to groups and organizations. In Proceedings of ICMAS'96, S.Francisco, June 1996, AAAI-MIT Press.

[Cas97a] C. Castelfranchi. Individual Social Action. In G. Holmstrom-Hintikka and R. Tuomela (eds.) Contemporary Theory of action. vol. II, 163-92. Dordrecht, Kluwer, 1997.

[Cas97b] Castelfranchi, C. Challenges for agent-based social simulation. The theory of social functions. IP-CNR, TR. Sett.97; invited talk at SimSoc'97, Cortona, Italy

[Cas98a] Castelfranchi, C., Modelling Social Action for AI Agents. Artificial Intelligence, (forthcoming).

[Cas98b] Castelfranchi, C., To believe and to feel: To embody cognition and to cognitize body The case for "needs". In 1998 AAAI Fall Symposium "Emotional and Intelligent: The Tangled Knot of Cognition."

[Coh90] P. R. Cohen and H. J. Levesque. Rational interaction as the basis for communication. in P R Cohen, J Morgan and M E Pollack (Eds): Intentions in Communication. The MIT Press, 1990.

[Con95] Conte,R. and Castelfranchi, C. Cognitive and Social Action, UCL Press, London, 1995.

[Con96] R. Conte and C. Castelfranchi. Mind is not enough. Precognitive bases of social interaction. In N. Gilbert (Ed.) Proceedings of the 1992 Symposium on Simulating Societies. London, University College of London Press, 1996.

[Den81] Dennet, Daniel C. Brainstorms. Harvest Press, N.Y 1981.

[Els82] J. Elster. Marxism, functionalism and game-theory: the case for methodological individualism. Theory and Society 11, 453-81.

[Fra96] S. Franklin and A. Graesser. "Is it an Agent, or just a Program?: A Taxonomy for Autonomous Agent", Proceedings of the 3rd International Workshop on Agent Theories, Architectures, and Languages, Springer-Verlag, 1996, 21-35.

[Gas98] L. Gasser. Invited talk at Autonomous Agents'98, Minneapoli May 1998.

[Gen94] M.R. Genesereth and S.P. Ketchpel, S.P. 1994. Software Agents. TR, CSD, Stanford University.

[Gro95] B. Grosz, Collaborative Systems. AI Magazine, summer 1996, 67-85.

[Hay67] F.A. Hayek, The result of human action but not of human design. In Studies in Philosophy, Politics and Economics, Routledge & Kegan, London, 1967.

[Kur97] S. Kurihara, S. Aoyagi, R. Onai. Adaptive Selection or Reactive/Deliberate Planning for the Dynamic Environment. In M. Boman and W. Van de Welde (Eds.) Multi-Agent Rationality - Proceedings of MAAMAW'97 , Berlin, Springer, LNAI 1237,1997, p.112-27

[Lev90] Levesque H.J., P.R. Cohen, Nunes J.H.T. On acting together. In Proceedings of the 8th National Conference on Artificial Intelligence, 94-100. Kaufmann. 1990

[Mac98] Macy, R. , In JASSS, I, 1, 1998.

[Mat92] M. Mataric. Designing Emergent Behaviors: From Local Interactions to Collective Intelligence. In Simulation of Adaptive Behavior 2. MIT Press. Cambridge, 1992.

[McD87] McDermott D. 1987. A critique of pure reason. In Computational Intelligence, 3, 151-60.

[McF83] McFarland, D. 1983. Intentions as goals, open commentary to Dennet, D.C. Intentional systems in cognitive ethology: the "Panglossian paradigm" defended. The Behavioural and Brain Sciences, 6, 343-90.

[Ros68] Rosenblueth, A. & N. Wiener 1968. Purposeful and Non-Purposeful Behavior. In Modern systems research for the behavioral scientist, Buckley, W. (ed.). Chicago: Aldine.

[Rus95] S.J. Russell and P. Norvig Artificial Intelligence: A Modern Approach. Prentice Hall, 1995.

[Sic95] J Sichman, Du Raisonnement Social Chez les Agents. PhD Thesis, Polytechnique - LAFORIA, Grenoble

[Sin91] M.P. Singh, Social and Psychological Commitments in Multiagent Systems. In Preproceedings of "Knowledge and Action at Social & Organizational Levels", Fall Symposium Series, 1991. Menlo Park, Calif.: AAAI, Inc.

[Ste90] L. Steels. Cooperation between distributed agents through self-organization. In Y. Demazeau & J.P. Mueller (eds.) Decentralized AI North-Holland, Elsevier, 1990.

[Suc87] Suchman, L.A. 1987. Plans and situated actions: The problem of human-machine communication. Cambridge: Cambridge University Press.

[Tha96] Thagard, P. 1996 Mind. Introduction to Cognitive Science. MIT Press.

[Tuo93] Tuomela, R. What is Cooperation. Erkenntnis, 38, 1993, 87-101.

[Tuo88] R. Tuomela and K. Miller. "We-Intentions", Philosophical Studies, 53, 1988, 115-37.

[Vir96] Virasoro, M.A. Intervista a cura di Franco Foresta Martin, SISSA, Trieste, 1996

[Wei97] Weisbuch G. 1997 Societies, cultures and fisheries from a modeling perspective. SimSoc'97, Cortona, Italy.

[Woo95a] M. Wooldridge and N. Jennings. Intelligent agents: Theory and practice. The Knowledge Engineering Review, 10(2): 115-52. 1995.

[Woo95b] Wooldridge M.J. and Jennings N.R. (Eds.) 1995 Intelligent Agents: Theories, Architectures, and Languages. LNAI 890, Springer-Verlag, Heidelberg, Germany.

The "Semantics" of Evolution: Trajectories and Trade-Offs in Design Space and Niche Space

Aaron Sloman

School of Computer Science, Univ. of Birmingham, Birmingham, B15 2TT, UK
A.Sloman@cs.bham.ac.uk
http://www.cs.bham.ac.uk/~axs/

Abstract. This paper attempts to characterise a unifying overview of the practice of software engineers, AI designers, developers of evolutionary forms of computation, designers of adaptive systems, etc. The topic overlaps with theoretical biology, developmental psychology and perhaps some aspects of social theory. Just as much of theoretical computer science follows the lead of engineering intuitions and tries to formalise them, there are also some important emerging high level cross disciplinary ideas about natural information processing architectures and evolutionary mechanisms and that can perhaps be unified and formalised in the future.

1 Introduction: Exploring Design Space

AI can be construed as the exploration of the space of possible designs for (more or less) intelligent agents, whether natural or artificial [4,13]. Designs are not all static. Some systems change aspects of their own design: they modify themselves, through learning, adaptation, or architectural development, e.g. from embryo to infant, and from infant to adult. Brain damage or disease can also produce design changes with deleterious consequences.

All these changes move a machine or organism from one region of design space to another. Possible routes through design space can be thought of as *trajectories* in the space.

Some regions of design space are not linked by possible trajectories for individual development. An acorn can transform itself into an oak tree, and by controlling its environment you can slightly modify what sort of oak tree (e.g. how big). But no matter how you try to train or coax it by modifying the environment, it will never grow into a giraffe. The acorn (a) lacks information needed to grow into a giraffe, (b) lacks the architecture to absorb and use such information, and (c) lacks the architecture required to modify itself into an architecture that can absorb the information.

Trajectories that are possible for an individual which adapts or changes itself will be called *i-trajectories*. Different sorts of i-trajectories could be distinguished according to the sorts of mechanisms of change, e.g. innately determined development, reinforcement learning, facilitation by repetition, and various kinds of self-organising processes partly driven by the environment.

Helder Coelho (Ed.): IBERAMIA'98, LNAI 1484, pp. 27–39, 1998.

Trajectories which are not possible for an individual machine or organism but are possible across generations of individuals subject to a particular type of evolutionary development will be called *e-trajectories*. Examples include development of humans and other animals from much simpler organisms and modifications of software structures by genetic algorithms. Conjectured e-trajectories leading to human minds are discussed in [5] and [18].

Whether two designs are linked by an e-trajectory or not will depend on the type of evolutionary mechanism available for manipulating genetic structures and the type of ontogenetic mechanism available for producing individuals (phenotypes) from genotypes. In biological organisms the two are connected: the ontogenetic mechanism can also evolve. Lamarckian inheritance would allow i-trajectories to form parts of e-trajectories.

There are also some changes to individuals that are possible only through external intervention by another agent, e.g. performing repairs or extensions, or debugging software. Such changes follow *r-trajectories* (repair-trajectories).

Viewing a species as a type of individual, e-trajectories for individuals form i-trajectories for a species, or a larger encompassing system, such as an ecology. Researchers in AI, Alife and evolutionary computation all contribute to the study of such trajectories. This study is in its infancy.

2 "Semantics of Evolution"

In computer science "semantics of computation" refers to abstract, mathematical, properties of programming languages, data structures and the processes which can occur in virtual machines of various sorts. Likewise a study of the most general features of evolutionary trajectories in design space addresses a topic that could be called "semantics of evolution" (though both differ from the more common use of the word "semantics" in linguistics).

Milner [9] noted that theoretical computer science follows the lead of engineering intuitions and tries to formalise them. Since the intuitions are often very subtle and complex the process of formalisation can lag far behind. Likewise attempts to study and formalise the space of possible designs and the various trajectories in design space will lag behind intuitive understanding gained from empirical research in biology, psychology, and computational explorations. This paper attempts to identify some of the phenomena to be formalised.

Many have attempted to formalise features of evolution, individual learning, development etc. Kauffman [7] describes mathematical laws which constrain biological mechanisms and processes in surprising ways. The ideas discussed below deal with phenomena which at present are too ill defined for mathematical formulation and computational modelling.

3 Generalising Fitness Landscapes

Evolutionary trajectories are often represented in a "fitness landscape" where a fitness value is associated with various locations in design space. If a class of designs can be specified by two parameters (e.g. length and stiffness of a spring), then there is a 2-D space of designs, and adding a measure of fitness of the spring for a particular purpose, produces a 3-D fitness landscape. Typically, design spaces are far more complex than this, and cannot be specified by a fixed number of parameters, e.g. designs for Prolog compilers vary in structure and complexity. Moreover, many designs have no single fitness measure: Prolog compilers vary according to their portability, the speed of compilation, the speed of compiled code, the size of compiled code, the kinds of error handling they support, etc.

A set of constraints and requirements for a design can be called a "niche". Fitness of designs for organisms and artefacts may be compared in relation to a niche. Requirements for a compiler can vary just as the requirements for a plant or insect can. So there is a space of possible niches: "niche space" ([13,15,17]).

Designs and niches are both abstract and can have different concrete instantiations. Designs don't presuppose a designer and requirements (niches) don't presuppose a requirer. There are different ways actual requirements can be generated: e.g. engineering goals vs biological needs and pressures.

Two insects in the same physical location can be in different niches, so niches are not determined by physical location. Neither are they simply in the eye of a beholder: niche-pressure can influence movement of individuals or a species in design space. This can happen in different ways. If the individual has adaptive capabilities it may move along an i-trajectory so as to fit a niche better. Alternatively the pressure may cause a gene pool, or a subset of a gene pool, to move along an e-trajectory.

There are many different sorts of causal relations: within an architecture, between architectures, between architectures and niches, between niches. Niches can interact with one another by producing pressure for changes in designs, which in turn can change niches, as in co-evolution of organisms. So there are trajectories in niche space as well as design space.

Where independent changes in different dimensions are possible, a complex niche can cause parallel design changes, e.g. making an organism both physically stronger and better able to recognize complex physical structures. Problems arise when the changes are not independent: e.g. increasing agility may conflict with increasing strength. Where there are pressures for incompatible changes, which one actually occurs may depend on subtle features of the total context, and two identical individuals may be pushed along divergent trajectories because of slight differences in context.

Feedback loops occur where changes in one individual or group alter the niche, and therefore the causal influences on another individual or group. Such feedback can lead to continual change, to oscillations, or to catastrophes.

4   Simple and Complex Fitness Relations

In the simplest case a design either fits or does not fit a niche. More generally the relation is more complex, and different designs may fit the same niche to

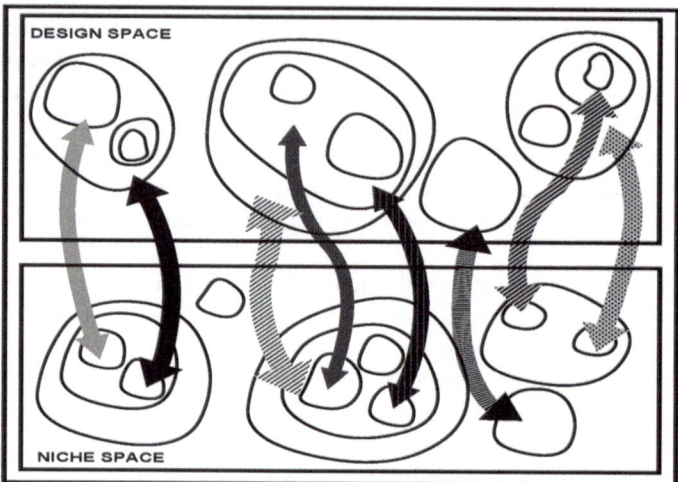

Fig. 1. Design space and niche space: Relations between designs and niches are complex and varied "fitness" descriptions, not numeric values. Trajectories are not shown.

different degrees. Besides being simply better or worse, designs may fit a niche in different ways – e.g. different combinations of speed, robustness, flexibility, etc. The different styles of arrows in Figure 1 are intended to indicate this.

If the fitness of designs solving a particular problem vary only in degree, then the search for a solution can be thought of as the search for a location in design space where the fitness value is highest. This is the familiar notion of a fitness landscape. A learning mechanism or an evolutionary process might pursue a trajectory in which the design is guided towards a fitness peak in the landscape. High peaks can be very hard to find.

We can now generalise this idea in a number of ways.

(a) Instead of a fixed niche determining the evaluation we consider a space of niches as well as the space of designs. A design can then be assessed in relation to many possible niches, so that it does not have only one fitness value. Kauffman [7, pp 221ff] allows for this by mentioning that the fitness values for particular designs, and therefore the landscape, can change if objects in the environment change. If those objects also have fitness landscapes then there are *coupled* fitness landscapes, each causing changes in the other. His notion of a fitness landscape changing corresponds to our notion of a design having different fitness descriptions in relation to different regions of niche space.

(b) Instead of each niche determining an evaluation function which yields a numeric fitness, or even a total ordering of designs, it may determine a collection of incommensurable criteria for assessing designs (like speed and error handling in a compiler, or protection from predators and from cold in a house). In general the comparison of a niche and a design will yield not a number but a description of the match ([8,11]). In simple cases this could be a vector of values. Sometimes there is a partial ordering of the descriptions, and sometimes not even that, because there is no way to combine the different dimensions of comparison. Design A might be better than B in one respect, B better than C in another and C better than A in a third. (Compare consumer reports.) Engineers are very familiar with such tradeoffs between designs.

(c) Different designs and different niches can vary in complexity. So also do the descriptions of fitness. Assessment of a spelling checker will be much simpler than assessment of an operating system.

(d) If fitness values are non-scalar, trajectories no longer lead uphill, downhill or horizontally. A path can lead to improvements in some respects and degradation in others. "Selection" becomes a problematic notion.

(e) Having separate fitness values allows different sorts of selection to occur in sequence, simplifying the evolutionary design task by decomposing it, as an engineer might. When the changes required to improve different features are not independent there may be no useful decomposition. The "divide and conquer" approach is not always applicable: sometimes a creative new design is needed.

(f) If identical individuals inhabit slightly different niches (e.g. because of different social roles or different neighbours) reproductive success might be favoured by different traits. E.g. in some farming communities physical strength may be more important than intelligence, whereas in a nearby industrialised region intelligence is more useful for acquiring resources to raise a family. Thus different e-trajectories can be explored in parallel within a population exposed to different niches. Functional differentiation within a social system can accelerate this. Since motivation and performance are linked we can expect diversity of tastes as well as abilities. This may explain why we have individuals both able and willing to be concert pianists, steeplejacks, brain surgeons, etc.

(g) Since designs have complex structures, a niche can change simply because of a change *within* a design, without anything changing in the environment. E.g. a change which increases running speed may alter energy requirements. So some aspects of a design determine requirements for other aspects. What you need is partly determined by what you've got. This can generate positive feedback loops driving designs along e-trajectories without any environmental changes.

(h) The effects of niche pressures change in character when organisms develop cognitive abilities which enable them to recognize their own and others' needs and abilities. If they can assess in advance the relevance of different physical characteristics or behaviours to filling those needs, then improvements in a useful trait may be selected both directly through differing abilities to provide for offspring, and indirectly through recognition of the trait by potential mates. Eugenic social policies are similar. Cognitive abilities can also influence co-evolution: if predators can tell in advance which prey are easier to catch, they can select victims in a herd. Thus recognition of signs of weakness can accelerate the elimination of weaker traits. So cognitive processes in organisms can make evolution and co-evolution more like a process of design.

From the standpoint described here, genetic algorithms which use a scalar "fitness function" are simply a special case. Moreover, in artificial evolution the designer often adds a separate selection function which uses the output of the fitness function. In natural evolution (and some Alife scenarios) selection and fitness are related in more subtle and varied ways.

We have seen that when organisms have cognitive abilities this can make evolution more like a design process. Perhaps we should think of the biosphere as a sort of super-organism struggling to develop itself and through the intelligence of its products becoming more like a designer.

5   Dynamics, Discontinuities and Inhomogeneities

Since niches and designs interact dynamically, we can regard them as parts of virtual machines in the biosphere consisting of a host of control mechanisms, feedback loops, and information structures (including gene pools). All of these are ultimately implemented in, and supervenient on physics and chemistry. But they and their causal interactions may be as real as poverty and crime and their interactions.

The biosphere is a very complex abstract dynamical system, composed of many smaller dynamical systems. Some of them are evanescent (e.g. tornados), some enduring but changing over diverse time scales (e.g. fruit flies, oak trees, ecosystems). Many subsystems impose constraints and requirements to be met or overcome by other subsystems: one component's design is part of another component's niche. Through a host of pressures, forces and more abstract causal relations, including transfer of factual information and control information, systems at various levels are constantly adjusting themselves or being adjusted or modified. Some of the changes may be highly creative, including evolution of new forms of evolution, and new mechanisms for copying and later modifying modules to extend a design.

These ideas may seem wild, but they are natural extensions of ideas already accepted by many scientists and engineers, e.g. [7,2].

Discontinuous e-trajectories. Both design space and niche space have very complex topologies, including many discontinuities, some small (e.g. adding a bit more memory to a design, adding a new step in a plan) some large (adding a new architectural layer, or a new formalism). Understanding natural intelligence may require understanding some major discontinuities in the evolutionary history of the architectures and mechanisms involved. This in turn may help us with the design of intelligent artefacts.

I suspect discontinuities in design space occur somewhere between systems that are able merely to perform certain tasks, and others which can use generalisations they have learnt about the environment to create new plans, i.e. between reactive and deliberative architectures. Discontinuities in e-trajectories can occur when an old mechanism is copied then modified: e.g. a mechanism which originally associates sensory patterns with appropriate responses could be copied then used to associate sensory patterns with predicted sensory patterns or with a set of available responses.

Discontinuities might also be involved in the evolution of the "reflective" abilities described below: not only being able to do X but having and being able to use information on how X was done, or why X was done, or why one method of doing X was used rather than another. (Compare [17,20].) What sorts of niche pressures in nature might favour such e-trajectories is an interesting biological question.

Design space and niche space are "layered": regions within them are describable at different levels of abstraction and for each such region different "specialisations" exist. Some specialisations of designs are called implementations. The philosopher's notion of "supervenience" and the engineer's notion of "implementation" (or realisation) seem to be closely linked, if not identical.

Both are inhomogeneous spaces: local topology varies with location in the space, since the minimal changes possible at various locations in the same space can be very different in type and number. Consider designs of different complexity: there are typically more ways and more complex ways, of altering a complex design than a simple design. So they have neighbourhoods of different structures. By contrast, in most multi-dimensional spaces considered by scientists and engineers (e.g. phase spaces), each point has the same number of dimensions, i.e. the same number and the same types of changes are possible at all points (unless limited by equations of motion).

Discontinuous i-trajectories. A system which develops, learns or adapts changes its design. I-trajectories, like e-trajectories can be discontinuous (e.g. cell division) and link regions in inhomogeneous spaces. The most familiar examples are biological: e.g. a fertilised egg transforming itself into an embryo and then a neonate. In many animals, including humans, the information processing architecture seems to continue being transformed long after birth, and after the main physiological structures have been established: new forms of control of attention, learning, thinking, deliberating, develop after birth. Ontogeny may partly recapitulate phylogeny: but cultural influences may change this.

Humans follow a very complex trajectory in design space throughout their lives. A good educational system can be viewed as providing a trajectory through niche space which will induce a trajectory in design space in self-modifying brains. A culture provides a set of developmental trajectories.

In general, following a trajectory in design space also involves a trajectory in niche space: the niches for an unborn foetus, for a newborn infant, a schoolchild, a parent, a professor, etc. are all different. Moreover, an individual can instantiate more than one design, satisfying more than one niche: e.g. protector and provider, or parent and professor. To cope with development of multi-functional designs we can include *composite niches* in niche space, just as there are composite designs in design space.

6   Trajectories for Virtual Machines in Software Systems

A distinction between i-trajectories and e-trajectories can be made for evolvable software individuals inhabiting virtual machines. A word processor which adapts itself to different users may or may not be capable of turning itself into a compiler through a series of adaptations. As in nature, there may be e-trajectories linking software designs that are not linked by i-trajectories.

Whether an e-trajectory exists from one software design to another in an artificial evolutionary system depends on (a) whether there is a principled way of mapping the features of the designs onto genetic structures which can be used to recreate design instances via an instantiation (ontogenetic) function, and (b) whether the structures can be manipulated by the permitted operators (e.g. crossover and mutation), so as to traverse a trajectory in "gene space" which induces a trajectory in design space via the instantiation function. Whether some sort of evaluation function or niche pressure can cause the traversal to occur is a separate question [10]. E-trajectories can exist which our algorithms never find.

7   Evolution of Human-Like Architectures

We have argued in [14] and elsewhere (*contra* Dennett's "intentional stance") that many familiar mental concepts presuppose an information processing architecture. We conjecture that it involves several different sorts of coexisting, concurrently active, layers, including an evolutionarily old "reactive" layer involving dedicated highly parallel mechanisms each responding in a fixed way to its inputs. These may come from sensors or other internal components, and the outputs may go to motors or internal components, enabling loops. Some reactive systems have a fixed architecture except insofar as weights on links change through processes like reinforcement learning. Insects appear to have purely reactive architectures implementing a large collection of evolved behaviours. As suggested in [18], sophisticated reactive architectures may need a global "alarm" mechanism to detect urgent and important requirements to override relatively slow "normal" processes. This can interrupt and redirect other subsystems (e.g. freezing, fleeing, attacking, attending).

A hybrid architecture, as shown in Figure 2, could combine a reactive layer with a "deliberative" layer which includes the ability to create new temporary structures representing alternative possibilities for complex future actions, which it can then compare and evaluate, using further temporary structures describing similarities and differences. This plan-construction requires a long term memory associating actions in contexts with consequences. After creating and selecting a new structure the deliberative system may execute it as a plan, and then discard it. Alternatively it may be able to modify itself permanently by saving some or all of the structure for future re-use. In humans the reactive architecture seems also to be extendable by re-use of plans, e.g. learning car driving or language comprehension may create new reactions.

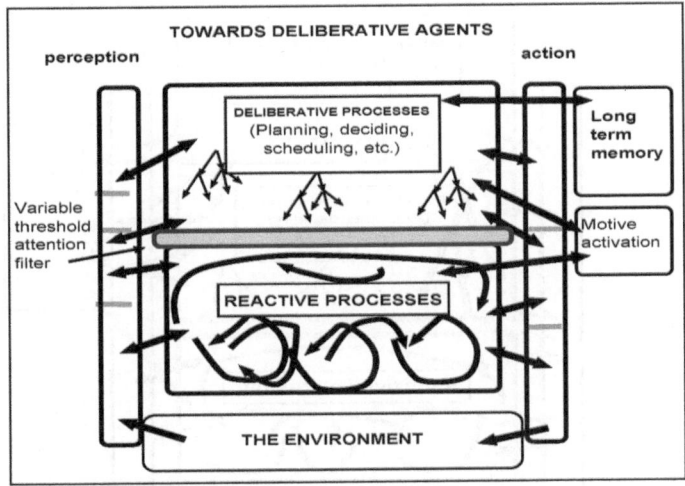

Fig. 2. A hybrid reactive and deliberative architecture. A global "alarm" mechanism could be added. See text.

As before, a global alarm mechanism may be needed for coping with dangers and opportunities requiring rapid reactions. In mammals this seems to involve the limbic system, and emotional processes [3,6].

A deliberative mechanism will (normally) be discrete, serial, and therefore relatively slow, whereas a reactive mechanism can be highly parallel and therefore very fast, and may include some continuous (analog) mechanisms, possibly using thresholds. Resource limits in deliberative mechanisms may generate a need for an attention filter of some kind, limiting the ability of reactive and alarm mechanisms to interrupt high level processing.

By analysing tradeoffs we may be able to understand how niche-pressures can lead to development of combined, concurrent deliberative and reactive architectures in organisms.

Everything that can be done by a hybrid architecture could in principle be done by a suitably complex reactive architecture e.g. a huge, pre-compiled lookup table matching every possible history of sensory inputs with a particular combination of outputs. However, pre-requisites for such an implementation may be prohibitive: much longer evolution, with more varied evolutionary environments, to pre-program all the reactive behaviours, and far more storage to contain them, etc. For certain agents the universe may be neither old and varied enough for such development nor big enough to store all the combinations required to match a deliberative equivalent with generative power. Perhaps evolution "discovered" this and therefore favoured deliberative extensions for some organisms.

A deliberative mechanism changes the niches for perceptual and motor mechanisms, requiring them to develop new layers of abstraction, as indicated in Figure 2. Likewise, development of new, higher level, abstractions in perceptual

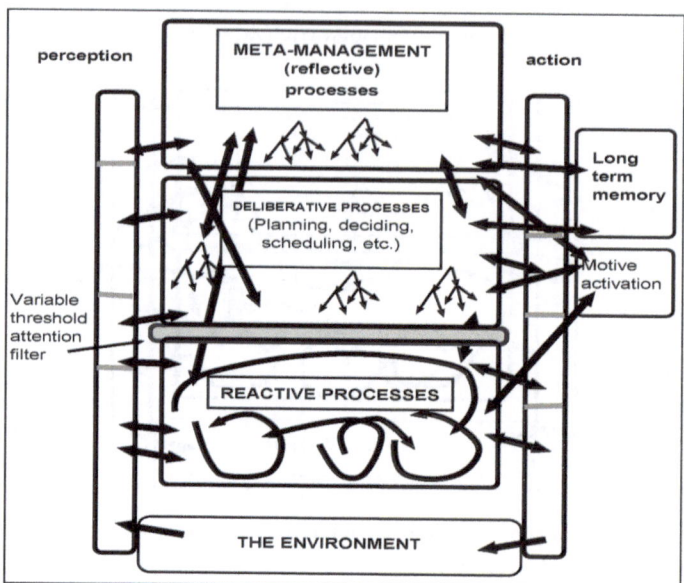

Fig. 3. A meta-management layer adds self monitoring, self-evaluation, etc. Three classes of emotions correspond to alarm mechanisms (not shown, to save clutter) acting on the three layers.

and motor systems may change the niches for more central mechanisms, e.g. providing new opportunities for learning and simplified planning.

Meta-management. Reflection on and retrospective evaluation of actions can often lead to future improvements. This is also true of *internal* actions. Thus besides abilities to perceive the environment and how external actions change it, there is a use also for internal self-monitoring, self-evaluation, self-modification (self-control) applied to *internal* states and processes. This could explain the evolution of a third architectural layer, as indicated in Figure 3.

Sensory "qualia" arise in self-monitoring mechanisms with access to intermediate sensory information structures not normally attended to. Different kinds of sensory qualia depend on different perceptual abstraction layers. Such "self-knowledge" is distinct from normal perception providing knowledge about the environment. "Meta-management" capabilities produce other sorts of qualia related to thinking processes, deliberation, desires, etc.

Robots with these capabilities might begin to wonder how their mental processes are related to their physical implementation, just as human philosophers do. Some of them, not fully understanding the notion of virtual machine functionality and the varieties of forms of supervenience, might even produce spurious but convincing arguments that they have conscious processes which cannot be explained by or fully implemented in physical processes. They may wonder whether humans are actually *zombies* with all the behavioural capabilities of conscious robots, but lacking their consciousness. I believe this solves the so-called "hard" problem of consciousness, see [1]. (Earlier work exploring these ideas can be found in [12,13,14,16,17,19])

Such agents (with a combination of reactive, deliberative and self-management sub-architectures) may combine to form social systems. Questions about trajectories in design space and niche space arise for social systems also. Human social systems develop information and rules which are transmitted to individuals, including rules that control meta-management (e.g. through guilt).

Accounting for all this needs a theory embracing computer science, theoretical biology, AI, psychology, neuroscience, anthropology, sociology, etc. Good software engineers and AI researchers are beginning to develop new intuitions about some of these things and it should be possible to find mathematical constructs that capture those intuitions, as computer science follows software engineering.

8   Further Work

We need to find more precise ways of describing architectures, designs, niches and their causal interactions, to improve on the high level concepts used only intuitively at present. This will involve both abstracting from domain specific details, so as to replace empirical concepts with mathematical concepts, and also enriching our understanding of the details of the processes, so that we can characterise and model the dynamics.

If the intuitive notions of niche, genotype etc. in biology can be made sufficiently precise to enable us to understand precisely the relationships between niches and designs for organisms, this may provide a better understanding of the dynamics and trajectories in biological evolution, including the evolution of evolvability.

This could lead to advances in comparative psychology. Understanding the precise variety of types of functional architectures in design space and the virtual machine processes they support, will enable us to describe and compare in far greater depth the capabilities of various animals. We'll also have a conceptual framework for saying precisely which subsets of human mental capabilities they have and which they lack. Likewise the discussion of mental capabilities of various sorts of machines could be put on a firmer scientific basis, with less scope for prejudice to determine which descriptions to use. E.g. instead of arguing about which animals, which machines, and which brain damaged humans have consciousness, we can determine precisely which sorts of consciousness they actually have.

We could also derive new ways of thinking about human variability and the causes and effects of mental illness, brain damage, senile dementia, etc. This could have profound practical implications.

Acknowledgements

The ideas reported here have been influenced by discussions with Margaret Boden, Chris Complin, Luc Beaudoin, Stan Franklin, William Langdon, Brian Logan, Riccardo Poli, Paul Marrow, Ian Millington, Rosalind Picard, Andy Pryke, Tim Read, Douglas Watt, Ian Wright, among many others.

References

1. David J Chalmers. *The Conscious Mind: In Search of a Fundamental Theory.* Oxford University Press, New York, Oxford, 1996. 37
2. Jack Cohen and Ian Stewart. *The collapse of chaos.* Penguin Books, New York, 1994. 32
3. Antonio R Damasio. *Descartes' Error, Emotion Reason and the Human Brain.* Grosset/Putnam Books, 1994. 35
4. Randall Davis. What are intelligence? and why? *AI Magazine,* 19(1):91–110, 1998. (Presidential Address to AAAI96). 27
5. D.C. Dennett. *Kinds of minds: towards an understanding of consciousness.* Weidenfeld and Nicholson, London, 1996. 28
6. Daniel Goleman. *Emotional Intelligence: Why It Can Matter More than IQ.* Bloomsbury Publishing, London, 1996. 35
7. Stuart Kauffman. *At home in the universe: The search for laws of complexity.* Penguin Books, London, 1995. 28, 30, 32
8. B. Logan and A. Sloman. Agent route planning in complex terrains. Technical Report CSRP-97-30, University of Birmingham, School of Computer Science, 1997. 31
9. Robin Milner. Semantic ideas in computing. In Ian Wand and Robin Milner, editors, *Computing Tomorrow: Future research directions in computer science,* pages 246–283. Cambridge University Press, 1996. 28
10. R. Poli and B. Logan. On the relations between search and evolutionary algorithms. Technical Report CSRP-96-07, School of Computer Science, The University of Birmingham, March 1996. 34
11. A. Sloman. How to derive "better" from "is". *American Phil. Quarterly,*, 6:43–52, Jan 1969. 31
12. A. Sloman. The mind as a control system. In C. Hookway and D. Peterson, editors, *Philosophy and the Cognitive Sciences,* pages 69–110. Cambridge University Press, 1993. 37
13. A. Sloman. Explorations in design space. In *Proceedings 11th European Conference on AI,* Amsterdam, 1994. 27, 29, 37
14. A. Sloman. Semantics in an intelligent control system. *Philosophical Transactions of the Royal Society: Physical Sciences and Engineering,* 349(1689):43–58, 1994. 34, 37
15. A. Sloman. Exploring design space and niche space. In *Proceedings 5th Scandinavian Conference on AI, Trondheim,* Amsterdam, 1995. IOS Press. 29
16. A. Sloman. Towards a general theory of representations. In D.M.Peterson, editor, *Forms of representation: an interdisciplinary theme for cognitive science.* Intellect Books, Exeter, U.K., 1996. ISBN: 1-871516-34-X. 37

17. A. Sloman. What sort of control system is able to have a personality. In Robert Trappl and Paolo Petta, editors, *Creating Personalities for Synthetic Actors: Towards Autonomous Personality Agents*, pages 166–208. Springer (Lecture notes in AI), Berlin, 1997. (Originally presented at Workshop on Designing personalities for synthetic actors, Vienna, June 1995). 29, 33, 37

18. A. Sloman. Damasio, descartes, alarms and meta-management. In *Proceedings International Conference on Systems, Man, and Cybernetics*. IEEE, 1998. 28, 34

19. A. Sloman. What sort of architecture is required for a human-like agent? In Michael Wooldridge and Anand Rao, editors, *Foundations of Rational Agency*. Kluwer Academic, 1998(forthcoming). 37

20. A. Sloman and B. S. Logan. Architectures and tools for human-like agents. In Frank Ritter and Richard M. Young, editors, *Proceedings of the 2nd European Conference on Cognitive Modelling*, pages 58–65, Nottingham, UK, 1998. Nottingham University Press. 33

Searching the World Wide Web: Challenges and Partial Solutions

Ricardo A. Baeza-Yates[*]

Depto. de Ciencias de la Computación, Universidad de Chile
Casilla 2777, Santiago, Chile
rbaeza@dcc.uchile.cl

Abstract. In this article we analyze the problem of searching the WWW, giving some insight and models to understand its complexity. Then we survey the two main current techniques used to search the WWW. Finally, we present recent results that can help to partially solve the challenges posed.

1 Introduction

The boom in the use of the World Wide Web (WWW) and its exponential growth are well known facts nowadays. Just the amount of textual data available is estimated in the order of one terabyte. In addition, other media, as images, audio and video, are also available. Thus, the WWW can be seen as a very large, unstructured but ubiquitous database. This triggers the need for efficient tools to manage, retrieve, and filter information from this database. This problem is also becoming important in large Intranets, where we want to extract or infer new information to support a decision process. This task is called data mining. We make the important distinction between data and information. The later is processed data that fulfills our needs.

In this article we outline the main problems of searching the WWW and some partial solutions to them. We focus on text, because although there are techniques to search in images and other non-textual data, they cannot be applied (yet) in large scale. We also emphasize syntactic search. That is, we search for WWW documents that have some words or patterns as content, which may (in most cases) or may not reflect the intrinsic semantics of the text. Although there are techniques to preprocess natural language and extract the text semantics, they are not 100% effective and they are also too costly for large amounts of data. In addition, in most cases they work with well structured text, a thesaurus and other contextual information.

We now mention the main problems posed by the WWW. We can divide them in two classes: problems of the data itself and problems of the user. The first are:

---

[*] This work was supported by CYTED Project VII.13: AMYRI.

Helder Coelho (Ed.): IBERAMIA'98, LNAI 1484, pp. 39–51, 1998.

- Distributed data: due to the intrinsic nature of the Web, data spans over many computers and platforms. These computers are interconnected with no predefined topology and with very different bandwiths.
- High percentage of volatile data: due to Internet dynamics, new computers and data can be added or removed easily. We also have relocation problems when domain or file names change.
- Large volume: the exponential growth of the WWW poses scaling issues that are difficult to cope with.
- Unstructured data: most people say that the WWW is a distributed hypertext. However, this is incorrect. Any hypertext has a conceptual model behind, which organizes and adds consistency to the data and the hyperlinks. That is hardly true in the WWW, even for individual documents.
- Quality of data: the WWW can be considered as a new publishing media. However, there is, in most cases, no editorial process. So, data can be even false, invalid (for example, because is too old), poorly written or, typically, with many errors from different sources (typos, grammatic mistakes, OCR errors, etc.)
- Heterogeneous data: in addition to having to deal with multiple media types and hence with multiple formats, when talking only about text, we also have different languages and, what is worse, different alphabets, some of them very large (for example, Chinese or Japanese Kanji).

Most of these problems are not solvable by just software improvements. For example, the cross-language or bad quality issues. Those will not change (and it should not in some cases!) or imply changing working habits. The second class of problems are faced by the user. Given the above, there are basically two problems: how to query and how to manage the answer of the query. Without taking in account the content semantics of a document, it is not easy to precisely specify a query, unless it is very simple. On the other hand, if we are able to pose the query, the answer might be a thousand of WWW pages. How do we handle a large answer? How do we rank the documents? (that is, how we select the documents that really are of interest for the user). In addition, a single document could be large. How do we browse efficiently in such documents?

So, the overall challenge is to, in spite of the intrinsic problems posed by WWW, circumvent all of them and answer the questions above, such that a good query could be sent to the search system, obtaining a manageable and relevant answer. The organization of this paper is as follows. We first describe and model the WWW. This is the first step to understand its complexity and being able to analyze possible solutions. Second, we outline the main ways used today to search the Web, giving some examples. Third, we outline several new results that should help in (partially) solving some of the problems outlined. Between them, we can mention compression techniques allowing random-access, use of available text structure, visual query languages and visual browsing. Some of the results presented are part of an Iberoamerican project funded by CYTED (AMYRI) which has as a goal the research and development of techniques and tools to search the WWW [13].

2   Measuring and Modeling the WWW

In an interesting article, already (sadly) outdated, Tim Bray [16] studied different statistical measures of the WWW. From simple questions as how many servers there are in the WWW to characterizing WWW pages. Currently, there are near one million servers, counting domain names starting with www. However, as not all WWW servers have the www prefix, the real number is higher. On the other hand, the number of independent institutions that have WWW information is much less, because many places have multiple servers. The exact percentage is unknown, but should be more than 30% which was the result back in 1995.

The most popular formats of WWW documents are HTML followed by GIF, TXT, PS, and JPG, in that order. How is a typical HTML page? First, most of them are not standard, meaning that they do not comply with all the HTML specifications.In addition, although HTML is an instance of SGML, HTML documents seldom start with a formal document type definition. Second, they are small, a few Kbs (around 6 to 10) and no images. The pages that do have images, use them for presentation issues as colored bullets and lines. The average page has between 5 and 15 references (links) and most of them are local (their own WWW server hierarchy). However, on average no external server points to it (commonly there are only are local links). In fact, in 1995, around 80% of the pages had less than 10 links to itself.

The top ten most referenced sites sites are Microsoft, Netscape, Yahoo!, and top US universities. In those cases we are talking about sites being pointed by at least ten thousand places. On the other hand, the site with most external links is Yahoo!. In some sense, Yahoo! is the glue of the WWW. Otherwise, we would have many isolated portions (this is the case with most personal WWW pages). If we assume that each HTML page has 6Kb and there are 100 pages per server, for one million servers we have at least 600Gb of text. The real volume should be larger.

Can we model the document characteristics of the whole WWW? We will make a first attempt. The first problem is the distribution of document sizes, which has been found to have self-similarity [19]. This can be modeled using a "heavy-tail" distribution. That is, the majority of documents are small, but there is non trivial number of large documents. This is intuitive for image or video files, but it is also true for HTML pages. The simplest "heavy-tail" distribution is called the Pareto distribution: the probability of a document of size x is $\alpha k^\alpha/(x^{1+\alpha})$ where k and α are parameters of the distribution. For text files, α is about 1.36, being smaller for images and other binary formats. In fact, for less than 50Kb, images are the typical files, from there to 300Kb we have audio files, and over that to several megabytes we have video files.

For text files, the second important thing is the number of distinct words or vocabulary of each document. We use the *Heaps' Law* [24]. This is a very precise law ruling the growth of the vocabulary in natural language texts. It states that the vocabulary of a text of n words is of size $V = Kn^\beta = O(n^\beta)$, where K and β depend on the particular text. K is normally between 10 and 100, and β is between 0 and 1 (not included). Some recent experiments [8,11] show that the most common values for β are between 0.4 and 0.6. Hence, the vocabulary of a text grows sublinearly with the text size, in a proportion close to its square root.

A first inaccuracy appears immediately. Supposedly, the set of different words of a language is fixed by a constant (e.g. the number of different English words is finite). However, the limit is so high that it is much more accurate to assume that the size of the vocabulary is $O(n^\beta)$ instead of $O(1)$, although the number should stabilize for huge enough texts. On the other hand, many authors argue that the number keeps growing anyway because of the errors

Another inconsistency is that, as the text grows, the number of different words will grow too, and therefore the number of letters to represent all the different words will be $O(\log(n^\beta)) = O(\log n)$. Therefore, longer and longer words should appear as the text grows. The average length could be kept constant if shorter words are common enough (which is the case). In practice, this effect is not noticeable and we can assume an invariable length, independent of the text size.

The third issue is how the different words are distributed inside each document. A much more inexact law is the *Zipf's Law* [38,23], which rules the distribution of the frequencies (that is, number of occurrences) of the words. The rule states that the frequency of the i-th most frequent word is $1/i^\theta$ times that of the most frequent word. This implies that in a text of n words with a vocabulary of V words, the i-th most frequent word appears $n/(i^\theta H_V(\theta))$ times, where

$$H_V(\theta) = \sum_{i=1}^{V} \frac{1}{i^\theta}$$

so that the sum of all frequencies is n. The value of θ depends on the text. In the most simple formulation, $\theta = 1$, and therefore $H_V(\theta) = O(\log n)$. However, this simplified version is very inexact, and the case $\theta > 1$ (more precisely, between 1.5 and 2.0) fits better the real data [8]. This case is very different, since the distribution is much more skewed, and $H_V(\theta) = O(1)$.

The fact that the distribution of words is very skewed (that is, there are a few hundreds of words which take up 50% of the text) suggest a concept which is frequently used in full-text retrieval: the *stopwords* [31]. A *stopword* is a word which does not carry meaning in natural language and therefore can be ignored (i.e. made not searchable), such as "a", "the", "by", etc. Fortunately, the most frequent words are stopwords, and therefore half of the words appearing in a text need not be considered. This allows, for instance, to significantly reduce the space overhead of indices for natural language texts.

3   Searching the WWW

There are basically three different approaches to search the WWW. Two of them are well known and used frequently. The first, is to use search engines that index all the WWW as a full-text database. The second, is to use Internet directories (catalogues or yellow pages). The third and not yet fully available, is to search the WWW as a graph. In the next paragraphs we outline and exemplify the two main approaches currently available.

3.1 Search Engines

Most search engines use the crawler-indexer architecture. Crawlers are pieces of software that traverse the WWW sending new or updated pages to a main server where they are indexed. That index is used in a centralized fashion to answer queries submitted from different places in Internet. The most large search engines in WWW coverage are Hotbot [3], Altavista [18], Northern Light [4], and Excite [1], in that order. According to recent studies the coverage of the WWW by these engines varies from 28 to 55% [5] or 14 to 34% [27], as the number of WWW pages is estimated from 200 to 320 million. More facts about search engines can be found in the last two references.

The WWW pages found by the search engine are ranked, usually using the number of occurrences of the query on each page. In most cases this is effective, in others may not have any meaning, because relevance is not fully correlated with query occurrence. The user can refine the query by constructing more complex queries based on the previous answer. As the users receive only a subset of the answer (the first 10 to 100 matches), the search engine should keep each answer in memory, such that is not necessary to recompute it if the user asks for the next subset. Search engines user interfaces in addition to words, allow to filter pages by using boolean operators, and geographic, language or date segmentation.

The main problem faced by these engines is the recollection of data, because of the highly dynamic nature of the WWW, saturated communication links and high loaded WWW servers. Another important problem is the volume of the data. Then, these schema may not be able to cope with WWW growth in the near future.

There other several variants of the crawler-indexer architecture. Between them we can mention Harvest [15] which uses a distributed architecture to gather and distribute data, being more efficient. However, the main drawback is that needs the coordination of several WWW servers. Another variant is WebGlimpse [29] that attaches a small search box to the bottom of every HTML page, and allows the search to cover the neighborhood of that page or the whole site, without having to stop browsing. We also have to mention search engines that specializes in specific topics. For example the Search Broker [28] or the Miner family [35]. Finally, we have the metasearchers. These are WWW servers that use several engines, collect the answers and unify them. Examples are Metacrawler [36] and SavvySearch [20].

3.2 WWW Directories

The best example of WWW directories is Yahoo! [2]. Directories are hierarchical taxonomies (trees) that classify human knowledge. The main advantage of this technique is that if we find what we are looking for, the answer will be in most cases useful. On the other hand, the main disadvantage is that the classification is not specialized enough and that not all WW pages are classified. The last problem is worse every day as the WWW grows. The efforts to do automatic classification in AI are very old. However, until today, natural language processing is not 100% effective to extract relevant terms from a document. Nowadays, classification is done by a limited number of people.

3.3   Finding the Needle in the Haystack

Now we give a couple of search examples. One problem with full-text retrieval is that although many queries can be effective, many others are a total deception. The main reason is that a set of words do not capture all the semantics of a document. There is too much contextual information that can be explicit or even implicit, which we understand when we read. For example, suppose that we want to learn oriental games as Shogi or Go. For the first case, searching for Shogi will give you very fast good WWW pages where we can find what Shogi is (a variant of chess) and its rules. However, for Go the task is complicated, because in opposition to Shogi, is not a unique word in English. We can add more terms to the query, as `game` and `japanese` but still we are out of luck, as the pages found are almost all about Japanese games written in English where the common verb go is used.

The following example taken from [9] explains better this problem, where the ambiguity comes from the same language. Suppose that we want to wind the running speed of the jaguar, a big South American cat. A first naive search in Altavista would be `jaguar speed`. The results are pages that talk about the Jaguar car, an Atari video game, a US football team, a local network server, etc. The first page about the animal is ranked 183 and is a fable, without information about the speed. In a second try, we add the term `cat`. The answers are about the Clans Nova Cat and Smoke Jaguar, LMG Entreprises, fine cars, etc. Only the page ranked 25 has some information on jaguars but not the speed. Suppose we try Yahoo!. We look at `Science:Biology:Zoology:Animals:Cats:Wild_Cats` and `Science:Biology:Animal_Behavior`. No information about jaguars there. We can try to do a more specific search, for example using LiveTopics. However here we also have a shortage of topics, so searching by jaguar only returns cars or football teams.

The lessons learned in the example are that search engines still return too much hay to find the needle while the directories do not have enough deepness to find the needle. So, we can use the following rules of thumb:

- Specific queries: look at an Encyclopedia.
- Broad queries: use directories.
- Vague queries: use search engines.

4   Improvements to Inverted Files

Most indices use variants of the inverted file. An inverted file is a list of sorted words (vocabulary), each one having a set of pointers to the pages where it occurs. As we mentioned before, a set of frequent words or stopwords are not indexed. This reduces the size of the index. Also, it is important to point out that a normalized view of the text is indexed. Normalizing operations include removal of punctuation and multiple spaces to just one space between each word, uppercase to lowercase letters, use of synonyms through a thesaurus, etc. For more information on Information Retrieval algorithms and data structures see [22].

State of the art techniques can reduce an inverted file to about 20% of the text (the Altavista index has around 200Gb and 16 DEC Alpha servers are used to answer the queries, each one with several processors and 8Gb -sic- of RAM). A query is answered by doing a binary search on the sorted list of words. If we are searching multiple words, the results have to be combined to obtain the final answer. This step will be efficient if each word is not too frequent.

Inverted files can also point to actual occurrences. However, that is too costly in space for the WWW, because then each pointer has to specify a page and a position inside the page (word numbers can be used instead of actual bytes). On the other hand, having the positions we can answer phrase searches or proximity queries, by finding words that are after each other or nearby in the same page, respectively.

Finding words starting with a prefix, are solved by doing two binary searches in the sorted list of words. More complex searches, like words with errors, arbitrary wildcards or in general, any regular expression on a word, can be performed by doing a sequential scan over the vocabulary. This may seem slow, but the best sequential algorithms for this type of queries can achieve near 5Mb per second and that is more or less the vocabulary size for 1Gb. Then, for several Gbs we can answer in a few seconds. For the WWW is still too slow (around three minutes for the Altavista index) but not completely out of the question.

Pointing to pages or to word positions is an indication of the granularity of the index. This can be less dense if we point to logical blocks instead of pages. In this way we reduce the variance of the different document sizes, by having all blocks to have roughly the same size. This not only reduces the size of the pointers (because there are less blocks than documents) but also reduces the number of pointers because words have locality of reference (that is, all the occurrences of a non-frequent word will tend to be clustered on the same block). This idea was used in Glimpse [30] which is the core of Harvest [15]. Queries are resolved in the same way in the vocabulary and then are sequentially searched in the corresponding block (exact sequential search can be done over 7Mb per second). Glimpse originally used only 256 blocks, which was efficient up to 200Mb for searching words that were not too frequent, using an index of only 2% of the text. However, tuning the number of blocks and the block size, reasonable space-time trade-offs can be achieved for larger document collections. In fact, in [11] we show that for searching words with errors we can have sublinear space and search time simultaneously. These ideas cannot be used (yet) for the WWW because sequential search cannot be afforded, as it implies a network access. However, in a distributed architecture where the index is also distributed, logical blocks make sense.

The last issue is compression. Inverted lists can be partly compressed, in particular list of occurrences with high granularity. In those cases, the list is a sequence of ascending integers where the differences are much smaller than the values itself. Therefore, we can store just the first value and a sequence of differences. This complicates a bit the query evaluation, but space gains are obtained. Compression can also be applied to the text. However, most compression schemes are context dependent. That is, to decompress we have to decompress the whole file. Nevertheless, by using Huffman byte-coding over words (not letters), compression ratios of 30% coupled with random access to the compressed file are achieved [32]. This compression technique can be combined with the logical block scheme, obtaining an 8-fold improvement over normal sequential search by searching the compressed query word over the compressed text. The improvements came from the fact that one third of the I/O is done and searching over a shorter file is much faster.

5   Visual Query Languages

Traditional systems used words and boolean operations (and, or, butnot) to retrieve information. However, common users many times are confused by these operators, partly due to how we use logical connectives in normal language. That problem still remains today, but search engines have improved the searching interfaces to make things more clear (for example, using "all of", "some of", or "none of" the words). Another solution is to use a visual metaphor to represent the boolean operations. For example, a spatial relation, where the horizontal axis specify groups of words that must be together while the vertical axis specify that a least one of the groups must be present.

Another way to enhance content queries is to use the structure of the document. For example, HTML structure. A query to find a word near an image can be much more precise than just searching the word. For this, the index must include structural elements, adding little space, as structure is usually sparse. There are several proposals for query languages over content and structure [14]. However, most of them are too complicated for the final user. This drawback can be circumvent by using a visual query language. This is very natural as structure is highly correlated with the layout of a document. So, specifying a word near an image using a palette of elements, is not too difficult.

A proposed metaphor for a simple visual query language is given in [12]. What the user usually sees is a page of text. So our visual language will be a page where the structure is composed from a set of predefined objects and the content is written where we want to find it. Each structure element will be a rectangle with its name in the top (using the special name Text if it is a content element). Each content element is placed inside the rectangle. Union of queries are obtained by putting rectangles besides each other. Inclusion is obtained by placing rectangles inside rectangles. Figure 1 shows a query where the Text element **a** must be inside a chapter and should not include documents having the content element **c**.

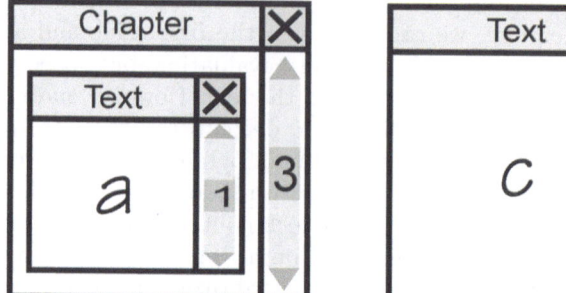

Fig. 1. Example of a visual query.

6   Visual Browsing

Most visual representations focus on some specific aspects. In text retrieval we can distinguish visualizations for a single document, several documents or queries. Most of the time only one of those elements is visualized. In the last years, several visual metaphors have been designed, for each element, describing next some of them.

6.1   Text Visualization

Possible text visualizations follow, in addition to the normal one, which is the text itself.

 - One possible view is a normal text window with an augmented scroll-bar (similar to [33] but in a different context) which has marks where the text positions appear in the document. The scroll-bar can be viewed as a complete compact view of the text [10].
 - The text itself is fish-eyed zooming where the query occurs given some adjacent lines to understand the context. The number of lines can be modified by the user. We call this an elastic text [10].
 - Only the text layout is given, in multiple columns [21]. Colored lines may indicate where the query occurs.

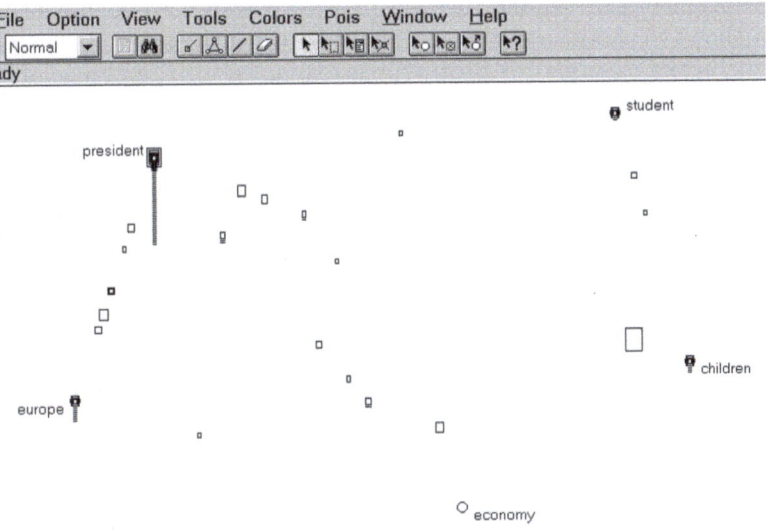

Fig. 2. Answer visualized by VIBE.

6.2   Document Visualization

Nowadays there are more than 20 proposals for visualizing a set of documents. The VIBE system [34] is based on user given points of interest of the query (using weighted attributes). These points (query words) act as gravitational forces that attract the documents according to the number of occurrences of each query (see Figure 2). Documents are displayed with different icon types and sizes.

Another metaphor for the document space based on inter-particle forces, as VIBE, is proposed in [17]. In [37] the document space is abstracted from a Venn diagram to an iconic display called InfoCrystal. One advantage of this scheme is that is also a visual query language. Visual tools in three-dimensions to handle the document space are presented in LyberWorld [26]. Visualization of occurrence frequency of terms in different text segments of a document is presented in [25].

Now we present a more elaborate metaphor for manipulating and filtering an answer given by a set of documents [10]. Figure 3 shows an instance of the visual analysis tool that we propose for advanced users. We use a "library" or "bookpile" analogy depending if the tool is used horizontally or vertically, because both are possible. Each document (seen as a book) is represented as a rectangle with a particular color, height, width and position into the set. Each one of this graphical attributes, including the order of the list, can be mapped to a document attribute (occurrence density, size, date, etc). In the example, the order and the color are mapped to the same attribute (for example, the creation date). These mappings allow to study different correlations of attributes on the document set, helping the user to select the desired documents. A select button allows to choose a document subset by using the mouse (the wide border rectangle in the example). A prototype is explained in [7] and available in [6].

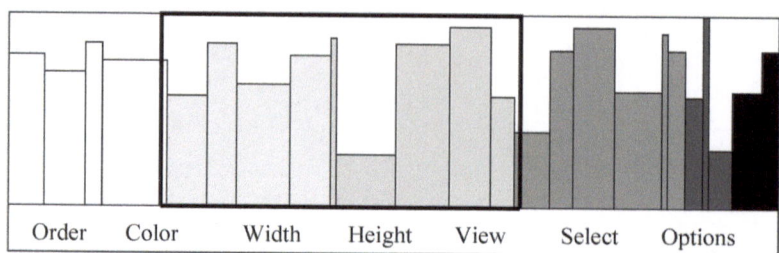

Fig. 3. Analyzing and selecting a document set.

The mapping of the attributes is selected by the menu buttons below the book list. The way the books are seen can also be changed. The set of documents can be forced to fit into the window (as in the example), presented using a predefined choice of maximal/minimal widths and heights (using a scroll-bar if bigger than the window). Another view is a fish-eye representation for large sets, focusing where the user wants (by clicking with the mouse the appropriate sector).

6.3   Query Visualization

The relations between query terms and the answer can also be visualized [10]. For example, a pie view showing the percentage of documents of the total database that were selected. Another possibility is to show the distribution of occurrences within terms of the query using boxes of different sizes. This view is useful to know what terms are the best filters in the given query. A third possibility, is to show the distribution of documents selected on the database logical or physical space. This view can show if there is any logical locality of reference associated with the query.

7   Conclusions

A careful integration of some of the new results presented here can help on partially solving the problems of searching the WWW. For example, a truly co-operative and distributed architecture similar to Harvest can diminish WWW traffic and extend the scalability of search engines. In each local index, compression and logical blocks can be used, obtaining smaller indices and documents. This is one of the goals of the AMYRI project [13] mentioned in the introduction. The first step will be a client-server architecture, followed by a distributed architecture for the search engine server.

50   Ricardo A. Baeza-Yates

Acknowledgments

We thanks the helpful comments of Gonzalo Navarro, in particular his contribution to Section 2.

References

1. Excite: Main page. http://www.excite.com, 1995. 43
2. Yahoo!: Main page. http://www.yahoo.com, 1995. 43
3. Hotbot: Main page. http://www.hotbot.com, 1996. 43
4. Northern Light: Main page. http://www.northernlight.com, 1997. 43
5. Search Engine Watch: Main page. http://www.searchenginewatch.com, 1997. 43
6. O. Alonso and R. Baeza-Yates. A bookpile applet. http://www.dcc.uchile.cl/-.˜.rbaeza/sem/visual/mio/Bucpil.html, 1997. 49
7. O. Alonso and R. Baeza-Yates. Visualizations of answers in WWW retrieval. Technical report, Department of Computer Science, Univ. of Chile, 1997. http://noval.cs.nvgc.vt.edu/ alonso/viswww.html. 49
8. M. Araújo, G. Navarro, and N. Ziviani. Large text searching allowing errors. In Proc. WSP'97, pages 2–20. Carleton University Press, 1997. 41, 42
9. R. Baeza-Yates. Modeling, browsing and querying large text databases. Technical Report DCC-94-2, Dept. of Computer Science, Univ. of Chile, 1994. 44
10. R. Baeza-Yates. Visualizing large answers in text databases. In Int. Workshop on Advanced User Interfaces (AVI'96), pages 101–107, Gubbio, Italy, May 1996. ACM Press. 47, 48, 49
11. R. Baeza-Yates and G. Navarro. Block-addressing indices for approximate text retrieval. In Proc. CIKM'97, pages 1–8, Las Vegas, USA, 1997. 41, 45
12. R. Baeza-Yates, G. Navarro, J. Vegas, and P. de la Fuente. A model and a visual query language for structured text. Santa Cruz, Bolivia, Sept 1998. IEEE CS Press. 46
13. R. Baeza-Yates and N. Ziviani. AMYRI: Main page. http://www.dcc.ufmg.br/-latin/amyri/, 1997. 40, 49
14. R.A. Baeza-Yates and G. Navarro. Integrating contents and structure in text retrieval. ACM SIGMOD Record, 25(1):67–79, March 1996. 46
15. C. Mic Bowman, Peter B. Danzig, Darren R. Hardy, Udi Manber, and Michael F. Schwartz. The harvest information discovery and access system. Computer Networks and ISDN Systems, 28:119–125, 1995. 43, 45
16. T. Bray. Measuring the web. In Fifth International World Wide Web Conference, Paris, May 1996. http://www5conf.inria.fr/fich..html/papers/P9/-Overview.html. 41
17. M. Chalmers and P. Chitson. BEAD: Exploration in information visualization. In ACM SIGIR'92, 1992. 48
18. Digital Equipment Corporation. Alta Vista: Main page. http://altavista.-digital.com, 1996. 43
19. M. Crovella and A. Bestavros. Self-similarity in World Wide Web traffic: Evidence and possible causes. In ACM Sigmetrics Conference on Measurement and Modeling of Computer Systems, pages 160–169, May 1996. 41
20. Daniel Dreilinger. Savvysearch home page. 1996. http://guaraldi.cs.-colostate.edu:2000. 43

21. Stephen Eick. Graphically displaying text. *Journal of Computational and Graphical Statistics*, 3(2):127–142, 1994. 47

22. W. Frakes and R. Baeza-Yates, editors. *Information Retrieval: Data Structures and Algorithms*. Prentice-Hall, 1992. 45

23. G. Gonnet and R. Baeza-Yates. *Handbook of Algorithms and Data Structures*. Addison-Wesley, 2nd edition, 1991. 42

24. J. Heaps. *Information Retrieval - Computational and Theoretical Aspects*. Academic Press, NY, 1978. 41

25. M. Hearst. Tilebars: Visualization of term distribution information in full text information access. In *ACM SIGCHI*, Denver, CO, May 1995. 48

26. M. Hemmje, C. Kunkel, and A. Willet. Lyberworld - a visualization user interface supporting text retrieval. In *17th ACM SIGIR*, Dublin, Jul 1994. 48

27. S. Lawrence and C.L. Giles. Searching the world wide web (in reports). *Science*, 280(5360):98, April 3 1998. 43

28. U. Manber and P. Bigot. Search Broker: Main page. `http://debussy.cs.-arizona.edu/sb/`, 1997. 43

29. U. Manber, M. Smith, and B. Gopal. Webglimpse: combining browsing and searching. In *Proc. of USENIX Technical Conference*, 1997. 43

30. U. Manber and S. Wu. GLIMPSE: A tool to search through entire file systems. In *Proc. USENIX Technical Conference*, pages 23–32. USENIX Association, Berkeley, CA, USA, Winter 1994. 45

31. G. Miller, E. Newman, and E. Friedman. Length-frequency statistics for written English. *Information and Control*, 1:370–380, 1958. 42

32. E. Moura, G. Navarro, N. Ziviani, and R. Baeza-Yates. Fast searching on compressed text allowing errors. In *Proc. SIGIR'98*, Melbourne, Australia, August 1998. ACM Press. 46

33. D. Olsen. Bookmarks: An enhanced scroll bar. *ACM Trans. on Computer Graphics*, 11(3):291–295, 1992. 47

34. K. Olsen, R. Korfhage, K. Sochats, M. Spring, and J. Williams. Visualization of a document collection: The VIBE system. *Information Processing and Management*, 29(1):69–81, 1993. 48

35. V. Ribeiro and N. Ziviani. Meta Miner: Main page. `http://canela.dcc.ufmg.-br:8080/metaminer.html`, 1997. 43

36. Erik Selberg and Oren Etzioni. Multi-service search and comparison using the MetaCrawler. In *Proceedings of the Fourth International World Wide Web Conference*, Boston, December 1995. `http://www.w3.org/pub/Conferences/WWW4/-Papers/169`. 43

37. A. Spoerri. Infocrystal: A visual tool for information retrieval and management. In *Information and Knowledge Management'93*, Washington D.C., 1993. 48

38. G. Zipf. *Human Behaviour and the Principle of Least Effort*. Addison-Wesley, 1949. 42

Groups and Societies: One and the Same Thing?

Eduardo Alonso*

Department of Computer Science, University of York
York YO10 5DD, United Kingdom
ea@minster.york.ac.uk

Abstract. To answer this question, we propose a general model of coordination in *Multi-Agent Systems*. Autonomous agents first recognise how they depend on each other (they may need or prefer to interact about the same or different goals), and then, in the negotiation phase, exchange offers in the form of commissive speech acts. Finally, agents adopt social, interlocking, commitments if an agreement is reached.
Joint plans are seen as deals and team activity as a special case of social activity in which, having agents the same common goal, every possible deal is profitable. Consequently, notions traditionally involved in *Cooperative Problem Solving* such as help and joint responsibility are applied to any social interaction. Therefore, the answer to our question is *yes*.

1 Introduction

The main concern in *Distributed Artificial Intelligence* (DAI) is how to design interaction protocols so that agents coordinate their behaviour. In *Multi-Agent Systems* (MAS), autonomous agents are devised by different designers, and have individual motivation to achieve their own goal and to maximise their own utility. Thus, no assumptions can be made about agents working together cooperatively. On the contrary, agents will cooperate only when they can benefit from that cooperation.

Most of the formal models presented in MAS are centered in analysing isolated aspects of the coordination problem, such as dependence nets [5,14], joint intentions [11,6], social plans [12], or negotiation models [17,18,10,15]. As far as we know, only Wooldridge and Jennings [21] have tried to represent the whole process in *Cooperative Problem Solving* (CPS) domains, where autonomous agents happen to have a common goal and then acquire social attitudes before forming a group.

A more comprehensive coordination framework has been presented in [3]: Agents with probably disparate and even conflict goals reason about their dependence relations and exchange offers following "social" strategies until they reach a deal. The resulting conditional commitments oblige them to abide by the agreements in societies. Therefore, there is no need for the agents to swear to act as a group in a team-formation stage.

---

* This research has been supported by the Ministerio de Educación y Cultura del Gobierno Español (EX 97 30605211).

Helder Coelho (Ed.): IBERAMIA'98, LNAI 1484, pp. 52–63, 1998.

The purpose of this paper is to prove that this model of coordination accounts for teams as well as for societies, and that the rules governing team action do not diverge from those controlling societies. We will illustrate that social notions traditionally related to CPS domains such as *help* or *joint responsibility* are applicable both to teams and societies. Therefore, all kind of groups can be represented with a single model.

The remainder of the paper is structured as follows. In the second section we introduce our concept of autonomous agent; in the third section an analysis of dependence relationships is presented; in the fourth section, the negotiation process is described; finally, we define societies as the result of the coordination process and show that the terms of the agreements explain any "social" concept. For simplicity, the model is presented in two-agents task oriented domains. Due to space restrictions we are not defining the language in full here, but readers are referred to [2].

2 Autonomous Agents

Agents are autonomous but probably no-autosufficient entities. Each agent is viewed as an independent "cognitive object" with his own beliefs, abilities, goal, and utility function. In our model goals are not fixed. Agents can compare and make decisions about plans and/or deals that satisfy different subgoals or that satisfy their goals only partially. This ability to relax one's goal opens up new opportunities for agreement, and enlarge the space of cooperation.

In order to model agents' behaviour we use a branching tree structure [7] (as it is common in MAS literature [12,20]), where each branch depicts an alternative execution path, π_i: Each node in the structure represents a certain state of the world and each transition an action. Formally, $\pi_i = (s_0, ..., s_{i-1}, a_i, s_i, ..., s_n)$. The set of actions associated to a path is defined as $\mathsf{act}(\pi_i) = \{a_1, ..., a_{n-1}\}$. We can identify goal/subgoal structures with particular paths through the tree, each leaf labeled with the utility obtained by traversing this path. Those leaves with the highest worth might be though of as those that satisfy the full goal, while others, with lower worth values, only partially satisfy the goal.

The rationality of a behaviour is understood according to its utility in the scale of preferences given a maximising policy. Nevertheless, in order to avoid un-contextualised decisions, utilities are defined with regard to agents' (sub)goals[1]. Following [13],

Definition 1. The utility of a (sub)path for an agent is the difference between the worth of the (sub)goal achieved executing this path and its cost. Therefore, if $\mathsf{GOAL}(x, \phi_i)$, $\mathsf{ACH}(\pi_i, \phi_i)$, and $\mathsf{cost}(x, \pi_i) = \{a_i : a_i \in \pi_i \wedge \mathsf{Ag}(a_i, x)\}$

$$\mathsf{utility}(x, \pi_i) = \mathsf{worth}(x, \phi_i) - \mathsf{cost}(x, \pi_i)$$

---

[1] Haddawy showed in [8] that for simple step utility functions, choosing the plan that achieves a goal leads to choose the plan that maximises utility.

Definition 2. The solution set for a goal: $\mathsf{Sol}(\phi_i) = \{\pi_i | \mathsf{ACH}(\pi_i, \phi_i)\}$. That is, $\mathsf{Sol}(\phi_i)$ defines the space of all possible solutions of ϕ_i. These solutions are ordered according to their utility in the scale of preferences.

3   Dependence Analysis

In the first phase of the coordination process agents try to recognise how they depend on each other. This recognition stage is crucial since it expresses agents' motivations and explains why they might be interested in coordinating their actions. Consequently, this dependence analysis establishes the rules under which deals are arranged and guides all the coordination process.

First, we consider agents' condition.

Definition 3. An agent is autosufficient for a given goal according to a set of paths if each path in this set achieves this goal and the agent is able to execute every action appearing in it.

Henceforth $\mathsf{Sol}(\phi_i) = \{\pi_1, ..., \pi_n\}$ and $\{\pi_w, ..., \pi_x\} \subseteq \{\pi_1, ..., \pi_n\}$,

$$\mathsf{AUTOSUFFICIENT}(x, \{\pi_w, ..., \pi_x\}, \phi_i) \text{ iff}$$
$$\forall \pi_i \in \{\pi_w, ..., \pi_x\} \ \ \forall a_i \in \mathsf{act}(\pi_i) \ \ \mathsf{Ag}(a_i, x)$$

On the other hand, there will probably other paths in the solution set of the goal such that the agent is not able to execute. For these paths, the agent is said to be deficient.

$$\mathsf{DEFICIENT}(x, \{\pi_w, ..., \pi_x\}, \phi_i) \text{ iff}$$
$$\forall \pi_i \in \{\pi_w, ..., \pi_x\} \ \ \exists a_i \in \mathsf{act}(\pi_i) \ \ \neg \mathsf{Ag}(a_i, x)$$

We define now how agents depend on each other: $\mathsf{N}(x, y, \{a_j, ..., a_k\}, \phi_i)$ and $\mathsf{W}(x, y, \{a_j, ..., a_k\}, \phi_i)$ mean that x needs or "weak" depends on y with regard to $\{a_j, ..., a_k\}$ for achieving ϕ_i. On the other hand, $\oplus$ and $\ominus$ are the "charge" of the relation: $\oplus$ means that the dependence relationship is about the execution of the actions related to ψ_i, whilst $\ominus$ is about its omission. There are four possible basic dependence relations[2]

1. $\oplus \mathsf{N}(x, y, \{a_j, ..., a_k\}, \phi_i) \leftrightarrow$
   $\forall \pi_i \in \{\pi_1, ..., \pi_n\} \mathsf{DEFICIENT}(x, \pi_i, \phi_i) \wedge$
   $\exists \delta_i = \{\alpha, \{a_j, ..., a_k\} \subset \mathsf{act}(\{\pi_1, ..., \pi_n\})\}$,
   That is, an agent needs positively the other agent to execute a set of actions if and only if he is not able to execute any subpath in his goal's solution set

---

[2] For simplicity, we have constrained the model to one relation each time, but agents can depend on each other in many different intermixed ways. For example, two agents with the same goal can need each other about two subpaths and depend weakly on one another about the rest of the path at issue. Moreover, different relations can arise if alternative paths are taken into consideration.

and there exists a deal such that y executes a subset of the actions associated with this goal.

This is a purposely vague definition, because the actions involved in the deal depends on how y is affected by x. The important thing is to realise that x needs y not only because of his own inefficiency but also because there is space for cooperation. The deal guarantees the required space of cooperation since every deal is supposed to be individual- rational, that is, it must improve both agents' position.

2. $\oplus W(x, y, \{a_j, ..., a_k\}, \phi_i) \leftrightarrow$
   $\text{AUTOSUFFICIENT}(x, \{\pi_w, ..., \pi_x\}, \phi_i) \wedge$
   $\exists \delta_i = \{\alpha, \{a_j, ..., a_k\} \subset \text{act}(\{\pi_1, ..., \pi_n\})\},$
   $\{a_j, ..., a_k\}$ can be the actions associated with any path in the solution set. The agreed path will be a subset of a path satisfying x's goal. The only condition is that $\text{utility}(x, \pi_k^{\delta_i}) > \text{utility}(x, \pi_i \in \{\pi_w, ..., \pi_x\}).$

3. $\ominus N(x, y, \{a_j, ..., a_k\}, \phi_i) \leftrightarrow$
   $\text{AUTOSUFFICIENT}(x, \{\pi_w, ..., \pi_x\}, \phi_i) \wedge$
   $\text{INHIBIT}(\{a_j, ..., a_k\}, \{\pi_w, ..., \pi_x\}) \wedge$
   $\exists \delta_i = \{\alpha, \neg\{a_j, ..., a_k\}\},$
   where a set of actions inhibits a set of paths if and only if there is no extension of these paths containing members of the set of actions. Probably, stand-alone paths are preferred to the ones resulting from the deal, but x has no choice. Therefore, $\{a_j, ..., a_k\}$ must be optional in y's goal solution set. Otherwise, there is an open conflict. Usually, these actions will be adopted to be used as threats.

4. $\ominus W(x, y, \{a_j, ..., a_k\}, \phi_i) \leftrightarrow$
   $\text{AUTOSUFFICIENT}(x, \{\pi_w, ..., \pi_x\}, \phi_i) \wedge$
   $\text{INHIBIT}(\{a_j, ..., a_k\}, \{\pi_j, ..., \pi_k\} \subset \{\pi_w, ..., \pi_x\}) \wedge$
   $\exists \delta_i, \delta_i = \{\alpha, \neg\{a_j, ..., a_k\}\},$
   In this case, the set of actions inhibits some of the autosufficient paths. However, there is a deal from which the inhibited paths can be executed and whose utility is greater than the utility of non-inhibited paths.

One significant feature of our model is that only bilateral relations are allowed. Unlike in [5,14,21], an agent cannot act in society according exclusively to its individual needs or preferences, or offer deals to achieve his goal without taking into account others' motivations. We can analyse the space of interaction according to the "charge" of the relations as follows:

1. We can say that *social interaction* takes place in three possible cases (a similar approach is presented in [13]):

   (a) a *cooperative* situation is one in which each agent welcomes the existence of the other agent. That is, when they depend positively on each other. This is usual in mutual relations (when agents share the same goal) because it is always profitable for both agents to share the load of executing the associated plan;

(b) a *compromise* situation is one in which both agents would prefer to be alone (they depend on each other negatively). However, since they are forced to cope with the presence of the other, they will agree on a deal. Typically when one agent's gain always entails the other's loss;

(c) a *neutral* situation is one in which one agent is in a cooperative situation and the other is in a compromise one.

2. On the other hand, we say that *social co-action* happens in two circumstances

(a) a *conflict* situation is one in which agents come across but there is no deal that resolve their possible interactions. For example, when agents have parallel goals or in killer-victim relations. In such cases, although they do depend on each other, their relation is not subject to coordination. It is true that they need to reason about each others' behaviour (the victim will try to anticipate the killer's behaviour in order to escape, and *vice versa*) but the nature of their dependence is a-social;

(b) agents are *independent* if there is at least one of them whose goal is not affected by other's goal. As an example, we have the *parasite* agent, who waits the other to achieve his goal.

According to the "weight" of each agent in the interaction, there are two types of social interaction: *Symmetric* situations, SYM, in which both agents need or "weak" depend on each other; or *Asymmetric* situations, ASYM, in which x needs y, and this second agent only "weak" depends on the first. In that case, it is said that y has power (POW) over x. Accordingly, an agent x has not power over other agent y just because y needs x (unlike in [4]), but the powerful agent must have some motivation to exploit his dominating status. If either of the agents is not interested in interacting, talking about dependence relationships is pointless.

If we compare now our model with others in MAS literature, we have that we enlarge substantially the space of cooperation, as

- we allow agents to negotiate in need or preference (only [21] studies both cases);
- agents can negotiate not only about common goals, but about disparate and even conflict goals. This is because agents are allowed to relax their initial goals and negotiate about subgoals and/or degrees of satisfaction of their respective goals. Imagine two hunters trying to get the same hare. They have common compatible subgoals, to catch the prey, but two parallel final goals, to eat it. So, they will cooperate about that subgoal (because coordinating their attack increases their chances), and then compete openly;
- deals can be about the execution or the omission of actions (the possibility of "non-negative contribution" is just pointed out in [9]).

4   Negotiation Process

Once agents have a model of the interaction situation, they exchange offers directly. Negotiation is a process through which in each temporal point one agent, say x, proposes an agreement from the negotiation set (NS), and the other agent, y, either accepts the offer or does not. If the offer is accepted, then the negotiation ends with the implementation of the agreement. Otherwise, the second agent then has to make a counteroffer, or reject x's offer and abandon the process.

We are not introducing here a detailed model of the negotiation procedure (see [3,2]). In this paper our only concern is about those aspects of the model that will help us to show that groups are just societies of agents that share a goal. One of these aspects has to do with how joint commitments are understood. We consider that in order to avoid references to irreducible "social" notions the contents of joint intentions must be tracked throughout the coordination process, and that the conditions of individual social commitments must be expressed as arguments in the offers.

We say that an agent x offers a deal if he requests the other agent y to be socially committed to execute some action and asserts that if y confirms such commitment, he will commit himself to execute another action. Formally (the speech acts operators come from [16]),

1. $OFF(x, y, \delta_i = \{\alpha, \beta\}) \equiv$
   $REQ(x, y, SOC - COM(y, x, \beta, \alpha)) \wedge$
   $ASS(x, y, (CONF(y, x, SOC - COM(y, x, \beta, \alpha)) \rightarrow SOC - COM(x, y, \alpha, \beta)).$
2. Using this definition, counteroffers are easily defined as a refusal followed by other offer.

The content of such commitments must specify the social conditions under which these engagements persist or are dropped out. We say that an agent is socially committed with other agent to execute an action if he has the intention of executing it until he believes that his part of the deal is true or will never be true, when he adopts the goal of having this situation mutually believed. Moreover, an agent's social commitment will be also abandoned if he believes that his pattern has failed in executing his part. In this case, the goal of having this fact mutually believed is interpreted as acknowledgement.

Definition 4. $SCOM(x, y, \alpha, \beta) =_{def}$
   $UNTIL \quad BEL(x, \neg SCOM - C(x, \alpha, \beta))$
   $INT(x, \alpha)$
   $WHEN \quad GOAL(x, MBEL(x, y, \neg SCOM - C(x, \alpha, \beta))),$

Definition 5. $SCOM - C(x, \alpha, \beta) \equiv$
   $[BEL(x, \alpha) \wedge BEL(x, \Box \neg \alpha) \wedge BEL(x, \Box \neg \beta)]$

where β is other agent's part. Therefore, social commitments are conditioned. This is because in MAS, where benevolence is not assumed, negotiation is only understood according to this *quid pro quo* policy. When an agent x makes an offer, the actions requested are those he believes he depends on y; on the other hand, the actions he promises to be committed to if y accepts the offer are those actions he believes y depends on him. That is, negotiation steps are created according to dependence relationships. Thus, unlike in Wooldridge and Jennings's proposal [21], there is no need for a team-formation phase.

To what agreements can agents come? As we study asymmetric relations, the only *a priori* condition for a bargain to be in the space of deals is that it has to be individual rational. It would be "unfair" to ask a dominant agent to accept a Pareto-Optimal deal if he can obtain more profit from another deal. By individual-rational we mean that both agents must improve their position with the deal. So, if an agent has a stand-alone plan, the deal must not decrease his utility; if the agent has no such an alternative to the negotiated agreement, the deal must give him non-negative utility. The search for "fair" deals is presented in two ways:

Strict Mechanism: Firstly, we define a "fairness" one-to-one function from the set of situations to the set of deals, $f : SIT \rightarrow NS$, giving the values depicted in **Fig.1.** (where SYMN means symmetric necessity relation, and so on):

$$1.f(SYMN(x, y, \alpha, \beta)) = \delta_i = \{\alpha, \beta\}$$

$$2.f(SYMW(x, y, \alpha, \beta)) = \begin{cases} \delta_i & \text{iff} \quad P - Opt_{\{x,y\}}(NS) = \delta_i \\ \delta_i & \text{iff} \quad P - Opt_{\{x,y\}}(NS) = \{\Delta\} \wedge \\ & r(\{\Delta\}) = \delta_i \end{cases}$$

$$3.f(POW(x, y, \alpha, \beta)) = \begin{cases} \delta_i & \text{iff} \quad greatest_x(NS) = \delta_i \\ \delta_i & \text{iff} \quad maximal_x(NS) = \{\Delta\} \wedge \\ & greatest_y(\{\Delta\}) = \delta_i \\ \delta_i & \text{iff} \quad maximal_x(NS) = \{\Delta\} \wedge \\ & flat(x, \{\Delta\}) \wedge r(\{\Delta\}) = \delta_i \end{cases}$$

Fig.1. The "fairness" function.

1. If the agents are in a symmetric situation and they need each other, then the only "fair" solution consists in exchanging the actions involved.
2. If the agents are in a symmetric situation and they depend weakly on each other, then the deal can be:
   2.1. Pareto-Optimal deal, if it is unique.
   2.2. If there are several Pareto-Optimal deals, then the resulting agreement will be a random variable among the set of "fair" deals. For example, when autosufficient agents with a common goal meet, they may be indifferent about how tasks should be distributed. Or when there are two Pareto-Optimal deals implying an odd number of actions
3. If one agent has power over the other, then the "fair" deal will be:
   3.1. The one maximising his utility, the greatest in his scale of preferences.

3.2. If it is not unique, then the "fair" deal will be the most preferred by the dominated agent among the dominant's set of maximals.

3.3. If the dominated agent is indifferent, then one of the deals in this set is chosen at random.

Tolerant Mechanism: It is more useful to apply a tolerant mechanism in dynamic environments in which failures in the execution of the agreements will occur quite often. We introduce a set of ordered deals $(\Delta, \leq)$ representing the "fair" deal associated to each possible situation derived from the actual one. As a result, agents agree not only on the specific deal which is carried out at the first time, but also about the deals *in reserve*. So, in case of failure agents will use the following automatic rule:

RENEG: In case of failure in the execution of a specific deal, eliminate it from the set of deals and apply the "fairness' function according to the situation generated.

Example 1. Imagine that the two agents share the same goal and that there is a SYMW *relationship between them. The deal is, therefore, assumed to be a simple task distribution. We have the following set of possible deals* $\Delta = \{\{\alpha, \beta\}, \{\beta, \alpha\}, \{\emptyset, (\alpha, \beta)\}, \{(\alpha, \beta), \emptyset\}\}$. *As agents depend weakly on each other, the "fair" deal must be Pareto-Optimal, one of the two first deals in* Δ. *Imagine that* $\{\alpha, \beta\}$ *is chosen by random and that* FAILS(x, α). *Then, there will be two possible deals left, namely* $\{\beta, \alpha\}$ *and* $\{\emptyset, (\alpha, \beta)\}$. *Moreover, the relation between the agents has changed, and now* y *will have power over* x. *Therefore, the first deal, the one maximising* y*'s utility, is chosen. We can go one step further, and suppose that* x *fails again executing* β. *In this case, the only possible deal to be carried out is* $\{\emptyset, (\alpha, \beta)\}$.

5   After Negotiation

In our proposal each agent is still considered independent after negotiation. Joint plans are understood as deals through which agents make social commitments to execute particular actions, not to act as a group. We can define now joint commitments simply as the conjunction of the social commitments involved.

Definition 6. JCOM(x, y, δ_i) $=_{\text{def}}$ SCOM(x, y, α, β) $\wedge$ SCOM(y, x, β, α)

Societies are seen as groups of agents with a joint commitment to execute the agreed deal. For us, a group of agents forms a society when they reach an agreement, not when they decide to act as such and try jointly to reach an agreement. That is, the notion of society is a result of coordination and not its condition.

Our approach explains certain unclear aspects of teamwork. It is common in MAS literature to refer to the team as a whole when there is no way of attaching individual attitudes to its members.

*Example 2. Consider a team of two pilots whose goal is to carry as many he-
licopters to a point as possible. Following the joint intentions framework it is
sufficient if the team reaches that point, ech individual need not do so individu-
ally. In so doing, the team is reified and the* task distribution enigma *arises [ ].
We think that our approach is more natural. In this case, we have three possi-
ble deals,* $\{\{\alpha, \beta\}, \{\alpha, \emptyset\}, \{\emptyset, \beta\}\}$, *where each part means an agent reaching that
point. The order of preference is* $\{\alpha, \beta\} > \{\alpha, \emptyset\} = \{\emptyset, \beta\}$. *The RENEG rule is
applied automatically, each deal satisfying the goal to some degree:* $\{\alpha, \beta\}$ *satisfies completely the goal, as all the pilots reach the point, whereas* $\{\alpha, \emptyset\}$ *and*
$\{\emptyset, \beta\}$ *satisfy the goal only partially. In any case, each agent achieves the goal if
one of the deals is accomplished.*

We adopt this individualistic approach to stress the bargaining nature of
social interactions, and that agents coordinate their behaviour and form societies
with regard to common interests, not to common goals, as their motivations can
be very disparate. From this point of view, agents do not agree and form groups
to achieve a goal, but to execute deals that will achieve (perhaps partially) their
(common or not) goals.

Therefore if the negotiation protocol ends in agreement agents will adopt a
joint commitment and form a society.

Definition 7. SOCIETY$(\{x, y\}, \delta_i) =_{\mathsf{def}}$
 MBEL$(x, y, \mathsf{SIT}(x, y, \sigma_i)) \wedge$
 MBEL$(x, y, f(\mathsf{SIT}) = \delta_i) \wedge$
 MBEL$(x, y, (\mathsf{JCOM}(x, y, \delta_i)))$

Of course, this notion of society is quite basic. Things are more complicated
in real environments, where team action can involve notions of social justice
and social welfare. In the end, groups will behave according to the ideology or
interests of the designer. However, it is worth pointing out that we are working
with systems (MAS) where the utilitarian point of view is closely related to
liberalism. If notions of global utility are taken into account, agents will stop
being autonomous, and some kind of community spirit will control our designs.

6   Groups

In this final section we exemplify how "help" and "joint responsibility" are understood in our model, and conclude that, all in all, both concepts are applicable
both to teams and societies.

According to Tuomela [ ] one of the most important notions of cooperative
activity is the one of *help*, in the sense of (extra) actions strictly contributing to
other participants performing their parts well. In MAS agents are not assumed
to be benevolent and will therefore cooperate and help each other when they can
benefit from that cooperation (that is, when the cost of "helping" actions does
not exceed the gains accruing from them). So, as far as agents have common
interests, they will keep executing RENEG. Since everything is arranged before
execution starts, no action can be interpreted as altruistic help.

Why are groups so special? We have seen in **Example 1** that when agents share a common goal their preferences are highly positively correlated. Whenever a collection of agents has the same goal, it is in their own interest to help each other. This is because in teams the problem of coordination is in practice the problem of how to distribute the goal tasks. Even if x is suddenly unable to execute any action, y will execute the entire plan, because he has nothing to lose: the deal will be equal to his stand-alone plan, the goal's plan-structure. He cannot refuse to execute it because of x's failure. Otherwise, he himself will not achieve the goal. Having a common goal they are in a situation in which they are destined to cooperate and act jointly. However, help is not unique to groups. In societies where agents have different goals, the renegotiation rule will be applied until the corresponding deal is not individual-rational.

What about *joint responsibility*? Agents with joint responsibility are supposed to be equally rewarded or blamed for the actions they execute as a collective.

Example 3. Imagine a football team playing a crucial match. Each player will receive a medal if the team wins or will be fired if they lose. Suppose that they have never played before, so that they agree on a set of deals, the first consisting of eleven actions meaning the usual distribution of tasks (goalkeeper, defender, sweeper, striker, etc...) and five different empty sets for the substitutes. Suppose now that the striker, number 9, is sent off, so that agents must apply the renegotiation rule and execute the second plan according to the new circumstances. For example, the wings must center their positions in the pitch and try to score. Then, if the team wins, should the number 9 be awarded? And, if they lose, should he be fired? Should the substitutes be awarded or blamed? The intuitive answer to these questions is "yes". Now, we have a model that explains why: as agents agreed on the other deals as part of the "general" deal, everyone in the team is responsible for the outcome.

7   Conclusions

In this paper we have presented a model of coordination in which agents first recognise how they depend on each other and then exchange offers and counteroffers until they reach an agreement. Agreements can be executed following a strict mechanism, or can involve the use of a renegotiation rule that provides different deals. In this last case, agents agree on a set of deals, so that deals are executed in a given order according to the changing conditions an the ability of the agents. Using this mechanism we have illustrated how notions linked to CPS, such as help and joint responsibility are explained without mentioning any social attitude. Everything is settled in the terms of the agreements. Therefore, we have concluded that there is no point in adopting different mechanisms of coordination for teams or societies. Any collective will follow the same coordination mechanism, regardless of whether agents share the same goal or not.

There are several issues to be addressed in future work, the most obvious of which is the need for refinement of the model. Moreover, the model should cope better with uncertainty: Agents can have incomplete knowledge and different points of view, so argumentation turns to be an essential part in coordination. Finally, the tolerant mechanism works well in games in which the rules are well-known, but real-life social interactions are usually far more complicated than a football match. The study of multiple-encounters and roles will hopefully allow us to identify and characterise the constant environmental factors required to find equilibria between efficiency and stability.

References

1. E. Alonso. An uncompromising individualistic formal model of social activity. In M. Luck, M. Fisher, d'Inverno M., N. Jennings, and M. Wooldridge, editors, *Working Notes of the Second UK Workshop on Foundations of Multi-Agent Systems (FoMAS-97)*, pages 21–32, Coventry, U.K., 1997. 60
2. E. Alonso. Agents Behaving Well: A Formal Model of Coordination in Multi-Agent Sytems. Technical Report YCS-98-?, Department of Computer Science, University of York, York, YO10 5DD (UK), July 1998. 53, 57
3. E. Alonso. How individuals negotiate protocols. In *Proc. ICMAS-98*. IEEE Computer Science Press, 1998. 52, 57
4. C. Castelfranchi. Social power: A point missed in Multi-Agent, DAI and HCI. In Y. Demazeau and J-P. Müller, editors, *Decentralized A.I.*, pages 49–62, Amsterdam, The Netherlands, 1990. Elsevier Science Publishers B.V. 56
5. C. Castelfranchi, M. Miceli, and A. Cesta. Dependence relations among autonomous agents. In E. Werner and Y. Demazeau, editors, *Decentralized A.I. 3, Proc. MAAMAW-91*, pages 215–227, Amsterdam, The Netherlands, 1992. Elsevier Science Publishers. 52, 55
6. P.R. Cohen and H.J. Levesque. Teamwork. *Nous*, 25:487–512, 1991. 52
7. E.A. Emerson and J. Srinivasan. Branching time temporal logic. In J.W. de Bakker, de Roever W.P., and G. Rozenberg, editors, *Linear Time, Branching Time, and Partial Models in Logics and Models for Concurrency*, pages 123–172, Berlin, Germany, 1989. Springer-Verlag. 53
8. P. Haddawy. *Representing plans under uncertainty*. Springer-Verlag, Berlin, Germany, 1994. 53
9. N.R. Jennings. On being responsible. In E. Werner and Y. Demazeau, editors, *Decentralized A.I. 3, Proc. MAAMAW-91*, pages 93–102, Amsterdam, The Netherlands, 1992. Elsevier Science Publishers. 56
10. S. Kraus, J. Wilkenfeld, and J. Zlotkin. Multiagent negotiation under time constraints. *Artificial Intelligence*, 75:297–345, 1995. 52
11. H.J. Levesque, P.R. Cohen, and J.H.T. Nunes. On acting together. Technical Report 485, SRI International, Menlo Park, CA 94025-3493, May 1990. 52
12. A.S. Rao, M.P. Georgeff, and E.A. Sonenberg. Social plans: A preliminary report. In E. Werner and Y. Demazeau, editors, *Proc. MAAMAW-91*, pages 57–76, Amsterdam, The Netherlands, 1992. Elsevier Science Publishers. 52, 53
13. J.S. Rosenschein and G. Zlotkin. *Rules of Encounter*. The MIT Press, Cambridge, MA, 1994. 53, 55
14. J.S. Sichman, R. Conte, Y. Demazeau, and C. Castelfranchi. A social reasoning mechanism based on dependence networks. In A. Cohn, editor, *Proc. ECAI-94*, pages 173–177. John Wiley and Sons, 1994. 52, 55

15. C. Sierra, N.R. Jennings, P. Noriega, and S. Parsons. A framework for argumentation-based negotiation. In M.P. Singh, A. Rao, and M.J. Wooldridge, editors, *Proc. ATAL-97*, pages 177–192, Berlin, Germany, 1998. Springer-Verlag. 52

16. I.A. Smith and P.R. Cohen. Toward a semantics for an agent communications language based on speech- acts. In *Proc. AAAI-96*, pages 24–31, Cambridge, MA, 1996. AAAI Press/MIT Press. 57

17. R.G. Smith and R. Davis. Frameworks for cooperation in distributed problem solving. *IEEE Transactions on Systems, Man and Cybernetics*, 11(1):61–70, 1981. 52

18. K.P. Sycara. Persuasive argumentation in negotiation. *Theory and Decision*, 28:203–242, 1990. 52

19. R. Tuomela. What is cooperation? *Erkenntnis*, 38:87–101, 1993. 60

20. M. Wooldridge. Coherent social action. In A. Cohn, editor, *Proc. ECAI-94*, pages 279–283. John Wiley and Sons, 1994. 53

21. M. Wooldridge and N.R. Jennings. Towards a theory of cooperative problem solving. In J.W. Perram and J-P. Müller, editors, *Proc. MAAMAW-94, Workshop on Distributed Software Agents and Applications*, pages 40–53, Berlin, Germany, 1996. Springer-Verlag. 52, 55, 56, 58

From Mental States and Architectures to Agents' Programming

Milton Corrêa[*] and Helder Coelho[**]

Abstract. Agents (in AI and DAI) are founded upon theories related to mental states and to the notion of architecture. However, there is still no consensus, or sufficient knowledge, to formulate a satisfactory theory which would define mental states, relating them to architectures and agent behaviour. The paper is located in this context and presents a theory in which a space of mental states is built up on types of mental states which are defined from a set of basic attributes which are: an External Content (a declaration about a situation in the world); criterions to determine the unsatisfaction, uncertainty, urgency, insistence, intensity and importance associated to a mental state; laws of causality through which a mental state can produce another; and mechanisms for provoking, selecting, suspending and interrupting the processing of a mental state.

A space for possible agents' architectures is built up on that mental states space. So, from these two spaces, the paper presents a methodology to define and compare agents' architectures and to understand and produce the corresponding agents behaviour. In addition, it is shown that this methodology is suitable for agent programming based on the Object Oriented Programming paradigm.

1. Introduction

There is still no consensus in regard to the entire list or the best choice of mental states. Over the last decade, several sub-lists have been proposed, which however, suffered restrictions either because of specific features of a problem domain or by the limitations of the chosen logical apparatus. There is also a current feeling of uneasiness related to the state of art concerning mental states in DAI. The definition of what an agent is remains not clear in view of disparate opinions [14]. Several attempts and models have been made to clarify these issues [4], in which dynamic aspects of reasoning based on the revision of beliefs and motivational attitudes are modeled in a compositional manner. Recently, Sloman[1996] advanced the theory of a table of mental states but without specifying how this is to be carried out. He argued that mental mechanisms are best considered in a global architecture context. We are

*Serviço Federal de Processamento de Dados, Rio de Janeiro, Brasil,
e-mail: correa@unisys.com.br .
** Departamento de Informática, Faculdade de Ciências, Universidade de Lisboa, Lisboa, Portugal, e-mail: hcoelho@di.fc.ul.pt .

Helder Coelho (Ed.): IBERAMIA'98, LNAI 1484, pp. 64-75, 1998.

convinced after Corrêa and Coelho[1993] and Corrêa[1994] that a complete functioning agent needs a specification based on the notion of architecture, but highlighted by the dynamics of mental reactions. The way all mental states move around and interact is carefully controlled, in a similar way to what occurs now with artificial chemical reactions [11]. The present contribution is a further step to clarify our holistic approach to mentality, that is the integration among mind, architecture and behaviour.

Our starting point is the observation that mental states (MS) as Beliefs, Desires and Intentions, are commonly defined as being structured on basic components (the same occurred with Mendeleev's periodic table of the elements in 1869). Cohen and Levesque[1990] defined Intention as being structured on "Choice" plus "Commitment", in other works "Commitment" is also thought as more basic than Intention [5], [20]. Werner[1991] treated Intentions as Strategies, and Bratman [1990] defined them as Plans. The components of Belief usually are a Proposition and a "true" or "false" value associated to it, or a degree of Certainty and can also have a degree of Importance [18].

On the other hand, Sloman[1990, 1996] pointed out that urgency, importance, intensity and insistence are behind agent's actions.

We argue that other mental states than Belief, Desires and Intentions can be necessary to understand and to explain the complexities of agents behaviour and a complete and consistent theory about agents' mental states has not only to explain and build the artificial agents but also to understand the natural ones[13].

For instance, Expectation is a mental state which enables more flexibility and more complex behaviours [17], [26], [9]. Expectations and Intentions can complement one another. Intentions can embody an agent's expectations that the agent act in ways to satisfy those intentions, while expectations can lead an agent to form intentions to check that those expectations are satisfied. The Expectation can be defined in terms of basic attributes as an External Content ("Romeo expects that Juliet will come back") , uncertainty ("Romeo expects that Juliet will come back, but he is not sure"), urgency ("Romeo expects that Juliet will come back urgently"), importance ('It is very important for Romeo that Juliet will come back"), intensity ("Romeo is intensively expecting that Juliet come back"), insistence ("Romeo continuously expects that Juliet will come back"), unsatisfaction ("Juliet still does not come back as Romeo expected"), control ("Juliet still does not come back, and Romeo cannot wait anymore so, he has to do something").

Our approach considers mental states as organizations of agent's internal processing of information related to their actions, and a fundamental feature of these organizations is that they are related to situations in the world (intentionality). Mental states are guides for agent's actions such that the agent behaviour can be explained on them and, on the other hand, mental states can interact to produce the agent behaviour. We assume that there is a limited set of basic attributes such that a mental state is defined in terms of some combination of them.

In Corrêa and Coelho[1997] it is proposed a framework to standardize the commonly notion of usual mental states as Beliefs, Desires and Intentions and other not so much used in DAI as Expectations. It is shown that from this framework the research and application to build agents with new other possible types of mental states (as Hopes) can be possible.

In the paper it is shown that this framework can be applied to agent programming based on the Object Oriented Programming paradigm. Our aim is to establish a methodology: 1) The mental states are characterized in terms of a small set of basic attributes; 2) we argue that these attributes are, at least, sufficient to define mental states; 3) other possible mental states could also be characterized by assigning them a set of those attributes; 4) This mental states model can explain agents' interactions; 5) An Agent Oriented Programming results from this mental states model.

2. A Framework for Mental States

In order to have a theoretical structure to define mental states we need to find an agreement about their basic components or attributes. This can be obtained by observing the conceptions and applications of the usual mental states and filtering a common set of them. On the other hand, these attributes must be put together and analised if they are capable to offer a base to define the usual mental states of DAI (Belief, Desires and Intentions) and other not well applied yet, although known from Psychology, Philosophy and Economics as relevant to explain human behaviour as Expectations, Hopes and Necessities. When we diversify applications and work within Social and Human Sciences we are forced to adopt such other mental states.

As a matter of fact assigning attributes to mental states can be validated according to the theories of Psychology, Cognitive Science and Philosophy [22], [23], [9], [13]. They must enable MS to explain agent actions and they must also allow, from the point of view of agent's engineering, the building of agents through the definition of architectures based on mental states. From these basic attributes it should be possible to understand the relationships among mental states and their dynamics behind agents' behaviours.

To make references to these attributes we organize them in three groups: the first called "nucleus" contains the mental state's external content and a set of criterions for unsatisfaction, uncertainty, urgency, intensity, insistence and intensity; the second called "laws" contains a set of possible causal relationships among mental states and the last called "controls" contains a set of controls to trigger, choose, suspend and cancel mental states.

2.1 Nucleus

These attributes define proper characteristics of MS that is, the MS with the same set of attributes are classified as the same type as shown in the paragraphs below, but every particular MS is distinguished, at least, by its external content.

Normally an MS is distinguished from other MS of same type by the attributes of the nucleus.

- External Content (Ex. Content)

The mental states have external significance; that is to say, they are linked to the world in terms of what they are about. This external content in terms of the Situation Theory formalism is a proposition: "situation s supports infons e_1, e_2..."[2], [12].

- Unsatisfaction

This attribute is related to the stimulation of actions or changes of mental states. As Russel[1971] pointed out the unsatisfaction is the first motor of action. Thus, we consider that this component is the central motivator of actions and the producer of other mental states.

The degree of unsatisfaction is a function $s_p(t)$ from a proposition p and time t to the set of real positive numbers. A factor ε_s ($\varepsilon_s \varepsilon 0$) is necessary as a limit to decisions regarding agent MS unsatisfaction. An MS is satisfied at time t if $s_p(t) < \varepsilon_s$, otherwise MS is unsatisfied. So, we need some criteria (or procedure) to decide if a MS is satisfied or not.

- Uncertainty

It is a measure of agent confidence regarding the situation that corresponds to the mental state.

The degree of uncertainty is a function $c_p(t)$ from a proposition p and time t to the set of real positive numbers. A factor ε_c ($\varepsilon_c \varepsilon 0$) is necessary as a limit to decisions related agent MS uncertainty. For example, $c_p(t)$ can be a probability associated to a proposition p.

- Urgency

It is a measure of how much time remains to the point the corresponding MS must be satisfied.

The degree of urgency, corresponding to a mental state X at time t, is a function $u_x(t)$ from a time t to the set of real positive numbers. A factor ε_u ($\varepsilon_u \varepsilon 0$) is necessary as a limit to decisions related to MS urgencies.

- Intensity

It is related to the agent's pledge and energy dedicated to an MS. For example, if an agent is trying to satisfy an MS, the intensity of this MS is connected to how actively or vigorously this satisfaction is pressed and adopted.

The degree of intensity, corresponding to a mental state X at time t, is a function $v_x(t)$ from a time t to the set of real positive numbers. A factor ε_v ($\varepsilon_v \varepsilon 0$) is necessary as a limit to decisions related to MS intensities.

- Importance

The importance is related to a valuation in terms of benefits and costs the agent has of a corresponding mental state situation.

The degree of importance, corresponding to a mental state X at time t, is a function $m_X(t)$ from a time t to the set of real positive numbers. A factor ε_m ($\varepsilon_m \; \varepsilon \; 0$) is necessary as a limit to decisions related to MS importance.

- Insistence

This attribute is related to how much dificult it is for an agent to abandon a MS. For instance, if the agent strongly insists on some goal, this goal will not be abandoned easily .

The degree of insistence, corresponding to a mental state X at time t, is a function $n_X(t)$ from a time t to the set of real positive numbers. A factor ε_n ($\varepsilon_n \; \varepsilon \; 0$) is necessary as a limit to decisions related to agent MS insistences.

2.2 Laws

The laws define how the mental states are combined to cause other mental states or agent's actions. For example, under certain conditions, a Belief and a Desire cause another Desire: an agent A's Desire to learn mathematics and the Belief that agent B knows mathematics and that B teaches A, cause A's Desire to learn mathematics from B. Another law is: a Desire and a Belief can cause an Intention: A's Desire to learn mathematics from B and A's Belief that in order to learn from agent B, there is a strategy as: 1) ask B if he/she wants to teach mathematics to A, 2) if so, A accepts B's instructions regarding mathematics. That is, A must know how to learn from another agent. Thus, there is an A's Intention to learn mathematics from B.

A collection of laws relating Belief, Desire, Intention and Expectation is presented in figure 1 according to Corrêa [1994]. Another demonstration of such mental states dynamics applied in a Tutor/Learner session is shown in Moussale et al. [1996].

2.3 Controls

These attributes define how and when an MS causes another, can be suspended, canceled or stayed active. An MS is active when it produces or influences another MS, causes an agent action or contributes indirectly to an agent action. An MS is suspended when it is temporarily inactive. A MS is cancelled when it is permanently inactive. An embrionary idea of the relationships among behaviour and goal-terminating and interrupting mechanisms as these controls was also introduced by Simon [1967], although he didn't use the concept of mental states in that paper.

Let X be a mental state and p the corresponding situation. The possible laws will be triggered if $s_p(t) \, \varepsilon \, \varepsilon_s$, and at least one of the conditions (C1 to C7) below occurs:

C1) $u_x(t) \, \varepsilon \, \varepsilon_u$ and $v_x(t) \, \varepsilon \, \varepsilon_v$ and $m_x(t) \, \varepsilon \, \varepsilon_m$

C2) $u_x(t) \, \varepsilon \, \varepsilon_u$ and $m_x(t) \, \varepsilon \, \varepsilon_m$

C3) $u_x(t) \, \varepsilon \, \varepsilon_u$ and $v_x(t) \, \varepsilon \, \varepsilon_v$

C4) $v_x(t) \, \varepsilon \, \varepsilon_v$ and $m_x(t) \, \varepsilon \, \varepsilon_m$

C5) $m_x(t) \, \varepsilon \, \varepsilon_m$

C6) $v_x(t) \, \varepsilon \, \varepsilon_x$

C7) $u_x(t) \, \varepsilon \, \varepsilon_u$

C8) Conflicts' solution for choosing, suspending and canceling conflicting mental states. For instance:

> If X and Y are active and conflicting MS then
>
> suspend X if $g_x(t) < g_y(t)$ and $g_x(t) \, \varepsilon \, \varepsilon_c$
>
> cancel X if $g_x(t) < g_y(t)$ and $g_x(t) < \varepsilon_c$
>
> suspend Y if $g_yt) < g_x(t)$ and $g_y(t) \, \varepsilon \, \varepsilon_c$
>
> cancel Y if $g_y(t) < g_x(t)$ and $g_y(t) < \varepsilon_c$

Where $g_x(t)$ and $g_y(t)$ are the interruption functions, defined in terms of urgency, intensity or importance of the corresponding MS, and ε_c is a real positive number to be used as a limit to decide if a MS will be suspended or cancelled.

We will not present here a specific definition of conflicting mental states. We consider that two MS of the same type are conflicting when they cannot coexist at the same time in the agent mind.

C9) Activation of a suspended mental state.

If X is a suspended MS and there is no other active MS conflicting with X then X is activated, unless if there is an active MS Y conflicting with X then X is activated if $n_x(t) \, \varepsilon \, \varepsilon_n$, X is maintained suspended if $g_x(t) \, \varepsilon \, \varepsilon_c$ or X is canceled.

C10) Finding a strategy to satisfy an MS.

If there is no strategy or means to satisfy a MS X then if "it is possible to find a strategy or means to satisfy X" then "find and adopt this strategy" else   if $g_x(t) \, \varepsilon \, \varepsilon_c$ X is suspended otherwise X is canceled.

C11) Find alternatives when an adopted strategy doesn't work anymore.

If K is an adopted strategy to satisfy an MS X and, and at some moment, it is not possible to satisfy X through K then find another strategy if possible and $n_X(t)$ ε $ε_n$, suspend X if $g_X(t)$ ε $ε_c$ or cancels X.

The controls C1 to C7 shown above act as trigger mechanisms, so that an MS X alone (or combined with another) will produce other mental states through its possible laws assigned in the table. The controls C8 and C9 act as filters to activate or suspend a MS. C10 and C11 govern MS directly depending on agents' actions. These controls (C8 to C11) are a meta-strategy that corresponds to the so-called "commitment" of a mental state [6], [5], [20].

The relationships among these attributes and six mental states, Beliefs (B), Desires (D), Intentions (I), Expectations (E), Hopes (H), Necessities (N) and Perceptions (P), are shown in the table of figure 1.

The attributes assigned to Beliefs, Desires and Intentions in the table, are according to the DAI specialized literature and also to Philosophy. Expectations are not extensively used in DAI and we conjecture that they have the attributes as shown in the table. We include also Hopes and Necessities as a test of our theory, because they were not considered in DAI until now. So, we suggest that these two MS could have the attributes assigned to them as in the table, but this is an open question requiring further discussion.

In figure 1 the types of mental states are indicated in the columns of the table and their corresponding attributes (marked with an x) are indicated in the rows. The group of rows labeled from L1 to L9 corresponds to the laws relating the mental states among them, that is, let W some MS indicated in a column, so if in this column a row labeled by "L1) B <=" is marked then a Belief can be caused by MS W (B <= W), the row labeled "L2) B <= B +" means that a Belief can be caused by another belief and W (B <= B + W) and similarly, "L3) D <=" means D <= W, "L4) D <= B+" means D <= D + W etc... The row labeled "L10) A <=" means that the mental state W can produce directly some action A of the agent (A <= W). The correspondence among the mental states and the controls C1, C2,...is also shown in the table. For example, the Beliefs (B) are defined by assigning them the atributes Ex. Content, Uncertainty, Insistence, Importance, L1, L2, L7, L8, L9, C8, and C9.

In the paper we are considering only individual mental states, however the notions of social mental states are also necessary for more precise and complete modeling of agents' interactions in a society [15], [25], [24], [7]. We are also developing these social notions according to our theory, but we don't have space to present these advances here.

3. The Space of Mental States and Agent Architectures

The table of figure 1 presents types of mental states relating them to a set of basic ttributes. The attributes selected define the type of mental state. In a more formal manner, type Z of a mental state is defined by a triple $<N_Z , L_Z, C_Z>$, where N_Z is a

	B	D	I	E	H	N	P
Ex. Content	x	x	x	x	x	x	x
Unsatisfaction		x	x	x	x	x	
Uncertainty	x		x	x	x		x
Urgency		x	x	x		x	
Importance	x	x	x	x	x	x	
Intensity		x	x	x		x	x
Insistence	x	x	x	x	x	x	
L1) B<=	x			x			x
L2) B <= B+	x			x			x
L3) D <=		x			x	x	
L4) D <= B+		x		x			
L5) I <=			x				
L6) I <=B+		x	x				
L7) E <=	x		x				
L8) H <=	x	x					
L9) P <=	x	x		x			
L10) A <=			x				x
Control C1		x	x	x		x	
Control C2		x	x	x		x	
Control C3		x	x	x		x	
Control C4		x	x	x		x	
Control C5		x	x	x	x	x	
Control C6		x	x	x		x	
Control C7		x	x	x		x	
Control C8	x		x	x			
Control C9	x		x	x			
Control C10			x				
Control C11			x				

Figure 1: Table of relationships among mental states Beliefs (B), Desires (D), Intentions (I), Expectations(E), Hopes (H), Necessities(N), Perceptions(P) and their possible attributes.

set of nucleus attributes excepting the External Content, L_z is a set of laws and C_z is a set of controls. A mental state X of type Z is a triple $<S_x, Z, F_x>$, where S_x is the External Content of X, Z is the triple defined above and F_x is a set of couples $<f_{ix}$, $\varepsilon_{ix}>$, such that f_{ix} is a function defined from time t to a set of real positive numbers, ε_{ix} is a real positive number and each couple F_{ix} $(F_{ix} \quad F_x)$ corresponds to an N_{iz} attribute $(N_{iz} \quad N_z)$. We denote by Z^x a triple $<S_x, Z, F_x>$ (a mental state X of type Z).

Let M represent the mental states space defined by the set of possible triples $<S_X, Z, F_X>$. An agent A architecture is a sub-set of mental states M space (A $\wp$ M). The space of possible agent architectures is M^*, the power set of M.

For example, the BDI architectures can be considered as sets $\{B^1, B^2,..., B^s, D^1, D^2,..., D^u, I^1, I^2,...,I^v\}$, where B is the Belief type, D is the Desire type and I the Intention type. This means that an implementation of that architecture would have all the attributes corresponding to Beliefs, Desires and Intentions.

The architecture (called SEM) presented in Corrêa and Coelho [1993] and Corrêa [1994] still includes the Expectation type (E) so, this architecture is defined by sets $\{B^1, B^2,..., B^s, D^1, D^2,..., D^u, I^1, I^2,...,I^v, E^1, E^2,..., E^w\}$. It was implemented on the basis of architectures $\{B^1, B^2,..., B^s\}$, $\{D^1, D^2,..., D^u\}$, $\{I^1, I^2,...,I^v\}$ and $\{E^1, E^2,..., E^w\}$(called sub-agents), such that $\{B^1, B^2,..., B^s\} \approx \{D^1, D^2,..., D^u\} \approx \{I^1, I^2,...,I^v\} \approx \{E^1, E^2,..., E^w\}$ is the agent architecture (global agent).

All that suggests a methodology for constructing agents' architectures by implementing sub-agents in such a way their architectures are defined by the sets $\{Z_k^1\}$ (k = 1,..., n; i = 1,..., n_k) and the global agent architecture is $\{Z_1^1\}\approx,... ,\{Z_k^1\}\approx,...,\approx\{Z_n^1\}$ (i = 1,..., m_k).

One of the advantages of defining the space of mental states and the space of architectures closely related is that when we are speaking about the agent's mental states we can also see which the processes and the flow of information envolved in these processes inside the architecture are.These processes are implicated in the mental states attributes. On the other hand, by seeing the processes and the flow of information inside an agent's architecture we can guess which mental states can be attributed to the agent.

4. Agent Programming

This methodology to build agents, to be useful, should not only be a guide to classify and make comparison among mental states agents' architectures since it provides a space to define them, but it should also be a guide to program agents. The approach of mental states as defined from the basic attributes shown in table of figure 1 is very adequate to map mental states to Classes and Objects of Object Oriented Programming (OOP) as shown below. Our experiments with agent programming according to the theory of the paper are currently in progress. In these testbeds the types of mental states are programmed as Classes in an OOP language as the Java programming language [1] and, a particular mental state is a particular object of the corresponding class. So, to program an agent we need to define their mental states as objects as sketched below:

```
Desire desire1 = new Desire(Extenal_Content_D1, eSD1, eUD1, eVD1, eND1, eMD1);
Desire desire2 = new Desire(Extenal_Content_D2, eSD2, eUD2, eVD2, eND2,
eMD2);
    ...
Belief belief1 = new Belief(External_Content_B1, eCB1, eMB1);
Belief belief2 = new Belief(External_Content_B2, eCB2, eMB2);
```

That is, desire1, desire2 are objects of class Desire and belief1, belief2 are objects of class Belief. The External_Content (D1, D2, B1, and B2) are Propositions. So, there are classes defined also to support the constructs of Situation Theory (infons, situations, inferences with situations etc...). The other parameters correspond to the mental states thresholds (see figure 1).

A programming sketch of the mental states desires from the framework of figure 1 can be:

```
import Proposition;
public class Desire extends Thread {
      public Situation External_Content;
public float eS, eU, eV, eN, eM;
public Desire(Proposition External_Content,  float eS, float eU, float eV, float eN,
float eM) {
        this.External_Content = External_Content;
        this.eS = eS;  this.eU = eU;  this.eV = eV;  this.eN = eN;  this.eM = eM;
      }
      public void run() { // the object desire runs concurrently with other mental states
      while (unsatisfaction() > eS & insistence() > eN)
        {// controls to trigger corresponding laws
        if ( urgency() > eU & importance() > eM & intensity() > eV)
        // trigger a law to produce another mental state
          triggerDesiresLaw(External_Content, eS, eU, eV, eN, eM);
        }
      }
      public float unsatisfaction() { //this is a method for a desires' unsatisfaction}
      public float urgency(){// this is a method for a desires' urgency}
      public float insistence() { // this is a method for a desires' insistence }
      public float importance() { // this is a method for a desires' importance}
      public float intensity() { // this is a method for a desires' intensity}
      public void triggerDesiresLaw(Situation EC, float eS, float eU, float eV, float eN,
float eM)
       { // this is a  method to trigger the desire corresponding laws to produce other
      mental states}
}// End of Desire
```

We have no space and it is not our intention to present here a complete nor a consistent programming of the mental state framework. We only wish to show in a very sketched way how the structure presented in figure 1 can be directly and easily described in a object programming language as Java. It is important to note that a desire object is implemented as a Java thread, that is, it runs concurrently with other mental states which, on the other hand, is also a thread. The other mental states can also be programmed similarly. So, the concurrent computing is a basis for this programming framework.

5. Conclusion

This article proposes a theory for defining two spaces, one for mental states and another for architectures. The mental states spaces may include more mental states, not only to analyse their validity but also their dynamics and influence on the agent behaviour.

Our theory also allows for the definition of the space of possible architectures in terms of mental state spaces. This is really an advantage because it offers tools for engineering and programming agents (in a Object Oriented Programming paradigm) and a methodology for the experimentation and the evaluation of the relations among mental states, architectures and agents behaviour.

So, modeling the actions of an agent and looking inside their mental sites (sequence of mental events) makes the design and the programming of agents easier.

References

[1] K. Arnold and J. Gosling. The Java Programming Language, The Java Series, Sun Microsystems, 1996.

[2 Perry, 1983] J. Barwise and J. Perry. Situation and Attitudes, A Bradford Book, The MIT Press, 1983.

[3] Michael Bratman. What is Intentions? In P. R. Cohen, J.L. Morgan and M. Pollack (eds.), Intentions in Communication, The MIT Press, Cambridge, MA, 1990.

[4] F. Brazier, B. Dunin-Keplicz, J.   Treur, R. Verbrugge. Modeling Internal Dynamic Behaviour of BDI Agents, Proceedings of MODELAGE Workshop, January, 1997.

[5] Cristiano Castelfranchi. Commitments: From Individual to Groups and Organizations, Proceedings of The First International Conference on Multi-Agent Systems (ICMAS-95), 1995.

[6] P. Cohen and H. Levesque. Intention is Choice with Commitment, Artificial Intelligence, 42:213-261, 1990.

[7] P. Cohen, H. Levesque and I. Smith. On Team Formation. In Contemporary Action Theory, G. Hintikka and R. Tuomela (editors), Kluvier Academic Pub, 1997.

[8] Milton Corrêa and Helder Coelho. Around the Architectural Agent Approach to Model Conversations, Proceedings of Modeling Autonomous Agents in a Multi-Agent World (MAAMAW-93), Nêuchatel, Switzerland, Springer-Verlag, 1993.

[9] Milton Corrêa. The Architecture of Dialogs of Distributed Cognitive Agents, Ph. D. Thesis (in Portuguese), Federal University of Rio de Janeiro, January, 1994.

[10] Milton Corrêa and Helder Coelho. A Framework for Mental States and Agent Architectures. In Multi-Agents Theory and Architectures Conference, MASTA97, Coimbra, 1997.

[11] R. Deeth. Chemical Choreography. New Scientis, July 5th, 1997.

[12] K. Devlin. Logic and Information, Cambridge University Press, 1991.

[13], Esther Frankel and Milton Corrêa. A Cognitive approach to Body-Psychotherapy. The Journal of Biosynthesis, Vol 26 N° 1, Abbotisbury Publications, April, 1995.

[14] S. Franklin and A. Graesser. Is it an agent, or just a program? a taxonomy for autonomous agents, Memphis University, Working Report, March, 1996.

[15] N. Jennings. Controlling cooperative problem solving in industrial multi-agents systems using joint intentions. Artificial Intelligence 75, 1995.

[16] Neila Moussale, Rosa Viccari and Milton Corrêa. Tutor-Student Interaction Modeling in an Agent Architecture Based on Mental States, Brazilian Symposium on AI (SBIA-96), Springer-Verlag, 1996 .

[17], I. Pörn. Action Theory and Social Science. Some Formal Models, Reidel Publishing Company, Dordecht-Holland, 1974.

[18] Milton Rokeach. Beliefs, Attitudes and Values, Jossey-Bass Inc, Pub., 1970.

[19] Bertrand Russel. The Analysis of Mind, George Allen&Unwin Ltd, 1971.

[20] Yohav Shoham. Agent-Oriented Programming, Artificial Intelligence, 60, 1993.

[21] Herbert Simon. Motivational and Emotional Controls of Cognition, Psychological Review, Vol. 74, N° 1, 1967.

[22] Aaron Sloman. Motives Mechanisms and Emotions, In M.A.Boden (ed.) The Philosophy of Artificial Intelligence, Oxford Readings in Philosophy Series, Oxford University Press, 1990.

[23] Aaron Sloman. What Sort of Architecture is Required for a Human-like Agent? Invited talk at Cognitive Modeling Workshop, AAAI96, Portland Oregon, August, 1996.

[24] Milind Tambe. Teamwork in Real-world, Dynamic Environments. International Conference on Multi-agents Systems, 1996.

[25] R. Tuomela. The Importance of Us. Stanford University Press, 1995.

[26] Bonnie Webber, N. Badler, B. Eugenio, C. Geib, L. Levison, M. Moore. Instructions, Intentions and Expectations, University of Pennsylvania, Computer and Information Department, June, 1993.

[27] Eric Werner. A Unified View of Information, Intention and Ability, In Decentralized Artificial Intelligence, Y. Demazeau and J. P. Mueller (eds.), Elsevier Science Pub., 1991.

Acknowledgment

PROJECTO PRAXIS XXI SARA 2/2.1/TIT/1662/95

Genetic Integration
in a Multiagent System
for Job-Shop Scheduling

Thierry Galinho[1], Alain Cardon[2], and Jean-Philippe Vacher[1]

[1] PSI-LIRINSA
Insa de Rouen
Place Emile Blondel, F-76130 Mont-Saint-Aignan
{Thierry.Galinho,Jean-Philippe.Vacher}@insa-rouen.fr
[2] LIP6 Paris VI
UPMC, Case 69
4, Place Jussieu, F-75252 Paris Cedex 05
Alain.Cardon@lip6.fr

Abstract. The Job-Shop scheduling problem constitutes a typical NP-Difficult problem. Determining an optimal solution is almost impossible, but trying to improve an existent solution is the way to lead to a tasks repartition which is better. We use Multi-Agents Systems (M.A.S.). These simulate the behavior of entities that are going to collaborate to accomplish actions on a Gantt diagram with the intention to better resolve a given economic function. Communications between global and local agents, components of the MAS, due to their actions, manage the appearance of agents of intermediate granularity and the global optimization in production scheduling. To have micro and meta-agents, a Multi-Objective Genetic algorithm is used, and especially on account of an ideal solution of such a problem which is a point where each objective function corresponds to the best (minimum) possible value. The genetic autonomy and the notion of motivation for an agent may lead to a drastically new kind of emergence phenomenon (different social behavior, auto-referring evaluation process, ...) in self-organizing multiagent systems. It is certainly a difficult task but it may set the seeds of a prolific approach concerning artificial life to optimize a Job-Shop Scheduling Problem.

1 Introduction

The Job-Shop scheduling problem constitutes a typical NP-Difficult problem. It becomes then impossible to determine an optimal solution (correspondent to a determined criterion) in a reasonable time. It invites therefore to use random techniques and or heuristics to determine a good quality solution. This solution being able to be an optimal solution. Nevertheless, seen the important number of possible solutions, it is very difficult that we determined rather an optimum place. The graphic representation of a solution is made under the form of a Gantt diagram.

Helder Coelho (Ed.): IBERAMIA'98, LNAI 1484, pp. 76–87, 1998.
© Springer-Verlag Berlin Heidelberg 1998

The problem consists to improve this representation so as to find a best therefore a new solution corresponding to a new optimum, by constraints satisfying that we have fixed. To do that, we employ a multiagent system (MAS) in order that agents that constitute it, according to the knowledge that they have been able to acquire [11], make evolve the Gantt diagram to a good solution. We present in this communication the multiagent systems in production's scheduling. Then, we will specify the model that we have used and finally the notion of granularity of agents coming from the agent's knowledge and from the reproduction between agents.

2   MAS in Scheduling

2.1   Representation of the Gantt Diagram

The representation level that we have fixed, is the operation. A job being constituted of several operations, it is necessary to minimize the maximum delay of all jobs [15][13]. According to a solution, good or bad, the Gantt diagram presents some characteristics as the presence of holes, operations of similarly nature dispersed on the graph, etc [10]. It represents the graphic interpretation of the scheduling of all jobs (See Fig. 1). The objective is to determine a best solution by minimizing the presence of holes (times die), by regrouping operations of similarly nature so as to reduce times of cleaning and preserie by taking into account the matric of costs. General manner, it is necessary to improve the Gantt diagram of horizontal manner. But the alone horizontal vision is not significant, even by respecting constraints. It is important to improve the Gantt diagram according to specificities, zones, that can be released, correspondent to similar characteristics. It appears therefore zones having special characteristics (zone of inactivity, ...). Therefore, agents must act on these zones so as to improve the Gantt diagram.

2.2   Objects Manipulated

As we have said it previously, the representation level that we have chosen is the operation. Therefore, objects that we manipulate will be operations. By extension, agents will act on groups of operations (or zones). Previously, we have introduced the notion of zones. A zone does not make reference necessarily in physical operations, the former can be potential as a hole that can correspond to a potential task of not activity.
Consequently, the goal of agents composing the MAS is to operate roundups of operations, in the respect of precedence constraints to the level of the Gantt diagram.

3   Objective of the MAS on the Gantt Diagram

By definition, MAS represent a subset emerging of the Artificial Intelligence that tend to put in evidence the two following principles :

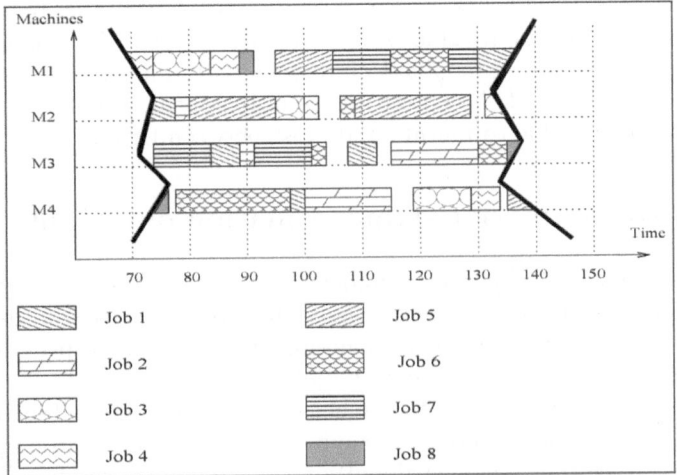

Fig. 1. A Gantt diagram representation

1. The complex system construction employing agent multiple,
2. Mechanisms for the coordination of independent agent behaviors.

Nevertheless, this definition is not generally accepted in AI, for purposes contained in our article, we consider an agent as being an entity with objectives, actions to accomplish and areas of knowledge, which is situated in its environment.

However, the ability to consider the coordination of the autonomous agent behavior is a new way among fields of the Distributed Artificial Intelligence (DAI). Therefore, because of the knowledge of agents, rules of actions, ..., the MAS will have for principal objective to group agents having similar behaviors to elaborate strategies to the jobs level, jobs of jobs, machines, machines of machines, etc. Thus, **it appears the notion of group.** The objective of the MAS is to improve the Gantt diagram, therefore it invites to establish the notion of group corresponding to elementary entities having common grinds and physical sameness (same capacity of machine, etc.) or interdependence.

We will use the notion of zone for the roundup of entities on the Gantt diagram while we will speak about the notion of group for the roundup of entities similarly or close nature.

Agents have to intervene on groups and elementary entities, the MAS will be then composed with micro and meta-agents. It is therefore important, for this evolution, to introduce agents having a character : the meta-agents of evolution. These meta-agents will have therefore as function to make evolve this organization by means a Genetic Algorithm establishing the sexued reproduction of agents . It is necessary to note that, traditionally, agents have as unique possibility only the cloning. But here, we use Genetic Algorithm for the physical evolution of agents. It appears therefore, in the course of the evolution, different sizes of agents: we will speak about agent's granularity. We have therefore micro and the meta-agents that are going to intervene, according to their size, on an entity or a group, by passing by intermediate levels. Thus, agents having a meta-knowledge are going be able to intervene on the macro-entities (group) as well as on some zones of the Gantt diagram. It appears therefore a distributed agent system being able to mutate and cross between them.

4   The Multidimesion Transformation of a Gantt Diagram

The representation of a planning under the form of a Gantt diagram in two dimensions does not allow to define the global characteristics or general of the former. By the former, we hearing the notion of quality, the respect of the master plan, etc. An operation, constituent of a job, makes emerge only the characteristics places (delay, advance, ...). Nevertheless, these local characters do not make show local information, nevertheless capital, aiming to obtain from global evaluations from predictions (they as global) of the commercial service. The roundup of operations by family, by taking account a macro-nomemclature, to which are made correspond the macro - programs for the realization of tasks corresponding to a family, is not visible. General manner, given the nature NP -Difficult of organizations, we plan to improve a Gantt diagram, according to an economic function. In order that, it is necessary us to transform the evaluated Gantt in a dynamic system whose:

1. views to the level place, correspondent to a structure such that the share, the operation, ... and
2. views to the level global, correspondent, they also to a structure (Gantt, etc).

These views are in interaction unite them by report to others by the dynamic function intermediary, which correspond to the evolution of an organization. The idea is to end to an organization of manipulated elements. This organization is in tension, that is to say that some elements "react" by putting in obviousness the fact that they not contribute to an improvement of the Gantt diagram. The goal of our system is "to slacken" it, to end to a global improvement of the Gantt without arrive to a "rupture". By rupture, we hear the fact that the Gantt no longer goes from the whole to satisfy production needs and to take account master plans of the enterprise. To make this, we plan to realize a colored transformation of the Gantt diagram to obtain a multi -dimensional representation of the former. We have chosen as formalism the decomposition of the specter of the white light to represent the n-uplet **Advance − Delay − Priority**. Thus, by playing on nuances, we can represent all possible cases n-uplet (See Fig. 2). However, some characteristics are not visible but have inevitably to appear in the coding (family of product, etc) so as to realize the crosscheck to determine strategies to implement for multiagent systems, composed of global agents (of trends) and local agents (operation on one or a group of tasks), could improve globally the Gantt diagram, while satisfying to respect of the population. Thereby, the radiation of an operation corresponds to its ability to make

show information clearly: activity to realize, time of cycle, machine to use, etc.
A 2–D Gantt diagram represents a discreet environment because of the presence of holes, consequently, it is not possible to consider as continuous space.
Topologies, generally defined, make reference to a continuous environment. Our
objective is to show that connexities ordinarily defined in a discreet space are
equivalent to the connexities of a continuous space. That will allow us to define
continuous totalities from totality discreet. A general manner, that returns to
make a decomposition of $\mathbb{R}^n$.

From the transformation of the Gantt diagram in discreet multi-dimension images, we can regroup identical information between them. By transforming our
Gannt diagram in multi-dimension image, we can have a more global vision of
the system on which agents will be able to intervene.

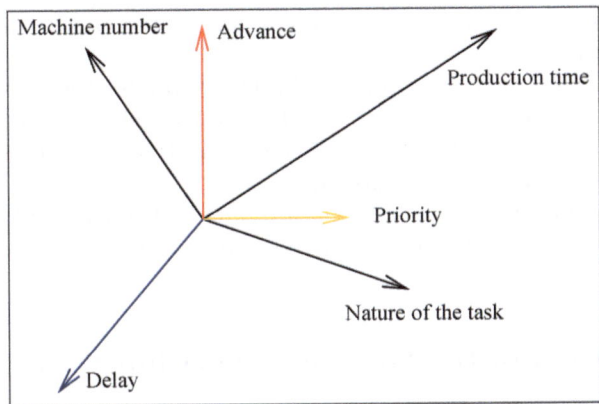

Fig. 2. Multidimension representation of a Gantt diagram

4.1 Mutation and Crossing Functions

Traditionally, agents of the MAS can only reproduce by cloning. Out here, we
introduce the notion of sexued reproduction. It is entirely possible to cross several
agents so as to give some new. To make this, we use a genetic algorithm.

The mutation will correspond to the change of a bit (1) [12], thus, we can use
switchboard operators.

$$1 \longrightarrow 0 \text{ and } 0 \longrightarrow 1 \tag{1}$$

Our constraint, at the mutation level, corresponds to have a correspondence between the bits string and the database. Thus, by changing the value of one bit,
we can introduce a new character. This will have a repercussion on the environment, but especially on its membership to a group. The communications it
has been able to have with other elements of the group will be, incontestably,
changed. For example, consider that the mutation introduces a certain aggres-
siveness at the agent level, then communications with the group are going to

change and the group, consequently, will probably loose some of its social cohesion. Therefore, in order to avoid the too abrupt upset of the social balance that can exist between individuals composing a group and the organization itself, the mutation interventions by genetic algorithms will need to be weak. Nevertheless, we can consider that at the beginning, the simulation of the organization, as at the beginning of a civilization, progress was rapid enough. Therefore, at the beginning, we can introduce an important number of mutations. We will use as distribution (2), for the number of mutation by generation, a curve of parameters (α, β) [1].

$$f : x \longrightarrow \frac{\beta}{x^\alpha} \text{ with } \beta \in \mathbb{R}^+ \text{ and } \alpha \in \mathbb{R}^{+*} \tag{2}$$

Thus, by using this type of distribution, we introduce a lot of mutations at the beginning of the simulation and few at the end in order to avoid the breaking of the process of evolution by deeply modifying characteristics of chromosomes, therefore of individuals.

Too many mutation in the systems would inexorably set the seeds of chaos. We have previously seen a possible distribution. Nevertheless, by using a Gaussian distribution to determine the probability of mutation, we preserve the switchboard concerning the Genetic Algorithm.

Also, mutation will not be done by a mathematical function at the end of the developpement but a meta-agent can be used to stoped the process if the system didn't give good results.

5   Description of the Genetic Algorithm Used

A MAS simulates the behavior of entities composing a social organization. The GA, as for it, simulates the biological evolution process, in the senses of Darwin, of entities composing an organization. That is to say that less effective individuals are going to disappear to the profit of individuals better adapted. It appears therefore an elitist system, style " law of the strongest " that is established.

The genetic algorithm used resumes the great lines described in works of D. Goldberg [7] and J. Holland [8,9]. Nevertheless, a Simple Genetic Algorithm (SGA) makes intervene only one function of performance. Here, we use the criterion of optimization of Pareto to establish our fitness function. We have a multicriterion optimization function [4]. The result is a multi-objectif genetic algorithm [6].

The ideal solution of such a problem is a point where each objective function corresponds to the best (minimum) possible value. The ideal solution, in most cases, does not exist because of the contradictory nature, rather contradictory objective functions: compromises have to be done. A different concept of optimality has to be introduced. Solving a multiobjective problem generally requires the identification of Pareto optimal solutions [14], a concept introduced by V. Pareto, a prominent Italian economist, at the end of the last century. A solution is said Pareto optimal, or non dominated, if starting from that point in the design space, the value of any of the objective functions cannot be improved without deteriorating at least one of the others.

5.1   Direct Multiobjective Problem's Solution

Directly solving the multiobjective problem has the advantage of finding a representative subset of the Pareto front in one shot; on the other hand, not many efficient methods exist which are capable of this approach. A Genetic Algorithm using the dominance criteria to drive the evolution of the population is one of these methods. The characterizing feature of the multi-objective GA is thus the introduction of the Pareto criteria in the method used for individuals selection [14]; by selecting individuals in the reproduction phase according to the domination criteria, a set of non dominated solutions can be developed. These are all possible alternative solutions to the problem, which meet the requirements at different level of compromise, and that approximate the Pareto front of the problem. In this way, the arbitrary choice regarding the weights to attribute to the different design criteria is avoided.

6   Going Deeply in the Relationships of GA and MAS

The use of GA in MAS is the beginning of what can be an interesting research area. There are clearly two kind of approaches, the first is centralized, in other words, some of the genetic is outside the agent. The function of selection is a good example of such out-of-the-agent feature [18][16][17].
However, we believe that if one wants to completely merge the genetic approach and MAS (See Fig. 3), we must make the agent a completely autonomous genetic entity. By that we mean that not only the genetic patrimony has to be "onboard" but also the functions of selection and crossing. An agent must choose which other agent it wants to reproduce with [17]. The location of the function of mutation is not clearly known since it is caused by the possible exposure to external events coming from the environment and during the genetic code replication phase.

If we also introduce the notion of motivated behavior for agents [2] we go deeply in the artificial life problematics. The genetic autonomy and the notion of motivation for an agent may lead to a drastically new kind of emergence phenomenon (different social behavior, auto-referring evaluation process, ...) in self-organizing multi-agent systems. It is certainly a difficult task but it may set the seeds of a prolific approach concerning artificial life.

7   Agent Modelisation

The goal of our problem is to improve a Gantt diagram corresponding to a Job-Shop Scheduling Problem. To do this, we use a simplified version of a real

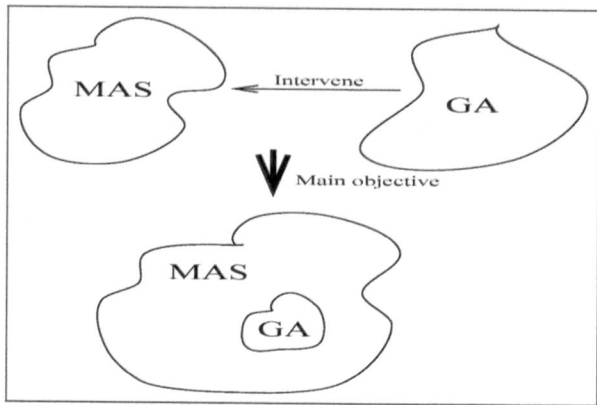

Fig. 3. MAS and GA in the environment

description of a workshop which have been defined in the system named FISIAS (Fast Interactive System for Intelligent Automated Scheduling). This development, made for an industrial structure, was not adapted to our case obviously. We have chosen to modify or to remove some elements of the model.

Generally speaking, the set of treatments refering to a schedule in quantity is not used here. On the same manner, we work with a finite loading. Therefore, we keep informations coming from the infinite loading as indicators, gauges for our system. In our development, we use finite loading but we use some results coming from MRP (infinite loading). At the level of the workshop, we use the linear time and not the calendar time.

7.1   Possible Roundups

Within workshop, we have some equivalent machines. To lead to an agents' representation, we must have roundups of entities. This entities will correspond to an "agent" for the future development of our problem. These entities can be an equivalent machine, a job, an operation, ...

Thus, coming from an independent set of equivalent machines, we made, according to criteria, roundups to obtain machines' group. After, these-ones will be divided in sub-groups according to the output, to the matrix cleaning time, to the loading/bottleneck, ... We made on the same manner for jobs, operations, ... In our model, a job can be characterised by its linear routing, the fact that it can be interrupted, divided and by dates (due date, availability, criticality, jamming, ...). An operation is characterised by the process time, ...

As we have groups of machines, we also have groups of jobs, operations, ..., and, each group have a set of sub-groups. We have sub-group by output, by matrix of cleaning/pre-series, etc. Therefore, how obtain coherent sub-groups?

To obtain coherent sub-groups, we use the refine technic. To define sub-groups, we coming from the biggest group and we refine these sub-groups to specialize them. At the end of the process, we lead a static representation.

At the level of the dynamic representation corresponding to the quality appearance, we use informations coming from the schedule with infinite loading as well as these coming from quality criteria. Thus, we obtain groups by using ressouces from the workshop and from the material.

7.2   Scheduling System by Agents

As we have groups of machines, we have also groups of jobs, operations, etc. Some agents have to accomplish actions on a part of the Gantt diagram or on a group. Our agents must evolve to do revelant actions and manage/modify/create specific groups. Our system do not use the scheduling itself but use the dynamic of our system. We don't put jobs, operations to relise on machines directly. This is agents that intervene to put operations on the Gantt diagram. These placing will be made according to timeliness, possibilities of agents.

As we can see on the figure 4, the scheduling is realised by agents. Therefore, as the scheduling evolve during the process, our system wants to have agents that evolve during the scheduling process. This evolution is done by a genetic feedback.

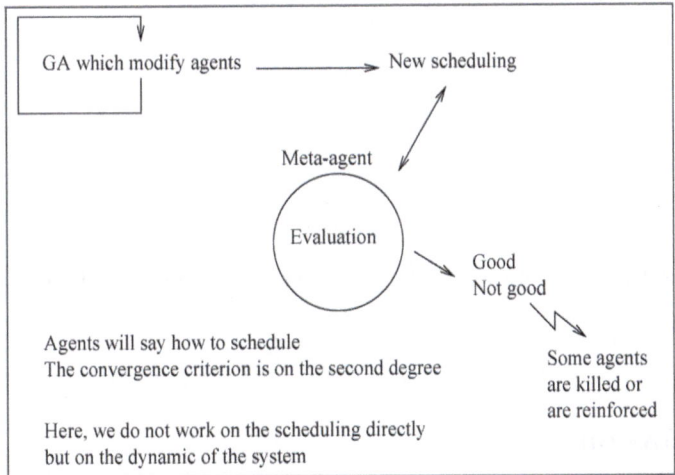

Fig. 4. Dynamic represensation by agents for our problem

8   Agent Representation

8.1   View of an Agent

Coming from the representation and the definition of an agent, which have been done by J. Ferber, we can have a simplified view of this-one.
An agent can be represented as follow:

- actions' function to lead to groups of agents.
- heuristics - strategies.
- homeostatic parameters to lead to behaviour's rules.
- a communication network

Therefore, an agent simulate the behaviour of a leaving organism. Thus, we can said that an agent have three statements: the peace, to intendto do something and the action (See Fig. 5).

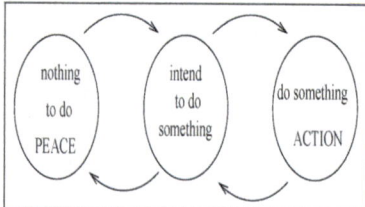

Fig. 5. The three statement of an agent

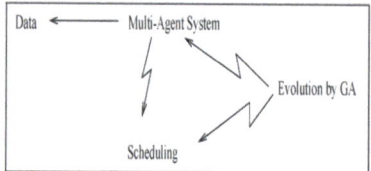

Fig. 6. Data representation between MAS and Gantt diagram

9   Conclusion

We have seen in this communication that a Multiagent System can be used with a Genetic Algorithm to minimize the delay of a Job-Shop Scheduling Problem. Determining an optimal solution is almost impossible, but trying to improve an existent solution is the way to lead to a tasks repartition which is better. Therefore, we use have used Multi-Agents Systems.

According to a solution, good or bad, the Gantt diagram presents some characteristics as the presence of holes, operations of similarly nature dispersed on the graph, etc. The MAS simulate the behavior of entities that are going to collaborate to accomplish actions on the Gantt with view to better resolving the given economic function. Therefore, we haven't one econmic function, it's why we use a Multi-Objective Genetic Algorithm to find an ideal solution. This solution is a point where each objective function corresponds to the best (minimum) possible value.

During the simulation process, agents granularity appears with the mutation behavior introduce by GA. At the end of the simulation, communications between global and local agents, due to their actions, manage the appearance of agents of intermediate granularity and the global optimization in production scheduling. This communication reflects the genetic integration in a multiagent system; the first results show that a MAS and a multi-objective GA are a way to optimize a Gantt diagram of a Job-Shop Scheduling Problem.

References

1. Bäck, T.:", Self-Adaptation in Genetic Algorithms, [19] (1992) 263–271 81
2. Cardon, A. and Lesage, F.: An Interpretation Process of Communication Between Actors in a Distributed System for Crisis Management, Proceedings of the Symposium of Informatic Economics, (1997) 82
3. Cardon, A. and Durand, S.: A Model of Crisis Management System Including Mental Representations, AAAI Spring Symposium, Stanford University, USA, March (1997)
4. Chankong, V. and Haines, Y. Y.: Multiobjective decision making: theory and methodology, North Holland series in system science and engineering, North Holland, New York, 8, (1983) 81
5. Ferber, J.: Les systèmes multi-agents, Vers une intelligence collective, Ed. InterEditions, Paris (1995)
6. Gass, S. and Saaty, T.: The computational algorithm for the parametric objective function, Naval research logistics quarterly, 2 (1955) 39–65 81
7. Goldberg, D. E.: Genetic Algorithms in Search, Optimization, and Machine Learning, Addison-Wesley, Reading, MA (1989) 81
8. Holland, J. H.: Adaptation in natural and artificial systems, University of Michigan Press, Ann Arbor, MI (1975) 81
9. Holland, J. H.: Adaptation in natural and artificial systems: an introductory analysis with applications in biology, control and artificial intelligence, **Complex adaptive systems**, MIT Press, Cambridge, MA(1992) 81
10. Lamy, P.: Ordonnancement et gestion de production, Hermes (1987) 77
11. Langton, C. G.: Artificial Life: the proceedings of an interdisciplinary workshop on the synthesis and simulation of living systems, Workshop held September, 1987 in Los Alamos, New Mexico, Addison-Wesley, Redwood City, CA, September (1989) 77
12. Michalewicz, Z.: Genetic algorithms + data structures = evolution programs, Springer, Berlin (1992) 80
13. Pécuchet, JP. & al: FISIAS, Fast Interactive System for Intelligent Automated Scheduling, Revue Automatique et Productique Appliquées, Hermes, 2(4), (1989) 23–38 77

14. Poloni, C.: Hybrid GA for multi objective aerodynamic shape optimisation, Genetic Algorithms in Engineering and Computer Science, by Winter G., Périaux J., Gálan M., Cuesta P., John Wiley & Sons Ltd, England, December (1995) 397–416 81, 82
15. Portmann, MC.: Méthodes de décomposition spatiale et temporelle en ordonnancement de production, Université de Nancy 1, Doctorat d'Etat, (1987) 77
16. Vacher, JP., Galinho, T. and Z. Mammeri, Z.: Une application des algorithmes génétiques à l'ordonnancement d'atelier, MOSIM'97, Actes de la première conférence francophone, Modélisation et simulation des systèmes de production et de logistique, by M. Itmi, JP. Pécuchet, H. Pierreval, Editions Hermes, Paris, (1997) 43–50 82
17. Vacher, JP., Cardon, A. and Galinho, T.: Genetic Algorithms in a Multi-Agent System, Proceeding of the EUROGEN'97 Conference, Trieste, Italy, Web site : http://eurogen.cira.it, (1997) 82
18. Vacher, JP., Cardon, A. and Galinho, T.: Heuristics Granularity in a Multi-Agents Systems (MAS): Application to the Production Management, Proceeding of the YOR10 conference, (1998) 82
19. Varela, F. J. and Bourgine P.: Towards a Pratice of Autonomous Systems: Proceedings of the First European Conference on Artificial Life, MIT Press, Cambridge, MA (1992) 86

A New Dynamic Model for a Multi-Agent Formation

Daniel Gonçalves[1], Pedro Machado[1], and Ana Paiva[2]

[1] Instituto Superior Técnico, Technical University of Lisbon
[2] Instituto Superior Técnico, Technical Univesity of Lisbon and INESC
djvg@gia.ist.utl.pt
pedro.machado@ip.pt
Ana.Paiva@inesc.pt

Abstract. Many systems have been already developed concerning agent teams in a world with obstacles. One of the problems of such systems lies on how to maintain a pre-defined formation when we have several agents moving in the world. In this paper we defend that, in order to have a robust and realistic system, a control model that includes the notions of mass and acceleration must be used. To prove that, we developed a control system based on the classic mechanical physics, which is a force-based model. From the results obtained we can see that, although some problems arise when using such realistic kind of model, they are solvable and the quality of the simulations performed by the system is significantly better than the simulations obtained using other control models.

Keywords: Multi-Agent Systems, Multi-Agent Formation

1 Introduction

Amongst several known problems in the field of mobile robotics, the most usually discussed is how to allow the robot to move autonomously in an unknown environment. This problem becomes worse when we consider not only a single robot, but a team of them given that a robot must consider not only the terrain topology, but also the positions and movements of the remaining robots, to prevent collisions and to stay out of their way. To handle such problem we must therefore establish a *group behavior* that allows the robots to perform in the right way.

Recently, these problems have been the object of study of the area of *software agents* [4] and multi-agent systems. One of the distinguishing features of this area is the fact that each agent is responsible for determining its own actions (resorting only to it's knowledge of the world, given by the sensors), not being controlled by any external process. This tries to mimic what we can find in nature, where no higher intelligence determines the individual actions. Rather, the overall behavior of the society of agents emerges from the individual decisions. The software agent's approach seems to be not only more adequate, but also more correct to deal with this problem.

Helder Coelho (Ed.): IBERAMIA'98, LNAI 1484, pp. 88–100, 1998.

In this area, several systems have already been developed. The most famous of these is undoubtedly, the *BOIDS* system, created by Craig Reynolds [3]. Based on the same approach other systems have been developed, such as, for example the system by Hodgins and Brogan [2] that simulates a herd of pogo-stick-like robots in a tri-dimensional world. One aspect of these systems is that they do not maintain any kind of formation or differentiate the agents and specify their desired positions in relation to each other. However, formations are important since they allow the team to use its sensory assets in a more efficient way than if the team was arranged randomly [1]. This paper focuses exactly in the formation control of a team of robots.

Moreover, we want for the formation to remain robust enough in the presence of unpredicted obstacles. One system that achieves these goals was created by Balch and Arkin [1]. It is based on a small number of robots able to maintain a pre-determined formation while moving towards a goal, even in the presence of obstacles. However, some limitations can be found on their approach, in particular its lack of realism.

In this paper we defend that such kind of system should have a more realistic dynamic model, thus, including the notions of mass and acceleration. The work here described introduces these notions through the use of a formation control system based on the classic mechanical physics, thus, a force-based model. We will show the problems that arise when using that realistic kind of model, and how we solved them.

This paper is organised as follows. In the next section, we will discuss the problem domain and the entities involved in it. Next, we will rapidly describe the main characteristics of Bach and Arkin's system [1], and explain the reasons behind the need for some improvements. Then, we will show what makes our system different from the existing ones and the results we achieved with it. Finally we will discuss the results and point out the conclusions our work led to.

2   The Problem Domain

The system created simulates a society where several agents can move in a world with obstacles, whilst trying to reach a goal position. Since this system can be seen as an extension of the original work by Balch and Arkin [1] we introduce the basic concepts involved very briefly.

2.1   The Formations

In order to make possible the definition of a formation, it is necessary to distinguish an agent from its companions. Thus, we attribute an unique number to each agent. A very large number of formations are, of course, possible. There are, however, four standard formations in military domains, depicted in Fig. 1:

Line: the robots travel side-to-side.
Column: the robots travel behind each other.

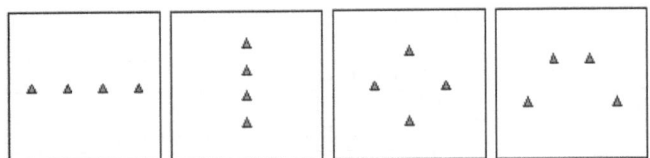

Fig. 1. Possible formations

Diamond: the position of the robots is that of the vertexes of a diamond.
Wedge: the robots are positioned in a "V" shape.

These formations, besides allowing the verification of the validity of the system in that domain, are rich enough to test a great amount of situations in simulation terms, each one having its own problems, as we will see below.

2.2   Reference Methods

There are three classical reference methods: in *relation to a given robot* , in *relation to a leader*, and in *relation to the formation's center of mass*. The first method is similar to the one used in BOIDS [3], with the difference that in BOIDS the position of a bird was dependent on those of its neighbors, which could be any other birds. In here, the robot from which the position is determined is given from the start. The definition of the desired position of a robot in relation to its reference point is given in terms of two values: an *angle* and a *distance*.

The angle must be measured not in relation to the horizontal, but in relation to the perpendicular of the movement of the reference point. This will allow the formation to maintain itself when not moving straightforward.

It's velocity vector, in the case of a single robot gives the direction of the movement of the reference point. In the case the reference point is the center of mass of the formation, the average of the individual velocity vectors is used.

2.3   The World

The world is a bi-dimensional square with arbitrary size, where several *obstacles* (columns with a given radius) can be found.

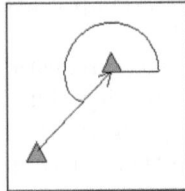

Fig. 2. Relative reference

Table 1. Motor Schemas

Motor schemas	Usefulness
Avoid-Static-Obstacle	Avoid collisions with static obstacles
Avoid-Robot	Avoid collisions with other robots
Move-To-Goal	Drive the robots towards the goals
Noise	Noise
Maintain-Formation	Force the robots to maintain the formation

Apart from the obstacles, the only other important points in the world are the *goals*. A goal is a point that represents the place the robots must go in order to fulfil their mission. In the case there are several goals in the world, the robots must get to them in a pre-specified order. The robots are considered to have achieved a goal when the center of mass of the formation is less than a given number of units from the goal.

2.4   The Motor-Schemas

The formation behaviors of the robots were implemented as motor-schemas (Table 1). These schemas are similar to the ones used by Balch and Arkin.

From each schema we have a vector (usually a force), ranging from zero to a preset maximum. All the resulting vectors are added, taking into account their relative gain. The resulting vector that determines, at each instant, how will the robot's movement be altered.

Avoid-Static-Obstacle and Avoid-Robot: these schemas' functions are used to prevent collisions with an obstacle or with other robots. The resulting vector will be in line with the line that joins the robot and the obstacle and the direction that will keep them both apart. The intensity of the vector will depend on two values: a *minimum* and a *maximum range*. If the distance between the robot and the obstacle is grater that the maximum range, then the intensity of the vector will be zero. If it is smaller than the minimum range, it will be the maximum permitted intensity. Otherwise, it will oscillate between those two values.

Move-To-Goal: this schema is the responsible to make a robot move in direction of it's objective. Its result is simply a vector with the maximum intensity and the direction of the goal.

Noise: to make the simulation more realistic, this schema results in a vector with random direction and intensity, thus introducing noise in the system.

Maintain-Formation: this is, perhaps, the most important schema, since it allows the robots to position themselves in the desired formation positions. First, the desired position is determined, in relation to the established reference point. Then according to the distance of the robot to that point, the intensity of the vector with its direction will vary.

Like in the avoidance schemas, two values are considered: a minimum and a maximum radius. In this case, however, if the distance to the desired point is greater than the maximum range, the intensity of the vector will be the greatest allowed. The desired point is then said to be in the *"ballistic zone"*. If the distance is smaller than the minimum radius, the intensity of the vector will be zero (*"dead zone"*). Otherwise, the desired point is in the *"controlled zone"* and the vector's intensity is proportional to the distance.

2.5   Limitations of the Existing Approach

The mechanisms we described until now were used in system developed by Balch and Arkin [1]. However, there are some limitations to their work. Firstly, the reference method that gives the desired position of a given robot in relation to that of another robot was not implemented. Secondly, and by far the most important omission of this work is that the simulation model is based only on the velocity, and not acceleration. This means that the vectors returned by the motor-schemas are, in fact, an indication of the desired velocity in the next instant. This makes the simulation very unrealistic, since it assumes there can exist infinite accelerations, that can radically change the speed vector of a body instantly. It also simplifies greatly the control problems, making the task of maintaining the formation a very easy one.

These limitations motivated the creation of our system, which will be described and evaluated in the following sections.

3   A Realistic Simulation Model

To overcome the limitations presented, a new system was created. Mainly, we have improved the existing system on three factors: new types of obstacles, new vector intensity decay models and a dynamic force-based control model.

3.1   New Types of Obstacles

In the real world, it is very unrealistic to assume that all the obstacles an agent will face are fixed in nature. Not only that but it is plausible that the agent would react differently when faced with different obstacles. It might, for instance, start to deviate from larger ones first (since they are circular in nature, they will occupy a greater area to avoid, requiring a larger deviation).

So, in the first place, we assumed our agents have some kind of "improved sensor" that can not only detect what is the distance to the nearer obstacles, but also the *curvature radius* of them. Our *avoid-static-obstacle* motor-schema will take this information into consideration, and the resulting vector will be proportional to the size of the obstacles.

Besides this change to the static obstacles, we also introduced another kind of obstacles: the *mobile obstacles*. These are other agents that, unlike the robots, are limited to roam the landscape in a pre-determined or random way, thus hampering the voyage of the robots. We created these obstacles in order to account for the multitude of unexpected features the robots might encounter on a real situation (people, animals, and so on). To deal with these obstacles, a different schema, *avoid-moving-obstacle*, was introduced.

3.2   Vector Intensity Decay Models

When determining what will be the intensity of the vector returned by a motor-schema, two radiuses are normally used. In the case of the *avoid-static-obstacle* scheme, for instance, when the distance between the obstacle and the robot is superior to a given radius, the intensity will be zero. If it is smaller than a certain value, the intensity will be the maximum allowed. Between those two values, the intensity will vary. In the original system, the variation of the intensity of that vector was *linear*. In our model, we have implemented a *quadratic* decay.

We found that often, this aspect added an "urgency feeling" to the robots, as the repulsion (or attraction, depending on the schema) will increase greatly in extreme situations, but will be moderate otherwise. Since we used an acceleration model, if, by any chance the robots get into one of those extremes, the response must be swift. In other cases, we do not want the robot to use very large accelerations since it would make the task of controlling it more difficult.

3.3   The Dynamic Model

In our system, we have implemented a control model where the vectors resulting from the motor-schemas are, in fact, force vectors. We call this control model the *acceleration model*. According to that mass of the robot, we generate an acceleration vector (up to a given maximum), that we will use to alter the movement of the robot at the next instant of time.

We also introduced *attrition* into the system. This was done by defining an attrition constant that generates a force with a direction opposite to that of movement in each time step. This makes it very difficult for the robots to saturate the system by getting to the *maximum speed*. This speed is still possible, but only temporarily and due to a very large acceleration which, as we have seen, occurs in extreme cases, using the geometric decay model. Thus, a robot falling behind it's desired position will, it the situation gets too bad, give an "extra push" that will be enough to compensate temporarily for the attrition and get in formation.

Likewise, even when travelling a long time in a straight line, the speed will not be at it's maximum, thus allowing for a correct change of direction.

All these problems, while relevant when simulating a real environment, do not occur in the velocity model (where the output of the schemas is a velocity vector, rather than a force).

3.4   Problems Introduced by the New Dynamic Model

The force-based dynamic model brought some new problems to the system. In the following paragraphs, we will briefly discuss them and analyze possible ways to solve them. This was done by carefully tuning a series of parameters that define how the system will behave.

Global Constants: the value of the *maximum acceleration* had to be chosen very carefully. A small value would not be enough to permit the robots to react quickly enough to a sudden need of change in direction (such as when taking a curve). Likewise, a very large *maximum speed* would result in a similar behaviour. Thus, it was necessary to choose these two values correctly in relation to each other, in order to have accelerations large enough to account for the speed of the robots, but not large enough to make them loose control at the slightest change in movement. This was related to the attrition constant that we chose (that ended up being 0.1).

Maintain-Formation Parameters: although this might not be evident, to make the force returned by this schema large in relation to that of the others (or to the maximum acceleration), might have ill effects.

For example, if when getting out of formation, a robot heads with great speed towards the desired position, once it reaches that position, it would not be able do decelerate fast enough to stay there. So, we will witness an oscillatory behaviour, where the robot will first move very fast towards the position in one direction, and then in the other (Fig. 3).

Move-To-Goal Parameters: the *move-to-goal* schema might not be so easy to define as it would seem. If the force produced by this schema is very large, the robots will try to head towards the goal no matter what lies in their path. This will hamper greatly the robots' capability to avoid obstacles.

Also, if the acceleration produced by this schema is very high, it will be difficult for the robots to change direction once they have reached a goal, towards another one. So, we must be very careful while choosing the value of the gain for thus schema.

Maintain-Formation vs. Move-to-Goal: another important trade-off was between the *maintain-formation* and the *move-to-goal* schemas. A situation that usually arises is that the robots, when travelling in a straight line towards a goal, tend to narrow the formation.

This occurs because the forces produced by the *move-to-goal* schema all point to the same place, and do not take into account that the actual "goal" to each robot is different according to it's position in the formation. Because the

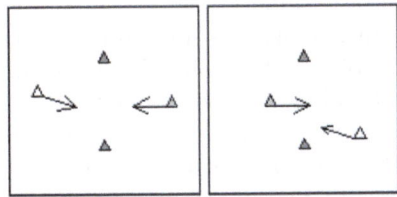

Fig. 3. Oscillatory behaviour

Table 2. Default parameters

Parameter	Value	Parameter	Value
Avoid-Static-Obstacle		Avoid-Moving-Obstacle	
Gain	3	Gain	1.5
Maximum Range	50	Maximum Range	50
Minimum Range	5	Minimum Range	5
Avoid-Robot		Maintain-Formation	
Gain	2.5	Gain	4
Maximum Range	10	Maximum Range	40
Minimum Range	5	Minimum Range	3
Move-To-Goal		Noise	
Gain	3	Gain	0.05

robots will travel for some time along a straight line, they will have time to greatly increase their speed towards the goal. So, if the *maintain-formation* force is not large enough, it will not suffice to avoid the narrowing effect.

Avoidance Schemas: we must take care with the forces resulting from these schemas, in order to allow the robots to attain a goal that lies behind an obstacle (if the repulsion is too large, they will never be able to pass beyond that point). We can adjust these schemas in two ways: with a large intensity on a small radius and vice-versa. With a small radius, the influence of the schema will be felt independently by each robot (since some of them might be inside the radius and others not). With a large radius, the influence of the schema is felt more uniformly on the entire formation.

Finally, the *avoid-robots* schema must only yield a force in extreme situations, since, otherwise, we risk losing control with the antagonism between this schema and *maintain-formation*.

4   Tests

We conducted some tests with the same velocity model as Balch and Arkin [1] and the results we got were similar. To perform the tests with the acceleration model, and taking into account the previous considerations, some values for the parameters were chosen (see Table 2).

The robots' maximum velocity was limited to 30 spatial units/time unit and they were given the mass of one. The robots' dimension varies in unrelated tests. Towards the objective of making the *avoid-robot* schema an emergency force, we gave it a gain of 2.5, an influence sphere of 15 and a minimum radius of 5.

In all tests, the world is similar, with a dimension of 1000x1000 spatial units and no mobile obstacles (to permit comparing the tests). The sample period was 0.1 time units and the value of noise gain was 10% of the maximum acceleration.

4.1   Statistical Evaluation

The main evaluation of the system is qualitative. Despite that, we tried to add some objective evaluation and some more concrete manner to compare the performance of the system with altered parameters or in different situations. Therefore we considered:

Path Ratio. This value is calculated dividing the robots' average traveled space by the distance between the various goals. This gives a notion of the deviation of the robots to the correct path. Notice that this ratio has a minimum of 1, and is normal in the simulations to have values substantial greater than this limit - some of the robots, in order to *maintain-formation*, have to perform same kind of external path regarding the line between goals;

Formation Error. Is the sum of the position error of each of the robots towards is ideal position in every instant of the simulation. This contains information about the formation maintenance;

Average Formation Error. Is the average of the above value;

Simulation Time. Length of the simulation, in time units or number of samples.

When defining a robot's position in the formation in relation to another robot it is important, in order to achieve good results, to consider carefully what robots should be related. The immediate option, defining one robot in relation to is nearest neighbor is not always the best solution.

4.2   Results Obtained

1. Column Formation A formation with 50 spatial units between the robots and a robot dimension of 10 was used. When using the definition of the position in relation to center of mass, the behavior, in qualitative terms, of the formation is good. The average formation error is low (36). Note that a very small change in the orientation of the reference point, either a robot or, in this particular case, the formation's center of mass, causes an enormous variation of the ideal position of the robot. The path ratio is around 1.07. This is explained by the tendency in performing the curves external to the rectilinear path between goals.

In case of formation relative to a leader, the error values are considerably larger (91.0 in the average and 421.2 to the maximum). This is because in this case the reference point (the leader) has quicker oscillations than the center of mass, introducing a non real error measure (the maximum error happen when in the end of a rectilinear path the leader suddenly change is orientation).

When facing an obstacles field, the robots in this formation, independently of it's definition, tend to follow the same path, like a snake.

2. Line Formation A formation with 50 spatial units between the robots and a robot dimension of 8 was used.

Table 3. Test results of the different formations

	Column		Line		Diamond			Wedge	
	Leader	CoM	Relative	CoM	Relative	Leader	CoM	Relative	CoM
Path Ratio	1.08	1.07	1.10	1.11	1.14	1.08	1.07	1.08	1.06
Formation Error									
Minimum	17.41	6.43	1	2	10	0	1	13	2
Average	91	36.3	583.3	152.3	200	166	72	341	225
Maximum	421.2	106.4	1790	427.2	570	450	251	836	839
Std. Dev.	70.6	25.7	435.5	96.7	121	124	50	214	181
Time	2581	1765	2198	3086	3087	2648	2693	2839	3216

This formation, when faced with a obstacle, produces a position error larger than the column formation. Take in account that in order to avoid an obstacle a robot must change it's movement perpendicularly to its actual direction.

In the case of a relative formation, the gain of the *maintain-formation* schema must be very small (0.4) to prevent an increasing oscillation, that, in ultimately makes the robots go around each other. We didn't find a set of value parameters that made the performance of this kind formation definition acceptable.

As an important note on the behavior of this formation is the narrowing that it suffers when approaching a goal.

3. Diamond and Wedge Formations In the diamond formation, the distance between the robots and the center of mass was fixed to 75 units, and the robots dimension to 10. The increase of this distance forced a relaxation of the goal achieving condition. Thus, the desired distance to a goal was incremented to 40.

The best results, with the formation in relation to a leader or in relation to the center of mass, were achieved with an avoid obstacles schema concentrated and powerful (with a gain of 9 gain and a radius of 20). On the other hand, in

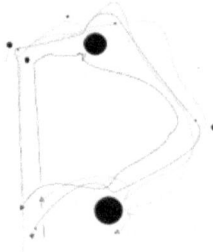

Fig. 4. Diamond formation defined in relation to a leader

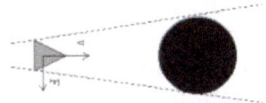

Fig. 5. Ideal avoid obstacle force.

formation relative to another robot, the best results were obtained with a long range schema and low gain (100 and 2 respectively).

Note that, in the formation defined in relation to a leader, if the leader robot turns, the others maybe go back a little or change their path in order to maintain the formation. Because the leader has no concern about the formation, he has a tendency to get to a goal faster than the others, and then have to wait for them.

On the Wedge formation, the results of the tests are similar.

5 Discussion

The results we found lead to some questions, both empirical and theoretical which will be discussed bellow.

5.1 Schemas Parameters

In all the cases, we encountered that a low radius but a strong gain of the *avoid-robots* schema produces the best results. In fact, this emergency force, in a trivial situation, is unnecessary: the *maintain-formation* schema will produce the desired repulsive force when the robots are approaching each other.

When concentrated, the *avoid obstacle* schemas produce a behavior where each robot travels along the obstacles' borders. Some times there is a transformation in this normal, and observed, behavior and the robots try to avoid the obstacles in an oscillatory manner - approaching and retreating quickly.

A particular situation occurs when a robot is following a path that crosses an obstacle's center. The force generated by this schema will only slow down the robot's velocity, but it will not induce a shift strong enough to make the robot contour the obstacle. Also, this force is maintained when the robot passes the obstacle, now with the form of a positive acceleration, like if the robot is running away from the obstacle.

One improvement to this schema, would be to make the force have an orientation somewhat different from the current. In the case of Fig. 5, for example, the ideal force was perpendicular to the movement.

One last observation: this schema's gain must be substantially larger than the *move-to-goal* schema gain, in order to prevent a deadlock situation.

When a robot achieves a goal it continues to suffer the effects of *move-to-goal* schema, until all the formation achieves that goal. This causes, particularly in leader referenced formations, where the leader is in the front, that the robot keeps an oscillatory movement around the goal. It's suggested as future work to keep the force of this schema as zero in the neighborhood of the goal.

This last schema is also responsible for the narrowing, and slow reaction in emergency situations. To restrain its influence to the essential, we suggest that this schema's gain should be proportionally inverse to the velocity of the robot.

5.2   Formation Definitions

In every formation, the narrowing increases proportionally to the space between robots. This introduces large error values. The relative defined formations work better when the *maintain-formation* schema uses a larger radius to limit the controlled zone. This type of formation has big error values, even if the formation is well formed (look at the minimum error values for these formations).

In a leader-defined formation, non-leader robots should have zero gain in the *move-to-goal* schema, thus, they should be limited to following the leader.

5.3   Statistical Evaluation

The *formation error* used is an ambiguous statistic, and should be used with great caution. For example, it can be a good method to compare different tests with the same formation, but it's not so good between different formation definitions. In order to quantify the oscillation that robots suffer, the energy spent in a simulation must be considered in a future work.

6   Conclusions

As shown by the performed tests, by using the new simulation model more realistic results are obtained. Indeed, the old model based only in the velocity of the agents is not only unrealistic, but also much more sensitive to noise, thus introducing more oscillations in the robots. It also, requires a careful-tuning of the schemas to prevent unlimited velocities. Aiming to create a system that can eventually be used in a real-world environment, a velocity model is evidently inadequate. When presented to different situations (different formations, for instance) it doesn't have the robustness we would desire, needing to be tuned differently for each case.

The acceleration model we have presented in this paper brings new advantages to the simulation but it also introduces some complexity in the control system. It is not evident what schemas should be considered. Also, the tuning of the several parameters is not evident. However, once it is tuned, it performs correctly in a wide range of situations as shown by the results presented.

References

1. T. Balch and C. Arkin. Motor schema-based formation control for multiagent robot teams. In *Proceedings ICMAS-95*, pages 10–16, 1995. 89, 92, 95
2. J. Hodgins and D. Brogan. Robot herds: Group behaviours for systems with significant dynamics. In *Proceedings Artificial Live IV*, pages 319–324. MIT Press, 1994. 89
3. C. Reynolds. Flocks, herds and schools: A distributed behavioral model. *Computer Graphics*, 4(21):25–34, 1987. 89, 90
4. Russel and Norvig. Intelligent agents. In *Artificial Intelligente: A Modern Approach*, pages 31–52, 1994. 88

A Case of Multiagent Decision Support: Using Autonomous Agents for Urban Traffic Control [*]

Sascha Ossowski[1], José Cuena[2] and Ana García-Serrano[2]

[1] Department of Computer Science, Rey Juan Carlos University of Madrid,
Camino de Humanes 63, 28936 Móstoles (Madrid), Spain
S.Ossowski@escet.urjc.es

[2] Department of Artificial Intelligence, Technical University of Madrid,
Campus de Montegancedo s/n, 28660 Boadilla del Monte (Madrid), Spain
{jcuena,agarcia}@dia.fi.upm.es

Abstract. This paper presents the experimental TRYSA$_2$ distributed decision support system, that has been designed for the management of the urban motorway network around Barcelona. It shows how different technologies in the area of intelligent agents can be combined to solve this real-world decision support problem: on the one hand, a pre-established distribution of the loci of decision-making and the nature of local traffic management tasks, suggested to apply "deliberate" problem-solving agents; on the other, the complexity of the co-ordination task called for an "emergent" approach, in order that the overall decision support functionality be the result of non-benevolent agent interactions. The paper sets out from a description of our particular traffic management problem. Subsequently, the architecture of TRYSA$_2$ is outlined, pointing out the design strategy followed and describing how the different design steps have been realised. Finally, we discuss the lessons learnt from building this multiagent application.

1. Introduction

The problem of coherent distributed decision-making is intrinsic to many complex real-world situations, where the behaviour of a complex dynamic system is regulated by human operators, who can perform particular control actions on different parts of the system. In the frame of the management of a computer network, for instance, different local administrators are responsible for reconfiguring certain sub-networks to improve aspects of local and global network performance; another example is traffic management in a road network, where an operator decides upon the sets of traffic signals to be set in different parts of the network, so as to overcome local traffic problems. In general, local decisions respecting control actions for one part of the system affect the effectiveness of others. In consequence, it is necessary to achieve

[*] Research supported by the Spanish Dirección General de Tráfico, and by the European Union through the HCM/TMR programme

Helder Coelho (Ed.): IBERAMIA'98, LNAI 1484, pp. 100-111, 1998.
© Springer-Verlag Berlin Heidelberg 1998

certain level of co-ordination to obtain a coherent set of local control decisions. In such a scenario, a *distributed decision support system* (DSS) is a software tool that assists operators in their decision-making, by automatically monitoring a dynamic system, warning about present or future undesired situations and suggesting appropriate coherent control actions to operators [5].

The nature of distributed decision support often "calls for" an architecture based on multiple cognitive agents: the structure of the agent society reflects the internal structure of the system to be controlled, thus coping with potential communication or privacy requirements, while the knowledge-based (i.e. "cognitive") approach allows to explicitly model the operators' expertise, so that they can *understand* the system's advice as well as the reasons that justify it. Still, the design of distributed DSSs of this type turns out to be a rather difficult task for two major reasons: first, co-ordination among the different loci of decision-making (and the corresponding support agents) becomes significantly harder when the size of the systems grows, fact which is especially important for real-world applications [9,12]; second, despite recent work in this direction [7,8,10], the lack of adequate design strategies and methodologies gives the design of such systems some flavour of a "black art".

This paper describes how these difficulties have been attacked in a real-world case: it presents the architecture of a distributed DSS in the domain of urban traffic management as an example of a practical application of decentralised multiagent technology. First, our particular traffic management problem in the urban motorway network of Barcelona is outlined. Then, the $TRYSA_2$ traffic management system is presented, describing our design strategy, the agent models that this strategy gave rise to, and the $ProsA_2$ agent architecture that operationalises these agent models. Finally, we discuss the lessons learnt from building this decentralised multiagent application.

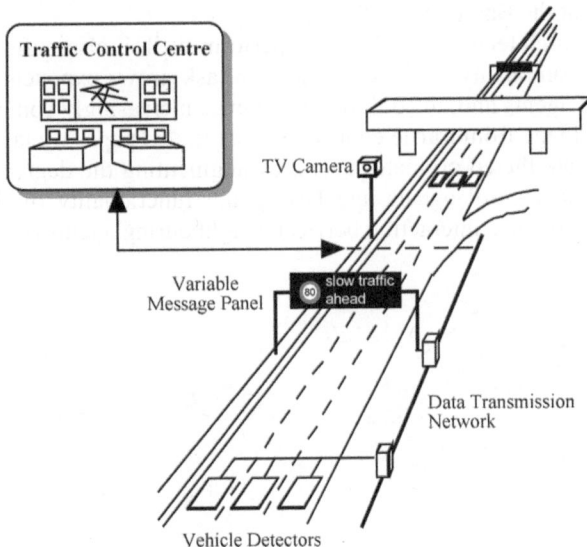

Figure 1. A traffic management infrastructure

2.   The Problem: Urban Traffic Control

In big cities, traffic control centres are in charge of managing urban transport, so as to maintain and restore the "smooth" flow of vehicles. In Barcelona, the local traffic control centre JPT is in charge of this job: traffic engineers continuously receive information about the traffic state, identify potential problems, and act upon control devices to overcome them. It has become particularly difficult for the JPT engineers to perform this job in real time, as in the follow-up of the 1992 Olympic Games the traffic management infrastructure in Barcelona has become increasingly complex. Nowadays, information about the traffic state of the urban motorway network, consisting of one ring-road and seven adjacent motorways, is provided by over 300 tele-metered sensors ("loop detectors") via fibre optics communication links. Control actions can be taken by means of 52 Variable Message Signals (VMS), 3 traffic lights for junction control, as well as by ramp metering on 7 ring-road drives. Figure 1 illustrates typical elements of this traffic management infrastructure.

The *TRYS* system has been developed to provide real-time decision support for JPT traffic controllers [3]. In line with the traffic engineer's logical subdivision of the road network into *problem areas*, TRYS relies on a set of knowledge-based traffic control *agents*, each responsible for traffic management in one such area. On the basis of sensor data, operator notifications and contextual information, each agent generates proposals of signal plans for control devices. Potential conflicts between agents (problem area usually overlap!) are resolved by a special co-ordinator agent, which receives control plans from the traffic control agents and harmonises them, so as to obtain globally consistent signal plans. These signal plans are presented to the operator who finally decides to enact or to modify them. TRYS has been installed and is being evaluated at the Barcelona test site [3].

Although this architecture has shown to perform well, it also suffers difficulties in *scalability*. The complexity of the co-ordination task grows exponentially in the size of traffic control agents and, in addition, it becomes increasingly complex to elicit co-ordination knowledge from traffic control experts. In this paper we tackle the problem of how to eliminate the co-ordinator agent, by augmenting the degree of local *autonomy* of the traffic control agents and having the functionality of the co-ordinator emerge as a consequence interaction between neighbouring agents (see Figure 2)

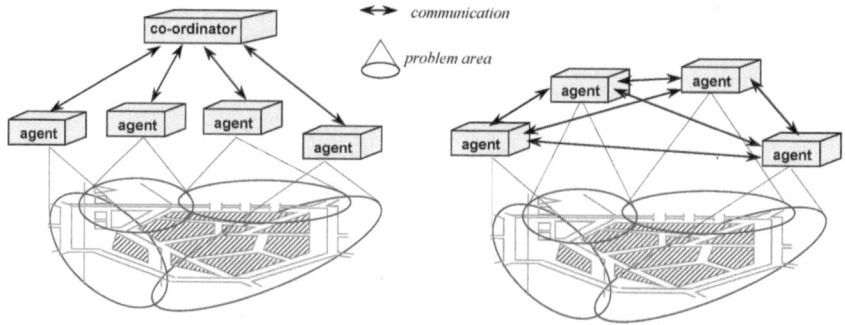

Figure 2. Centralised (TRYS) y decentralised co-ordination (TRYSA$_2$)

3.   The TRYSA$_2$ System

In this section we present the TRYSA$_2$ system (TRYS Autonomous Agents), in which autonomous traffic control agents co-ordinate their signal plans in a decentralised fashion. TRYSA$_2$ augments local problem-solving capacities of TRYS agents by a model of self-interested pursuit of (local) goals, thus converting the original "benevolent" TRYS agents into autonomous agents. So, in the follow-up of the problem area decomposition of the TRYS approach, the TRYSA$_2$ experimental system consists of 11 traffic control agents that jointly manage the traffic in the motorway network around Barcelona (Figure 3).

In the sequel we first outline the design approach that we followed when developing the TRYSA$_2$ system. Subsequently, its application to the design of TRYSA$_2$ agents is outlined. Finally, we sketch the implementation and operation of the system.

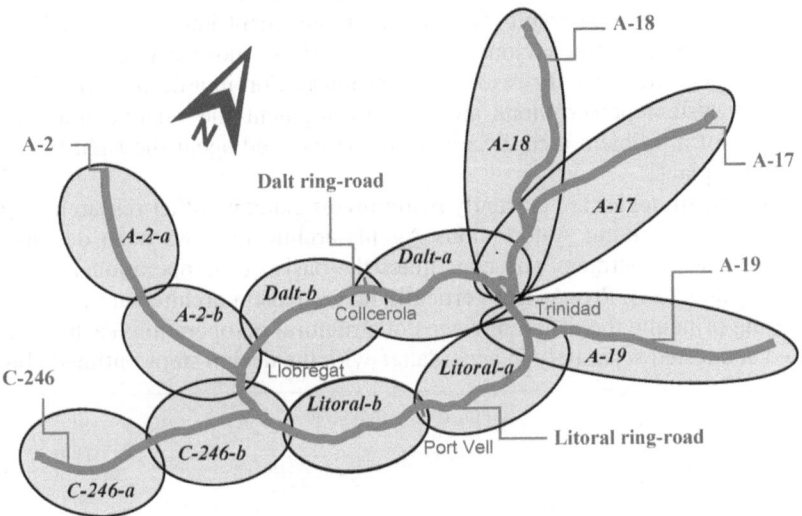

Figure 3. Autonomous traffic agents for Barcelona

3.1 The design process

Problem-solving and co-ordination in TRYSA$_2$ rely on the mechanism of *structural co-operation* [13,14], that has been developed to achieve co-ordination within societies of autonomous problem-solving agents. Within structural co-operation, the functionality of an agent system is determined by the agents' local goals, the dependence relations [16] that their environment implies, as well as normative prescriptions [2]: norms bias agent interactions, which influence self-interested agent behaviour so as to make it instrumental with respect to a global functionality [12]. In accordance with this mechanism, multiagent system design is a three stage process.
1. Individual stage: design of local problem-solving.

Agents are endowed with a "motivation" on the basis of which they generate individual goals in response to certain undesired situations; they are provided with problem-solving mechanisms that enable them to achieve (or: "head towards") these goals. No reference to potential interference with other agents is made. The traffic control agents of the original TRYS system are precisely of this type.

2. Social stage: modelling of autonomous agent interaction.
   The possible interdependencies between the agent's problem-solving actions are determined, giving rise to the multiple possibilities of conflict and synergy between them. Self-interested agent behaviour is to be modelled on this basis (e.g. when to ask others for help and when to grant or deny help [15]), and its impact on society level is determined. In the TRYSA$_2$ system we use a model from bargaining theory (the Nash solution), accept it as the outcome of self-interested agent interaction, and perform distributed search for the corresponding solution.

3. Normative stage: design of a functional normative bias.
   The "equilibrium" that results from autonomous agent interaction need not correspond to a functional behaviour at society level. So, normative prescriptions have to be designed that bias the result of agent interaction in a desired direction. In the TRYSA$_2$ system prescriptions are used to augment the relative importance (or "power") of a problem area, by giving the associated agent the right to enact certain signal plans.

Similar design strategies are currently being investigated by other researchers [6]. The ProsA$_2$ (Problem-solving Autonomous Agent) architecture has been developed that supports this design strategy and constitutes the basis of the operationalisation of the TRYSA$_2$ system [13]. ProsA$_2$ is a vertically layered agent architecture [11], reflecting the layering principle the different stages of structural co-operation: each layer can be designed and tested separately in accordance with the design steps outlined above.

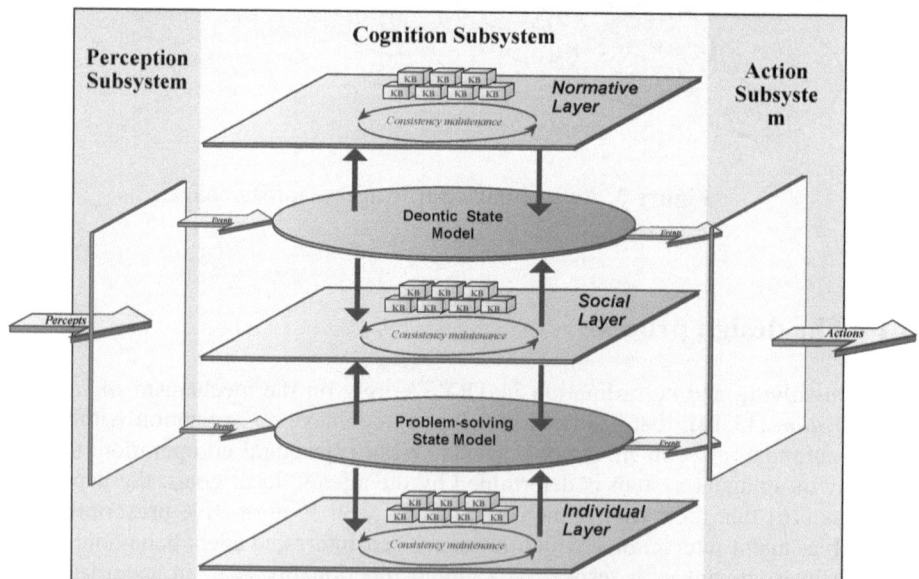

Figure 4. ProsA$_2$ agent architecture

The general architecture of a ProsA$_2$ agent is depicted in Figure 4. It comprises three subsystems. The *perception subsystem* is endowed with perceptors that capture stimuli of the outside world. In the TRYSA$_2$ system it is in charge of perceiving data from the road sensors as well as messages from its acquaintances.

The result of the perception process is passed to the *cognition subsystem*, where the (problem-solving and deontic state) information models are updated. This new information provided by perceptors can bring them into an "inconsistent" state. The three layers of the cognition subsystem are in charge of reacting to these changes by restoring model consistency. Based on their particular layer knowledge, they all run different instantiations of the same three phase control loop: first, significant changes in the information models are detected (e.g. new data from some sensors); second, the reasons for such inconsistency are determined; third, the adequate model updates are determined (e.g. generating new local signal plans). Each layer is responsible for maintaining the consistency of particular parts of the information models. In TRYSA$_2$ agents, the individual layer generates alternative signal plans on the basis of available traffic data (and ranks them so as to maximise their positive impact in the traffic flow of the agent's *local* problem area). The social layer sets out from the interdependencies between the agents' local signal plans, modifies these local proposals and/or their ranking accordingly, and indicates pertinent messages to be sent. On the basis of contextual information, the normative layer deduces permissions or prohibitions to use certain control devices and, in consequence, to enact certain signal plans.

Finally, the *action subsystem* checks for changes in the information models and manipulates the agent's effectors accordingly. In the case of TRYSA$_2$ agents, it is in charge of sending messages to other agents and of informing about newly proposed road signal plans.

The core functionality of ProsA$_2$ agents is provided by the knowledge units (KUs) [4] of each of its layers. Figure 5 shows the knowledge endowment of the layers of TRYSA$_2$ agents. In the sequel, we will describe each layer, paying special attention to the contents of each of these KUs and describing how this knowledge is articulated in the layers' reasoning cycles.

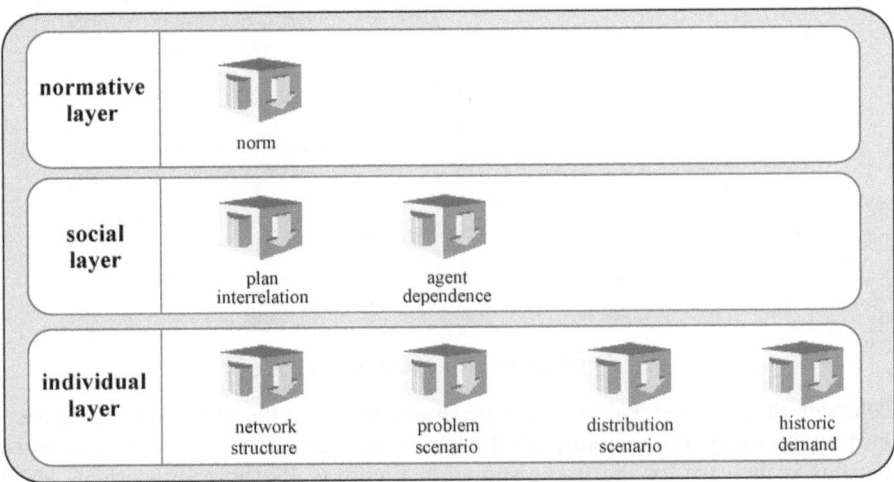

Figure 5. Knowledge units of the TRYSA$_2$ layers

3.2   Individual stage

The individual stage of the design process corresponds to the TRYSA$_2$ agents' local problem-solving and is implemented through the individual layer.

Every couple of minutes, a TRYSA$_2$ agent receives temporal series of magnitudes such as traffic speed, flow and occupancy from the road sensors of its area. This raw data is initially pre-processed in order to filter out noisy and erroneous data. Subsequently, data abstraction is performed, calculating aggregate magnitudes such as temporal and spatial gradients for the different sections. Both tasks are performed by means of the physical network structure KU. The agent updates its problem-solving model with this completed traffic information.

In step two, problem identification (and also some part of problem diagnosis) is performed by matching the abstracted traffic data against the frames in the problem scenario KU. Figure 6 shows one such frame that matches the abstracted traffic data. Suppose that as a result of data abstraction low speed and high occupancy are identified in *Ronda de Dalt en Diagonal* and medium to high speed and low occupancy in *Ronda en d'Eslugues*. These facts match the frame shown in Figure 6, so that an incident in the central lane of Diagonal road is identified, which manifests itself as a traffic excess (with respect to the road's capacity) of 2200 veh/h between *Diagonal* and *Llobregat* in the *Dalt* ring-road. Traffic from *Collcerola* to *Llobregat* and, in a minor degree, from *Diagonal* heading towards *Llobregat* contributes to this excess.

Step three, the control recommendation phase, adheres to the following line of reasoning: first, the historic traffic demand between nodes is retrieved and the contribution of each path to the problem in the critical section calculated. This is done by matching the current abstract traffic state and the state of the control devices against the distribution scenario frames.

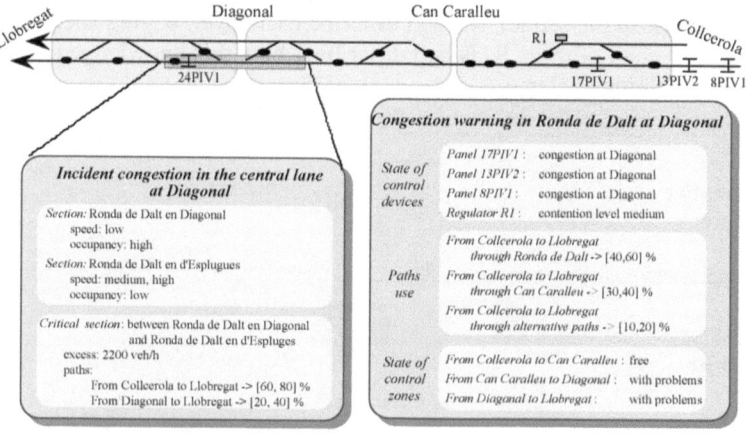

Figure 6. An example scenario

Coherent alternative signal plans are generated by using the distribution scenario KU once again: every frame applicable to the current situation is pre-selected. Assume that this is the case for the frame shown in Figure 6. Its short term effects are estimated by simulating its impact on the current traffic situation. This is done by using the physical network structure knowledge to assign traffic to the road network in accordance with the distribution of traffic volume among paths that it specifies. The frame in the example specifies that about one half of the traffic volume from *Collcerola* to *Llobregat* will pass through the *Dalt* ring-road, while a smaller amount chooses a path through *Can Caralleu* or other alternative paths, if the corresponding signal plan is set. If the simulation shows a reasonable decrease of excess in the critical section, the frame's signal plan constitutes one recommendation of the system. In the example, it is suggested to display congestion warnings at *Diagonal* for panels *17PIV1*, *13PIV2* and *8PIV1*, while setting the contention level of regulator *R1* to medium.

Signal plan recommendations are ranked according to their *utility*, i.e. by their expected reduction of (local) traffic excess. They constitute the individual action alternatives and are stored in the agent's information model.

3.3   Social stage

In the social stage agents take signal plan interrelation into account, reconsidering their choice of alternative local signal plans so as to achieve maximum alleviation for congestions in their *local* problem areas. Plan interrelation can be of logical or physical nature: either one local signal plan proposal influences the effectiveness of another (e.g. by deviating traffic from one problem, thereby increasing the traffic demand in the other, already congested area); or some local signal plans intend to set the same control device in different, incompatible states (e.g. by displaying different messages at the same VMS).

For this enterprise, an agent keeps track of the current local signal plans of its acquaintances in its information model. The three step control cycle of the social layer is driven by this information: when messages arrive, indicating that some acquaintance has switched to another local signal plan ("value" messages) or that certain combinations of local plans are illegal ("no-good" messages), the agent checks whether its currently most preferred local signal plan is still consistent. If not, it tries to find its most preferred local signal plan that re-establishes consistency, and informs interested agents about this change by sending "value"-messages. If there is no such plan, it sends "no-good" messages, inducing other agents to switch to another local signal plan. Once one agent detects that all agents are in a consistent state, it stores the current set of local signal plans as a potential solution. At the end of this process, one solution is chosen in accordance with the underlying bargaining model.

In order to reject or modify inconsistent local plans, the social layer is endowed with the *plan interrelation* KU, which expresses dependencies between plans and possible ways of dealing with them in terms of states of control devices. This knowledge is represented by rules, that obey to the following format:

$$[cdev_1 \, , \quad \ldots \, , \quad cdev_n \,] \Rightarrow [cdev_m \, , \quad \ldots \, , \quad cdev_j \,] \qquad \text{or}$$
$$[cdev_1 \, , \quad \ldots \, , \quad cdev_n \,] \Rightarrow [nogood \,]$$

The operational semantics of such a rule determines that the control device states of the antecedent can be substituted by those of consequent without any important changes in the effect of the signal plans (e.g. by merging different messages "congestion at A" and "congestion at B" to be displayed on the same VMS into one "congestion at A and B" message). If control devices are merely incompatible, the consequent is the constant *nogood*.

The above knowledge defines relations between *plans*. The *agent dependence* KU hosts knowledge about relations between *agents* in the shape of rules of the form

$$[cdev_1 , \ldots , cdev_n] \Rightarrow [\alpha_1 , \ldots , \alpha_m]$$

If all control devices $cdev_1$ to $cdev_n$ switch to new states, then this concerns the agents α_1 to α_m. Note that these rules actually compile knowledge about the capabilities of an agent's acquaintances upon the background of possible plan relations. For instance, if agent α_i may set a message M_i on VMS P, and α_j possibly displays a message M_j on the same panel, while both messages are incompatible, then the knowledge base of α_i's dependence KU will contain a rule stating that setting M_i on VMS P concerns agent α_j. The KU serves two purposes: when used with forward inference, it allows an agent to deduce which agents are to be informed about changes in its local signal plans; using backward inference, it enables an agent to determine its "social strength", by deducing the acquaintances that can affect the executability or the outcome of local signal plans.

From a *global* point of view, the agent behaviour outlined above implies a distributed multi-stage constraint optimisation algorithm, based on ideas of asynchronous weak commitment search [17]. In the sequel, we will just sketch this algorithm: In stage 1, setting out from the local sets of alternative signal plans, agents repeatedly exchange messages, so as to determine the set of undominated consistent local signal plans. This is done in an asynchronous distributed fashion, that allows for local and temporarily incompatible views of the overall state. The agent that detects the termination of stage 1, takes the initiative in stage 2. On the basis of the outcome of stage 1 it computes an (approximate) probability with which each of the sets of consistent local signal plans shall be enacted, so as to maximise the product of local agent utilities (i.e. of local traffic excess reduction). Finally, in stage 3 a set of signal plans is selected at random in accordance with the outcome of stage 2, and the agents are urged to enact the corresponding local signal plans accordingly.

In TRYSA$_2$, this process shows anytime properties: in time critical situation the distributed search phase can be interrupted and a potential signal plan is enacted directly. A more detailed analysis of the algorithm can be found in [13]. Note that the above procedure allows calculating the outcome of *self-interested* agent interaction by *co-operative* distributed search.

3.4   Normative stage

The normative stage of the design process biases the overall behaviour of TRYSA$_2$ in a desired direction, by letting the normative layer issue prescriptions in relation to specific traffic situations. As Figure 5 indicates, the *norm* KU is in charge of hosting and enacting this knowledge.

In TRYSA$_2$, normative situations are supposed to vary with the traffic demand structure. In consequence, the norm KU qualifies normative situations temporally by means of frames. In the "temporal" section of these frames, the current date and time is classified in terms of two categories: *type of day* and *type of season*. Values for the former are either *Working day*, *Sunday*, *Saturday* or *Holiday*. Rules specify how the value *holiday* is derived. The category season may be instantiated to *Xmas*, *Easter*, *Summer*, or *Normal*. Again, the values are related to the current date and time by means of rules. The "normative" section describes a normative structure as a function of the above information. A normative structure is defined by two categories: *prohibitions* and *permissions*. Each of these categories may be instantiated by a set of control device states.

We require the knowledge bases of the agents' norm KUs to be globally consistent: if one agent is allowed to use a control device, all others that might access it are prohibited to use it. The associated reasoning method first classifies the current date and time, in order to match the resulting temporal categories against the normative patterns. By means of this method the agent can infer the normative situation which is pertinent to it.

3.5   The system

The TRYSA$_2$ system has been implemented experimentally on networked workstations. The TRYSA$_2$ agents constitute separate Prolog processes (with some extensions in C++), which communicate via sockets. The Barcelona test site is simulated by the AIMSUN traffic simulator [1]. AIMSUN is endowed with a precise description of the traffic management infrastructure at the test site, including detailed models of the road network, the sensors, control devices etc., and performs microscopic ("car by car") simulation of traffic flows. A special observer agent has been implemented in Tcl/Tk in order to visualise the problem-solving process and its results. Figure 7 shows a snapshot of the interface window of the observer agent.

The dynamics of the system may be illustrated by the typical lines of reasoning within TRYSA$_2$, which are determined by the three classes of events that may cause agent activation:

- If new data about the current traffic state arrives, an agent's *individual* layer generates a set of local signal plans. The change in the information model triggers the social layer which starts a social interaction process. Messages are sent and received in accordance with the distributed algorithm outlined above, and the agents adapt their local signal plans accordingly.
- The *normative* layer deduces a new normative situation, when the current temporal context has changed. If necessary, the acquaintances are informed about this, otherwise the local information model is updated. If the social layer detects a change in the set of potential signal plans, it initiates a social interaction process as above.
- Finally, when messages from an agent's acquaintances are received, the corresponding changes in the information model trigger the *social* layer. The layers reacts to this by restoring local consistency and sending messages. Again, agent behaviour follows the distributed algorithm outlined above.

4.   Conclusions

In this paper we have presented the architecture of the TRYSA$_2$ distributed decision support system that has been designed experimentally for the management of the urban motorway network around Barcelona. We have reported our design strategy for this type of system and presented an agent architecture to operationalise it. This approach lead to a knowledge-based multiagent system that combines deliberate local problem-solving with emergent co-ordination.

The TRYSA$_2$ systems shows that the principled design of distributed DSSs on the basis of a cognitive multiagent architecture is feasible and adequate. By comparing this approach, which relies on decentralised, "emergent" co-ordination model, to the original TRYS system, we conclude that the present approach promotes scalability. When a new acquaintance enters the system, agents still need to be informed about its capabilities and, if the newcomer may enact previously unknown signal plans, the interrelation of these plans with existing control actions is to be added to the agents' knowledge bases. Still, the introduction of the new agents produces a shift in the social equilibrium, leading to a new base-line co-ordination without any further modifications to the agent knowledge. In the centralised approach, however, this effect can only be achieved by completely reconsidering the priority relations that a distinguished co-ordinator agent is endowed with.

In future work we will further refine the normative knowledge within the TRYSA$_2$ system. The different effects of particular types of prescriptions in real-world traffic situations will be examined by means of experimental studies. In addition, we are thinking of applying multiagent learning techniques to this task.

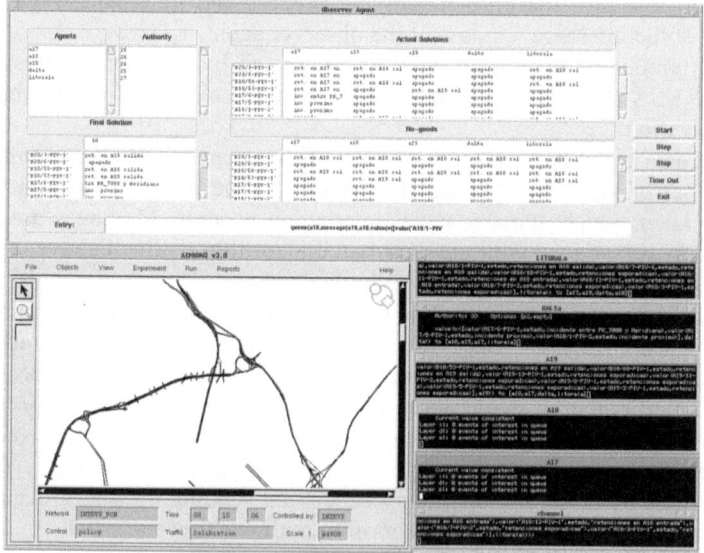

Figure 7. TRYSA$_2$ interface

References

1. Barceló J., Ferrer J., Grau R.: "AIMSUN2 and the GETRAM Simulation Environment". *Proc. 13th EURO Conference*, 1994
2. Conte R., Castelfranchi C.: *Cognitive and Social Action*, UCL Press, 1995
3. Cuena J., Hernández J., Molina M.: "Knowledge-oriented Design of an Application for Real Time Traffic Management: the TRYS System". *Proc. ECAI-96*, 1996
4. Cuena J., Molina M.: "KSM: An Environment for Design of Structured Knowledge Models". In: *Knowledge-based Systems: Advanced Concepts, Techniques and Applications* (Tzafestas, ed.), World Scientific, 1997
5. Cuena J., Ossowski S.: "Distributed Models for Decision Support". To appear in: *Introduction to Distributed Artificial Intelligence* (Weiss & Sen, eds.), AAAI/MIT Press, 1998
6. Demazeau, Y.: "Towards Multi-agent Logic Programming". *Slides of a Ph.D. course delivered at the Technical University of Madrid*, 1997
7. Glaser N.: *Contribution to Knowledge Modelling in a Multi-Agent Framework*. Ph.D. thesis, Henri Poincaré University at Nancy, 1996
8. Iglesias, C., Garijo M., González J.: "Metodologías orientadas a agentes". In: *Inteligencia Artificial – Revista Iberoamaricana sobre IA*. Special Issue on DAI (García-Serrano & Ossowski, eds.), 1998
9. Jennings N.: "Coordination Techniques for Distributed Artificial Intelligence". In: *Foundations of DAI* (O'Hare & Jennings, eds.), Wiley, 1996
10. Moulin B., Brassard M.: "A scenario-based design method and an environment for the development of multiagent systems". In: *DAI Architectures and Modelling* (Zhang & Lukose, eds.), Springer, 1995
11. Müller J., Pischel M., Thiel M.: "Modeling Reactive Behaviour in Vertically Layered Agent Architectures". In: *Intelligent Agents* (Wooldridge & Jennings, eds.), Springer, 1995
12. Ossowski S., García-Serrano A.; Cuena J.: "Emergent Co-ordination of Flow Control Actions Through Functional Co-operation of Social Agents". *Proc. ECAI-96*, 1996
13. Ossowski S.: *Contribución al Estudio Funcional de las Sociedades Artificiales de Agentes – Coordinación Emergente de Agentes Software Autónomos*. PhD thesis, Technical University of Madrid, AI Dept., 1997
14. Ossowski S., García-Serrano A.: "Social Structure in Artificial Agent Societies: Implications for Autonomous Problem-solving Agents". To appear in: *Proc. ATAL-98*, 1998
15. Sekaran M., Sen S.: "To help or not to help". *Proc. 17th Conf. of the Cognitive Science Society*, 1995
16. Sichman J., Demazeau Y.: "Exploiting Social Reasoning to deal with Agency Level Inconsistencies". *Proc. ECAI-94*, 1994
17. Yokoo M.: "Asynchronous Weak Commitment Search for Solving Distributed Constraint Satisfaction Problems". *Proc. CLP-95*, 1995

Lazy Learning Algorithms for Problems with Many Binary Features and Classes

Werner Winiwarter

Instute of Applied Computer Science and Information Systems
University of Vienna
Liebiggasse 4/3, A-1010 Wien, Austria
winiwarter@acm.org
http://www.ifs.univie.ac.at/~ww/

Abstract. We have designed several new lazy learning algorithms for learning problems with many binary features and classes. This particular type of learning task can be found in many machine learning applications but is of special importance for machine learning of natural language. Besides pure instance-based learning we also consider prototype-based learning, which has the big advantage of a large reduction of the required memory and processing time for classification. As an application for our learning algorithms we have chosen natural language database interfaces. In our interface architecture the machine learning module replaces an elaborate semantic analysis component. The learning task is to select the correct command class based on semantic features extracted from the user input. We use an existing German natural language interface to a production planning and control system as a case study for our evaluation and compare the results achieved by the different lazy learning algorithms.

1 Introduction

In this paper we introduce several new lazy learning algorithms, which are especially useful for learning problems with a large number of binary features and classes. We define *binary features* as features which possess only the two values 0 and 1. A value of 1 encodes the situation that an instance contains the feature; otherwise the value equals 0.

Such learning tasks are typical for *machine learning of natural language* but also can be found in many other applications. In particular for machine learning of natural language there exists some empirical evidence [16] that the abstractions achieved by using model-based algorithms adds no additional predictive power. On the contrary, even limited forms of generalization can harm the performance of the algorithm due to the many subregularities and exceptions that are characteristic of linguistic problems.

In our work we consider two subgroups of lazy learning: instance-based learning and prototype-based learning. *Instance-based learning* approaches represent the learned knowledge simply as collection of training cases or instances. A new

Helder Coelho (Ed.): IBERAMIA'98, LNAI 1484, pp. 112–124, 1998.

case is classified by finding the instance with the highest similarity and by using
its class as prediction [9]. Instance-based algorithms need only a very small training effort but a large amount of memory and processing time for classification
because the algorithm has to compare new cases with all existing instances.

An alternative to instance-based approaches is *prototype-based learning*,
which creates a prototype for each class during training [10,5]. These prototypes
are then used for the comparison with new cases. This has the big advantage
that there is no longer the necessity to store any training instances as learned
knowledge. In addition, the number of required comparisons during classification
is reduced to the number of existing classes.

We have developed the lazy learning algorithms as part of our machine learning workbench, which also includes several algorithms for decision tree learning, rule-based learning, and hybrid approaches [15]. All of these algorithms
have been implemented by means of the deductive object-oriented database
ROCK & ROLL [3]. The use of the available powerful programming language enables the efficient implementation of a large variety of different learning
paradigms. It also gives the user a convenient integrated tool, which assists him
in applying the algorithms to the data collection stored in the same database
(see also [6]).

The learning task we chose for our algorithms concerns *natural language
database interfaces*. One of the main obstacles to the efficient use of natural
language interfaces is the often required high amount of manual knowledge engineering (see [2] for a recent survey). This time-consuming and tedious process
is often referred to as the infamous "knowledge acquisition bottleneck". It may
require extensive efforts by experts highly experienced in linguistics as well as
in the domain and the task [8]. Therefore, natural language interfaces represent
a domain that is very well suited for the application of lazy learning algorithms
to automate the acquisition process of linguistic knowledge.

The rest of the paper is organized as follows. First, we introduce the lazy
learning algorithms in detail before we present the learning task: the application
of machine learning to natural language database interfaces. Finally, we explain
the set-up of an extensive case study and discuss the results from the evaluation.

2   Lazy Learning Algorithms

2.1   Instance-Based Learning

The different proposed instance-based learning algorithms vary in how they assess the similarity (or distance) between two instances. Two very popular methods are *IB1* [1] and *IB1-IG* [4]. IB1 applies the simple approach of treating all
features as equally important whereas IB1-IG uses the information gain [7] of
the features as weighting function to take account of the different relevance of
the individual features.

Besides implementing these two benchmark algorithms, we have developed a
new algorithm called *BIN-CAT* for binary features with class-dependent weighting and asymmetric treatment of the feature values. In BIN-CAT we calculate

the similarity between a new case X and a training case Y using the following formula:

$$
\begin{aligned}
\mathrm{SIM}(X, Y) = {} & \sum_{i=1}^{n} p\left(D_i, C_Y\right) \cdot w_i \cdot \sigma\left(x_i, y_i\right) - \\
& \sum_{i=1}^{n} p\left(D_i, C_Y\right) \cdot w_i \cdot \delta_Y\left(x_i, y_i\right) - \\
& \sum_{i=1}^{n} \left[1 - p\left(D_i, C_Y\right)\right] \cdot w_i \cdot \delta_X\left(x_i, y_i\right) \ .
\end{aligned}
\tag{1}
$$

Here, n indicates the number of features, D_i the collection of those instances that have value 1 for the ith feature, and C_Y the class of the training case Y. The term $p(D_i, C_Y)$ then denotes the proportion of instances in D_i that belong to class C_Y to the total number of training cases for C_Y. $\sigma(x_i, y_i)$, $\delta_Y(x_i, y_i)$, and $\delta_X(x_i, y_i)$ are determined as follows:

$$
\sigma\left(x_i, y_i\right) = \begin{cases} 1 \text{ if } x_i = 1 \wedge y_i = 1 \\ 0 \text{ otherwise} \end{cases}
$$

$$
\delta_Y\left(x_i, y_i\right) = \begin{cases} 1 \text{ if } x_i = 0 \wedge y_i = 1 \\ 0 \text{ otherwise} \end{cases}
$$

$$
\delta_X\left(x_i, y_i\right) = \begin{cases} 1 \text{ if } x_i = 1 \wedge y_i = 0 \\ 0 \text{ otherwise} \end{cases}
\tag{2}
$$

so that we rate the second sum in (1) higher for a larger number of occurrences of feature i for class C_Y whereas we rate the third sum lower. In other words, if the training case Y contains a certain feature but the new case X does not, then we rate the difference the stronger the more often the feature occurs for class C_Y. For features occurring in the case X but not in Y we apply the opposite principle.

Finally, w_i represents the weight of feature i. We calculate its value by introducing the following weighting function:

$$
w_i = \frac{1}{c} \cdot \sum_{j=1}^{c} 1 - 4 \cdot p(D_i, j) \cdot \left[1 - p(D_i, j)\right] \ .
\tag{3}
$$

The term under the summation symbol represents the selectivity of feature i for class j. It equals 1 if either all or none of the instances have value 1 for this feature. In this case, all instances for class j either possess or do not possess this feature, which makes it a very discriminating characteristic. The opposite extreme is that $p(D_i, j)$ equals 50 % because then the feature possesses no information for the prediction of the class and the term under the summation symbol becomes 0.

2.2 Prototype-Based Learning

We have developed the prototype-based algorithm *BIN-PRO* for binary features. For each class C we compute $|D_C|$, the number of instances that belong to class C, as well as $|D_{C,f}|$. The latter restricts the set of instances D_C to those instances that have value 1 for feature f.

As similarity function between a new case X and a class C we introduce the following formula:

$$\text{SIM}(X,C) = \sum_{f \in X} |D_{C,f}| \cdot w_f - \frac{1}{|D_C|} \cdot \sum_{f \notin X} |D_{C,f}| \cdot w_f \ . \tag{4}$$

In this formula we consider both features that are present in the new case X and features that are important for class C but missing in X. However, we give more emphasis to the former by dividing the second sum by $|D_C|$. As weighting function w_f we use (3) again.

To further improve the performance of BIN-PRO in comparison with BIN-CAT (see Sect. 4), we have added an iterative adaptive component to BIN-PRO. The resulting algorithm *BIN-PIA* iteratively adapts the values $|D_{C,f}|$ to increase the *fitness* of the algorithm, i.e. the proportion of correctly classified training instances.

Figure 1 shows the applied algorithm in detail. For each wrong classification of a training instance X and all features $f \in X$, it decrements $|D_{C_{\text{pred}},f}|$ for the wrong predicted class C_{pred} by 1 and increments $|D_{C_{\text{corr}},f}|$ for the correct class C_{corr} by 1. This adaptation of the $|D_{C,f}|$ is repeated in several iterations for all training instances until either the fitness reaches 100 % or the number of iterations exceeds a certain limit.

3 Learning Task

The learning task in natural language database interfaces is to select the correct command class based on semantic features extracted from the user input. Therefore, it can be modeled as classification problem with a large number of binary features and classes. For that purpose we have developed the interface architecture displayed in Fig. 2. The *morpho-lexical analyzer* transforms the user input into a *deep form list (DFL)*, which indicates for each word token its surface form, category, and semantic deep form (see [12] for more details).

For database interfaces unknown values contained in the input possess particular importance for the meaning of a command [13]. Therefore, we treat the unknown values separately in the *unknown value list (UVL) analyzer*. This module checks the data type of unknown values and looks them up in the database to find out whether they represent identifiers of existing entities. In such a case

```
Program Iterative-Adaptation
begin
    repeat
        set number of correctly classified instances |Dcorr| to 0;
        foreach instance X in training collection D do
        begin
            calculate predicted class Cpred with maximum similarity according to (4);
            if Cpred = correct class Ccorr then
                increment |Dcorr|;
        else
                foreach feature f do
                    if f ∈ X then
                    begin
                        decrement |D Cpred,f|;
                        increment |D Ccorr,f|;
                    end
        end
        assign |Dcorr| / |D| to fitness;
    until fitness = 1.0 or number of iterations > limit;
end
```

Fig. 1. Algorithm for iterative adaptation

the entity type is indicated in the resulting UVL, otherwise we use the data type instead. UVL and DFL represent the input to the *machine learning (ML) classifier*. It assigns a ranked *command class list (CCL)* to the input sentence according to the learned classification knowledge. As last step we use the CCL and UVL to *generate database commands*.

For the encoding of the training data we only make use of the semantic deep forms contained in the DFL. We use English concepts as deep forms and map them to binary features, i.e. a certain feature has the value 1 if the deep form is a member of the DFL, otherwise it equals 0. For the elements of the UVL we apply a more detailed encoding, which maps the number and the type to binary features. Figure 3 shows an example of the feature encoding for a German input sentence. Besides a German morpho-lexical analyzer, we also developed modules for the processing of English and Japanese input [14]. All components of the interface architecture are implemented in ROCK & ROLL by taking advantage of the available powerful deductive object-oriented programming language.

4   Evaluation

As a case study for the evaluation of the lazy learning algorithms we use them within a German natural language interface to a *production planning and control system (PPC)*. The task of the PPC is the mean-term scheduling of products and

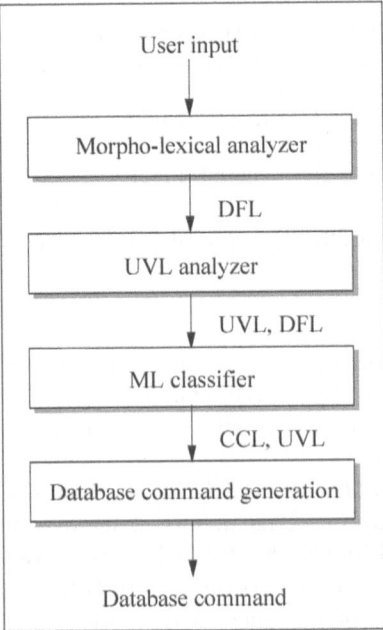

Fig. 2. Interface architecture

resources involved in the manufacturing processes, i.e. material, machines, and labor. The output of the PPC is the master production schedule, which is needed for the coordination of related business services, e.g. engineering, manufacturing, and finance. The modeled enterprise produces precision tools by applying job order production and serial manufacture as basic strategies.

The efficient realization of the high demands of this application exceeds by far the available power of relational database technology. Therefore, the PPC represents an excellent choice for taking full advantage of the extended functionality of deductive object-oriented database systems. Furthermore, the complex requirements justify the effective use of a natural language front-end.

During previous research [11] we developed a natural language interface based on 1000 input sentences, which had been collected from users by means of questionnaires. The input sentences were then mapped to 100 command classes (10 sentences for each class). The mapping was performed by elaborate semantic analysis; for the development of the underlying rule base we spent several man-months.

Therefore, we were eager to see if we could replace this extensive effort by a machine learning module, which learns the same linguistic knowledge automatically. As result of the encoding of the complete data collection of 1000 sentences we identified the large number of 317 features, 290 for the DFL and 27 for the UVL. For the evaluation of the different machine learning algorithms we used

User input	St 37 H kostet nun 1.7 Schilling (St 37 H costs now 1.7 Schilling)
DFL	cost, now, schilling
UVL	1 material, 1 real

Fig. 3. Example of feature encoding

the success rate and the top-3 rate as performance measures. The *success rate* indicates the proportion of correctly classified test cases whereas the *top-3 rate* shows the proportion of cases for which the correct classification is among the first three predicted classes.

We performed *10-fold cross-validation* to test the machine learning algorithms' predictive accuracy. This means that we randomly divided the data collection into 10 equal blocks. Each block in turn was used as test set whereas the remaining blocks formed the training set. Table 1 shows the achieved mean and standard deviation of the success rate and top-3 rate for the 5 different learning algorithms.

Table 1. Test results

	SUCCESS RATE		TOP-3 RATE	
	MEAN	STDEV	MEAN	STDEV
IB1	81.3 %	2.50 %	94.5 %	1.65 %
IB1-IG	89.0 %	3.71 %	98.4 %	1.17 %
BIN-CAT	95.2 %	1.62 %	99.9 %	0.32 %
BIN-PRO	92.5 %	3.17 %	99.6 %	0.70 %
BIN-PIA	94.7 %	3.40 %	99.7 %	0.67 %

The test for the statistical significance of the performance differences between the different algorithms resulted in the significance matrix displayed in Table 2 (for a significance level of 5 %). For each cell of the matrix it shows the significance of the performance difference between the algorithm written as column label A_C and the algorithm written as row label A_R:

1. +: A_C is significantly better than A_R,
2. −: A_C is significantly worse than A_R,
3. ∼: there is no significant difference between A_C and A_R.

Each entry shows first the result for the success rate and then for the top-3 rate, e.g. the entry +/∼ between BIN-CAT and BIN-PRO means that BIN-CAT

Table 2. Significance matrix

	IB1	IB1-IG	BIN-CAT	BIN-PRO	BIN-PIA
IB1		+/+	+/+	+/+	+/+
IB1-IG	−/−		+/+	+/+	+/+
BIN-CAT	−/−	−/−		−/∼	∼/∼
BIN-PRO	−/−	−/−	+/∼		∼/∼
BIN-PIA	−/−	−/−	∼/∼	∼/∼	

did significantly better than BIN-PRO regarding the success rate but that there was no significant difference with respect to the top-3 rate.

Figure 4 gives a clearer picture by ranking the algorithms according to the achieved success and top-3 rates. In this figure the brackets represent a significant difference between two algorithms. In other words, all algorithms inside of a bracket possess no significant difference, e.g. the first bracket on the left shows that BIN-CAT did significantly better than BIN-PRO but that there were no significant differences between BIN-CAT and BIN-PIA or between BIN-PIA and BIN-PRO.

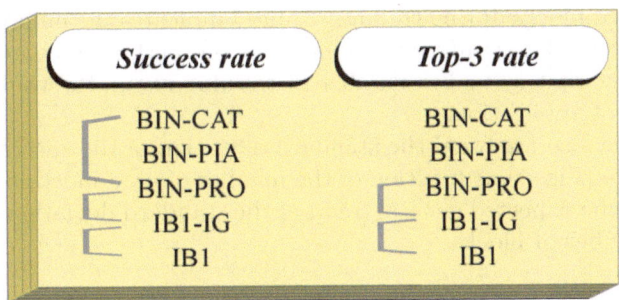

Fig. 4. Ranking of algorithms

If we compare the results for the different algorithms, we can see that the three algorithms of the BIN group clearly outperform IB1 and IB1-IG. BIN-CAT is only significantly better than BIN-PRO concerning the success rate whereas BIN-PIA shows no significant inferiority with respect to both performance measures. This outstanding performance of both BIN-PIA and BIN-PRO is remarkable if one considers the much more condensed representation of the learned knowledge by the use of prototypes.

To estimate the computational overhead of BIN-PIA in comparison with BIN-PRO we monitored the number of required iterations, which was only 3.5 on average. Figure 5 plots the average fitness of BIN-PIA after each iteration; it shows the excellent convergence of the algorithm.

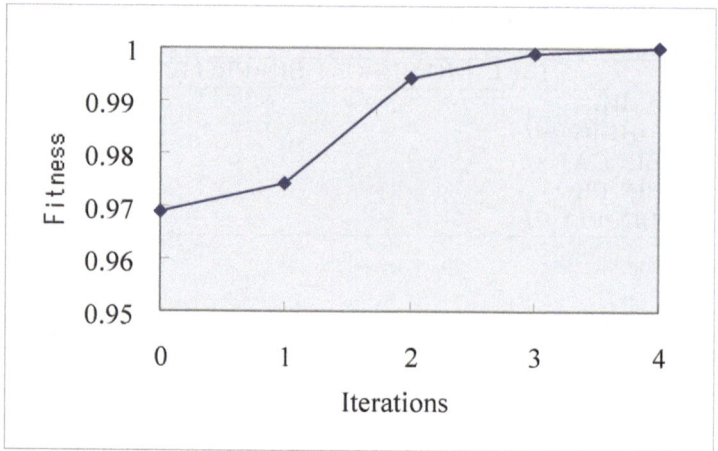

Fig. 5. Fitness function of BIN-PIA algorithm

In the last part of our evaluation we generated learning functions, which show the decrease of the success rate (Fig. 6) and the top-3 rate (Fig. 7) for a smaller number of used blocks during training. Table 3 indicates the number of blocks for which we observed a significant reduction of the performance measures. These results suggest that a smaller number of training examples would be sufficient for this type of application.

Finally, we also analyzed the standard deviation of the success rate (Fig. 8) and top-3 rate (Fig. 9) as function of the number of used blocks during training, which shows the expected general trend of the standard deviation to increase for a smaller number of blocks.

5   Conclusion

Our empirical results were surprisingly good if one considers the complexity of the task, which included many similar classes that were very difficult to distinguish even for human experts. In any case, we could show that lazy learning algorithms represent a sound alternative to manual knowledge acquisition for the application in natural language database interfaces.

The results also show that the prototype-based algorithms are competitive with instance-based learning. By using the technique of iterative adaptation we could observe results that showed no significant inferiority to the best instance-based algorithm BIN-CAT. This behavior of BIN-PIA is remarkable if one considers the large reduction of required memory and processing time for classification by the use of prototypes.

Future work will concentrate on the important point of testing our learning algorithms on standard benchmark machine learning datasets and other typical

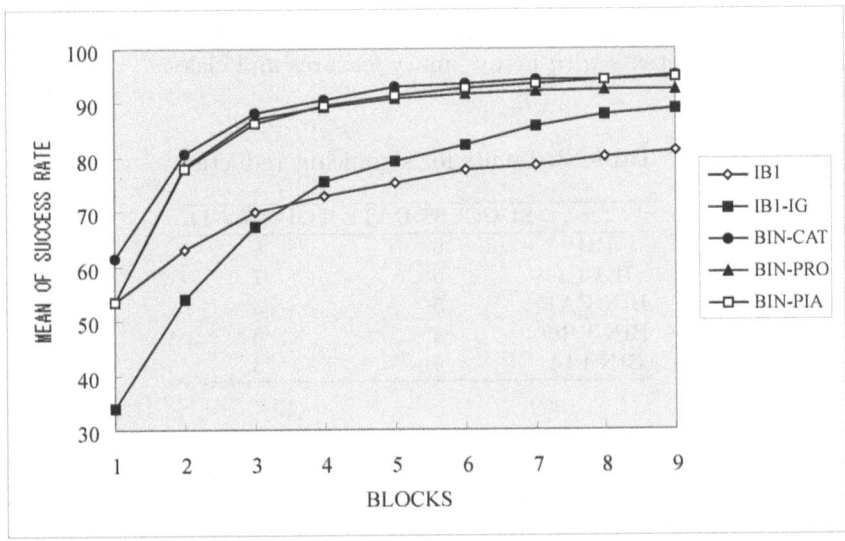

Fig. 6. Learning functions for success rate

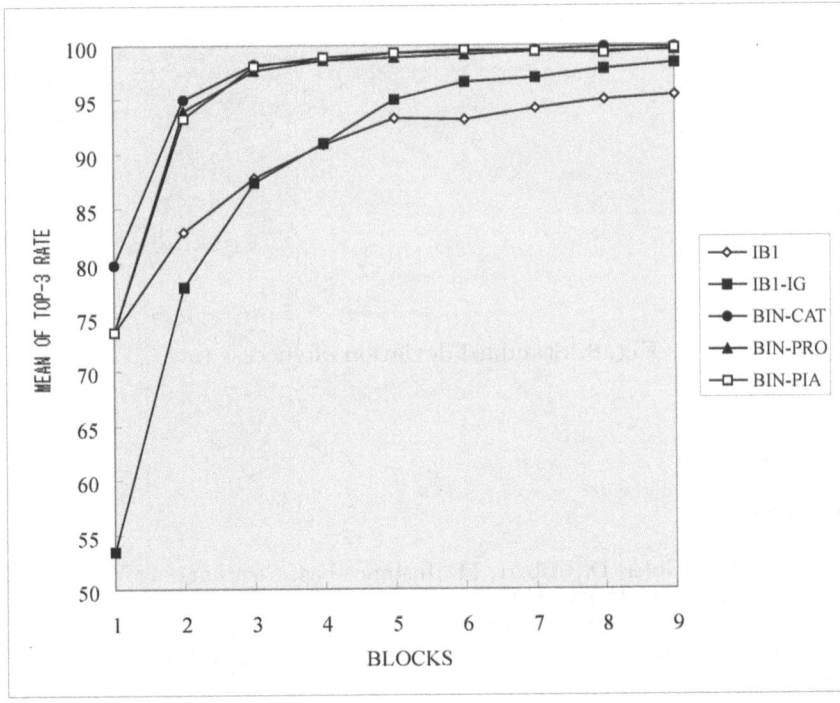

Fig. 7. Learning functions for top-3 rate

datasets for machine learning of natural language. This will provide more experimental evidence to show that the presented methods are generally valid also in other learning contexts with many binary features and classes.

Table 3. Limits for significant reduction

	SUCCESS RATE	TOP-3 RATE
IB1	6	6
IB1-IG	6	7
BIN-CAT	5	5
BIN-PRO	4	3
BIN-PIA	5	3

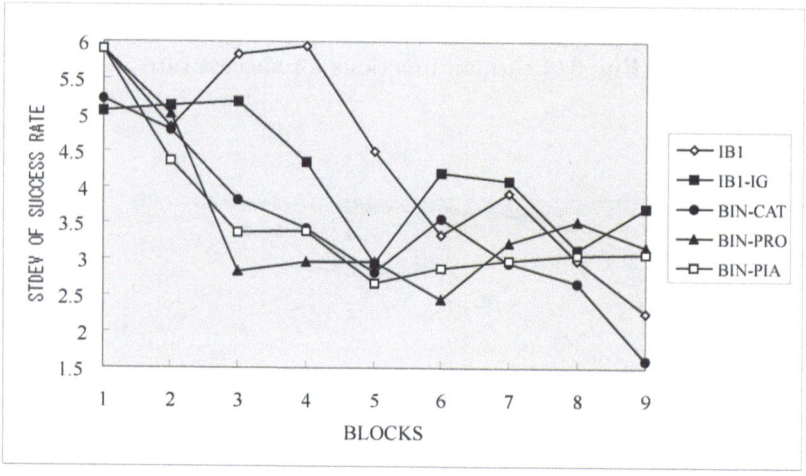

Fig. 8. Standard deviation of success rate

References

1. Aha, D. W., Kibler, D., Albert, M.: Instance-based learning algorithms. Machine Learning **7** (1991) 37–66   113
2. Androutsopoulos, I., Ritchie, G. D., Thanisch, P.: Natural language interfaces to databases – an introduction. Journal of Natural Language Engineering **1:1** (1995) 29–81   113
3. Barja, M. L. et al.: An effective deductive object-oriented database through language integration. Proc. of the Intl. Conf. on Very Large Data Bases (1994) 463–474   113

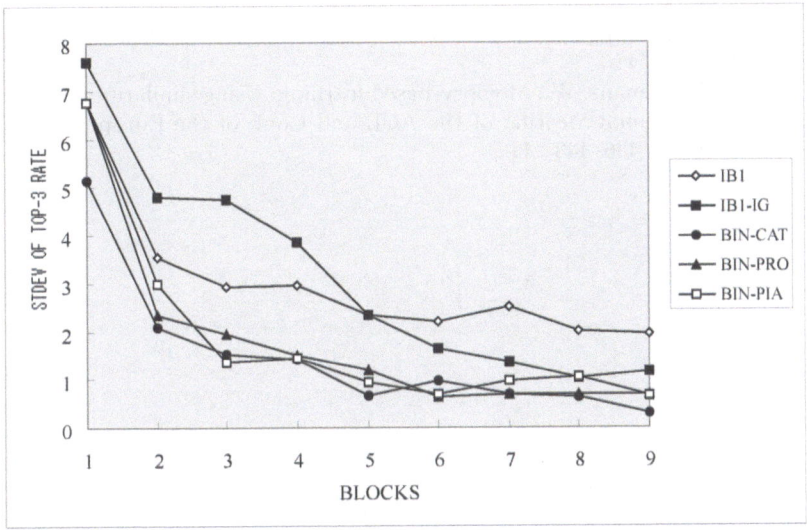

Fig. 9. Standard deviation of top-3 rate

4. Daelemans, W., van den Bosch, A.: Generalisation performance of backpropagation learning on a syllabification task. Drossaers, M., Nijholt, A. (eds): TWLT3: Connectionism and Natural Language Processing. Twente University Press, Enschede (1992) 27–37   113
5. Datta, P., Kibler, D.: Learning prototypical concept descriptions. Proc. of the Intl. Conf. on Machine Learning (1995) 41–45   113
6. Imielinski, T., Mannila, H.: A database perspective on knowledge discovery. Communications of the ACM **39:11** (1996) 58–64   113
7. Quinlan, J. R.: Induction of decision trees. Machine Learning **1** (1986) 81–206 113
8. Riloff, E., Lehnert, W.: Information extraction as a basis for high-precision text classification. ACM Transactions on Information Systems **12:3** (1994) 296–333 113
9. Tversky, A.: Features of similarity. Psychological Review, **84:4** (1977) 327–352 113
10. Uehara, K., Tanizawa, M., Maekawa, S.: PBL: Prototype-based learning algorithm. 113
    Wess, S., Althoff, K.-D., Richter, M. M. (eds): Topics in Case-Based Reasoning. Springer-Verlag, Berlin (1994)
11. Winiwarter, W.: The Integrated Deductive Approach to Natural Language Interfaces. Ph.D. thesis, University of Vienna (1994)   117
12. Winiwarter, W.: MIDAS – the morphological component of the IDA system for efficient natural language interface design. Proc. of the Intl. Conf. on Database and Expert Systems Applications (1995) 584–593 115
13. Winiwarter, W.: Unknown value lists and their use for semantic analysis in IDA – the integrated deductive approach to natural language interface design. Proc. of the Australasian Database Conf. (1996) 194–203   115
14. Winiwarter, W., Kambayashi, Y.: A comparative study of the application of different learning techniques to natural language interfaces. Proc. of the Workshop on Computational Natural Language Learning (1997) 125–135   116

15. Winiwarter, W., Kambayashi, Y.: A machine learning workbench in a DOOD framework. Proc. of the Intl. Conf. on Database and Expert Systems Applications (1997) 452–461 113
16. Zavrel, J., Daelemans, W.: Memory-based learning: Using similarity for smoothing. Proc. of the Annual Meeting of the ACL and Conf. of the European Chapter of the ACL (1997) 436–443 112

GD: A Measure Based on Information Theory for Attribute Selection*

Javier Lorenzo, Mario Hernández, and Juan Méndez

Dpto. de Informática y Sistemas
Univ. de Las Palmas de Gran Canaria, Campus Univ. de Tafira
35017 Las Palmas, Spain
{jlorenzo,mhernandez,jmendez}@dis.ulpgc.es

Abstract. In this work a measure called *GD* is presented for attribute selection. This measure is defined between an attribute set and a class and corresponds to a generalization of the Mántaras distance that allows to detect the interdependencies between attributes. In the same way, the proposed measure allows to order the attributes by importance in the definition of the concept. This measure does not exhibit a noticeable bias in favor of attributes with many values. The quality of the selected attributes using the GD measure is tested by means of different comparisons with other two attribute selection methods over 19 datasets.

Keywords: Machine learning, Intelligent information retrieval, Feature selection

1   Introduction

In many Machine Learning problems, the induction algorithms have to deal with attributes that are not relevant to the definition of the class. The irrelevant or redundant attributes do not affect the ideal Bayesian classifier because the addition of new attributes never decreases the performance of the classifier. However, many practical classifiers decrease its performance when irrelevant or redundant attributes arise. To overcome this problem, different approaches have been proposed to select the more relevant attributes that define a class. Some works on attribute selection were the WINNOW algorithm proposed by Littlestone [15], the FOCUS algorithm proposed by Almuallim and Dietterich [3] and the Relief algorithm proposed by Kira and Rendell [11]. All these algorithms share as a common characteristic that they do not include the performance of the classifier as a measure to guide the selection of the attributes. John et al. [10] propose the *wrapper* approach that utilizes the performance of the classifier to carry out the selection of the attributes. There is much evidence that wrapper method give good results [1,10]. However, due to its computational cost, wrapper methods can only be applied in combination with classifiers of low complexity. An

---

* This work was supported in part the Spanish Ministry of Education under project TAP95-0288

Helder Coelho (Ed.): IBERAMIA'98, LNAI 1484, pp. 124–135, 1998.

intermediate approach proposed by Scherf and Brauer [21] performs the feature selection in two steps. The first step is a filter approach whose result is a set of different attribute subsets and the second step is a wrapper approach over the resultant subsets in the first step.

The method proposed in this work utilizes a measure based on Information Theory to guide the selection of the attributes. The use of concepts of Information Theory in feature selection is not recent. Quinlan [20] proposed a measure called Gain Ratio that corresponds to the ratio between mutual information and the entropy [24]. Another approach based on Information Theory is proposed by López de Mántaras [16], where a distance measure is defined and its relationship with the Gain Ratio measure proposed by Quinlan is analyzed. Wettschereck and Dieterich [23] demonstrated that the performance of the k-NN and Nearest-Hyperrectangle classifiers increases when the attributes are weighted by mutual information. Daelemans [7] reaches similar conclusions when the features used in the Exemplar-based Generalization algorithm are weighted with the mutual information in a problem of assignment of syllable boundaries in Dutch.

In the previous works the attributes are considered independent, they do not take into account the possible relations between them. In this work a measure called *GD*, between an attribute subset and the class is proposed. This measure, unlike the Gain Ratio, tries to get the possible interdependence among attributes and is based on a quadratic form of the distance proposed by López de Mántaras and a matrix called *Transinformation Matrix*.

The organization of the rest of this paper is as follows. In section 2 some concepts of Information Theory are reviewed. Then in section 3, the distance proposed by López de Mántaras is analyzed. The GD measure is defined in section 4, and a comparison with two other selection attribute methods on several datasets is presented in section 5. The selection of the attributes is carried out from a set of labeled samples. Each sample of the data set is composed of a n dimensional vector of attributes $X = \{X_1, X_2, \ldots, X_n\}$ and a label Y which indicates the class the sample belongs to.

2   Review of Some Concepts on Information Theory

As the measure we propose in this work is based on Information Theory, before introducing the measure itself, a review of some previous concepts of the Information Theory is included. The different concepts will refer to the attributes and the class because they can be considered as random variables and so the concepts can be defined on them.

Let $H(X_i)$ the entropy of attribute X_i with values $\{x_i^1, \ldots, x_i^k\}$, with definition:

$$H(X_i) = -\sum_{i=1}^{k} P(x_i^k) \log P(x_i^k) \tag{1}$$

where $P(x_i^k)$ is the probability that value x_i^k occurs. According to the expression, the entropy measures the average of uncertainty of the attribute and it is non negative [6]. In the same way that we have defined the entropy of an attribute, we can define the entropy of the class Y.

When one attribute is known, the amount of uncertainty of the class is decreased. A measure that reveals the information given by an attribute X_i over a class Y is the mutual information, $I(X_i; Y)$. The expression of the mutual information is:

$$I(X_i; Y) = H(Y) - H(Y/X_i) = \sum_k \sum_j P(y_j, x_i^k) \log \frac{P(y_j, x_i^k)}{P(y_j)P(x_i^k)} \qquad (2)$$

In equation (2), $H(Y/X_i)$ represents the entropy of Y when X_i is known. This entropy is called conditional entropy and it is non negative and less or equal to $H(Y)$ [6], so the mutual information is greater or equal to zero and commutative.

From the joint entropy of an attribute and the class $H(X_i, Y)$ and from the mutual information $I(X_i; Y)$, the *entropy distance* [18] is defined as:

$$d(X_i, Y) = H(X_i, Y) - I(X_i; Y) \qquad (3)$$

The entropy distance measures the information that the attribute X_i gives about a class. Because, the more information the attribute gives, the greater the mutual information is and therefore the smaller the distance is.

3   Mántaras Distance

A measure that is conceptually very close to the measure proposed in this work is the Mántaras distance proposed by López de Mántaras [16], so we are going to give a short description of it before to define the GD distance.

The Mántaras distance is a distance measure between two partitions to select the attributes associated with the nodes of a decision tree. In each node, it is chosen the attribute that produces the partition closest to the correct partition of the samples subset in the examples.

The Mántaras distance has the following expression:

$$d_{LM}(P_A, P_B) = H(P_A/P_B) + H(P_B/P_A) \qquad (4)$$

Where $H(P_A/P_B)$ and $H(P_B/P_A)$ correspond to the entropy in each partition when the another is known. It is possible to demonstrate the following properties [16]:

1. $d_{LM}(P_A, P_B) \geq 0$ and equal iff $P_A = P_B$
2. $d_{LM}(P_A, P_B) = d_{LM}(P_B, P_A)$
3. $d_{LM}(P_A, P_B) + d_{LM}(P_B, P_C) \geq d_{LM}(P_A, P_C)$

If we change the references to partitions by attributes and class in the definition of the Mántaras distance, we get the following expression for the Mántaras distance

$$d_{LM}(X_i, Y) = H(X_i/Y) + H(Y/X_i) \tag{5}$$

and using equation (2) and the relation

$$H(Y/X_i) = H(Y, X_i) - H(X_i) \tag{6}$$

equation (5) can be transformed in

$$d_{LM}(X_i, Y) = H(X_i, Y) - I(X_i; Y) = d(X_i, Y) \tag{7}$$

which corresponds to the expression of the entropy distance and shows that the entropy distance is a metric distance function.

4   GD Measure

The use of the Gain Ratio and the Mántaras distance has the drawback of operating over isolated attributes. Therefore, these methods do not detect the possible dependencies that there could be between attributes. A manner to get into account the interdependencies between attributes is to compute the mutual information for each pair of attributes $I(X_i; X_j)$. These interdependencies of attributes can be represented with the aid of the *Transinformation Matrix T*, a square matrix of dimension n (number of attributes) where each element $t_{i,j}$ of the matrix is the mutual information between attributes *i-th* and *j-th*.

$$T = [t_{i_j}]_{i,j=1,n} = [I(X_i; X_j)]_{i,j=1,n}$$

Some properties hold for this matrix whose demonstrations can be found in [17].

1. $t_{i,i} \geq t_{i,j}$, $i, j = 1 \ldots n$ and $i \neq j$
2. $t_{i,j} \geq 0$, $i, j = 1 \ldots n$
3. $t_{i,j} = t_{j,i}$, $i, j = 1 \ldots n$

Proposition 1. *Given an attribute set* $\{X_1, X_2, \ldots, X_n\}$ *and its associated transinformation matrix T, if for any row* i *it is established that*

$$\exists j : t_{i,i} = t_{i,j}$$

Then the attribute X_j *is redundant with respect to* X_i *and it can be removed from the set without any information lost.*

Proof. From the definition of the transinformation matrix and the expression (2) of the mutual information:

$$t_{i,i} = I(X_i, X_i) = H(X_i) - H(X_i/X_i) = H(X_i)$$
$$t_{i,j} = I(X_i, X_j) = H(X_i) - H(X_i/X_j)$$

So, if $t_{i,i} = t_{i,j}$

$$I(X_i; X_i) = I(X_i; X_j) \Rightarrow H(X_i) = H(X_i) - H(X_i/X_j) \Rightarrow H(X_i/X_j) = 0 \quad (8)$$

$H(X_i/X_j) = 0$ means that the knowledge of X_j decreases to zero the uncertainty of X_i, and therefore attribute X_j holds the whole information over X_i and one of them can be removed without any information lost.

Once the transinformation matrix has been defined, it is necessary to find an expression for the GD measure that includes the transinformation matrix and the distance (3). This expression must be defined in such a way that subsets of attributes with high dependencies between attributes yield lower values than other ones without these high dependencies. A solution comes from the analogy to significance level between the transinformation matrix and the covariance matrix (Σ) of two random variables. This analogy can be established because both matrices measure interrelation between variables. In the Mahalanobis distance [9], the covariance matrix is utilized to correct the effects of cross covariances between two components of a random variable. The expression of the Mahalanobis distance [9] between two samples (X, Y) of a random variable is:

$$d_{Mahalanobis}(X,Y) = (X - Y)^t \Sigma^{-1}(X - Y) \quad (9)$$

where $d_{Mahalanobis}(X, Y)$ corresponds to the Euclidean distance if Σ is the identity matrix.

Therefore the GD measure can be defined in a similar way to the Mahalanobis distance, using the transinformation matrix instead of the covariance matrix and the distance (3) instead of the Euclidean distance. The GD measure $d_{GD}(X, Y)$ between the set of attributes X and the class Y is expressed as:

$$d_{GD}(X,Y) = D(X,Y)^t T^{-1} D(X,Y) \quad (10)$$

where $D(X,Y) = [d_{LM}(X_1, Y), \ldots, d_{LM}(X_n, Y)]^T$ is a vector whose i-th element is the Mántaras distance (equivalent to the entropy distance) between the attribute X_i and the class, and T is the transinformation matrix of the set of attributes X. From the equation (3) we can observe that the elements of the $D(X, Y)$ vector are smaller as the information that the attribute gives about the class is greater.

Given a set of attributes and the associated transinformation matrix, the GD measure fulfills the following properties:

1. $d_{GD}(X,Y) \geq 0, \forall X, Y$ and $d_{GD}(X,X) = 0$
2. $d_{GD}(X,Y) = d_{GD}(Y,X), \forall X, Y$

The demonstration of the two previous properties is trivial if we take into account the properties of the Mántaras distance and the properties of the transinformation matrix. The triangle inequality property has not been demonstrated

Table 1. Results of experiments to detect the influence of the number of values of an attribute

Data Set		GR	$1\text{-}d_{LM}$	d_{GD}
1	m=2	0.0012	0.0006	3.9903
	m=5	0.0021 (75%)	0.0015 (150%)	4.7216 (18%)
	m=10	0.0032 (166%)	0.0025 (316%)	5.5559 (39%)
2	m=2	0.0012	0.0007	2.9563
	m=5	0.0021 (75%)	0.0016 (128%)	3.9559 (33%)
	m=10	0.0033 (175%)	0.0027 (285%)	4.8589 (64%)
3	m=2	0.0049	0.0015	10.9777
	m=5	0.0084 (71%)	0.0042 (180%)	9.1349 (-16%)
	m=10	0.0133 (171%)	0.0079 (426%)	9.2887 (-15%)

for the GD measure yet, and so it can be considered as a semi-metric distance function [4].

The GD measure satisfies the *monotonicity* property that states that the distance increases with dimensionality. Therefore, only subsets with the same cardinality can be compared between them.

After the redundant attributes have been filtered according to proposition 1, the use of GD measure for feature selection is based on the fact that the distances $d(X_i, Y)$ decreases as the information of an attribute subset about the class increases. On the other hand, if an element of the transinformation matrix is large (it indicates that the interdependence between two attributes is high) then the GD measure increases. Therefore it can be concluded that lower values of GD measure between an attribute subset and the class indicate that the attributes give a lot of information about the class and that there is no high interdependencies between the attributes.

In the GD measure an important aspect is the singularity of the transinformation matrix. In [17] has been analytically demonstrated that the transinformation matrix is non singular for dimension two and three. An analytical demonstration have not been found for greater dimensions yet, but all the matrices generated in the examples of section 5 were found non-singular.

The GD measure does not exhibit a noticeable bias in favor of attributes with large numbers of values as Gain Ratio and Mántaras distance do [24]. To test the previous statement, we performed the experiments presented in [24] by White and Liu. These experiments consist of three synthetic data set, each one with three attributes with 2, 5 and 10 values respectively. The attributes have not any relation with the classes which are distributed in each data set as follows: two equiprobable classes, two classes with an odds ratio of 4:1 and five equiprobable classes.

Table 1 shows the obtained values of the Gain Ratio (GR), the Mántaras distance (d_{LM}) and the GD measure (d_{GD}). In the table the relative increment with respect to the smallest dimension appears in brackets. The relative increment of the GD measure is low unlike the Gain Ratio and the Mántaras distance that have a relative increment of two orders of magnitude.

Table 2. Results obtained with the Naive Bayes classifier

	d_{GD}		$ReliefF$			d_{LM}		
	# attr.	Acc.	# attr.	Acc.	Concl.	# attr.	Acc.	Concl.
BW	10	96.30±0.22	7	96.74±0.23	<	10	96.30±0.22	=
GL	8	48.08±1.04	8	48.08±1.04	=	3	49.18±1.10	=
G2	4	69.92±1.10	4	65.11±1.10	>	2	61.67±1.10	>
HD	8	85.04±0.62	11	85.45±0.65	=	12	85.15±0.62	=
IR	2	96.00±0.49	2	96.00±0.49	=	2	96.00±0.49	=
LD	6	55.58±0.82	3	59.45±0.91	<	6	55.58±0.82	=
PI	6	75.67±0.46	2	76.60±0.50	<	4	75.70±0.47	=
WI	6	97.53±0.34	13	97.43±0.34	=	12	97.59±0.35	=
PO	1	70.49±1.68	1	71.18±1.64	<	1	69.47±1.67	>
TT	6	72.12±0.43	6	73.00±0.43	<	6	73.02±0.44	<
VO	1	95.63±0.28	1	95.63±0.28	=	1	95.63±0.28	=
LE	7	74.99±0.44	7	74.99±0.44	=	7	74.99±0.44	=
P5	1	45.13±0.24	1	44.84±0.24	=	1	45.13±0.24	=
BC	4	74.09±0.80	8	74.13±0.73	=	7	74.05±0.79	=
CR	1	86.37±0.37	1	86.37±0.37	=	1	86.37±0.37	=
M1	1	75.00±0.60	3	75.00±0.60	=	3	75.00±0.60	=
M2	1	67.14±0.74	1	67.14±0.74	=	1	67.14±0.74	=
M3	2	97.22±0.23	2	97.22±0.23	=	4	97.22±0.23	=
ZO	7	93.65±0.74	8	93.75±0.73	=	8	93.75±0.73	=

5   Experiments

In this section we compare the quality of the selected attributes by the GD measure with the selected attributes by other two methods. The other two methods chosen in this comparative study are the Mántaras distance and the ReliefF method. On the one hand, the Mántaras distance has been chosen because it has a conceptual resemblance with the proposed method. On the other hand, the ReliefF method has been chosen because it has been widely referenced in the bibliography [5,22,12]. The ReliefF method is a version of the Relief method due to Kononenko [14] that permits attributes with missing values and multiclass problems. The quality of each selected attribute was tested by means of the accuracy that three classifiers yields. As we are interested in comparing the selection methods, we do not make any optimization in the classifiers to avoid the introduction of a bias in the accuracy due to the optimizations. The classifiers were: the Naive Bayes classifier [9], a decision tree induced with the ID3 method [20] and the IB1 algorithm [2]. The implementation of the induction algorithms was done using the $\mathcal{MLC}$++ library [13] and the comparative was performed with 19 databases of the UCI Machine Learning Databases Repository [19]. The databases used in the experiments were the following ones: Breast Cancer Ljubljana (BC), Breast Cancer Wisconsin (BW), Credit Card (CR), Glass (GL), Glass2 (G2), Heart Disease (HD), Iris (IR), Led (LE), Liver Disorder (LD), Monk1, Monk2, Monk3 (M1,M2,M3), Parity5+5 (P5), Pima Indian Diabetes (PI), Post-operative (PO), Tic-Tac-Toe (TT), Voting (VO), Wine (WI), Zoo (ZO).

GD: A Measure Based on Information Theory for Attribute Selection

Table 3. Results obtained with the ID3 classifier

	d_{GD}		$ReliefF$			d_{LM}		
	# attr.	Acc.	# attr.	Acc.	Concl.	# attr.	Acc.	Concl.
BW	2	95.32±0.23	3	95.46±0.23	=	10	94.72±0.29	>
GL	6	69.72±0.96	6	69.72±0.96	=	8	69.27±0.98	=
G2	5	82.56±0.96	3	83.42±0.95	=	6	88.20±0.81 2	<
HD	4	79.07±0.71	5	81.41±0.72	<	8	78.96±0.75	=
IR	2	95.93±0.49	2	95.93±0.49	=	2	95.93±0.49	=
LD	4	64.37±0.78	4	64.37±0.78	=	5	63.51±0.75	=
PI	8	70.65±0.49	8	70.65±0.49	=	8	70.65±0.49	=
WI	3	94.61±0.49	5	95.28±0.53	=	3	94.61±0.49	=
PO	4	70.56±1.62	1	71.18±1.64	=	1	69.47±1.67	=
TT	9	85.46±0.33	9	85.46±0.33	=	9	85.46±0.33	=
VO	1	95.63±0.28	1	95.63±0.28	=	1	95.63±0.28	=
LE	7	73.44±0.42	7	73.44±0.42	=	7	73.44±0.42	=
P5	8	99.96±0.04	5	100.0±0.00	=	8	99.96±0.04	=
BC	4	75.77±0.70	1	72.50±0.80	>	4	75.05±0.77	=
CR	1	86.37±0.37	1	86.37±0.37	=	1	86.37±0.37	=
M1	5	99.93±0.07	3	100.0±0.00	=	5	99.93±0.07	=
M2	5	77.80±0.69	5	77.80±0.69	=	5	77.80±0.69	=
M3	5	100.0±0.00	6	100.0±0.00	=	5	100.0±0.00	=
ZO	9	96.42±0.59	8	96.03±0.60	=	8	96.03±0.60	=

As the GD measure is not defined for attributes with missing values, the databases were chosen with few missing values. All the previous ones have less than 10% of samples with missing values and these samples were removed from the dataset. With respect to the continuous attributes, they were discretized with the simple equal width discretization method with 10 intervals. The process followed to test the quality of the attributes selected with the GD measure was the following. For all datasets, we selected the best attribute subset according to each of the three methods being compared. Then we estimate the accuracy yielded by each classifier yields using the selected attributes. The accuracy was estimated taking the mean of ten runs of a 10 k-fold cross validation [8].

To search the subset with minimum value of GD measure, a Sequential Forward Search (SFS) was implemented, adding in each step the attribute that gave the lower increase of the measure value. For the ReliefF algorithm we sorted the attributes in decreasing order of relevance and took in each case the number of attributes we were considering. With the Mántaras distance we did the same but sorting the attributes in increasing value of the distance. The best results obtained for each classifier are shown in the tables 2 , 3 and 4.

To assess the obtained results, two paired t statistical tests with a confidence level of 90% were realized. Under the null hypothesis of the first statistical test, the two methods have the same accuracy, which means that $accuracy_{d_{GD}} = accuracy_{ReliefF}$ or $accuracy_{d_{GD}} = accuracy_{d_{LM}}$. If the null hypothesis of this statistical test is rejected, and another statistical test is performed in which the null hypothesis is that the accuracy of proposed method is lower or equal to

Table 4. Results obtained with the IB1 classifier

	d_{GD}		$ReliefF$			d_{LM}		
	# attr.	Acc.	# attr.	Acc.	Concl.	# attr.	Acc.	Concl.
BW	9	95.81±0.23	5	96.38±0.21	<	7	95.90±0.23	=
GL	6	76.53±0.89	6	76.53±0.89	=	9	68.59±0.99	>
G2	5	87.85±0.73	5	87.85±0.73	=	4	86.68±0.83	=
HD	11	80.78±0.69	5	79.30±0.73	=	8	76.52±0.71	>
IR	4	95.73±0.50	4	95.73±0.50	=	4	95.73±0.50	=
LD	5	66.01±0.81	5	66.01±0.81	=	5	66.01±0.81	=
PI	8	70.63±0.44	8	70.63±0.44	=	8	70.63±0.44	=
WI	11	97.54±0.37	11	96.69±0.41	>	9	98.26±0.32	<
PO	1	50.08±2.37	2	56.52±1.69	<	1	54.76±2.74	<
TT	9	80.77±0.38	8	81.98±0.37	<	8	81.94±0.37	<
VO	14	93.98±0.33	10	93.77±0.33	=	10	93.84±0.39	=
LE	7	64.81±0.66	7	64.81±0.66	=	7	64.81±0.66	=
P5	8	99.92±0.05	5	100.0±0.00	=	8	99.92±0.05	=
BC	6	73.53±0.73	8	74.03±0.72	=	7	74.08±0.75	=
CR	11	83.49±0.43	9	82.92±0.40	=	1	82.31±1.23	=
M1	5	99.79±0.12	3	100.0±0.00	<	5	99.79±0.12	=
M2	5	67.01±0.70	5	67.01±0.70	=	5	67.01±0.70	=
M3	5	99.66±0.15	2	96.94±0.28	>	5	99.66±0.15	=
ZO	11	97.71±0.44	10	97.03±0.48	=	13	97.51±0.48	=

the another method, which that means that $accuracy_{d_{GD}} \leq accuracy_{ReliefF}$ or $accuracy_{d_{GD}} \leq accuracy_{d_{LM}}$. The results of these statistical tests appear in the tables 2, 3, 4 under the column labeled "Concl.".

If we consider all the possible results that we get using the three selection methods (GD measure, ReliefF and Mántaras distance) and the three classifiers (Naive Bayes, ID3 and IB1) with the 19 databases we get 114 results. Now we are going to analyze these 114 obtained results to get some conclusions out about the performance of the different methods.

In 9 (7.9%) of the 114 cases, the set of attributes selected by the GD measure yields better accuracy than the two other methods. In 90 (78.9%) of the 114 cases, the set of attributes selected by the GD measure yields a accuracy that is equal to the two other methods. Considering the comparative with the two methods separately we get that with respect to the ReliefF method in 4 (7%) of the cases the set of attributes selected by the GD measure is better than the selected by ReliefF and in 43 (75.4%) is equal. On the other hand, with respect to the Mántaras distance in 5 (8.8%) of the cases the results obtained by the GD measure improve the results of the Mántaras distance, and in 47 (82.4%) cases the results are equal.

Taking into account the nature of the attributes of the selected databases, the databases can be grouped in four groups: continuous attributes (BW, GL, G2, HD, IR, LD, PI and WI databases), nominal attributes (PO, TT and VO databases), boolean attributes (LE and P5 databases) and mixed attributes (BC, CR, M1, M2, M3 and ZO databases). If we compare the results obtained in

Table 5. Number of nodes of the tree generated by ID3

	d_{GD}		*ReliefF*			d_{LM}		
	# attr.	# nodes	# attr.	# nodes	Concl.	# attr.	# nodes	Concl.
BW	2	62.16±0.34	3	84.66±0.68	<	10	49.18±0.38	>
GL	6	83.74±0.49	6	83.74±0.49	=	8	78.92±0.49	>
G2	5	39.92±0.26	3	43.74±0.34	<	6	34.60±0.38	>
HD	4	73.22±0.39	5	84.66±0.38	<	8	120.20±0.66	<
IR	2	14.66±0.15	2	14.66±0.15	=	2	14.66±0.15	=
LD	4	173.40±0.92	4	173.40±0.92	=	5	156.04±0.83	>
PI	8	231.66±0.93	8	231.66±0.93	=	8	231.66±0.93	=
WI	3	16.28±0.22	5	16.22±0.23	=	3	16.28±0.22	=
PO	4	131.15±1.64	1	4.00±0.00	>	1	4.00±0.00	>
TT	9	327.34±2.38	9	327.34±2.38	=	9	327.34±2.38	=
VO	1	4.00±0.00	1	4.00±0.00	=	1	4.00±0.00	=
LE	7	159.94±0.26	7	159.94±0.26	=	7	159.94±0.26	=
P5	8	321.30±7.07	5	63.00±0.00	>	8	321.30±7.07	=
BC	4	105.33±1.21	1	4.00±0.00	>	4	37.42±0.07	>
CR	1	3.00±0.00	1	3.00±0.00	=	1	3.00±0.00	=
M1	5	69.98±2.07	3	41.00±0.00	>	5	69.98±2.07	=
M2	5	145.90±0.34	5	145.90±0.34	=	5	145.90±0.34	=
M3	5	19.00±0.00	6	19.00±0.00	=	5	19.00±0.00	=
ZO	9	22.54±0.08	8	26.62±0.10	<	8	26.62±0.10	<

each kind of databases, it can be noticed that GD measure gives better results in databases with continuous and mixed types of attributes. However in the databases with nominal attributes, the GD measure has a lower performance. Finally, the results obtained with the three methods is the same in the databases with boolean attributes.

After the previous global evaluation of the results, we are going to focus on two databases: BW and CRX. The BW database has a completely irrelevant attribute that is the identifier of each sample. This attribute has been the last selected attribute by ReliefF and the GD measure whereas the Mántaras distance selects it firstly. In the CRX database, the attributes A4 and A5 are completely correlated and one of them has been removed in some distributions of this database. This correlation between attributes A4 and A5 is detected by the GD measure and selects the A5 attribute in last position, however ReliefF and the Mántaras distance do not take into account the correlation between the attributes and they select both of them before other attributes.

In table 3, it can be noticed that in general the attribute selection methods do not improve significantly the performance of the induced decision tree as it has been mentioned by other authors. On the contrary, the main advantage of attribute selection methods is the reduction of the reduction of the induced tree because the presence of irrelevant or redundant attributes increase the size of the tree. The GD measure seems to follow the same trend that the other methods in reference to the accuracy, but the size of the tree is reduced in certain cases.

In the table 5 the number of the nodes of the induced trees is presented along with the results of two statistical tests similar to the used with the accuracy but now making reference to the number of nodes. If we focus on the databases of the table 3 whose accuracies are not statistically different and we compare the number of nodes of the trees, we observe that in 4 (11.8%) cases the trees induced with the attribute set obtained using the GD measure has less nodes than the obtained with the attributes selected by the other two methods, and in 22 (64.7%) the number of nodes is equal.

6   Conclusions

In this paper, a measure, called GD measure, for attribute selection based on Information Theory have been presented. Unlike other measures of based on Information Theory, the GD measure does not only select the most relevant attributes but also takes into account the interdependencies between attributes to detect redundant attributes.

From the comparative study carries out, we can conclude that the results obtained with the GD measure and ReliefF method are very similar with respect to the accuracy, although the dimensionality of the attribute sets selected with the GD measure have a slightly lower dimensionality than the selected with the Relief method.

On the other hand, the use of the GD measure for feature selection seems to improve the results obtained with the Mántaras distance and with fewer attributes. This can be due to the introduction of the transinformation matrix that detect the dependencies between attributes. It is important to point out that GD measure works well in problems where the attributes are continuous or where there are several different types of attributes.

Finally, the GD measure does not seem to exhibit a noticeable bias in favor of attributes with large number of values like other measures based on Information Theory have. This fact was probed empirically following the experiments proposed by Liu.

References

1. David W. Aha and Richard L. Bankert. Feature selection for case-based classification of cloud types: An empirical comparison. In *Proc. of the 1994 AAAI Workshop on Case-Based Reasoning*, pages 106–112. AAAI Press, 1994. 124
2. David W. Aha, Dennis Kibler, and Marc K. Albert. Instance-based learning algorithms. *Machine Learning*, 6:37–66, 1991. 130
3. H. Almuallim and T.G. Dietterich. Learning with many irrelevant features. In *Proc. of the Ninth National Conference on Artificial Intelligence*, pages 547–552. AAAI Press, 1991. 124
4. Michael R. Anderberg. *Cluster Analysis for Applications*. Academic Press Inc., New York, 1973. 129
5. Rich Caruana and Dayne Freitag. Greedy attribute selection. In *Proc. of the 11th International Machine Learning Conference*, pages 28–36, New Brunswick, NJ, 1994. Morgan Kaufmann. 130

6. T. M. Cover and J. A. Thomas. *Elements of Information Theory*. John Wiley & Sons Inc., 1991. 126

7. Walter Daelemans and Antal van den Bosch. Generalization performance of back-propagation learning on a syllabification task. In *Proc. of the Third Twente Workshop on Language Technology*, pages 27–38, 1992. 125

8. P. A. Devijver and J. Kittler. *Pattern Recognition: A Statistical Approach*. Prentice-Hall, Englewood Cliffs, New Jersey, 1982. 131

9. R. Duda and P. Hart. *Pattern Classification and Scene Analysis*. John Willey and Sons, 1973. 128, 130

10. G. H. John, R. Kohavi, and K. Pfleger. Irrelevant features and the subset selection problem. In W. William and Haym Hirsh, editors, *Procs. of the Eleventh International Conference on Machine Learning*, pages 121–129. Morgan Kaufmann, San Francisco, CA, 1994. 124

11. Kenji Kira and Larry A. Rendell. The feature selection problem: Traditional methods and a new algorithm. In *Proc. of the 10th National Conf. on Artificial Intelligence*, pages 129–134, 1992. 124

12. Ron Kohavi and George H. John. Wrappers for feature subset selection. *Artificial Intelligence*, 97(1-2):273–324, December 1997. 130

13. Ron Kohavi, Dan Sommerfield, and James Dougherty. Data mining using MLC++: A machine learning library in C++. In *Tools with Artificial Intelligence*, pages 234–245. IEEE Computer Society Press, 1996. Received the best paper award. 130

14. Igor Kononenko. Estimating attributes: Analysis and extensions of relief. In F. Bergadano and L. de Raedt, editors, *Machine Learning: ECML-94*, pages 171–182, Berlin, 1994. Springer. 130

15. Nick Littlestone. Learning quickly when irrelevant attributes abound: A new linear-threshold algorithm. *Machine Learning*, 2:285–318, 1988. 124

16. R. Lopez de Mántaras. A distance-based attribute selection measure for decision tree induction. *Machine Learning*, 6:81–92, 1991. 125, 126

17. Javier Lorenzo and Mario Hernández. Sobre el uso de conceptos de teoría de la información en la selección de características. Technical Report GIAS-TR-006, Grupo de Inteligencia Artificial y Sistemas, Dpto. de Informática y Sistemas, Univ. de Las Palmas de Gran Canaria, 1996. 127, 129

18. David J.C. MacKay. Information theory, inference and learning algorithms. http://wol.ra.phy.cam.ac.uk/mackay/itprnn/book.ps.gz, 1997. 126

19. C. J. Merz and P.M. Murphy. *UCI Repository of machine learning databases*. Irvine, CA: University of California, Department of Information and Computer Science., 1996. 130

20. J. R. Quinlan. Induction of decision trees. *Machine Learning*, 1:81–106, 1986. 125, 130

21. M Scherf and W. Brauer. Feature selection by means of a feature weighting approach. Technical Report FKI-221-97, Institut fur Informatik, Technische Universitat Munchen, 1997. 125

22. Dietrich Wettschereck and David W. Aha. Weighting features. In *Proc. of the First Int. Conference on Case-Based Reasoning*, pages 347–358, 1995. 130

23. Dietrich Wettschereck and Thomas G. Dieterich. An experimental comparison of the nearest-neighbor and nearest-hyperrectangle algorithms. *Machine Learning*, pages 5–27, 1995. 125

24. Allan P. White and Wei Zhong Liu. Bias in information-based measures in decision tree induction. *Machine Learning*, 15:321–329, 1994. 125, 129

Robust Incremental Clustering with Bad Instance Orderings: A New Strategy

Josep Roure[1] and Luis Talavera[2]

[1] Departament d'Informàtica i Gestió
Escola Universitària Politècnica de Mataró
Avda. Puig i Cadafalch 101-111
08303 Mataró, Catalonia, Spain
roure@eupmt.upc.es

[2] Departament de Llenguatges i Sistemes Informàtics
Universitat Politècnica de Catalunya
Campus Nord, Mòdul C6, Jordi Girona 1-3
08034 Barcelona, Catalonia, Spain
talavera@lsi.upc.es

Abstract. It is widely reported in the literature that incremental clustering systems suffer from instance ordering effects and that under some orderings, extremely poor clusterings may be obtained. In this paper we present a new general strategy aimed to mitigate these effects, the Not-Yet strategy which has a general and open formulation and it is not coupled to any particular system. Unlike other proposals, this strategy maintains the incremental nature of learning process. In addition, we propose a classification of strategies to avoid ordering effects which clarifies the benefits and disadvantages we can expect from the proposal made in the paper as well from existing ones. A particular implementation of the Not-Yet strategy is used to conduct several experiments. Results suggest that the strategy improves the clustering quality. We also show that, when combined with other local strategies, the Not-Yet strategy allows the clustering system to get high quality clusterings.

Keywords: Machine Learning, Data mining, Incremental clustering, Order effects.

1 Introduction

Ideally, intelligent agents should possess the ability of adapting their behavior to the environment over time through learning. Thus, learning methods should be able of updating a knowledge base in a continual basis as new experience is gained. Particularly, if an agent performing a *clustering* task [6] should be able of using its learned knowledge to carry out some performance task at any stage of learning, the conceptual scheme should evolve as every new instance is observed without simultaneously processing previous instances. This sort of clustering is often referred to as *incremental clustering*. As noted by Langley [9], there can be several interpretations of incremental learning. In the remainder of this paper,

Helder Coelho (Ed.): IBERAMIA'98, LNAI 1484, pp. 136–147, 1998.

we will assume that a clustering method is incremental if inputs one instance at a time, does not reprocess previous instances and maintains a single conceptual structure in memory.

Incremental clustering, as defined above, has to rely on some sort of hill climbing strategy which triggers small modifications of the knowledge base as new instances are observed. This way of incorporating single instances into the cluster structure makes incremental systems to be sensitive to instance order, as widely reported in the clustering literature [2,5,7,8,9,10].

We say that incremental clustering algorithms exhibit ordering effects when they may yield different cluster structures when the same instances are presented in different orders. In some cases, they even can produce very poor quality clusterings. The problem lies in that a hill climbing strategy may narrow too much the search through the clustering space in a manner that initial observations may lead to a clustering scheme which does not reflect the real structure in the domain. In the worst case, the system might never be able of reaching a good clustering despite of gaining new experience.

2   Avoiding Ordering Effects

Research in incremental clustering has approached the ordering effects problem by using several strategies. In this section, we will give a classification of strategies to avoid ordering effects with regard to two different dimensions, namely, the stage in the clustering process in which they are applied and the scope. Our aim is to clarify the potential benefits and limitations that a given strategy can provide and also, to provide a general framework to place in our own research.

If we divide the strategies according to the stage in the clustering process in which they are applied, we can distinguish among three application points: before, during and after clustering. Methods which are applied *before clustering* can only be used when all or a great amount of data is known beforehand. The idea is to arrange the instance order in such a way that favors the system search process to reach the best classification. It is seen that when dissimilar objects are consecutively presented, the resulting classification is much better than when similar objects are presented together [5,7]. This occurs because, in the former case, initial observations are from different areas of the description space leading initial clusters to reflect these areas, while in the later, a skewed cluster structure may evolve. Thereafter, the clustering system may not be able to recover when further instances from other parts of the description space are observed. A typical example of preprocessing are *seed selection* methods which select 'seed' observations from data growing clusters around them [2,11].

When constructing a cluster structure in an incremental fashion, only two basic operators are needed, one to *create* a new cluster given an instance and another to *incorporate* an instance to an existing cluster. Theoretically, using these two operators, any clustering structure could be built. However, once an object is consolidated into the structure, the clustering system cannot move it using these two basic operators, therefore the system cannot easily recover from

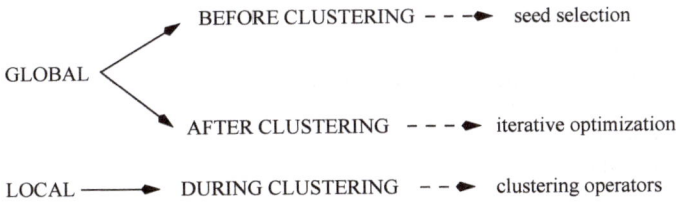

Fig. 1. Classification of strategies to avoid order effects and some examples

previously taken bad decisions when further experience is gained. The clustering system may be provided with additional operators to be applied *during clustering* in order to be able of recovering from bad instance orders. These operators can be viewed as providing some sort of backtracking capabilities to the system without having a memory of previous knowledge structures. A classical example of clustering operators are the *merge* and *split* operators of COBWEB [4].

Finally, we can tackle with ordering effects using *after clustering* strategies. These strategies are intended to act upon a previously obtained clustering in order to improve it. Iterative optimization algorithms are well suited to this approach. Usually, they exploit the gained clustering to redistribute observations or clusters and lead to an improved clustering according to some objective function. After clustering strategies rely on a continuous reprocessing of the clustering structure so they violate the requirements of incremental learning.

¿From another point of view, we can distinguish strategies according to the scope of their application and effects. For a *global strategy* we mean a method which uses information about the whole domain and, therefore, needs to know a significant amount of data in advance, possibly including an extensive reprocessing of instances. In contrast, a *local strategy* acts upon a small piece of knowledge assuming that small, local changes will contribute to improve global clustering quality. Usually, this sort of strategies will be triggered only by new observations. Figure 1 shows the classification of strategies discussed so far. Clearly, global strategies are expected to give significantly better results than local ones since we cannot guarantee local changes to have a sufficiently strong effect upon the global knowledge structure. However, global strategies may be undesirable under the incremental learning assumption because they extensively reprocess the instances in the dataset.

3   The Not-Yet Strategy

Since our goal is to solve the instance ordering problem while maintaining the incremental nature of clustering systems, we propose a solution to be applied during the clustering process. This is a local strategy and so implies a trade-off between the degree of clustering quality improvement and the preservation of the incremental properties of a system.

Let I be an instance
Let P be a partition
Let E be the expected utility/confidence of adding I to P
Let α be the Not-Yet threshold value
if $E \geq \alpha$ **then** add(P,I)
   else add_NY_buffer(I)
endif

Table 1. Not-Yet control strategy

Our solution is based on a simple and intuitive idea. We refer to it as the *Not-Yet* strategy and it has a general and open definition. The strategy states that the incorporation of instances will be deferred if they are in either one of the following two cases, a) it is not expected the utility of the resulting clustering, after incorporating the instance, to be improved, and b) there is not confidence enough about how the instance should be included in the existing clustering. The Not-Yet strategy assumes the existence of a buffer which stores instances that have not been incorporated into the clustering. In order to apply the strategy to a particular clustering system, three issues need to be specified. Firstly, we need some measure to decide whether an instance should be included in the buffer. Secondly, a criterion to determine how buffered instances are reprocessed is also needed. And finally, we can consider how to order the instances into the buffer. Since our aim is to propose a general enough framework to fit into several approaches we will not specify any particular solution for these questions at this point. In the experiments, however, we will propose an example of how the Not-Yet strategy could be effectively implemented.

In Table 1 an algorithmic formulation of the Not-Yet control strategy is shown. We assume the existence of an *add* operator in the original clustering algorithm which given a partition and an instance incorporates the instance to the partition. This operator is embed into a new conditional estructure containing the α threshold, which constraints the amount of utility or confidence required for an instance in order to be incorporated into a clustering. It is worthy to note that if we assume the E value to be always positive, when α is 0, the Not-Yet control strategy simply reduces to the original clustering algorithm, which becomes a particular case of a more general strategy. This fact demonstrates the generality of the strategy proposed.

Figure 2 shows a typical running of a clustering system on two extreme cases of instance ordering. The graph shows the evolution of the value of a clustering quality function with every new observed instance. When instance ordering is good, the graph reveals that high quality clusters are initially constructed because instances cover very different clusters underlying the domain which are easy to discriminate by the system. Later, the system clustering gracefully converge to the quality global maximum. This maximum is below the initial obtained scores since additional instances may present a more uncertain cluster member-

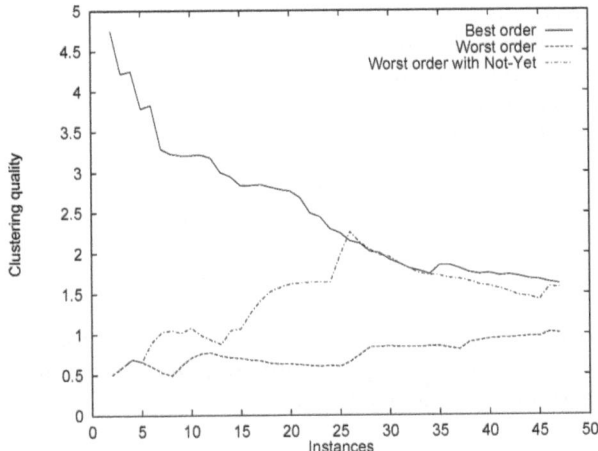

Fig. 2. An example of the Not-Yet strategy effect on clustering quality

ship, so that initial confidence is reduced. Bad orderings have the opposed effect. Low quality clusterings are created at the beginning which strongly condition the rest of the process. We added a third curve reflecting the evolution of the clustering quality when using the Not-Yet strategy with a bad ordering. At the beginning, the system behaves in the same manner that the original algorithm, but as it buffers some instances –around the fifth instance– the cluster quality increases. When quality reaches its maximum, it converges with the good ordering curve. The graph clearly shows how our strategy tries to reach the same 'good learning path' starting from a different learning point. Note, that the horizontal axis measures the number of instances effectively incorporated into the cluster structure. So, when using the Not-Yet strategy, a quality maximum is reached around the 25th instance but, at this point, other instances may have been observed and buffered as well. In fact, in the particular case of the graph shown, only around 25 instances passed the Not-Yet 'filter' the first time they were observed, the rest of them being buffered. When incorporating buffered instances a decrease of the clustering quality is observed but this behavior is similar to that of the system with a good ordering. It is worth to notice that the discussed graph shows a selected example of an optimal behavior of the Not-Yet strategy for illustration purposes.

Complexity when using our strategy will vary from system to system depending on the cost of effectively incorporating an instance and computing the expected utility or confidence of adding the instance. However, most clustering systems use some quality function to decide the best choice when an instance is observed, so it is likely that this function is a good candidate to measure the amount of utility/confidence. Also, we can assume the buffer reordering to be random and hence, of linear cost. If this is the case, complexity is augmented by a constant factor. This factor is dependent on the times every instance is con-

Let I be an instance and P be a partition
Let $M1, M2$ be the best and second best CQF
Let α be the Not-Yet threshold value
if $(1 - M2/M1) \geq \alpha$ **then** add(P,I)
  else add_NY_buffer(I)
endif

Table 2. Implementation of the Not-Yet control strategy for the experiments.

sidered for incorporation into the cluster structure. Obviously, given the open formulation of the Not-Yet strategy, more complex criteria might be used, becoming computational complexity harder.

4   Experiments

In order to empirically evaluate the Not-Yet strategy we conducted several experiments using four well-known datasets of the UCI repository [12]. Since the clustering task is an unsupervised learning task, we have treated labels just as another attribute. In the experiments we assume a general model of hierarchical incremental clustering using two basic operators, one for creating a new class and another to incorporate an instance to an existing class. A concept hierarchy grows incrementally as new instances are observed after applying one of these operators according to the value of some *cluster quality function* (*CQF*). This is a typical model of incremental clustering using a hill climbing strategy which estimates the goodness of applying the available operators and chooses the best option, without reconsider any decision made. Particularly, this model corresponds to the one used in the COBWEB system [4]. The measure of *category utility* used in this system is also used in the experiments as the *CQF*. We used a COBWEB-like clustering strategy because it is simple, well-known and it has been applied (or augmented) in several learning systems [1,8].

In addition, we considered an augmented version of this basic procedure by adding the *merge* and *split* operators used in COBWEB. Briefly, the merge operator modifies a hierarchy by combining two existing clusters while the split operator breaks existing clusters into smaller ones. Split and merge operators provide a sort of backtracking to the clustering system. Since these operators constitute a well known strategy, they may be taken as a basis for evaluating the Not-Yet results. Moreover, as both strategies represent a different approach, it is possible to investigate a combined approach as we will discuss later.

As stated before, we embed the basic control procedure into another one implementing the Not-Yet strategy. The strategy does not incorporate an instance to a cluster structure if there is not evidence enough to decide between the available operators. As shown in Table 2, for each instance, a ratio between the second best *CQF* and the best one is computed. We consider that an operator does not yield a significant better clustering than others if the confidence is below the α threshold, which is in the [0,1] range. Also, as we mentioned before, we can select some method to reorder the instances in the buffer prior to reprocessing. Instead of relying on simply maintaining the order of insertion in the buffer, we chose to randomize the instances.

We tested our strategy with the basic and the augmented clustering models, under two different experimental conditions. In the first experiment, the criterion to reprocess instances was simply to flush the buffer at the end of the clustering process. Therefore, an unlimited size of the buffer was assumed. Actually, in practice, the size was limited by the total number of instances of each tested dataset. As we will discuss later, this criterion may appear to be counterintuitive under an strict incremental learning environment. So, a second type of experiments were conducted limiting the buffer size, with instance reprocessing being fired as soon as the buffer becomes full.

4.1   Experiments with Unlimited Buffer

Experiments were performed on both random and worst case orderings. Table 3 shows the results obtained with both orderings using several values of the α parameter for the Not-Yet strategy. The zero value for this parameter corresponds to the original algorithm without buffering any instance. These experiments assume that the main goal of clustering is to discover a top level partitioning of data of high quality and so we give the CQF scores of the first level.

Results demonstrate that instance ordering has a critical effect in cluster quality. When bad orderings are presented, the quality of discovered clusterings significantly drops compared to the results obtained with random orderings. Results from the augmented version of the algorithm show the limitations of the plain version even with random orderings. Moreover, they give an idea of the CQF values that we could reasonably expect to obtain with each dataset. Results suggest that although the additional operators improve the behavior of the system, their impact is still limited. This is possibly due to the fact that they constitute a local strategy and are only triggered by new observations.

The Not-Yet strategy does not appear to change the behavior of the clustering procedure in results with random orderings, neither with the basic nor with the augmented algorithms. With bad orderings, the strategy improves results with both algorithms. However, in the case of the basic procedure the CQF values are still lower than those obtained with random orderings. We could expect to match the random ordering results by using the Not-Yet strategy since the buffer is randomized and a large number of instances is buffered in many cases. The difference in the results seems to suggest that only few instances may strongly influence the rest of the clustering process. This problem is overcome by using the additional operators and the Not-Yet strategy simultaneously, which results in high quality clusterings. This result can be explained by the fact that the Not-Yet strategy and the clustering operators are complementary approaches. While the former consistently detects bad orderings and rearranges the instance ordering to solve the problem, the later allows to modify the hierarchy at the cluster level. So, although operators may theoretically deeply change the cluster

		Basic				Augmented			
		CQF		Buffered inst.		CQF		Buffered inst.	
	α	Rand.	Worst	Rand.	Worst	Rand.	Worst	Rand.	Worst
soyb. small	0.0	1.49 (0.14)	0.91 (0.11)	0.00	0.00	1.62 (0.01)	1.12 (0.19)	0.00	0.00
	0.05	1.52 (0.12)	0.99 (0.13)	0.03	0.46	1.61 (0.03)	1.42 (0.17)	0.21	0.37
	0.10	1.49 (0.15)	1.02 (0.17)	0.11	0.80	1.60 (0.05)	1.52 (0.10)	0.52	0.80
	0.15	1.48 (0.15)	1.04 (0.12)	0.40	0.88	1.60 (0.04)	1.58 (0.05)	0.69	0.89
	0.20	1.46 (0.12)	1.10 (0.11)	0.81	0.90	1.61 (0.04)	1.58 (0.06)	0.83	0.90
	0.25	1.48 (0.13)	1.12 (0.11)	0.93	0.91	1.61 (0.03)	1.59 (0.05)	0.93	0.93
soyb. large	0.0	1.00 (0.10)	0.63 (0.14)	0.00	0.00	1.17 (0.02)	0.95 (0.14)	0.00	0.00
	0.05	1.03 (0.09)	0.65 (0.14)	0.02	0.06	1.16 (0.03)	1.06 (0.11)	0.22	0.40
	0.10	1.05 (0.10)	0.72 (0.10)	0.09	0.81	1.16 (0.03)	1.13 (0.07)	0.52	0.74
	0.15	1.07 (0.10)	0.73 (0.08)	0.31	0.96	1.16 (0.03)	1.16 (0.03)	0.82	0.96
	0.20	1.05 (0.11)	0.76 (0.08)	0.75	0.98	1.17 (0.02)	1.16 (0.03)	0.90	0.98
	0.25	1.01 (0.11)	0.77 (0.09)	0.92	0.99	1.16 (0.03)	1.16 (0.03)	0.96	0.99
house	0.0	1.29 (0.28)	0.85 (0.19)	0.00	0.00	1.61 (0.00)	1.43 (0.12)	0.00	0.00
	0.05	1.33 (0.26)	0.82 (0.17)	0.00	0.01	1.61 (0.00)	1.50 (0.11)	0.01	0.30
	0.10	1.35 (0.25)	0.84 (0.15)	0.01	0.09	1.60 (0.05)	1.53 (0.10)	0.06	0.48
	0.15	1.34 (0.25)	0.83 (0.16)	0.08	0.72	1.60 (0.04)	1.58 (0.07)	0.17	0.80
	0.20	1.37 (0.25)	0.83 (0.13)	0.29	0.98	1.61 (0.01)	1.60 (0.01)	0.38	0.93
	0.25	1.35 (0.27)	0.85 (0.13)	0.64	0.98	1.61 (0.00)	1.60 (0.01)	0.66	0.99
zoo	0.0	1.05 (0.12)	0.67 (0.17)	0.00	0.00	1.17 (0.03)	0.95 (0.14)	0.00	0.00
	0.05	1.06 (0.12)	0.67 (0.14)	0.02	0.10	1.17 (0.03)	1.05 (0.10)	0.13	0.39
	0.10	1.05 (0.13)	0.73 (0.11)	0.06	0.54	1.17 (0.03)	1.10 (0.08)	0.30	0.67
	0.15	1.03 (0.15)	0.77 (0.12)	0.19	0.87	1.16 (0.03)	1.15 (0.05)	0.53	0.87
	0.20	1.00 (0.17)	0.76 (0.08)	0.45	0.92	1.17 (0.03)	1.16 (0.03)	0.70	0.93
	0.25	1.03 (0.17)	0.78 (0.09)	0.78	0.93	1.16 (0.03)	1.16 (0.03)	0.83	0.94
mush	0.00	1.11 (0.22)	0.52 (0.13)	0.00	0.00	1.38 (0.00)	0.81 (0.24)	0.00	0.00
	0.05	1.16 (0.21)	0.53 (0.16)	0.00	0.01	1.38 (0.00)	1.18 (0.19)	0.03	0.51
	0.10	1.17 (0.20)	0.52 (0.16)	0.01	0.10	1.38 (0.00)	1.29 (0.11)	0.18	0.67
	0.15	1.17 (0.23)	0.65 (0.08)	0.07	0.99	1.38 (0.00)	1.38 (0.01)	0.46	0.98
	0.20	1.16 (0.22)	0.71 (0.06)	0.35	0.99	1.38 (0.00)	1.38 (0.00)	0.81	0.99
	0.25	1.15 (0.19)	0.73 (0.06)	0.77	0.99	1.38 (0.00)	1.38 (0.00)	0.90	0.99

Table 3. Clustering results. Averages and standard deviations over 50 trials

structure, they are not triggered by ordering conditions. On the other hand, the Not-Yet strategy has not the ability to directly modify the cluster structure despite of correctly detecting bad orderings.

Table 3 shows that the number of buffered instances increases as the α value does, and also that this increment is faster with bad orderings. This demonstrates the ability of the Not-Yet strategy for detecting bad instance orders. In addition, clustering quality tends to improve as we use higher α values. This result could be expected given that, in this case, the number of instances being reordered is larger. Despite of this, an α value around 0.20 seems to perform reasonably well in all tested datasets.

Buffer		α					
		0.10	0.20	0.30	0.35	0.40	0.45
100	CQF	1.11 (0.21)	1.12 (0.20)	1.23 (0.17)	1.22 (0.16)	1.23 (0.15)	1.23 (0.16)
	Buff.ins.	0.32	0.64	0.74	0.97	0.99	0.99
200	CQF	1.11 (0.23)	1.21 (0.22)	1.26 (0.15)	1.31 (0.08)	1.31 (0.08)	1.32 (0.07)
	Buff.ins.	0.35	0.69	0.82	0.99	0.99	0.99
300	CQF	1.20 (0.21)	1.22 (0.21)	1.28 (0.15)	1.32 (0.11)	1.32 (0.11)	1.32 (0.11)
	Buff.ins.	0.44	0.64	0.76	0.99	0.99	0.99
400	CQF	1.25 (0.14)	1.27 (0.14)	1.27 (0.13)	1.31 (0.07)	1.31 (0.08)	1.31 (0.08)
	Buff.ins.	0.51	0.85	0.91	0.99	0.99	0.99
500	CQF	1.26 (0.14)	1.24 (0.14)	1.26 (0.12)	1.24 (0.16)	1.24 (0.16)	1.23 (0.16)
	Buff.ins.	0.50	0.93	0.98	0.99	0.99	0.99
600	CQF	1.29 (0.12)	1.36 (0.09)	1.36 (0.09)	1.37 (0.02)	1.37 (0.02)	1.37 (0.02)
	Buff.ins.	0.56	0.65	0.81	0.99	0.99	0.99
700	CQF	1.29 (0.11)	1.38 (0.01)	1.37 (0.03)	1.38 (0.01)	1.38 (0.00)	1.37 (0.04)
	Buff.ins.	0.62	0.83	0.93	0.99	0.99	0.99
800	CQF	1.30 (0.11)	1.38 (0.00)	1.38 (0.00)	1.38 (0.00)	1.38 (0.00)	1.38 (0.00)
	Buff.ins.	0.64	0.89	0.99	0.99	0.99	0.99
900	CQF	1.30 (0.12)	1.38 (0.00)	1.38 (0.00)	1.38 (0.00)	1.38 (0.00)	1.38 (0.00)
	Buff.ins.	0.63	0.97	0.98	0.99	0.99	0.99

Table 4. Clustering results for the augmented algorithm with worst orders and different buffer sizes. Averages and standard deviations over 50 trials.

4.2   Experiments with Limited Buffer

In the previous experiments, the most important improvements are obtained at the expense of maintaining a big buffer, i.e., with high α values. It may appear counterintuitive with the idea of incremental learning to maintain a buffer of more than 90% of the instances in the dataset and flush the buffer at the end of the process. Strictly speaking, in an incremental learning environment, the system never achieves a final state so it is not clear in which moment the buffer has to be flushed. A natural solution is to limit the Not-Yet buffer in a way that it would be flushed several times during learning, without assuming any final state in the learning process.

Table 4 shows results from the *mushroom* dataset with worst orderings and different buffer sizes. We chose this dataset because it has a large number of instances and it is expected to give more relevant results. In these experiments instance reprocessing is fired as soon as the buffer is full. Comparing these results with the ones from Table 3, it can be observed that buffer sizes in the 600-900 range give similar results to the ones obtained with unlimited buffer size and same α values. Reducing the buffer size, for α values around 0.20, that gave optimal results in the previous experiments, we also got a reduction of the CQF scores. However, it is interesting to note that for these smaller buffer sizes, higher CQF values can be achieved increasing the α threshold. Probably, this occurs because flushing the –randomized– buffer during the learning process, results in a partial cluster structure of reasonable quality. So, when new instances are considered, the α value does not constrain enough their incorporation into the clustering. These claims are supported by the data in Table 4, where it is observed that smaller buffer sizes tend to reduce the number of stored instances compared to larger buffer sizes for the same α values.

5   Related Work

Several works have approached the ordering problem in incremental clustering, although this research has mainly benefited from two particular approaches. Lebowitz first introduced the idea of *deferred commitment* within the framework of his UNIMEM conceptual clustering system [10]. Our proposal extends Lebowitz's work by decoupling the buffering strategy from any particular system. Also, we have introduced the α parameter, that allows to see the original algorithm as a particular case of the new control strategy. We think that this formulation should help in applying the strategy to any existing algorithm without any major changes.

The second related work (from which the Not-Yet name is borrowed) is the application of this strategy to the LINNEO$^+$ clustering system [2,13]. This work contains the basic ideas proposed here, but again the application is tuned for an specific system and the problems studied are deeply related to a particular clustering strategy.

Although devoted to global methods, we have to mention relevant Fisher's work on iterative optimization of clusterings [5]. This work explores several methods for iteratively improving clustering quality, showing that among these methods some exhibit an optimum performance. But recall that these methods often operate reprocessing the whole dataset and violate the constraints stated for incremental clustering. This sort of strategies are useful from the viewpoint of a data analysis task in which the entire dataset is available in advance so that we are not limited by strict incremental constraints.

6   Conclusions and Future Work

We have presented a classification of strategies to avoid ordering effects in clustering with regard to two related dimensions, namely, the point of the clustering process in which they are applied and the scope of the strategy. This classification aims to clarify the benefits and disadvantages we can expect from the application of existing or newly proposed strategies.

A new local strategy has been proposed to deal with ordering effects. We think that the formulation of the strategy is simple and open in the sense that it is not coupled with any particular evaluation function or algorithm. As a local strategy, it has a limited impact over the entire conceptual structure as the experiments have shown. It is difficult to assess the quality of this improvement beyond the simple quantitative analysis in terms of the CQF. For some applications it can suppose an important improvement in terms of understandability or performance while for other it may be imperceptible. On the other hand, when coupled with another local strategy such as the merge/split operators, the Not-Yet strategy allows the clustering system to reach an optimum quality clustering even with worst orderings.

We have noted that the most significant benefits are obtained at the expense of maintaining a large Not-Yet buffer. Since an incremental system has to be able of using the acquired knowledge for some performance task at any learning stage, we have to assume that the system has also to be able of quickly reincorporate the buffered instances before actuating. Our experiments demonstrate that it is possible to use the Not-Yet strategy and maintain the strict incremental nature of the clustering process by means of using limited buffer sizes. In practice, buffer size will be limited by the amount of instances that the system can manage in a reasonable amount of time before entering in 'performance mode'. This time will be dependent on the particular application.

It is unclear how the proposed procedure scales up to large datasets such as those typically referred to in *data mining* tasks [3]. However, we think that the Not-Yet strategy may be an inexpensive and effective way of avoiding ordering effects since it is unlikely that a whole large dataset would present a bad order. Rather, it probably will have bad ordered subsets, so that a large enough Not-Yet buffer will be able to deal with the problem. Note that the size which could be considered large for the buffer in the experiments, may be simply a small part of a very large dataset of thousands of instances. We plan to explore these issues in future work.

Finally, it is worth to remark that the experiments conducted used a relatively simple implementation of the Not-Yet strategy. Extensions studying the order of instances in the buffer, the criterion to reprocess instances or the number of times instances may be reprocessed appear to be promising topics for further research.

References

1. J. R. Anderson and M. Matessa. Explorations of an incremental, bayesian algorithm for categorization. *Machine Learning*, (9):275–308, 1992. 141
2. J. Béjar. *Adquisición automática de conocimiento en dominios poco estructurados*. PhD thesis, Facultat d'Informàtica de Barcelona, UPC, 1995. 137, 145
3. U. Fayyad, G. Piatetsky-Shapiro, and P. Smyth. Knowledge discovery and data mining: towards a unifying framework. In *Proceedings of the Second International Conference on Knowledge Discovery and Data Mining, KDD96*, Portland, OR, 1996. AAAI Press. 146
4. D. H. Fisher. Knowledge acquisition via incremental conceptual clustering. *Machine Learning*, (2):139–172, 1987. 138, 141
5. D. H. Fisher. Optimization and simplification of hierarchical clusterings. *Journal of Artificial Intelligence Research*, (4):147–180, 1995. 137, 145

6. D. H. Fisher and P. Langley. Conceptual clustering and its relation to numerical taxonomy. In W. A. Gale, editor, *Artificial Intelligence and Statistics*. Addison-Wesley, Reading,MA, 1986. 136
7. D. H. Fisher, L. Xu, and N. Zard. Ordering effects in clustering. In *Proceedings of the Ninth International Conference on Machine Learning*, pages 163–168, 1992. 137
8. J. H. Gennari, P. Langley, and D. Fisher. Models of incremental concept formation. *Artificial Intelligence*, (40):11–61, 1989. 137 , 141
9. P. Langley. Order effects in incremental learning. In P. Reimann and H. Spada, editors, *Learning in humans and machines: Towards an Interdisciplinary Learning Science*. Pergamon, 1995. 136, 137
10. M. Lebowitz. Deferred commitment in unimem: waiting to learn. In *Proceedings of the Fifth International Conference on Machine Learning*, pages 80–86, 1988. 137 , 145
11. R. S. Michalski and R. E. Stepp. Learning from observation: Conceptual clustering. In R. S. Michalski, J. G. Carbonell, and T. M. Mitchell, editors, *Machine Learning: An Artificial intelligence approach*, pages 331–363. Morgan Kauffmann, San Mateo, CA, 1983. 137
12. P.M. Murphy and D.W. Aha. Repository of machine learning. *University of California at Ivrine. URL: http://www.ics.uci.edu/mlearn/MLRpositoru.html.* 141
13. J. Roure. Study of methods and heuristics to improve the fuzzy classifications of LINNEO+. Master's thesis, Facultat d'Informática de Barcelona, UPC, 1994. 145

Distributed Reinforcement Learning in Multi-agent Decision Systems

J. Ignacio Giráldez and Daniel Borrajo

Universidad Carlos III de Madrid
c/ Butarque, 15
28911 Leganés, Madrid, Spain
{giraldez,dborrajo}@ia.uc3m.es

Abstract. Decision problems can be usually solved using systems that implement different paradigms. These systems may be integrated into a single distributed system, with the expectation of obtaining a group performance more satisfactory than individual performances. Such a distributed system is what we call a Multi Agent Decision System (MADES), a special kind of Multi Agent System, that integrates several heterogeneous autonomous decision systems (agents). A MADES must produce a single solution proposal for the problem instance it faces, despite the fact that its decision making is distributed, and every agent produces solution proposals according to its local view and to its idiosyncrasy. We present a *distributed reinforcement algorithm* for learning how to combine the decisions the agents make in a distributed way, into a single group decision (solution proposal).

Topics: Multi Agent Systems, Machine Learning, Distributed Artificial Intelligence

1 Introduction

Two kinds of learning techniques are usually found in Multi Agent Systems (MAS): *local learning* and *distributed learning* [4]. *Local learning* is carried out by an agent on its own, without the need of the participation of other agents. This implies that the only available view of the world comes from the agent's standpoint. *Distributed Learning* is carried out as a result of the joint action of several agents of the MAS. This means that *distributed learning* can not be accomplished as a result of the isolated action of one agent. In *distributed learning* tasks, agents may need to observe other agents, or use knowledge facilitated by other agents [5]. In these situations, the agent's view of the world may be qualitatively different from the view of the world that the agent perceives in *local learning*. Every agent observes the world from a different standpoint, and interprets this view according to its own insight. The concurrence of the agents individual actions gives rise to a group behaviour. Learning appropriate group behaviours is the most common distributed learning task (e.g. [2], [4]).

Some complex decision problems can be solved by several different monolithic decision systems, based on different machine learning or problem solving

Helder Coelho (Ed.): IBERAMIA'98, LNAI 1484, pp. 148–159, 1998.
© Springer-Verlag Berlin Heidelberg 1998

paradigms. When the quality of the results obtained separately by these systems is not satisfactory, they can be united in a *Multi Agent DEcision System (MADES)*, with the expectation of obtaining a joint performance superior to the performance obtained using the monolithic systems in an isolated way. A MADES is a Multi Agent System built for decision making, where a single decision is output by the system as a group, although internally many decisions may be made locally by the component agents [1]. These decisions may be incompatible, and even contradictory. But in spite of this, a single decision has to be made by the system to solve the problem at hand. How to incorporate these individual local decisions, into a single group decision, poses a group behaviour learning problem for the MADES. In this work, we propose a distributed reinforcement learning algorithm to solve this problem. A simplified version of this algorithm was implemented, tested, and experimental results reported in [1]. Here we present the formalization of the full algorithm, and discuss the full range of its potential. We also formalize the concept of Multi Agent Decision System (MADES).

Section 2 summarizes the IAO architecture[1]. Section 3 presents an ordered stepwise procedure for the solution of problems using the IAO distributed reinforcement learning algorithm in MADES. Section 4 discusses the two ways in which this algorithm can influence behaviors in MADES. Sections 5 and 6 reproduce some results obtained with a simplified and restricted version of the algorithm presented here. We conclude with section 7 where we discuss important topics.

2   The Intelligent Agents Organization

The Intelligent Agents Organization (IAO) is a Multi Agent Decision System architecture aimed at solving complex decision problems [1]. Figure 1 shows a high level view of this architecture:

- One agent, known as the *referee*, is in charge of the overall system control. It broadcasts problem instance descriptions (service requests), and control signals to the rest of the team. It then receives the respective replies from the rest of the agents. These replies may be either advice, or problem solving proposals. The relationship among the referee and the rest of the agents can be regarded as a client-server relationship. The services the referee may request to an agent are either the solution proposal synthesis (only to worker agents), or an advice request (only to advisor agents). These service requests are scheduled in a way that maximizes parallelism (every agent runs on a different machine), so the MAS response time is minimized.
- A *worker agent* receives problem descriptions from either the referee, or another worker, and replies with solution proposals. Worker agents work in parallel on a solution proposal to the same problem instance, and are capable of autonomous decision making. Any of them could be the basis

---

[1] a more complete description of it can be found in [1]

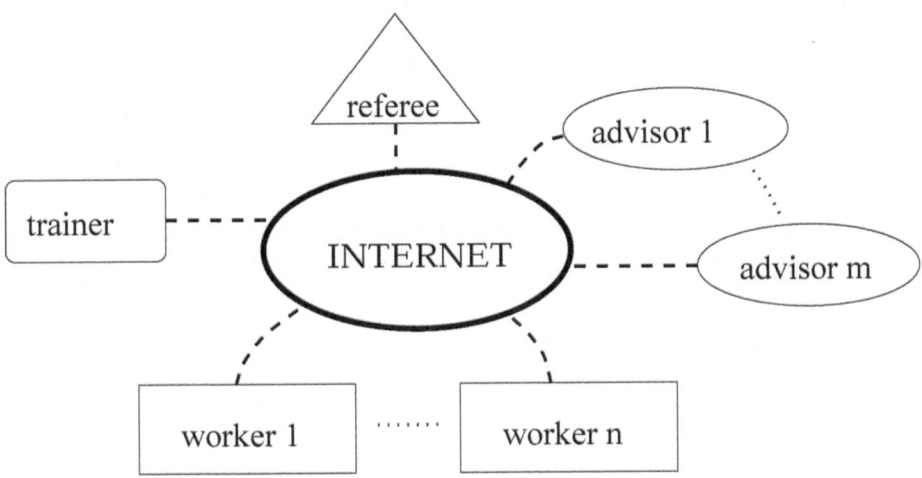

Fig. 1. A schematic view of the IAO Architecture.

of a monolithic system aimed to solve each problem. The only restriction imposed on workers is that they should adhere to the client-server protocol. Other than that, there is a total freedom for the system designer to use any agent he/she wishes as a worker. Due to this flexibility, the IAO model is widely applicable.

– Several agents play the role of *advisors*. They are contacted by, either the referee or a worker agent, and receive a problem instance as input. They reply to the requester with the identification of the worker agent that they expect to be the most competent of the group, in the solution of the aforementioned problem instance. The referee will use this advice, when one of the proposals the worker agents provide has to be selected. A worker agent may use this advice to ask the worker, that the advisor indicated, for its cooperation in the solution of the problem instance.

– A *trainer* agent produces problem instances that are used for training and testing. Problem generation can be made either randomly, or using an "ad hoc" scheme. The criteria for problem synthesis affects the success of the learning effort, as it is widely known.

3   The IAO Distributed Reinforcement Learning Algorithm

The purpose of this algorithm is to enable the agents to improve their collective behaviour themselves. It is applicable to any MADES that follow the role differentiation specified by the IAO model. Next, we describe the steps to be followed for problem solving with the IAO model.

3.1   Problem Modeling

The domain is modeled as a problem space:

$$World = (S_w, A)$$

  where

- S_w is the state space, whose representation depends on the problem at hand.
- A is the action set, whose elements are all the possible actions that can be executed on states.

  A *Multi Agent Decision System* is modeled as

$$MADES = (S_M, i, A_M, A_r, A_w, A_a, A_t, g)$$

where

- S_M is the set of states of the world as the MADES perceives them.
- i is the input function, that translates from the external to the internal state representation,

$$i : S_W \rightarrow S_M$$

  In decision problems, i is usually the unit function, so S_M is usually equal to S_W.
- A_M is the set of actions that the MADES can execute on the world, which is usually equal to A.
- A_r is a single element set formed by an autonomous agent that controls the ordered execution of the system's decision making algorithm, and is known as the referee.
- A_w is the set of workers, autonomous agents that receive problem descriptions and reply with a proposal of the decision to be made to solve the problem. We use w to denote the number of workers in the MADES.
- A_a is the set of advisors, autonomous agents whose mission is to observe the worker agents, to learn their competencies, and to inform other agents about their findings.
- A_t is the set of trainer agents, whose mission is to sinthesize problem instances for the MADES to train on.
- g is the group behaviour, a control policy that specifies how to produce a single group decision from the agents decision proposals A_g^w,

$$g : S_M \times A_g^w \rightarrow A_M$$

  An autonomous agent is modeled as

$$agent = (S_g, A_g, i_g, C_g, S'_g, S_I, b)$$

where

- S_g is the set of the possible inputs the agent may receive.

- A_g is the set of the actions the agent can execute. In MADES, the typical actions are decision making and adaption.
- i_g is the agent's input function,

$$i_g : S_M \to S_g$$

- C_g is the set of the communication's acts that the agent can perform. In MADES, they are usually either the request of a decision making service to another agent (i.e. a consultation), or the reply to a decision request with the results.
- S'_g is the set of all the data the agent receives from another agents (e.g. a classification petition).
- S_I is the set of the agent's internal states.
- b is the agent's behaviour function,

$$b : S_g \times S'_g \times S_I \to A_g$$

3.2 Partitioning of the State Space

If an advisor based on reinforcement learning is used for the estimation of which worker (say $worker_i$) is the most competent of the group for the solution of a given problem instance ($problem_i$), then you need to store a huge reinforcement table of the form $(problem_i, worker_i)$. The storage of this table is unaffordable in sufficiently complex problems. If all the problem instances with some qualitative similitude, were handled best by the same worker, then we might build reinforcement tables associating the appropriate worker to the set containing this collection of similar problem instances. Now the reinforcement table has much fewer entries, and it is of the following form $(set_i, worker_i)$. In order to obtain a set description of the state space we partition it as it is explained next.

The state space S is partitioned in s subsets: $S = \bigcup_{i=1}^{s} S_i$ such that $S_i \cap S_j = \emptyset$ when $i \neq j$. Similar problem instances should be contained within the same subset, because the algorithm works assuming the following hypothesis: if one worker is more competent for the solution of a given problem than the rest of the workers, then it will also be more competent than its peers in the solution of problem instances similar to the aforementioned (i.e. in the solution of problem instances that lie in the same subset of the partition). Unsupervised classification methods may be used for this task. The problem lies in finding and adequate distance function in S: a good function requires that the person that builds it have deep knowledge about the problem domain, and about which are the most predictive features in the problem representation.

The indexed characteristic function locates the subset of the partition that contains a given problem instance:

$$c : S \to N/x \epsilon S, c(x) = i \Rightarrow x \epsilon S_i$$

A cumulative reinforcement table $T_i = [r_1 \ldots r_w]$, where w is the number of workers, is assigned to every S_i. The meaning of the ith entry of T_i is the cumulative reinforcement received by the ith worker as a result of its past decisions. The reinforcement tables T_i, form the rows of the cumulative reinforcement matrix

$$M = \begin{bmatrix} r_{1,1} & \cdots & r_{1,w} \\ \vdots & & \vdots \\ r_{s,1} & \cdots & r_{s,w} \end{bmatrix}$$

where $r_{i,j}$ is the cumulative reinforcement received by agent j, as a result of its intervention in the solution of problems that belong to S_i.

3.3   Problem Solving Trace

Some problems require that the decision system make a series of decisions before the problem can be considered as solved (as in robotics problems or games). In these problems, the "world" evolves following a series of states,

$$Trace = [s_1 \ldots s_n]$$

as a result of a series of actions/decisions taken by the MADES,

$$SystemTrace = [D_1 \ldots D_n]$$

The MADES makes decision D_i based on the local decisions made by the agents at time i: $d_{i,1} \ldots d_{i,n_a}$ where n_a is the number of autonomous agents in the MADES.

3.4   Distributed Credit Assignment

When the outcome of the problem solving episode is finally known, the decision system is reinforced according to the desirability of this outcome. Since the decisions were made by a MADES, in a distributed fashion, the credit assigned will also have to be distributed among the agents that participated in the decision. Let us consider that the world is in the state s_i, and the agents propose decisions/actions $d_{i,1} \ldots d_{i,n_a}$, and the resulting group's decision is D_i. The distributed credit assignment algorithm distributes credit in a twofold way: on the one hand, credit is distributed in time (because early distant states influence less the outcome than recent states), on the other hand, credit is also distributed "spatially" among the agents that take part in the distributed decision making procedure, according to their opposition/support to the decision that the MADES finally produced. Thus, the distributed credit assignment function depends on the iteration i, the desirability of the final outcome o, and the participation of the agents that compose the MADES (which is represented by the local assesments/decisions they forward $d_{i,1} \ldots d_{i,n_a}$),

$$dca : N \times \Re \times A_g \ldots A_g \rightarrow \Re^w$$

the output of the distributed credit assignment function dca is used as the reinforcement vector at time step i,

$$\boldsymbol{RV}(i) = dca(i, o, d_{i,1} \ldots d_{i,n_a})$$

so we get a series of reinforcement vectors, $\boldsymbol{RV}(1) \ldots \boldsymbol{RV}(n)$.

3.5   Reinforcement Tables Update

The cumulative reinforcement tables $T_j, j = 1 \ldots s$, are updated with the proper reinforcement vectors:

$$T_{c(s_i)} = T_{c(s_i)} + \boldsymbol{RV}(i)$$

4   The Use of Distributed Reinforcement Learning in a MADES

The distributed reinforcement learning algorithm we present can improve the group's behaviour in two ways:

1. It is a way to learn the workers competencies. This means that by comparing the cumulative rewards of the workers for a given problem, the advisors can determine which worker is expected to handle that problem best. This results in a group behaviour's improvement.
2. Workers can evolve in a way that maximizes their future rewards, which produces a "local" adaptation.

5   An Instance of a MADES

We have chosen checkers endgames as the problem domain for our experiments. These endgames contain 8 pieces at most, and the majority pose a considerable difficulty for human players [3]. We have solved the problem following the steps outlined in section 3. The details are shown next.

The world is modeled as

$$World = (S, A)$$

where

- S is composed by all the legal checkers situations with eight pieces at most. We use the following notation, $s_j = (c_1 \ldots c_{32})$ such that $c_i \epsilon \{w, p, b, m, e\}$ where w denotes a white man, p a white king, b a black man, m a black king and e an empty space.
- A is composed of a single type of action, the move of a piece from one box of the board to another, observing the rules of checkers. We denote it like this: $mov(x_1, y_1, x_2, y_2, Capture, CaptureList)$ which represents an action that moves the piece at location (x_1, y_1) to (x_2, y_2), removing from the board all pieces whose locations are specified in $CaptureList$ when $Capture$ is bounded to yes.

The *Multi Agent Decision System* is modeled as

$$
\begin{aligned}
MADES = (&S, 1, \{observe, move\}, \{Ref\}, \\
&\{alphaAG, bayesAG, backpropAG, c4.5AG, hybridAG\}, \\
&\{reinf, rote\}, \{ctrainer\}, g)
\end{aligned}
$$

where

- Since the input function is the unit function, no preprocessing is done upon the observed state.
- $Ref = (S, \{move\}, 1, \{ask, listen\}, \{A_w \bigcup S^w\}, \{\sigma_i, i = 1 \ldots 6\}, b_{ref})$ which means that the input the referee receives is the aforementioned set of the legal checkers situations (S). The action it can execute is a legal move on the checkers board. Again, the input function is the unit function. The only communication acts it can perform are asking for something to another agent, and listening to its reply. The internal σ_i states are described in the following control algorithm that specifies the behaviour b_{ref} of the referee. The referee is at internal state σ_i when the step i of the algorithm is being executed.
  1. get current state description (the current board's situation)
  2. broadcast it to the rest of the agents
  3. receive their replies (the move they would execute on that situation)
  4. choose one of the proposals the agents forwarded
  5. execute that action (i.e. make a move on the board)
  6. if a final state has not yet been reached, then repeat control cycle
- $A_W = \{alphaAG, bayesAG, backpropAG, c4.5AG, hybridAG\}$ is the set of workers. $alphaAG$ is a simple alpha-beta searcher. $hybridAG$ is an alpha-beta searcher, that consults the $reinf$ advisor at leaf nodes, and receives from it the identification of the worker that is expected to solve best that situation. Then, $hybridAG$ contacts that worker and requests its collaboration to evaluate the node. If that collaboration is not possible, the node is evaluated locally. The rest of the workers are classifiers that make decisions based on what they have learnt during their training. The specification of all the workers is quite similar. The input set is the same for all the workers: the set of legal checkers situations. The input function is different for every worker, because they do not share internal representations. The behavior function provides a proposal according to decision making formalism of the agent (feed-forward neural network, decision tree or whatever).
- $A_a = \{reinf, rote\}$ The $reinf$ advisor learns the competencies of the workers, and represents them in reinforcement tables. The reinforcement a worker obtains for the solution of a certain class of problems is used by other agents as an indication of how good the worker is at the task. The $rote$ advisor keeps track of who is the worker that best solves a given problem by means of rote learning. Since it cannot generalize, it is not useful in problems with huge state spaces like this one, so we discontinued its use after some testing.
- $A_a = \{asses, reply, ask, listen\}$ An agent can produce a decision as result of an assesment (compute next move), can communicate the decision back to the requester, or it may ask another agent for some service (decide on which of the workers is the competent to solve this checkers situation, or recommend a move to perform next, or evaluate a checkers situation)
- $A_t = \{trainer\}$ is a special agent built to produce checkers problems of tunable difficulty.
- The group behaviour is the result of a voting mechanism. Every worker votes for a move (the workers supported by the advisors get extra votes), and the winning move is the one the MADES outputs.

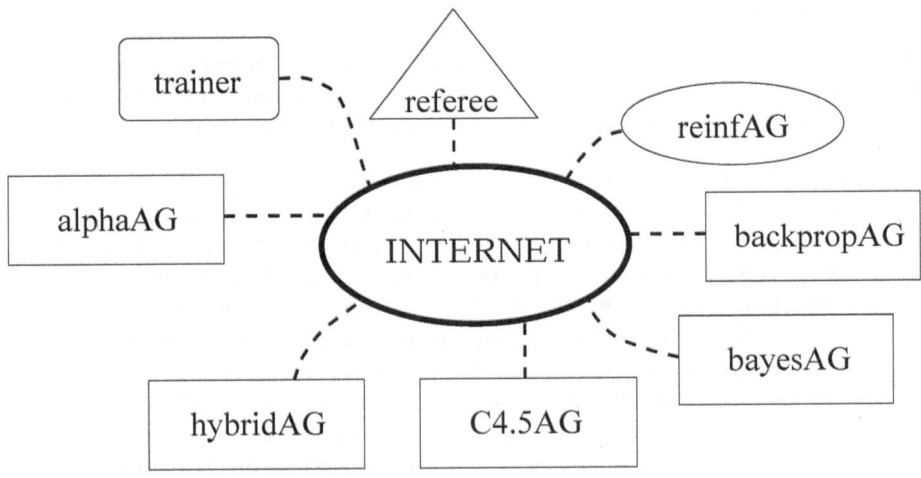

Fig. 2. Architecture of our Multi Agent DEcision System.

5.1 Partitioning of the State Space

The space of legal checkers situations is partitioned according to the following criteria:

- number of white men
- number of black men
- number of white kings
- number of black kings
- existence of capture opportunities for white
- existence of capture opportunities for black
- existence of crowning opportunities for white
- existence of crowning opportunities for black

The indexed characteristic function $c(x)$ counts these 8 indexes to locate the subset of the partition where x lies.

As an example, we show the cumulative reinforcement table for the subset whose indexes are (1, 0, 2, 1, yes, no, no, yes):

$$T_{(1,0,2,1,yes,no,no,yes)} =$$
$$[backprop(0.3333), bayes(-0.2053), c4\_5(-0.0625), alpha(-0.5357), hybrid(0)]$$

If the *reinf* advisor were consulted about who is the expected most competent worker, to make decisions when the current state belongs to the aforementioned subset, the advisor would reply with the *backpropAG* identifier, since this is the worker with highest cumulative reward.

5.2   Problem Solving Trace

A trace is kept of the series of successive checkers situations, along with the identification of the workers that supported the decision (action) that leads to the next state. As an example a part of a sample trace is shown:

```
credit(proposal(e, m, e, e, e, e, e, e, b, e, p, e, e, e, w, e, e,
e, e, e, e, e, w, e, e, e, p, b, e, e, e, e), [alpha]).
credit(proposal(e, m, e, e, e, e, e, e, b, w, p, e, e, e, e, e, e,
e, e, e, e, e, w, e, e, e, p, e, e, e, e, m), [c4_5, alpha]).
credit(proposal(e, m, e, e, e, e, e, e, e, w, e, e, e, b, p, e, e,
e, e, e, e, e, w, e, e, e, p, e, e, e, e, m), [c4_5, bayes]).
credit(proposal(e, m, e, e, e, e, e, e, e, w, e, e, e, e, p, e, b,
e, e, e, e, e, w, p, e, e, e, e, e, e, e, m), [alpha]).
credit(proposal(e, m, e, e, e, e, e, e, e, w, e, e, e, e, p, e, e,
e, w, e, b, e, e, p, e, e, e, e, e, e, e, m), [backprop]).
```

5.3   Distributed Credit Assignment

The aforementioned problem solving trace, is used to determine which workers agree with the main variation at every node of the game tree. The tree is traversed from leaves to root, assigning credit to the workers at every node. At a node at depth $CurrentDepth$, the workers receive the following reinforcement:

$$Reinf(worker) = Result \cdot Agree \cdot \frac{CurrentDepth}{NMoves}$$

where $NMoves$ is the total amount of moves executed by the MADES in the endgame. $Result$ is equal to $+1$ if the MADES won the game, and -1 otherwise. $Agree$ is equal to $+1$ if $worker$ agreed with the main variation, and 0 otherwise (no credit assigned). The discounting mechanism is implemented in the $CurrentDepth$ variable, agents are assigned less credit in the final outcome when their decisions are made at shallow nodes. This formula computes the entries of the reinforcement vector. The indexed characteristic function is used to locate the subset the current node belongs to. Then the reinforcement table associated to this subset is fetched, and upddated with the reinforcement vector. This algorithm is repeated for every node along the main variation.

6   Results

The MADES played test games against every one of its workers, with the following results:

opponent	MADES advantage
c4.5AG	21%
backpropAG	17.5%
bayesAG	17%
hybridAG	2%
alphaAG	2%

To explain how the MADES advantage percentage is computed, let's use the test against *alphaAG* as a reference. A 2% advantage of the MADES over *alphaAG* means that the MADES wins 4% more test endgames than it loses. So, its real advantage is 4% / 2 = 2%, because if the opponent (alphaAG) won 2% more endgames its score would be incremented in 2% and the MADES' score would be diminished by 2%, so both would be even. This can be mathematically expressed by this formula:

$$s = \frac{[w(G) - l(G)] \times 100}{2 \times G}$$

where s is the score percentage, G is the number of played games, $w()$ is the number of won games, and $l()$ is the number of lost games.

These results show that the MADES beats any of its members, and this justifies integrating the workers into the MADES. They have been obtained taking advantage of only one of the adaptation opportunities that the distributed reinforcement learning algorithm provides: reinforcement tables have been used for competencies' learning, but have not been used for the workers' "local" adaptation (which is now underway).

Some previous results are also worth mentioning. The MADES' score has evolved from -20% (when it had only played 300 training games) to +2.03% (after 10832 training games). This improvement has been mainly due to the learning of the workers competencies. But to a lesser extent it has been due to worker replacements. The flexibility of the IAO model allows the replacement of a worker by another, and the adaption of the rest of the system to the new MADES composition, thanks to the adaptive behaviour of the advisors. We replaced two workers during the MADES' lifetime, the first replacement improved the MADES' score 1.7 points, and the second 1.17 points.

7   Discussion

Distributed reinforcement learning can play a double role in Multi Agent Decision Systems. On the one hand, control information can be learnt in the form of a competencies map, that is a map of the state space where it is specified which worker is expected to handle best every kind of problem instance. Since it may be known which worker is the most trustworthy for the solution of a problem instance, the distributed decision making procedure takes this worker's proposal with a special consideration. So the group's decision making procedure is adapted following the predictions of the competencies map.

On the other hand, the cumulative reinforcement the worker agents receive provides an indication that can be used for local adaption, which will eventually be noticeable in the group's behaviour, and in how the advisors characterize them. The use of a different reinforcement table for every subset of the partition, provides an indication of how the adaption should be directed in a more detailed way than in other reinforcement learning proposals.

References

1. J. I. Giráldez and D. Borrajo. A distributed model for the combination of heterogeneous knowledge based agents. In *J. Hunt, R. Milnes (eds.) "Research and Development in Expert Systems XIV"*, December 1997. Proc. of ES97, ppl75-184, SGES Publications. 149

2. Thomas Haynes and Sandip Sen. Evolving behaviorial strategies in predators and prey. In *G. Weiss, S. Sen (eds.), Adaption and Learning in Multi Agent Systems, Proc. of the IJCAI 95 Workshop, Springer*, 1996. 148

3. Jonathan Schaeffer, Robert Lake, Paul Lu, and Martin Bryant. Chinook, the world man-machine checkers champion. *AI Magazine*, 17(1):21-29, Spring 1996. 154

4. G. Weiss. Learning to coordinate actions in multi-agent systems, august 1993. Proc. IJCAI, Chambery, France, volume 1, pp311-316. 148

5. G. Weiss. Some studies in distributed machine learning and organizational design. Technical Report FKI-189-94, Institut für Informatik, Technische Universität München,1994. 148

Dynamic Discretization of Continuous Attributes

João Gama, Luis Torgo, and Carlos Soares

LIACC, FEP - University of Porto
Rua Campo Alegre, 823, 4150 Porto, Portugal
Phone: (+351) 2 6001672, Fax: (+351) 2 6003654
{jgama,ltorgo,csoares}@ncc.up.pt
http://www.up.pt/liacc/ML

Abstract. Discretization of continuous attributes is an important task for certain types of machine learning algorithms. Bayesian approaches, for instance, require assumptions about data distributions. Decision Trees, on the other hand, require sorting operations to deal with continuous attributes, which largely increase learning times. This paper presents a new method of discretization, whose main characteristic is that it takes into account interdependencies between attributes. Detecting interdependencies can be seen as discovering redundant attributes. This means that our method performs attribute selection as a side effect of the discretization. Empirical evaluation on five benchmark datasets from UCI repository, using C4.5 and a naive Bayes, shows a consistent reduction of the features without loss of generalization accuracy.

Keywords: Discretization, Feature Selection, Continuous Attributes

1 Introduction

Discretization is a process that divides continuous numeric values into a set of intervals that can be regarded as discrete categorical values. There are two main reasons why discretization is an important task in machine learning. The first one is related to the Bayesian formalism. Methods based on this formalism require for each test example, the computation of the conditional probability of the class given the example: $p(Cl_i|Example)$. For nominal attributes this probability can be estimated with frequencies obtained from the training data. For continuous attributes a strong assumption about the data distribution is needed. Usually, in the absence of other information, we assume a normal distribution. As such, the conditional probability is given by the probability density function $p(x) = \frac{1}{\sqrt{2\pi\sigma^2}}e^{-(x-\mu)^2/2\sigma^2}$. Several authors (see for instance [3,7]) note that this assumption is a very severe limitation of learning algorithms based on the Bayes formalism.

The second motivation for performing attribute discretization is related to computational complexity. As it was mentioned by Catlett [1] and others, the

Helder Coelho (Ed.): IBERAMIA'98, LNAI 1484, pp. 160–169, 1998.

performance of tree based learners is strongly conditioned by the sorting of continuous attributes' values. This is an operation that on average takes $O(n * Log\ n)$. Using profiling tools Catlett observed on several large domains that most of the CPU time was spent on sorting. This means that processing continuous attributes is a bottleneck to efficient induction on very large training sets.

Literature on attribute discretization abounds. A major reference in this subject is the work of Fayyad and Irani [5]. These authors proved that the limits of the obtained intervals are always in the boundary between examples of different classes. However, their approach has a limitation: it doesn't take into account the interdependencies between attributes. This is the main advantage of our work: the discretization of each attribute takes into account the discretization of the other continuous features.

Dougherty and his colleagues [4] define three different axis upon which we may classify discretization methods: *supervised vs. unsupervised, global vs. local* and *static vs. dynamic. Supervised methods* use the information of class labels while *unsupervised methods* do not. *Local methods* like the one used by C4.5, produce partitions that are applied to localized regions of the instance space. *Global methods* such as binning are applied before the learning process. In *static methods* attributes are discretized independently of each other, while *dynamic methods* take into account the interdependencies between them.

The following section of this paper, reviews the related work, identifying the main problems of the discretization of continuous features. Section three presents our method in detail, stressing the search for the interdependencies between attributes. On section four we perform an empirical evaluation of the method using two well known algorithms, C4.5 and a naive Bayes on five benchmark datasets from the UCI repository. Finally, we present some conclusions and future work.

2   Related Work

2.1   Main Problems

Three main problems are addressed in the existing literature on discretization. The following sections present a brief discussion of these issues.

How Many Intervals to Consider? We can find in the literature several approaches: those that fix the number of intervals in advance and those in which k is automatically set. As examples of the former, C4.5 sets the number of intervals to 2, and in [3] the number of intervals is fixed to 10. As examples of the latter, k can be computed taking into account the number of distinct values observed on the training set, for instance $k = max(1, 2 * log\ l)$ ([4]), or using *Cross Validation* [12].

This last strategy has one advantage: given a dataset with several continuous features, the number of intervals of each feature depends on the number of different values observed on the training set. As such, different features can be discretized with different number of intervals.

How to Allocate an Observed Value to an Interval? The simplest discretization procedure, often used, is known as *Equal interval width*. It divides the rank of observed values for a feature into k equally sized bins. The only advantage of this unsupervised method is its simplicity. The main drawback is the influence of outliers.

Another simple discretization procedure, *Equal frequency intervals*, divides a continuous feature into k bins where (given m instances) each bin contains m/k values. A variation of this method, known as *Maximal marginal entropy*, starts with equal frequency intervals and adjusts the boundaries to decrease the entropy of each interval.

A more sophisticated approach is known in the literature as *k-means*. The distribution of the values over the k intervals minimizes the intra-interval distance and maximizes the inter-interval distance. It begins with an *equal width* distribution of the observed values over the k intervals, followed by an iterative process where the values near the boundaries change between intervals while this process improves the criterion mentioned above.

How to Choose the Representative Value for Each Interval? The usual method chooses the *mean* of the values that fall on this interval. Due to the influence of *outliers* some authors prefer to use the *median*.

2.2 Other Systems

We now briefly describe some of the existing discretization systems.

Unsupervised Methods The ChiMerge system [9] begins by placing each observed real value into its own interval and proceeds by using the χ^2 test to determine when adjacent intervals should be merged.

The StatDisc [10] method also uses statistical tests as a means of determining discretization intervals. This is also a bottom-up method that creates a hierarchy of discretization intervals using the ϕ measure as a criterion for merging intervals. StatDisc can merge N adjacent intervals at a time. Merging of intervals continues until some ϕ threshold is achieved. The final hierarchy of discretizations can be explored and a suitable final discretization automatically selected.

Supervised Methods The 1R system, presented by Holte [6], attempts to divide the domain of every possible continuous variable into pure bins, each containing a strong majority of one particular class. This method works reasonably well when used in conjunction with the 1R induction algorithm.

Catlett [2] has explored the use of entropy based discretization in decision tree algorithms. Empirical studies have shown an impressive increase in induction speed on very large datasets. This work was the precursor of Fayyad and Irani's [5] recursive entropy minimization heuristic for discretization. To control the number of intervals produced over the continuous space they use a *Minimum*

Description Length criterion. In the original paper, this method was applied locally at each node during tree generation. Some other authors have used the method as a global discretization with good results [4].

Robnik-Sikonja and Kononenko [11] have applied the ReliefF algorithm to discretization tasks. ReliefF is a method for estimating the probability that two near examples of the same class have the same value for an attribute and that two near examples from different classes have the same value for the attribute. The ReliefF is a heuristic measure to decide which of two discretizations is the "best".

3   Our Method

We can look at all possible discretizations of a continuous feature as a hierarchy. The most general discretization is at the top of this hierarchy, and consists of one interval containing all the observed values. At the bottom of the hierarchy we have the most specific discretization which is a set of intervals, each containing a single value. For more than one feature we have a set of hierarchies. Static discretization methods consider that the discretization of one feature is independent from the discretization of the others. Our proposal is to perform a search over all the hierarchies of possible discretizations for all the attributes. By proceeding this way the discretization of one feature depends on the discretization of other features. Thus we are able to explore inter-dependencies between features.

The available data is split into two disjoint datasets. The first one, referred to as the *training set*, is used to build the hypothesis of possible discretizations. The second one, the *validation set*, is used to evaluate the hypothesis[1].

For each continuous attribute, the *boundary cut-points* are collected from the training set. A *cut point* is defined as the midpoint between each successive pair of values in the sorted sequence of attribute values. A *boundary cut-point* is a *cut point* involving examples of different classes. As proved by Fayyad and Irani [5] the *minimum* of any entropy based measure must occur at a *boundary cut-point*.

Our approach performs an A^* search over the set of hierarchies defined by the *boundary cut-points* of each attribute. The basic goal of the search is to determine the number of intervals into which each attribute will be divided.

3.1   The Search Space

The search space is defined by all the possible combinations of attribute discretizations.

It consists of $n_1 * n_2 * ... * n_n$ states, where n_i is the number of em boundary cut points of attribute i and n is the number of continuous features.

A state on this search space can be described by a vector of integers, $[v_1,..,v_n]$, where v_i is the number of intervals used to discretize attribute i. If $v_i = 1$ this

---

[1]   In the experimental study, we use 30% of the data for the validation set.

means that attribute i does not contribute to class discrimination. Attribute i is irrelevant and will be ignored.

The most general discretization corresponds to the vector $[1, ..., 1]$ and the most specific corresponds to the vector $[n_1, ..., n_n]$. The search space can be seen as a lattice:

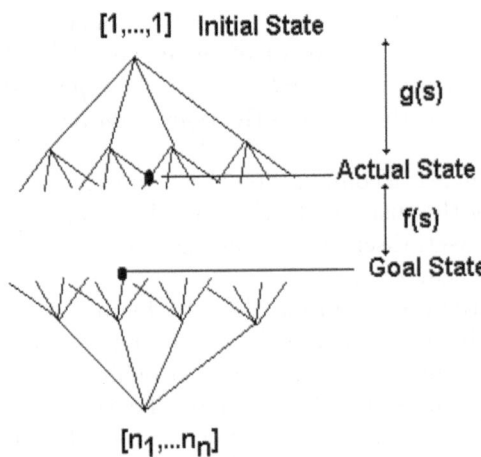

Fig. 1. The search space lattice

The initial state of the search engine consists of the vector $[1, ..., 1]$ meaning that no continuous attribute contributes to class discrimination. Each state of the search lattice defines a discretized dataset. We evaluate each state of discretization by calling the target learning system with the corresponding discretized dataset. The learned theory is evaluated in the *validation set*, and the obtained score is taken as a quality assessment of the tried discretization.

The search through the space of discretizations is done with a specialization operator. On the search tree, each node has n descendants. On each descendant, the number of intervals of one attribute grows by a user defined parameter.

Consider, for example, a problem with 3 continuous attributes. Each state is given by a 3 dimensional vector, for example, $[4, 2, 6]$ meaning that the first continuous attribute was divided into 4 intervals, the second attribute was divided into 2 intervals and the third attribute was divided into 6 intervals. Assuming that the interval increment is set to 2, this node will have three descendants:

$$[6, 2, 6], [4, 4, 6] \text{ and } [4, 2, 8].$$

The next node to expand is the one not yet expanded and with lowest value of an *objective function* which will be described bellow.

3.2   States Evaluation

The evaluation of a candidate set of intervals is done as follows. The training and the validation data are discretized using the candidate set. This means that for each example the value of a continuous attribute is replaced by the representative value of the interval where the attribute-value falls.

To discretize a dataset, we need to know not only the number of intervals but also their limits. We apply a *k-means* procedure to the *boundary cut-points* vector of each continuous attribute. For the attribute i, the k parameter, i.e. the number of intervals, is given by the v_i of the vector of the current hypothesis. The output of the *k-means* procedure are the *boundaries* and the *representative values* of each interval. Presently we use the *mean* as the *representative value* for each interval.

The objective function we minimize is a combination of two functions: f and g. The first one, function f, measures the distance to the goal. It is computed as the error rate on the validation dataset, discretized using the actual hypothesis. Obviously the goal is an error rate near zero.

The second function measures the distance from the initial state. It is computed as $g(\boldsymbol{v}) = \frac{1}{k} \sum_{i=1}^{n} log\ v_i$, where k is a user-defined parameter to avoid the dominance of g in the objective function. The intuition behind the use of function g is that between two different states that evaluate the same value for function f we prefer the one which minimizes the number of intervals. The set of intervals is computed from the values observed on a learning set. If there is a large number of intervals, small variations on the training set will be propagated on to the set of intervals. By minimizing the number of intervals, we are also reducing the dependence of the set of intervals from the training set. This fact will have positive influence on the *variance* of the generated classifier.

3.3   Terminal Conditions

There are two terminal conditions. The first one occurs if the evaluation of function f returns 0.

The second condition occurs when, for several iterations of the state's expansion, there is no improvement of the objective function. Presently we use the following heuristic: after 3 expansions without improving the objective function, the system linearly increases the step. After 3 new expansions without improvement, the discretization process stops.

3.4   Discussion

The proposed method requires one sort operation for each continuous attribute. A normal Decision Tree requires one sort operation for *each node* and each continuous attribute.

At each evaluation of the search procedure, we apply a *k-means* procedure that has no proof of convergence, although it appears to always converge in a finite number of iterations [8]. It also can be computationally more expensive than the sort operation. For large datasets the described procedure requires much more time than generating a single Decision Tree.

Another problem occurs when all or almost all the continuous attributes are relevant for class discrimination. In this case the starting point is far from any solution. Solutions for those two problems are presented in the next section.

3.5 Extensions for Large Datasets

For large datasets, we can consider that we have enough data points. The *k-means* procedure is a *heavy artillery* and useless. Instead of using the iterative standard procedure we apply one single convergence step, that reduces the complexity to $O(n)$ in the worst case.

The lattice in the figure 1, suggest a search strategy that could solve the second problem. We can consider, on one hand an ascendent branch that goes from the most general to the most specific, and on the other hand a descendent branch that goes from the most specific to the most general. The initial state, for the ascendent branch, consists on the vector $[1, ..., 1]$. The initial state, for the descendent branch, consists on the vector $[V_1, ..., V_n]$. The ascendent search works the same way as the descendent one, only in the opposite direction. On the example of the previous section, the state $[4,2,6]$ will have three descendants: $[6,2,6],[4,4,6]$ and $[4,2,8]$ if it is on the ascendent branch, or $[2,2,6],[4,1,6]$ and $[4,2,4]$ if it is on the descendent branch.

The search engine can skip from the ascendent branch to the descendent branch, because the next node to expand is the one not yet expanded and with lowest value of the *objective function*.

4 Empirical Evaluation

The method was evaluated on 5 well known datasets from the UCI repository. Table 1 shows some basic dataset characteristics. In the last column we present the sum of boundary cut-points for all continuous attributes in the dataset, providing a hint on the size of the search space. The evaluation was done using 10 fold cross validation. For each fold, the dataset is split into a training set and an independent test set.

Dataset	Nr.Examples	Classes	Attributes	Continuous	Nr. Boundary cut-points
Australian	690	2	14	6	862
Diabetes	768	2	8	8	1048
German	1000	2	24	7	209
Heart	270	2	13	7	317
Iris	150	3	4	4	111

Table 1. Datasets Characteristics

The training set is used by our algorithm, *Discretizer*, to generate the set of intervals as explained before. Internally, this dataset is divided into a *train* and a *validation* set. *Discretizer* outputs for each continuous attribute a set of *interval boundaries* and the *representative value* of each interval. This output is used to discretize both the training set and the test set.

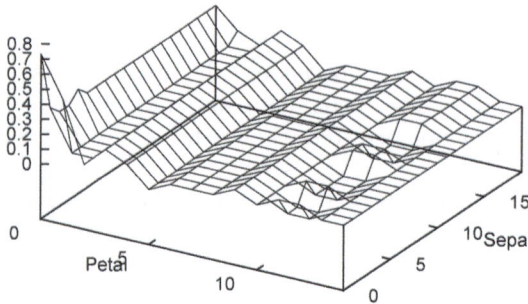

Fig. 2. A simplification of the search space for the *Iris* problem

Tables 2 and 3 respectively present the results of applying C4.5 and naive Bayes to both the original and discretized datasets.

For each dataset we show both error rates, the significance of the difference of the means from *t-paired tests*, under the *null hypothesis* that the mean of the errors are equal, and the last column shows the mean number of used attributes in the discretized version of the dataset.

Dataset	C4.5	Discretizer	*ttest*	Used Attributes Mean
Australian	14.9 ±2.6	12.5 ±3.2	-97%	2.5
Diabetes	25.9 ±3.3	25.3 ±3.8	-40%	4.5
German	28.9 ±4.4	27.2 ±3.1	-91%	3.5
Heart	22.2 ±6.1	25.6 ±8.1	79%	3.6
Iris	4.0 ±4.7	5.3 ±4.2	65%	3.0
Means	19.2	19.0		

Table 2. Error rates using C4.5 from 10 *Cross Validation*

With respect to *error rates*, the trend indicated by these results is that learning on the discretized dataset competes well against learning on the original dataset. Three times we observed an improvement, with statistical significance confidence levels, on *Australian* and *German* datasets using C4.5, and on *Australian* data using Bayes. Only once we observe a significant degradation of the error rate, *German* data using Bayes. Most important is the effect on feature

Dataset	Bayes	Discretizer	ttest	Used Attributes Mean
Australian	22.5 ±4.9	14.2 ±3.4	-100%	2.4
Diabetes	26.3 ±6.4	25.8 ±6.3	25%	5.5
German	25.8 ±4.4	26.3 ±3.6	99%	3.3
Heart	15.9 ±6.1	16.7 ±8.1	27%	4.0
Iris	4.0 ±5.0	6.7 ±4.2	56%	3.6
Means	18.9	18.7		

Table 3. Error rates using Bayes from 10 *Cross Validation*

reduction. In almost all the experiments, redundant features are determined and eliminated from the discretized dataset. In some folds of the cross validation procedure, all the continuous features are removed. Most of the times, only half of the original continuous features are considered to be relevant.

Figure 2 visualizes part of the search space for a simplified version of the *Iris* dataset. We only consider two attributes: petal and sepal width. For different number of discretization intervals we plot the *error rate* obtained using C4.5. The minimum error rate is obtained using 5 intervals for *petal width* and is independent of the attribute *sepal width*.

5   Conclusions

According to Dougherty's terminology, the method we propose is global, supervised and dynamic. Global means that it is used as a pre-processing method. Discretization is performed previously to the learning phase. The method is supervised because the possible intervals are defined in terms of *boundary cut points*. And it is dynamic because all attributes are discretized in an interdependent way.

In the empirical evaluation carried out, we only observed once a significant error rate degradation, while a significant increase of performance occurred three times.

The most significant aspect of the proposed method is related with its ability to perform feature selection while discretizing continuous features. For instance, on the *Australian* dataset, we observed a significant increase of performance using only 2 or 3 from the 6 original continuous attributes. The dynamic discretization, which looks for interdependencies between features, detects redundant attributes and performs feature selection as a side effect. The proposed method seems to be effective on detecting irrelevant features.

The formulation that we have described of the search procedure, is naturally extended for parallel computation. Instead of setting one or two starting points, we can have several points distributed over the search space, and perform a parallel search. The search engine is not restricted to A^* algorithms. We intend to use *Genetic algorithms* to perform the search.

Acknowledgments

Gratitude is expressed to the support given by the FEDER and PRAXIS XXI projects and the Plurianual support attributed to LIACC.

References

1. J. Catlett. Megainduction: a test flight. In *Machine Learning: Proceedings of the 8 International Conference*. Morgan Kaufmann, 1991. 160
2. J. Catlett. On changing continuous attributes into ordered discrete attributes. In Y. Kodratoff, editor, *European Working Session on Learning -EWSL91*. LNAI 482 Springer Verlag, 1991. 162
3. P. Domingos and M. Pazzani. Beyond independence: Conditions for the optimality of the simple bayesian classifier. In L. Saitta, editor, *Machine Learning Proc. of 13th International Conference*. Morgan Kaufmann, 1996. 160, 161
4. J. Dougherty, R. Kohavi, and M. Sahami. Supervised and unsupervised discretization of continuous features. In A. Prieditis and S. Russel, editors, *Machine Learning Proc. of 12th International Conference*. Morgan Kaufmann, 1995. 161, 163
5. U. Fayyad and K Irani. Multi-interval discretization of continuous-valued attributes for classification learning. In *13th International Joint Conference of Artificial Intelligence*, 1993. 161, 162, 163
6. R.C. Holte. Very simple classification rules perform well on most commonly used datasets. *Machine Learning, Vol, 11*, 1993. 162
7. R. Kohavi and M. Sahami. Error-based and entropy-based discretization of continuous features. In *Proceedings of KDD 96*, 1996. 160
8. B. Moret and H. Shapiro. *Algorithms from P to NP - Design and Efficiency, Vol. 1*. The Benjamin Publishers, 1990. 165
9. Kerber R. Chimerge: discretization of numeric attributes. In *Proceedings of the 10 National Conference on Artificial Intelligence*. MIT Press, 1992. 162
10. M. Richeldi and M. Rossoto. Class driven statistical discretization of continuous attributes. In S. Wrobel and N. Lavrac, editors, *Machine Learning: ECML-95*. LNAI 912, Springer Verlag, 1995. 162
11. M. Robnik-Sikonja and I Kononenko. Discretization of continuous attributes using relieff. In *Proceedings of RK95*, 1995. 163
12. L. Torgo and J. Gama. Search-based class discretization. In *Proceedings ECML-97*. LNAI 1224, Springer Verlag, 1997. 161

Intelligent Collaborative Information Retrieval

Joaquin Delgado, Naohiro Ishii, and Tomoki Ura

Department of Intelligence & Computer Science
Nagoya Institute of Technology
Gokiso-cho, Showa-ku, Nagoya 466-8555 JAPAN
{jdelgado,ishii,tomkey}@ics.nitech.ac.jp

Abstract. The next generation of intelligent information systems will rely on **cooperative agents** for playing a fundamental role in actively searching and finding relevant information on behalf of their users in complex and open environments, such as the Internet. On the other hand, the relevance of such information is a user-dependent notion within the scope or context of a particular domain or topic. Previous work, mainly in information retrieval (IR), focuses on the analysis of the **content** by the means of keyword-based metrics. Some recent algorithms apply social or **collaborative** information filtering to improve the task of retrieving relevant information and for refining each agent's particular knowledge. In this paper, we combine both approaches developing a new content-based filtering technique for learning up-to-date users' profiles that serves as basis for a novel collaborative information-filtering algorithm. We demonstrate our approach through a system called *RAAP* (Research Assistant Agent Project) devoted to support collaborative research by classifying domain specific information, retrieved from the Web, and recommending these "bookmarks" to other researchers with similar interests.

1 Introduction

Undoubtedly, in the next generation of intelligent information systems, cooperative information agents will play a fundamental role in actively searching and finding relevant information on behalf of their users in complex and open environments, such as the Internet. *Relevance,* on the other hand, can only be defined for a specific user, and under the context of a particular domain or topic. Because of this, the development of intelligent, personalized, content-based, *document classification* systems is becoming more and more attractive now Furthermore, learning profiles that represent the user's interests within a particular domain, later used for *content-based filtering*, has been shown to be a challenging task. This becomes more difficult if the relevant set of attributes for each class *changes in time*, what makes the problem even not suitable for traditional, fixed-attribute machine learning algorithms.

Helder Coelho (Ed.): IBERAMIA'98, LNAI 1484, pp. 170-182, 1998.
© Springer-Verlag Berlin Heidelberg 1998

Documents, as well as user's profiles, are commonly represented as keyword vectors[1] in order to be compared or learned. With the huge variety words used in natural language, we find ourselves with a noisy space that has extremely high dimensionality (10^4 - 10^7 features). For a particular user, it is reasonable to think that processing a set of correctly classified relevant and irrelevant documents from a certain domain of interest, may lead to identify and isolate the set of relevant keywords for that domain. Later on, these keywords or features can be used for distinguishing documents belonging to that category from others. Thus, these user-domain specific sets of relevant features, that we will call *prototypes,* may be used to learn to classify documents. It is interesting enough to say that these prototypes may change over time, as the user develops a *particular view* for each class. The problem of personalized learning of text classification, is in fact, similar to the one of on-line learning, from examples, when the number of relevant attributes is much less than the total number of attributes, and the concept function changes over time, as described in [1].

From a different perspective, cooperative multi-agent systems implicitly share "social" information, which can be potentially used to improve the task of retrieving relevant information, as well as refining each agent's particular knowledge. Using this fact, a number of "word-of-mouth" *collaborative information filtering[2]* systems, have been implemented as to *recommend* to the user things of interest. This is done based on the ratings that other *correlated users* have assign to the same object. Usually this idea has been developed for specific domains, like "Music" or "Films" as in Firefly[a] and Movie Critic[b], or for introducing people (matchmaking) as in Yenta[2]. A mayor drawback of these systems is that some of them completely deny any information that can be extracted from the content. This can be somehow convenient for domains that are hard to analyze in terms of content (such as entertainment), but definitely not suitable for textual content-driven environments such as the World-Wide Web (WWW). Besides, these systems usually demand from the user, a direct intervention for both classifying and/or rating information.

In this paper we describe a multi-agent system called *RAAP* (Research Assistant Agent Project) that intends to bring together the best of both worlds – Content-based and Collaborative Information Filtering. In *RAAP*, personal agents helps its users (researchers) to classify domain specific information found in the Web, and recommends these URLs to other users with similar interests. This eventually brings benefits for all the users within an organization, as information re-discovery is avoided and only peer-reviewed documents are recommended among them. This is particularly useful while involved in information and knowledge intensive collaborative work, such as scientific research.

---

[1] This is called the Vector Model and has been widely used in Information Retrieval (IR) and AI.

[2] Also called Social Filtering [3]

[a] http://www.firefly.net

[b] http://www.moviecritic.com

2   Description of *RAAP*

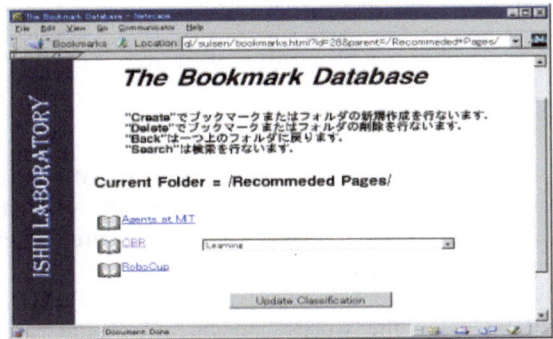

Figure 1 Agent's Suggestion

The Research Assistant Agent Project (*RAAP*) is a system developed with the purpose of assisting the user in the task of classifying documents (bookmarks), retrieved from the World Wide Web, and automatically recommending them to other users of the system, with similar interests. In order to evaluate the system, we narrowed our objectives to supporting a specific type of activity, such as *Research &Development (R &D)* for a given domain. In our experiment, tests were conducted using *RAAP* for supporting research in the *Computer Science* domain.

RAAP consists of a bookmark database with a particular view for each user, as well as a software agent that monitors the user's actions. Once the user has registered an "interesting" page, his agent suggests a classification among some predefined categories, based on the document's content and the user's profiles (Fig. 1). Then the user has the opportunity to reconfirm the suggestion or to change classification into one, that he or she considers best for the given document as shown in Fig.2.

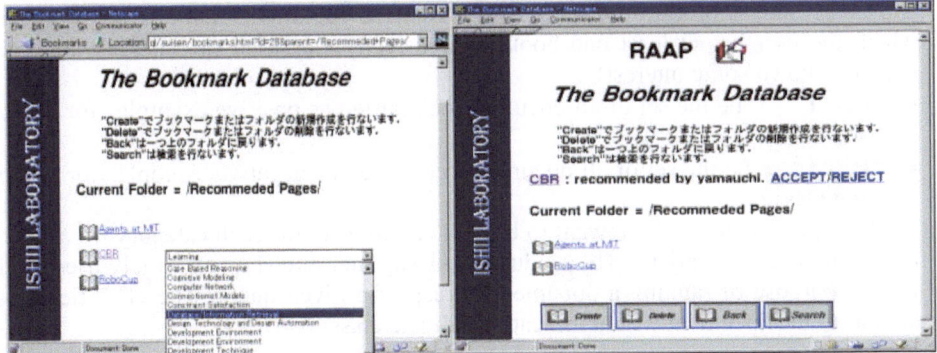

Figure 2 Classification   **Figure 3 Recommendation**

In parallel, the agent checks for newly classified bookmarks, and recommend these to other users that can either accept correct them when they eventually login the system and are notified of such recommendation, as illustrated in Fig.3.

During the first time registration into the system, the user is asked to select his/hers research areas of interest. This information is used to build the initial profile of that user for each class. The agent updates the user's profile for a specific class every time certain number k of documents are successfully classified into it. In that way, *RAAP* only uses up-to-date profiles for classification, reflecting always the latest interests of the user. During this process the agent learns how to improve its classification and narrow the scope of the people to whom it recommends in a way we shall explain in the following sections.

3   Learning to Classify

In our system, a **document** belonging to a user u_i, s as a finite list of terms, resulting of filtering out a stoplist of common English words, from the original document fetched from the WWW using its URL. These documents are either explicitly "bookmarked" or "accepted" by the user. In case of being "rejected", sometimes it can also be "saved" by the user's agent as negative example. Under this notion, and from now on, we will be using the words "document", "page" and "bookmark" without distinction. We will also be using "class", "category" and "topic" in the same way.

Because we are trying to build a document classification system that learns, it is of our interest to keep track of the positive and negative examples among the documents that have been already classified. In *RAAP*, **positive examples** for a specific user u_i and for a class c_j, are the documents *explicitly registered* or *accepted* by u_i and classified into c_j. Note that accepting a recommended bookmark is just a special case of registering it. On the other hand, **negative examples** are either *deleted* bookmarks, *misclassified* bookmarks or *rejected* bookmarks that happens to be classified into c_j. In the case of rejected bookmarks the document is only classified by the agent – we don't ask the user to reconfirm the classification for rejected bookmarks. In this sense, and as measure of precaution, we only take rejected bookmarks that fall into a class in which the user has at least one bookmark correctly classified (a class in which the user has shown some interest).

- Let $C_{i,j}^{+}$ be the set of all documents classified as positive examples for user u_i and class c_j
- Let $C_{i,j}^{-}$ be the set of all documents classified as negative examples for user u_i and class c_j

Now for a given user, we want to build a classifier Q for each category, as a list of terms, in order to apply the dot product similarity measure (Eq. 1), widely used in IR for the purpose of ranking a document D respect a given query. The classifier most similar to the document would indicate candidate class.

$$(1) \qquad sim\,(Q,D) = \sum_{\tau \in Q} w(\tau, Q)\, w(\tau, D)$$

For term weighting, we chose TF-IDF (Eq. 1.1), as it is one of the most successful and well-tested term weighting schemes in IR. It consists of the product of $tf_{\tau d}$, the term-frequency (TF) of term τ in the document d, by $idf_\tau = log_2(N/dt_\tau) + 1$, the inverse document frequency (IDF), where N is the total number of documents of collection and dt_τ is the total number of occurrences of τ in the collection. Note that we maintain a different collection for each user.

(1.1)

$$w(\tau, d) = \frac{tf_{\tau,d}\left[\log_2\left(\frac{N}{df_\tau}\right) + 1\right]}{\sqrt{\sum_i\left(tf_{\tau_i,d}\left[\log_2\left(\frac{N}{df_{\tau_i}}\right) + 1\right]\right)^2}}$$

3.1 Relevance Feedback

Given the unique terms in Q, $P=\{\tau_1, \tau_2, \tau_3,..., \tau_r\}$, named P as for Prototype, it is it easy to see that both Q and D can be represented as numerical vectors, containing the respective weights of these terms in Q and D, denoted as $\vec{Q}$ and $\vec{D}$ respectively. Their dot product[3] is, in fact, the similarity measure explained before. We can also express Q and D as numerical vectors, containing the term frequency of each elements of P within them, denoted respectively, as:

$$Tf(D) = <tf_{\tau_1,D}, tf_{\tau_2,D}, tf_{\tau_3,D},..., tf_{\tau_r,D}>$$

and

$$Tf(Q) = <tf_{\tau_1,Q}, tf_{\tau_2,Q}, tf_{\tau_3,Q},..., tf_{\tau_r,Q}>$$

We can now describe mathematically a very simple approach to the process of relevance feedback as:

(2) $Tf(Q^{i+1}) = Tf(Q^i) + \alpha Tf(D)$

Where $\alpha = 1$ if $D \in C_{i,j}^+$

$\alpha = -1$ if $D \in C_{i,j}^-$

And then, recalculate $\vec{Q}^{i+1}$ based on the values of $Tf(Q^{i+1})$.

Another approach found in the literature, is the Rocchio's Algorithm [3]:

(2.1) $\vec{Q} = \frac{\beta}{\left|C_{i,j}^+\right|}\sum_{j \in C_{i,j}^+}\vec{D}_j - \frac{\gamma}{\left|C_{i,j}^+\right|}\sum_{j \in C_{i,j}^+}\vec{D}_j$

Note that $\left|\overline{C_{i,j}^+}\right| \neq C_{i,j}^-$

Usual values are:
$\beta=4$ and $\gamma=4\beta$

The basic problem of these algorithms and the main reason why we couldn't use them for our system is that *they do not take into account the possibility that the dimension of the vectors and may change in time.* In other words, that unique terms listed in P can be added or deleted in order to reflect the user's current interests (feature selection).

Perhaps Rocchio's algorithm can be adapted to be recalculated each time a unique term is added or deleted to P, but the computational cost would be very high. This is without mentioning the size of the complement of the positive examples, used to calculate the negative part of the formula.

---

[3] The dot-product between the numerical vectors of Q and D is denoted as $(\vec{Q} \circ \vec{D})$.

Instead, we propose a new algorithm for incrementally building in order to reflect effectively the user's current interests. We shall give at first a couple of useful definitions:

Definition 1: *We define **positive prototype** for a class c_i, user u_j at time t,*

$$P_{i,j}^{(t)+} = \{\tau_1, \tau_2, \tau_3, ..., \tau_r\}$$

as a finite set of unique indexing terms, chosen to be relevant for c_i, up to time t (see feature selection).

Definition 2: *We define **negative prototype** for a class c_i, user u_j at time t,*

$$P_{i,j}^{(t)-} \subseteq P_{i,j}^{(t)+} / \forall \tau \in P_{i,j}^{(t)-}, \exists d \in C_{i,j}^- \wedge (tf_{\tau,d} > 0)$$

as a subset of the corresponding positive prototype, whereas each one of its elements can be found at least once in the set of documents classified as negative examples for class c_i.

Now we construct the vector of our positive prototype as follows,

---

At time $t+1$

if $(P_{i,j}^{(t+1)+} = P_{i,j}^{(t)+})\{$

     $Tf(Q_{i,j}^{(t+1)+}) = Tf(Q_{i,j}^{(t)+}) + Tf(D_{i,j}^{(t)+})$

     Up date $\vec{Q}_{i,j}^{(t+1)+}$, based on $Tf(Q_{i,j}^{(t+1)+})$

$\}$ else$\{$

     forall $\tau \in P_{i,j}^{(t+1)+} - P_{i,j}^{(t)+}$ do$\{$

         calculate $w(\tau, d)$ for the n-most recently processed

         documents $\in C_{i,j}^+$ and update these values in $\vec{Q}_{i,j}^{(t+1)+}$

$\}\}\}$

Where n is the number of documents used as basis for feature selection.

This algorithm is to be applied in the same way for the negative prototype. We can now re-define the similarity measure between a class c_j and a document D as:

(3) $\quad sim_i^t(c_j, D) = (\vec{Q}_{i,j}^{(t)+} \circ \vec{D}_{i,j}^{(t)}) - (\vec{Q}_{i,j}^{(t)-} \circ \vec{D}_{i,j}^{(t)})$

Expressing this equation in words, we should say that for a given user u_i, the similarity between a class c_j and an incoming document D at time t, is equal to the similarity of D, with respect of the classifier of the corresponding positive prototype minus the similarity of D, with respect of the classifier of the corresponding negative prototype. This intuitively says that a document is similar to a class if its similar to the class positive prototype and not similar the class negative prototype. It is important to say that the initial positive prototype for each class is a list of selected core keywords from that domain that were integrated into the system to provide at least an initial classification.

Finally, we use a heuristic for *RAAP's* ranking. This heuristics states that *it is more likely that a new document is to be classified into a class in which the user has shown some interest before.* We chose the class with the highest ranking among these.

3.2 Feature Selection

Automatic feature selection methods include the removal of non-informative terms according the corpus statistics. In comparative studies on feature selection for text categorization [4], information gain (IG) is shown to be one of the most effective for this task. Information gain is frequently employed as a term-goodness criterion in the field of machine learning [5].

Given all these interesting properties we decided to use IG for selecting informative terms from the corpus. We re-define the expected information gain that the presence or absence of a term τ gives toward the classification of a set of pages (S), given a class c_j and for a particular use*r* user u_i as:

$$E_{i,j}(\tau,S) = I(S) - [P(\tau = present)I(S_{\tau=present}) + P(\tau = absent)I(S_{w=absent})$$

(4)   *where,*

$$I_{i,j}(S) = \sum_{c \in \{C_{i,j}^+, C_{i,j}^-\}} - P(S_c)\log_2(p(S_c))$$

In Eq. 4, $P(\tau=present)$ is the probability that τ is present on a page, and $(S_{\tau=present})$ is the set of pages that contain at least one occurrence of τ and S_c are the pages belonging to class c.

Using this approach, in RAAP, the user's agent finds the k most informative words from the set S of the n most recently classified documents. As in Syskill & Webert [6] we chose $k=128$ and arbitrary selected $n=3$ for our experiments.

Out of the selected 128 terms, 28 are to be fixed, as they constitute the core list of keywords or a basic ontology for a topic, given for that class as an initial classifier. Within the rest 100 words, we adopt the following scheme for adding or replacing them in the positive prototype:

1. Perform *stemming* over the most informative in order to create the list of terms.
2. Replace only the terms that are in the prototype but not in the list of the most informative terms.
3. As shown in the algorithm for constructing the classifier, update the weights of the newly added or replaced terms with respect of the n documents processed by the agent for this purpose.

We conclude this section saying that even if IG is a computationally expensive process, in RAAP this is drastically improved both by having n low and only updating the weights for the selected terms only with respect of these documents. We also provide a mechanism in which the "memories" of the terms that repeat in time, are left intact, given that their accumulated weight and information value is high.

4   Learning to Recommend

For the purpose of learning to recommend a page saved by the user, the agent counts with two matrixes. They are the *user vs. category* matrix M_{mxn} and the *user's confidence* factor, where m is the number of users in the system and n the number of categories. The first one is

	John	Kato	Ishii	Joao	Gina
Information Retrieval	7	7	3	4	7
Temporal Reasoning	4	3	2	0	4
CBR	1	3	7	2	3
Distributed AI	2	5	3	7	2

Table 1 User-Category Matrix

automatically constructed by counting, for that user, the number of times a document is successfully classified into a certain class. During the initial registration in *RAAP*, the matrix is initialized to one for the classes that the user has shown interest.

The first idea was the user-category matrix to calculate the correlation between a user u_x and the rest, using the Pearson-r algorithm (Eq. 5). Then recommend the newly classified bookmarks to those with highest correlation.

$$(5) \quad correl\,(u_x, u_r) = \frac{\sum_{i=1}^{n} u_{x,i} - \overline{u}_{x,i})(u_{r,i} - \overline{u}_{r,i})}{\sqrt{\sum_{i=1}^{n}u_{x,i} - \overline{u}_{x,i})^2 \sum_{i=1}^{n}(u_{r,i} - \overline{u}_{r,i})^2}}$$

$$\text{where } \overline{u}_{j,i} = \frac{\sum_{i=1}^{n} u_{j,i}}{n}; j \in \{x,r\}$$

One problem with this approach is that the correlation is only calculated as an average criterion of likeness between two users, regardless of the relations between the topics. That is, if the agent decides to recommend a bookmark classified into a class x, but it happens to be that its user is highly correlated to another user based on the values in the matrix respect other classes, then the bookmark would be recommended to that user anyway. These classes can be presumably unrelated to the class of the bookmark, which is undesirable since we only want the agents to recommend bookmarks to people that have interest in the topics to which it belongs or in related ones.   What we really want is to give more weight in the correlation between users to those classes more related to the class of the bookmark that is going to be recommended. For this reason we introduce the concept of similarity between two classes for a user u_i at time t, as the dice coefficient between the positive prototypes of the classes.

$$(6) \quad rel_i^t(c_m, c_n) = \frac{2 \times \left|P_{i,m}^{(t)+} \cap P_{i,n}^{(t)+}\right|}{\left|P_{i,m}^{(t)+}\right| + \left|P_{i,n}^{(t)+}\right|}$$

Where $|A \cap B|$ is the number of common terms, and $|A|$ is the number of terms in A.

Given the class of the bookmark c_j, the class similarity vector is defined as:

(6.1) $\vec{R}_j = < rel_i^t(c_j, c_1), rel_i^t(c_j, c_2), ..., rel_i^t(c_j, c_n) >$

where $n = \#$ of classes

Now we multiply this vector by the user-category matrix obtaining a weighted, user-category matrix.

(7) $WM = \vec{R}_j \times M$

Using this new User-Category matrix similar to the one shown in Table 1, but with modified (weighted) values, we proceed to calculate the weight between the subject user u_x (who recommends) and the others u_i (candidates to receive the recommendation) as the correlation between them multiplied by the confidence factor between them.

(8) $Weight(u_x, u_i) = correl(u_x, u_i) * confidence(u_x, u_i)$

In Eq. 8, the confidence factor of user u_i with respect u_j, is a function with a range between 0.1 and 1. It returns 1 for all new users respect others, and it decreased or increased by a factor of 0.01 every time a bookmark recommended by user u_x is accepted or rejected by u_i respectively. Note that $confidence(u_x, u_i) \neq confidence(u_i, u_x)$. This means that the confidence is not bi-directional, but differs for every combination of pair of users.

For deciding to who recommend we used a threshold of 0.5 for the minimum weight, as well as recommending to at most to $f(n) = \lceil 1/(n-264)) + 5 \rceil$ number of users, where n is the total number of users in the system. We use $f(n)$ to maintain a reasonable proportion of the number of users that are selected as recipients for the recommendation, respect the number of registered users that at some moment of time can be huge.

To avoid circular references in the recommendation chain, the agents verify that the recommended document is not already registered in the target's database.

5   Experimental Results

In order to evaluate the system we set up an experiment with 9 users in our laboratory. They were asked to interact freely with *RAAP* during one week, registering home pages only with content relevant to their current research interests. An update of the users' prototype for a certain class was executed every 3 bookmarks classified into that class.

- **Bookmark Classification**

A number of 72 bookmarks were registered and classified by the agents/users into a total of 9 different classes. We give the results of the classification in Table 2.

User ID	Correct	Incorrect	Total	Accuracy (%)	# of Updates
23	4	3	7	57.1	0
25	3	0	3	100.0	0
26	3	7	10	30.0	1
27	12	6	18	66.7	4
28	7	10	17	41.2	2
30	0	2	2	0.0	0
31	4	2	6	66.7	0
32	1	0	1	100.0	0
34	2	6	8	25.0	0

Table 2 Document Classification Accuracy

The first thing we should notice is that results were quite different for each user. The usage of the system also varied quite a lot. In this experiment only 2 users (ID=27,28) received 2 or more updates of there profiles, having also the largest amount of registered bookmarks. For ID=27, an average of 66.7% of accuracy was achieved while 4 profile updates occurred. This should be compared with ID=28 that had a somewhat low average of 41.2% of accuracy with 2 updates and ID=26 with 30.0% and only 1 update. This growing pattern suggests that when more updates occur, better classification is achieved. For the cases where there was no updating at all, an average of more than 55% of accuracy was obtained. But we should be very carefull with this result, since the initial, predefined, selection of keywords for each class was no guarantee for a correct classification. More learning was supposed to occur in order to make a better evaluation.

- **Bookmark Recommendation**

As we can see in Table 3, the overall acceptance rate was quite high for the majority of the users. In total, there were 74 recommendations, 52 (70%) of which were accepted. Comparing this with the results in bookmark classification, it is easy to realize that, in general, the acceptance rate was lower for those users that didn't receive any update in their profile such as ID=23, 34.

User ID	Accept	Reject	Total	Accuracy (%)
23	3	8	11	27.3
25	6	0	6	100.0
26	9	1	10	90.0
27	13	2	15	86.7
28	7	3	10	70.0
30	8	1	9	88.9
31	2	1	3	66.7
32	4	5	9	44.4
34	0	1	1	0.0

Table 3 Recommendation Acceptance Rate

Out of 70 registered bookmarks only 42 were unique, which means that 30 of them (41.7% of all the bookmarks) actually came from recommendations. This indicates that intelligent information sharing and collaborative filtering occurred in high degree.

As for the amount of data used for the experiment we should recognize it falls short but it gave us a general idea of the behavior of the system.

Finally, for a more general evaluation, we must point out that for *RAAP* there was no training data available, other than the bookmarks itself. The learning was performed on-line and incrementally throughout the interaction with the system. Thus, *RAAP* cannot be directly compared with traditional of-line, text categorization algorithms. In spite of this, our classification algorithm showed to be satisfactory, to the extent that in the majority of the cases the user didn't even need to rectify the agent's suggestion. The relatively high percentage of accepted recommendations showed that its not only feasible to support collaborated filtering on content-based filtering, but also that with the increase of *relevant* data as product of the recommendations, the classification accuracy is very likely to improve.

6   Related Works

There are a several related works that intend to filter and recommend to the user "interesting" Web pages. We can classify them into those using content-based filtering techniques and those using collaborative filtering.

Among the content-based filtering systems we can mention *Syskill & Webert* [6], a system that builds user's profile using Expected Information Gain, and compares the effectiveness of several Machine Learning algorithms for the task of classifying a page as interesting or not for the user. A main difference with our system is that, in *Syskill & Webert*, the domains of the set of web pages used for training and testing the algorithms are previously decided. In other words, this system only recommends to the user pages within a specific topic, extracted from a previously decided online directory, or a list of pages that result from a query to search engine such as LYCOS. It does not perform text categorization of a new document -- at least not among the domains; nor it gives any advice about whether the domain itself is in fact interesting or not for the user! Another difference is that the user's profile is built only once and is not automatically updated afterwards. Learning is performed off-line, with the need of training set with previously rated pages. An another similar system is *WebWatcher* [7], which recommends hyperlinks within a Web page, using the TF-IDF document similarity metrics also used in our system.

Collaborative filtering systems are more rare in the literature and currently oriented more to commercial systems that perform recommendations in the entertainment domain, such as *Movie Critic* and *Firefly*, as we mentioned in the introduction. Some more classical systems are *Ringo* [8], a music recommending system (upon which *Firefly* is based) and *Grouplens* [9], a system that personalized selection of Netnews. Both systems employ Pearson-*r* correlation coefficients to determine similarity between users, regardless of the content of the information being recommended. In any case the user is asked to rate the content, using some predefined scale, in order to calculate this correlation.

Up to the time of the writing of this paper, there have been few reported systems that try to combine both techniques. In the matchmaking domain, that is, recommending people, instead of recommending documents, we can mention *Yenta* [2], and *Referral Web* [10]. These systems somehow perform keyword based textual analysis of private and public documents in order to refine their recommending algorithms that are originally based on collaborative filtering techniques. *RAAP* differs to these systems in several ways, being the objective to filter documents and performing on-line learning of user's profiles. These profiles are later used not only to match similarities among people but also among personal domains of interests.

7   Conclusion and Future Work

The contributions of this paper are threefold:
1) We proposed the combination of content-based information filtering with collaborative filtering as the basis for multi-agent collaborative information retrieval. For such purpose the system RAAP was explained in detail.
2) A new algorithm for active learning of user's profile and text categorization was introduced.
3) We proposed a new algorithm for collaborative information filtering in which not only the correlation between users and also the similarity between topics is taken into account.

Some experimental results that support our approach were also presented. As future work we are looking forward test *RAAP* in broader environments and to compare it with other similar systems, as well as improve the efficiency of both the classification and recommendation processes. Larger amount of data will be collected in subsequent experiments in order to obtain a better evaluation.

Acknowledgements

This work was supported by the Hori Foundation for the Promotion of Information Science and the Japanese Ministry of Science, Culture and Education (Monbusho).

References

1. Blum, A., "On-line Algorithms in Machine Learning" (a survey). Dagstuhl workshop on On-Line algorithms (June 1996).
2. Foner, L., "A Multi-Agent Referral System for Matchmaking", in *Proceedings of the First International Conference on the Practical Applications of Intelligent Agent Technology (PAAM'96)*, London (April 1996).
3. Maes, P.:,"Agents that Reduce Work and Information Overload", *Comm ACM*, 37, No7 (1994).

4.   Yang, Y., Pedersen, J. "Feature selection in statistical learning of text categorization", *Proceedings of the Fourteenth International Conference on Machine Learning (ICML '97)*, (1997).
5.   Mitchell T., "Machine Learning" McGraw Hill, 1996
6.   Pazzani,M.,Muramatsu,J.,and Billsus, D., "Syskill & Webert: Identifying interesting websites", In *Proceedings of the American National Conference on Artificial Intelligence (AAAI'96)*, Portland, OR. (1996)
7.   Armstrong, R., Frietag, D., Joachims, T. and T.M. Mitchell: "WebWatcher: a learning apprentice for the world wide web" In *Proceedings of the 1995 AAAI Spring Symposium of Information Gathering from Heterogeneous, Distributed Environments*, Stanford, CA, 1995. AAAI Press.
8.   Shardanand, U. and Maes P.: "Social Information Filtering: Algorithms for Automation "Word of Mouth"": *ACM/CHI'95*.
     http://www.acm.org/sigchi/chi95/Electronic/documnts/papers/us_bdy.htm
9.   Resnick, P., Iacovou N., Sushak, M., Bergstrom, P., Riedl, J.: "GroupLens: An Open Architecture for Collaborative Filtering of Netnews", in the *Proceedings of the CSCW 1994 conference*, October 1994.
10. Kautz, H., Selman, B. and Shah, M.: "The Hidden Web", AI Magazine, Summer 1997. AAAI Press.

Analysis of Agent Programs Using Action Models

José and M. Ramírez

Dept. de Computación
Universidad Simón Bolívar
Apartado 89000, Caracas 1080-A, Venezuela
jramire@ldc.usb.ve

Abstract. The use of action models for the analysis of control programs can be useful for two reasons. First, it promises to deliver better tools for the simulation, verification and synthesis of control programs, and second it presents challenging problems for theories of action and knowledge. In this paper we use a theory of actions and knowledge developed elsewhere to analyze control programs for navigation tasks. We model both physical and sensing actions and establish conditions under which different control programs are executable and lead the agent to the intended goal.

Motivation

Consider a rectangular environment with an agent trying to reach a goal object . The agent has a position and orientation and can either move forward or rotate. He has also sensing capabilities that allow him to determine the position of the target object within certain constraints: e.g., that no other object is on the way, that the distance or angle to the goal object is within his reach, etc.

Program 1 Rotate and Move to Goal

$$reached(goal) \rightarrow done$$
$$see(goal) \land facing(goal) \rightarrow move$$
$$see(goal) \rightarrow rotate$$

Intuitively if these constraints are met, a simple control loop expressed as the sequence of condition-action pairs in Program 1 should lead the agent to the goal. Methodologies for building agent control programs of this form have been proposed by Brooks [4], Nilsson [14] and others. Such programs are normally tested on simulated worlds or in the real world. Here we aim to show that such programs can also be tested over sufficiently rich action models. An action model is a description of the effects of actions on both the envieonment (e.g., [8]) and

Helder Coelho (Ed.): IBERAMIA'98, LNAI 1484, pp. 183–194, 1998.

the agent's internal state or knowledge [12,15]. Since a control program is a mapping from knowledge to actions, an action model can be used to predict whether a control program is executable and whether it will lead the agent to its intended goal (see also [11,2]).

An action model is a good standpoint for the evaluation of the executability of a program, determining if the constraints associated with the actions are met, the conditions for the execution of the actions are achieved, and if such conditions can be evaluated. In some agent programming approaches the executability is guaranteed by imposing restrictions on the evaluation mechanism [13], establishing consistency rules [17] or providing mechanisms of detection of abnormal situations and fallback [5]. The verification that the program will lead the agent to its goal is also possible given an accurate action model that supports the assumption that the goal condition is reachable and that the actions performed will eventually make *true* that condition.

Action Theories

The model for actions below is a variation of a model reported in [3], which in turn is an extension of [8]. It comprises a *language* for describing actions in the form of a logical theory, and a *semantics* that maps such theories into sets of state trajectories s_0, s_1, s_2, ... where each s_i represents the state of the world at time i. The modeling language is built up from constant, function and predicate symbols distinguished by certain semantic properties:

1. *fixed symbols* have denotations that are fixed and *known* across time
2. *fluent symbols* have denotations that tend to persist
3. *action symbols* are used to denote actions

Fixed symbols include symbols like '3', '+', '=','$\sqrt{}$', etc., whose denotation is fixed and standard, and other symbols that we call *identifiers* that we regard as self-denoting.

For simplicity we assume that action symbols are *propositional symbols* denoting *actions*, and fluents are either constant or function symbols of arity one. Thus a relation like on(x,y) in the blocks world is modeled by an equality like loc$(x) = y$. Moreover, each functional fluent f will have a *type* of the form $D_f \rightarrow R_f$ meaning that the function denoted by f takes elements from D_f and maps them into R_f. The fluent loc for example may have a type $BLOCKS \rightarrow R$, where $BLOCKS$ is a set of block identifiers (*block_A*, *block_B*, etc) and R is the real line. The domain D_f of the functions denoted by functional fluents is assumed to be given by a set of identifiers. Terms, atoms, and formulas are defined from the constant, function, and predicate symbols in the standard way, except that the only terms of the form $f(t)$ when f is a fluent are the ones in which t belongs to D_f. Such terms, as well as the constant fluent symbols, are called *fluent terms*.

Action Rules The *action rules* are rules of the form

$$A \wedge C \to L$$

where A is an *action*, C is a formula not involving action symbols, and L is an *assignment* of the form $F := t$, where F is a fluent term and t is a term. For example, the action rules:

$$hit \wedge h > \Delta \to h := h - \Delta$$
$$hit \wedge h \leq \Delta \to h := 0$$

say that after hitting a nail with a hammer, its distance to the wall decreases by a fixed constant Δ if its original distance was greater than Δ, and to zero otherwise.

Definitions

New *terms* and *atoms* can be introduced in the language by means of *definitions*. For example, the atom close($block\_A$) can be defined to be true just when $|\mathsf{pos}(block\_A)| \leq 0.1$ is true, and similarly the term dist($block\_A$) can be defined as the value of the term $\mathsf{pos}(block\_A) - \mathsf{pos}(me)$. New terms t are defined by expressions of the form:

$$t \overset{\text{def}}{=} t'$$

meaning that the denotation (value) of t is the denotation of the term t'. Similarly, new atoms p can be defined by expressions of the form:

$$p \overset{\text{def}}{=} A$$
$$p \ \textbf{if} \ A$$

Defined terms and atoms can be used anywhere as long as they do not introduce circularities in the definitions.[1]

An *action theory* T is a triplet of the form $\langle D, A, O \rangle$, where D is a *domain theory* containing action rules and definitions, A is set of timed actions, and O is a set of observations. A timed action is an expression of the form $p[i]$, where p is an action symbol and i is a time point (a non-negative integer). An observation is an expression of the form $F[i]$, where F is a non-action formula and i is a time point. For example, the rules above about hitting a nail together with the actions $A = \{hit[0], hit[1], hit[2]\}$ and the observation $\mathsf{h}[0] = 5$ constitute an action theory. The semantics of such theories is given below. Provided that the value of the fixed symbol Δ is 2, this action theory for instance yields the conclusion $\mathsf{h}[3] = 0$.

---

[1] Circularities in the definitions mean circular chain of dependencies, where a defined expression *depends* on a second defined expression when the second appears in the definition of the first.

Semantics

The semantics maps an action theory into a set of state trajectories s_0, s_1, ...where s_i stands for the *state* of the world at time i.

States

Each state s is an *interpretation* over a domain D that assigns a denotation x^s to each expression x in the language in the standard way:

- $c^s \in D$, if c is a constant symbol
- $f^s \in D^n \to D$, if f is a function symb. with arity n
- $[f(\mathbf{t})]^s = f^s(\mathbf{t}^s)$
- ...

For standard symbols x (numerals, arithmetic operators and predicates, etc.), x^s is the standard denotation of x, while for identifiers $x^s = x$.

For terms t defined as $t = t'$, t^s is defined as t'^s, while for atoms p defined as $p = A$, p^s is defined as A^s.

Similarly, for atoms p defined by a collection of clauses of the form p **if** A, p^s is true iff A^s is true for some such clause. A state s *satisfies* a formula F, written $s \models F$, if $F^s = \mathbf{true}$.

Trajectories

A trajectory t is an infinite sequence of states s_0, s_1, ..., s_i, ... over a common domain D.

A trajectory s_0, s_1, ... is *admissible* relative to a given *domain theory* if the changes in every transition s_i to s_{i+1}, for $i \geq 0$, are supported by the rules; i.e.,

- $f^{s_{i+1}} = t^{s_i}$ if $f := t$ is supported in s_i, else $f^{s_{i+1}} = f^{s_i}$
- $f^{s_{i+1}}(c) = t^{s_i}$ if $f(c) := t$ is supported in s_i, else $f^{s_{i+1}}(c) = f^{s_i}(c)$ for each $c \in D_f$.

An assignment $f(t) := t'$ (f :=t) is supported in a state s_i when for some rule $F \to f(t) := t$ ($F \to f := t$) its antecedent F is true in s_i.

Models

The *models* of an action theory $T = \langle D, A, O \rangle$ are the admissible trajectories (relative to D) that are *compatible* with both the actions A and the observations O. A trajectory s_0, s_1, ... is *compatible* with the observations if for each expression $F[i] \in O$, F^{s_i} is true, and is *compatible with the actions* A iff for each action symbol p, p^{s_i} is true iff $p[i] \in A$ (i.e., actions not in A are assumed to be false).

For the example above, it is simple to check that a transition from a state s_i to a state s_{i+1} is admissible if:

- $h^{s_{i+1}} = h^{s_i}$, when hit^{s_i} is false or $h^{s_i} = 0$,
- $h^{s_{i+1}} = 0$, when hit^{s_i} is true and $h^{s_i} \leq \Delta$, or $h^{s_i} = 0$
- $h^{s_{i+1}} = h^{s_i} - \Delta$, when $h^{s_i} > \Delta$ and hit^{s_i} is true

In the resulting models s_0, s_1, $\ldots$, of the theory $h^{s_0} = 5$, $h^{s_1} = 3$, $h^{s_2} = 1$, and $h^{s_3} = 0$.

Control Theories

Control theories are similar to action theories except that actions are replaced by control programs. In other words, a control theory has the form $C = \langle D, P, O \rangle$, where D and O are as above, and P is a control program. A control program is a finite sequence of condition-action pairs:

$$c_1 \to a_1 \; ; \; c_2 \to a_2 \; ; \; c_3 \to a_3 \; ; \; \ldots$$

where each a_i is an action and each c_i is a formula which does not involve any actions. That sequence is evaluated from scratch at every time point $i \geq 0$, and the first action whose condition is true is executed. Later on we will consider two conditions such programs must satisfy: namely, the agent must have the *knowledge* to evaluate the conditions c_i, and if c_i is the first condition that evaluates to true, the *preconditions* of a_i must be true as well. The *models* of a control theory $T = \langle D, P, O \rangle$ are the admissible trajectories (relative to D) that are *compatible* with both the observations O and the program P where:

Definition 1. *A trajectory s_0, s_1, $\ldots$ is compatible with program P if for each state s_i and each action a, a is true in s_i if and only if $a = a_j$ and $c_j \to a_j$ is the first condition-action pair in P whose condition c_j is true in s_i.*

Going back to the example above, it is simple to check that the effect of the actions $hit[0]$, $hit[1]$ and $hit[2]$ can be achieved by the simple program $h > 0 \to hit$. Moreover, the program will achieve the effect $h = 0$ for *any* initial value of h as long as it can evaluate the condition $h > 0$ (see below).

Action Constraints

So far we have ignored that actions often have preconditions which may prevent the action to be executed. For example, a agent cannot move forward when facing a close obstacle, he cannot pick up an object if he does not have an empty hand, etc. We accommodate preconditions by extending action and control theories with a fourth component: *action constraints*. Action constraints are expressed by formulas of the form:

$$a \supset C$$

where a is an action, and C is a formula expressing a *precondition* for a.

The semantics of action constraints is very simple and follows the Strips model [ ]: an action theory is *executable* when no model of the theory contains a state s_i that violates an action constraint. For example, if *move* $\supset$ clear_front is a constraint, a theory in which a *move* is performed when clear_front is false is *non-executable*.

Knowledge

The executability of control theories is a bit more subtle than the executability of simple actions as the agent has to be able to *evaluate* the conditions in the program. A condition-action pair may be $facing(goal) \rightarrow move$, yet the agent may not *know* whether it is facing the goal or not (say because of limited visibility, presence of obstacles, etc). In such case the program is not executable.

In order to characterize the executability of programs we need to model what the agent *knows*. For that purpose we introduce an intensional operator K so that $K(x)$ for a term or (objective) formula x means that *the denotation of x is known* (see [7] for details, and [12] and [15] for related approaches). The knowledge of the agent will be grounded in the definitions in the theory and in the expressions x whose denotation are *observable* (e.g., the time of the day is observable when looking at the clock).[2] We express that the denotation of a term or formula x is observable to the agent by writing $obs(x)$. The conditions C that make certain terms or expressions x observable are encoded by means of defining clauses of the form (see Section 2)

$$obs(x) \textbf{ if } C$$

that indicate that $obs(x)$ is true when some such formula C is true. The truth of the epistemic expression $K(x)$ in a state s is determined by the denotation of x in all states s' that are possible from s given the definitions and *observables* that are true in s (i.e., the expressiones x s.t. $obs(x)$ is true in s):[3]

Definition 2. $K(x)$ *is true in s iff $x^s = x^{s'}$ for all states s' that are accessible from s, where s' is accesible from s if for all expressions x observable in $s, x^{s'} = x^s$.*

For example, if the atom *high* is defined in the theory as $h > 10$, the truth of the atom *high* will be *known* if the fluent h is *observable* (i.e., $K(high)$ follows from $obs(h)$). This is because for *all* states s' accessible from s we must have $h^{s'} = h^s$ (because h is observable), and hence $(h > 10)^{s'} = (h > 10)^s$.

More generally all observable expressions are always *known,* and if an expression x (atom or term) is defined in terms of expressions y that are known, x will be known as well. Provided with this model of knowledge, the *executability* of a program relative to a given domain theory can be characterized as follows:

Definition 3. *A program is executable if in every state s_i of every model s_0, s_1, ...1) all action constraints are satisfied, 2) all conditions c_0, c_1, ..., c_j up to and including the first condition that is true in s_i are known.*

In all programs that we consider, the action a_1 associated with the first condition c_1 will be the special action **done** that has no effects. We will be able to say that a program P *achieves* a formula (goal) G if in every model the action **done** becomes true at some point, and at such point G is true.

---

[2] The model of knowledge below is a simplification of the model in [3] which assumes that the agent also knows the rules in the theory.

[3] Notice that all states automatically satisfy the definitions.

Analysis of Simple Navigation Programs

Situation 1

We are ready to analyze the Program 2, an extended version of the program discussed in Section 1. For that we need to model each of the conditions and actions involved in the program.

Program 2 Amble and Move to Goal

$$reached(goal) \rightarrow done$$
$$see(goal) \land facing(goal) \rightarrow move$$
$$see(goal) \rightarrow rotate$$
$$\neg blocked \rightarrow move$$
$$\mathbf{true} \rightarrow rotate$$

First we assume a set of object identifiers OBJ, containing the identifier *goal* for the goal object, and a coordinate system with origin in the bottom-left corner of the rectangular environment shown in Figure 1. The position and orientation of the agent will be represented by three fluents xpos, ypos and angle. Following the denotation suggested by Latombe in [9] and assuming that the agent is a rigid *free-flying* object; xpos and ypos are the coordinates of the center of the agent with respect to the origin of the environment, and angle is the angle between the x-axis of the agent and the environment, restricted to the interval $(0, 2\pi]$ with modulo 2π arithmetic. The effects of the two actions on these fluents are captured by the rules:

$$rotate \rightarrow \mathsf{angle} := \mathsf{angle} + \delta angle$$
$$move \rightarrow \mathsf{xpos} := \mathsf{xpos} + \delta dist \cos(\mathsf{angle})$$
$$move \rightarrow \mathsf{ypos} := \mathsf{ypos} + \delta dist \sin(\mathsf{angle})$$

where $\delta angle$ and $\delta dist$ are two known constants standing for the angular and linear step sizes. The agent has no information about the absolute location of the objects (or itself), yet it can determine the *relative* positions $dist(obj)$ and angles $angle(obj)$ of the objects obj he can 'see' (this is the so-called *indexical* information [10]). Given that the *absolute* position of the objects is captured by the fluents xloc and yloc, their position and angles relative to the agent can be defined as follows:

$$dist(obj) \stackrel{\text{def}}{=} \sqrt{(\mathsf{xpos} - \mathsf{xloc}(obj))^2 + (\mathsf{ypos} - \mathsf{yloc}(obj))^2}$$
$$angle(obj) \stackrel{\text{def}}{=} \mathsf{angle} + \theta(obj)$$
$$\theta(obj) \stackrel{\text{def}}{=} \sin^{-1} \frac{\mathsf{ypos} - \mathsf{yloc}(obj)}{dist(obj)}$$

where *obj* stands for each of the identifiers in the set OBJ.

With these definitions, some of the conditions in the program can be modeled by the schemas:

$$facing(obj) \overset{\text{def}}{=} angle(obj) \leq \delta angle$$

$$reached(obj) \overset{\text{def}}{=} facing(obj) \wedge close(obj)$$

$$close(obj) \overset{\text{def}}{=} dist(obj) \leq \delta dist$$

The condition *see(goal)* in the program is special because it aims to model the *perceptual* machinery of the agent. If we want to predict how the agent is going to behave, we have to provide a model for the condition *see*.[4] A very simple model assumes that the agent is going to *see* any object that is within a certain maximal distance (*vdist*) and a certain maximal angle (*vangle*):

$$see(obj) \overset{\text{def}}{=} dist(obj) \leq vdist \wedge angle(obj) \leq vfield$$

We assume that the *effect* of 'seeing' an object is to make its relative distance and an angle *observable:*

$$obs(dist(obj)) \overset{\text{def}}{=} see(obj)$$

$$obs(angle(obj)) \overset{\text{def}}{=} see(obj)$$

In addition, the agent always knows whether it's seeing an object or not:

$$obs(see(obj)) \overset{\text{def}}{=} \textbf{true}$$

Finally we assume that the action *move* has the precondition

$$move \supset \neg blocked$$

where *blocked* is defined by the collection of clauses:

$$blocked \textbf{ if } facing(obj) \wedge close(obj)$$

obtained by replacing *obj* by each identifier in OBJ, including the walls that are modeled as abstacles.

We are ready to prove that under some conditions, the program (2) will be *executable* and will *achieve* the goal *reached(goal)*. The conditions that we assume are: $OBJ = \{goal\}$ (no other object but the goal; in particular no walls or obstacles), $vfield = 360^0$ (full visibility in all directions), *initially dist(goal)* $\leq$ *vdist* (goal object is initially within the linear visibility range). Two other natural conditions that we assume are $\delta angle < vfield/2$ and $\delta dist < vdist$.

---

[4] Note that *see* is modeled as a 'defined condition' rather than as a 'knowledge gathering action' as in [15]. In this way, the agent continously gathers information from its surrounding (when certain conditions hold) without requiring its active participation in the form of deliberate actions.

We prove first that the action constraint $move \supset \neg blocked$ is satisfied in all states s_i of every model s_0, s_1, ... of the resulting control theory. Indeed, since there is only one object $goal$, $blocked$ is true iff $heading(goal)$ and $close(goal)$ are true. Yet that means that $reached(goal)$ is true, and then, that $move$ is false. Thus, $move \supset \neg blocked$ is always satisfied. We prove now that the agent has always the *knowledge* to evaluate the conditions in the program. Let us prove first that the truth of $reached(goal)$ is always known. We consider two cases: when $see(goal)$ is true and when $see(goal)$ is false. In the second case, $reached(goal)$ must be false because the restrictions $\delta angle < vfield/2$ and $\delta dist < vdist$ guarantee that $\neg see(goal)$ implies $\neg close(goal) \vee \neg facing(goal)$. Likewise, in the first case, $dist(goal)$ and $angle(goal)$ must be known, and hence, the atoms $close(goal)$ and $facing(goal)$, as well as $reached(goal)$, must be known too. As a result, we get that if $see(goal)$ is false, $reached(goal)$ must be false, and if $see(goal)$ is true, $reached(goal)$ must be known. Since the state of the atom $see(goal)$ is always known, this means that the state of $reached(goal)$ will be known too. Similar arguments suffice to prove that the other conditions ($facing(goal)$ and $\neg blocked$) will also be known.

We are left to show that, under the assumptions above, the program will lead the agent to a state where $reached(goal)$ is true. Actually, under those assumptions $see(goal)$ must be initially true. Furthermore, since there is full angular visibility, and the agent only moves in the direction of the goal, once $see(goal)$ becomes true, it remains true throughout. That means, among other things, that the agent cannot be rotating forever as, eventually, the condition $facing(goal)$ will become true. Yet once this condition becomes true, the agent will move towards the goal, and every time the agent moves, $dist(goal)$ will decrease [5]. This does *not* mean, however, that once $facing(goal)$ becomes true it remains true until $goal$ is reached. Yet, even if $facing(goal)$ becomes false, the distance to the goal decreases and the program will bring back the agent to a state where $facing(goal)$ is true again. Thus, eventually, in a finite number of steps, $reached(goal)$ will be true.

Situation 2

If the assumption that the visibility range is 360^0 is changed and a limited range is used instead, the Program (2) remains executable but does not necessarily lead the agent to the goal. This is because, in the new context, it is no longer true that once $see(goal)$ is true, it remains true throughout. Indeed, if the agent is not facing the goal, it will rotate, and at certain point $see(goal)$ may become false. At that point, the agent will move away from the goal and won't come back (since we are assuming that there are no other objects such as walls).

There is however a simple modification to the program that avoids this problem. It consists in the introduction of two different rotations, a left rotation and a right rotation. Under the conditions above, even with a limited visibility range,

---

[5] this involves some trigonometrical arguments based on the fact that the maximum $\delta angle$ must be 60^0

Program 3 Specialization of the action *rotate*

$$reached(goal) \rightarrow done$$
$$see(goal) \wedge facing(goal) \rightarrow move$$
$$see(goal) \wedge on-left(obj) \rightarrow rotate\text{-}l$$
$$see(goal) \wedge on-right(obj) \rightarrow rotate\text{-}r$$
$$\neg blocked \rightarrow move$$
$$true \rightarrow rotate\text{-}l$$

---

the new program leads the agent to the goal. The action rules for the two new actions are:

$$rotate\text{-}r \rightarrow \mathsf{angle} + \delta angle$$
$$rotate\text{-}l \rightarrow \mathsf{angle} - \delta angle$$

and the definitions of the new conditions are:

$$on\text{-}left(obj) \stackrel{\mathrm{def}}{=} 0 \leq angle(obj) \leq vfield/2$$
$$on\text{-}right(obj) \stackrel{\mathrm{def}}{=} (360 - vfield/2) \leq angle(obj) \leq 360$$

Situation 3

In the presence of other objects, i.e., when OBJ includes other objects besides *goal*, the situation changes significantly. First of all, the program (1) is not executable, as in certain situations a *move* can be triggered in situations in which the precondition $\neg blocked$ is false. This however is easy to fix: we just need to introduce the condition $\neg blocked$ among the conditions for *move*.

The other problem (or feature!) is that the way that the model defines $see(obj)$ implicitly assumes that all objects are *transparent*; namely, the visibility of the agent (i.e., the definition of $see(goal)$) depends only on the linear and angular distance to the goal; without taking into account the presence of objects that can be on the way.

This all implies that if $see(goal)$ is always true (say because the parameters $vfield$ and $vdist$ are sufficiently large), the agent will *move* only when $facing(goal)$ and $\neg blocked$ are both true, and will *rotate* otherwise. However, when the obstacle in the way is perpendicular to the line that joins the agent to the goal, rotations alone cannot establish the conjunction $facing(goal) \wedge \neg blocked$ (because in such arrangement $facing(goal)$ will be true exactly when $facing(obst)$ is true, where *obst* is the obstacle identifier). Thus in this case, the program will be make the robot *rotate* forever. A solution to this problem can be obtained by replacing the third line of the Program 2 with the line:

$$see(goal) \wedge \neg will\_block \rightarrow rotate$$

where $will\_block$, defined as:[6]

$$will\_block \text{ if } close(obj) \wedge angle(obj) \leq 2\delta angle$$

detects rotations that will make the condition $blocked$ true, and in those cases, make the agent take a step away from the obstacle.

Using the resulting program the agent exhibits the typical behavior of a fly trying to get pass a window [7]. The correctness of the resulting program is slighlty complex and depends on some topological constraints on the set of objects (the presence of separations among the objects, etc).

The modeling of 'opaque' objects as opposed to transparent objects requires a redefinition of $see(obj)$ to:

$$see(obj) \stackrel{\text{def}}{=} dist(obj) \leq vdist \wedge$$
$$angle(obj) \leq vfield(obj) \wedge \neg occluded(obj)$$

where the $occluded$ predicate must be defined in terms of the 'cells' occupied by the objects in OBJ and the location $\{\mathsf{xpos}, \mathsf{ypos}\}$ of the agent. In the presence of such objects, the agent can be trapped in trajectories in which the goal object is never visible, and thus, in which the program will not lead the robot to the goal. This can be seen using the simulator built to experiment with the theories, models and programs posed in this work.

Conclusions and Related Work

We have used a theory of actions and knowledge to analyze control programs for navigation tasks, modeling both physical and sensing actions and establishing the conditions under which different programs are executable and lead the agent to the goal. The use of action models can also be useful for the *construction* of control programs. Nilsson's [14], for example, advocates a methodology for writing teleological control programs in which the actions in one line are supposed to contribute to the realization of the conditions in the preceding lines. This design criterion can be formalized in this framework as:

Definition 4. *A program P is teleoreactive if in all models s_0, s_1, s_2, ..., every state s_i that makes $c_j \rightarrow a_j$ for $j > 0$ the first applicable condition-action pair in s_i, is followed after a finite number of time points by a state $s_{i+\Delta}$ that makes $c_k \rightarrow a_k$ the first applicable condition-action pair where $k < j$.*

Our analysis shows clearly that, even in simple programs as program 1, that satisfies the *Universal* property of TeleoReactive programs [13], there are conditions that violates the TeleoReactive principle, since once the robot start moving, $facing(goal)$ may become temporarily false. However, these execution errors won't prevent (in this case) that the goal condition will ultimately be achieved.

---

[6] For the condition $will\_block$ to be known, $2\delta angle$ should be smaller than $vfield$.

[7] This can be observed using the simulator available at `http://www.ldc.usb.ve/~92-24791/TR/`; snapshots were not included due to space limitations.

For this type of models to be useful for the analysis of real robot plans, however, both richer control structures (e.g., see [11,7,2]) and uncertainty (e.g., [1,16,7]) would need to be accommodated. We plan to explore some of these issues, as well as the automatical construction of robot plans, elsewhere.

References

1. F. Bacchus, J. Halpern, and H. Levesque. Reasoning about noisy sensors in the situation calculus. In *Proceedings IJCAI-95*, pages 1933–1940, 1995. 194
2. C. Baral and T. Son. Relating theories of actions and reactive robot control. In *Proc. AAAI 96 Workshop on Theories of action, Planning and Robot Control: Bridging the gap*, 1996. 184, 194
3. Blind. A model for actions knowledge and contingent plans. submitted to AAAI-97, 1997. 184, 188
4. R. Brooks. The behavior language user's guide. Technical report, AI Lab., MIT, 1989. 183
5. R.A. Brooks. The behavior language; user's guide. Technical report, MIT AI Lab, 1990. 184
6. R.E. Fikes and N. Nilsson. STRIPS: a new approach to the application of theorem proving to problem solving. *Artificial Intelligence*, 2:189–208, 1971. 187
7. H. Geffner and J. Wainer. Towards a practial model of actions and knowledge. Submitted, 1998. 188, 194
8. M. Gelfond and V. Lifschitz. Representing action and change by logic programs. *J. of Logic Programming*, 17:301–322, 1993. 183, 184
9. J.C. Latombe. *Robot Motion Planning*. KAP, 1991. 189
10. Y. Lesperance and H. Levesque. Indexical knowledge and robot action. *Artificial Intelligence*, 73:69–116, 1995. 189
11. H.J. Levesque. What is planning in the presence of sensing? In *Proc. AAAI 96 Workshop on Theories of action, Planning and Robot Control: Bridging the gap*, 1996. 184, 194
12. R. Moore. A formal theory of knowledge and action. In J. Hobbs and R. Moore, editors, *Formal Theories of the Commonsense World*. Ablex Publishing Co., Norwood, N.J., 1985. 184, 188
13. N. Nilsson. Teleo-reactive programs for agent control. *JAIR*, 1:139–158, 1994. 184, 193
14. N. Nilsson. Teleoreactive programs for agent control. *Journal of Artificial Intelligence Research*, 1:139–158, 1994. 183, 193
15. R. Scherl and H. Levesque. The frame problem and knowledge producing actions. In *Proceedings of AAAI-93*, pages 689–695. MIT Press, 1993. 184, 188, 190
16. M. Shanahan. Noise and the commonsense informatic situation for mobile robot. In *Proceedings AAAI-96*, pages 1098–1103, 1996. 194
17. Y. Shoham. Agent oriented programming. Technical report, Robotics Lab, Computer Science Department, Stanford University, 1993. 184

Bayesian Networks for Reliability Analysis of Complex Systems

José Gerardo Torres-Toledano[1] and Luis Enrique Sucar[2]

[1]Instituto de Investigaciones Eléctricas, Unidad de Procesos Térmicos
Apdo.Postal 1-475 C.P. 62001, Cuernavaca, Morelos, México
jgtorres@iie.org.mx.
[2]ITESM - Campus Morelos., Departamento de Computación
Apdo.Postal 99-C, C.P. 62050, Cuernavaca, Morelos, México
esucar@campus.mor.itesm.mx.

Abstract. This paper presents an extension of Bayesian networks (BN) applied to reliability analysis. We developed a general methodology for reliability modeling of complex systems based on Bayesian networks. A reliability structure represented as a reliability block diagram is transformed to a Bayesian network representation, and with this, the reliability of the system can be obtained using probability propagation techniques. This allows for modeling complex systems, such as a bridge type, and dependencies between failures, which are difficult to obtain with conventional reliability analysis techniques. The relation between a BN and fault tree, and some advantages of BN for modeling system reliability are shown. We present some examples of the application of this methodology in solving difficult cases, which occur in reliability analysis of power plants.

1. Introduction

Complex industrial plants and equipment for critical applications, such as power plants, require a high reliability, i.e., a very low probability of failure. For this, there are statistical techniques that can predict the reliability of a complex system based on its structure and the reliability of each component. Some traditional techniques for reliability analysis have several important limitations, including the assumption that all the failures are independent and that the rate of failure is constant (exponential model). Also, building the model used to calculate the reliability of the system is a difficult and complex task, so an expert reliability engineer is usually required.

In general, failure prediction is a difficult problem. However, for a given time period (mission time), the probability of failure can be obtained by applying probability theory. In the context of this work, reliability is the probability that the equipment performs its intended functions satisfactorily or without failure, for a

Helder Coelho (Ed.): IBERAMIA'98, LNAI 1484, pp. 195-206, 1998.

mission time, under specific design and environmental conditions. The reliability of complex equipment depends on the individual reliability of its elements.

The motivation for developing this work is to obtain a computational method that can incorporate explicitly dependencies between failures and include the effects of maintenance in the reliability analysis of complex systems in operation. A Bayesian network is used to represent the system reliability structure, and obtain its reliability via probability propagation. With this representation the limitations of other techniques are avoided, so it is possible to manage dependencies and non-exponential distributions.

This paper is divided in seven parts. The second part summarizes the theory of Bayesian networks, and the third one, general aspects of reliability analysis. The fourth part focuses on dependency between failures in reliability analysis and the fifth part presents a procedure for systems reliability modeling supported by Bayesian networks. The following part presents an application to reliability analysis of power plants. Finally, the conclusions and future work are presented.

2. Bayesian Network

Bayesian networks are directed acyclic graphs (DAG), see figure 1, in which the nodes represent propositions (or variables), the arcs signify direct dependencies between the linked propositions, and the strength of these dependencies are quantified by conditional probabilities [8]. Such graphical structures, known also as belief networks, are used for representing expert knowledge. The graph represents a set of random variables and its dependency and independency relations. It is used to estimate the posterior probability of unknown variables given other variables (evidence), through a process known as *probabilistic reasoning*. This generates recommendations or conclusions about a particular problem, and can be used for explanation, the process of communicating the relevant information to the user.

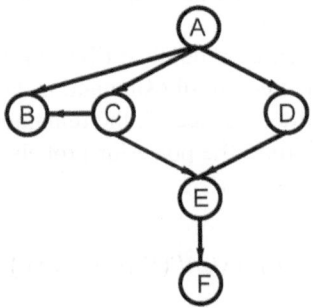

Fig. 1. Example of a directed acyclic graph

2.1 Probability Propagation

The topology of a Bayesian network represents the dependency relations between the variables implicated. It represents which variables are conditionally independent given another variable. Following figure 1, C is conditionally independent of D, given E if:

$$P(C|D,E)=P(C|E)$$

An advantage of Bayesian networks is that they provide a compact representation of the joint probability distribution of the variables. This probability can be expressed as a product of the conditional distributions of each node given its direct influences (parents) in the graph. Hence, letting $pa(t)$ denote the parents of node t, the graph implies that the joint distribution $P(T)$ has the form:

$$P(T) = \prod_{t \in T} P(t|pa(t)) \tag{1}$$

This is also known as a recursive model with respect to some DAG. Thus, for example, the model for figure 1 is equivalent to:

$$P(A,B,C,D,E,F) = P(F|E) \cdot P(E|C,D) \cdot P(D|A) \cdot P(C|A) \cdot P(B|C,A) \cdot P(A) \tag{2}$$

The reasoning mechanism is called probabilistic reasoning. It consists in instantiating the input variables (symptoms or evidences) and propagating their effect through the network to update the probability of the hypothesis variables. The propagation procedure is based on Bayes theorem and the structure of dependencies of the network.

Propagation in trees. A tree structured network has only one node, called root node, without parents and the rest of the nodes have only one parent.

In a tree, any node (C) can be a point of division in two independent sub-trees. A sub-tree contains as root the node of division and is denoted by (-), the data contained in this sub-tree represents the evidence V^-, the remainder of the tree is denoted by (+) with evidence V^+ [7]. Therefore, the posterior probability of any variable (C) can be obtained by Bayes theorem as:

$$P(C_i|V)=P(C_i)P(V^+,V^-|C_i)/P(V) \tag{3}$$

But since both sub-trees are independent, and with Bayes theorem further applied, we have:

$$P(C_i|V) = \propto P(C_i|V^+)P(V^-|C_i) \tag{4}$$

Where α is a normalization constant. If we define:

$$\pi(C_i) = P(C_i \mid V^+) \tag{5}$$

$$\lambda(C_i) = P(V^-|C_i) \tag{6}$$

Replacing the equations (5) and (6) in (4), we obtain:

$$P(C_i \mid V) = \propto \pi(C_i)\ \lambda(C_i) \tag{7}$$

The above equation offers a way to update the probabilities of any node C as a product of the predictive evidential support (π) from all non-descendant nodes of C mediated by C's parent, and the retrospective evidential support (λ) from C's descendants.

The propagation procedure can be implemented through communications between neighboring nodes, by local operations, and by sending messages between connected nodes in the network [9].

Propagation in polytrees or simply networks connected. A polytree is a network in which a node can have more than one parent, without multiple paths between nodes (figure 2).

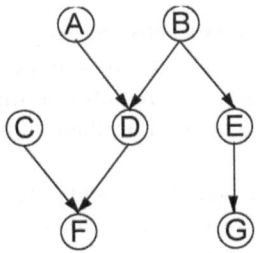

Fig. 2. Example of a polytree

The propagation of probabilities in polytree structures is very similar to the case of tree networks [7]. The principal difference is that polytrees require the conditional probability of each node given all its parents nodes. In a similar way that for tree structured networks, for the case of polytrees an expression to obtain the probability of any node given some evidence can be deduced [9].

Consider a typical fragment of a singly-connected network, consisting of a node B_i, the set of all parents of B_i, $V^+ = \{V_1^+, \cdots V_n^+\}$, and the set of all children of B_i, $V^- = \{V_1^-, \cdots V_m^-\}$. As before, let V be the total evidence obtained, so that:

$$P(B_i|V) = \alpha P(B_i|V_1^+, \cdots V_n^+) P(V_1^-|B_i) \cdots\cdots P(V_m^-|B_i) \tag{8}$$

Dividing the polytree in two parts, V^+ and V^-, it is possible to obtain a mechanism for local probability propagation similar to the one for trees.

The algorithm for probability propagation in polytrees is very efficient, so the computation time required is nearly proportional to the diameter (largest path) of the network. For multiconnected networks probability propagation is more complex and there are several algorithms based con clustering, conditioning and stochastic simulation [9, 7].

3. Reliability Analysis

In reliability analysis, we can distinguished three characteristic types of failures which may be inherent in the behavior of the equipment [1]. First, there are the failures which occur early in the life of a component. These are called *early failures* and in the majority of the cases are the result of a poor manufacturing and quality control techniques during the production process. Second, there are failures which are caused by wear out of parts. These occur in equipment only if it is not properly maintained or not maintained at all. Third, there are the so called "chance" failures. These failures are caused by sudden cumulative stress beyond the design strength of the component. Chance failures occur at random intervals, irregularly and unexpectedly.

Reliability analysis differentiates between early, wear out, and chance failures for two main reasons. First, each one of these types of failures follows a specific statistical distribution and therefore requires a different mathematical treatment. Second, different methods must be used for their elimination or correction.

In reliability analysis of a complex system, is nearly impossible to model the complete system. The logical process to accomplish this is to divide the system in smaller elements, units, subsystems, or components. The main assumption is that every entity has two states, success and failure (although some times three or more states are needed). The subdivision generates a "block diagram" that is similar to the description of systems in operation [3]. The models are then fixed to this structure, and they utilize probabilistic techniques to calculate the reliability of the system in terms of the reliability of the subdivisions [10].

To evaluate the adequate performance, an observation of inadequate performance in operation is required, therefore, the frequency at which malfunctions and failures occurs it is used as a parameter for a mathematical formulation of reliability. This parameter is called *failure rate*; it is usually measured in number of failures per unit operating hour. Its reciprocal value is called the ***mean time between failures*** and this is measured in hours [1].

4. Dependency between Failures in Reliability Analysis

Our objective is to build a versatile computational tool capable of evaluating the reliability of complex systems during its useful life or wear. Traditionally, fault trees [3] are used for reliability analysis. However, this technique has its limitations. It usually assumes independent events and it is difficult to model dependencies between events or faults.

Dependent events can be found in reliability analysis in the following cases:

1) **Common causes**. A condition or event which provokes multiple elemental failures is called a common cause. For instance, fire or flood may cause simultaneous failures of sets of components. Thus, under these conditions, component failures are no longer independent. Other sources of common cause are aging, human error and system environment.

2) **Mutually exclusive primary events**. Consider the basic events: "switch fails to close" and "switch fails to open". These two basic events are *mutually exclusive*, i.e., the occurrence of one basic event precludes the other. Thus, we encounter dependent basic events when a fault tree involves mutually exclusive basic events.

3) **Standby redundancies.** When an operating component fails, a standby component is put into operation, and the redundant configuration continues to function. Thus, components failures are not statistically independent, since the failure of an operating component causes a standby component to be more susceptible to failure.

4) **Components supporting loads**. Assume that a set of components supports loads such as stress, current, etc. A failure of one component increases the load supported by the other components. Consequently, the remaining components are more likely to fail, and we can not assume statistical independence of these components.

Bayesian networks allow to represent explicitly dependencies between failures as above mentioned. We suggest to employ this approach to solve reliability analysis of complex systems, in particular when there are dependent failures.

5. Procedure for System Reliability Modeling

The procedure for reliability analysis based on Bayesian networks consists in defining the conditional probability matrix equivalent to the series and parallel configurations of simple systems, as the AND/OR gates utilized in fault trees. Being the reliability block diagram a methodology commonly used for reliability analysis, we will refer it to introduce the representation with BN. Reliability analysis begins with the construction of a reliability block diagram of the system. This is a graphic representation where every component is represented as a block or rectangle connected to other components, in series or in parallel form.

Considering a series or parallel system with only two components, figure 3, its representation as a Bayesian network is shown in figure 4, with one additional node, X. We use circles for representing series systems and squares for parallel systems. The X node is a binary variable that represents the system state, success or fault.

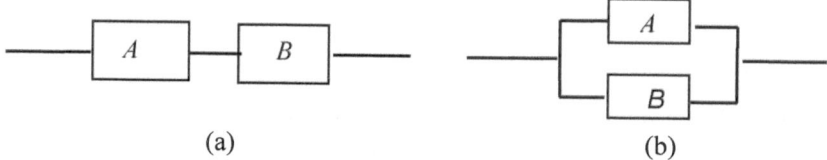

(a)   (b)

Fig. 3. System reliability block diagram: (a) series, (b) parallel

(a)   (b)

Fig. 4. Bayesian network for two components: (a) series system, (b) parallel system

According to equation (1), the joint probability of the series system is:

$$P(X,A,B) = P(X/A,B)\ P(A,B) \tag{9}$$

where the elements of the columns of the conditional probability matrix, $P(X/A,B)$, are the combination of the parent nodes states: A,B are operating, A is operating and B is failed, A is failed and B is operating, and A, B are failed. The first row represents the success probability of the system given the information of A and B. This matrix is equivalent to an AND gate used in fault trees:

$$P(X/A, B) = \begin{bmatrix} 1 & 0 & 0 & 0 \\ 0 & 1 & 1 & 1 \end{bmatrix} \qquad (10)$$

The elements of the $P(A,B)$ matrix are taken from the marginal probability $P(A)$ and $P(B)$, for example $P(a'\,b)$ is the probability that component A is in a failure state and component B in an operating state.

$$P(A, B) = \begin{bmatrix} a\,b \\ a'\,b \\ a\,b' \\ a'\,b' \end{bmatrix} \qquad (11)$$

In the parallel case only the conditional probability matrix is modified, such matrix is equivalent to an OR gate [11]:

$$P(X/A, B) = \begin{bmatrix} 1 & 1 & 1 & 0 \\ 0 & 0 & 0 & 1 \end{bmatrix} \qquad (12)$$

Following the above scheme, the generalization for multiple components is not difficult. For instance, for a three component system, which requires at least two components functioning, the system representation using a BN is shown in figure 5, and the probability matrix will be:

$$P(X/A, B, C) = \begin{bmatrix} 1\,1\,1\,1\,0\,0\,0\,0 \\ 0\,0\,0\,0\,1\,1\,1\,1 \end{bmatrix} \qquad (13)$$

Thus, for simple systems (series/parallel combination without dependent failures) we obtain a BN that has an inverted tree structure (polytree). This is equivalent to a fault tree and will give the same results. However, the BN model could be extended to represent more complex systems, that are difficult, if not impossible, to model with fault trees.

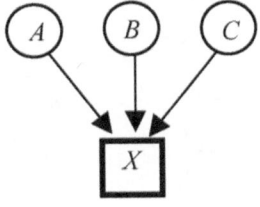

Fig. 5. Bayesian network for a series 3 component system

6. Applications to Reliability Analysis

6.1 Complex Combination of Series-Parallel System

In order to exemplify the advantages of using BN, consider the schematic reliability block diagram in figure 6. This system is known as bridge type. The system is operable if at least one of the paths AC, BD, AED o BEC is good.

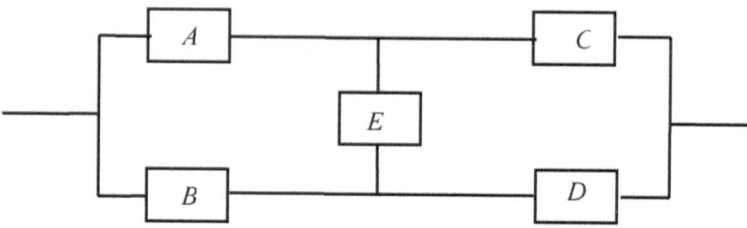

Fig. 6. Reliability block diagram

The usual method to compute the reliability of a bridge system is selecting a component, and consider two alternatives: the component is working (good) or the component has failed (bad) [1]. In this case the E element is chosen, which is the best choice to simplify the solution. The system is divided in two subsystems, one when E is considered as good and other where E has failed.

When a set of subsystems are defined utilizing series-parallel connected configurations, the total reliability could be evaluate applying Bayes' theorem. The probability of success of the complete system in terms of conditional probabilities is $P(X) = P(X/E= good) P(E=good) + P(X/E=bad) P(E=bad)$.

The previous method is laborious. However, using a BN approach the solution is simplified so the system reliability can be obtained from single network. A graphic representation for the bridge system in the scheme of BN is shown in figure 7.

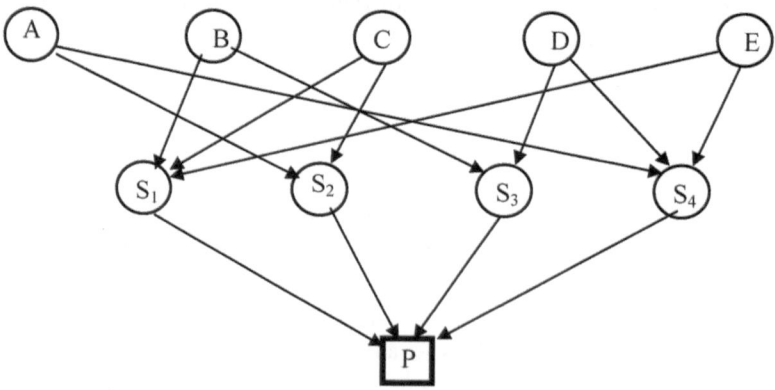

Fig. 7. Bayesian Network of a complex system

For example, if the A,B,C,D, and E components have 0.1 as success probability value, the system reliability is **0.9785** and its failure probability **0.0215**. To obtain these values, we apply probability propagation techniques (in this case, it is a multiconnected network) to the network in figure 7, obtaining the probabilities for the intermediate nodes (S_i) and for the complete system (P). For this particular case, the results for the subsystems are:

$$P(S_1) = P(S_4) = (0.729, 0.271)$$
$$P(S_2) = P(S_3) = (0.810, 0.190)$$

We have developed an algorithm for building automatically a BN representation from the reliability block diagram [6].

6.2. Reliability of Dependent Components

Suppose three independent sources of shock are present in the environment [2]. A shock from source 1 destroys component 1; it occurs at a random time U_1, where $P[U_1 > t] = e^{-\lambda_1 t}$. A shock from source 2 destroys component 2; it occurs at random time U_2, $P[U_2 > t] = e^{-\lambda_2 t}$. Finally a shock from source 3 destroys *both* components, it occurs at random time U_{12}, where $P[U_{12} > t] = e^{-\lambda_{12} t}$. Thus the random life length T_1 of component 1 satisfies:

$$T_1 = min(U_1, U_{12}),$$

while the random life length T_2 of component 2 satisfies:

$$T_2 = min(U_2, U_{12})$$

A BN model for this example of dependent failures is shown in figure 8, where S_i represents the *i-th* source and C_i the *i-th* component. The system states are assigned to X. In this case, all the conditional probability matrix are defined equivalent to AND gates, because a series system is considered.

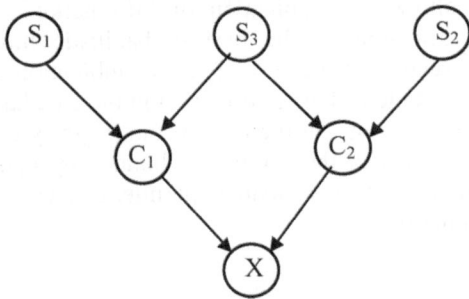

Fig. 8. Bayesian network of a system with common cause failures

The reliability and failure probability of the system are obtained by applying the conventional procedure for probability propagation for multiconnected networks [7]. Reliability results for particular values are shown in table 1.

Node	Reliability
S_1	0.9417
S_2	0.9048
S_3	0.9980
C_1	0.9398
C_2	0.9030
X	**0.8504**

Table 1. Reliability (probability of success) for a system with common cause failures

7. Conclusions

Bayesian networks are an alternative technique for the systems reliability analysis with an ample potential of application. They are based on the management of conditional probability and on probability propagation. BN have a strong similarity to fault trees. In fact, fault trees could be viewed as a particular case of BN. One of the advantages of using Bayesian networks is the explicit representation of dependencies.

In this paper we have presented a general methodology for modeling reliability of complex systems based on Bayesian networks. A reliability structure represented as a reliability block diagram can be transformed to a Bayesian network representation, and with this, the reliability of the system can be obtained using probability propagation techniques. This allows for modeling complex systems, such as a bridge type, and dependencies between failures, which are difficult to represent with conventional reliability analysis techniques.

This approach also allows a combination of information sources (objective and subjective) and the selection of the best probabilistic model according to the distribution and the structure of the system. The combination of information sources could be applied to avoid the lack of information in the data bases of certain areas for reliability analysis. For example, in the case of the majority of the power plants, the information is augmented with the estimates obtained by operators or maintenance personal. The combination of these sources permits to increase the precision of the system reliability estimation.

Another future direction for research is to use this type of models for design. In this case, we can set the desired reliability of the system and obtain the required reliability of each compnent, using the same probability propagation techniques.

References

[1] Igor Bazovsky, (1961). Reliability Theory and Practice. Prentice Hall.
[2] R. E Barlow and R.F. Proschan, (1975). Statistical Theory of reliability and Life Testing Probability Models. Holt, Rinehart and Winston, Inc.
[3] Ralph R. Fullwood and Robert E. Hall, (1988). Probabilistic risk Assessment in the nuclear power industry, Fundamentals & Applications. Pergamon Press.
[4] E. J. Henley and H. Kumamoto, (1992). Probabilistic risk Assessment. IEEE Press.
[5] IEEE, (197). IEEE Guide for General Principles of Reliability Analysis of Nuclear Power Generating Station Safety Systems. ANSI/IEEE, Std 352-1987.
[6] G. Mojica-Ortiz, G. Torres-Toledano, L.E. Sucar, Intelligent System for Reliability Analysis using Bayesian Networks, 4th WCES, 641-648, 1998.
[7] Richard E. Neapolitan, (1990). Probabilistic Reasoning in Expert Systems, theory and algorithms. John Wiley & Sons.
[8] Judea Pearl, (1986). Fusion, Propagation, and Structuring in Belief Networks. Artificial Intelligence 29(3), 241-288.
[9] Judea Pearl, (1988). Probabilistic Reasoning in Intelligent Systems: Network of Plausible Inference. Morgan Kaufmann.
[10] Martin L. Shooman, (1968). Probabilistic Reliability: An Engineering Approach. McGraw-Hill.
[11] M. Schwarzblat, J. Arellano, G. Martínez, (1980). Análisis de confiabilidad en el IIE, Seminario sobre confiabilidad en plantas termoeléctricas, Instituto de Investigaciones Eléctricas, México (in Spanish).

Temporal Representation and Reasoning for Dynamic Environments

Eva Onaindia and Miguel Rebollo

Dpto. Sistemas Informaticos y Computacion
Universidad Politecnica de Valencia
Camino de Vera s/n 46071 Valencia, Spain
onaindia@dsic.upv.es

Abstract. Most of real AI applications developed under dynamic environments have to interact with the external world, deal with imprecision of data and make estimations about the possible data occurrence at different instants of time. A temporal model suitable for this type of domains must provide a representation framework able to capture external observations, update this information in the internal state application and deduce how these changes influence the application evolution. Reasoning processes for dynamic domains are generally quite complex due to the imprecision and variability of data. This usually leads to situations where the available time to update all the necessary information before processing the following change is not enough. When this occurs the internal model is not more consistent with the external world thus leading to dysfunctions in the system.

This paper presents a suitable temporal model for applications running under dynamic environments. The proposed framework allows to keep the world model consistent with the external world as well as the prediction of future consequences. All reasoning algorithms are designed as a search process between two time-points allowing to obtain approximate responses for a temporal query instead of optimal long time-consuming solutions.

Content Areas: Temporal Reasoning, Knowledge Representation

1 Introduction

Most of real AI applications developed under dynamic environments are used to model the behaviour of applications that interact with the external world. Three main features define the behaviour of these applications:

a) The necessity of relating data to a clock time in order to time-stamp external observations with its acquisition date.
b) The problem of keeping the world model consistent with the external world and to predict the possible future consequences that may derive from the application evolution.

Helder Coelho (Ed.): IBERAMIA'98, LNAI 1484, pp. 207–218, 1998.
© Springer-Verlag Berlin Heidelberg 1998

c) The necessity of efficient data management procedures to assert, remove, update or retrieve temporal information at any time.

First item states the necessity of dealing not only with qualitative constraints [9] but also with metric information [2] [3]. This expressiveness sometimes needs to be augmented to include the possibility of expressing alternative situations that may arise in the application evolution. The Temporal Constraint Networks (TCN) [3] is the most popular approach to handle with disjunctive temporal constraints. But the problem of checking consistency in a general TCN is NP-hard [5] and even algorithms for local consistency may result in exponential costs. In the particular environment we are concerned to the possibility of expressing disjunctive situations is important but this issue can be tackled by choosing an appropriate representational framework which allows for efficient reasoning algorithms.

Other approaches as temporal graphs or time-map managers [2] seem more adequate for applications which handle large amounts of information and where data updatings are frequently produced [10]. This is because algorithms for temporal graphs do not perform an explicit propagation of the information. In this way, the design of uniform search procedures is a more difficult task and therefore a constant response time in a recovery process can not be ensured; but the saving time in the assertion of new information compensates the lack of achieving responses in constant time. Different reasoning mechanisms have been devised for temporal graphs in order to reduce complexity in temporal operations [4].

The probabilistic temporal models have been specially developed to deal with dynamic applications. Probability is used to represent data under uncertainty [6] or to estimate the probability for a certain data to hold at a particular instant of time [7]. In this way, data are associated to a certain probability of occurrence so the application can form different clusters of information according to this probability. However, the inherent complexity of probabilistic inference makes impracticable to compute these operations within a certain range of time. Additionally, these models require to dispose of an exhaustive knowledge about the application behaviour in order to be able to estimate every element which may influence in the problem.

This paper presents a suitable temporal model for applications running under dynamic environments. The paper is structured as follows: section 2 presents the internal time model, section 3 describes how this model is applied to represent the data application, section 4 explains the temporal inference process by means of an example, section 5 specifies the reasoning algorithms and section 6 concludes.

2   Internal Time Model

The proposed temporal model follows an object-oriented approach based on the reified formalisms [8] [1] and is composed of a discrete set of time-points. This approach permits to have an explicit representation of time, to separate the temporal and non-temporal part of data, to constraint data over the time line and to associate data with a temporal interval to represent its validity.

2.1   Basic Concepts

The temporal model uses time-points as elementary primitives to represent the beginning and ending of data (temporal facts).

Definition 1 (temporal fact). *A temporal fact tf_i is a tuple $\langle o_i, s_i, v_i, b_i, e_i \rangle$ where o_i is a symbol associated to an application object, s_i is a temporal slot of the object which takes different values along the time and v_i is the value associated to s_i between the beginning point b_i and ending point e_i.*

By default e_i is always after b_i. Both b_i and e_i stand for the temporal validity of value v_i for slot s_i. When a new value v_j is acquired for the same slot in the object, a new temporal fact is created, $tf_j = \langle o_i, s_i, v_j, b_j, e_j \rangle$, and e_i and b_j will denote the same instant of time, thus indicating tf_i precedes tf_j.

Definition 2 (event). *An event ev_i is a tuple $ev_i = \langle o_i, s_i, v_i, t_i, or_i \rangle$ where o_i is the object and s_i the slot subject to the modification incorporated by the event; v_i is the new value to be attached to the slot, t_i is the time instant at which the event is produced and or_i represents the event origin, either external or internal.*

Events are used to represent the temporal data evolution and denote the changes produced in temporal facts. An external event is a value acquired from the external world (for instance through sensors) and an internal event is a value generated by the reasoning system which is controlling the application. In the following, and for the sake of simplicity, we will not make distinctions in the treatment of both types of events.

2.2   Temporal Constraints

Time-points are seen as symbolic variables where temporal constraints can be posted. A time-point tp_i is represented as an interval $[l_i, r_i]$ where $l_i, r_i \in \mathbf{Z}$ represent the earliest and the latest occurrence date for tp_i. This interval $[l_i, r_i]$ is called *temporal window* of tp_i. Date(tp_i) is defined as a function that returns the temporal window of time-point tp_i. Two additional functions are defined to recover the earliest and latest occurrence date of time-point tp_i:

$$\mathsf{LeftLim}(\mathsf{Date}(tp_i)) = l_i$$
$$\mathsf{RightLim}(\mathsf{Date}(tp_i)) = r_i$$

If left and right limit of tp_i are unknown then temporal window is given by $[-\infty, +\infty]$. When the occurrence date of tp_i is perfectly known, the left and right limit refer to the same time instant ($l_i = r_i$).

Definition 3 (temporal constraint). *A binary temporal constraint is a tuple $\langle tp_i$ before|after d_k $tp_j \rangle$ where tp_i and tp_j denote time-points, $d_k \in \mathbf{Z}$ and after|before denote the type of temporal relation between both time-points.*

The meaning of a temporal constraint can be stated as follows:

- $\langle tp_i$ after d_k $tp_j \rangle$ indicates that $\mathsf{Date}(tp_i)$ must occur after d_k units of time from $\mathsf{Date}(tp_j)$. i.e., $\mathsf{LeftLim}(\mathsf{Date}(tp_i)) = l_j + d_k + 1$ and $\mathsf{RightLim}(\mathsf{Date}(tp_i)) = +\infty$. This temporal constraint computes the first instant of time where tp_i can occur with respect to tp_j
- $\langle tp_i$ before d_k $tp_j \rangle$ indicates that $\mathsf{Date}(tp_i)$ must occur before d_k units of time from $\mathsf{Date}(tp_j)$, i.e., $\mathsf{RightLim}(\mathsf{Date}(tp_i)) = r_j + d_k - 1$ and $\mathsf{LeftLim}(\mathsf{Date}(tp_i)) = -\infty$. This temporal constraint computes the latest instant of time where tp_i can occur with respect to tp_j.

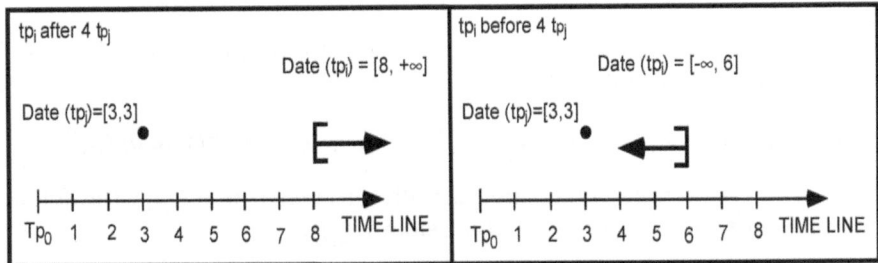

Fig. 1. Temporal constraints

Two special time-points Tp_0 and now are used in the model. The former represents the initial time of the clock system ($\mathsf{Date}(Tp_0) = [0, 0]$). now represents the current time ($\mathsf{Date}(now) = [l_{now}, r_{now}]$), where $l_{now} = r_{now}$ is the number of time units elapsed from $\mathsf{Date}(Tp_0)$ until the current moment. In fact, for a time-point tp_i, l_i and r_i represent the minimum and maximum number of time units that must elapse from $\mathsf{Date}(Tp_0)$ to know the exact occurrence date of tp_i.

Equality relation between two time-points tp_i, tp_j is represented as the conjunction of two temporal constraints: tp_i after -1 tp_j and tp_i before 1 tp_j. Symbolic constraints between two time points can be easily represented by setting d_k equal to 0. In this way, "tp_i occurs before tp_j" would be represented by means of temporal constraint $\langle tp_i$ before 0 $tp_j \rangle$.

Let c be a temporal constraint of the form $\langle tp_i$ after d_k $tp_j \rangle$ or $\langle tp_i$ before d_k $tp_j \rangle$. The following functions are defined over the set of temporal constraints:

- $\mathsf{Source}(c) = tp_j$ is the time-point reference on which the temporal constraint is applied to.
- $\mathsf{Distance}(c) = d_k$ is the temporal distance defined in c.
- $\mathsf{Relation}(c) = \mathsf{after}|\mathsf{before}$ is the type of the temporal relation in c.

2.3   Properties of the Internal Time Model

Some of the most relevant properties of the internal time model are:

Property 1: finite in the beginning $\forall tp_i$, $\langle Tp_0$ before 1 $tp_i \rangle$

Property 2: symmetry

$$\forall tp_i, tp_j, d_k : \langle tp_i \text{ after } d_k \ tp_j \rangle \rightarrow \langle tp_j \text{ before } -d_k \ tp_i \rangle$$
$$\forall tp_i, tp_j, d_k. : \langle tp_i \text{ before } d_k \ tp_j \rangle \rightarrow \langle tp_j \text{ after } -d_k \ tp_i \rangle$$

Property 3: transitiveness

$$\forall tp_i, tp_j, tp_k, d_k : \langle tp_i \text{ before } d_k \ tp_j \rangle \wedge \langle tp_j \text{ before } d_l \ tp_k \rangle \rightarrow$$
$$\langle tp_i \text{ before } d_k + d_l - 1 \ tp_k \rangle$$

Property 4: reflexiveness $\quad \forall tp_i, d_k > 0 : \langle tp_i \text{ before } d_k \ tp_i \rangle$
Property 5: partial order

$$\forall tp_i, tp_j, d_k : \langle tp_i \text{ before } d_k \ tp_j \rangle \rightarrow \forall d_l \geq d_k, \ \langle tp_i \text{ before } d_l \ tp_j \rangle$$

To denote two time-points are partially ordered ($tp_i \preceq tp_j$) the following temporal constraint can be used: $\langle tp_i \text{ before } 1 \ tp_j \rangle$.

2.4 Time-Point Representation

Definition 4 (time-point). *A time point tp_i is defined as a tuple $\langle l_i, r_i, S_i \rangle$ where l_i and r_i stand for the earliest and latest occurrence date of tp_i and S_i is the set of all temporal constraints posted on tp_i. S_i is defined as a disjunction of sets of temporal constraints $(S_{i1}, S_{i2}, \ldots, S_{in})$ where each S_{ik} represents a possible temporal occurrence for tp_i.*

Definition 5 (group of constraints). *A particular set $S_{ik} \in S_i$ is defined as a group of temporal constraints over tp_i. A group of temporal constraints S_{ik} defines a temporal interval in the following way:*

$$\mathsf{LowerBound}(S_{ik}) = \{a | a \in \mathbf{Z},$$
$$a = max_c(\mathsf{Distance}(c) + \mathsf{LeftLim}(\mathsf{Source}(\mathsf{Date}(c))) + 1),$$
$$\forall c \in S_{ik}, \mathsf{Relation}(c) = \mathsf{after}\}$$
$$\mathsf{UpperBound}(S_{ik}) = \{a | a \in \mathbf{Z},$$
$$a = min_c(\mathsf{Distance}(c) + \mathsf{RightLim}(\mathsf{Source}(\mathsf{Date}(c))) - 1),$$
$$\forall c \in S_{ik}, \mathsf{Relation}(c) = \mathsf{before}\}$$

Proposition 1. *Let c_1, c_2 be two temporal constraints of the form $\langle tp_i$ after $d_k \ tp_j \rangle$ and $\langle tp_i$ before $d_l \ tp_j \rangle$ respectively which belongs to a group S_{ik}. Temporal constraints c_1 and c_2 are consistent if and only if $d_l \geq d_k + 2$.*

The demonstration is trivial by following properties of symmetry, transitiveness and reflexivity. Let's show the above proposition by an example. Let $tp_j = \langle 3, 3, () \rangle$ be a time-point with no constraints defined over it and whose occurrence date is at time instant 3, and $tp_i = \langle x, y, (S_{i1}) \rangle$ where $S_{i1} = \{\langle tp_i \text{ after } 2 \ tp_j \rangle,$

$\langle tp_i$ before 3 $tp_j \rangle \}$. There exists only one group of constraints for tp_i which is composed of two constraints applied to tp_j. By computing Lower and Upper bounds of S_{i1} we obtain LowerBound $(S_{i1}) = 2 + 3 + 1 = 6$ and UpperBound $(S_{i1}) = 3 + 3 - 1 = 5$ thus resulting in an inconsistent interval $[6,5]$. In this way, the distance of a before temporal constraint must be at least two time units greater than the temporal distance of an after temporal constraint in the same group of constraints applied to the same time-point.

Definition 6 (joining of constraints). *Let $S_i = (S_{i1}, S_{i2}, \dots, S_{in})$ for time-point tp_i. The final temporal window for tp_i is calculated according to the lower and upper bound of each S_{ik}. Hence:*

$$\mathsf{LeftLim}(\mathsf{Date}(tp_i)) = \{\ d | d \in \mathbf{Z}, d = min(\mathsf{LowerBound}(S_{ik}))\ \forall k \in 1, \dots, n \}$$
$$\mathsf{RightLim}(\mathsf{Date}(tp_i)) = \{\ d | d \in \mathbf{Z}, d = max(\mathsf{UpperBound}(S_{ik}))\ \forall k \in 1, \dots, n \}$$

Temporal information is represented in a graph where nodes correspond to time-points and edges denote temporal constraints.

Each edge or each path with combinable edges (transitiveness property) between two nodes gives rise to a temporal constraint between them. Let CA_{ij} and CB_{ij} be the set of all temporal constraints connecting tp_i and tp_j through the temporal relation after and before respectively. For each temporal constraint c which belongs to one of those sets, Distance(c) is calculated by successively applying property of transitiveness over the time-points which make up the path in the graph.

3 Temporal Data Representation

3.1 Temporal States

A temporal fact can be in one of these states: past, current or future. Recall that the special time-point *now* represents the current time, i.e. the number of time unit elapsed from Tp_0 (initial time at which the application execution starts) until the current moment.

Definition 7. *A temporal fact $tf_i = \langle o_i, s_i, v_i, b_i, e_i \rangle$ is a past fact if the temporal constraint $\langle e_i$ before 1 now$\rangle$ holds.*

For a past temporal fact it also holds $\langle b_i$ before 0 now$\rangle$. This means that both, $Date(b_i)$ and $Date(e_i)$ are precise dates, concrete instants of time preceding the current time *now* (or equal to *now* in the case of the ending time-point).

Definition 8. *A temporal fact $tf_i = \langle o_i, s_i, v_i, b_i, e_i \rangle$ is a current fact if temporal constraints $\langle b_i$ before 1 now$\rangle$ and $\langle e_i$ after 0 now$\rangle$ hold. The beginning time of a current temporal fact is a perfectly known date and its ending time is only partially known.*

Definition 9. *A temporal fact $tf_i = \langle o_i, s_i, v_i, b_i, e_i \rangle$ is a future fact if temporal constraints $\langle b_i$ after 0 now$\rangle$ and $\langle e_i$ after 0 now$\rangle$ hold. In this case, both are imprecise dates.*

3.2   Events

Events are used to model the temporal changes in temporal facts. There are two main modifications that may occur in temporal facts: a current fact may become past or a future temporal fact may become current.

Definition 10. *Let* $tf_i = \langle o_i, s_i, v_i, b_i, e_i \rangle$ *be a current temporal fact at the current moment (now);* tf_i *will become a past fact in a future time* $t' > now$ *if an event* $ev_j = \langle o_i, s_i, v_j, t', or_j \rangle$ *occurs (the event brings about a new value for the temporal slot* s_i *in the object* o_i *where* $v_i \neq v_j$).

The condition that must hold for an event $ev_j = \langle o_i, s_i, v_j, t', or_j \rangle$ to produce a current-to-past modification in temporal fact tf_i is: $\mathsf{LeftLim}(\mathsf{Date}(e_i)) \leq t' \leq \mathsf{RightLim}(\mathsf{Date}(e_i))$. In this case ev_j confirms the date for the end of tf_i and $\mathsf{Date}(e_i)$ is set to $[t', t']$.

Definition 11. *Let* $tf_i = \langle o_i, s_i, v_i, b_i, e_i \rangle$ *be a future temporal fact at the current moment (now);* tf_i *will become a current fact in a future time* $t' > now$ *if an event* $ev_i = \langle o_i, s_i, v_i, t'_i, or_i \rangle$ *occurs (the event confirms the future value* v_i *of slot* s_i *in the object* o_i).

The condition that must hold for an event $ev_i = \langle o_i, s_i, v_i, t', or_i \rangle$ to produce a future-to-current modification in temporal fact tf_i is: $\mathsf{LeftLim}(\mathsf{Date}(b_i)) \leq t' \leq \mathsf{RightLim}(\mathsf{Date}(b_i))$. In this case ev_i confirms the prediction and $\mathsf{Date}(b_i)$ is set to $[t', t']$.

4   Temporal Causality

Causal relations are represented in the model by means of temporal constraints. The principle of causality states that the effects of a causal relation hold if and only if all the causes in the relation already hold in the knowledge base. In other words, the beginning time of temporal facts representing the consequences of a causal relation can never occur before the beginning time of their causes. This statement of causality is extended in our model by allowing to infer new information on the basis of future temporal facts. The new deduced temporal fact will hold as future data until all the premises are confirmed, i.e. until the temporal facts used for deduction become current facts. This means the model can perform inferencing based on future data aimed at advancing what is expected to occur in the application evolution. Let's take an example of a possible causal relation in the block's world domain. The classical action of picking up a block is stated as follows:

```
if      (?block status free ?b1 ?e1)   and
        (robotarm status free ?b2 ?e2)
then
        (?block status holding)
```

The identifier ?block is a variable to be instantiated to the corresponding block and values instantiated in ?b1 ?e1 ?b2 ?e2 are the time-points associated to the beginning and ending points of temporal facts that satisfy each premise. Let tf_1 and tf_2 be the temporal facts that match the first and second premise of the causal relation respectively. The situations that may arise are the following:

- If tf_1 is a past temporal fact and tf_2 is a current or future fact (or inversely) then it is clear both conditions will never hold simultaneously because by the time the *robotarm* is free the block's top is not free any more; in this case the system can never infer the block's status is holding.
- If, at the time the operator is being evaluated, both tf_1 and tf_2 are current temporal facts then we can ensure that both conditions currently hold so the block can be held *now*.
- If any of the temporal facts is future (and the other is current or future too) the system will not be able to deduce the block is held *now*. However, it may be possible to conclude that *blockA* will be held sometime in future. The system will infer such an information if there exists at least one future instant of time where both temporal facts may hold simultaneously as current facts. This is calculated by computing the test of temporal intersection.

Definition 12 (temporal intersection). *Let $T = tf_1, tf_2, \ldots, tf_n$ be the set of temporal facts that match the premises of a causal relation. It is said there exists temporal intersection among the temporal facts at the current time now if the following condition holds:*

$$\forall i, j \in [1, \ldots, n], i \neq j, \langle e_i \text{ after } 0 \ b_j \rangle \wedge \langle e_i \text{ after } 0 \text{ now} \rangle$$

This test determines if temporal facts matching the premises currently hold or may hold simultaneously in a future time. If the result of the test is true then the model computes the temporal interval where the conclusions are expected to occur or are actually occurring; in the latter case the left and right bounds of this interval will be equal and will represent a time instant before or equal *now*.

Let $tf_1 = \langle blockA, status, free, b_1, e_1 \rangle$ and $tf_2 = \langle robotarm, status, free, b_2, e_2 \rangle$ be the two temporal facts that fulfill the premises of the causal relation and $\mathsf{Date}(now) = [3, 3]$. Assuming both tf_1 and tf_2 are future temporal facts with $\mathsf{Date}(b_1) = [4, 10]$ and $\mathsf{Date}(b_2) = [5, 9]$, the conclusion will be a future temporal fact $tf_3 = \langle blockA, status, holding, b_3, e_3 \rangle$. The exact occurrence date for tf_3 will depend on the last temporal fact, between tf_1 and tf_2, which becomes current. This gives rise to three possible different situations (corresponding to situations S_{31}, S_{32} and S_{33} in Fig. 2): 1) tf_1 is the last temporal fact to become current, therefore *blockA* will be held when its top is free, 2) tf_2 is the last temporal fact to become current, so *blockA* will be held when the *robotarm* is free or 3) both tf_1 and tf_2 become current at the same time.

Time-point b_3 is defined as $\langle 5, 10, (S_{31}, S_{32}, S_{33}) \rangle$ what means that the earliest time instant where *blockA* can be held is at 5 and the latest at 10.

Let's assume that $Date(now) = [6, 6]$ and the first event acquired from the external world confirms *robotarm* is free at the current time [6,6] ($ev_j =$

$\langle robotarm, status, free, 6, or_j \rangle$). Then tf_2 becomes a current fact with $\mathsf{Date}(b_2) = [6,6]$. The model updates the temporal window for b_3 (Fig. 3.).

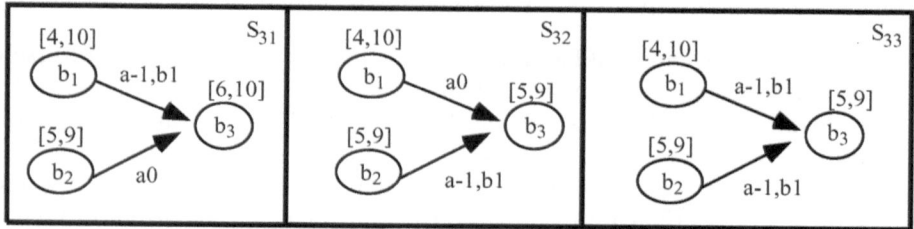

Fig. 2. Groups of constraints for time-point b_3

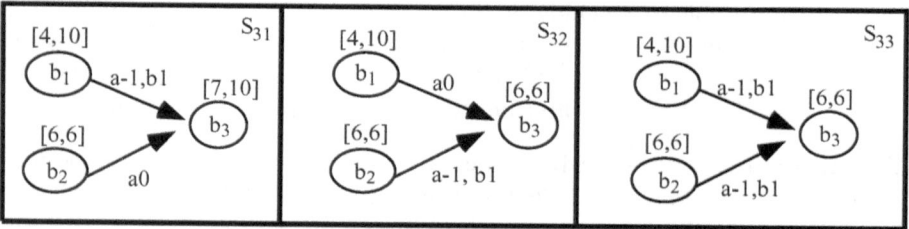

Fig. 3. Updating temporal window for time-point b_3

Since $Date(now) = [6,6]$ and $blockA$ is not holding now, the only consistent group for b_3 is S_{31} and then $b_3 = \langle 7, 10, (S_{31}) \rangle$. This indicates that $blockA$ can be held at 7 as the earliest time instant. Let's assume that two time units have elapsed and $Date(now) = [8,8]$. An external event reports that $robotarm$ is occupied at that time. Then tf_2 becomes a past fact with $\mathsf{Date}(e_2) = [8,8]$. It is obvious the model can not infer yet that $blockA$ will be held. But we need to add some information in order to detect this situation.

The test of temporal intersection requires to check that every ending time-point occurs after the beginning time-point of each temporal fact. This is a *temporal relation* which must be satisfied in order to infer the conclusions, but it is not possible to represent such a relation by posting a temporal constraint between the two time-points. In other words, a temporal constraint states a temporal-causal relation between two time-points and constrains the temporal window of a time-point according to the updatings in the temporal window of the other time-point.

The desired effect is achieved by setting a temporal constraint between the beginning of the conclusion and the ending of each of the causes ($\langle b_3$ before 0 $e_1 \rangle$, $\langle b_3$ before 0 $e_2 \rangle$). These temporal constraints are used to denote that the exact ocurrence date for b_3 should be known before dates for e_1 and e_2.

5   Temporal Reasoning

This section describes the reasoning algorithms of the temporal model. Tasks to be performed are asserting, deleting, updating and recovering of the information. Updating and deletion requires from a propagation process in the graph. Assertion and consults are carried out by means of a search process.

5.1   Recovery Process

The recovery process consists in retrieving the sufficiently restricted (according to the constraint expressed in the query) temporal constraint between two nodes in the graph. By obtaining existing edges or combinable paths between two nodes the recovery process can return three types of answers: TRUE, FALSE or POSSIBLE. Following, we provide definitions for a before query while answers for an after query can be obtained by applying property 2 on the next definitions:

Definition 13. $\mathsf{q\_bef}(tp_j, d_k, tp_i) = TRUE \leftrightarrow \exists c \in CB_{ij}, \mathsf{Distance}(c) \leq d_k$

Definition 14. $\mathsf{q\_bef}(tp_j, d_k, tp_i) = FALSE \leftrightarrow \exists c \in CA_{ij}, \mathsf{Distance}(c) \geq d_k - 1$

Definition 15. $\mathsf{q\_bef}(tp_j, d_k, tp_i) = POSSIBLE \leftrightarrow \forall c_1 \in CB_{ij}, c_2 \in CA_{ij}, \mathsf{Distance}(c_1) > d_k \wedge Distance(c_2) < d_k - 1$

A TRUE response is obtained for a query when there already exists a path in the graph which represents that temporal constraint. A FALSE answer is obtained when the contrary restriction is found in the graph. A POSSIBLE answer is obtained when there are no paths which confirm neither a TRUE nor a FALSE response.

5.2   Consistency Test

The consistency test checks whether the new temporal constraint to be asserted is consistent with the rest of information in the graph. To carry out this proof the model checks one of the following two conditions, depending on the temporal relation type of the constraint:

Definition 16. *A constraint of the form* $\langle tp_i$ before $d_k\ tp_j \rangle$ *is consistent if* $\forall c \in CA_{ij}, d_k > \mathsf{Distance}(c) + 1$

Definition 17. *A constraint of the form* $\langle tp_i$ after $d_k\ tp_j \rangle$ *is consistent if* $\forall c \in CB_{ij}, d_k < \mathsf{Distance}(c) - 1$

From the above definition it can be easily deduced that the graph is consistent if and only if there are not path-cycles composed of edges after whose distance is ≥ 0 or path-cycles composed of edges before whose distance is ≤ 0.

Proposition 2 (consistency). *A temporal graph is consistent if and only if* $\forall tp_i, \langle tp_i$ before $d_k\ tp_j \rangle \rightarrow d_k > 0$ *and* $\forall tp_i, \langle tp_i$ after $d_k\ tp_j \rangle \rightarrow d_k < 0$

5.3   Search Procedure

The search process is carried out in two phases: a) an *interval phase* where a response is obtained by consulting the left and right limits of time-points and b) and *expansion phase* where a search is performed from the source node to the destination by combining temporal constraints. The *interval phase* consists in obtaining a first response to a particular temporal query by substracting the left and right limits of the two involved time-points. For a specific time point tp_i, a list with all nodes which constitute the most restrictive path between tp_i and Tp_0 is maintained. This is a useful information for two reasons:

- if a temporal search involves two time-points in the same restrictive path, minimal/maximal optimal distance separating both nodes can be obtained by simply substracting their left/right limits.
- if the two time-points are not found in the same restrictive path then an approximate solution can be obtained by substracting their left-right limits.

In this second case, there is no guarantee that the obtained solution is optimal. If the resulting distance does not respond TRUE or FALSE to our query, the *expansion phase* is activated. This is based on a A^* search algorithm where parallel differences between time points (substracting both left and right limits) is used as an heuristic evaluation. The algorithm is implemented by following [11] thus permitting the obtention of linear search costs in practice.

Let tp_i and tp_j be two time-points. The maximum **before** distance of tp_j with respect to tp_i is $r_j - l_i + 1$ since r_j is the latest ocurrence date for tp_j and l_i is the earliest ocurrence date for tp_i. Consequently, this distance can be used as an upper bound in the process of computing a q_bef between the two nodes. That is, the goal of the search process is to minimize that distance and the solution is progressively refined as a new shorter distance is found in the expansion phase. This can also be applied to an **after** constraint by obtaining a lower bound on substracting limits l_j and r_i ($l_j - r_i - 1$).

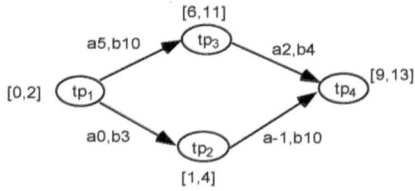

Fig. 4. An example of temporal graph

Let's take the graph in Fig. 4 and the query q_aft($tp_4, 8, tp_1$). By comparing l_4 and r_1 the response would be POSSIBLE ($9 - 2 - 1 < 8$). However, there exists a path connecting tp_4 and tp_1 through tp_3 which responds TRUE to our query ($5 + 2 + 1 = 8$); that is, the combination of constraints which determine the left limit of tp_4 constitute the most restrictive path from Tp_0 to tp_4 ($\mathsf{Date}(Tp_0) = [0,0], l_4 = 0 + 8 + 1 = 9$). Since tp_1 is found on that path, the optimal distance between tp_1 and tp_4 can be obtained by computing $l_4 - l_1 - 1$. In summary, when a time-point tp_i is on the most restrictive path from Tp_0 to another time-point tp_j, the optimal after/before distance between both time-points is computed by substracting their left/right limits.

The advantage of the proposed method is that the first phase allows to achieve a very rapid response which may be the optimal one in some cases. Otherwise, the *expansion phase* can find a more refined solution as more computation time is given to the algorithm.

6   Conclusions

The main contributions of the presented work are: a) the definition and design of a representation framework specially adapted for dynamic environments with the ability of reasoning about past, current and future data, b) the specification of an internal time model which allows to handle any temporal requirement by means of temporal constraints, thus facilitating the temporal data management and c) the design of the reasoning algorithms are based, as far as possible, on simple arithmetic operations on the limits of time-points, thus being possible the computation of an approximate response very rapidly. This is an important requirement in dynamic environments as in real-time systems.

References

1. Barber F.A. "A metric Time-point and Duration-Based Temporal model". SIGART-ACM Bulletin Vol.4, No.3, pp. 30-49 (1993)   208
2. Dean T.L., McDermott D.V. "Temporal Data Base Management". Artificial Intelligence 32, pp. 1-55 (1987)   208
3. Dechter R., Meiri I., Pearl J. "Temporal constraints networks". Artificial Intelligence 49, pp. 61-95 (1991)   208
4. Gerevini A., Schubert L. "Efficient algorithms for qualitative reasoning about time". Artificial Intelligence 74(2), pp. 207-248. (1995)   208
5. Golumbic M.C., Shamir R. "Complexity and algorithms for reasoning about time: A graph-theoretic approach". Journal of ACM Vol. 40, pp. 1108-1133 (1993)   208
6. Haddawy P. "Representing Plans Under Uncertainty. A logic of Time, Chance, and Action". Lecture Notes in Artificial Intelligence. Springer-Verlag 770. (1994)   208
7. Hanks S., McDermott D. "Modeling a dynamic and uncertain world I: symbolic and probabilistic reasoning about change". Artificial Intelligence 66, pp. 1-55. (1994) 208
8. Shoham Y.: "Reasoning about change". MIT Press. (1988)   208
9. Van Beek P."Reasoning about Qualitative Temporal Information". Proc. AAAI-90, pp. 728-734, Boston, MA. (1990)   208
10. Yampratoon E., Allen J.F. "Performance of Temporal Reasoning Systems". University of Rochester. Computer Science Department. TRAINS Technical Note 93-1. (May 1993)   208
11. Korf R.E. "Linear-space best-first search". Artificial Intelligence 62, pp. 41-78. (1993)   217

Heuristics for Improving the Non-oblivious Local Search for MaxSAT

G. De Ita[1], D.E. Pinto[2], and M. Nuño[1]

[1] Facultad de Ciencias de la Computación, B.U.A.P
[2] Universidad Popular Autónoma del Estado de Puebla U.P.A.E.P
{gdeita,mnuno}@fcfm.buap.mx
DPinto@sun1.pue.upaep.mx

Abstract. We determine special cases where the behaviour of the non-oblivious local search is worse than the behaviour of the classical local search. We propose some modifications to the non-oblivious objective function in order to cover these cases. We present an empirical analysis and comparative results among the analysed algorithms. This empirical analysis shows that non-oblivious local search (that uses the new objective function introduced here) combined with tabu strategy and the use of the complemented value of the last local optimum as a mechanism for re-starting the search, obtains in practice, better solutions than the classical local seach or non-oblivious local seach alone.

1 Introduction

The objective of Automatic Theorem Proving (ATP) is to design efficient algorithms to demonstrate the validity of a logical formula. In the case of propositional logic, it is well known that the Satisfiability problem (SAT) and the Maximum Satisfiability problem (MaxSAT) are computationally hard problems, in such a way that any known algorithms that solve them require in the worst of the cases an exponential number of steps over the length of the input.

The SAT problem consists of deciding whether a Boolean conjunctive form F is satisfiable. The SAT problem is NP-complete even when it is restricted to instances with exactly three literals per clause (3-SAT problem). Its optimized version, MaxSAT problem, computes the maximum number of simultaneously satisfiable clauses in F. MaxSAT problem is NP-complete even for formulas with at least two literals per clause.

Both SAT and MaxSAT problems are central problems for ATP and for complexity theory. The interest in SAT and MaxSAT is also motivated by the important role that they play as representative problems of their complexity class. Therefore, there is a great interest in the design of efficient algorithms for the resolution of these problems.

Recently, there has been a renaissance in the study of effective heuristic algorithms based on local search. Starting from the late eighties, both discrete and continuous-based greedy algorithms have been proposed (see [2]). Of course, it is not our purpose to present an exhaustive list of these algorithms. Instead,

Helder Coelho (Ed.): IBERAMIA'98, LNAI 1484, pp. 219–229, 1998.

we present a new objective function that improves the general behaviour of the non-oblivious 1-local search.

We also present different strategies in order to improve the general behaviour of the algorithms based on a local search paradigm. We add to the local search a tabu search strategy with the purpose of speeding up the phase to reach a local optimum, and we proposed the use of the complement value of the local optimum found previously as a mechanism for determining a 'good' point to re-start the search after arriving at a local optimum and in order to avoid review paths already explored.

The empirical analysis and the comparative results among these algorithms show that the non-oblivious local search with the tabu strategy and the use of complemented values have robust behaviour and obtain in practice better solutions than the non-oblivious local search alone.

1.1 Preliminary Definitions

Let $\mathbf{X} = \{x_1, \ldots, x_n\}$ be a set of n Boolean variables. Let $Lit(\mathbf{X})$ be the set of literals: $Lit(\mathbf{X}) = \mathbf{X} \cup \{\overline{x_1}, \ldots, \overline{x_n}\}$.

A *clause* C is a disjunction of literals. For a natural number k, a $k-$clause is a clause consisting of exactly k literals. We'll denote the number of literals of the clause C with $|C|$. A *conjunctive form (CF)*, or *formula* is a conjunction of clauses. A $k-$CF is a CF containing only $k-$clauses.

An *assignment* A is a function, $A : X \to \{true, false\}$. There are 2^n different assignments that can be defined over a set $\mathbf{X}$ with n Boolean variables. We will also consider an *assignment* A as a set of literals. The sign in which the literal appears in A is the logical value that the assignment A gives to the variable x. Note that there are no duplicate variables in an assignment.

A clause is true if at least one of its literals is true. A CF is true if each of its clauses is true.

For any assignment $A \subset Lit(\mathbf{X})$, let $c(F, A)$ be the number of clauses satisfied by A, i.e.:

$$c(F, A) = |\{i \le m | \exists j \in [1, k_i] : l_{ij} \in A\}|,$$

evidently, each CF F with m clauses is *satisfiable* iff there is an assignment A such that $c(F, A) = m$. *MaxSAT* is the problem that, given a CF, obtains an assignment $A_0 \subset Lit(\mathbf{X})$ such that $c(F, A_0) = \text{Max}\{c(F, A) | A \subset Lit(\mathbf{X})\}$.

Let $P(\cdot, \cdot)$ be a prototypical NP *optimization problem*:

Instance: A real function $f : D \to R$.
Solution: A point $x_0 \in D$ such that $f(x_0) = \text{Max}\{f(x) | x \in D\}$.

Let $Sol(P(f, D))$ be the set of solutions of $P(f, D)$. And Let $A : (f, D) \mapsto A(f, D) \in D$ a procedure that proposes for any instance (f, D) a candidate to be an element of $Sol(P(f, D))$. We say that the algorithm A *approximates* the problem P with *performance ratio* $r \in R$ if for each instance (f, D) of P we have $|f(A(f, D))| \ge r \cdot |f(\mathbf{x})|$ for some solution $\mathbf{x} \in Sol(P(f, D))$, in other words, the maximized value proposed by the algorithm is within a ratio r of the actual maximized value.

Any polynomial time algorithm A approximating the optimization problem and which for any instance (f, D) delivers a solution of value at least within a ratio r of the optimal value is said to be a $r-approximation\ algorithm$ (PTAA). The performance ratio r is usually called *the guarantee factor* of the algorithm. There arise several possibilities:

1. There is a sequence of algorithms $\{A_n\}_n$ such that each A_n is a PTAA of ratio r_n and the sequence $\{r_n\}_n$ is such that $r_n \to_{n \to +\infty} 1$. In this case the collection of algorithms $\{A_n\}_n$ is said to be a *polynomial time approximation scheme* (PTAS).
2. There is a PTAA only for some ratio $r < 1$.
3. For any r there is no PTAA.

There is, naturally, the problem of characterizing the optimization problems falling in each one of the above categories.

For many optimization problems, algorithms with small worst-case ratios were quickly found. In some other cases, the problem of finding a worst-case ratio r algorithm, for any constant $r \in [0, 1]$, was proved to be as hard as finding an optimal solution. For example, it is known that there is a constant threshold $c < 1$ such that if MaxSAT could be approximated in polynomial time with a guarantee factor better than c then P=NP. One explicit constant threshold know for Max2SAT is $\frac{95}{96}$ and $\frac{26}{27}$ for Max3SAT [3].

However, it is also important to analyse the properties of the MaxSAT problem, with the objective of determining the best guarantee factor r that can be reached in polynomial time.

2   Local Search Paradigm

Among the approximation procedures, a technique that has proved to be efficient to find assignments that satisfy a satisfiable Boolean formula, is the local search technique [12]. Local search or local optimization is a primitive form of continuous optimization in discrete search space. It was one of the early techniques proposed to cope with the challenging computational intractability of NP-hard combinatorial optimization problems.

The local search method can be analysed through the structure $< x_0, f, H >$, where:

x_0 - is the point used in order to start the search,

f - is the function that we want to minimize or maximize and,

H - is the real-value distance function or metric between points in search space.

For the MaxSAT problem, the search procedure operates over the discrete space D of possible assignments of the Boolean formula. Usually, the local search starts with a randomly-generated solution x_0 and the 'Hamming' distance H is used as the metric (The Hamming distance $H(x, y)$ between two binary strings x and y is given by the number of bits that are different between both strings).

A δ−neighborhood of a point $x \in D$, denoted by $N_\delta(x)$, is: $N_\delta(x) = \{y \in D | H(x,y) \leq \delta\}$. Then, two points x and y in D are δ−neighboring if $H(x,y) \leq \delta$. We will denote $N_1(x)$ with $N(x)$.

Given a current solution x, a δ−local search algorithm proceeds to review all $N_\delta(x)$ and then to choose the one which produces the best solution according to f, or to seek only until finding the assignment that improves the value of f. We decide to move immediately to the neighbor that improves the objective function, since in practice, we have seen that both strategies reach similar solutions, but this option clearly reduces the complexity of the average time of the algorithm.

The classical local search paradigm, (or *oblivious local search* (LS) as it is called by Khanna), uses as its objective function f, the function that gives, for each current assignment, the number of clauses satisfied by this assignment. It is also common to use as its objective function the polynomial function that result by arithmetization of the formula given (see for example [5],[8]).

A typical δ−local search which starts from the initial solution x_0, looks for a point $x_{i+1} \in N_\delta(x_i)$ so that $f(x_{i+1}) < f(x_i)$ (or $f(x_{i+1}) > f(x_i)$ if the objective is maximized). If such a point exists, it becomes the new current solution and the process is iterated. Otherwise, x_i is retained as a *local optimum*.

Even though local search has been demonstrated to be an efficient strategy to solve SAT and MaxSAT when the Boolean formula F has several satisfiable assignments, the procedure has the serious problem that is blocked on local optimums, but yet more serious; the fact is that the approximation ratios that guarantee this paradigm are still far from the theoretical threshold which can be reached in polynomial time.

For example, the classical δ−local search has a guarantee factor of $\frac{k}{k+1}$ [9][11] although δ may take any positive integer $\delta = o(n)$, where n is the number of variables and k is the minimum number of literals contained in any clause of the formula, i.e. for the Max2SAT problem, the guarantee factor that provides the classical local search is $2/3$.

3   Non-oblivious Local Search

In the design of efficient approximation algorithms for MaxSAT, a recent approach of interest is based on the use of *non-oblivious functions*, which was introduced in [1] and [11].

The objective function in local search has been traditionally expressed as a function that tries to maximize the number of clauses satisfied by the current assignment. But different types of local search can be obtained by using different objective functions to direct the search, including functions that originally do not show the natural option of maximizing the number of clauses that are satisfied by an assignment.

Given an assignment x, let S_i be the set of clauses in which exactly i literals are true, and let $w(S_i)$ be the total weight associated with the clauses in S_i, i.e. $w(S_i) = |S_i|$ - cardinality of S_i. Khanna introduced the objective function: $f_{NOB} = \sum_{i=1}^{k} c_i w(S_i)$ where the differences between two consecutive coefficients

$\Delta_i = c_i - c_{i-1}$, satisfies:

$$\Delta_i = \frac{1}{(k-i+1)\binom{k}{i-1}} \left[\sum_{j=0}^{k-i} \binom{k}{j} \right]. \tag{1}$$

Note that this formulation permits us to determine the values for each $c_i, i = 1, ..., k$. Khanna remarked that the value chosen for c_0 was not relevant to the behaviour of non-oblivious local search. Despite this idea, we will show that the value chosen for c_0 is important in order to improve the general behaviour of the non-oblivious local search (NV-LS).

A local optimum in the classical local search is not necessarily a local optimum in NV-LS, and in fact, the f_{NOB} objective function could 'jump' over the local optimums of the classical local search, causing different behaviour of the search strategy.

For example, Khanna proposed for the Max2SAT problem, the non-oblivious objective function $f_{NOB} = 3/2w(S_1) + 2w(S_2)$. Using this objective function, it has been shown that a 1-local search achieves a guarantee factor of 3/4. And in general, using the objective function $f_{NOB} = \sum_{i=1}^{k} c_i w(S_i)$ that obeys (1), any 1-local search for Max-kSAT ensures a guarantee factor of $\frac{2^k-1}{2^k}$ [11].

Therefore, the NV-LS improves the guarantee factor of the LS even if the search is restricted to reviewing few neighbors. In fact, the guarantee factor reached by NV-LS is the same as that wich can be reached using the Johnson's greedy algorithm [10][13].

Although Feige et al. [6] have proposed a randomized approximation algorithm based on *semidefinite programming* to resolve Max2SAT, with an approximation ratio of 0.931, the generalization of this technique for MaxSAT has not yet been resolved.

Analyzing the solutions obtained by programs that implement the classical local search as well as the non-oblivious local search, we detected instances of Max-kSAT in which the classical local search reaches a better solution than applying NV-LS.

A simple example of this case is the family of formulas of the type: $F = \{\{x_i, x_j\} | 1 \leq i < j \leq n\} \cup \{\{\overline{x}_1, \overline{x}_2\}\}$. Considering $n = 5$ and as the current solution $x = (1, 1, 1, 1, 1)$ then $f_{NOB}(x) = 3/2(0) + 2\left(\binom{5}{2}\right) = 20$ and, in fact, x is a local optimum that does not satisfy F because for every 1-neighbor x', $f_{NOB}(x) \geq f_{NOB}(x')$, i.e. with $x_1 = (0,1,1,1,1)$, $f_{NOB}(x_1) = 3/2(5) + 2(6) = 19.5$. Although x is a local optimum under NV-LS, its neighbor x_1 is a better solution since x_1 satisfies F.

Although NV-LS has a better guarantee factor than LS, the classical local search from the same current assignment $x = (1, 1, 1, 1, 1)$ obtains a better solution because it finds that x_1 is the local optimum.

In order to correct this situation, we determined a new non-oblivious objective function for Max2SAT defined as:

$$f_{NOB} = 2w(S_2) + 3/2w(S_1) - w(S_0). \tag{2}$$

We have defined this objective function in order to consider the number of unsatisfied clauses that appear in each evaluated assignment. Note that the values of the coefficients $c_i, i = 1, ..., k$ could be used to differentiate among assignments that have the same number of satisfied clauses, but the coefficient c_0 is critical in order to consider the number of unsatisfied clauses that appear in each evaluated assignment.

Let $f_{NOB} = \sum_{i=0}^{k} c_i w(S_i)$ the objective function for the NV-LS, without loss of generality, we assume that the variables have been renamed such that each unnegated literal is assigned the true value. And let $P_{i,j}$ and $N_{i,j}$ the number of clauses in S_i containing the literals x_j and $\bar{x}_j$ respectively. Considering x as 1-local optimum and denoting with $\frac{\delta f}{\delta x_j}$ the current change in f_{NOB} when the value of the variable x_j is flipped, i.e. when x_j changes from 1 to 0. And let us consider m to be the total number of clauses of the instance.

As x is a 1-local optimum, then for $1 \leq j \leq n$.

$$\frac{\delta f}{\delta x_j} = \sum_{i=2}^{k} \Delta_i N_{i-1,j} - \Delta_k P_{k,j} - \sum_{i=1}^{k-1} \Delta_i P_{i,j} + \Delta_1 N_{0,j} \leq 0$$

Then $\frac{\delta f}{\delta x_j} = \sum_{i=1}^{k-1} \Delta_{i+1} N_{i,j} + \Delta_1 N_{0,j} - \Delta_k P_{k,j} - \sum_{i=1}^{k-1} \Delta_i P_{i,j} \leq 0$.

Thus, $\Delta_1 N_{0,j} \leq \Delta_k P_{k,j} + \sum_{i=1}^{k-1} (\Delta_i P_{i,j} - \Delta_{i+1} N_{i,j})$.

Summing over all values of j and using the fact that $\sum_{j=1}^{n} P_{i,j} = iw(S_i)$ and $\sum_{j=1}^{n} N_{i,j} = (k-i)w(S_i)$, we obtain the following inequality:

$$k \Delta_k w(S_k) + \sum_{i=1}^{k-1} (i\Delta_i - (k-i)\Delta_{i+1}) w(S_i) \geq k \Delta_1 w(S_0). \qquad (3)$$

(Note a small difference with the summation low index obtained by Khanna[11]). For example, for the Max2SAT case, formula (3) is written as,

$$2\Delta_2 w(S_2) + (\Delta_1 - \Delta_2) w(S_1) \geq 2\Delta_1 w(S_0). \qquad (4)$$

Thus, we want to determine values for c_0, c_1, c_2 in such way that Δ_1 will be a big positive integer while Δ_2 and $\Delta_1 - \Delta_2$ will both be, small positive integers. For example, if we determine that the relation $w(S_1) \leq w(S_0)$ always holds for a class of formulas, then defining $c_0 = -1; c_1 = \frac{3}{2}; c_2 = 2$ (as in (2), we obtain that $\Delta_1 = \frac{5}{2}$ and $\Delta_2 = \frac{1}{2}$. Then (4) is transformed in to

$$w(S_2) + 2w(S_1) \geq 5w(S_0). \qquad (5)$$

Let us denote the number of unsatisfied clauses with $w(S_0) = $ UNSAT and, with the number of satisfied cluases $w(S_1) + w(S_2) = $ SAT. Then SAT + UNSAT $= m$. From(5) we determine that SAT$+w(S_0) \geq$ SAT$+w(S_1) \geq$ 5·UNSAT, obtaining the inequality SAT $\geq$ 5·UNSAT$-$UNSAT $= 4$·UNSAT, and obtaining a guarantee factor of $\frac{4}{5}$ for this class of instances.

In order to improve the approximation factor that can be reached using non-oblivious local search over Max2SAT instances, we must analyse the ratios $\frac{w(S_1)}{w(S_0)}$

and $\frac{w(S_2)}{w(S_0)}$. For example, if we can find that for a given instance $w(S_1) \leq p \cdot w(S_0)$ always hold, then we can find adequate values for the coefficients c_0, c_1, c_2, in such way that the coefficient of each term on the left hand side of the inequality (4) will be minimum (Khanna looks for the unity in each term) while the coefficient on the right hand side will be maximum.

Of course, we do not know the value for p until the algorithm finishes processing the given instance. Therefore, we believe that the definition of the coefficients $c_i, i = 0, \dots, k$(at least for the coefficient c_0) should be defined in a dynamic way, so they can be adjusted during the execution of the NV-LS, with the objective of reaching the maximum approximation factor for each instance.

In order to improve the general behaviour of the algorithm, it is adequate to use strategies that permit us to speed up the search, 'jump' over local optimums and determine a 'good' point for re-starting the search after a local optimum is found.

4   History-Based Heuristics

In order to improve the general behaviour of our implemented algorithm based on the non-oblivious local search paradigm, we added a tabu search strategy used in order to speed up the phase of reaching a local optimum. Moreover, we used the complement of the last local optimum found in order to avoid review paths already explored and as a mechanism for determining a 'good' point to 're-start' the search process after arriving a local optimum.

Analyzing the behaviour of the local search paradigm, we can see that the process of search could be divided into two phases. In the first phase, called 'ascent-hill', wich occurs relatively quickly, a neighbor can be found to the current solution that improves the objective function. This phase is relatively short [7] and it is followed by a second phase, called 'Plateu'. In this second phase it is hard to find a neighbor that improves the objective function, therefore it is usual to visit points that maintain the same value of the function. It is in this second phase that the greatest quantity of time in the search process generally is invested.

One of the strategies that traditionally has been applied to improve the behaviour of the paradigm of the local search is the tabu heuristic. In [5] and [9], a tabu search has been used as an additional strategy to speed up the search for a local optimum during the 'Plateu' phase.

In both methods, the tabu strategy is based on the use of an array that maintains the direction of the ascents found during the flips of variables. The values of the array are used in order to forbid inverse movements, at least during a fixed number of iterations of the algorithm. An array is introduced to indicate which variables give positive changes for the objective function in the search process. When a variable gives a positive change in the objective function, the difference of the change is stored in the position of this variable. Local changes in the ascending direction are performed while the value of the position of this variable is zero.

For example, a positive value in the position j of the array indicates a positive local change in the variable j; therefore in the next e (assuming that this positive change was e) iterations of the algorithm, the reverse move is forbidden in this position.

The use of the array to store the ascending directions is useful to reduce the number of tested points and speed up the search for local optimums.

4.1   Use of Complemented Values to Restart the Search

Different history-based heuristics have been proposed to continue local search schemes beyond local optimality. These schemes help to intesify the search in promising regions and to diversify the search into uncharted territories by using the information collected from the previous phase of the search [2].

Our search tabu proposal proceeds as follows; we assume that the configuration is currently locally optimal. Then only in this situation, a perturbation or 'kick' is applied to the optimal point in order to generate a new point to restart the search, in such way that the search 'jumps' from one local optimum to another.

The difference between the tabu search and the probabilistic searchs as the 'annealing heuristic', where the test of 'accept/reject' is applied in each point that obeys a probabilistic parameter, is that in our tabu search we only jump until arriving at a local optimum.

In this plan, it is convenient to use an array where we can store the local optimums that were found, in order to avoid to falling into a loop. Tracing the list of local optimums that where found under the algorithm, we observe that sometimes a same local optimum was obtained, indicating that the search goes over regions previously explored. This effect can be avoided, if we can define appropiately way the new 'restart' point of search, after it has arrived at a local optimum.

For example, if we suppose that x_0 is a local optimum, then a 'kick' can be applied to it to make the control of the search jump to a new point x_1 that defers significantly of x_0. We use the complement of last local optimum found as a point to 're-start' the search, and if this new point belongs to an already visited path, then a new point can be built that defers to each one of the local optimums that have been kept in the array of local optimums.

The use of complemented values of the last local optimum for restarting the search permits us to diversify the area of search with the intention of avoiding review paths already explored. Furthermore the use of the local optimum array avoid falling in loops, obtaining heuristic that turns out to be a robust search and, according to the results of the empirical analysis, that improves the behaviour of the non-oblivious local search.

Finally, the success of this algorithm is determined, first by its ability to move successfully through the 'Plateu' phase, reducing the time of this phase, and second, by the use of the complement of the last local optimum found as a new point to restart the search, giving amplitude to the search.

5   Computational Results

For experimental purposes, we have realized a brief empirical analysis and compared the results obtained by local search (LS), non-oblivious local search as defined by Khanna (NV-LS), and our non-oblivious local search, (NTA-LS) which is combined with the two heuristics presented here (tabu strategy and use of complements). The three algorithms were executed for small instances of formulas in Conjunctive Form (CF) that were randomly built. Each CF is characterized by n,m and k, where n is the number of variables, m is the number of clauses and k is the number of literals in each clause. In our case, we are considering only instances of 2-FC, so that k is always fixed to 2. We assume that no clause is a tautology. The method we have followed to build the random formulas is as described in [7] and [8].

We have also programmed an exact algorithm for Max2SAT in order to know how close the various heuristics get to the true optimum. The maximum number of trials for each algorithm is bounded by similar values, in such a way that each algorithm had similar running times (particularly, bounded in polynomial time).

For each one of the three algorithms and for a given instance, we generated 10 random initial points and solved each one of these instances 10 times. The ten values obtained for each instance were averaged and this is the average number of satisfied clauses Z for such an instance. We then estimated the ratio between Z and the true optimum. This ratio is calculated for each one of the ten instances that conform a group, the mean of the ten ratios is calculated and it is the approximation ratio that we are plotting for each n and m fixed.

It should be noted that we are considering small instances that cover the area known as phase transition for Max2SAT problem, i.e. $m \in [n, 5n]$, an area where it is assumed that the instances are typically much more difficult to solve than others away from this phase transition [4]. This region is generally considered to be a good source of hard instances for MaxSAT (and SAT) and has been the focus of recent experimental effort.

The experimental analysis shows that in the practice, the algorithm based on our non-oblivious local search with tabu strategy and the use of complemented values gives the closest solutions to the optimal true value.

The graphs in figures 1, 2 and 3 show the average of the approximation factor obtained for each one of the three algorithms, where $n = 15, 20$ *and* 25 and m goes from $[25, 100], [25, 100]$ *and* $[50, 125]$ respectively.

6   Conclusions

It is possible to improve the approximation factor obtained using non-oblivious local search over Max-kSAT instances. If we can find, for a given instance, a relation between $w(S_i) \leq p \cdot w(S_0)$ for some $i = 1, \ldots, k$ then by exploiting this

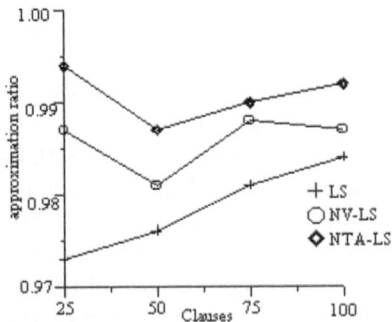

Fig. 1. Graph with the means of the approximation ratio for each algorithm for instances 2-CF, with n=15 variables.

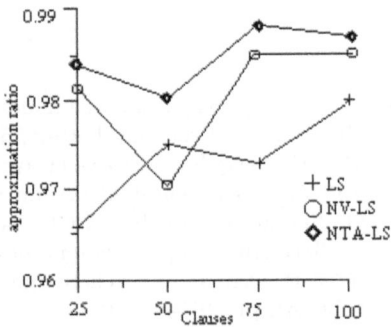

Fig. 2. Graph of the average approximation ratio for each algorithm for instances 2-CF, with n=20 variables.

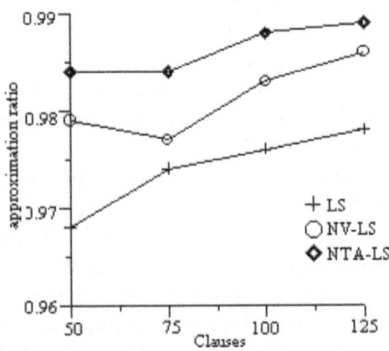

Fig. 3. Graph of the average ratio appproximation for each algorithm for instances 2-CF, with n=25 variables.

relation, it is possible to define appropiate values of the coefficients $c_i, i = 1, \ldots, k$ for the non-oblivious objective function in order to achieve the best aproximation factor for this instance.

We present different strategies that preserve the polynomial-time complexity of the proposed algorithms and improve the general behaviour of the non-oblivious local search. Mainly, we added a tabu search heuristic with the purpose to speed up the phase to reach a local optimum, and we proposed the use of complemented values as a mechanism for restarting the search after arriving at a local optimum in order to avoid reviewing paths already explored.

The empirical analysis and the comparison of the results of these algorithms, show that the non-oblivious local search (that uses the new objective function introduced here) combined with the tabu strategy and the use of the complemented value of the last local optimum for restarting the search, has a robust behaviour and obtains in practice better solutions than the non-oblivious local search alone.

References

1. Alimonti P., New local search approximation techniques for maximum generalized satisfiability problems, Information Procesing Letters, 57(3) , 1996, 151-156.
2. Battiti R., Protasi M., Reactive search, a history-sensitive heuristic for MAX-SAT, to appear in ACM Journal of Experimental Algorithmics, 1997.
3. Bellare M., Goldreich O., Sudan M., Free bits, PCP and non-approximability Towards tight results, Proc. 36th An. Symp. on Found. of Comp. Sc.(FOCS), 1995.
4. Cheeeseman P., Kanesfsky B., Taylor W., Where the really hard problems are, Proceedings of the 12th IJCAI, pp. 163-169. 1991.
5. De Ita G., Morales G., Heurísticas para mejorar la búsqueda local en el tratamiento del problema de máxima satisfactibilidad, (Iberamia96), 1996.
6. Feige U., Goemans M., Approximating the value of two prover proof systems with applications to MAX 2SAT and MAX DICUT, Proceeding 32 Symp. on foundations of Computer Science, pp.182-189, 1995.
7. Gent I.P., Walsh T., An empirical analysis of search in GSAT, Jour. of Artificial Intelligence Research 1, pp.47-59, 1993.
8. Gu J., Global optimization for Satisfactibility (SAT) Problem, IEEE Transaction on Knowledge and Data Engineering, Vol. 6, No.3, 361-381, June 1994.
9. Hansen P., B Jaumard, Algorithms for the Maximum Satisfiability Problem, Computing 44, 279-303, 1990.
10. Johnson D., Approximation algorithms for combinatorial problems, Journal of Computer and System Sciences 9, 256-278, 1974.
11. Khanna Sanjeev, R. Motwani, M. Sudan and U. Vazirani, On Syntactic versus Computational Views of Approximability, TR95-023 ECCC 1995
12. Selman B., Kautz H., Cohen B., Local search strategies for Satisfiability testing, Second DIMACS Challenge on Cliques, Coloring, and Satisfiability, Oct. 1993.
13. Yannakakis M., On the Approximation of Maximum Satisifiability, Journal of Algorithms, Vol. 17, pp. 475-502, 1994.

Integrating the Completion and the Well Founded Semantics

Mauricio Osorio[1] and Bharat Jayaraman[2]

[1] Universidad de las Americas
Departamento de Ingenieria en Sistemas Computacionales
Sta. Catarina Martir, Cholula, Puebla, 72820 Mexico
osorio@cs.buffalo.edu
[2] Department of Computer Science
State University of New York at Buffalo
Buffalo, NY 14260, USA
bharat@cs.buffalo.edu

Abstract. The three most well-known semantics for negation in the logic programming framework are Clark's completion [Cla78], the stable semantics [GL88], and the well-founded semantics [vGRS91]. Clark's completion (COMP) was the first proposal to give a formal meaning to *negation as failure*. However, it is now accepted that COMP does not always captures the meaning of a logic program. Despite its computational and structural advantages, the well-founded semantics (WFS) is considered much too weak for real applications. The stable semantics (STABLE), on the other hand, is so strong that many programs become inconsistent. We present in this paper examples to support these claims, and we introduce a new semantics, called CWFS, which is as powerful as COMP in inferring positive literals and as powerful as WFS in inferring negative literals. Due to its particular construction, CWFS helps to understand the relationship among COMP, WFS, and STABLE. We also discuss some implementation issues of CWFS.

Keywords: Knowledge Representation, Non-monotonic Reasoning, Well Founded Semantics, Stable Semantics, Clark's Completion, Normal Programs, Logic Programming.

1 Introduction

In the field of logic programming, a 'normal program clause' is defined as a definite program clause with possibly negated literals ($\neg$) in the antecedent of the clause [Llo87]. Negation here is interpreted as *negation as failure*, and thus we have a departure here from classical logic to a nonmonotonic logic. The first proposal to provide a plausible declarative semantics for negation-as-failure appeared nearly 20 years back [Cla78], and it is now referred to as the Clark's completion semantics. However, it is now accepted that Clark's completion is often too weak and does not always capture the intended meaning of logic programs, especially for knowledge representation tasks ([BG94, BD96b]). Hence it became

Helder Coelho (Ed.): IBERAMIA'98, LNAI 1484, pp. 230–241, 1998.
© Springer-Verlag Berlin Heidelberg 1998

necessary to find new approaches for specifying the semantics of logic programs. This led to the discovery of two quite dominant approaches: the well-founded semantics (WFS) [vGRS91], and the stable semantics (STABLE) [GL88]. Despite its computational and structural advantages, it has been observed that WFS has as the drawback that it does not infer all atoms that one would expect to be true (see [AB94,Sch92]).

Let us consider the following example considered in [AB94,BLM90,Dix95a], which is representative for the problems with *reasoning by cases*. Let P be

$a \leftarrow \neg b$

$b \leftarrow \neg a$

$p \leftarrow a$

$p \leftarrow b$

The authors in [AB94,BLM90] argue that since neither a nor b can be derived in any semantics based on two-valued models, the disjunction $a \vee b$, and hence also p, should be true. WFS(P) does not fulfill this as pointed out in [AB94,Dix95a]. But observe that STABLE as well as COMP derive p. Our proposed semantics CWFS also derives p. Consequently, lots of extensions of WFS have been defined in recent years to address this situation.

STABLE on the other hand is inconsistent for many programs. Consider the following program P:

$b \leftarrow a$

$a \leftarrow b$

$a \leftarrow \neg b$

Then P does no have any stable model. One can argue by reasoning by cases (on b) that a should be a consequence of P. Once accepted this fact we observe that b is also a consequence of the program. So, the intended model of P is $\{a, b\}$. This is what COMP(P) defines. And CWFS behaves as COMP for this program.

We argue that COMP is very weak to infer negative literals but not so to infer positive literals. On the other hand, WFS is strong enough to infer many negative literal but very weak to infer positive atoms. In general, STABLE derives many literals and so it becomes inconsistent in cases where we argue that there is an intended model.

We agree that "the diversity of different approaches in semantics of negation suggests that there is probably not a unique intended semantics for logic programs. Which semantics should be used depends on concrete applications. To be able to chose the "right" semantics among different ones, it is of great importance to understand the inherent relations between them" [Dun95].

Based on these observations, we define a new semantics called CWFS which combines WFS and COMP in a suitable way. Roughly speaking, CWFS uses the WFS power to derive negative literals and the COMP power to derive positive literals. We prove that CWFS lies "in between" WFS and STABLE, namely, that WFS $\leq_k$ CWFS $\leq_k$ STABLE (where $\leq_k$ is the knowledge ordering to be defined in section 2). Due to the particular construction of CWFS (based on a confluent calculus for WFS and COMP) and our results of CWFS, we are not only suggesting a new semantics but we are contributing to understand better the relationship between COMP, WFS and STABLE. The unique aspect of CWFS respect to the different semantics invented so far (as for instance [Dix95a, Dun95, Sch92]) is that (to our knowledge) this is the only proposal that is given that combines two well known semantics to get as a result a semantics that fits so well in between WFS and STABLE. In addition, our current research suggests that CWFS can be used to provide a direct semantics to the class of programs studied in [JOM95, OJ96, OJ97]. A formal discussion about this claim is outside the scope of this paper, nevertheless we give a simple example of this nature in section 3. We restrict our attention to programs P, such that $ground$(P) is finite ($ground$ is defined in section 2). The generalization to consider any program is possible but involves several technical difficulties that could hide the main idea, and therefore we left it out of this paper.

Our paper is structured as follows. Section 2 gives the general background required in the paper. Section 3 gives examples about the problems of COMP, WFS and STABLE. In section 4 we introduce CWFS and we show how CWFS overcomes the problems mentioned in section 3. Finally, in section 5 we present conclusions and discuss some implementation issues related to CWFS.

2   Background

We first review the definition of propositional classic logic.

A signature $\mathcal{L}$ is a finite set of elements that we call *atoms*. Classical propositional calculus can be defined over the set of well formed formulas defined using a signature and the two logical connectives $\neg$ and $\rightarrow$; the rule of modus pones and the three axiom schemas:

a1) $\alpha_1 \rightarrow (\alpha_2 \rightarrow \alpha_1)$
a2) $(\alpha_1 \rightarrow (\alpha_2 \rightarrow \alpha_3)) \rightarrow ((\alpha_1 \rightarrow \alpha_2) \rightarrow (\alpha_1 \rightarrow \alpha_3))$
a3) $\neg\neg\alpha_1 \rightarrow \alpha_1$

It is not hard to show that classical logic needs a1, a2 and a3; We use $\vdash_m$ to denote provability in the restricted formal system with just a1 and a2.

We now review general concepts related to logic programming. We assume that the reader has familiarity with standard notions as terms, atoms, literals and formulas. A *literal* is an atom or the negation of an atom a that we denote by $\neg a$. Given a set of atoms $\{a_1, \ldots, a_n\}$, we write $\neg\{a_1, \ldots, a_n\}$ to denote $\{\neg a_1, \ldots, \neg a_n\}$. We may denote a normal clause C as usual [Llo87]: $a :\text{-} l_1, \ldots, l_n$, where a is an atom and each l_i is a literal; or by $a \leftarrow \mathcal{B}^+, \neg\mathcal{B}^-$, where $\mathcal{B}^+$ contains all the positive body atoms and $\mathcal{B}^-$ contains all the negative body atoms. We also use $body(C)$ to denote $\mathcal{B}^+ \cup \neg\mathcal{B}^-$. A program is a finite set of clauses. Sometimes we will consider the logical constants **t** and **f** with their intended interpretation. By $ground$(P) we mean the Herbrand instantiation of the program P. An interpretation based on a signature $\mathcal{L}$ is a disjoint pair of sets $< I_1, I_2 >$ such that $I_1 \cup I_2 \subseteq \mathcal{L}$. Given two interpretations $I = \langle I_1, I_2 \rangle$, $J = \langle J_1, J_2 \rangle$, we define $I \leq_k J$ iff $I_i \subseteq J_i$, $i = 1, 2$. Clearly $\leq_k$ is a partial order. We may also see an interpretation $\langle I_1, I_2 \rangle$ as the set of literals $I_1 \cup \neg I_2$. When we look at interpretations as sets of literals then $\leq_k$ corresponds to $\subseteq$.

2.1 Semantics of Normal Programs

The semantics of normal programs have a departure from classic logic. The logic programming community has decided to use *negation as failure* (NF): if A is a ground atom

the goal $\neg A$ succeeds if A fails, and

the goal $\neg A$ fails if A succeeds

This is clearly not justifiable for classical negation, at least not relative to the given program P; the fact that A fails from P does not mean that one can prove $\neg A$. For example, if P is

$$A \leftarrow \neg B$$

then B fails and so $\neg B$ succeeds and therefore A succeeds. But A is not a logical consequence of P. For the reasons that are given for the preference of NF over classical negation, see [Sch92a]. Since NF is defined in terms of the operational semantics, and as we said before, in principle, a programmer should be only concerned with the *declarative meaning* of her program, it becomes important to provide a convincing declarative semantics to NF. The first proposal was given 1978 and it is called the Clark's completion. The main idea is that, to deduce negative information from a normal program, we could "complete" the program by adding the only-if halves of the definitions of the predicate symbols. For example, the completion of $A \leftarrow \neg B$ is $A \leftrightarrow \neg B$, and also $\neg B$ only if there is no definition for B. (For the details about Clark's completion, see [Llo87].) However, it is now accepted that the Clark's completion does not always capture the intended meaning of logic programs. Let us consider the well-known **Unreachable** program. Let P be as follows:

```
edge(a, b).    edge(c, d).    reachable(a).
reachable(X) ← reachable(Y), edge(Y, X).
unreachable(X) ← ¬reachable(X).
```

Here, edge(a,b) means that there is a directed edge from a to b.

We obviously expect vertices c,d to be unreachable, and indeed, Clark's semantics implies it, i.e.,

$comp(P) \models$ unreachable(c) and $comp(P) \models$ unreachable(d)

Suppose we add to P the clause edge(d, c) and call the resulting program P'. Although we still expect that c and d are to be unreachable, the Clark's semantics of P' does not imply that c and d are unreachable. This example illustrates well why COMP is weak to infer negative literals. Moreover, by the compactness theorem, no first-order formula can express the concept of *transitive closure*. This result imposes a fundamental restriction of any semantics based only in the notion of logical consequence.

Hence it became necessary to find new forms for specifying the semantics of logic programs. A new approach emerged that now is known as the *canonical model* approach.

2.2   Canonical Models

This approach was initiated by the idea of *stratification* [ABW88]. A program
is *stratified* if there is no recursion through negation. With the stratified semantics, our program example P' is broken in two parts (called *strata*) P'_1 and P'_2,
where P'_1 is:

   edge(a, b).   edge(c, d).   edge(d, c).
   reachable(a).   reachable(X) ← reachable(Y), edge(Y, X).
and P'_2 is the single clause: unreachable(X) ← ¬reachable(X).
Then we first compute the minimal model of P'_1. The result will fix the semantics of the predicates of this stratum, i.e. we will get the semantics for edge and
reachable. Then we compute the minimal model of P'_2 with the interpretation
of the "lower" level predicates (in this case edge and reachable) fixed. The resulting semantics agrees with the intended meaning. Since not every program is
stratified, this idea had to be extended in a number of ways, such as *local stratification*, *weak stratification*, *modular stratification* and *effective stratification*, see
([AB94,BG94].

   The *stable* semantics [GL88] and *well-founded* semantics [vGRS91], are general approaches to assigning semantics to a logic program that generalize the
approaches based on stratification. We will briefly describe the *stable semantics*
(SM) and *well-founded semantics* (WFS) for (possible) infinite ground programs.

   Say that a Herbrand model M of a program P is *supported* if for every
atom $A \in M$ there exists a clause whose consequent is A and whose antecedent
is true in M. Say that a Herbrand model M of P is *well-supported* if it is
supported and there exists a well-founded partial ordering $\leq$ on M such that
for any atom $A \in M$ there exists a clause in P with consequent A and for
every positive literal B in the antecedent of the clause, we have $B < A$. For any
normal program P, the well-supported models of P are defined to be the *stable
models* of P. When the program has a unique stable model then it becomes the
stable declarative semantics of the program, otherwise the declarative semantics
of the program is undefined. Since many programs could considered inconsistent
by having several stable models, it is useful to adopt the the *sceptical* view of
the stable semantics, which consists in defining a literal l as a consequence of
STABLE if l is true in every stable model of the program. Only to be congruent
with two-valued classic logic, we say that STABLE derives every literal when P
lacks STABLE models. (In a real problem we would perhaps prefer to say for
this case that STABLE derives no literal at all, i.e. the empty set.)

   We now discuss the *well-founded semantics* of a program P. First we define
a *partial interpretation* I as a consistent set of literals (i.e., not both a and $¬a$
belong to I) whose atoms are in the Herbrand base of P. We say a literal is
true in I if it is in I, and we say it is *false in I* if its complement is in I. Let
the Herbrand base H of P and its partial interpretation I be given. We say
$A \subseteq H$ is an *unfounded set (of P) with respect to I* if each atom $p \in A$ satisfies
the following condition: For each clause R of P whose head is p, (at least) one
of the following holds: (i) Some (positive or negative) subgoal q of the body is
false in I, (ii) Some positive subgoal of the body occurs in A. Now, the *greatest*

unfounded set (of P) with respect to I, denoted by $U_P(I)$, is the union of all sets that are unfounded with respect to I.

To define the well-founded semantics, three transformations T_P, U_P and W_P are defined as follows: (i) $p \in T_P(I)$ iff there is some instantiated clause R of P such that R has head p, and each subgoal literal in the body of R is true in I; (ii) $U_P(I)$ is the greatest unfounded set of P with respect to I; and (iii) $W_P(I) = T_P(I) \cup \neg U_P(I)$. Let α range over all countable ordinals. The sets I_α and I^∞, whose elements are literals in the Herbrand base of a program P, are defined recursively as follows: For limit ordinal α, $I_\alpha = \bigcup_{\beta < \alpha} I_\beta$. Note that $I_0 = \emptyset$. For a successor ordinal $\alpha = \beta + 1$, $I_{\beta+1} = W_P(I_\beta)$. Finally, define $I^\infty = \bigcup_\alpha I_\alpha$. The *well founded semantics* of a program P is the "meaning" represented by the limit I^∞.

To study in detail several issues related to semantics for normal programs as as well as current extensions of WFS, see [Dix95a, BD96b, BG94, DO97b, DO97c]. To our knowledge, our proposal is different to any other idea presented so far.

2.3 Semantics of Programs

Following [Llo87], a program is a finite set of program statements, each of which has the form $a \leftarrow W$, where the head a is an atom and the body W is an arbitrary first order formula. We follow [Llo87] and consider them as macros of normal programs. Such approach has been followed by [HL94], [Nai86]. In [Pet97] this approach (with some variants in the translation) is studied respect to the stratified, WFS and STABLE semantics.

3 Problems of COMP, WFS and STABLE

Example 1:. We have seen in section 2.1 how COMP fails to give the intended meaning to the **Unreachable** program. It was unable to derive the negative literals $\neg$ `unreachable(c)`, $\neg$ `unreachable(d)`. The WFS semantics gives the intended semantics to this program since the notion of unfounded sets is strong enough to derive the intended negative literals. Our proposed semantics CWFS agrees with WFS in this case.

Example 2:. Our example here is taken from [vGRS91]. Let P be the program:
$$p \leftarrow \neg p, \neg q$$
Then comp(P) is inconsistent. Let us add to P the "harmless" clause $p \leftarrow p$ and call this program P_1. Now comp(P_1) is consistent and derives p as well as $\neg q$. On the other hand, if we add to P the "harmless" clause $q \leftarrow q$ and call this program P_2 it turns out that comp(P_2) infers q as well as $\neg p$. The main criticism of [vGRS91] is that it should not be the case that the semantics of the three "similar" programs P, P_1 and P_2 differs that much. STABLE adopts a "uniform" position in the sense that it gives the same answer to the three programs, that in this case corresponds to define no intended model for any of them (i.e., STABLE lacks of STABLE models). Here, CWFS behaves as STABLE.

As already said, the main problem with WFS is that it is considered much too weak for real applications. Let us consider again the following example used in the introduction.

Example 3:. This example is representative for the problems with *reasoning by cases*. Let P be

$$a \leftarrow \neg b$$
$$b \leftarrow \neg a$$
$$p \leftarrow a$$
$$p \leftarrow b$$

As mentioned before, one can argue that p should be derivable. WFS(P) does not fulfill this as pointed out in [Dix95a]. When WFS can not infer any negative literal, its power to derive positive literals reduces to the power of the inference system $\vdash_m$ (defined in section 2) that indeed is very weak. STABLE as well as COMP derive p. So thus our proposed CWFS semantics.

The following two examples illustrate problems in WFS as well as STABLE.

Example 4: Consider the program P

$$c \leftarrow c$$
$$b \leftarrow a$$
$$a \leftarrow b$$
$$a \leftarrow \neg b, \neg c$$

Then P does no have stable models and WFS(P)=$\emptyset$. Our following argument explains that $\{a, b, \neg c\}$ could be considered as the intended model of P. First, we should be able to remove tautologies without changing the semantics of the program, getting:

$$b \leftarrow a$$
$$a \leftarrow b$$
$$a \leftarrow \neg b, \neg c$$

Since c does not occur as the head of any clause of the program, by "negation as failure" we can infer $\neg c$ and so we also infer $a \leftarrow \neg b$. By the pair of clauses:

$$a \leftarrow b$$
$$a \leftarrow \neg b$$

and *reasoning by cases* we can derive a. Finally, by *modus ponens* applied to a and $b \leftarrow a$, we get b. So, the intended model of P is $\{a, b, \neg c\}$. CWFS behaves in this way.

4   Definition of CWFS

We remind the reader that our (normal as well as general) programs P have the restriction that $ground(P)$ is finite. We need the following transformation rules (see [Dix95a,BD97,BZF97]) that we will apply to $ground(P)$:

RED$^+$: This transformation can be applied to P, if there is an atom a which does not occur in HEAD(P). RED$^+$ transforms P to the program where all ocurrences of $\neg a$ are removed.

RED⁻: This transformation can be applied to P, if there is a clause $a \leftarrow \ \in P$. RED⁻ transforms P to the program where all clauses that contain $\neg a$ in their bodies are deleted.

TAUT: *(Tautology)* Suppose P contains a clause which has the same atom in its head and in its body. Then we remove the given clause.

Success (S): Suppose that P includes a fact a and a clause $q \leftarrow Body$ such that $a \in Body$. Then we replace the clause $q \leftarrow Body$ by $q \leftarrow Body \setminus \{a\}$.

Failure (F): Suppose that P includes a fact a and a clause $q \leftarrow Body$ such that $a \notin HEAD(P)$. Then we erase the given clause.

Loop Detection (Loop): We say that P_2 results from P_1 by $Loop_A$ iff there is a set A of atoms such that for each clause $a \leftarrow Body \in P_1$, if $a \in A$, then $Body \cap A \neq \emptyset$, $P_2 := \{a : -Body \in P_1 : Body \cap A = \emptyset\}$, $P_1 \neq P_2$.

It has been shown that **Loop + RED⁻ + RED⁻ + S + F** defines a confluent and terminating calculus over finite *ground* programs [BZF97]. The normal form of this program is called *remainder*. It is not hard to see that if we extend the system by adding the **Taut** reduction the calculus remains confluent and terminating. We call this new normal form *rem*.

What are the minimal requirements we want to impose on a semantics? Certainly we want that facts, i.e. clauses with empty bodies are true. Dually, if an atom does not occur in any head, then its negation should be true. This gives rise to the following definition, that we can also call the explicit semantics of a program.

Definition 1 (SEM$_{min}$).
For any program P we define $HEAD(P) = \{a| \ a \leftarrow \mathcal{B}^+, \neg \mathcal{B}^- \ \in P\}$ — the set of all head-atoms of P. We also define

$$SEM_{min}(P) = \langle P^{true}, P^{false} \rangle, \ where$$

$$P^{true} := \{p| \ p \leftarrow \ \in P\}, \quad P^{false} := \{p| \ p \in \mathcal{L}_P \setminus HEAD(P)\}$$

Showing WFS(P)=SEM$_{min}$($ground(remainder(P))$) is one of the main results of [BZF97]. This result holds if we use *rem* instead of *remainder*.

Definition 2 (Definition of def and sup).
Let P be ground normal program and let a be an atom, by the definition of a in P, we mean the set of clauses: $\{a \leftarrow body \in P\}$, that we denote by $def(a)$. We define

$$sup(a) := \begin{cases} \mathbf{f} & if \ def(a) = \emptyset \\ body_1 \vee \ldots \vee body_n & if \ def(a) = \{a \leftarrow body_1, \ldots, a \leftarrow body_n\} \end{cases}$$

Definition 3 (COMP(P) ([Cla78])).
For any ground normal program P and a set of atoms A we define $COMP(P)$ over A[1] as the classical theory $\{a \leftrightarrow sup(a) : a \in A\}$.

---

[1] In the classical definition of COMP(P), A is the Herbrand Base of P

Definition 4 (CWFS(P)).

*Let P be a normal program, we define COMP-WFS(P):=
COMP(rem(ground(P)), where COMP is defined over the Herbrand Base of P.
A Herbrand model of COMP-WFS(P) is called an intended model of P with
respect to CWFS. The basic CWFS semantics of P is defined as the unique intended model of P with respect to CWFS. When there many or none intended
models, we say that the program is inconsistent. The scenario CWFS semantics
of P is defined as the set of intended models of P. Finally, the sceptical CWFS
semantics of COMP-WFS(P), denoted as CWFS(P), is defined as*

$\{l : COMP\text{-}WFS(P) \vdash l,$ where l is a ground literal of $COMP\text{-}WFS(P)\}$

Note that the sceptical CWFS is inconsistent only when it lacks of intended
models. In this case it proves every ground literal. (But we could redefine this
notion and state that in this case it derives no ground literal at all.) Unless
stated otherwise, we assume the sceptical view of the CWFS semantics.

4.1   Examples.

We explain how to find the CWFS semantics by using some examples from
section 3. To simplify the presentation we only consider propositional normal
programs here. Therefore $ground(P)=P$.
We start with example 2. We apply the **RED$^+$** reduction to get:

$p \leftarrow \neg p$

Since we can not apply any other reduction, this is the $rem(P)$ normal form of P.
Now, COMP$(rem(P)) = \{p \leftrightarrow \neg p, \neg q\}$. Thus, the program is inconsistent. If we
consider program P_1, we have to apply **Taut** and **RED$^+$** to obtain $rem(P_1)$.
So, $rem(P_1)=rem(P)$ and we can check that $rem(P_1)= rem(P)= rem(P_2)$. So,
for CWFS the three programs are inconsistent. The same situation occurs with
STABLE. Both STABLE and CWFS avoid the irregular behavior of COMP that
gives very different semantics to the three similar programs.

We now consider example 3. Here, no reduction can be applied and so we
only need to complete the program to get $\{a \leftrightarrow \neg b, b \leftrightarrow (\neg a, p \leftrightarrow a \vee b)\}$.
Therefore CWFS(P)=$\{p\}$.

We now consider example 4. Here, we can apply **Taut**, **Red$^+$** to get the
normal form $red(P)$:

$b \leftarrow a$

$a \leftarrow b$

$a \leftarrow \neg b$

And the completion of the program is $\{b \leftrightarrow a, a \leftrightarrow (b \vee \neg b)\}$. Therefore CWFS(P)
$= \{a, b, \neg c\}$.
The following result is immediate by the construction of CWFS (due to lack
of space we omitt the proofs).

Theorem 1 ((closure properties of CWFS)).

*CWFS is closed under each transformation **Loop**, **RED$^-$**, **RED$^+$**, **S**, **F**, **Taut**.*

Theorem 2 ((STABLE models are intended models WRT CWFS)).
For every normal program P, if M is a stable model of P then M is an intended model of P with respect to CWFS.

The following theorems assume the sceptical approach of the given semantics.

Theorem 3 ((CWFS is consistent in more cases than STABLE)).
For every normal program P, STABLE(P) is consistent implies that CWFS(P) is consistent, but the reciprocal is false.

Theorem 4 ((CWFS is in between WFS and STABLE)).
For every normal program P, WFS(P) $\leq_k$ CWFS(P) $\leq_k$ STABLE(P). Moreover, the inequalities are strict.

For (general) programs, we define CWFS(P) := CWFS(*trans-to-normal*(P)), where *trans-to-normal* is the translation given in chapter 4 of [Llo87].

5   Conclusions and Further Work

Several authors have pointed out some shortcomings of COMP, STABLE and WFS. We review some program examples and present new ones that support this claim. COMP lacks for a good machine to derive negative literals, while WFS tends to be too weak while STABLE too strong. We propose the new semantics CWFS that tries to reduce the problem by adopting a stronger form than WFS but staying weaker than STABLE. Our research suggests that CWFS can be used to model aggregation, where WFS is too weak but STABLE is too strong, see [OJ97]. This is however, material for a future paper. Moreover, CWFS is closed under well known tranformations such as **Taut, S, F**, etc. Thanks to confluence and termination, these transformation rules have both a declarative and an operational meaning. ¿From the declarative point of view, they tell us that our semantics is closed under the given transformation rule. From an operational point of view the transformations are computable functions that can be applied to simplify the program. With regard to implementation issues, it may be noted that computing *ground*(P) is a very costly operation. In [BZF97] it is shown that to compute *remainder*(*ground*(P)) we can start with a subset of *ground*(P) that we can compute more efficiently. Their result also applies to *rem*. The same authors explain in [BZF97a] that "in any practical implementation, one would not apply the transformation to the entire set of clauses but partition the program clauses according to the strongly *connected components* of its static dependency graph". They also present a strategy of transformation applications that provides an efficient form to make the entired reduction. The algorithm is polynomial time w.r.t. to size of the EDB. For several programs *rem*(*ground*(P)) is already a set of fact and so we can immediately compute CWFS skiping the completion part. Then, as shown in [BD95], we can compute CWFS by doing hyperresolution on *rem*(*ground*(P)). Another idea, could be to transform *rem*(*ground*(P)) into a set of constraints and to use linear programming as explained in [BNNS93] to compute the minimal models of the completion of the program.

References

ABW88.   Krzysztof R. Apt, Howard A. Blair, and Adrian Walker. Towards a theory of declarative knowledge. In Jack Minker, editor, *Foundations of Deductive Databases*, chapter 2, pages 89–148. Morgan Kaufmann, 1988. 234

AB94.   Krzysztof R. Apt, and Roland N. Bol Logic Programming and Negation: A Survey. *Journal of Logic Programming*, 19,20:9-71, 1994 231, 234

BD95.   Stefan Brass and Jürgen Dix. Disjunctive Semantics based upon Partial and Bottom-Up Evaluation. In Leon Sterling, editor, *Proceedings of the 12th Int. Conf. on Logic Programming, Tokyo*, pages 199–213. MIT Press, June 1995. 239

BD97.   Stefan Brass and Jürgen Dix. Characterizations of the Disjunctive Stable Semantics by Partial Evaluation. *Journal of Logic Programming*, 32(3):207–228, 1997. (Extended abstract appeared in: Characterizations of the Stable Semantics by Partial Evaluation *LPNMR, Proceedings of the Third International Conference, Kentucky*, pages 85–98, 1995. LNCS 928, Springer.). 236

BD96b.   Gerhard Brewka and Jürgen Dix. Knowledge representation with logic programs. Technical report, Tutorial Notes of the 12th European Conference on Artificial Intelligence (ECAI '96), 1996. Also appeared as Technical Report 15/96, Dept. of CS of the University of Koblenz-Landau. Will appear as Chapter 6 in *Handbook of Philosophical Logic*, 2nd edition (1998), Volume 6, Methodologies. 230, 235

BNNS93.   C. Bell, A. Nerode R. Ng, and V.S. Subrahamanian Implementing Stable Semantics by Linear Programming. in L. M. Pereida and A. Nerode editors *Logic Programming and Nonmonotonic Reasoning,* pages 23-42, MIT Press 1993. 239

BG94.   Chitta Baral and Michael Gelfond. Logic Programming and Knowlege Representation. *Journal of Logic Programming*, 19-20, 1994. 230, 234, 235

BZF97.   Stefan Brass, Ulrich Zukowski, and Burkhardt Freitag. Transformation Based Bottom-Up Computation of the Well-Founded Model. In J. Dix, L. Pereira, and T. Przymusinski, editors, *Nonmonotonic Extensions of Logic Programming*, LNAI 1216, pages 171–201. Springer, Berlin, 1997. 236, 237, 239

BZF97a.   Stefan Brass, Ulrich Zukowski, and Burkhardt Freitag. Improving the Alternating Fixpoint: The Transformation Approach. In J. Dix, U. Furbach, and A. Nerode, editors, *Logic Programming and Nonmonotonic Reasoning, LNAI 1265,* pages 40-59. Springer, Berlin, 1997. 239

Cla78.   Keith L. Clark. Negation as Failure. In H. Gallaire and J. Minker, editors, *Logic and Data-Bases*, pages 293–322. Plenum, New York, 1978. 230, 237

BLM90.   Chitta Baral, Jorge Lobo, and Jack Minker. Genelalized Well-founded Semantics for Logic Programs. In M. E. Stickel. editor *.10th International Conference on Automated Deduction, LNAI 449,subseries LNCS,* pages1102-116. Springer,J. Siekmann, July 1990. 231

Dix95a.   Jürgen Dix. A Classification-Theory of Semantics of Normal Logic Programs: I. Strong Properties. *Fundamenta Informaticae*, XXII(3):227–255, 1995. 231, 232, 235, 236

DO97b.   Jürgen Dix and Mauricio Osorio Provability Closures in Logic Programming. Proc. of the *International Symposium of Computer Science in Mexico*, Instituto Politecnico Nacional editors, 1997. 235

DO97c.   Jose Arrazola, Jürgen Dix and Mauricio Osorio Confluence Rewriting Systems for Logic Programming Semantics. Research Report 27-97. University of Koblenz, Germany. 235

Dun95.   P. M. Dung. An Argumentation-theoric Foundation for Logic Progamming *The Journal of Logic Programing*, 151-177, 1995. 231, 232

GL88.   Michael Gelfond and Vladimir Lifschitz. The Stable Model Semantics for Logic Programming. In R. Kowalski and K. Bowen, editors, *5th Conference on Logic Programming*, pages 1070–1080. MIT Press, 1988. 230, 231, 234

HL94.   P. M. Hill and J. W. Lloyd The Gödel Programming Language. *MIT Press*, 1994. 235

JOM95.   B. Jayaraman, M. Osorio and K. Moon, "Partial Order Programming (revisited)", *Proc. AMAST, LNCS 936*, pages 561-575. Springer-Verlag, July 1995. 232

Llo87.   John W. Lloyd. *Foundations of Logic Programming*. Springer, Berlin, 1987. 2nd edition. 230, 233, 235, 239

Nai86.   L. Naish. Negation and Quantifiers in NU-Prolog. in *Proc. of the Third Int. Conf. on Logic Programming, LNCS 225*, pages 624-634. Springer-Verlag, 1986. 235

OJ96.   Mauricio Osorio and Bharat Jayaraman. Towards a Broader Basis for Logic Programming Memorias de IBERAMIA 96, Cholula, Mexico, 1996. 232

OJ97.   Mauricio Osorio and Bharat Jayaraman. Aggregation and WFS$^+$. In J. Dix, L. Pereira, and T. Przymusinski, editors, *Nonmonotonic Extensions of Logic Programming*, LNAI 1216, pages 71–90. Springer, Berlin, 1997. 232, 239

Pet97.   Vyacheslav Petukhin Programs with Universally Quantified Embedded Implications. In J. Dix, U. Furbach, and A. Nerode, editors, *Logic Programming and Nonmonotonic Reasoning, LNAI 1265,* pages 309-323. Springer, Berlin, 1997. 235

Sch92.   John S. Schlipf. Formalizing a Logic for Logic Programming. *Annals of Mathematics and Artificial Intelligence*, 5:279–302, 1992. 231, 232

Sch92a.   John S. Schlipf. Logics for Negation as Failure. *Logic for Computer Science*, MSRI Publications21, Springer-Verlag 1992. 233

vGRS91.   Allen van Gelder, Kenneth A. Ross, and John S. Schlipf. The well-founded semantics for general logic programs. *Journal of the ACM*, 38:620–650, 1991. 230, 231, 234, 235

Recognition of Partially Occluded Flat Objects

Carlos Orrite, Angel Alcolea and Alfonso Campo

Departamento de Ingenería Electrónica y Comunicaciones.
Universidad de Zaragoza. María de Luna 3, 50015 Zaragoza, Spain
e-mail: corrite@posta.unizar.es

Abstract. This paper is focused on the object recognition problem in computer vision under partial occlusion. The approach followed to carry out this goal is the alignment method described exhaustively in the literature. In this approach the recognition process is divided in two stages: in a first stage, the transformation in space between the viewed object and the model object is determined. In a second stage the model that best matches the viewed object is found. Given four points in the image, it is necessary to find the four corresponding points in the model. This problem involving combinatorial search is resolved by means of a genetic algorithm. The occlusion problem has been dealt with special attention, so a new method has been proposed consisting of three processes: identification, grouping and verification. The recognition algorithm proposed here has been tested in several examples obtaining good results.

1 Introduction

Object recognition is one of the most important aspects of visual perception. The problem of shape-based object recognition can be approached in different complexity levels, depending on the restrictions place upon the scene configuration:

- The objects considered are flat and rigid, moving in the plane and scaling.
- Flat objects which are not restricted to move in the plane, but are allowed to move and rotate in three-dimensional space.
- Three-dimensional objects (rather than flat) in rigid transformations. This case can be further subdivided according to whether the visible contours are "sharp", such as the edges of a cube, or smooth, such as the projected silhouette of a cylinder or a sphere.
- Articulated objects, that is, objects containing movable parts, such as a pair of scissors or the human body.
- Many real objects can undergo more complicated transformations, such as bending, stretching, and other types of distortions.

This paper examines the case of flat objects in three-dimensional space with possible occlusions. A large number of different methods have been proposed in the

Helder Coelho (Ed.): IBERAMIA'98, LNAI 1484, pp. 242-252, 1998.
© Springer-Verlag Berlin Heidelberg 1998

literature, but the different approaches can be classified into three main classes: recognition by invariant properties, recognition by object decomposition into parts, and alignment methods [1].

The first approach is not appropriated in the case of objects partially occluded. Invariant properties are in most of cases related to the global analysis of the object to recognize. Obviously in presence of occlusions it is impossible to compute the mentioned properties.

Recognition by object decomposition into parts is related to a theory presented by Biederman [2], named Recognition by Components (RBC). The RBC is a theory of human image understanding from the field of psychology. Following this theory, the perceptual recognition of objects is considered to be a process in which the input image is segmented at regions of deep concavity into an arrangement of simple geometric components, such as blocks, cylinders, wedges, and cones. The fundamental assumption of the RBC theory is that a modest set of generalized-cone components, called geons can be derived from contrasts of five readily detectable properties of edges in a two-dimensional image: curvature, collinearity, symmetry, parallelism, and cotermination. The usefulness of this theory lies in the assumption that the detection of this properties is generally invariant over viewing position, and consequently, robust object perception is carried out when the image is projected from a new point of view. In the case presented here, where we are considering only flat objects, the image segmentation takes place in the T-junction points formed by contour occlusions.

Some authors propose the contour segmentation at negative curvature minima previous to the recognition process [3], and others segment the curves in concave-convex segments [4]. These approaches have not been taken into account since we are considering a general contour without any restrictions, which may present no negative curvature minima or inflexion points. Moreover, curvature maxima are not invariant points under projective transformations, although in most cases they are.

Alignment methods are other approach to visual object recognition [5]. In this approach the recognition process is divided into two stages. The first one determines the transformation in space that is necessary to bring the viewed object into alignment with possible object models. The second stage determines the model that best matches the viewed object.

The approach presented here is based on the image segmentation into parts by the localization of the T-junction points. The new segments so generated, will be identified following an alignment method under consideration of projective transformation.

In the following section we discuss this approach in more detail, reviewing the main approaches implemented up to date. In section 3 the shape matching algorithm proposed by us, and based in Genetic Algorithms is presented, being in section 4 where the occlusion problem is taken into account. Section 5 shows two experiments of object recognition in presence of occlusion based in the proposed method and a discussion of the results. Finally, in section 6 we present our conclusions.

2 The Alignment Approach

If V denotes the object view which is under analysis for recognition, Mi is a object model in the database, and Tij is the set of allowed transformations that can be applied to object model Mi, then the process of recognition requires to find the best transformation Tij that applied to the Mi model, maximize a given function F of fit quality between the model and the object.

The alignment approach can be decomposed in two stages. In a first stage, the transformation between the object view and the model object, for all candidate models, is determined. Afterwards, the object model that best matches the object view is selected. The first step is known as alignment stage. The transformations allowed are projective transformations.

Since the projective plane has three homogeneous coordinates, the transformation is represented by a 3x3 matrix with 8 essential parameters. The general projective transformation from one projective plane, Π, to another, π, is represented as:

$$\begin{bmatrix} x_1 \\ x_2 \\ x_3 \end{bmatrix} = \begin{bmatrix} t_{11} & t_{12} & t_{13} \\ t_{21} & t_{22} & t_{23} \\ t_{31} & t_{32} & t_{33} \end{bmatrix} \begin{bmatrix} X_1 \\ X_2 \\ X_3 \end{bmatrix} \qquad (1)$$

the coordinates before the transformation are represented in capital letters, while the coordinates after the transformation are represented in small letters. Cartesian coordinates are obtained from the previous expression according to the equations:

$$x = \frac{x_1}{x_3} = \frac{t_{11}X + t_{12}Y + t_{13}}{t_{31}X + t_{32}Y + t_{33}}$$

$$y = \frac{x_2}{x_3} = \frac{t_{21}X + t_{22}Y + t_{23}}{t_{31}X + t_{32}Y + t_{33}} \qquad (2)$$

In the previous equations the parameter t33 does not affect neither x coordinate nor y coordinate, then it is considered as an arbitrary scale factor that does not affect the Cartesian coordinates, so we can choose t33=1.

The projective transformation matrix T requires eight independent parameters to define a unique mapping. Since each point in the plane provides two Cartesian coordinate equations, it is necessary to find four point correspondences, provided that no three of them are collinear, between two projectively transformed planes to define the transformation matrix uniquely.

The resulting linear system of equations is:

$$\begin{bmatrix} X_1 & Y_1 & 1 & 0 & 0 & 0 & -x_1X_1 & -x_1Y_1 \\ 0 & 0 & 0 & X_1 & Y_1 & 1 & -y_1X_1 & -y_1Y_1 \\ X_2 & Y_2 & 1 & 0 & 0 & 0 & -x_2X_2 & -x_2Y_2 \\ 0 & 0 & 0 & X_2 & Y_2 & 1 & -y_2X_2 & -y_2Y_2 \\ X_3 & Y_3 & 1 & 0 & 0 & 0 & -x_3X_3 & -x_3Y_3 \\ 0 & 0 & 0 & X_3 & Y_3 & 1 & -y_3X_3 & -y_3Y_3 \\ X_4 & Y_4 & 1 & 0 & 0 & 0 & -x_4X_4 & -x_4Y_4 \\ 0 & 0 & 0 & X_4 & Y_4 & 1 & -y_4X_4 & -y_4Y_4 \end{bmatrix} \begin{bmatrix} t_{11} \\ t_{12} \\ t_{13} \\ t_{21} \\ t_{22} \\ t_{23} \\ t_{31} \\ t_{32} \end{bmatrix} = \begin{bmatrix} x_1 \\ y_1 \\ x_2 \\ y_2 \\ x_3 \\ y_3 \\ x_4 \\ y_4 \end{bmatrix} \quad (3)$$

Ayache and Faugeras [6] present an method to identify and locate objects lying on a flat surface. This approach known as HYPER analyzes real scenes with randomly oriented and partially occulted flat industrial parts. The model position is defined by a transformation T, which takes into account a rotation in the plane, a scaling and a translation. The description of the model and the scene primitives is carried out by approximating the contour by polygons, more exactly, by a set of linear segments, where every segment is described by four parameters, x, y, l and a, where x and y are the coordinates of the segment midpoint, l is the segment length and a is the segment orientation measured relatively to the horizontal axis. The hypotheses generation is based in locally compatibility defined as angles difference and length of segments once the transformation T has been estimated. The evaluation process takes place by updating the model position following a recursive least square technique (Kalman filter) in order to update the estimate transformation T.

The main difference in relation to our proposal lies in the paradigm employed to set up the hypotheses generation and evaluation. Ayache and Faugeras use a linear approach due to the restrictions place upon the scene configuration, i.e., rotation in the plane of the image. In our case, it is not possible to follow a linear method, as the previous one, because of the non-linear characteristic of our approach, rotation of the object in 3D space. So, we employ a paradigm based on genetic algorithms to solve the problem of searching the optimun solution in non-linear processes.

Zisserman et al. [7] obtain four distinguished points based on properties that are preserved under projection, such as incidence properties (like tangency and points of tangency). This approach is not useful in the case of occlusion because the points obtained from the input image following the procedure described by Zisserman, are not equivalent to those obtained by the same method in the model view.

Huttenlocher and Ullman [8] implement an application based on the alignment approach in order to recognize flat objects, like rigid machine parts that were allowed to translate, rotate in space and change of scale. The recognition system identifies a small number of salient and stable points such as strong maxima in curvature, deep concavities and the centres of closed or almost closed blobs. The method proposed by Huttenlocher and Ullman is based on three points to determinate the transformation that have been carried out by specifying six parameters: three for rotation, two for the translation (under orthographic projection) and one for scaling. In this paper, we are considering four points because the transformations allowed are not restricted to be orthographic, but they can be projective.

In the case of projective transformations, it is difficult to identify stable points. For example, maxima in curvature points used by Huttenlocher and Ullman are not in general stable ones. For instance, a circle can be viewed as an ellipse with two maxima of curvature or vice versa, an ellipse can be transformed in a circle losing these extreme points. On the other hand, the most important difference lies in the possibility of occlusion by other objects.

If we consider visual recognition as a problem involving search in a large space, i.e., given a viewed object, the best match is sought in the space of all stored object models and all of their possible views, a method that resolve combinatorial optimization must be used in order to obtain a solution in a reasonable time. In this work we proposed the used of Genetic Algorithms as the paradigm to follow.

3   Genetic Algorithms for Shape Matching

First proposed by John Holland in 1975, genetic algorithms are computational models based on the mechanics of natural selection and natural genetics [9]. They provide a powerful paradigm in order to solve combinatorial optimization problems. As opposed to other optimization techniques which work with a single point in the search space, the genetic algorithm maintains a large population of configurations and combs the search from a multitude of points.

In the present decade, genetic algorithms have experimented a widespread use as optimization techniques to solve problems in a wide variety of domains, including structural shape matching [10]. In this paper we are concerned with a genetic algorithm (GA) for the problem of finding the best matching between a candidate shape and its corresponding model in a data base.

Basically, the so called simple genetic algorithm has been implemented, although a scaling mechanisms has been carried out in order to avoid premature convergence, and dynamic techniques are used [11]. The process consists in the selection of four no-collinear points in the input image and the localization of these points in the different object models.

The structure of the GA implemented is as follows:

```
program Genetic (MAX)
   initialization;
   evaluation;
   scaling;
   repeat
     generation;
     evaluation;
     scaling;
   until number of generations = MAX;
end.
```

The *initialization* function creates and initializes a population.

The *evaluation* function computes the fitness of the individuals in a population. It consists of the following steps:

Decoding the binary strings to obtain the corresponding values in pixels.

Calculation of the transformation matrix following the process described in the previous section.

Application of the transformation matrix to the model.

Arrangement of the pixels in the input image under consideration and the model in order to compare both.

Normalization process in order to compensate for the transformations prior to comparing the viewed object with potential models.

Fitness function evaluation.

A simple matching measure similar to the Hamming distance used by other authors like Ullman has not been followed because of the inherent inaccurate of the process. Instead of the Hamming distance we have used a fitness function evaluation that takes into account the correlation of the x's and y's co-ordinates between the observation and the model, as well as, the mean of the Euclidean distance. This fitness function has the following expression:

$$fit = 0.2 \cdot corrcoef(x) \cdot 0.2 \cdot corrcoef(y) + 0.6 \cdot mean$$

(4)

Where de corrcoef(x) is a matrix of correlation coefficients formed from array x

Scaling of fitness values involves readjustment of string fitness values in order to avoid premature convergence. A linear scaling has been implemented to ensure that the maximum number of offspring allocated to a string is 2.

The *generation* function creates a new offspring population according to:

- Selection of the parents.
- Perform crossover and mutation.
- Generation of a new population.
- Encoding the solutions as binary strings.

The previous algorithm has been implemented in MATLAB and set up in a PC based on a PENTIUM processor at 150Mhz. The computational cost C of the algorithm (expressed in seconds) is given by de equation 5 where the linear behavior of all variables is stated.

$$C = 10^{-4} \cdot f \cdot (6.45 \cdot b \cdot m + 2.5 \cdot m + 119 \cdot m \cdot x + n \cdot [7.4 \cdot b \cdot m + 2.5 \cdot m + 119 \cdot m \cdot ;$$

(5)

where the parameters f, n, b, m and x are defined as:

f = number of objects.

n = number of generations.

b = number of bits in the codification.

m = number of individuals in the population.

x = number of pixels of the contour to approximate.

The genetic parameters as crossover probability, mutation probability, population size and number of generations have been chosen experimentally. The population has a size of 100 individuals, i.e., string of bits, the crossover probability is equal to 0.6 and the mutation probability is 0.003. Just only 20 generations has been found sufficient to reach a good solution.

4 The Problem of Occlusion

In this point we regard with the problem of partial descriptions of the data and cope with the problem of matching partial descriptions to complete descriptions of the models. By partial data we refer to curve segments which are bounded by a pair of T-junction points. The method proposed consists of three processes: identification, grouping and verification. During the identification process, isolated curve segments extracted from the input image are compared and associated with features of the object models. The final result is a list of relations between every curve segment in the input image and the associated models which have been identified as possible solutions. The figure 1 shows a list of segments corresponding to occluded contours and pointers to models they may belong to, that we have called identification tree.

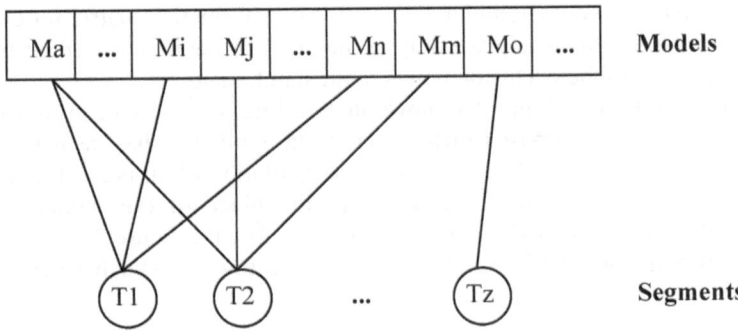

Fig. 1. Identification tree.

Once all segments have been classified, a grouping process is carried out. In this process open isolated segments that may belong to the same model object are grouped in a new segment hypothesis. Finally, a verification of the groupings formed in this way takes place. This verification consists in the simultaneous recognition of both segments by means of the estimation of the transformation matrix for the grouping, and the evaluation of the fitness function.

5 Results and Discussion

The figure 2 shows the model database used in order to test the proposed algorithms.

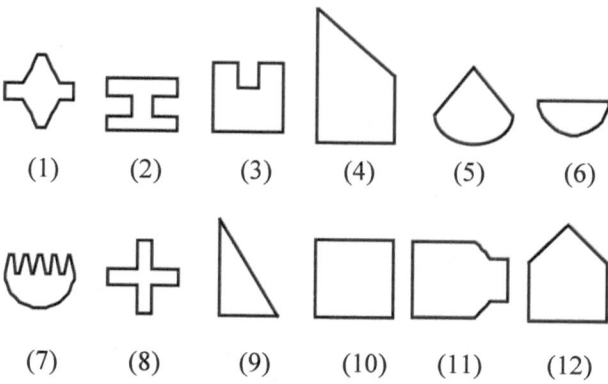

Fig. 2. Model data base.

As mentioned previously, the alignment method considers four points in the occluded view of the object, two of them being the T-junction points formed due to the occlusion of the contour, and determine the transformation matrix for every model. The matching process takes place only in the piece of the model contour between the equivalent points to the occlusion points in the input image.

As an example, the figure 3A shows in fine line, the view of an object partially occluded. Once the proposed method has been applied, it has been found that the view displayed in figure 3B represents the best solution of all presented in the model data base. The figure 3C corresponds to the piece of the model contour that corresponds to the view under consideration. Finally, the figure 3A shows in dashed line the best transformation given by the GA application that matches very closely.

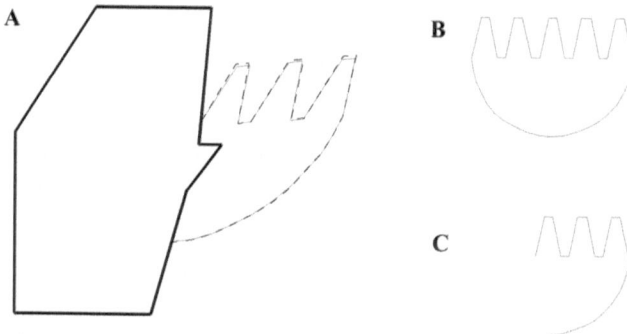

Fig. 3. Example of occlusion.

In the previous example, the recognition process took place without any problem since the piece of the original contour exhibited sufficient and significant information in order to determinate the accurate model with no ambiguity. However, in more realistic examples, we can find a lack of precision in the recognition process since it is very common to find several acceptable models corresponding to the input image, each with different transformation matrix. This is due to the great flexibility exhibited by the projective transformation to change the shape of the objects. The figure 4 is an example of this. In the left side a view painted in fine line has been obtained from the model, in thick line, just applying the following transformation:

$$x = 2X + 0.2Y + 600$$
$$y = 2Y - 0.5X + 400$$

If we consider now this view occluded by another object, as represented on the right side of the same image, it results in two isolated contour pieces labelled A and B.

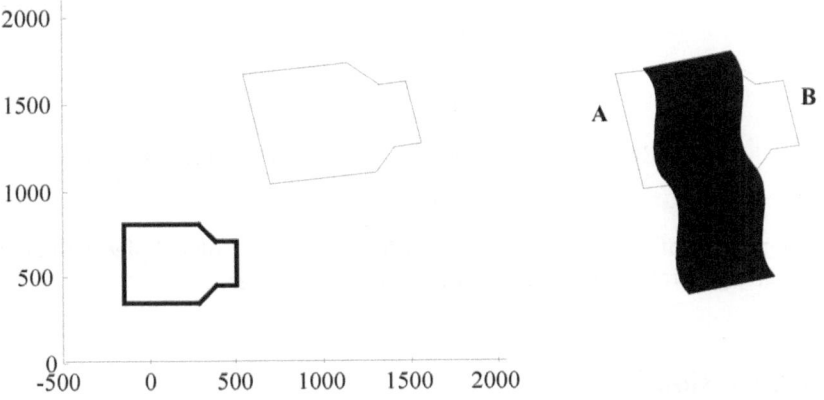

Fig. 4. An occlusion generating two isolated pieces.

As we have referred in the previous section, the procedure begins identifying the models in the data base at which every one of the non occluded piece of the contour can belong. In the present example, it has been found that the piece A can correspond to the model objects 2, 3, 4, 8, 10, 11 and 12. On the other hand, the piece B can correspond to the models objects 1, 3, 4, 9, 10, 11 and 12. There are five common solutions that have to be verified independently. Four of them, the corresponding to the objects 3, 4, 10 and 12 are quickly rejected since there are pixels in one of the pieces, A or B, that coincide with the pixels in the other piece, B or A. So, there is only one solution left that has to be verified following the described process, i. e., given the four occlusion points, the transformation matrix is calculated and the fitness function is computed for this solution.

The final result is depicted in the figure 5. In 5A both pieces of the contour are shown, as well as the same pieces, in dashed line, computed according to the transformation matrix found. In 5B the respective pieces are painted in thick line over the model identified.

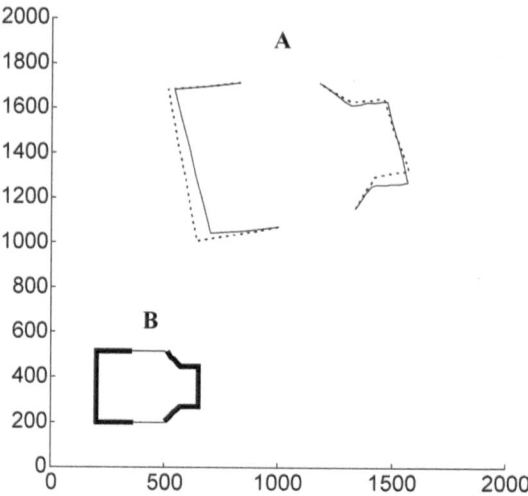

Fig. 5. Recognition of isolated pieces of the contour partially occluded.

The process of verification carried out only with two isolated pieces of contour can be directly generalized with an arbitrary number of pieces.

6 Conclusions

This paper is focused on the object recognition problem, more precisely, on the recognition of partially occluded flat objects. This issue is very important in industrial applications where we can find flat objects in 3-D space under possible occlusions. The method developed in this work is based on two different approaches that together provide a powerful framework to solve this problem. These approaches are recognition by object decomposition into parts, and alignment methods.

The alignment approach has been carried out taking four non-collinear points in the input image and looking for the corresponding points in every model in the image database. Two of the alignment points correspond to the T-junction points between the contour of the object under consideration and the contour of the object or objects occluding the previous one.

Due to the huge flexibility exhibited by the projective transformation, we have found a problem in the frequent lack of uniqueness in the identification of an occluded contour. This leads to a multiple identification of models. Anyway, this problem has been solved in part thanks to the simultaneous identification of several occluded contours by means of the so called identification tree proposed in this work.

The results provided by the present algorithm applied to a limited image database have been completely satisfactory, so we are encouraged to follow this line by testing the proposed approach in the recognition of flat objects in real images.

The main problem in this approach is the computational time necessary to get a solution due to the kind of transformations allowed and the lack of restrictions imposed in the solution of the problem. Anyway, we have verified the lineal condition of the considered approach in reference to the number of models presented in the model data base.   For a realistic implementation we are considering the implementation of the algorithms in a massively parallel architecture that takes into account the inherent parallelism exhibited by the GA.

References

1. D.W. Murray, "Strategies in object recognition", Gec Journal of Research, Vol. 6, No. 2, pp. 80-95, 1988.
2. I. Biederman, "Recognition-by-Components: A Theory of Human Image Understanding", Psychological Review, Vol. 94, No 2, pp. 115-147, 1987.
3. K. Siddiqi and B.B. Kimia, "Parts of Visual Form: Computational Aspects", IEEE Trans. Pattern Anal. Machine Intell., Vol. 17, No. 3, pp. 239-251, 1995.
4. C. Orrite and A. Alcolea, "Identifying Perceptually Salient Segments on Planar Curves", Pattern Recognition and Image Analysis, Preprints of the VII National Symposium on Pattern Recognition and Image Analysis, pp. 419.424, Published by Centre de Visió per Computador, Universitat Autònoma de Barcelona, Spain, 1997.
5. S. Ullman, "Aligning pictorial descriptions: An approach to object recognition", Cognition, Vol. 32, pp. 193-254, 1989.
6. N. Ayache and O.D. Faugeras, "HYPER: A New Approach for the Recognition and Positioning of Two-Dimensional Objects", IEEE Transactions on Pattern Analysis and Machine Intelligence, vol. PAMI-8, No. 1, pp. 44-54, January 1986.
7. A. Zisserman, D.A. Forsyth, J.L. Mundy and C.A. Rothwell, "Recognizing General Curved Objects Efficiently", in book Geometric Invariance in Computer Vision, pp. 228-251, The MIT Press, 1992.
8. D.P. Huttenlocher and S. Ullman, "Object Recognition using alignment", MIT AI Memo 937.
9. D. E. Goldberg, "Genetic Algorithms in Search, Optimization and Machine Learning", Addison-Wesley Publishing Company, Inc. 1989.
10. M. Singh, A. Chatterjee and S. Chaudhury, "Matching Structural Shape Descriptions using Genetic Algorithms", Pattern Recognition, Vol. 30, No. 9, pp. 1451-1462, 1997.
11. M. Srinivas and L.M. Patnaik, "Genetic Algorithms: A survey", Computer, pp. 17-26, June 1994.

Estimating 3D Shape from the Optical Flow of Photometric Stereo Images

José R.A. Torreão

Instituto de Computação/CAA
Universidade Federal Fluminense
24210-240 Niterói, RJ, Brazil
jrat@caa.uff.br

Abstract. Photometric stereo (PS) images are obtained from a single camera under different illuminations, and have traditionally been employed for the estimation of surface gradient in computer vision. Recently, it has been suggested that such images can also be matched to yield relevant depth cues both in human and in artificial vision. Here, we analyse the optical flow information carried by pairs of PS images taken under slightly different illuminations: By modelling the displacement of the irradiance pattern over the imaged surfaces, due to the illumination change, as a rotation plus a small translational correcting factor, we are able to obtain good 3D surface reconstructions through a structure-from-motion least-squares approach. Our framework for shape estimation does not require knowledge of the reflectance map function, which is at the core of the traditional approach to photometric stereo.

1 Introduction

Photometric stereo (PS) images are obtained from a single camera under different illuminations, and have traditionally been employed for the estimation of surface gradient in computer vision [1,2]. Recently, it has been suggested that such images can also be matched to yield relevant depth cues both in human and in artificial vision. In [3], for instance, a relation was found between the disparity field obtained by matching PS images along a fixed direction, and the shape of the imaged surface. Here we extend that approach, by considering the shape information carried by the optical flow associated with a pair of PS images captured under slightly different illuminations. Such optical flow, which results from the displacement of the irradiance pattern over the imaged surface, due to the change in illumination, can be related to the surface function if a plausible model is assumed for the underlying movement. As we show in the following section, essentially the same relation as in [3] can be obtained when we model such movement as a rotation plus a small translational component along the optical-axis direction. Our approach has the advantage of being completely independent of the reflectance map function, which is the basis for the traditional PS estimation and also for the work in [3]. We present reconstructions yielded by our optical-flow approach to photometric stereo (OFPS), both for synthetic and for real images of surfaces with lambertian plus quasi-specular reflectance.

Helder Coelho (Ed.): IBERAMIA'98, LNAI 1484, pp. 253–261, 1998.

2   Photometric Stereo and Optical Flow

Let us consider a pair of photometric stereo images, I_1 and I_2. It is known that the image intensities can be expressed as [4]

$$I_i(x, y) = R_i(p, q), \quad i = 1, 2 \tag{1}$$

where $p = \frac{\partial z}{\partial x}$ and $q = \frac{\partial z}{\partial y}$ are the gradient components of the imaged surface, $z(x, y)$, and where the reflectance map functions R_1 and R_2 correspond to the two illumination directions, $\hat{S}_1$ and $\hat{S}_2$. If those directions are not far apart, and if the surface is smooth, we can attempt to match the two images to obtain a disparity map, $D(s) = (D_X(s), D_Y(s))$, such that $I_1(s) \approx I_2(s + D(s))$ at each image point, $s = (x, y)$. Employing a Taylor-series expansion on the right-hand side of such equation, we find that the PS disparity map satisfies the relation

$$\Delta I(s) \approx D_X(s) \frac{\partial I_2}{\partial x} + D_Y(s) \frac{\partial I_2}{\partial y} \tag{2}$$

which is the standard optical-flow constraint equation, with $\Delta I(s) \equiv I_1(s) - I_2(s)$ playing the role of the time-derivative of the image intensity, and with the disparity vector playing the role of the flow velocity [5].

The PS disparity field - or optical flow field -, $D(s)$, results from the displacement of the irradiance pattern over the imaged surface, and carries information about its shape. Such information can be recovered via a structure-from-motion scheme, if some assumption is made about the underlying movement. We propose to model such movement essentially as a rotation, allowing for a correction factor in the form of an arbitrary translation along the $z-$axis (optical axis direction). As it is known, under orthographic projection such a translation does not affect the optical flow (see Section 4).

Calling $\Theta = (A, B, C)$ the rotation vector, and $V(x, y)$ the translation along the $z-$direction, the equation of motion for the irradiance pattern, given in terms of a coordinate system fixed with respect to the camera, becomes

$$\Delta R = \Theta \times R + V(x, y) \tag{3}$$

where ΔR is the displacement of an infinitesimal irradiance patch initially located at point $R = (x, y, z)$ in the scene. From (3), we obtain the equations

$$\Delta x \equiv D_X = Bz - Cy, \quad \Delta y \equiv D_Y = Cx - Az, \quad \Delta z = V(x, y) + Ay - Bx \tag{4}$$

where the first two identities follow from the assumption of orthographic projection.

The first two equations in (4) relate the observed optical flow to the surface function $z(x, y)$ and to the rotation components A, B and C. The third relation, on the other hand, involves the unobservable translational component, $V(x, y)$, and takes part in a further constraining relation: since we are assuming that the irradiance pattern moves, due to the illumination change, as if sliding over the imaged surface, we must impose the condition that the displacement vector, ΔR, should be, at each point, perpendicular to the local surface normal, i.e.,

$$\Delta R.\hat{n} = 0 \tag{5}$$

where

$$\hat{n} = \frac{(-p, -q, 1)}{\sqrt{p^2 + q^2 + 1}} \tag{6}$$

is the unit normal vector. Thus, from (5), and using the third relation in (4), we easily obtain the constraint equation

$$V(x, y) = D_X p + D_Y q + Bx - Ay \tag{7}$$

The first two relations in (4), along with equation (7), form the basis of our shape estimation strategy: we will try to determine the surface function and the rotation parameters which best satisfy the former, while minimizing the translational factor, $V(x, y)$, in the latter. We propose a least-squares estimation from the functionals

$$\mathcal{F}_1 = \int \int [D_X + Cy - Bz]^2 + [D_Y - Cx + Az]^2 dx dy \tag{8}$$

and

$$\mathcal{F}_2 = \int \int [D_X p + D_Y q + Bx - Ay]^2 dx dy \tag{9}$$

which come from (4) and (7), respectively.

Minimization of the integrand in (8) with respect to z immediately yields

$$z(x, y) = \frac{BD_X - AD_Y + C(By + Ax)}{A^2 + B^2} \tag{10}$$

Employing (10) back in (8) and minimizing $\mathcal{F}_1$ with respect to A, we obtain

$$A = \gamma B \tag{11}$$

with

$$\gamma = \frac{\alpha \pm \sqrt{\alpha^2 + 4\beta^2}}{2\beta} \tag{12}$$

where

$$\alpha = \int \int [(D_X + Cy)^2 - (D_Y - Cx)^2] dx dy \tag{13}$$

and

$$\beta = \int \int [(D_X + Cy)(D_Y - Cx)] dx dy \tag{14}$$

Equation (10) may therefore be rewritten as

$$z'(x, y) \equiv Bz(x, y) = \frac{(D_X + Cy) - \gamma(D_Y - Cx)}{(\gamma^2 + 1)} \tag{15}$$

giving an estimate of the imaged surface, up to a multiplicative constant, in terms only of the photometric disparity field and the rotation component C. As such component cannot be obtained independently of z', we then proceed as follows: assuming $C = 0$ in equations (12) to (15), we arrive at an initial estimate for z'. From this, we may update the C value: assuming $z(x, y)$ fixed, and minimizing $\mathcal{F}_1$ with respect to C, we get

$$C = \frac{\int \int [z'(\gamma x + y) + D_Y x - D_X y] dx dy}{\int \int (x^2 + y^2) dx dy} \tag{16}$$

Plugged back into equations (12) to (14), this in turn gives a new estimate for γ, and thus for z' through (15). The whole process can then be repeated, and has been found to converge in a few iterations.

Now, we can also estimate B through our second functional: rewriting $\mathcal{F}_2$, in equation (9), in terms of $p' = \frac{\partial z'}{\partial x}$ and $q' = \frac{\partial z'}{\partial y}$, and minimizing the resulting expression with respect to B, yields

$$B^4 = \frac{\int \int (D_X p' + D_Y q')^2 dx dy}{\int \int (\gamma y - x)^2 dx dy} \tag{17}$$

which completes our estimation of $z(x, y) \equiv z'(x, y)/B$.

We obtain two pairs of maps for z, due to the double value for γ in (12), and to the plus and minus signs for B in (17). One of these maps is usually a plausible reconstruction of the imaged surface.

It is interesting to remark that, in such reconstruction, the reflectance map functions R_i, which are at the core of the traditional approach to photometric stereo [1,2], play no part. Also, with an optical flow constraint slightly modified, for taking into account the fact that there may not be conservation of intensities if the reflecting properties of the surfaces are non-uniform, our approach to PS has yielded good reconstructions for surfaces with a position-dependent albedo. In such cases, we based the optical flow estimation on a constraint of the form

$$a_t \Delta I(s) \approx a_x D_X(s) \frac{\partial I_2}{\partial x} + a_y D_Y(s) \frac{\partial I_2}{\partial y} \tag{18}$$

where

$$a_i = \frac{1}{\eta \Delta I_i^{max} + \Delta I_i^{avg}} \tag{19}$$

for $i = x, y$ or t.

In (19), ΔI_i^{max} and ΔI_i^{avg} denote the maximum and the average values, in a small window centered on site s, of the absolute intensity differences, along the x, y and t dimensions, of the PS image pair. Thus, the a_i's essentially modulate the values of the associated derivatives in (18) - recall that $\Delta I(s) \equiv I_1(s) - I_2(s)$ plays the role of a time derivative - by the reciprocal of a measure of the intensity variations in the neighborhood of the considered point, thereby somewhat shielding the optical flow estimates from the influence of the inhomogeneities in surface albedo. The form of the a_i's, with η a free parameter, has been chosen so that (18) remains invariant under linear transformations of the input images.

3   Experiments

Figures 1 to 3 show results of surface estimation experiments with our optical flow approach to photometric stereo. Each figure depicts a pair of PS input images and the reconstructed surface. In all the experiments, the illumination vectors were of the form $\hat{S} = (\sin \sigma, 0, \cos \sigma)$; the flow field, $D(s)$, was obtained through Horn and Schunck's iterative algorithm [5] and then employed in equation (10) - with A, B and C estimated as described - to yield $z(x, y)$.

In the first experiment, the inputs were four pairs of synthetic images of a lambertian ellipsoid, obtained for the illumination directions (σ values) $(-30^o, -10^o)$, $(-10^o, 0^o)$, $(0^o, 10^o)$ and $(10^o, 30^o)$, and $D(s)$ was taken as the sum of the flow fields resulting for each image pair.

In the second experiment, we considered a sphere with lambertian plus quasi-specular reflectance, and non-uniform albedo (the central stripe has lower albedo than the rest of the surface). A single synthetic image pair was used (illumination directions -30° and 30°), and the modified constraint form (18) was employed, instead of (2), in Horn and Schunck's optical flow estimation algorithm.

Lastly, the third experiment deals with reconstructing the shape of a real vase, of approximately lambertian reflectance, from two input image pairs, obtained for the illumination directions $(-10^o, 0^o)$ and $(0^o, 10^o)$.

4   Discussion

We have introduced a process of shape estimation from the optical flow associated with pairs of photometric stereo images obtained under slightly different illuminations. Such flow results from the displacement of the irradiance pattern over the scene, which we have modelled as a rigid-body rotation coupled with a small position-dependent translation along the optical-axis direction. This choice has been motivated by an analogy with a situation where the illumination is kept fixed, but the observer rotates about the scene. For a surface symmetrical about the rotation axis, such movement would give rise to the same optical flow field as would result, for a fixed observer, from an equal rotation of the illumination source in the opposite direction. Since a rotation of the observer under fixed illumination will also be, in this case, equivalent to an opposite rotation of the surface, along with its initial irradiance pattern (as if the irradiance pattern had been painted on the imaged surface), we may conclude that, for such symmetrical surfaces, the optical flow resulting from a change of illumination can be exactly described as arising from a rotation of the 3-D irradiance pattern on the scene.

This is certainly not true for a general asymmetrical surface, but when the change in illumination direction is small and the surface is smooth, we have found that we are still able to model the irradiance pattern movement as a rotation, provided that we allow for a correction factor in terms of a position-dependent translation along the optical-axis direction (direction z). As it is known, under orthographic projection any such translation does not contribute to the optical

258   José R.A. Torreão

flow; therefore, for any assumed rotation, there will be an infinite number of
surfaces, differing by the translational factor, which will be equally consistent
with the observed irradiance displacement field. The translational factor thus
represents an extra degree of freedom, which allows us to consider the estimation
of a great variety of shapes through a very simple model: given the optical flow of
the PS image pairs, we try to determine the surface rotation which best explains
such flow and which, at the same time, minimizes the unobservable translational
factor along z.

Such framework has led to an expression for the surface function in terms
only of the parameters of the movement, which are estimated via a least-squares
approach. It is interesting to compare this expression (equation (10)) with the
corresponding relation obtained when matching the PS images along a fixed
direction, as in [3]. There, the surface function is recovered as

$$\hat{z}(x,y) = \frac{(k_1 D_X + k_2 D_Y)I_2(s) - k_0(k_1 x + k_2 y) + F(k_2 x - k_1 y)}{k_1^2 + k_2^2} \quad (20)$$

where k_0, k_1 and k_2 are the linear coefficients of the reflectance map for the
difference image, $I_1 - I_2$, and F is an arbitrary function. It is easy to see that
the C-factor in (10) corresponds to the function F in (20). Moreover, if we take
as our surface estimate, instead of the z in (10), a $\overline{z}$ given by

$$\overline{z}(x,y) = z(x,y) + \frac{\Delta z}{2} \quad (21)$$

(which amounts to taking, as the depth value at the point (x,y), the average of
the estimates at that point and at the matched point $(x + D_X, y + D_Y)$), there
results, by neglecting the factor $V(x,y)$, essentially the same functional relation
as (10), i.e.,

$$\overline{z}(x,y) = \frac{BD_x - AD_y + (A^2 + B^2)(Ay - Bx)/2 + C(By + Ax)}{A^2 + B^2} \quad (22)$$

Acknowledgment

This work was partially supported by the Project Finep/Recope 0626/96-SAGE.

References

1. Lee, K.M., Kuo C.-C.: Shape reconstruction from photometric stereo. Procs.
   ICCV'92 (1992) 479-484 253, 256
2. Woodham, R.J.: Photometric method for determining surface orientation from multiple images. Optical Engineering, vol. 19(1) (1980) 139-144 253, 256
3. Fernandes, J.L., Torreão, J.R.A.: Estimating depth through the fusion of photometric stereo images. Procs. ACCV'98, Lect. Notes Comp. Sci. 1351 (1998) 64-71 253,
   258
4. Horn, B.K.P.: Understanding image intensities. Artificial Intelligence, vol. 8(11)
   (1977) 201-231 254
5. Horn, B.K.P., Schunck B.G.: Determining optical flow. Artificial Intelligence, vol.
   17 (1981) 185-203 254, 257

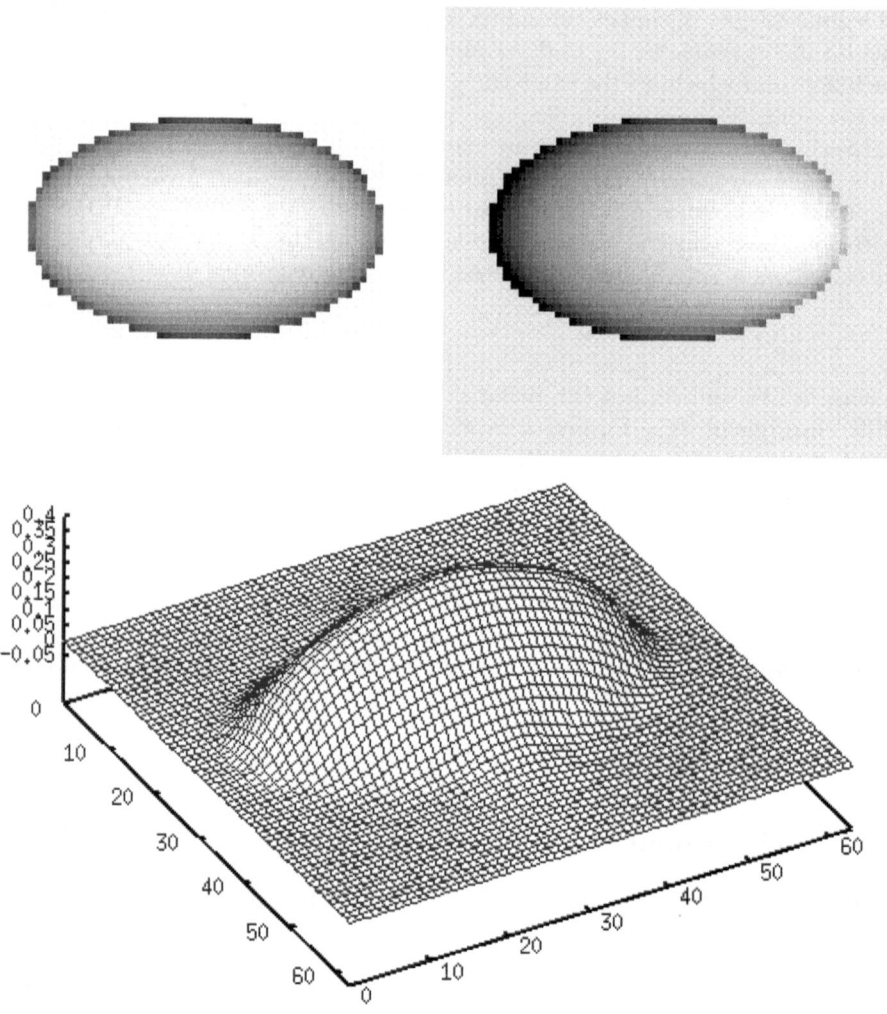

Fig. 1. OFPS Shape Estimation. Top: Input image pair. Bottom: Estimated depth map

260   José R.A. Torreão

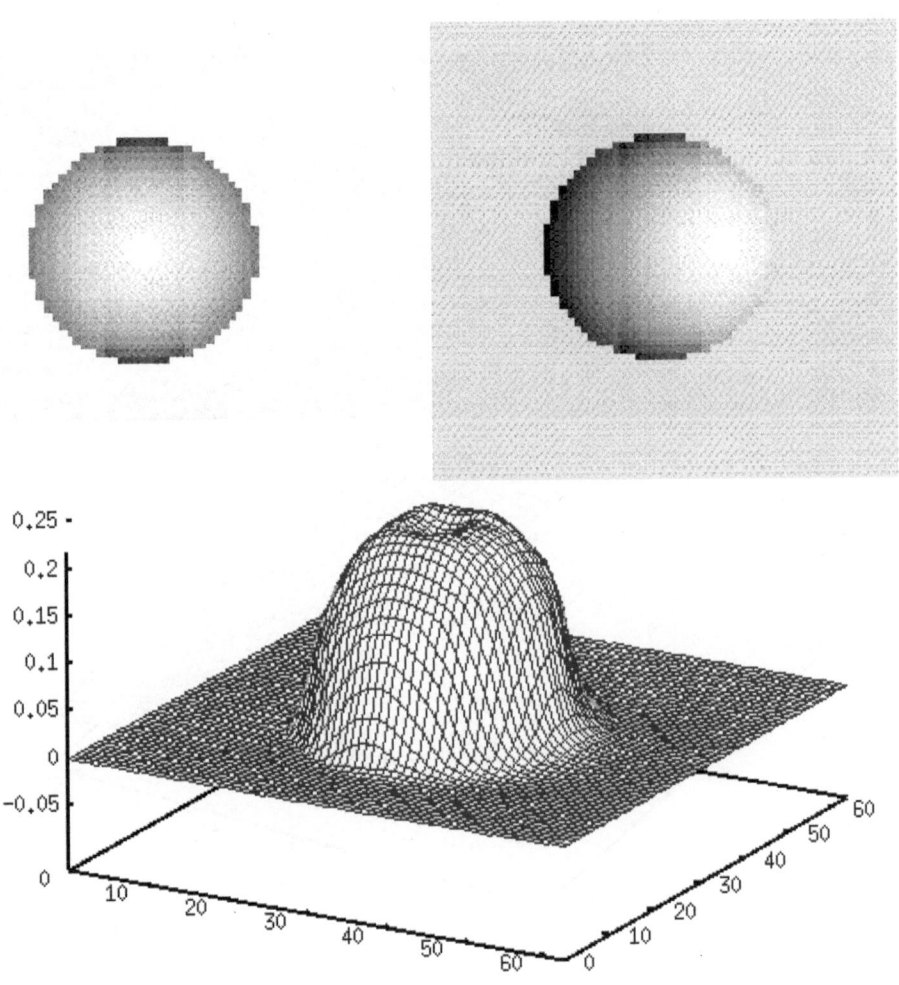

Fig. 2. OFPS Shape Estimation. Top: Input image pair. Bottom: Estimated depth map

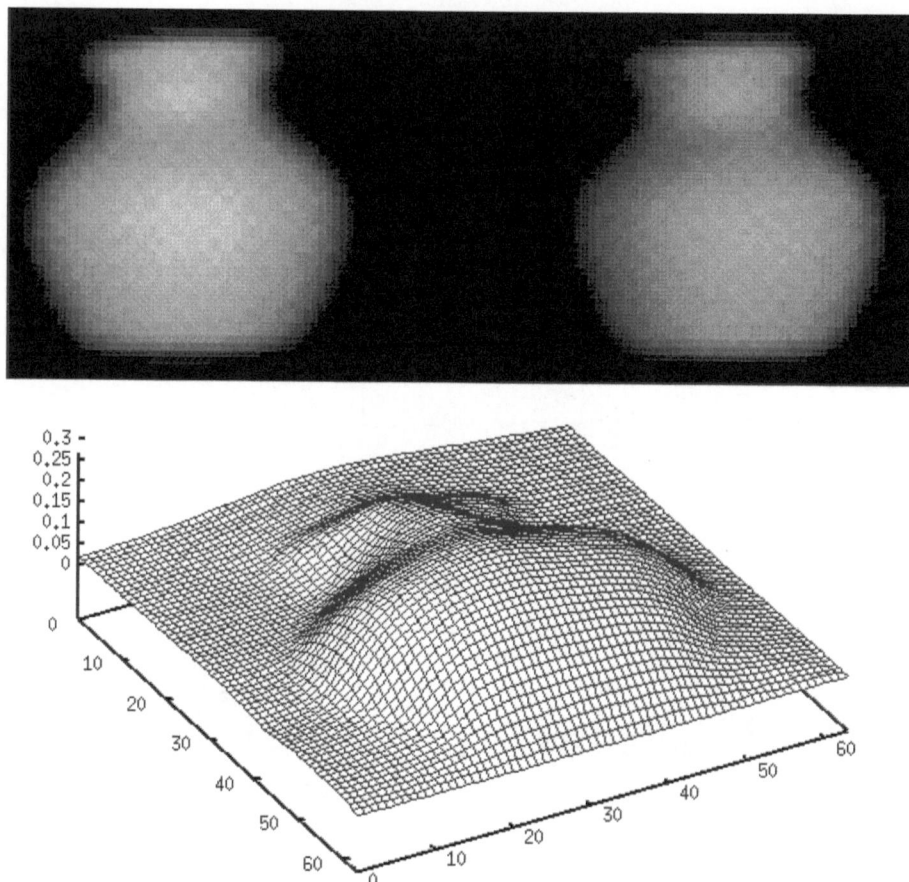

Fig. 3. OFPS Shape Estimation. Top: Input image pair. Bottom: Estimated depth map

Computer Vision Interaction for Virtual Reality

Homero V. Ríos Figueroa and Joaquín Peña Acevedo

Laboratorio Nacional de Informática Avanzada, A.C.
Rébsamen 80, c.p. 91090, Xalapa, Veracruz, México
{hrios,jpena}@xalapa.lania.mx

Abstract. As virtual reality evolves towards more natural interfaces, new contact less interaction based on gesture recognition is unfolding. This interaction is supported on geometric, dynamic and cognitive modelling of gestures. As well as other branches of artificial intelligence, computer vision plays an important role in this modelling.
The purpose of this paper is to describe how computer vision is helping to develop virtual reality and present some interfaces developed in our laboratory.

1 Introduction

During 1945, Vannevar Bush conceived the use of computers beyond calculation and thought about them as a fundamental tool for transforming human thought and creative activity [2]. He anticipated the use of computers for multimedia processing.

Since Bush's time many technological breakthroughs have occured, but computers are still limited in their multimedia understanding [18]. This means that we have increased the effective bandwidth of information from computers to humans, by sending audio, images, audio, graphics, haptic data, but the same rate of improvement has not happened in computer understanding. Most computers still receive input from low bandwidth devices like keyboards or mouse. Only few interfaces are able to understand application related domains of audio, visual or haptic information [7].

Several researchers have identified this unbalance and are working on more intuitive interfaces like virtual reality, speech recognition, image understanding and multimodal interfaces [3,18]. In the rest of this paper we will concentrate on image understanding techniques which are relevant for virtual reality.

The main conceptual components of a virtual reality system are: a) *inmmersion*, the ability to experience a 3D world as a reality, b) *viewpoint*, refers to the point of observation of the user, c) *navigation*, which allows to change viewpoint and d) *manipulation*, the capacity to interact and change the relative position of objects in the environment [14].

Another important component of virtual reality (VR) is *tracking*, since it helps to establish the correct position of the user in the environment, and therefore provides the appropriate visualization and interaction [36]. There are many

Helder Coelho (Ed.): IBERAMIA'98, LNAI 1484, pp. 262–274, 1998.

technologies which help in tracking body part and they are based on electric, magnetic, ultrasonic, infrared, optic or image analysis principles [3]. In this paper, we are interested in this last type of tracking.

Since visual perception allows many organisms to interact successfully with their surroundings it is natural to think that computer vision (CV) might help to bring closer people and computers. This interaction would be based on the interpretation of body language, through *gesture recognition*. This new research topic is bringing together people with backgrounds on computer vision, human computer interaction, psychology, and artificial intelligence.

In the rest of this paper we will concentrate on gesture recognition as it applies to human computer interaction in general, and virtual reality in particular. Also, we will present a general methodology which emerges from related works worldwide. Finally, we will describe the main interfaces developed in our lab, and how they compare to other similar systems.

2   Computer Vision and Virtual Reality

At first glance, computer vision and virtual reality do not seem related, in fact they look opposite. CV attempts to reconstruct surfaces, recognize objects and provide motion information of objects from images. That is, it goes from images to objects. In contrast, computer graphics and VR work from object models to images. So in certain sense, they are complementary [22]. However, the boundary between these areas is becoming thinner as many people realize that the solution to key problems in both areas involve a close interaction between the physics of image formation, geometric and mechanical modelling of object shape, deformation and motion [33,34,8]. As well as cognitive modelling of actions and behaviour to express agents or organism responses to visual stimuli [9].

Other problems that are of special interest to both fields but with with different points of view are stereoscopic vision and object tracking. In the case of CV the problem of stereopsis is object reconstruction from two images of the object. For VR, the problem is how to obtain two different images of a scene composed of objects, so they are appropriate for visualization in devices like head mounted displays. The common link is that of stereoscopic visualization as achieved by the human brain [16].

The problem of object tracking is very important for both areas, because in the case of VR, helps to track body parts to provide the appropriate feedback of change in position of the user or objects in the virtual environments. Also, real time tracking is vital for proper visualization and reducing the so called "lag time" [36].

In the case of computer vision, object tracking is also very important in the context of time varying imagery, real time vision systems and robotic systems with visual capacity [8]. In addition, object tracking is very important for organism to follow predators and prey.

Recently, CV and VR have come closer as many people realize that more natural interfaces can be built by using CV to provide object tracking. That is following body parts or providing gesture recognition, without having to wear any special equipment. This has the advantage to provide more freedom of movement and makes the computer to adapt to humans, rather that the other way around.

Another close interaction between CV and VR has come from what is called *augmented reality* [1]. The idea is to register in a common environment, real and virtual objects. That is, in these systems it is possible to see the real world augmented with computer generated objects. For example, a surgeon during an operation will be able to see an MRI volume superimposed with the images of the actual patient [13].

CV is also helping to animate VR specially when the environment incorporates autonomous agents. Some simulation programs of artificial life use synthetic vision as a sensor for organisms, so they can react to the presence of other beings, for instance approaching or receding [30].

2.1   Related Works

We are interested in research works which use computer vision as a general human computer interface. The more general context in which we find this concept is in what is called *smart rooms* and *smart clothes* [23]. The idea is to have many cameras and computers in a network which are continuously analysing the images of people. These cameras can be in different places in a room, street, or they can be attached to human clothes. As a result of the analysis, people can be recognized, tracked, or communicate with computers and decisions can be made.

Other works are more specific and involve face recognition [31], emotions recognition [23], sign language understanding [32], teleoperation in virtual reality robotics environments [20], tracking of the whole human body for surveillance applications   [5],   hand   tracking   [10,25,15],   iris   tracking   and   recognition [41,17,27,24,40] and head tracking for general human computer interaction [26,4,39].

2.2   Framework to Relate VR and CV

From the analysis of works which involve CV and human computer interaction, we have obtained a framework which helps to understand previous work, and also as a guide to develop new interfaces (Figure 1).

In computer graphics and virtual reality we have a database of 3-D models which are used for rendering and visualization. In these systems, the user navigate or interacts with the environment through a graphical user interface (GUI), or directly with special hardware (data glove, HMD, etc.). In any case, the actions of the user modify the database of graphics objects and this in turn changes the visualization.

What is relatively new in VR, is telemanipulation and augmented reality where the graphic objects in the database have some correspondence with actual objects in the real world. In this case, by moving one graphics object, for instance a 3-D model of a robot arm, it is possible to move a real robot, possibly in a distant location [20]. Also, in augmented reality the correspondence and registration is more critical, since virtual and real object have to appear as sharing the same space [1]. Vision techniques have an important role in helping to provide proper registration and in maintaing the consistency and correspondence of real and virtual worlds [20,13].

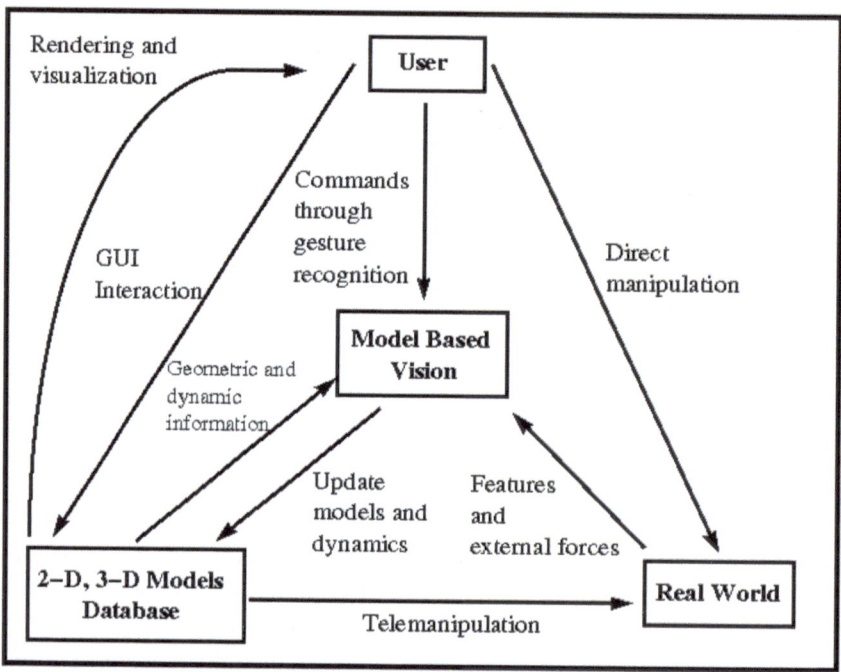

Fig. 1. Model based vision can be an important part of a virtual reality system.

In the case of direct, contactless, human computer interaction through gesture recognition, the vision systems plays a more active role, since it allows the user to communicate with the computer, without having to wear any special hardware [23]. Since the system must have a representation of the gesture to recognize or track, we can think this representation as geometric and dynamic model information that fetched by the model based vision module guides its search through the image data. This model can be implicit in the system or explicitly represented and could be stored in a 2-D or 3-D model database.

The images are analyzed and features and external forces are extracted which drive model matching, and the vision module updates the model parameters and dynamics for the best fit [6,33,34,8].

3   Trackers Developed in Our Laboratory

As a result of our literature review we have defined the objective of our research group as the study of computerized visual perception as a mean of interaction between human and computers, and robots or agents (bots) with real or virtual environments. Until now, our work has been concentrated on developing human computer interfaces through computer vision in general, and in particular for virtual reality systems (Figure 2). Our graphics interfaces are original and also some of the tracking methods that we have developed. In the next subsections we will describe the features of our iris, hand and glasses tracker, and the GUIs that have been implemented for manipulation and navigation in virtual reality systems.

Fig. 2. Work environment

3.1   Iris Tracker

The novelty of our iris tracker is that we do not need to attach the camera to the user's head, or provide the initial position of the head as in other works [17,41]. We do not provide the eyes rotation, but we are able to obtain the center, and radius of a pair of circles which are fitted to each iris [27], as is illustrated in Figure 3. Taking the mid point of the segment that joints the centers of the circles, we define a visual cursor that can be employed for activating buttons in GUIs. By using visual fixation, and if both iris remain in the same position in several frames (5 in our implementation), we interpret this behaviour as the location of a point of interest, and we can associate it with the "click" of a button.

Our iris detector works by applying edge detection to each frame, followed by thinning and search of circles using a Hough transform. The most promising pair of circles are selected by applying heuristics [27]. The performance of this tracker is between 3-5 frames/second running on a Indy, SGI workstation. For our algorithms to work properly, it is important to have a good illumination that generates good contrast in the images and the edges appear well defined. We have found this experimental condition as the most critical for our implementation.

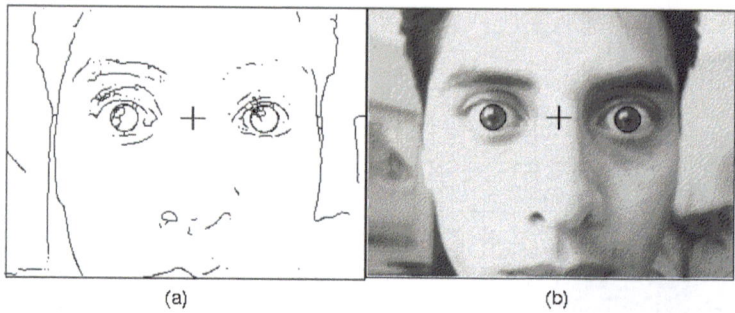

(a)   (b)

Fig. 3. Iris detector. (a) Edges on the image. (b) The mark represents the visual cursor which is defined by the position of the eyes.

3.2   Hand Tracker

Our approach for the hand tracker is not as powerful and general as in other works [10,25,15], but we provide simpler solutions for tracking a hand with extended fingers [24,28].

Our method uses edge detection and frame differences to extract moving features with high gradients. Then, we apply a thinning algorithm, followed by a Hough transform to detect lines [12]. Finally, we extract the most meaningful segments which correspond with the fingers to obtain a global centroid from all the segments. This centroid provides a reference position for a cursor (Figure 4). The changing size of the segments provides cues about the proximity (approaching or receding) of the hand from the camera. The performance of the hand tracker is also between 3-5 frames/second on the same platform as described above.

3.3   Glasses Tracker

Some types of stereoscopic glasses do not provide head tracking, so we decided to develop one using computer vision. Since the model that we have (Crystal eyes,

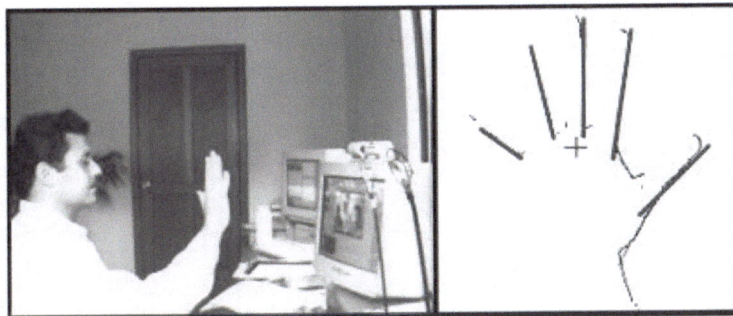

Fig. 4. Hand detector. This image shows how to establish communication with the computer, using a cursor defined by the position of the segments that approximate the fingers.

Stereoscopic corp.) has a rectangular frame, the idea was to fit parallelograms to the different images. Since a rectangular shape can deform into a trapezoidal shape under perspective transformation, in this case we use an affine approximation, an under these conditions a rectangle deforms into a parallelogram. For this method to work, the perspective effect should remain small, so it is important that the glasses do not get too close to the camera during side view.

For each frame the method searches for high gradient points, and from them, a contour following algorithm is applied [12]. Only closed contours and those that satisfy a shape criteria are preserved. If two contours remain that approximate the shape of the glasses, these are fitted with an affine transformation using the method of normalization, provided with the DIAS software [35,37]. ¿From the affine deformation of the rectangle into a parallelogram, it is possible to work out the 3-D rotation of the glasses in space [39]. The lines shown in Figure 5 are the projections of a spacial line segment in direction of the line of sight.

Our implementation of this algorithm using the DIAS software [35], has a performance of 10 frames/sec using images of 160 x 120 pixels on a Pentium PC (200 MHz) [39]. We have not found similar works related to glasses tracking, but only to head tracking [4,26]. We think that our method can be more accurate for head tracking than those reported in the literature, because we track specific, well defined features (glasses in our case), but we cannot make definite claims until we perform a formal experimental analysis.

4   Graphical User Interfaces Developed in Our Laboratory

The graphical user interfaces that we have developed allow the manipulation of 2-D and 3-D objects with hand or eyes movements. It is possible to select different objects, change their orientation in space, bring closer or move away the object, navigate in a 3-D environment or change the relative position of objects [24]. The first interface is used to manipulate objects so that they move according to the movements of the user head (Figure 6).

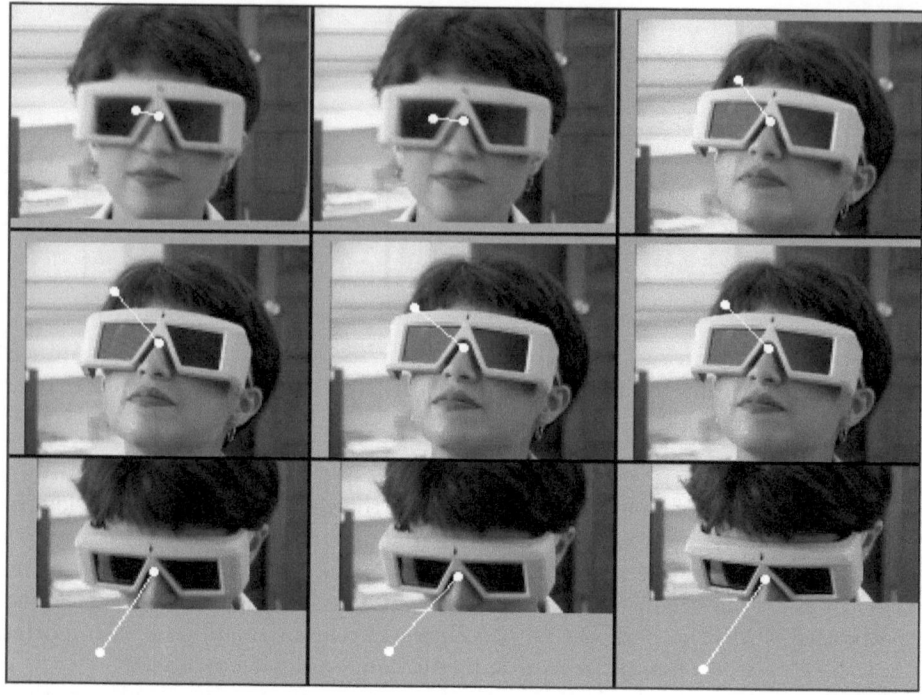

Fig. 5. Determination of the line of sight from the parallelogram that fits the glasses. The image point corresponding to the center of the glasses is shifted into the center of the image.

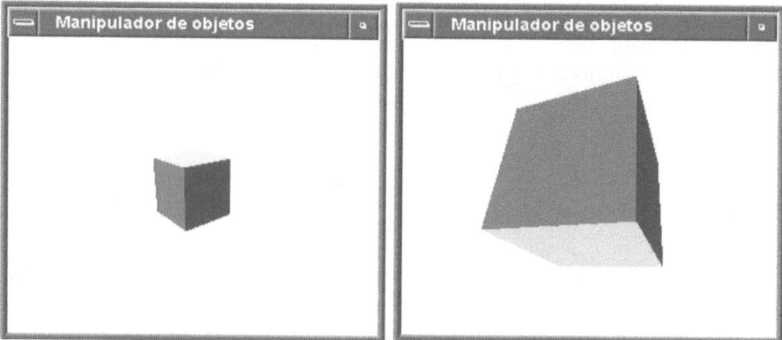

Fig. 6. The cube changes its position and orientation while the user head is moving.

Another graphical user interface works as a visualization tool for 3-D objects. It uses the cursor defined by the iris detector to activate some buttons which serve to select, rotate, or bring near or far an object (Figure 7). The iris must be detected at least five times to activate a button.

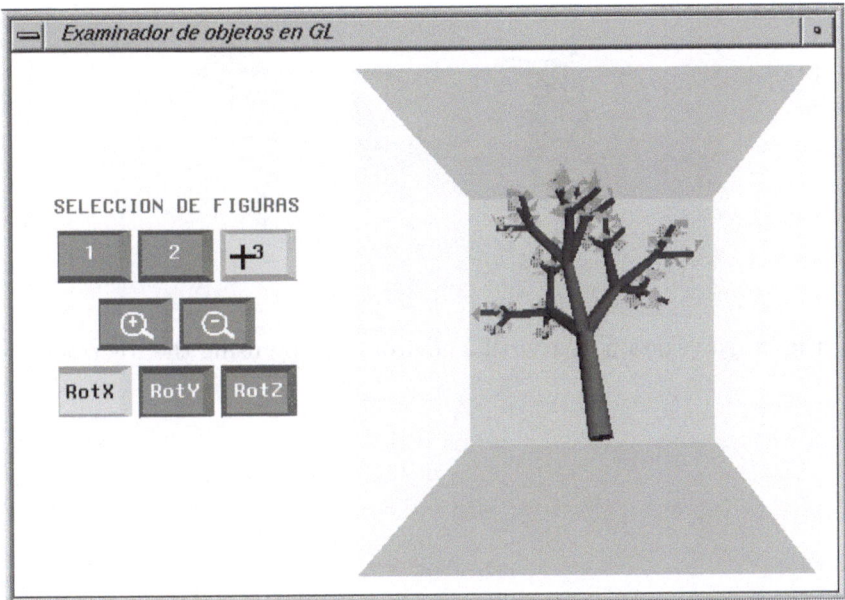

Fig. 7. Examinator of 3-D objects. The button number 3 is selected.

Figure 8 shows another interface. We can move in the virtual environment only by translations. They are in correspondence with the translations of the defined cursor with regard to its initial position.

Besides of navigation, we implemented the selection of objects contained in the virtual environment (Figure 9).

5   Conclusion and Future Work

We have analyzed works in the literature that relate computer vision and virtual reality and as a result we have proposed a framework to understand present and future works. Also, we presented the contribution of our group in developing eyes, hand and glasses trackers and their graphical user interfaces.

Our ongoing work in collaboration with the National Autonomous University of Mexico (UNAM) and the University of Houston-Downtown (UH-D) involves the creation of cooperative virtual environments with gesture recognition interfaces and autonomous, intelligent agents, and will be reported in future academic events.

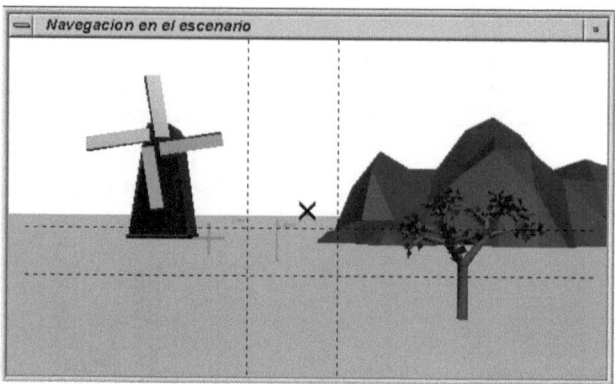

Fig. 8. Navegation in a virtual environment by using the iris tracker.

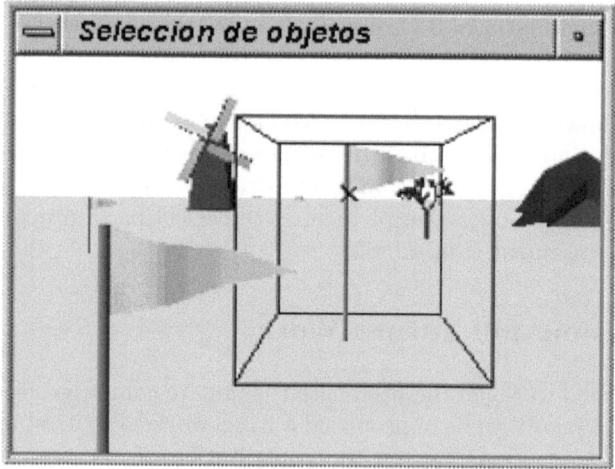

Fig. 9. The frame box around the flag indicates that this object has been selected.

Acknowledgements

This work has been funded by the Mexican National Council of Science and Technology (CONACYT) as project ref. C098-A "Distributed simulation of gesture recognition interfaces and intelligent agents for virtual environments".

References

1. Aliaga, D.G. (1997). "Virtual objects in the real world". *Communications of the ACM*, Vol. 40, No. 3, pp. 49-54. 264, 265
2. Baecker, R.M. and Buxton, W.A.S. (1987). "A historical and intellectual perspective of human-computer interaction". In *Readings in Human-Computer Interaction, a multidisciplinary approach*, Baecker, R.M. and Buxton, W.A.S. (Eds.), Morgan Kaufmann. 262
3. Barfield, W. and Furnes, T.A. (1995). *Virtual Environments and Advanced Interface Design*. Oxford University Press. 262, 263
4. Basu, S., Essa, I. and Pentland, A. (1996). "Motion regularization for model-based head tracking". *MIT Media Laboratory Perceptual Computing Section*, Technical Report No. 362. 264, 268
5. Baumberg, A.M. and Hogg, D.C. (1993). "Learning flexible models from ' image sequences". Report 93.36, Research Report Series, School of Computer Studies, University of Leeds, U.K. 264
6. Blake, A. and A. Yuille (Eds.). (1992). *Active Vision*, MIT Press. 265
7. Bolt, R.A. (1985). "Conversing with computers". *Technology Review*, 88 (2), 35-43. 262
8. Brown, C.M. and Terzopoulos (Eds.) (1994). *Real-time Computer Vision*. 263, 265
9. Buxton, H. (1997). "Visual interpretation and understanding". Cognitive Science Research Paper 452, School of Cognitive and Computing Sciences, University of Sussex, U.K. 263
10. Cipolla, R., Okamoto, Y. and Kuno, Y. (1993). "Robust structure from motion using motion parallax". Proceedings of the International Conference on Computer Vision, IEEE Press. 264, 267
11. Faugeras, O. (1993). *Three-Dimensional computer vision, a geometric viewpoint*. MIT Press.
12. Gonzalez, R.C. and R.E. Woods. (1992). *Digital Image Processing (3rd ed.)*, Addison-Wesley. 267, 268
13. Grimson, W.E.L. (1995). "Medical applications of image understanding". *IEEE Expert, Intelligent systems and their applications*, Vol. 10, No. 5, pp. 18-28. 264, 265
14. Hayward, T. (1993). *Adventures in Virtual Reality*. QUE corp. 262
15. Heap, T. and Samaria, F. (1995). "Real-time hand tracking and gesture recognition using smart snakes". Technical Report, Olivetti Research Limited, U.K. 264, 267
16. Hubel, D.H. (1988). *Eye, Brain and Vision*, Scientific American Library 263
17. Lam, K.M. and Yang, H. (1996). "Locating and extracting the eye in human face images". *Pattern Recognition*, Vol. 29, No. 5, pp. 771-779. 264, 266
18. Maybury, M.T., (Ed.). (1993). *Intelligent Multimedia Interfaces*. MIT Press. 262
19. Mundy, J.L. and Zisserman, A. (Eds.). (1992). *Geometric Invariance in Machine Vision*. MIT Press.

20. Natonek, E., Zimmerman, T., Fluckiger, L, "Model based vision as feedback for virtual reality robotics environments". *Virtual Reality, Annual International Symposium '95*, IEEE 264, 265

21. Ohzu, H. and Habara, K. (1996). "Behind the scenes of virtual reality: vision and motion". Proceedings of the IEEE, Vol. 84, No. 5, pp. 782-798.

22. Page, I. (1988). "The disputer: a dual-paradigm parallel processor for graphics and vision". In Page, I. (Ed.), *Parallel Architectures for Computer Vision*, Oxford University Press. 263

23. Pentland, A.P. (1996). "Smart rooms". *Scientific American*, April 1996, pp. 54-62. 264, 265

24. Peña, J., Rios, H.V., y Barradas, P. (1997). "Interacción con escenarios 3D por medio de ademanes y movimientos oculares", *Memorias del Congreso Computación Visual 97*, pp. 213-219, Facultad de Ciencias, UNAM, México. 264, 267, 268

25. Rehg, J.M. and Kanade, T. (1993). "DigitEyes: vision-based human hand tracking", School of Computer Science, Carnegie Mellon University, Technical report number: CMU-CS-93-220. 264, 267

26. Rekimoto, J. (1995). "A vision-based head tracker for fish tank virtual reality" *Virtual Reality, Annual International Symposium '95*, IEEE 264, 268

27. Rios, H.V. y Barradas, P.D. (1996). "Interacción Hombre-Máquina por medio de movimientos oculares". *Memorias del V Congreso Iberoamericano de Inteligencia Artificial*, pp. 492-501. 264, 266, 267

28. Rios, H.V., Figueroa, J.M. y Barradas, P.D. (1997). "Visión por computadora en interfaces Hombre-Máquina", *Soluciones Avanzadas*, No. 42, febrero 1997, pp. 51-56. 267

29. Rothe, I., Suesse, H. and Voss, K. (1996). "The method of normalization to determine invariants", *Pattern Analysis and Machine Intelligence*, Vol. 18, No. 4, pp. 366-376.

30. Winter, S. y Rudomin, I. (1997). "Synthetic computer vision for autonomous agents in distributed partitioned environments". Memorias del Congreso Computación Visual 97, pp.157-166 , Facultad de Ciencias, Universidad Nacional Autónoma de México. 264

31. Schwartz, E.I. (1995). "A face of one's own". *Discover* the world of Science, vol. 16, no.2, December 1995, pp. 78-87. 264

32. Starner, T. and Pentland, A. (1996). "Real-time American sign language recognition from video using hidden Markov models". *MIT Media Laboratory Perceptual Computing Section*, Technical Report No. 375. 264

33. Terzopoulos, D., Witkin, A. & Kass, M., "Constraints on Deformable Models: Recovering 3D Shape and Nonrigid Motion", Artificial Intelligence, Vol. 36 (1988), pp. 91 - 123. 263, 265

34. Terzopoulos D. (1991). "Visual Modelling", Proceedings of the British Machine Vision Conference, BMVA. 263, 265

35. Towersoft. (1995). *DIAS, Dialog and Programming System for Digital Image Analysis.* User reference manual, version 4.0, Towersoft, Berlin, Germany. 268

36. Vince, J. (1995). *Virtual Reality Systems*. Addison-Wesley. 262, 263

37. Voss, K. and Suesse, H. (1997). "Invariant fitting of planar objects by primitives". *Pattern Analysis and Machine Intelligence*, Vol. 19, No. 1, pp. 80-84. 268

38. Voss, K. (1993). *Discrete Images, Objects and Funciones in Z^n*. Algorithms and Combinatorics 11, Springer-Verlag.

39. Voss, K., Ríos, H.V. and Peña, J. (1998). "Head tracking by glasses detection". *Computación y Sistemas*, Revista Iberoamericana de Computación, No. 3, pp. 170-178, Centro de Investigación en Computación, Instituto Politécnico Nacional, México. 264, 268

40. Wildes, R.P. (1997). "Iris recognition: an emerging biometric technology". *Proceedings of the IEEE*, Vol. 85, No. 9, pp. 1348-1364. 264

41. Young, D., Tunley, H. and Samuels, R. (1995). "Specialized Hough transform and active contour methods for real-time eye tracking". Cognitive Science Research Paper, No. 386, University of Sussex, England, U.K. 264, 266

Placing Artificial Visual Landmarks in a Mobile Robot Workspace

Joaquin Salas[1] and Jose Luis Gordillo[2]

[1] CICATA-IPN Unidad Querétaro
José Siurob 10, Col Mercurio, Querétaro, Qro., México CP 76040
salas@sisnet.com.mx
[2] Centro de Inteligencia Artificial, ITESM Campus Monterrey
Garza Sada Sur 2501, Monterrey, N.L., México CP 64849
gordillo@campus.mty.itesm.mx

Abstract. Recently, research on mobile robotics has been focused on achieving reliable performance on autonomous systems. We believe that one possible way to do this is by using landmarks to bound uncertainty during the path planning and navigation stages. In this paper, we present an algorithm to compute the position of artificial visual landmarks in a mobile robot workspace. We aim to maximize the region in the workspace from where a landmark can be seen, *i.e.*, to define the position of the landmarks in the workspace. After pointing out that this problem is combinatorial in nature, we propose a simulated annealing type of technique to find the optimal landmark arrangement.

1 Introduction

There is a growing interest to make autonomous robot technology available in current human environments. Nevertheless, this poses certain difficulties that have not been settled by our current state of knowledge in the areas of perception, real-time control and reasoning [6]. It has been argued that it is because human environments carry on cultural information that provide humans with cues that facilitates navigation and goal execution. Researchers [2] have proposed enginnering the environment, via the use of artificial landmarks, to reduce the complexity of the model of the environment. In this way, a robot could use its computing resources to solve a commanded task within a required time frame. Nowdays, the use of artificial landmarks for navigation and self localization is widespread. This is why, we feel that an study of how to place them optimally in the robot workspace is worth pursuing.

In this paper, we study the landmark placing problem, defined as computing the position of the landmarks in the workspace that maximize their joint coverage. In a recent paper, Tashiro *et al.* [9] studied this problem using a signboard landmark made of four LEDs. In their approach, they have a model of the localization error of the robot with respect to the landmark. Their objective is to minimize the maximum localization error. We feel that this approach may offer advantages when preattentive visual capabilities are available.

Helder Coelho (Ed.): IBERAMIA'98, LNAI 1484, pp. 274–282, 1998.
© Springer-Verlag Berlin Heidelberg 1998

The landmark placing problem may be seen as a generalization of the art gallery problem [8] where restrictions apply to the perceptual capabilities of the guards. Theory says that in two dimensions, $\lfloor n/3 \rfloor$ guards are sometimes sufficient and always necessary to cover a polygon of n sides. In this case, the assumption is that the guards have complete peripheric perception and can detect features in the environment that are either infinitely far or arbitrarily close. From another interesting perspective, the landmark placing problem can be reformulated in terms of a sensor placement problem exchanging landmarks by sensors. Then, the problem may be to cover the maximum possible area with the minimum number of sensors. Clearly, the outcome depends on the model of the sensor used. Consider, for instance, Zhang's [10] studies about how to place optimally accoustic transceivers in a two dimensional space.

The use of artificial landmarks is widespread in problems such as navigation, localization and path planning. For instance, Bessiere, P., *et al.* [3] and Lazanas and Latombe [6] describe methods for path planning based on the assumption that landmarks exist in the environment. We see our research on the landmark placing problem as complementary to these techniques.

The problem of selecting an optimal arrangements among different possibilities is combinatorial in nature. In order to solve it, we use a simulated annealing algorithm [5]. In §2, we describe the landmark placing algorithm. Then in §3, we present experimental results. Finally, we conclude discussing the implications of our results and point out research directions.

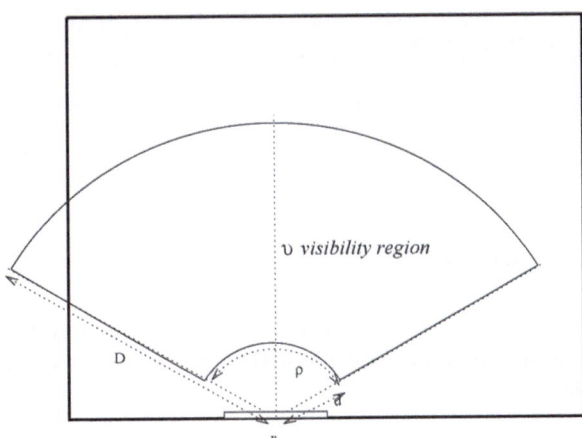

Fig. 1. Idealization of a landmark visibility region. A landmark on a wall at position **r** can be observed from a distance x, $d < x < D$ spanned over an angle ρ.

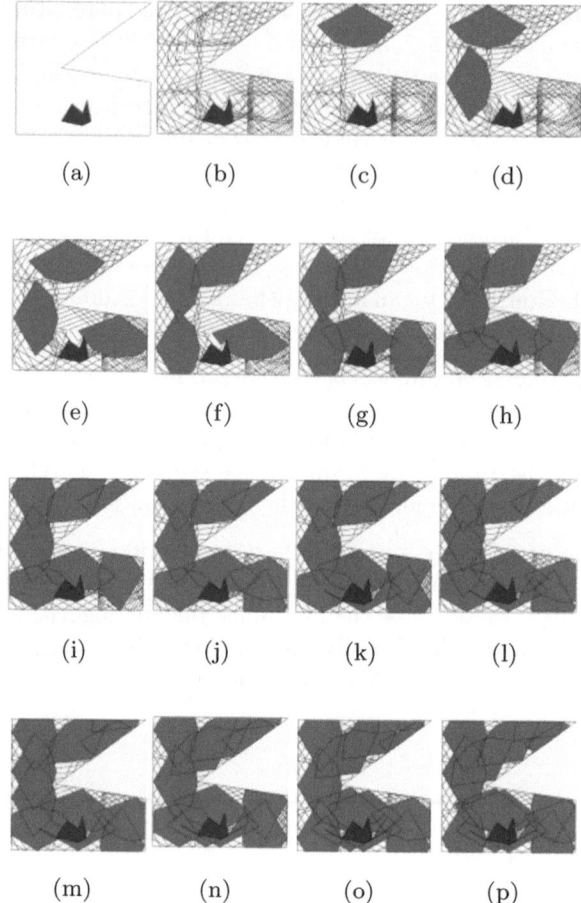

Fig. 2. Results of the algorithm for 1-14 landmarks in a workspace.

2   Placing Landmarks

Firstly, we define the constraints, suppositions and objective function, and then we propose a simulated annealing algorithm to find the optimal value of the objective function.

2.1   Landmark Configurations

Let us define the robot workspace $\mathcal{W}$ as a polygonal region in $\Re^2$. Suppose that the workspace contains a set $\mathcal{B}$ of polygonal obstacles. A *landmark visibility region* $\mathcal{U}(\mathbf{p})$ is a subset of $\mathcal{W} - \mathcal{B}$ from where the robot can potentially detect a landmark in $\mathbf{p}$. Suppose that the robot has a visual system such that

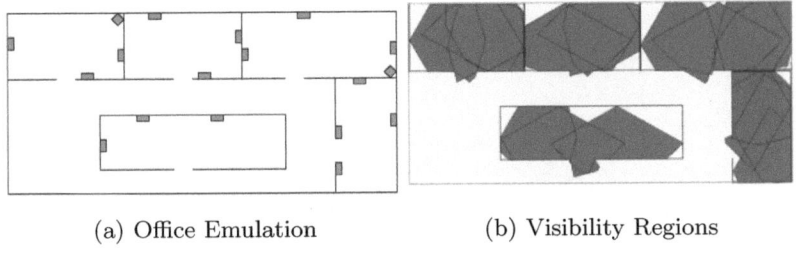

(a) Office Emulation   (b) Visibility Regions

(c) Robot enters a Room

Fig. 3. We emulate an office-like environment with cardboard walls. Landmarks are placed at each gray box (a). The landmark visibility regions are shown in (b). In (c), the landmarks with ID number 0 and 1 are aside the doorway.

once a landmark is detected it can compute some geometric information such as the position of the robot with respect to the landmark. The reliability of the collected information depend, among other things, on the relative positions of the robot and the landmark, the capabilities of the robot visual system, and the landmark structure. Loosely speaking, the geometry of $\mathcal{U}$ is defined by the range of distances and the range of angles from where the visual system can extract information from a landmark. In our case, reliability may be thought as a property that tell us how close is a parameter to its true value. One may hypothetize that the visibility region for each parameter, and each landmark, is different because they are all based on different image analysis. For instance, the distance may be inferred from the apparent size of the projected landmark, while the orientation may be computed from the apparent image distortion of the landmark. In all cases, the error is different and as a consequence generate a different visibility region. Nevertheless, a visual system would have difficulties to extract useful information if it is too close or too far from the landmark center. Also, some problems will be experimented if the visual system line of sight is too deviated from the landmark normal. For simplicity, we idealize $\mathcal{U}(\mathbf{p})$ as a section of a circular ring (see Fig 1) spanning an angle $\rho \in (\phi(\mathbf{u}) - \Delta, \phi(\mathbf{u}) + \Delta)$

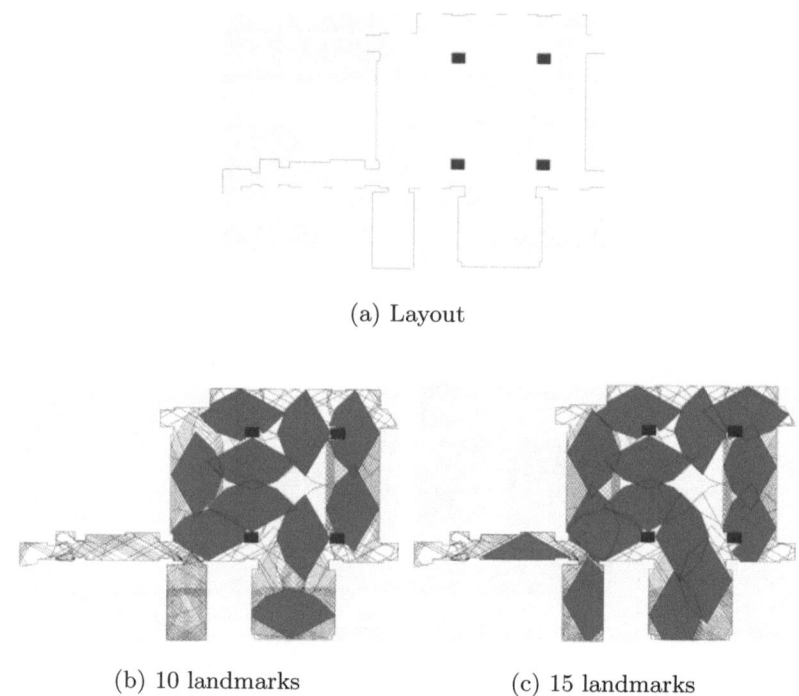

(a) Layout

(b) 10 landmarks   (c) 15 landmarks

Fig. 4. Layout and examples of landmark placing for a portion of our lab.

and radius $r \in (d, D)$, where $\phi(\mathbf{u})$ is the angular orientation of the vector $\mathbf{u}$ and the angle Δ and lengths d, D are parameters that characterize the visual system. Also, we assume that a landmark is a plannar patch that can be pasted on plannar walls. In order of taking into account the workspace boundaries and the existence of obstacles, we define the *working visibility region* $\mathcal{V}$ as the intersection of $\mathcal{U}$ with the workspace minus the obstacles. In other words,

$$\mathcal{V}(\mathbf{p}) = (\mathcal{W} \bigcap \mathcal{U}(\mathbf{p})) - \mathrm{T}(\mathcal{B}, \mathcal{U}(\mathbf{p})) \tag{1}$$

where T returns the region that contains all the points in the landmark's visibility area $\mathcal{U}$ such that for the line that goes from one of these points to $\mathbf{p}$ there is at least one point contained in the obstacle $\mathcal{B}$. That is,

$$\mathrm{T}(\mathcal{B}, \mathcal{U}, \mathbf{p}) = \{\mathbf{q} \mid \mathbf{q} \in \mathcal{U}, \mathbf{t} \in \overline{\mathbf{pq}} \Rightarrow \mathbf{t} \in \mathcal{B}\} \tag{2}$$

Given a certain workspace, we define a *configuration* $\mathcal{P}$ as the set of n landmarks placed on points $\{\mathbf{p}_1, \ldots, \mathbf{p}_n\}$ along the boundary of $\mathcal{W}$ or $\mathcal{B}$. Under such conditions, the function to optimize is the area of the union of the working visibility regions $\bigcup_{i=1}^{n} \mathcal{V}(\mathbf{p}_i)$ for a given configuration $\mathcal{P}$.

$$A(\bigcup_{i=1}^{n} \mathcal{V}(\mathbf{p}_i)) = \sum_{i=1}^{n} B(\mathcal{V}(\mathbf{p}_i)) - \sum_{i=1}^{n-1} \sum_{j=i+1}^{n} B\left(\mathcal{V}(\mathbf{p}_i) \bigcap \mathcal{V}(\mathbf{p}_j)\right) + O_3() \quad (3)$$

where $O_3()$ is the resulting area of intersecting three or more working visibility regions $\mathcal{V}(\mathbf{p}_k)$ and B is a function that computes the area of a polygon. We will dismiss the term $O_3()$ assuming that the landmarks will be well spread and as a result the intersection of three or more working visibility areas will be small. The area of a polygon can be efficiently computed considering only the vertex points as follows. Let $\mathcal{A}$ be a polygon with vertex $\{\mathbf{a}_1, \mathbf{a}_2, \ldots, \mathbf{a}_v\}$ sorted in counterclockwise order (also assume that $\mathbf{a}_1 = \mathbf{a}_{v+1}$). A vertice $\mathbf{a}_i$ has coordinates $<x_i, y_i>$. The area $B(\mathcal{A})$ is,

$$B(\mathcal{A}) = 1/2 \sum_{i=1}^{v} (y_i + y_{i+1})(x_i - x_{i+1}) \quad (4)$$

In a nutshell, given the size $n = |\mathcal{P}|$ of the landmark configuration, we look for the places $\mathbf{p}_1, \ldots, \mathbf{p}_n$ that maximize the working visibility area (see Eq (3)). We use a simulated annealing algorithm to achieve this.

2.2   Simulated Annealing

Kirkpatrick *et al.* [5] noted that *"There is a deep and useful connection between statistical mechanics and multivariate or combinatorial optimization."*. Statistical mechanics deals with the problem of interpreting the properties of large aggregations of atoms. One of its fundamental questions is what happens to the matter when the system reaches its limit low temperature. When the temperature is high, the atoms will present high mobility. As the temperature cools off, the atoms find arrangements where they still keep a certain kinetic energy. An appropriate annealing scheme will cause the aggregation of atoms to align in structures of low energy. A certain configuration can be weighted by its Boltzmann probability factor, $\exp\left(\frac{-E}{kT}\right)$, where E is the energy at temperature T and k is Boltzmann's constant that relates temperature with energy. Metropolis *et al.* [7] suggested the following annealing procedure. The particles move at random within a hypersphere of known radius centered at the current particle position. The change in the energy ΔE of the system is calculated. If $\Delta E < 0$, then the system is in a state of lower energy and the configuration is accepted. If $\Delta E > 0$ then the new configuration is accepted with probability $\exp\left(\frac{-\Delta E}{kT}\right)$. After a certain number τ_c of changes have taken place or a certain number τ_n of trials are done the temperature is reduced by a factor ΔT. There is a finite number of temperature changes τ_t.

In our case, the energy E and constant k are factors related to the size of the working visibility area of a certain configuration $\mathcal{P}$. The initial temperature is set to one, $T \leftarrow 1$. At each temperature step the temperature is reduced by a multiplicative factor $\Delta_T = 0.97$, as $T \leftarrow T\Delta_T$. There is a maximum of 100 temperature steps τ_t. An initial configuration $\mathcal{P} = \{\mathbf{p}_1, \ldots, \mathbf{p}_n\}$ is generated at random such that $\mathbf{p}_i \neq \mathbf{p}_j$ for $i \neq j$. The Metropolis loop for the landmark placing problem runs as follows. A binary vector $C = \{c_1, \ldots, c_n\}$ of changes is computed at random. If $c_k = 1$, it means that another location, selected at random, will be tried for the landmark currently at $\mathbf{p}_k$. Otherwise the landmark stays where it is. A new configuration is computed at random taking into account the values in vector C and making sure that $\mathbf{p}_i \neq \mathbf{p}_j$ for $i \neq j$. The current configuration $\mathcal{P}$ is evaluated using Eq (3), thus obtaining the current objective function value α_i. If there is an improvement in the objective function, *i.e.*, $\alpha_i > \alpha_{i-1}$, then the new configuration is accepted. If there is no improvement then the new configuration is accepted with probability $\exp\left(\frac{\alpha_i - \alpha_{i-1}}{kT}\right)$. There are a number of trials at any temperature step. The Metropolis scheme suggests to pass to the next temperature step, *i.e.*, to reduce the temperature, when a maximum number of combinations τ_n is reached (currently $100 \times n$) or when a number of successful changes τ_c on the configuration have been applied (currently $10 \times n$). The algorithm passes to the next temperature step and the cycle is repeated until a certain maximum number of temperature steps τ_t are made.

3   Experimental Results

In Fig 2, we sketch the output of our placing algorithm with a simulation where a polygonal workspace $\mathcal{W}$ that includes an obstacle $\mathcal{B}$ is used. The working visibility region $\mathcal{V}(\mathbf{p}_i)$ is computed when the algorithm selects to place a landmark on position $\mathbf{p}_i$.

Our placing algorithm can be used in conjunction with path planning algorithms that assume the existence of landmarks by providing the regions within the workspace from where sensing in possible. For instance, Lazanas and Latombe [6] proposed a motion planning algorithm of polynomial time complexity. The idea is that with the use of artificial landmarks one can bound the uncertainty in the robot's position. We built an emulation of an office-like environment with cardboard walls, the cardboard's height is approximately 4 feet. Fig 3(a) shows the layout of the workspace. It also signals the approximate position and orientation of the 18 landmarks placed. In Fig 3(c), we show a picture of the the robot when it is entering a room. The landmarks are used to signal special places in the environment. For instance, we mark people's desks, the fridge, the coffee maker machine and so on. Our work and Lazanas and Latombe's work are complementary. Our algorithm provides a certain landmark configuration while Lazanas and Latombe's algorithm provides a path to go from the current to a goal position provided that the path exists.

In a third experiment, we run the landmark placing program in a portion of a map of our lab. Fig 4(a) shows the layout of a portion of the robot workspace. The central rectangles correspond to columns of the building. We run our algorithm for landmark placing. Fig 4(b) shows the result when the number of landmarks is 10. The algorithm reports that 51% of the area has been covered and that on the average each visibility region covers 96% of what it can cover, *i.e.*, they are well widespread. The landmark configuration is distributed mainly in the open area. Fig 4 (c) shows the result when the number of landmarks is 15. The algorithm reports that 69.8% of the area has been covered and that on the average each visibility region covers 87.6% of what it can cover. At this moment one of the offices and the corridor starts being covered.

Conclusion

One of the main problems in visual perception for mobile robots is the efficient use of limited computing resources. Some arguments against the use of artificial landmarks involve the high cost of engineering the environment and the disruption caused by the introduction of symbols in an otherwise harmonious decoration. However, we must point out that with few exceptions [4], the robots' workspaces are primarily designed with humans in mind as the primary users. In this case, human environments convey a lot of cultural information [1] that people use as landmarks to move and localize themselves and it is still not obvious how this information will be given to the robots.

This paper presents an algorithm for computing the place where landmarks should be placed to increase their joint coverage of the workspace. However, depending on the application on may need to increase the number of terms in Eq. (3) to obtain more accurate results, although at the expense of increasing computing time. In this document, we assumed a particular geometry for the visibility region $\mathcal{U}_i$. However, the shape of $\mathcal{U}_i$ changes depending on the type of parameter that one needs to recover. An observation model for each type of parameter that is going to be recovered can be incorporated into the computation of the landmark placement. This model can take into account a particular shape and a probabilistic model for each type of parameter and each landmark.

One may say that the use of artificial landmarks will become obsolete with the arrival of better computing technology. However, advances in computing technology must be accompanied by effective algorithmic development or otherwise they will be fruitless. Furthermore, we believe that there will be always a place for the study of symbols in the context of autonomous systems. A clear example: Although humans are a fairly sophisticated autonomous entities, symbol recognition plays an important role in our everyday lives, as for instance when we recognize traffic symbols on the streets.

Acknowledgments

We would like to express our sincere gratitude to Carlo Tomasi for his help, support and ideas.

References

1. Philip E. Agree and Ian Horswill. Cultural Support for Improvisation. In *Proceedings of the Tenth National Conference on Artificial Intelligence*, pages 363–368. American Association for Artificial Intelligence, AAAI Press, July 12-16 1992. 281
2. Craig Becker, Joaquin Salas, Kentaro Tokusei, and Jean-Claude Latombe. Reliable Navigation Using Landmarks. In *IEEE International Conference on Robotics and Automation*, pages 401–406, 1995. 274
3. P. Bessière, J.-M. Ahuactzin, E.-G. Talbi, and E. Mazer. The Ariadnes Clew Algorithm: Global Planning with Local Methods. In *IEEE International Conference on Intelligent Robots and Systems*, volume 2, pages 1373–1380, 1993. 275
4. Shigeki Ishikawa, Hideki Kuwamoto, and Shinji Ozawa. Visual Navigation of an Autonomous Vehicle Using White Line Recognition. *IEEE Transactions on Pattern Analysis and Machine Intelligence*, 10(5):743–749, 1988. 281
5. S. Kirkpatrick, C. D. Jr. Gelatt, and M. P. Vecchi. Optimization by Simulated Annealing. Technical Report 41093, International Business Machines Corporation (IBM), 1982. 275, 279
6. Anthony Lazanas and Jean-Claude Latombe. Landmark-Based Robot Navigation. Technical Report STAN-CS-92-1428, Department of Computer Science. Stanford University, 1992. 274, 275, 280
7. Nicholas Metropolis, Arianna W. Rosenbluth, Marshall N. Rosenbluth, Augusta H. Teller, and Edward Teller. Equation of State Calculations by Fast Computing Machines. *Journal of Chemical Physics*, 21(6):1087–1092, June 1953. 279
8. Joseph O'Rourke. *Art Gallery Theorems and Algorithms*. New York: Oxford University Press, 1987. 275
9. Kenji Tashiro, Jun Ota, Yeuan C. Lin, and Tamio Arai. A Design of the Optimal Arrangement of Artificial Landmarks. In *IEEE International Conference on Robotics and Automation*, pages 407–413, 1995. 274
10. Hong Zhang. Two-Dimensional Optimal Sensor Placement. *IEEE Transactions on Systems, Man, and Cybernetics*, 25(5):781–792, 1995. 275

Selection Analysis in Genetic Algorithms

José Galaviz-Casas

Instituto de Matemáticas, UNAM
Área de la Inv. Científica
Circuito Exterior, C.U., México, D.F., cp. 04510
jose@matem.unam.mx
http://www.matem.unam.mx/~jose

Abstract. This paper describes a formal framework for the analysis of genetic algorithms. The model is based on the idea that over the space of populations an equivalence relation can be defined, as well as a metric on the space of equivalence classes induced by this relation. With this tools it can be proved that selection in a GA causes some kind of convergence and entropy reduction. The model is not restricted to a particular kind of selection.

Keywords: genetic algorithms, Hamming distance, partition, poset, metric space, convergence, entropy.

1 Introduction

Since its introduction by Holland in 1960's, genetic algorithms (GA's) have motivated several efforts to develop a formal model where they can be explained. Holland itself gives the first step in his book ([7]), and provides the well known *schema theorem*. Although such theorem have recently been subject of much critical discussion, because is based only in destructive effects of crossover and mutation operators. Also the framework provided by Holland is restricted to a particular kind of GA with proportional selection, 1-point crossover and uniform mutation.

Other approaches have been proposed such as those based on statistical mechanics ([13,16]), and the very successful approach based on Markov chain analysis ([12,3,4], [15]), and its derivations related with dynamical systems ([17,18]).

In this paper a different framework is proposed for the analysis of GA's. As a first step towards a comprehensive approach, a GA with selection only is analyzed. The model presented here is more general than others because no particular kind of selection is not assumed. Such operator is described as generally as possible.

The theoretical framework is based on a partition of the populations set and the definition of a metric in such space. A partial order is defined on the set of partitions in order to prove some kind of convergence, if the GA operates only by iterated application of selection.

The convergence caused by selection has been analyzed in the past [10]. In this work a new approach is introduced, and is established that selection causes

Helder Coelho (Ed.): IBERAMIA'98, LNAI 1484, pp. 283–292, 1998.
© Springer-Verlag Berlin Heidelberg 1998

the population of a GA tends to a populations subset characterized by the same set of genotypes. Furthermore the presence of global maximum in such set of genotypes depends on the kind of selection rather than selection itself. As is mentioned above the analysis does not consider a particular kind of selection.

With the tools provided by the framework described, an analysis of general entropy behavior is done and is shown that, in general, selection forces leads to a decrease of entropy. The information theory approach has been presented before as in [11], but in a different way.

In the second section some concepts and notation, that will be used in the rest of paper, are defined. In the third section the fundamental tools are developed, based on metric spaces and the partition of the populations set. In the fourth section the analysis of selection is done by means of tools related with metric spaces. In section five the behavior of entropy is analyzed, and finally some conclusions and pointers to future research are exposed.

2   Basic Definitions

In this paper are used genetic algorithms whose individuals are binary strings, or equivalently integers encoded in binary, of length ℓ. Every individual in a population is in $\mathbb{B}_\ell = \{0, 1, \ldots, 2^\ell - 1\}$.

A genetic algorithm operates over populations with a finite number of those strings.

Definition 1. The number of binary strings contained in a population is the *population size*.

Note that the previous definition does not consider the number of different strings, only the number of strings, repeated or not, in the population. In order to count the number of different structures contained in the population the following definition is used:

Definition 2. The number of different binary strings contained at least once in a population P is the *number of genotypes* or the *cardinality of population* denoted by $\mathcal{C}(P)$. Note that $\mathcal{C}(P) \leq 2^\ell$

In the following N denotes the size of a finite population of binary strings. The set of all possible populations of size N of binary strings of length ℓ is denoted by $\mathbb{P}_N(\mathbb{B}_\ell)$ or in short $\mathbb{P}_{N,\ell}$.

Any population with a finite number of individuals can be described by means of the proportion of every binary string in the population.

Definition 3. Let f_i be the number of times (frequency) that $i \in \mathbb{B}_\ell$ appears in a population $P \in \mathbb{P}_{N,\ell}$. P is described by a vector $\mathbf{P} = (p_0, p_1, \ldots, p_{2^\ell-1}) \in [0,1]^{2^\ell}$, where $p_i = f_i/N$. $\mathbf{P}$ is the *proportions vector*.

The degree of variation in a population is then described by means of the following:

Definition 4. The *variation vector* of a population is $\mathbf{V}(\mathbf{P}) = (b_0, b_1, \ldots, b_{2^\ell - 1})$ where:

$$b_i = \begin{cases} 1 & if\ p_i > 0 \\ 0 & if\ p_i = 0 \end{cases}$$

The variation vector has an entry i equal to 1 if and only if the genotype i is represented by at least one instance in the population. Note that the set of all the variation vectors is equivalent to the set of integers $\{0, 1, \ldots, 2^{2^\ell} - 1\}$ encoded in binary.

Definition 5. The *variation coefficient* of the population $\mathbf{P}$, denoted by $v(\mathbf{P})$ is the number of ones in $\mathbf{V}(\mathbf{P})$. Note that this is the number of different *genotypes* represented in $\mathbf{P}$ by at least one string, that is $\mathcal{C}(\mathbf{P})$.

Definition 6. Let $\mathbf{P}$ and $\mathbf{Q}$ be two populations in $\mathbb{P}_{N,\ell}$. The *separation coefficient* between $\mathbf{P}$ and $\mathbf{Q}$, denoted by $H(\mathbf{P}, \mathbf{Q})$ is the number of positions where $\mathbf{V}(\mathbf{P})$ and $\mathbf{V}(\mathbf{Q})$ have different values. $0 \leq H(\mathbf{P}, \mathbf{Q}) \leq 2^\ell$.

Note that $H(\mathbf{P}, \mathbf{Q})$ is the traditional Hamming distance as is defined in [6]. In what follows $n = 2^\ell$.

3   The Populations Set Partition

Now is needed to define a partition in the space $\mathbb{P}_{N,\ell}$, in order to do it, is defined a equivalence relation as appears in [14] (chapter 2) for example.

Theorem 1. $H(\mathbf{P}, \mathbf{Q}) = 0$ *defines an equivalence relation in* $\mathbb{P}_{N,\ell}$

Proof: $\mathbf{P}$ is related with $\mathbf{Q}$ (denoted by $\mathbf{P} \sim \mathbf{Q}$) if and only if $H(\mathbf{P}, \mathbf{Q}) = 0$. It is needed to prove the relation is reflexive, symmetric and transitive:

- $\mathbf{P} \sim \mathbf{P}$, because the number of positions where $\mathbf{V}(\mathbf{P})$ differs from $\mathbf{V}(\mathbf{P})$ is zero, then $H(\mathbf{P}, \mathbf{P}) = 0$
- if $\mathbf{P} \sim \mathbf{Q}$ then the number of positions where $\mathbf{V}(\mathbf{P})$ differs from $\mathbf{V}(\mathbf{Q})$ is zero then $H(\mathbf{P}, \mathbf{Q}) = H(\mathbf{Q}, \mathbf{P}) = 0$ then $\mathbf{Q} \sim \mathbf{P}$
- if $\mathbf{P} \sim \mathbf{Q}$ and $\mathbf{Q} \sim \mathbf{R}$ then $H(\mathbf{P}, \mathbf{Q}) = H(\mathbf{Q}, \mathbf{R}) = 0$, the number of positions where $\mathbf{V}(\mathbf{P})$ is different from $\mathbf{V}(\mathbf{Q})$ and the number of positions where $\mathbf{V}(\mathbf{Q})$ and $\mathbf{V}(\mathbf{R})$ are different is zero, then $\mathbf{V}(\mathbf{P}) = \mathbf{V}(\mathbf{Q}) = \mathbf{V}(\mathbf{R})$, then $H(\mathbf{P}, \mathbf{R}) = 0$, that is $\mathbf{P} \sim \mathbf{R}$

□

The relation defined above induces a partition of the space where it is defined, $\mathbb{P}_{N,\ell}$. Every equivalence class is identified by means of the variation vector of any population in the class, given that such variation vector is the same for every population in that class. Then definition 4 can be extended to the set of classes and talk about the variation vector of a class rather than the variation vector of a particular population only. In what follows $\mathbb{C}_\ell$ denotes the set of all the populations classes of length ℓ strings.

Definition 7. Let i_2 be the nonnegative integer i encoded in binary. The class $C_i \in \mathbb{C}_\ell$ is:

$$C_i = \{\mathbf{P} \in \mathbb{P}_{N,\ell} | \mathbf{V}(\mathbf{P}) = (b_0, b_1, \ldots, b_{n-1}) \text{ with } i_2 = b_0 b_1 \ldots b_{n-1}\}$$

And

$$\mathbf{V}(C_i) = (b_0, b_1, \ldots, b_{n-1})$$

is the *variation vector* of the class C_i.

Definition 8. The number of ones in the variation vector of the class $C_i \in \mathbb{C}_\ell$ is the *variation coefficient* of C_i denoted by $v(C_i)$

So, two populations $\mathbf{P}$ and $\mathbf{Q}$ are in the same equivalence class if and only if they have the same genotypes. C_i denotes the class of all the populations whose variation vector corresponds to the integer i encoded in binary. H will be redefined.

Definition 9. $H(C_i, C_j)$ is the number of positions where $\mathbf{V}(C_i)$ and $\mathbf{V}(C_j)$ have different values.

Theorem 2. *H is a metric for $\mathbb{C}_\ell$.*

Proof: Let C_i and C_j be two classes of populations, H is the Hamming distance between two class variation vectors $\mathbf{V}(C_i)$ and $\mathbf{V}(C_j)$, and H is a true metric as proved in [1], then H is a metric for $\mathbb{C}_\ell$. □

Now is defined a Cauchy sequence in the metric space $\langle \mathbb{C}_\ell, H \rangle$ as appears in [14] and [5] (chapter 3).

Definition 10. A sequence $\{C\}^i$ in $\mathbb{C}_\ell$ is a *Cauchy sequence* if and only if for any real number $\varepsilon > 0$ there exists a nonnegative integer N such that for every $k, m > N$:

$$H(C^k, C^m) < \varepsilon$$

The previous definition provides the elements needed to demonstrate the following theorem. The definition of complete metric space can be found in [14] and [5] (chapter 3).

Theorem 3. *$\langle \mathbb{C}_\ell, H \rangle$ is a complete and bounded metric space.*

Proof: In order to demonstrate completeness is needed to show that any Cauchy sequence in $\mathbb{C}_\ell$ converges.

Let $\{C\}^i$ be a Cauchy sequence, then for any $\varepsilon > 0$ there exists an integer N such that for every $k, m > N$:

$$H(C^k, C^m) < \varepsilon$$

In particular for

$$\varepsilon = 1$$

Then exists N such that for every $k, m > N$:

$$H(C^k, C^m) < 1$$

This implies that $H(C^k, C^m) = 0$ because this is the only possible value for H less than 1, then C^k and C^m are the same string. And this string is in $\mathbb{C}_\ell$.

H can only take values in $\{0, 1, \ldots, 2^\ell\}$ then H is a bounded metric.   □

4   Convergence of Generic Selection

In this section is shown that a genetic algorithm, which operates only by selection (i.e. the probabilities of mutation and crossover are both zero), converges. Similar result has been demonstrated before [10], with the use of other techniques.

The algorithm converges to a class of populations rather than to a particular population. Every generation of a GA belongs to a class, looking the evolution of the algorithm from the classes point of view, it is possible to see that such evolution points to some particular class.

The following defines a partial order relation ([9, 8]) in $\mathbb{C}_\ell$.

Definition 11. Let C_i and C_j be two populations in $\mathbb{C}_\ell$. C_i is a *reduction* of C_j ($C_i \preceq C_j$) if and only if in every position where $\mathbf{V}(C_i)$ has 1, $\mathbf{V}(C_j)$ also has 1. This is, any class C_i is a reduction of other class C_j if and only if all the genotypes represented in C_i are also represented in C_j.

With the previous definition $\mathbb{C}_\ell$ constitutes a partially ordered set (poset), in fact the set is a lattice (any two classes are reduction of some other class and a class can be found that is reduction of both classes), the supremum element is $(1, \ldots, 1)$ and infimum element is $(0, \ldots, 0)$. An alternative lattice definition can be found in [9] (ch. 1). A poset $\langle L, \leq \rangle$ is a lattice if and only if the supremum and infimum exist for any finite nonvoid subset $S \subseteq L$.

Using the previous demonstrated theorem and the lattice definition mentioned above it is possible to prove the following theorem.

Theorem 4. *Let $\{C\}^i$ be an infinite sequence of elements in $\mathbb{C}_\ell$ such that*

$$C^i \preceq C^{i-1}$$

(monotonically decreasing), then $\{C\}^i$ converges to some class $I \in \mathbb{C}_\ell$ where $I = \inf\{C\}^i$

Proof: $\mathbb{C}_\ell$ has exactly 2^{2^ℓ} elements, then $\{C\}^i$ has a finite number of different terms $\Omega \subseteq \mathbb{C}_\ell$. By the lattice definition Ω has an infimum element I such that:

$$I \preceq C \quad \forall C \in \Omega \tag{1}$$

Let M be the smaller integer such that $C^M = I$. Given that $\{C\}^i$ is monotonically decreasing then for every $k \geq M$ occurs $C^k = I$. So for every $\varepsilon > 0$ there exists a $N = M$ such that for every $k, r > N$

$$H(C^k, C^r) = 0 < \varepsilon$$

So $\{C\}^i$ is a Cauchy sequence and converges for theorem 3.

Also for every $\varepsilon > 0$ if $r > M$ then

$$H(I, C^r) = 0 < \varepsilon$$

so $\{C\}^i$ converges to I.

$\square$

The meaning of *selection* can be formulated in general terms as follows.

Definition 12. Let $\mathbf{P}_i \in \mathbb{P}_{N,\ell}$ be a population in a class $C_k \in \mathbb{C}_\ell$. *Selection* is a function $S : \mathbb{P}_{N,\ell} \mapsto \mathbb{P}_{N,\ell}$ such that:

$$S(\mathbf{P}_i) = \mathbf{P}_{i+1}$$

where $\mathbf{P}_{i+1} \in C_r$ and $C_r \preceq C_k$

That is: selection can not increase the number of genotypes represented in any population. The result of applying selection to any population is other population with, at most, the same set of genotypes.

Definition 13. Let $\Phi : \mathbb{P}_{N,\ell} \mapsto \mathbb{C}_\ell$ be a function that assign to every population $\mathbf{P}$ the class where $\mathbf{P}$ lives. That is, if $\mathbf{P} \in C_k$ then $\Phi(\mathbf{P}) = C_k$.

The iterated application of selection in any population induces a monotonous decreasing sequence (as defined in [14], chapter 3) of the classes where such populations are. Given that the set of classes with H is a complete metric space, such sequence converges in $\mathbb{C}_\ell$. $S^k(\mathbf{P})$ denotes the k-th iterated application of selection to the population $\mathbf{P}$. Now the set of tools needed to prove following theorem is complete, analogous to the respective theorem for $\mathbb{R}$ (theo. 3.14 [14]):

Theorem 5. *Let $\mathbf{P}_0 \in \mathbb{P}_{N,\ell}$ be an initial population. The sequence:*

$$\dots \Phi(S^k(\mathbf{P}_0)) \preceq \dots \preceq \Phi(S^2(\mathbf{P}_0)) \preceq \Phi(S(\mathbf{P}_0)) \preceq \Phi(\mathbf{P}_0)$$

converges to some class $C \in \mathbb{C}_\ell$.

Proof: By theorem 4 this is true.

$\square$

5   Entropy Analysis

With the convergence result proved it is possible to analyze the behavior of entropy in the generic evolution of populations.

Definition 14. Let $\mathbf{P} = (p_0, p_1, \dots, p_{n-1})$ be a population in $\mathbb{P}_{N,\ell}$. The *entropy* of $\mathbf{P}$, denoted by $\mathcal{H}(\mathbf{P})$ is:

$$\mathcal{H}(\mathbf{P}) = \sum_{i=0}^{n-1} p_i \log_2 \left(\frac{1}{p_i} \right)$$

The entropy of a population with only one genotype is 0 because such genotype (i) has $p_i = 1$ and $p_j = 0$ for every $j \neq i$.

In a population of size N, with $k \leq n$ equally probable genotypes, the probability of each genotype is:

$$p_i = \frac{\frac{N}{k}}{N} = \frac{1}{k}$$

The entropy of a population with this condition is maximum:

$$\mathcal{H}(\mathbf{P}) = k \, \frac{1}{k} \, \log_2 (k) = \log_2 (k) \tag{2}$$

Then the greatest entropy of any population in $\mathbb{P}_{N,\ell}$ is ℓ because the total amount of possible genotypes is 2^ℓ. In summary:

$$0 \leq \mathcal{H}(\mathbf{P}) \leq \ell \quad \forall \, \mathbf{P} \in \mathbb{P}_{N,\ell}$$

Theorem 6. *Let $\mathbf{P} \in \mathbb{P}_{N,\ell}$ be a population whose variation coefficient is $v(\mathbf{P})$ then:*

$$\mathcal{H}(\mathbf{P}) \leq \log_2 (v(\mathbf{P}))$$

Proof: The entropy is maximum when all the genotypes are equally probable, applying the equation 2 with $k = v(\mathbf{P})$ the desired result is obtained.   □

It is useful to do an extension of the definition of population entropy to define the entropy of a class in $\mathbb{C}_\ell$.

Definition 15. Let $C \in \mathbb{C}_\ell$ be a class of populations, the *entropy* of C is defined as:

$$\mathcal{H}(C) = max \, \{\mathcal{H}(\mathbf{P}) \mid \mathbf{P} \in C\}$$

With this definition and theorem 6 the following corollary can be formulated:

Corollary 1. $\mathcal{H}(C) = \log_2 (v(C))$

Proof:

$$\mathcal{H}(C) = max \, \{\mathcal{H}(\mathbf{P}) \mid \mathbf{P} \in C\}$$

Every population $\mathbf{P} \in C$ has the same variation coefficient. Then, by theorem 6:

$$\mathcal{H}(C) = \log_2 (v(\mathbf{P})) \quad \forall \, \mathbf{P} \in C$$

and the variation coefficient of every population in C is the variation coefficient of C itself.   □

Corollary 2. *Let* $\mathbf{P}, \mathbf{Q} \in \mathbb{P}_{N,\ell}$ *be two populations such that:*

$$S(\mathbf{P}) = \mathbf{Q}$$

then:

$$\mathcal{H}(\Phi(\mathbf{Q})) \leq \mathcal{H}(\Phi(\mathbf{P}))$$

Proof: Since (def. 12):

$$\Phi(\mathbf{Q}) \preceq \Phi(\mathbf{P})$$

then the number of ones in $\mathbf{V}(\mathbf{Q})$ is less or equal that the number of ones of $\mathbf{V}(\mathbf{P})$ and:

$$\log_2\left(v(\Phi(\mathbf{Q}))\right) \leq \log_2\left(v(\Phi(\mathbf{P}))\right)$$

By the previous corollary:

$$\mathcal{H}(\Phi(\mathbf{Q})) = \log_2\left(v(\Phi(\mathbf{Q}))\right)$$

and

$$\mathcal{H}(\Phi(\mathbf{P})) = \log_2\left(v(\Phi(\mathbf{P}))\right)$$

So:

$$\mathcal{H}(\Phi(\mathbf{Q})) \leq \mathcal{H}(\Phi(\mathbf{P}))$$

□

Now the following theorem can be formulated:

Theorem 7. *Let* $\mathbf{P}_0 \in \mathbb{P}_{N,\ell}$ *be an initial population. The sequence:*

$$\{\mathcal{H}(\Phi(S^k(\mathbf{P}_0)))\}$$

is monotonically decreasing, bounded and convergent.

Proof: The monotony and decreasing features are obvious by the corollary 2. The lower bound is 0 and the upper bound is the entropy of the class where the initial population is. This sequence is in $\mathbb{R}$, that is a complete metric space, thus it converges to some real number. □

6   Conclusions and Future Research

The framework shown here is a new and useful approach for the analysis of GA's. With the tools provided by such a framework some features of selection have been proved. Also the analysis is more general that those reached by the use of some other methods.

The essential feature of selection has been isolated, the feature that is present in all the different kinds of this operator: selection can not increase the number of different genotypes present in a population. This is the sufficient condition that assures the convergence of a GA with selection only.

Also the behavior of entropy has been analyzed along the iterated application of selection to an initial population. It can be concluded that, from a global point of view, selection reduces entropy. Entropy can increase from one generation to the next but, in the long term, entropy will decrease and converge to a limit closer to zero as small is the number of different genotypes present in populations.

To demonstrate the usefulness of this framework it remains to apply it to all the other common genetic operators: mutation and crossover. Currently only some intuitive features have been proved. But is possible to speculate that if this method is applied to mutation, for example, the result will be that, in the limit, the sequence of classes where the generations are, tends to be in a neighborhood of some other class, the radius of such neighborhood will be greater proportionally to the probability of mutation and will also be affected by the distribution of genotypes present in the population.

It could be interesting to consider the mutation operator as noise in a channel. A population **P** before mutation will be transmitted through a noisy channel to another population **P'** and some of the symbols present in **P** will be modified to others that were originally not present.

Also is interesting the application of the method to the analysis of some particular kinds of selection as are presented in [2].

References

1. Adámeck, Jiři. *Foundations of Coding*. John Wiley & Sons. 1991. 286
2. Bäck, T. and F. Hoffmeister. Extended Selection Mechanisms in Genetic Algorithms. *Proceedings of 4th International Conference on Genetic Algorithms and their Applications*. Morgan Kaufmann. 1991. 291
3. Davis, T. E. and C. Principe. A Markov Chain Framework for the Simple Genetic Algorithm. *Evolutionary Computation*. 3(1). 1993. 283
4. De Jong, K. A. W. M. Spears and D. Gordon. Using Markov Chains to Analyze GAFO's. *Proceedings of Third Foundations of Genetic Algorithms Workshop (FOGA)*. Morgan Kaufmann. 1994. 283
5. Dieudonné, J. *Foundations of Modern Analysis*. Academic Press. 1960. 286
6. Hamming, Richard W.*Coding and Information Theory*. Prentice Hall Inc. 1980. 285
7. Holland, John. *Adaptation in Natural and Artificial Systems*. The University of Michigan Press. 1975. 283
8. Birkhoff, Garrett. *General Lattice Theory*. American Mathematical Society (Dept. of Mathematics, Harvard University). 1963. 287
9. Grätzer, George. *General Lattice Theory*. Academic Press. 1978. 287
10. Estivil-Castro, Vladimir. The Role of Selection *Proceedings of the First International Workshop on Frontiers on Evolutionary Algorithms*. Third Joint Conference in Information Sciencies. Vol. 1: Fuzzy Logic, Intelligent Control and Genetic Algorithms. March 2-5. 1997. 283, 287
11. Kargupta, Hillol. Information Transmission in Genetic Algorithm and Shannon's Second Theorem. *IlliGAL report 93003*. University of Illinois at Urbana-Champaign . 1993. 284

12. Nix, A. E. and M. Vose. Modeling Genetic Algorithms with Markov Chains. *Annals of Mathematics and Artificial Intelligence.* 5. 1992. 283
13. Prügel-Bennett, A. and J. L. Shapiro. Analysis of Genetic Algorithms using Statistical Mechanics. *Physical Review Letters.* 9(72). February 1994. 283
14. Rudin, Walter. *Principles of Mathematical Analysis.* 3rd edition. Mc Graw Hill. 1976. 285, 286, 288
15. Rudolph, Günter. Convergence Analysis of Canonical Genetic Algorithm. *IEEE Transactions on Neural Networks.* 5(1). Special Issue on evolutionary computation. 1994. 283
16. Stephens, C. R. and H. Waelbroeck. Analysis of Effective Degrees of Freedom in Genetic Algorithms. Instituto de Ciencias Nucleares, UNAM. *Preprint ICN-UNAM-96-08.* October 1996. 283
17. Vose, M. D. Modeling Simple Genetic Algorithms. *Evolutionary Computation.* 4(3). 1995. 283
18. Vose, M. D. and G. E. Liepins. Punctuated Equilibria in Genetic Search. *Complex Systems.* 5. 1991. 283

Human Face Identification Using Invariant Descriptions and a Genetic Algorithm[*]

R. Pinto-Elías[1][**] and J.H. Sossa-Azuela[2]

[1] Centro Nacional de Investigación y Desarrollo Tecnológico
Prolongación Av. Palmira S/N, Col. Iternado Palmira
Cuernavaca, Morelos, C.P. 62490, México
rpinto@infosel.net.mx
[2] Centro de Investigación en Computación-IPN
Av. Juan de Dios Bátiz esquina con M. Othón de Mendizábal
Unidad Profesional Adolfo López Mateos, México, D.F. C.P. 07730, México
hsossa@pollux.cic.ipn.mx

Abstract. A new method to automatically identify a human face onto a 2D gray level image is presented. The method uses an invariant description of the face and a genetic algorithm to accomplish the task. The features used are the first four translation, rotation and scale moment invariants proposed by Hu [1]. In a first step, an image possibly containing a face is first divided into small cells of fixed size of 5×5 pixels. For each cell, the ordinary moments are next computed. From these, the corresponding Hu's invariants are then derived. Human face identification is thus accomplished by grouping individual cells using a genetic algorithm by fitting a specific cost function. This cost function corresponds to the invariant description of a human face given in terms of the detected image features.

1 Introduction

The human face is a complex pattern. Finding human faces automatically in a scene is a difficult yet significant problem. In recent years this problem has attracted considerable attention [2], [3], [4], [5], [6], [7] and [8] although it still remains an open problem [9] and [10]. It is the first important step in a fully automatic human recognition system [4]. The solution to this problem is important in many applications such as videoconferencing, multimedia and internet video communication. It would be thus desirable to count with a methodology that allows the location of a face in an automatic way.

---

[*] This research was supported by the Consejo Nacional de Ciencia y Tecnología de México (CONACyT), the Consejo del Sistema Nacional de Educación Tecnológica de México (COSNET) and the Centro de Investigación en Computación of the IPN (CIC-IPN) and the Centro de Investigación y de Estudios Avanzados of the IPN (CINVESTAV-IPN).

[**] R. Pinto is a Ph.D. student at the Sección de Control Automático of the CINVESTAV-IPN.

Helder Coelho (Ed.): IBERAMIA'98, LNAI 1484, pp. 293–302, 1998.
© Springer-Verlag Berlin Heidelberg 1998

The technique here proposed consist on doing segmentation and recognition at the same time as follows. Given an input image possibly containing a face: 1) divide this image into small cells of size of 5×5 pixels, 2) compute the ordinary moments (those used in mechanics) for each cell, 3) from these moments, derive the corresponding Hu's invariants [1], and 4) accomplish human face detection by grouping individual cells by using a genetic algorithm by fitting a specific cost function. This cost function corresponds to the invariant description of a human face in terms of the detected image features.

In the solution of this problem, in this work, the next four suppositions are assumed:

1. The number of human faces in the image is unknown.
2. Their size, is also unknown, and
3. Their location and orientation are unknown too.
4. Small pan and tilt rotations and changes of facial expressions are also allowed.

The remaining of the paper is organized as follows. In section 2 each one of the steps composing the proposed methodology are described. In section 3 the features used to describe a face are presented. The guided searching algorithm and the technique to swap the space of solutions are given in sections 4 and 5, respectively. Some experimental results with the aim to test the performance of the proposed methodology are next presented in section 6. Some conclusions and directions for future research are finally given in section 7.

2 The Methodology

The proposed methodology to automatically identify a human face in a 2D image has two main steps: human face description and human face identification. Each of these two steps is next described.

2.1 Human Face Description

The human face can be considered as a pattern. As such, it can be described as a vector in terms of a set of invariant features as follows:

$$O_i = [\psi_1 \ \psi_2 \ , ..., \ \psi_K] \tag{1}$$

with

$$\psi_k = f_k(O_i), 1 \leq i \leq n, 1 \leq k \leq K \tag{2}$$

where

$$O_i \qquad is \quad face \quad number \quad i$$

$$\psi_k \qquad is \quad feature \quad number \quad k$$

$$f_k(O_i) \qquad \begin{matrix} is & the & generator & function \\ of & feature & number & k \end{matrix}$$

$$n \qquad is \quad the \quad number \quad of \quad faces$$

$$K \qquad is \quad the \quad number \quad of \quad features$$

To obtain O for each person a CCD camera is placed in front of the subject trying to keep him/her always into the visual field of the sensor. In each case, the corresponding face is next manually segmented. For each segmented region the ψ_k's are next computed (see section 3). A feature vector is finally obtained in terms of the describing features. A face is thus represented by a unique feature vector, $O_i, i = 1, ..., n$.

2.2 Human Face Identification

Using the feature vectors obtained in the last section a references, the identification process can be started. It consists of two steps as follows:

1. **Confidence Function Definition.** Define a function involving f_k, $C(f_k)$ to guide the searching process of a face (its description) into the representation space E. For a given image, E is composed as the union of all possible values of f_k, this is:

$$E = \bigcup_{r=1}^{R} f_k(r), \quad k = 1, 2, ..., K \tag{3}$$

   where R is the total number of disjoint pixel regions in the image.
2. **Searching process.** Swap the representation space E by means of a guided searching process until obtaining the best approximation of f_k by merging and by spliting fixed sized regions in the image. This will be done by a genetic algorithm as explained in section 5. The final result will be a region enclosing the object of interest (a face in this case).

3   Invariant Descriptors Used

Lots of features have been used in the past to derived the model of an object. The features actually used in this work are those proposed by Hu [1]. These features have been chosen because they have proven to be very nice features in shape recognition [1], [11], [12], and [13]. Only the first four are used. According to the proposed methodology in section 2 a face can thus be described as follows:

$$O_i = \begin{bmatrix} \phi_1 & \phi_2 & \phi_3 & \phi_4 \end{bmatrix} \tag{4}$$

To be used in the content of this work, these invariant features must be described in terms of the ordinary moments and not in terms of the central moments. For example, first Hu's invariant ϕ_1 can be expressed as:

$$\phi_1 = \frac{(m_{20} + m_{02}) \cdot m_{00} - (m_{10}^2 + m_{01}^2)}{m_{00}^3} \tag{5}$$

The reason to do this is because the ordinary moments can be directly added because they are referred to the same point (the origin of the coordinate frame); the central moments are referred to different points (the centroids of each cell). If we would like to use the central moments of each cell to obtain the invariant moments of bigger regions, it would be thus necessary to first recompute the centroids of each cell and then obtain the invariant moments for these new centroids.

Thus, if a region R of interest is divided into n subregions, $R_i, i = 1, ..., n$, the standard moments of R can be obtained as the summation of the standard moments of each subregion as:

$$m_{pq}(R) = \sum_{i=1}^{n} m_{pq}(R_i) \tag{6}$$

For each subregion, the standard moments are computed by means of the following expression [1]:

$$m_{pq}(R_i) = \sum_{(x,y) \in R_i} \sum x^p y^q f(x, y) \tag{7}$$

Let's suppose now that the entire image is divided into cells of the same size by using a fixed reticule as shown in figure 1 (a), and that for each cell the standard moments are computed using 7. An object in the image, when the reticule is applied, can be thus seen as subdivided in regions as shown in figure 1 (b). This way, the same object a different sizes, will include more or less cells.

The identification (segmentation) problem can thus be seen as an optimization problem: **find the set of contiguous cells best fitting the value of a descriptive function**. In our case, the descriptive function is a feature vector whose components are the first four Hu's invariants as shown in equation 4.

4   Guided Searching Algorithm

Now, if $O_{interest} = \begin{bmatrix} \phi_1 & \phi_2 & \phi_3 & \phi_4 \end{bmatrix}$ corresponds to the description of a face desired to be verified into an image, then the problem is reduced to find the set of cells whose image region invariant descriptors $\begin{bmatrix} \phi_1' & \phi_2' & \phi_3' & \phi_4' \end{bmatrix}$ obtained by combining the standard moments of each cell according to 5, 6 and 7 best fit the feature vector describing $O_{interest}$.

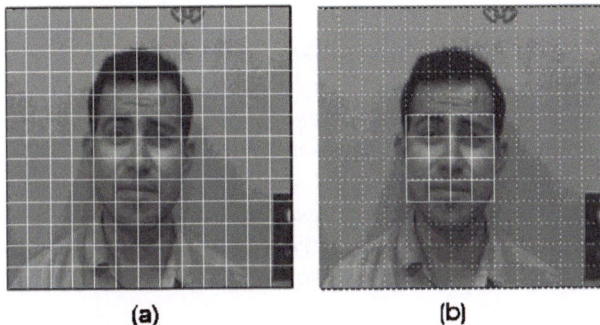

Fig. 1. (a) An image divided into cells of the same size by using a fixed reticule. (b) The object of interest subdivided into cells.

The cell grouping process is done by means of a genetic algorithm which will allows us to swap the representation space by using a confidence function $C(f_k)$. It is next described.

5   Genetic Algorithm

A genetic algorithm (GA) [14] has been chosen because as it was shown in [15,16,17], GAs have proven to be very useful tools in many problems including pattern recognition. The main features of the genetic algorithm used [14] are the following:

- A chromosome equals the grouping of a set of contiguous cells.
- The initial population contains only individual cells.
- New generations are obtained by recombining new and old populations.
- The crossing and mutation probabilities are fixed to be 70% and 5%, respectively.
- The size population is fixed to be 100.
- Multiple crossing point are used.
- The fitness function of each chromosome is obtained as:

$$fit = \left| \frac{\phi_i - \phi_d}{\phi_i + \phi_d} \right| \cdot f_f$$

where

$$fit \quad is the fitness of the chromosome$$

$$\phi_i \quad \begin{array}{l} are the values of the invariants \\ of the interest face \end{array}$$

$$\phi_d \quad \begin{array}{l} are the values of the invariants \\ of the image region specified \\ by a chromosome \end{array}$$

$$f_f \quad \begin{array}{l} is a shape factor defined as: \\ f_f = \max\left(\frac{A_M}{A_m}, \frac{A_m}{A_M}\right) \end{array}$$

$$A_M \quad \begin{array}{l} is the size of the major principal axe \\ of the face \end{array}$$

$$A_m \quad \begin{array}{l} is the size of the minor principal axe \\ of the face \end{array}$$

– The confidence or cost function to be minimized is defined as:

$$C(f_k) = \frac{\phi_i - \phi_d}{\phi_i + \phi_d}$$

where ϕ_i, ϕ_d and f are, respectively, the invariants searched for, the region invariants and the value of the function to be optimized.

The GA starts by generating a initial population containing only individual cells. Each chromosome represents thus an individual cell. The next population is obtained by crossing and/or mutating the chromosomes of the initial population. This population will contain chromosomes corresponding to regions composed of two or more cells. This process is repeated until the best minimization of the cost function is obtained.

A complete description of the GA algorithm is fully given in [14].

6   Experimental Results

In this section some experimental results are shown. To test the proposed methodology the set of faces shown in figure 2 was used. Each image is of 200×200 pixels and has 16 gray levels.

6.1   Human Face Description

For each person shown in figure 2 an image called *reference image* was taken. Each reference image was obtained by placing a CCD camera in front of the subject trying to keep him/her always into the visual field of the sensor.

Fig. 2. The set of images used.

Each face was next segmented as explained in section 2, the corresponding describing vectors were thus obtained as explained also in section 2. With these reference vectors the performance of the genetic algorithm as a face detector and recognizer was tested. The results are next shown.

6.2   Face Detection and Recognition

The performance of the GA was tested with a set of 300 images: 19 for each of the twelve people (228) and 72 containing other things than people. The first 228 images were obtained by placing again a CCD camera in front of the subject at different distances with regard to him trying to keep him always into the visual field of the sensor. Again, he or she was asked to rotate his/her face a little and to change his facial expression to obtain different samples

The experiment consisted in selecting at random from the 300 test images 50 trying to find in them each one of the 12 faces previously described. The search was individual, one face at the time. 600 tests were thus performed.

During testing, the GA satisfactorily found in 71% the desired face, in 21%, it failed, i.e. the GA identified a subimage not containing a face as the face, and in 8%, it gave false positives (the GA said that the face found in the image was that looked for when in reality it was not present in the image). Figure 3 shows some examples of the segmentation results obtained during the experiments. The results are summarized in table 1. For this table:

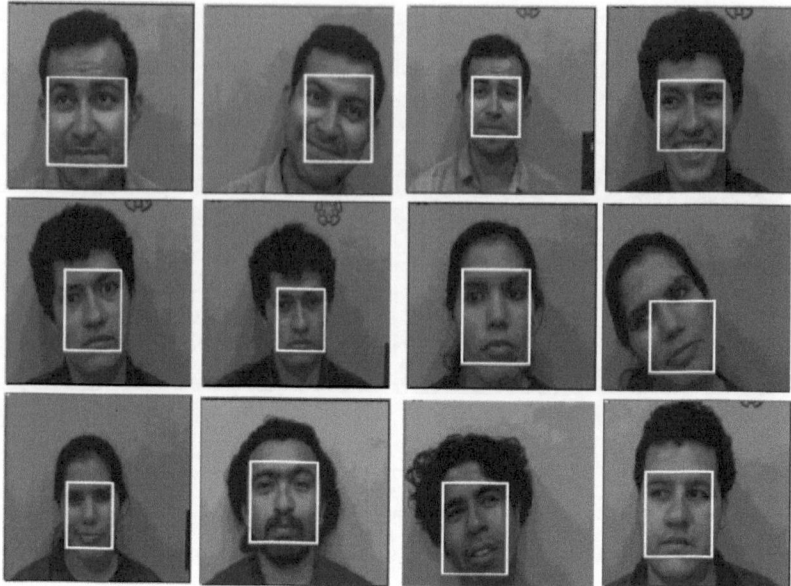

Fig. 3. Segmentation results.

- % of false positives is the percentage of cases in which the segmented face does not correspond to the desired one.
- % of lost faces is the percentage of cases in which the desired face was not found when it was really present in the image.
- % of found faces is the percentage of cases in which the desired face was satisfactorily found.

7   Conclusions and Future Research

A technique for the automatic identification of a human face onto a 2D gray level image was presented. The technique uses an invariant description of the face and a genetic algorithm to accomplish this task. The invariants used are the first four feature invariants proposed by Hu [1]. In a first step, an image possibly containing a face is first divided into small cells sized in 5×5 pixels. In a second step, for each cell, the ordinary moments are next computed. From these, the corresponding Hu's invariants are then derived. Human face segmentation and identification was thus accomplished by grouping individual cells using a genetic algorithm by fitting a specific cost function. This cost function corresponds to the invariant description of a human face.

The use of the proposed methodology to segment a face avoids the application of an exhaustive process over each image point. In the case of an exhaustive process, for each image point, windows of different sizes have to be evaluated,

Face No.	% found faces	% lost faces	% false positives
1	76	18	6
2	78	15	7
3	66	25	9
4	72	18	10
5	82	10	8
6	65	26	9
7	62	31	7
8	66	24	10
9	62	31	7
10	69	24	7
11	78	13	9
12	76	18	6

Table 1. Experimental rsualts in terms of the search efficiency of the GA.

and for each one of these windows the specified vector of descriptors has to be computed and compared with the interest model vector. Instead, the GA swaps the entire image only by considering interest regions guided by a confidence function.

We are planning to combine our method with other techniques to do cooperative object recognition. The goal is to put a set of different face detectors to work onto the same image, take their opinion about the image and fusion their results into a unique module that will give the final result. The aim, of course, is to see if the combination of several detectors give a better performance.

References

1. M. K. Hu, Visual pattern recognition by moment invariants, IRE Transactions on Information Theory, 8:179-187, 1962. 293, 294, 295, 296, 300
2. V. Govindaraju, D. B. Sher, R. K. Shrihari and S. N. Shrihari, Lociationg human faces in newspaper photographs, Proc. IEEE Conf. of Computer Vision and Pattern Recognition, 549-554, 1989. 293
3. V. Govindaraju, S. N. Shrihari and D. B. Sher, A computational model for face location, Proc. IEEE 3rd Int. Conference on Computer Vision, Japan, 718-721, 1990. 293
4. G. Yang and T. S. Huang, Human face detection in a complex bakcground, Pattern Recognition, 27(1):53-63, 1994. 293
5. G. Burel and D. Carel, Detection and localization of faces on digital images, Pattern Recognition Letters, 15:963-967, 1994. 293
6. Y. Dai and Y. Nakano, Extraction of facial images from complex backgroun using color inofrmation and SGLD matrices, Int. Workshop on Automatic face and Gesture Recognition, 238-242, 1995. 293
7. B. Takacs and H. Wechsler, Face location using a dynamic model of retinal feature extraction, Int. Workshop on Automatic face and Gesture Recognition, 243-247, 1995. 293

8. S. H. Lin, S. Y. Kung and L. J. Lin, Face recognition/detection by probabilistic decision-based neural network, IEEE Transactions on Neural Networks, 8(1);114-132, 1997. 293

9. K. Ch. Yow and R. Cipolla, Feature-based human face detection, Image and Vision Computing, 15:713-735, 1997. 293

10. S. Gutta and H. Wechsler, Face recognition using hybrid classifiers, Pattern Recognition, 30(4):539-553, 1997. 293

11. S. A. Dudani, K. J. Breeding and R. B. Mcghee, Aircraft identification by momnt invariants, IEEE Transactions on Computers, 26(1):39-46, 1977. 295

12. J. Boyce and W. Hossack, Moment invariants for patter recognition, Pattern Recognition Letters, 1:451-456, 1983. 295

13. Z. Mingfa, S. Hasani, S. Bhattarai and H. Singh, Pattern recognition with moment invariants on a machine vision system, Pattern Recognition Letters, 9:175-180, 1989. 295

14. D. E. Goldberg, Genetic algorithms in search, optimization and machine learning, Addison Wesley Publishing Company, Inc., 1989. 297, 298

15. C. A. Ankenbrandt, B. P. Buckles and F. E. Petry, Scene recognition using genetic algorithms with semantic nets, Pattren Recognition Letters, 11:235, 1990. 297

16. S. Bandyopadhyay, C. A. Murthy and S. K. Pal, Pattern classification using genetic algorithms, Pattern Recognition Letters, 16:801, 1995. 297

17. S. K. Pal and P.P. Wang, Genetic algorithms for pattern recognition, CRC Press, Inc. 1996. 297

Using the Min-Max Method to Solve Multiobjective Optimization Problems with Genetic Algorithms

Carlos A. Coello Coello*

Engineering Design Centre
University of Plymouth
Plymouth, Devon PL4 8AA, UK
ccoello@soc.plym.ac.uk

Abstract. In this paper, a new multiobjective optimization technique based on the genetic algorithm (GA) is introduced. This method is based in the concept of min-max optimum, taken from the Operations Research literature, and can produce the Pareto set and the best trade-off among the objectives. The results produced by this approach are compared to those produced with other mathematical programming techniques and GA-based approaches using a multiobjective optimization tool called MOSES (Multiobjective Optimization of Systems in the Engineering Sciences). The importance of representation is hinted in the example used, since it can be seen that reducing the chromosomic length of an individual tends to produce better results in the optimization process, even if it's at the expense of a higher cardinality alphabet.

1 Introduction

Engineering optimization has been a very fertile area of research in the last few years, but the normal trend has been to deal with a single objective at a time, and use ideal and unrealistic problems, rather than real-world applications. Assuming only one objective is generally unrealistic for engineering optimization problems, since most real-world problems have several (possibly conflicting) objectives. The common practice, therefore, has been to let the designer to make decisions based on his/her experience, instead of using some well-defined optimality criterion.

Over the years, the Operations Research community has produced more than 20 mathematical programming techniques to deal with multiple objectives. However, the main focus of these approaches is to produce a *single* trade-off based on some notion of optimality, rather than producing several possible alternatives from which the designer may choose. More recently, the genetic algorithm (GA), an artificial intelligence search technique based on the mechanics of natural selection, has been found to be effective on some scalar optimization problems. In

---

* Part of this work was developed by the author while visiting LANIA (Laboratorio Nacional de Informática Avanzada) in Xalapa, Veracruz, México

Helder Coelho (Ed.): IBERAMIA'98, LNAI 1484, pp. 303–313, 1998.
© Springer-Verlag Berlin Heidelberg 1998

order to extend the GA to deal with multiple objectives, the structure of the GA has been modified to handle a vector fitness function.

This paper will review some of the previous work in multiobjective optimization using GAs, and a new approach, proposed by the author, will be introduced. Also, MOSES (Multiobjective Optimization of Systems in the Engineering Sciences), a system developed as a testbed for multiobjective optimization techniques by the author, will be briefly described together with an example of its use. The new approach, based on the notion of min-max optimum, is able to generate the Pareto set and better trade-offs than any of the other techniques included in MOSES. The importance of using alphabets of cardinality higher than two will be emphasized, and the results found with this alternative representation will be shown to be better than those produced using a traditional binary representation, both for single and multiobjective optimization.

1.1 Statement of the Problem

Multiobjective optimization (also called multicriteria optimization, multiperformance or vector optimization) can be defined as the problem of finding [13]:

a vector of decision variables which satisfies constraints and optimizes a vector function whose elements represent the objective functions. These functions form a mathematical description of performance criteria which are usually in conflict with each other. Hence, the term "optimize" means finding such a solution which would give the values of all the objective functions acceptable to the designer.

Formally, we can state it as follows:

Find the vector $\bar{x}^* = [x_1^*, x_2^*, \ldots, x_n^*]^T$ which will satisfy the m inequality constraints:

$$g_i(\bar{x}) \geq 0 \quad i = 1, 2, \ldots, m \tag{1}$$

the p equality constraints

$$h_i(\bar{x}) = 0 \quad i = 1, 2, \ldots, p \tag{2}$$

and optimize the vector function

$$\bar{f}(\bar{x}) = [f_1(\bar{x}), f_2(\bar{x}), \ldots, f_k(\bar{x})]^T \tag{3}$$

where $\bar{x} = [x_1, x_2, \ldots, x_n]^T$ is the vector of decision variables.

1.2 Min-Max Optimum

The idea of stating the *min-max optimum* and applying it to multiobjective optimization problems, was taken from game theory, which deals with solving conflicting situations. The min-max approach to a linear model was proposed by Jutler and Solich and was been further developed by Osyczka [11], Rao [14] and Tseng & Lu [18].

The min-max optimum compares relative deviations from the separately attainable minima. Consider the ith objective function for which the relative deviation can be calculated from

$$z_i'(\bar{x}) = \frac{|f_i(\bar{x}) - f_i^0|}{|f_i^0|} \tag{4}$$

or from

$$z_i''(\bar{x}) = \frac{|f_i(\bar{x}) - f_i^0)|}{|f_i(\bar{x})|} \tag{5}$$

It should be clear that for (4) and (5) we have to assume that for every $i \in I$ and for every $\bar{x} \in X$, $f_i(\bar{x}) \neq 0$.

If all the objective functions are going to be minimized, then equation (4) defines function relative increments, whereas if all of them are going to be maximized, it defines relative decrements. Equation (5) works conversely.

2   Multiobjective Optimization Using GAs

Some of the most important GA-based multiobjective optimization techniques will be briefly explained in this section.

3   VEGA

David Schaffer [16] extended Grefenstette's GENESIS program [8] to include multiple objective functions. Schaffer's approach was to use an extension of the Simple Genetic Algorithm (SGA) that he called the Vector Evaluated Genetic Algorithm (VEGA), and that differed of the first only in the way in which selection was performed. This operator was modified so that at each generation a number of sub-populations was generated by performing proportional selection according to each objective function in turn. Thus, for a problem with k objectives, k sub-populations of size N/k each would be generated, assuming a total population size of N. These sub-populations would be shuffled together to obtain a new population of size N, on which the GA would apply the crossover and mutation operators in the usual way. Schaffer realized that the solutions generated by his system were non-inferior in a local sense, because their non-inferiority is limited to the current population, and while a locally dominated individual is also globally dominated, the converse is not necessarily true [16].

4   Lexicographic Ordering

The basic idea of this technique is that the designer ranks the objectives in order of importance. The optimum solution is then found by minimizing the objective functions, starting with the most important one and proceeding according to the order of importance of the objectives [15]. Fourman [6] suggested a selection scheme based on lexicographic ordering. In a first version of his algorithm, objectives were assigned different priorities by the user and each pair of individuals were compared according to the objective with the highest priority. If this resulted in a tie, the objective with the second highest priority was used, and so on. A second version of this algorithm, reported to work surprisingly well, consisted of randomly selecting the objective to be used in each comparison. As in VEGA, this corresponds to averaging fitness across fitness components, each component being weighted by the probability of each objective being chosen to decide each tournament [5]. However, the use of pairwise comparisons makes an important difference with respect to VEGA, since in this case scale information is ignored. Therefore, the population may be able to see as convex a concave trade-off surface, depending on its current distribution, and on the problem itself.

5   Weighted Sum: Hajela's Method

Hajela and Lin [9] included the weights of each objective in the chromosome, and promoted their diversity in the population through fitness sharing. Their goal was to be able to simultaneously generate a family of Pareto optimal designs corresponding to different weighting coefficients in a single run of the GA. Besides using sharing, Hajela and Lin used a vector evaluated approach based on VEGA to achieve their goal. They proposed the use of a utility function of the form:

$$\bar{U} = \sum_{i=1}^{l} W_i \frac{F_i}{F_i^*} \tag{6}$$

where F_i^* are the scaling parameters for the objective criterion, l is the number of objective functions, and W_i are the weighting factors for each objective function F_i. In MOSES's implementation, a min-max approach was used to determine the utility function, so that the scaling factor was the ideal vector.

Hajela's approach also uses a sharing function of the form:

$$\phi(d_{ij}) = \begin{cases} 1 - \left(\frac{d_{ij}}{\sigma_{sh}}\right)^{\alpha}, & d_{ij} < \sigma_{sh} \\ 0, & \text{otherwise} \end{cases} \tag{7}$$

where $\alpha = 1$ for this work, d_{ij} is a metric indicative of the distance between designs i and j, and σ_{sh} is the sharing parameter, which is typically chosen between 0.01 and 0.1. The fitness of a design i is then modified as:

$$f_{s_i} = \frac{f_i}{\sum_{j=1}^{M} \phi(d_{ij})} \tag{8}$$

where M is the number of designs located in vicinity of the i-th design.

Hajela incorporates weight combinations into the chromosomic string, and under his representation, a single number represents not the weight itself, but a combination of them. For example, the number 4 (under floating point representation) could represent the vector $X_w = (0.4, 0.6)$ for a problem with two objective functions. Then, sharing is done on the weights. Finally, a mating restriction mechanism was imposed, to avoid members within a radius σ_{mat} to cross.

6   MOGA

Fonseca and Fleming [4] have proposed a scheme in which the rank of a certain individual corresponds to the number of chromosomes in the current population by which it is dominated. Consider, for example, an individual x_i at generation t, which is dominated by $p_i^{(t)}$ individuals in the current generation. Its current position in the individuals' rank can be given by [4]:

$$rank(x_i, t) = 1 + p_i^{(t)} \tag{9}$$

All non-dominated individuals are assigned rank 1, while dominated ones are penalized according to the population density of the corresponding region of the trade-off surface. See Fonseca and Fleming [4] for details.

7   NSGA

The Non-dominated Sorting Genetic Algorithm (NSGA) was proposed by Srinivas and Deb [17], and is based on several layers of classifications of the individuals. Before the selection is performed, the population is ranked on the basis of nondomination: all nondominated individuals are classified into one category (with a dummy fitness value, which is proportional to the population size, to provide an equal reproductive potential for these individuals). To maintain the diversity of the population, these classified individuals are shared with their dummy fitness values. Then this group of classified individuals is ignored and another layer of nondominated individuals is considered. The process continues until all individuals in the population are classified. A stochastic remainder proportionate selection was used for this approach. Since individuals in the first front have the maximum fitness value, they always get more copies than the rest of the population. This allows to search for nondominated regions, and results in quick convergence of the population toward such regions. Sharing, by its part, helps to distribute it over this region.

8   NPGA

Horn and Nafpliotis [10] proposed a tournament selection scheme based on Pareto dominance. Instead of limiting the comparison to two individuals, a number of other individuals in the population was used to help determine dominance. When both competitors were either dominated or non-dominated (i.e., there was a tie), the result of the tournament was decided through fitness sharing [7]. The pseudocode for Pareto domination tournaments assuming that all of the objectives are to be maximized can be found in Horn and Nafpliotis [10].

9   An Approach Using a Min-Max Strategy

The idea of this approach is to generate the individuals in such a way that they all constitute feasible solutions. This can be ensured by checking that none of the constraints is violated by the solution vector encoded by the corresponding chromosome, and by designing special operators. Then the user has to provide a vector of weights, which are used to spawn as many processes as weight combinations are provided (normally this number will be reasonably small). Each process is really a separate GA in which the given weight combination is used in conjunction with a min-max approach to generate a single solution. After the n processes are terminated (n=number of weight combinations provided), a final file is generated containing the Pareto set, which is formed by picking up the best solution from each of the processes spawned in the previous step. Since this approach requires knowing the ideal vector, the user is given the opportunity to provide such values directly (in case he/she knows them) or to use another GA to generate it.

10   Example

To illustrate the use of MOSES and the efficiency of the new technique proposed, one engineering design example were selected from the literature [3]. Since it is generally intractable to obtain an analytical representation of the Pareto front, it is usually very difficult to measure the performance of a multiobjective optimization technique. For the purposes of this paper the results were compared only in terms of the best trade-offs that could be achieved. For that sake, the following expression was used

$$L_p(f) = \sum_{i=1}^{k} w_i \left| \frac{f_i^0 - f_i(x)}{\rho_i} \right| \tag{10}$$

where k is the number of objectives, $\rho_i = f_i^0$, or $f_i(x)$, depending on which gives the maximum value for $L_p(f)$, and w_i refers to the weight assigned to each objective (if not known, equal weights are assigned to all the objectives). A sketch of the Pareto front produced by each technique can actually be obtained with MOSES, but due to space limitations such graphs won't be included in this paper.

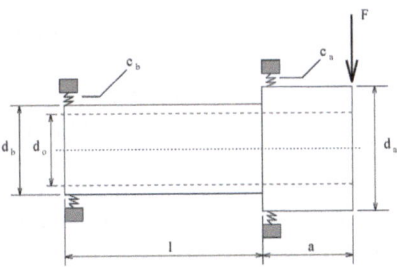

Fig. 1. Fig. 1 Sketch of the machine tool spindle used for the example.

10.1   Design of a Machine Tool Spindle

Consider the problem of a preliminary design of a machine tool spindle as presented in Figure 1 (taken from Eschenauer et al. [3]). The formulation of the multiobjective optimization problem is to minimize $f_1(x)$ and $f_2(x)$ as defined below [3].

$$f_1(x) = \frac{\pi}{4} \left[a(d_a^2 - d_o^2) + l(d_b^2 - d_o^2) \right] \tag{11}$$

$$f_2(x) = \frac{Fa^3}{3EI_a} \left(1 + \frac{l}{a} \frac{I_a}{I_b} \right) + \frac{F}{c_a} \left[\left(1 + \frac{a}{l} \right)^2 + \frac{c_a a^2}{c_b l^2} \right] \tag{12}$$

$$I_a = 0.049(d_a^4 - d_o^4), \quad I_b = 0.049(d_b^4 - d_o^4) \tag{13}$$

$$c_a = 35400 |\delta_{ra}|^{\frac{1}{9}} d_a^{\frac{10}{9}}, \quad c_b = 35400 |\delta_{rb}|^{\frac{1}{9}} d_b^{\frac{10}{9}} \tag{14}$$

$$\begin{aligned} g_1(x) &= l - l_g \le 0 \\ g_2(x) &= l_k - l \le 0 \\ g_3(x) &= d_{a1} - d_a \le 0 \end{aligned} \tag{15}$$

$$\begin{aligned} g_4(x) &= d_a - d_{a2} \le 0 \\ g_5(x) &= d_{b1} - d_b \le 0 \\ g_6(x) &= d_b - d_{b2} \le 0 \\ g_7(x) &= d_{om} - d_o \le 0 \end{aligned} \tag{16}$$

$$\begin{aligned} g_8(x) &= p_1 d_o - d_b \le 0 \\ g_9(x) &= p_2 d_b - d_a \le 0 \end{aligned} \tag{17}$$

$$g_{10}(x) = |\Delta_a + (\Delta_a - \Delta_b)\frac{a}{l}| - \Delta \le 0 \tag{18}$$

For this example, it is assumed that d_a must be chosen from the set $X_3 = \{80, 85, 90, 95\}$, and d_b from the set $X_4 = \{75, 80, 85, 90\}$. Additionally, the following constant parameters are assumed:

$$d_{om}=25.00 \text{ mm} \qquad d_{a1}=80.00 \text{ mm}$$
$$d_{a2}=95.00 \text{ mm} \qquad d_{b1}=75.00 \text{ mm}$$
$$d_{b2}=90.00 \text{ mm} \qquad p_1=1.25$$
$$p_2=1.05 \qquad l_k=150.00 \text{ mm}$$
$$l_g=200.00 \text{ mm} \qquad a=80.00 \text{ mm}$$
$$E = 210,000.0 \text{ N/mm}^2 \qquad F = 10,000 \text{ N}$$
$$\Delta_a = 0.00540000 \text{ mm} \qquad \Delta_b = -0.00540000 \text{ mm}$$
$$\Delta = 0.01000000 \text{ mm} \qquad \delta_{ra} = -0.00100000 \text{ mm}$$
$$\delta_{rb} = -0.00100000 \text{ mm}$$

11   Comparison of Results

The ideal vector that each method generates will be compared with the best results reported in the literature [3]. The two Monte Carlo methods included in MOSES were used, together with Osyczka's multiobjective optimization system [12] to obtain the ideal vector. Also, several GA-based approaches will be tested using the same parameters (same population size and same crossover and mutation rates). If niching is required, then the niche size will be computed according to the methodology suggested by the developers of the method.

Method	x_1	x_2	x_3	x_4	f_1	f_2
Monte Carlo 1	59.08	189.17	90	75	**606667.43**	0.032467
Monte Carlo 1	26.26	193.29	90	85	1457744.67	**0.019242**
GA (Binary)	60.00	200.00	80	75	**466532.80**	0.038087
GA (Binary)	25.00	190.09	95	90	1640191.80	**0.016613**
GA (FP)	56.16	194.49	95	90	**312430.43**	0.017951
GA (FP)	25.35	189.58	95	90	1641135.80	**0.016615**
Literature	63.89	183.29	85	80	**531059.80**	0.030182
Literature	66.45	183.36	95	85	694101.00	**0.023078**

Table 1. Comparison of results computing the ideal vector of the example (design of a machine tool spindle). For each method the best results for optimum f_1 and f_2 are shown in **boldface**.

The ideal vector of this problem was computed using the two Monte Carlo Methods included in MOSES (generating 100 points), and a GA (with a population of 100 chromosomes running during 50 generations) using binary and floating point representation. The corresponding results are shown in Table 1, including the best results reported in the literature [3]. The results for Monte Carlo Method 2 are the same than for Method 1. Notice that since Osyczka's multiobjective optimization system is not able to handle discrete variables, no

results are available for the min-max method using Osyzcka's system. The GA
using both binary and floating point representation found the ideal vector with
a procedure to adjust its parameters that has been described somewhere else [1]
(the results shown are the best after 81 runs). As can be seen in the results, the
best result for the first objective was found using floating point representation,
and the best result for the second objective was found using binary representation, although the difference for this second objective is not really significant
with respect to the difference for the first objective. The use of this floating
point representation in various single and multiobjective optimization problems
has been found to be superior (in general) to the binary representation, mainly
as we increase the number of variables or their respective allowable ranges [1]. In
terms of the multiobjective optimization problem, the new technique introduced
in this paper produces a better overall result than any of the other existing approaches, including the mathematical programming techniques. As it turns out,
this technique also produces the best sketch of the Pareto front and is able to
keep it for as many generations as necessary, contrasting with the other GA-
based techniques that either lose the front very quickly (e.g., VEGA, NSGA,
and Hajela's method) or aren't able to find it at all (e.g., GALC and the Lexicographic method). The only two approaches with which the new technique can
really compete in terms of finding the Pareto front are NPGA y MOGA, not
only in this but in most of the other problems analyzed by the author [2].

12   Conclusions

A new multiobjective optimization method based on the min-max optimization
approach has been proposed. This approach is very robust because it transforms
the multiobjective optimization problem into several single objective optimization problems, and it works very well independently of the representation scheme
used. However, a floating point representation seems to work better for numerical optimization applications. The main drawback of the new approach is that it
requires the ideal vector and a set of weights to delineate the Pareto set. Nevertheless, when the ideal vector is not known, a set of target (desirable) values for
each objective can be provided instead. Also, finding proper weights is normally
an easy task, since not many of them are required to get reasonably good results.

13   Future Work

Much additional work remains to be done, since this is a very broad area of
research. For example, it is desirable to do more theoretical work on niches
and population sizes for multiobjective optimization problems to verify some of
the empirical results obtained by the author. In that sense, it is expected that
MOSES may be useful as an experimentation tool for those interested in this
area. To talk about convergence in this context seems a rather difficult task, since
there is no common agreement on what optimum really means. However, if we use
concepts from Operations Research such as the min-max optimum, it should be

Method	x_1	x_2	x_3	x_4	f_1	f_2	$L_p(f)$
Ideal Vector					312430.43	0.01662	0.00000
Monte Carlo 1	56.67	190.22	85	80	728581.78	0.02647	1.92555
Monte Carlo 2	26.26	193.29	90	85	1457744.67	0.01924	3.82407
GALC (B)	42.27	187.83	95	90	1386131.13	0.01696	3.45719
GALC (FP)	42.78	188.01	95	90	1377893.38	0.01697	3.43203
Lexicographic (B)	62.02	200.00	95	85	856072.60	0.02184	2.05486
Lexicographic (FP)	61.98	190.91	95	80	709307.00	0.02619	1.84682
VEGA (B)	54.63	200.00	90	85	987526.38	0.02124	2.43936
VEGA (FP)	54.45	191.11	95	90	1151553.50	0.01775	2.75405
NSGA (B)	65.22	200.00	90	85	708412.19	0.02439	1.73510
NSGA (FP)	62.00	197.36	95	90	985238.13	0.01884	2.28746
MOGA (B)	65.52	200.00	90	85	699786.88	0.02453	1.71643
MOGA (FP)	67.75	189.34	95	90	800608.63	0.02011	1.77289
NPGA (B)	57.92	200.00	90	75	654768.06	0.03223	2.03595
NPGA (FP)	43.53	187.86	95	90	1363536.50	0.01701	3.38794
Hajela (B)	59.87	188.12	95	80	757841.81	0.02498	1.92946
Hajela (FP)	61.19	188.10	95	90	975296.19	0.01861	2.24167
GAminmax (B)	66.99	200.00	90	85	656950.38	0.02532	1.62676
GAminmax (FP)	71.98	188.17	95	90	672894.56	0.02169	1.45917

Table 2. Comparison of the best overall solution found by each one of the methods included in MOSES for the example given. GA-based methods were tried with binary (B) and floating point (FP) representations. The following abbreviations were used: GALC = Genetic Algorithm with a linear combination of objectives using scaling. In all cases, weights were assumed equal to 0.5 (equal weight for every objective).

possible to develop such a theory of convergence for these kinds of problems. Also, it is highly desirable to be able to find more ways of incorporating knowledge about the domain into the GA, as long as it can be automatically assimilated by the algorithm during its execution and does not have to be provided by the user (to preserve its generality).

References

1. Carlos A. Coello Coello, Filiberto Santos Hernández, and Francisco Alonso Farrera. Optimal design of reinforced concrete beams using genetic algorithms. *Expert Systems with Applications : An International Journal,* 12(1), January 1997. 311
2. Carlos Artemio Coello Coello. *An Empirical Study of Evolutionary Techniques for Multiobjective Optimization in Engineering Design,* PhD thesis, Department of Computer Science, Tulane University, New Orleans, LA, apr 1996. 311
3. Hans Eschenauer, Juhani Koski, and Andrzej Osyczka, editors. *Multicrite-ria Design Optimization.* Springer-Verlag, Berlin, Germany, 1990. 308, 309, 310

4. Carlos M. Fonseca and Peter J. Fleming. Genetic Algorithms for Multi-objective Optimization: Formulation, Discussion and Generalization. In Stephanie Forrest, editor, *Proceedings of the Fifth International Conference on Genetic Algorithms*, pages 416-423, San Mateo, California, 1993. University of Illinois at Urbana-Champaign, Morgan Kauffman Publishers. 307

5. Carlos M. Fonseca and Peter J. Fleming. An overview of evolutionary algorithms in multiobjective optimization. Technical report, Department of Automatic Control and Systems Engineering, University of Sheffield, Sheffield, U. K.. 1994. 306

6. M. P. Fourman. Compaction of symbolic layout using genetic algorithms. In *Genetic Algorithms and their Applications: Proceedings of the First International Conference on Genetic Algorithms*, pages 141-153. Lawrence Eribaum, 1985. 306

7. David E. Goldberg and J. Richardson. Genetic algorithm with sharing for multimodal function optimization. In J. J. Grefenstette, editor, *Genetic Algorithms and Their Applications: Proceedings of the Second International Conference on Genetic Algorithms*, pages 41-49. Lawrence Eribaum, 1987. 308

8. J. J. Grefenstette. GENESIS: A system for using genetic search procedures. In *Proceedings of the 1984 Conference on Intelligent Systems and Machines*, pages 161-165. 1984. 305

9. P. Hajela and C. Y. Lin. Genetic search strategies in multicriterion optimal design. *Structural Optimization*, 4:99-107, 1992. 306

10. J. Horn and N. Nafpliotis. Multiobjective Optimization using the Niched Pareto Genetic Algorithm. Technical Report IlliGAl Report 93005, University of Illinois at Urbana-Champaign, Urbana, Illinois, USA, 1993. 308

11. A. Osyczka. An approach to multicriterion optimization for structural design. In Proceedings of International Symposium on Optimal Structural Design. University of Arizona, 1981. 305

12. Andrzej Osyczka. *Multicriterion Optimization in Engineering with FORTRAN programs*. Ellis Horwood Limited, 1984. 310

13. Andrzej Osyczka. Multicriteria optimization for engineering design. In John S. Gero, editor, *Design Optimization*, pages 193-227. Academic Press, 1985. 304

14. S. Rao. Game theory approach for multiobjective structural optimization. *Computers and Structures*, 25(1):119-127. 1986. 305

15. S. S. Rao. Multiobjective optimization in structural design with uncertain parameters and stochastic processes. *AIAA Journal*, 22(ll):1670-1678,nov 1984. 306

16. J. David Schaffer. Multiple objective optimization with vector evaluated genetic algorithms. In *Genetic Algorithms and their Applications: Proceedings of the First International Conference on Genetic Algorithms*, pages 93-100. Lawrence Eribaum. 1985. 305

17. N. Srinivas and K. Deb. Multiobjective optimization using nondominated sorting in genetic algorithms. Technical report, Department of Mechanical Engineering, Indian Institute of Technology, Kanput, India, 1993. 307

18. C. H. Tseng and T. W. Lu. Minimax multiobjective optimization in structural design. *International Journal for Numerica Methods in Engineering*, 30:1213-1228, 1990. 305

A New Genetic Operator for the Traveling Salesman Problem

Néstor Carrasquero[1] and José A. Moreno[2]

[1]Grupo de Optimización Combinatoria Emergente, Facultad de Ingeniería,
Universidad Central de Venezuela
telf: 58-2-6053030 Caracas. Venezuela.
nestor@neurona.ciens.ucv.ve
[2]Laboratorios de Computación Emergente, Facultades de Ciencias e Ingeniería,
Universidad Central de Venezuela
telf:58-2-6053030 Caracas. Venezuela.
jose@neurona.ciens.ucv.ve

Abstract. This paper describes a new approach to the generation of good solutions to the TSP using evolution programs. A novel genetic crossover operator is introduced, which generates a single offspring without explicitly preserving particular characteristics like position, order or adjacency. A geometrical explanation of the heuristic lies on the fact that a good TSP tour does not have crossing edges (or knots). The crossover technique aims to untie the knots and consequently, the evolutionary search is executed over populations of lesser knotted solutions. This operator, that we have called knot-cracker, always produces legal offspring's avoiding repairing techniques. Experiments were performed over the same benchmarks used by the authors of the Enhanced Edge Recombination operator (EER) in their seminal publication. An enhanced version of the knot-cracker is also proposed, which improves previous results, reaches high quality solutions with high consistency and shows a better performance than the EER.

1   Introduction

The TSP is a problem in combinatorial optimization that involves finding the shortest Hamiltonian cycle in a complete graph of n nodes. It can be simple stated as follows; a traveling salesman must plan his itinerary to visit each of n cities exactly once and returning to the starting point, minimizing the total cost of the tour. In its Euclidean version the total cost of a solution is the length of the route measured with the Euclidean distance. The TSP is a classical example of a NP-hard problem. For problems of this class, it is theoretically possible to enumerate all permutations, evaluating each with respect to the stated objective and retaining the optimal. For not small n this exhaustive search procedure will fail because of time requirements: the number of combinations grows exponentially with n. As alternative resolution

Helder Coelho (Ed.): IBERAMIA'98, LNAI 1484, pp. 315-325, 1998.
© Springer-Verlag Berlin Heidelberg 1998

methods many heuristics, inspired in different fields, have been proposed. Some of them rely on analogies to natural processes, such as neural networks, ant colonies, simulated annealing and genetic algorithms. This paper focuses on the genetic algorithm (GA) approach, an application that has been of modest success [5].

The GA community interested in the TSP has emphasized the importance of designing efficient genetic operators, particularly crossover operators, strongly dependent on the genetic representation of the solutions. The canonical binary codification of chromosomes has not been well suited for sequencing problems [3], thus special representations had been proposed. One of the most natural and widely used is the path representation, where an n-tuple of integers represents the visiting sequence of the cities, the cycle is closed by linking the last city visited to the first. For this representation several crossover operators have been developed, they generally emphasize the inheritance of at least one of three typical characteristics in this kind of problems: position, order and adjacency. T. Stackweather et al. [4] made a performance comparison between six genetic sequencing operators to an instance of the TSP and to a scheduling problem. Their results indicate that the effectiveness of different operators is dependent on the problem domain. For the TSP they found that the EER proposed by D. Whitley et al. [5], that explicitly preserves mostly of the adjacency information of one of the parents, had the best performance. They conclude that the key difference between the operators' performance is the kind of information that each attempts to preserve during recombination and, for the TSP, the important information would seem to be the adjacency information [5]. In this paper we introduce a new crossover operator for the TSP that was designed with no preserving idea in mind.

The organization of this paper is as follows. In section 2 we explain the basics behind the proposed operator. In section 3 the workings of the operator is described. Section 4 explains the implementation and experimentation process and shows the results obtained with a first version of the knot-cracker over the 30 cities Oliver's problem [5]. Section 5 describes an enhancement of the operator and the results obtained over the complete benchmark [5]. Finally, there is a concluding section.

2   The Basic Ideas Behind the Operator

There are two basic ideas behind the proposed operator, one of them can be geometrically explained and the other is based on a physical similarity established by F. Marín [4]. Figure 1 illustrates the former; a global improvement in the cost of a TSP tour can be attained by undoing the crossing of two edges. The result is shown in the figure with dashed lines.

The cross-product of the position vector of two consecutive cities can be used in an indirect way, to establish the existence of crossing edges (or knots for simple) in a two-dimensional TSP. As shown in figure 2, the transition from one city a to another city b, can be seen as a rotation of the position vectors of the corresponding cities around the reference point k. The sense of this rotation is indicated by the sign of the cross-product of the position vectors. Thus, a sign change of this cross-product when considering successive transitions can be a hint of knot existence. The cross-product of the position vectors in the transition from a to b (see figure 2) has a positive sign, indicating a counterclockwise rotation around the reference point k. Whereas the cross-product of the position vectors in the transition from b to c has a negative sign indicating now a clockwise rotation. This successive change of sign of the cross-product is indicative of the presence of knots. It is important to note that not every change of sign of the cross-product necessarily means that there is a knot present. This can be seen in figure 3.

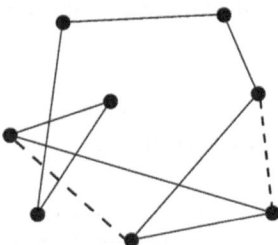

Fig. 1. The dashed lines show the effect of undoing the crossing of two edges on the total length of a TSP tour.

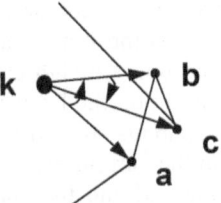

Fig. 2. A successive change of sign of the cross-product can be indicative of the presence of knots.

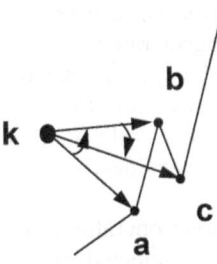

Fig. 3. Not every change of sign of successive cross-product means there is a knot present.

On the other hand, there is a physical motivation for the proposed operator. In 1996 F. Marín [2] introduced an order parameter for the TSP by making an analogy with a classical particle traveling around a closed trajectory. The order parameter proposed by Marín is proportional to the sum of the cross-products of the position vectors of the cities and is not dependent on the origin of coordinates. He solved, applying the simulated annealing technique, several instances of the TSP in special configuration (cities equally spaced in a circumference). It was observed that the values of this parameter fluctuate around zero at high temperatures when the system is highly disordered (large number of knots). On the other hand, at low temperatures, when the system is less disordered, the sign of the parameter remains unchanged and its value saturates in a manner which is instance dependent. The author established a transition temperature where the order parameter drastically changes its behavior suggesting that the starting point for the annealing schedule should be just above that transition temperature.

3   How the Knot-Cracker Works?

The knot-cracker, as we named the proposed operator, is essentially of crossover type. It produces an offspring by selecting subtours from one parent providing it preserves the current turning sense (i.e. the sign of the cross-product). We call the parent from which the last city has been taken the current parent and the other parent is the alternate one. The length of the subtour to be inherited from any parent depends on its capacity for retaining the turning sense. At the moment that the former subtour changes its turning sense, the following subtour can be inherited from the alternate parent. The shift from one parent to the other can be stated as follows. If the city proposed by the current parent produces a sign change in the cross-product and the next city in the alternate parent does not, the latter is included in the offspring. In that case the alternate and the current parents shift. If none of the parents offers a solution to a suspicious link, the city from the current parent is include in the offspring. Then a possible knotted sequence is inherited and the current and alternate parents remain unshifted. As usual, every city included in the offspring must be deleted from both parents.

In the experiments two opposed effects are observed, allowing in the first case just one parent shift in a recombination (like in the one-point crossover) or in the second case, all the possible parent shifts that can be made (a multiple-point crossover). In the latter case we observed an accelerated convergence at the early stages of the run and a premature diversity lost. The opposite behavior is observed in the former case, a slower initial convergence rate and more diversity and better values at the end. As a compromise solution we adopted, as rule of thumb, to randomly allow all possible parents shifts with a probability that linearly decreases along the run. Otherwise just one shift is allowed.

At the beginning of the crossover operation, the current parent, the starting city and the turning sense of the tour are selected at random. The reference point for the position vectors of the cities with which the cross-product is to be evaluated is also randomly selected. This point is chosen in the plane containing all the cities defined by the extremal ones, and is changed for each application of the operator. The first edge to be placed in the offspring is defined by the starting city and its successive neighbor in the selected turning sense. In the following example the way the operator works is illustrated. Let's take two parents:

P1: a b c d e f g h
P2: a b c g h e f d

and let's suppose the initial current parent to be P1, the starting city is b and the cross-product is negative. The offspring begins with:

O: b c

To point out where each city comes from and deletion, we shall underline the cities in the parent from which it is inherited and we shall strike through it in the alternate parent, as follows:

P1: a b̲c̲ d e f g h
P2: a b̶c̶ g h e f d

The next city suggested by P1 is d and the following in P2 is g. Suppose that the cross-product involving c (the last city placed in the offspring) and d keeps the turning sense, the offspring grows as follows:

O1: b c d

and

P1: a b̲c̲d̲ e f g h
P2: a b̶c̶ g h e f d̶

Accordingly to P1 the next city is e and to P2 is a. Suppose that the cross-product involving d and e is positive and the one involving d and a is negative, then P2 becomes the current parent and P1 the alternate one. The individuals are:

O1: b c d a
P1: a̶ b̲c̲d̲ e f g h
P2: a̲ b̶c̶ g h e f d̶

The next city in P2 is g and e is the next from P1. If the turning sense is kept up when selecting g, the three individuals are now

O1: b c d a g
P1: a̶ b̲c̲d̲ e f g̶ h
P2: a̲ b̶c̶ g̲ h e f d̶

From the current parent P2 the next city is h, the same from P1. If the turning sense when going from g to h is not kept up, P2 remains the current parent and the offspring is possible knotted:

O1: b c d a g h
P1: a̶ b̲c̲d̲ e f g̶h̶
P2: a̲ b̶c̶ g̲h̲ e f d̶

Finally, let's suppose that the original sense of turning remains unchanged by including the last two cities from P2, the three individuals are then:

O1: b c d a g h e f
P1: a̶ b̲c̲d̲ e̶f̶g̶h̶
P2: a̲ b̶c̶ g̲h̲ e f d̶

It can be observed that the subtour bcd is inherited from P1 and the subtour ghef comes from P2. The knot-cracker induces, as most sequencing crossover operators, an intrinsic mutation from the point of view of the adjacency. In this example the new links ag and fb, that were not present in any parent, have been introduced in the offspring.

Last but not least, from the previous explanation of the offspring building process follows that the knot-cracker always produces legal offspring's, and does not requires time consuming repairing techniques.

4   First Version: Implementation and Results

All results reported in this paper were obtained with a steady-state-without-duplicates GA, which replaces the lowest ranked individual in the current population with the newest offspring. The initial population is randomly generated, the parents selection is roulette-wheel-based and the fitness is linear normalized. The first experiment to compare the performances of the EER and the knot-cracker was performed over the Oliver's 30 cities problem, the same used by the authors of the EER in their seminal publication [5].

In order to make a fair comparison with our GA, we attempted to optimize the operators performance by tuning the population size. This parameter seems to be of paramount importance for both operators, in view of the fact that the two other parameters like the selective pressure is fixed for the fitness technique and the number of trials is large enough. To evaluate the Euclidean distance between two cities we follow the function proposed in [5]. The best known solution for this problem is 420 units long.

Results of 20 runs of 50000 trials appear in table 1. There we compare the population size required, the mean of trials to reach the best solution, the average of the length of the best tour and the worst solution found. In this problem the EER and the knot-cracker found the best known solution 20 out of 20 times, but the latter does it with 43% less iterations and a population 10 times smaller. In the figure 4 the evolution of the mean of the best values obtained over 20 runs can be observed. Note the difference of the slopes of both operators at the early stages of the run, which shows the ability of the knot-cracker to quickly make arise good solutions.

	EER	Knot-cracker
Population size	1000	100
Trials allowed	50000	50000
Mean of trials to best found	17744	12154
Average	420	420
Worst solution	420	420

Table 1. Results on the Oliver's 30 cities problem over 20 runs.

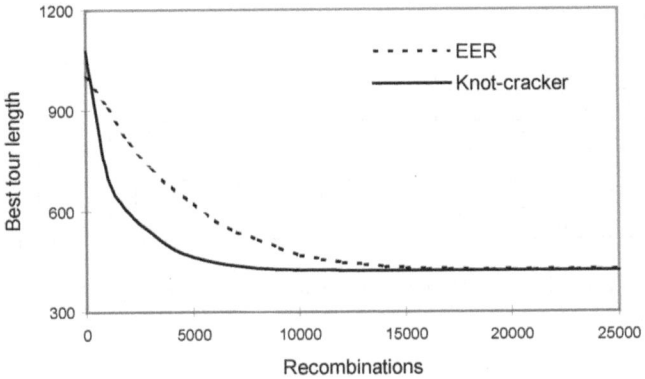

Fig. 4. Best results average over 20 runs of the Oliver's 30 cities problem.

5   Enhancing the Operator: Results

A modification that enhances the knot-cracker performance can be easily included. To determine the turning sense we calculate the sign of the cross-product and, of course, its magnitude. This magnitude represents the area of the parallelogram whose sides are the position vectors from the reference point as shown in figure 5. In most cases the smaller this area is the closer the cities are. This idea was used in the knot-cracker enhanced version to select the city to be included in the offspring when no parent solves the change of turning sense. This modification adds a greedy touch to the operator with no additional effort.

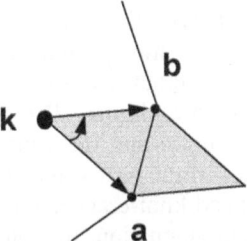

Fig. 5. The magnitude of the cross-product represents the area of the shaded parallelogram.

   Table 2 shows the performance of the enhanced knot-cracker over the same 30 cities problem. The average of recombinations needed to reach the best value is 33% of those required by the EER and only 47% of those of the previous version of the operator. For these results no loss of consistency nor population size increment was necessary. Figure 6 illustrates the mean of the best values over 20 runs for the three operators. Here again the slopes shows that the heuristic behind the knot-cracker increases the convergence rate without stagnation in spite of the smaller population size it requires.

	EER	Knot-cracker	E. knot-cracker
Population size	1000	100	100
Trials allowed	50000	50000	50000
Mean of trials to best found	17744	12154	5707
Average	420	420	420
Worst solution	420	420	420

Table 2. Results on the Oliver's 30 cities problem over 20 runs.

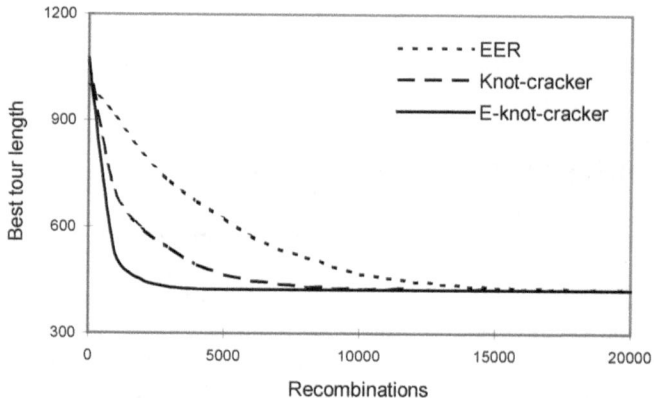

Fig. 6. Best results average over 20 runs of the Oliver's 30 cities problem.

Other experiments were made with the enhanced knot-cracker and the EER. Table 3 shows the results for Eilon's 50 cities problem [5]. The mean of trials to find the best solution of the enhanced knot-cracker is 17% bigger than the one of the EER and the averages of those solutions are similar. The worst value found by the EER is 2.58% over the best known solution and the enhanced knot-cracker is only 1.41%. Figure 7 illustrates the behavior of the best values over 20 runs. The slopes show that the heuristic behind the enhanced knot-cracker increases the convergence rate at the early stages of the runs without stagnation, in spite of the smaller population size it requires. The best known solution for this problem is 426 units long.

The results for Eilon's 75 cities problem [5] are shown in tables 4. In this problem the mean of trials to find the best solution of the enhanced knot-cracker is 11% smaller than the one of the EER and the averages are similar. The worst value found by the EER is 3.17% over the best known solution and the enhanced knot-cracker is 2.80% above. The evolution of the best values over 20 runs is shown in figure 8. Here again the slopes show the higher convergence rate of the enhanced knot-cracker. The best known solution for this problem is 535 units long.

	EER	E. knot-cracker
Population size	1000	300
Trials allowed	100000	100000
Mean of trials to best found	49146	57579
Average	427.75	427.45
Worst solution	437	432

Table 3. Results on Eilon's 50 cities problem over 20 runs.

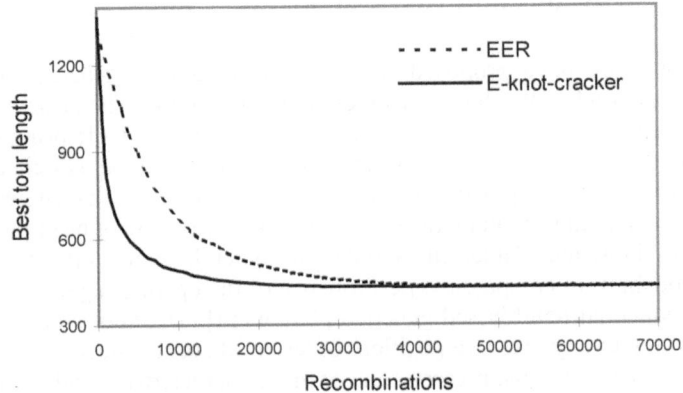

Fig. 7. Best results average over 20 runs of the Eilon's 50 cities problem

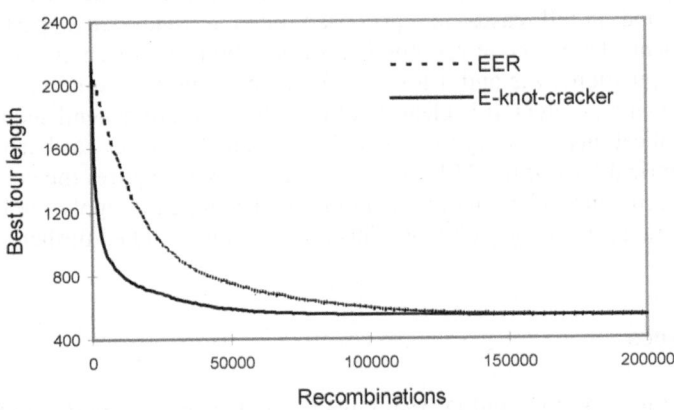

Fig. 8. Best results average over 20 runs of the Eilon's 75 cities problem.

	EER	E. knot-cracker
Population size	2000	500
Trials allowed	200000	200000
Mean of trials to best found	162722	146236
Average	542.05	542.90
Worst solution	552	550

Table 4. Results on Eilon's 75 cities problem over 20 runs.

6   Conclusions and Discussion

In this paper we have proposed two versions of a new genetic operator for the generation of good TSP solutions with evolution programs. The basic heuristic behind the proposed operators is to try to produce lesser knotted offspring's by mean of preserving a given turning sense. Since a turning sense can be associated to a sign of the cross-product of the position vectors of consecutive cities, a change of sign of this product can be a hint of knot existence. These operators do not need the evaluation of the cost of individual "inter-cities links" as other heuristic operators do [1]. This reason brought us to compare the performance of the operator against the EER, one of the best sequential non-biassed genetic operators [4]. The knot-cracker was designed without trying to any preserve position, order or adjacency, nevertheless the obtained results suggest that it must preserve one of those characteristics (adjacency at least). If this assumption is true it is just a consequence of the way the operator was built.

Experiments were performed over the same benchmarks used by the authors of the EER in [5]. In the Oliver's 30 cities problem, both versions of the knot-cracker have shown better performance than the EER and the enhanced knot-cracker did best. In the Eilon's 50 and 75 cities problems the enhanced knot-cracker was compared with the EER and in all cases the proposed operator had better performance. This improvement stands on fewer number of iterations to reach good solutions with smaller population sizes and a lower dispersion of the best solutions found (i.e. our operator stagnates later). It is clear that the EER is a more general sequential operator whose applicability goes beyond the TSP. The knock-cracker has been designed with the geometrical idea of the TSP in mind; that is why it requires the coordinates of the cities. It seems that other analogies should be developed to apply the knot-cracker to more general sequencing problems. This point is being studied further.

References

1.   P. Jog, J. Y. Suh and D. Van Gucht, The Effects of Population Size, Heuristic Crossover and Local Improvement on a Genetic Algorithm for the Traveling Salesman Problem. In Proc. of the Third International Conference on Genetic Algorithms. J. D. Schaffer editor. Morgan Kauffmann Publishers. Los Altos. CA, 1989.

2.   F. P. Marín, A new monitoring parameter for the traveling salesman problem. Phys. Rev. Lett. 77, 5149, 1996.

3.   Z. Michalewicz, Genetic Algorithms + Data Structures = Evolution Programs. Second edition. Springer-Verlag, Berlin, 1994.

4.   T. Starkweather, S. McDaniel, K. Mathias, D. Whitley and C. Whitley, A Comparison of Genetic Sequencing Operators. In Proc. of the Fourth International Conference on Genetic Algorithms. R. K. Belew and L. B. Booker editors. Morgan Kauffmann Publishers. Los Altos. CA, 1991.

5.   D. Whitley, T. Starkweather and D'A. Fuquay, Scheduling Problems and Traveling Salesman: The Genetic Edge Recombination Operator. In Proc. of the Third International Conference on Genetic Algorithms. J. D. Schaffer editor. Morgan Kauffmann Publishers. Los Altos. CA, 1989.

Decision Queue Classifier for Supervised Learning Using Rotated Hyperboxes

Jesús Aguilar, José Riquelme and Miguel Toro

Departamento de Lenguajes y Sistemas Informáticos.
Facultad de Informática y Estadística. Universidad de Sevilla.
E-mail: {aguilar, riquelme, mtoro}@lsi.us.es

Keywords: data mining, supervised learning, genetic algorithms.

Abstract. This article describes a new system for learning rules using rotated hyperboxes as individuals of a genetic algorithm (GA). Our method attempts to find out hyperboxes at any orientation by combining deterministic hill-climbing with GA. Standard techniques, such as C4.5, use hyperboxes that are aligned with the coordinate axes. The system uses the decision queue (DQ) as method of representing the rule set. It means that the obtained rules must be applied in specific order, that is, an example will be classify by the i-rule only if it doesn't satisfy the condition part of the i-1 previous rules. With this policy, the number of rules is less because the rules could be one inside of another one. We have tested our system on real data from UCI repository. Moreover, we have designed some two-dimensional artificial databases to show graphically the experiments. The results are summarized in the last section.

1 Introduction

Supervised learning (SL) is used when the data samples have known outcomes that the user wants to predict. This type of learning is the more common form because data are usually collected with some outcome in mind. Human problem solving is normally an exercise in studying input conditions to predict a result based upon previous experience with similar situations. SL algorithms tend to emulate that sort of human behavior.

Decision trees (DT) are a particularly useful tool in the context of machine learning

Helder Coelho (Ed.): IBERAMIA'98, LNAI 1484, pp. 326-336, 1998.
© Springer-Verlag Berlin Heidelberg 1998

techniques because they perform classification by a sequence of simple, easy-to-understand tests whose semantics is intuitively clear to domain experts. Some techniques, like C4.5, construct decision trees selecting the best attribute by using a statistical test to determine how well it alone classifies the training examples [9]. This class of DTs may be called axis-parallel, because the tests at each node are equivalent to axis-parallel hyperplanes in the space. Others techniques build oblique decision trees (ODT), as OC1[7], that tests a linear combination of the internal attributes at each node, for that, these tests are equivalent to hyperplanes at an oblique orientation to the axes.

At this point, we must remember that, in a domain with N training examples, each described using a k real-valued attributes, there are at most $2^k \binom{N}{k}$ distinct k-dimensional oblique splits; however, for axis-parallel splits, there are only $N \times k$ distinct possibilities, for that reason, it could exhaustively search the best split at each node.

Anyway, to find out the smallest DT (axis-parallel or oblique) is a NP-hard problem [2]. Both methods use hill-climbing, that is, the algorithm never backtracks; therefore, it could be converging to locally optimal solutions that are not globally optimal.

Simpson [12] introduced the idea of using hyperboxes to cluster or classify spatial data. Each hyperbox is viewed as a fuzzy cluster, a fuzzy set in which all of the elements within the hyperbox have membership 1.0 for being in that set, and elements outside the hyperbox can have a positive membership in the set depending on a fuzzy membership rule for that set. Simpson used a deterministic procedure to place and appropriately size hyperboxes to describe data. Hyperboxes were created and sized by considering the data in an ordered sequence. A hyperbox was placed around preliminary data. As subsequent data was added, either the present hyperbox was grown to include the new data, or a new hyperbox was added and the process continued. This procedure was of limited efficacy because it required trial-and-error setting of operator parameters and the final solution depended on the order of presentation of the data, even when the data possessed only spatial an not sequential characteristics. Fogel and Simpson used evolutionary programming to optimize the position of hyperboxes to cluster data in light of a minimum description length criterion (MDL). First, the experiments were restricted to evolving hyperboxes that were aligned with coordinate axes; and afterwards, they included the capability to rotate the hyperboxes. At this point, it is important to note that Fogel's method try to solve the clustering problem, that is, unsupervised learning.

Genetic algorithms (GA) employ a randomized search method to seed a maximally fit hypothesis [3, 4]. This search is quite different from other learning methods, like mentioned above. The GA search can move much more abruptly, replacing a parent hypothesis by an offspring less likely to fall into the same kind of local minima that can happen with the other methods.

In previous works, we presented a system to classify databases by using hyperboxes (axis-parallel). This system used a GA to search the best solutions and produced a hierarchical set of rules. The hierarchy means that an example will be classify by the i-rule if it does not satisfy the conditions of the i-1 precedent rules. The rules are sequentially obtained until the space is totally covered. The behavior is similar to a queue, for that reason we have called decision queue (DQ) to the produced rule set. This concept is based on the k-DL, the set of decision lists with conjuntive clauses of size at most k at each decision [11]. A decision list is a list L of pairs where each f_j is a term in C_k^n, each v_i is a value in $\{0,1\}$, and the last function f_r is the constant function true.

$$(f_1, v_1),...,(f_r, v_r) \tag{1}$$

A decision list L defines a boolean function as follows: for any assignment $x \in X_n$, L(x) is defined to be equal to v_j where j is the least index such that $f_j(x)=1$ (such an item always exists, since the last function is always true).

DQ is based on DL. Really, DQ is a DL-generalization because it permits codifying functions f_i of continuous attributes and the values v_i can belong to any set.

Futhermore, DQ does not have the last constant function true. However, we could interpret that last function as unknown function, that is, we do not know to which class the example belongs to. Therefore, it may be advisable to say "unknown class" instead of taking an erroneous decision.

In the sense mentioned above, our system has a measure, called unknowledge, to indicate how many test examples have not an associated class. As the number of rules or the allowed error rate (relaxing coefficient) can be given by the domain expert, some unnecessary mistakes could be avoided if the rule set does not assign to the test example a class. Incrementing the relaxing coefficient the unknowledge will be less, but the number of misclassified examples will be higher. The expert, based on experimentation, must determine such parameter.

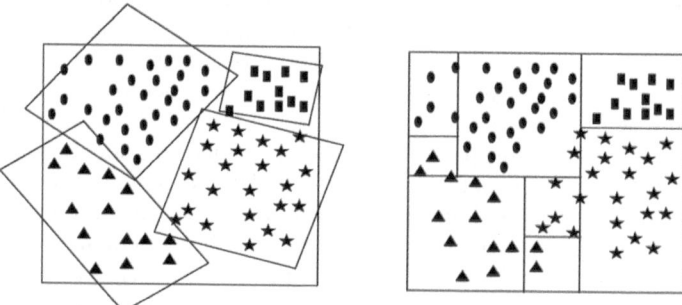

Fig. 1. Rotated versus axis-parallel hyperboxes.

In this paper, we propose to hold the primitive structure of our early works [1,10], but changing the shapes that models the search space. That is to say, current work extends these previous efforts by including the capability to rotate the hyperboxes.

We show in figure 1 an example, in which rotated hyperboxes can find out better solutions than axis-parallel hyperboxes they do. Decision queue policy is applied in order to reduce the number of rules.

With this DQ-method, there is no problem if the regions are overlapped. An extreme case is presented in the next figure.

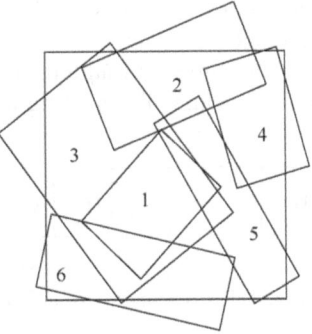

Fig. 2. Decision queues for overlapped regions.

In the other hand, if we use axis-parallel techniques, the number of rules is very high. When does it apply one technique or the other one? In principle, it is not possible to know it, but it could be a good solution to explore the search space with axis-parallel and, increasingly, to try to rotate the best solutions.

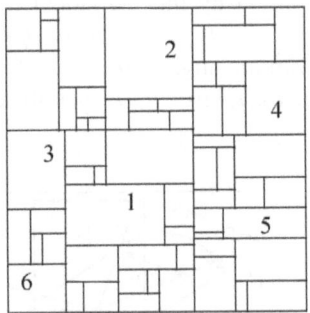

Fig. 3. Axis-parallel solution to the figure 2.

The number of rules, in figure 3, is very high. The numbers represents parts of the regions found out by using rotated hyperboxes, as shows figure 2.

2 Description

2.1 Environment

In order to apply GAs to a learning problem, we need to select an internal representation of the space to be searched and define an external function that assigns fitness to candidate solutions. Both components are critical to the successful application of the GAs to the problem of interest. Information of the environment comes from a data file, where each example has a class and a number of attributes. The GA uses real codification; that is, an individual is formed by an n-tuple of real. If k is the dimension, an individual has exactly $3 \times k$ values: $2 \times k$ for the boundaries of each dimension; $k - 1$ for the angles of rotations, in radians, anti-clockwise around the hyperbox centre; and 1 for the class. The next figure shows a n-tuple:

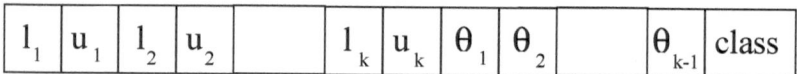

Fig. 4. Representation of an individual.

where l_i and u_i represent the lower and upper bounds of the individual, respectively, for every dimension; θ_i is the rotation angle; and class. In 2-dimension is possible to put an hyperbox at any orientation by using only one rotation; in k-dimension it is necessary k-1 rotations.

We consider that an example belongs to the area determined for an individual if it satisfies its condition part. Thus, let an example be given by $P_j=(p_1, p_2, ..., p_k, c)$ then it will be into the defined region by the individual (or equivalently, a rule will be covered by the rule) $ind_h = (l_1, u_1, l_2, u_2, ..., l_k, u_k, \theta_1, \theta_2,..., \theta_{k-1}, class)$ if rotating the example $P=(p_1, p_2, ... , p_k)$ with the angles $-\theta_1, -\theta_2,...,-\theta_{k-1}$ with relation to the centre of the hyperbox defined by $(l_1, u_1, l_2, u_2, ... , l_k, u_k)$, then the result P' belongs to this hyperbox.

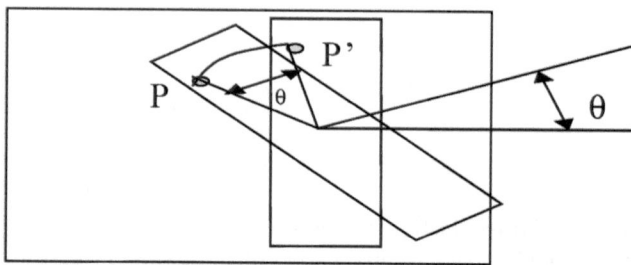

Fig. 5. Rotation of R the angle θ is equivalent to rotate P the angle $-\theta$ around the centre of R.

For example, in three dimensions the example (p_1, p_2, p_3, c) will be covered by the rule $(l_1, u_1, l_2, u_2, l_3, u_3, \theta_1, \theta_2, class)$ if P' satisfies

$$l_1 \le p'_1 \le u_1 \wedge l_2 \le p'_2 \le u_2 \wedge l_3 \le p'_3 \le u_3 \qquad (2)$$

where P' is obtained as follows:

Let $(m_1, m_2, m_3) = ((l_1 + u_1)/2, (l_2 + u_2)/2, (l_3 + u_3)/2)$ be the centre of the hyperbox defined by the rule, then the coordinates of P' are:

$$(p'_1, p'_2, p'_3) = (p_1 - m_1, p_2 - m_2, p_3 - m_3) \begin{pmatrix} 1 & 0 & 0 \\ 0 & \cos\theta_1 & -\text{sen}\theta_1 \\ 0 & \text{sen}\theta_1 & \cos\theta_1 \end{pmatrix} \begin{pmatrix} \cos\theta_2 & -\text{sen}\theta_2 & 0 \\ \text{sen}\theta_2 & \cos\theta_2 & 0 \\ 0 & 0 & 1 \end{pmatrix} + (m_1, m_2, m_3) \tag{3}$$

and it will be correctly classify if its class is equal to c.

2.2 Algorithm

The algorithm is a typical sequential covering GA [6]. It chooses the best individual of the evolutionary process, transforming it into a rule, which is used to eliminate data from the training file [13]. In this way, the training file is reduced for the following iteration. A termination criterion could be reached when more examples to cover do not exist.

The method of generating the initial population consists of randomly selecting for every individual of the population an example from the training file. After, it is obtained an interval to which the example belongs adding and subtracting a random quantity from the values of the example. Moreover, the angles are randomly generated between zero and $\pi/2$. Sometimes, the examples very near to the boundaries are hard to cover during the evolutionary process. For solving it, the search space is increased (actually, lower bound is decreased 5%, and upper bound is increased 5%). For example in 1-dimension, let a and b be the lower and upper bounds of the attribute; then, the range of the attribute is b-a; now, we randomly choose an example $(x_1,$ class) from the training file; last, a possible individual of the population could be:

$$(x_1 - range * k_1, x_1 + range * k_2, class) \tag{4}$$

where k_1 and k_2 are random values belonging to [0,1], and class is the same of that of the example.

The evolution module includes elitism: the best individual of every generation is replicated to the next one. A set of children is obtained from copies of the parents, randomly selecting it, but depending on their fitness values. The remainder is formed through crossovers. Afterwards, mutation is applied depending on a probability. Crossovers are specifically designed, choosing a value among one of the three segments formed inside the interval of the attribute by putting the two values of the individual as cross points. That is, for every attribute, an individual has two values, and then those values are partitioning the interval in three segments. We select randomly a value inside of a segment also randomly chooses. The next figure shows the procedure:

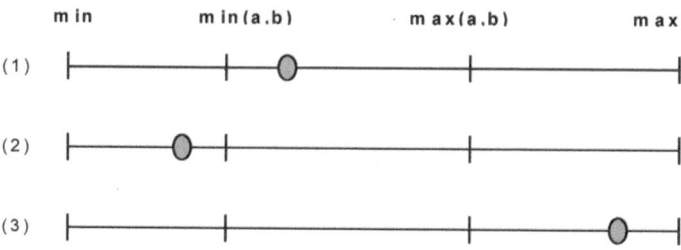

Fig. 6. Crossover operator.

One of the three types of crossover operator could be applied, depending on a probability. The first one is more conservative and second and third ones are more explorative. When the crossover is applied to any angle location, the first one is always used.

Mutation is applied in two different ways: if the location corresponds to a value of the interval, then a quantity is subtracted or added, depending on whether it is the lower or the upper bound, respectively (the distance actually is the lower euclidean distance between any two examples); if the location corresponds to an angle, it is randomly generated another one.

Furthermore, it is advisable to explore the space with the best individual, because we cannot know what angles are the best, and we cannot either know if an angle is going to be better than other is. In this way, we are using hill-climbing technique, what could find out best solutions; despite of inconveniences said in the introduction. The method consists of exploring close rotated regions with the same centre. The angles of the exploration belongs to the interval $[-\pi/6, \pi/6]$, with an increment of $\pi/30$. Then, every best rule explores the search space with other ten regions around the same centre for each attribute. However, in order to reach better fitness value, the interval is also modified the same quantity as mutation used.

To improve the best individual is a difficult task. If the fitness value is better, then the new angle replaces to the old, and one value of one attribute is modified as mentioned above. This method allows rotating an hyperbox using only one dimension. To explore 10 new orientations at the beginning (the first generations) can produce the typical problems of the hill-climbing methods. For that, we recommend to use few explorations at the start and increase it toward the final. Thus, the last generations explore more than the first ones.

We next show an overview of the DQ-Classifier.

```
While exists examples in training file

Step 1. Initialize population

Step 2. Repeat num_generations times
```

```
         Step 2.1. Evaluation

         Step 2.2. Select the best

         Step 2.3. Replication

         Step 2.4. Crossover and Mutation

         Step 2.6. Improve the best

   Step 3. Put the best one in Decision Queue

   Step 4. Eliminate the covered ones by the best one
```

Fig. 7. Overview of DQ-Classifier.

A possible criterion to implement the mutation operator consists of distinguishing between mutation of values and mutation of angles, as two independent operators. Mutation of values could be a higher probability of application than mutation of angles, and also, to incorporate to the evaluation function the distance from the individual (rule) to the closer example of the same class. Thus, we can penalty the rotated rules with wrong angles; that is, the new individual is not going near to the closer example of the same class.

2.3 Fitness Function

The evolutionary algorithm minimizes the fitness function f for each individual. It is given by

$$if\ G(i)*RC<=CE(i)\ then\ CE(i)=0 \tag{5}$$

$$f(i) = \frac{V}{T} + \frac{G(i)}{1 + CE(i)}$$

where T is the cardinality of the training file, V is a new factor called coverage (the rule coverage is the side of a k-dimensional hypercube which volume is equivalent to the volume of the covered k-dimensional region by the rule); $CE(i)$ is the class errors, which are produced when the i example belongs to the region defined by the rule, but it does not the same class; $G(i)$ is the number of goals of the rule; RC is the relaxing coefficient. Every rule can quickly expands for finding more examples due to V in the fitness function.

2.4 Relaxing Coefficient

Databases uses as training files have not areas clearly differentiated, for that, to obtain a rule system totally coherent involves a high number of rules. We show in previous paper [1] a system capable of producing a rule set exempt from error rate; however sometimes, it is interesting to reduce the number of rules for having a rule set which may be used like a comprehensible linguistic model. When databases present a distribution of examples very hard to classify, then it is advisable to use a relaxing coefficient [10]. Many times, we are more interested in understanding the structure of the databases than in the error rate. In this way, it could be better a system with less cardinality (despite some errors) than too many rules (with 0% of error rate). Then, it may be interesting to introduce the *relaxing coefficient* for understanding the behavior of databases by decreasing the number of rules. RC indicates what percentage of examples inside of a rule can have different class to the rule. RC behaves like the upper bound of the error with respect to the training file, that is, as an allowed error rate.

To deal efficiently with noise and find a good value for RC, the expert should have an estimate of the noise percentage in its data.

3   Application

3.1   Ex Profeso Databases

We have designed some databases of varying complexity to show graphically the experiments. These databases are shown in the fig. 8. Results are in table 1.

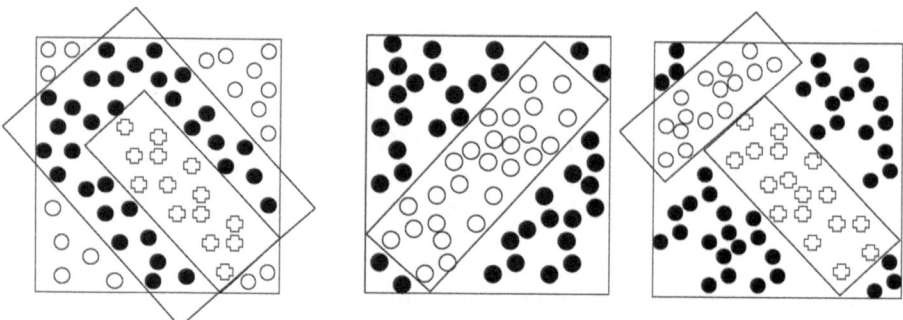

Fig. 8. Ex profeso databases named DB1, DB2 and DB3.

3.2   Databases from UCI Repository

The experiments described in this section are from UCI Repository [7]. We use five cross validation in all our experiments to estimate classification accuracy. This cross validation experiment consists of the following steps: randomly divide the data into two disjoint partitions (70% an 30%); build a rule set using 70% of data and test the rule set with 30% of data; for each partitions the number of correct classification of the rule set are all counted and divided it by the number of instances of the test file to compute the classification accuracy; the five values are summed and divided by five; report one hundred minus this accuracy multiplies by 100 and the average of the number of rules. We have chosen C4.5 to compare the results, also with five experiments and cross validation which are shown in Table 2.

DATABASE	C4.5		DQ-CLASSIFIER-RH	
	ERRO R RATE	NUMBER OF RULES	ERROR RATE	NUMBER OF RULES
DB1(200,2,2)	12.9	17	3.3	3
DB2(200,2,2)	16.25	12.5	2.7	2
DB3(200,2,2)	12.13	11	6.6	3

Table 1. The results of artificial databases.

DATABASE	C4.5		DQ-CLASSIFIER-RH	
	ERRO R RATE	NUMBER OF RULES	ERROR RATE	NUMBER OF RULES
IRIS (150, 4, 3)	6.3	4.4	4.83	3.6
BREAST CANCER (683, 9,	13.8	5.2	5.38	2.2
PIMA (768, 8, 2)	28.4	77.6	26.35	17.4
WINE (178, 13, 3)	7.2	5.0	10.1	6.4

Table 2. Databases (number of examples, dimension, number of classes).

It is very important to note that every execution has been realized with a population of 50 individuals and 50 generations. Very low numbers considering the number of examples and number of dimensions of the databases.

Decision queue is very relevant in relation to the number of rules.

4 Conclusions

A supervised learning tool to classify databases with rotated hyperboxes is presented in this paper. It produces a decision queue where conditions of each rule indicate if an example belongs to a rotated hyperbox. The number of rules is reduced with regard to other systems, like C4.5; and improves the flexibility to construct a classifier varying the relaxing coefficient.

References

[1] Aguilar, J. and Riquelme, J. COGITO: Un sistema de Autoaprendizaje basado en Algoritmos Genéticos. III Jornadas de Informática, pp. 79-88, Cádiz, 1997.
[2] Blum, A. and Rivest, R. L. Training a 3-node neural network is np-complete. In Proceedengs of the First ADM Workshop on the Computational Learning Theory, pp. 9-18, Cambrige, MA, 1988.
[3] Ghozeil, A. and Fogel, D.B. Discovering Patterns in Spatial Data Using Evolutionary Programming. Genetic Program Conference 96.
[4] Goldberg, D. Genetic Algorithms in search, optimization and machine learning. Addison-Wesley Publishing Company, Inc. 1989.
[5] Michalewicz, Z. Genetic Algorithms + Data Structures = Evolution Programs. Second Edition, Springer-Verlag, 1994.
[6] Mitchell, T. Machine Learning. MacGraw-Hill, 1997.
[7] Murphy, P. and Aha, D.W. UCI Repository of Machine Learning Databases. Dept. of Information and Computer Science. University of California, Irvine, 1994.
[8] Murthy, S. K., Kasif, S. and Salzberg, S. A system for induction of oblique decision trees. Journal of Artificial Intelligence Research, 1994. Morgan Kaufmann Publishers.
[9] Quinlan, J. R. C4.5: programs for Machine Learning. Morgan Kaufmann Pub.,1993.
[10] Riquelme J. and Aguilar, J. COGITO 2.0: Una herramienta para obtener un Clasificador Jerárquico en Apredizaje Supervisado. Conferencia de la Asociación Española para la Inteligencia Artificial. CAEPIA'97. pp. 489-498, Málaga, 1997.
[11] Rivest, R.L. Learning Decision Lists. Machine Learning, 87. pp. 229-246.
[12] Simpson, P.K. Fuzzy Min-Max Neural Networks. II. Clustering. IEEE Trans. Fuzzy Systems, Vol. 1:1,32-45.
[13] Venturini, G. SIA: a Supervised Inductive Algorithm with Genetic Search for Learning Attributes based Concepts.

SpADD: An Active Design Documentation Framework Extension Applied to Spatial Layout Design Problems

Claudio Lourenço da Silva[1] and Ana Cristina Bicharra Garcia[2]

[1] Pontifícia Universidade Católica, Departamento de Informática, Rua Marquês de São Vicente 225, Rio de Janeiro, RJ, Brasil
claudiol@inf.puc-rio.br , claudiol@cfch.ufrj.br
[2] Universidade Federal Fluminense, Departamento de Ciência da Computação, Praça do Valonguinho, s/n, Niterói, RJ, Brasil
bicharra@dcc.uff.br

Abstract. Spatial layout design problems are related to grouping objects with similar properties, assigning objects to pre-defined groups, positioning objects in a constrained space, as well as finding a path connecting certain objects in a tri-dimensional world. Representation, reasoning and documentation for spatial layout design problems are expensive, inconsistent, incomplete and imprecise. This paper proposes a framework called SpADD (Spatial Active Design Documentation) to assist designers in spatial layout design tasks, from a set of objects and a set of spatial constraints relating these objects. SpADD is based on an ADD (Active Design Documentation) approach extension, a canonical parametric network model, an engineering decision-making model and an object oriented class model applied to spatial layout design tasks. Initial results of using an implemented version of SpADD for preliminary design of oil pipeline layout in deep water oil fields are discussed.

1 Introduction

Many problems in engineering design involve grouping objects with similar properties, assigning objects to pre-defined clusters, positioning objects in a constrained space, as well as finding a path connecting certain objects, respecting a set of constrains and following a set of criteria. This tasks are known as SLDP (spatial layout design problems). Generally, the world surrounding the objects involved in SLDP is complex, dynamic and overloaded with information. As the size of the universe grows, the number of relevant parameters to be considered drastically increases, impoverishing the designers' perception of the problem. In addition, thresholds and horizon effects are seldom noticed by designers.

Even for ordinary designs, the complexity of representation, reasoning and documentation for SLDP in a constantly changeable world overloaded with spatial information is large. In addition, treatment of spatial issues as cyclic dependencies and

Helder Coelho (Ed.): IBERAMIA'98, LNAI 1484, pp. 337-348, 1998.

canonical parametric networks is very difficult due to the overwhelming amount of information.

In this work we propose a framework called SpADD (S̲patial A̲ctive D̲esign D̲ocumentation) to enhance GIS (G̲eographic I̲nformation S̲ystems) with intelligent mechanisms to deal with spatial layout design tasks in a domain where the world surrounding the objects is complex, dynamic and overloaded with information.

The main objectives of this research are:

- study the issues related to SLDP;
- create a framework to support spatial layout design reasoning which extends ADD (A̲ctive D̲esign D̲ocumentation) approach [5]; and
- implement a SpADD prototype to show its feasibility to deal with SLDP.

Two main approaches have been used to treat problems involving spatial reasoning: quantitative and qualitative. The quantitative approach [2] emphasizes a precise description of the objects geometry. The qualitative approach [9] [6] describes the relations among objects by a finite set of symbols. For example, the set of symbols {North, South, East, West} denotes a system of qualitative directions. The semantics of these symbols can vary, depending on the context and the scale. The need for precision in layout design calculation led us to follow the quantitative approach in modeling the domain. However, since any active document must generate decision's explanation to users, qualitative relations, such as further, greater, and less expensive, are employed to provide them.

This paper gives an overview of our research starting by presenting in Section 2 the issues related to SLDP and illustrating the problem with an example. Since SpADD is an ADD's extension, Section 3 presents an overview of the main aspects of ADD's approach. Section 4 presents the SpADD framework and Section 5 demonstrates ADDSUB, an SpADD's working prototype for oil pipeline design. The remaining Sections are concerned with related work and conclusions.

2 Spatial Layout Design

Design problems can be described as a complete specification of a set of components and their relations so as to satisfy a set of constraints [3]. In SLDP, the design specification consists of the list of selected objects, their clustering, their specific position and the path connecting them. Consequently, the SLDP design task consist of:

- *object clustering* [8] [7] [1]: the task of grouping similar objects respecting a set of constraints and following a set of criteria;
- *object assigning*: the task of assigning an object to a cluster;
- *object positioning*: the task of locating objects in a constrained space; and
- *route-finding* [10]: the task of finding the shortest path among located objects in a constrained world.

In SLDP, the decision order affects the design context. For example, if object A is positioned before object B, the location of object A is considered obstacle (constraint) to the position of object B. In the other hand. if object B is positioned before object A, the location of object B is considered obstacle (constraint) to the position of object A. This fact is valid to anyone of the type of decisions in SLDP.

The oil pipeline layout in deep water oil fields illustrate spatial layout design. Oil fields in deep water exploration needs a special process. The oil is pumped and drained to offshore platforms where it is treated to be exported to land. Given a set of wells with their target regions (objectives) and a number of oil exploration units (platforms), the oil pipeline layout task consists of:

- Find the best grouping of wells, considering the distance between the objectives' geometric centers (GC);
- Assign each platform to a well suited cluster, considering the maximum platform capacity and the maximum platform number of risers to receive the oil;
- Locate the well heads in each objective, in order to minimize the distance to the platform the well is associated;
- Locate each platform in a free area as close as possible to its cluster's GC;
- Define the pipeline routing that drains the oil from each well to the assigned platform, considering the existing obstacles.

Partial grouping, assigning, wells' and platforms' positions may be an input data too. Consequently, they may impose constraints to the process. The decision ordering also influence the process. Fig. 1 illustrates a submarine arrangement resulting from the process described above for two platforms and six oil wells.

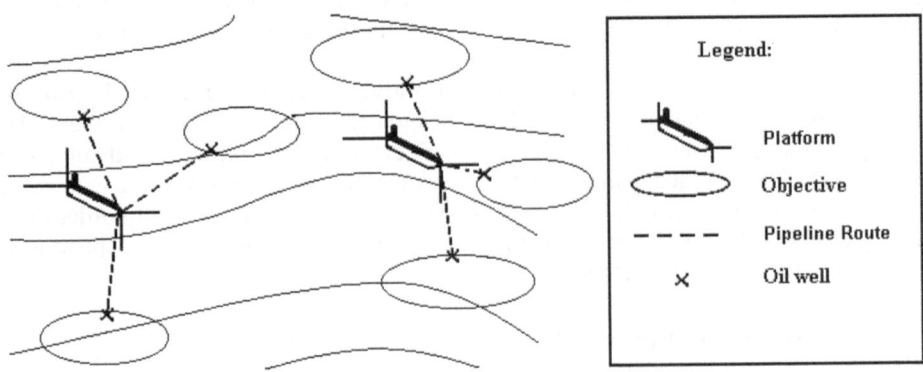

Fig. 1. Representation of a oil pipeline layout design.

The complexity of SLDP in a constantly changeable world overloaded with spatial information motivates our efforts in the creation of a framework (SpADD) to assist designers in such problems. Since SpADD is an ADD's extension, Section 3 presents an overview of the main aspects of ADD's approach.

3   The ADD Approach

The ADD (Active Design Documentation) approach uses the apprentice metaphor. Let's assume that a company hires an apprentice to observe and record a designer developing a project. The apprentice knows the basic engineering knowledge. He observes the designer and creates a project model with enough information to explain it even without the designer. While the apprentice expectations of the designer's decisions match, no interruption is needed.

The ADD (Active Design Documentation) approach uses the apprentice metaphor. Let's assume that a company hires an apprentice to observe and record a designer developing a project. The apprentice knows the basic engineering knowledge. He observes the designer and creates a project model with enough information to explain it even without the designer. While the apprentice expectations of the designer's decisions match, no interruption is needed.

Whenever the apprentice's expectation fails, he interrupts the designer to learn or to advise the designer of a constraint violation. Since this apprentice has limited knowledge, he can be substituted by a knowledge base and a knowledge acquisition procedure. ADD is this assistant agent that integrates design and documentation.

ADD uses a parametric network to represent domain knowledge. Nodes are design parameters and arcs are dependencies among them. Parameters represent the context and dependencies represent which are the parameter's sub-parameters, i.e., those parameters whose values need to be known before the calculation of a parameter's value. A parameter only can be calculated if all its sub-parameters have been already calculated.

The parameters can be of three types: primitive, derived or decided. A primitive parameter owns an independent value associated to a specific case of project. The derived parameter is a variable derived through deterministic formula (mathematics or heuristics). The decided parameter is a variable where alternatives are generated, constraints are applied to eliminate alternatives and criteria are applied to order them. Derived and decided parameters own a reference to the parameters they depend to be calculated, their sub-parameters.

4   The SpADD Framework

SpADD is an ADD extension including a canonical representation model and a object oriented class model to support spatial reasoning needed in spatial layout design problems. Section 4.1 presents the SpADD's knowledge base, emphasizing its characteristics to deal with the issues identified in layout design, and Section 4.2 presents SpADD's reasoning process, emphasizing the additional features added to the original ADD model.

4.1   SpADD's Knowledge Base

The SpADD's knowledge base involves three issues:
- An ADD's knowledge base extension to treat spatial reasoning problems
- A canonical knowledge model to treat spatial layout design problems;
- An object oriented class model applied to the SpADD's knowledge base and reasoning.

SpADD's ADD Knowledge Base Extension. The ADD knowledge base has information about the project domain and about the ADD's decision process. The original ADD knowledge base is linear, discrete and static. It has some limitations that hinder its use to deal with multiple methods for alternative design generation, cyclic dependencies, dynamic dependencies and canonical parameters and dependencies.

Multiple methods for alternative design generation. Some layout design decisions, such as objects' clustering, have more than one alternative generator method for the same parameter. For example, different clustering methods generally produce different solutions based on the same input data [1]. It would be interesting to run more than one program and to analyze and compare the resulting classifications. ADD uses only one method for alternative design generation for each parameter. SpADD allows the use of multiple methods for alternative design generation for each parameter. Thus it can also be used as a tool for evaluating different methods of alternative design generation.

Cyclic dependencies. ADD has references only to acyclic dependencies. Acyclic dependencies appears when one parameter influences another in a only way. However, spatial information treatment requires cyclic dependencies. Cyclic dependencies appears when one parameter influences another and vice-versa. In the oil pipeline layout domain, a well is positioned at the location as closest as possible to its assigned platform. On the other hand, a platform is located at the GC of the wells' locations, configuring a net of cyclic dependencies.

Dynamic dependencies. In layout design, dependencies may become known during the decision process. For example, a well depends of the platform's position to whom it will be assigned to be positioned. However, its platform only is known after the assigning decision of platforms to groups, in execution time. Therefore, parameter's dependencies can be classified in static or dynamic. The parameter's static dependencies are known previously by the parametric canonical model and are always present during the parameter's time-life. The parameter's dynamic dependencies are known during the decision process and are set by a parameter's static derived sub-parameter.

Canonical parameters and dependencies. In layout design, canonical parts of the parameter network can be reproduced dynamically in execution time, i.e., dependencies may become known during the decision process, and parameters or dependencies may be created during the data input. For example, even though a object description knowledge is available, each problem has a different number of objects: parameters and dependencies will be created during the data input. SpADD uses a canonical knowledge network to represent what parameters and dependencies exist previously or will be created during the data input or reasoning process. It is presented following.

SpADD's Knowledge Network Model. SpADD canonical parametric network's model (Fig. 2) is a quantitative model applied to SLDP, allowing the decisions' explanations. In Fig. 2 the parameters represent the context (the space, the existing objects , the forbidden regions) and the spatial layout decisions (object clustering , assigning, positioning and path finding).

SpADD canonical network considers the existence of two types of world objects, differentiated by their possibility to be assigned to cluster: the simple objects (those that cannot be assigned to clusters) and the composite objects (those that can be assigned to clusters).

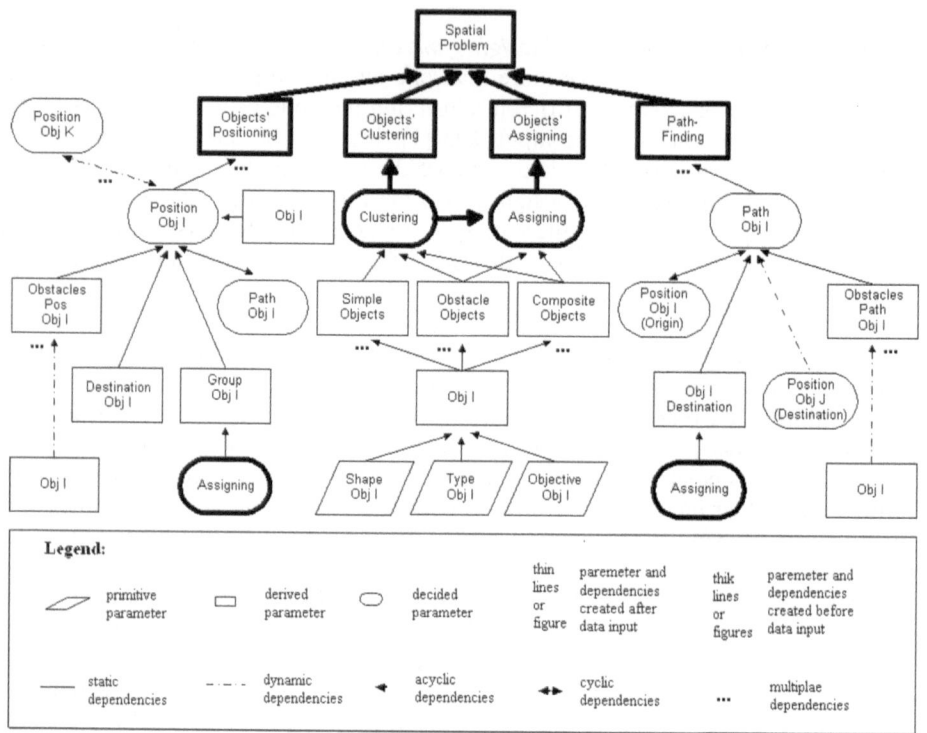

Fig. 2. SpADD knowledge network model.

The derived parameter *Obj*$_i$ represents a object of the spatial problem. It has as sub-parameters its relevant properties, such as shape, type, area and objective. The primitive parameter *Shape Obj*$_i$ represents the shape of the Obj$_i$ The primitive parameter *Type Obj*$_i$ represents the type of the Obj$_i$. The primitive parameter Objective *Obj*$_i$ represents the area in which the Obj$_i$ can be positioned.

The derived parameter *Simple Objects* concentrates as sub-parameters all type-simple objects. The derived parameter *Composite Objects* concentrates as sub-parameters all type-composite objects. The derived parameter *Obstacle Objects* concentrates as sub-parameters all type-obstacle objects.

The derived parameter *Spatial Problem* is a parameter whose function is to concentrate as sub-parameters all decisions of a spatial problem such as, such as: objects' clustering, assigning, positioning and path finding. The derived parameter *Objects' Positioning* is a parameter whose function is to concentrate as sub-parameters all objects' positioning decisions. The derived parameter *Objects' Clustering* is a parameter whose function is to have as sub-parameter the clustering decision. The derived parameter *Objects' Assigning* is a parameter whose function is to have as sub-parameters the assigning decision. The derived parameter *Path-Finding* is a parameter whose function is to concentrate as sub-parameters all decisions of finding a path between a object and the composite object assigned to the cluster where the object is.

The decided parameter *Position Obj$_i$* represents the position of a given object. It depends on the object itself, the other objects' positions (attracting objects), the path between the object and its destination and the world existing obstacles. The cyclic dynamic dependence between the parameter *Position Obj$_i$* and its attracting objects is carried dynamically when the position in being calculated. These dependencies are represented by a hatched line. The obstacles in the positioning decision time is obtained in the parameter *Obstacles Pos Obj$_i$*. The occupied space is dynamically obtained consulting the objects already positioned.

The decided parameter *Clustering* represents a set of objects sharing similar properties. The clustering process depends upon the obstacles and the simple and composite objects. In the clustering decision several clustering methods can be applied. This methods can be initially classified into two kinds, namely partitioning and hierarchical methods [7]. A partitioning method constructs a single partition with a defined number of clusters. Hierarchical algorithms deal with all number of clusters, from 1 to the number of objects, in the same run. The objects will be clustered are always the type-simple objects. If the clustering type is partitioning the number of clusters is defined by the number of type-composite objects.

The decided parameter *Assigning* represents the selection of composite objects to each cluster obtained. The assigning process depends upon the clustering, the obstacles and the available composite objects. Each object is assigned only to one cluster.

The decided parameter *Path Obj$_i$* represents the path between Obj$_i$ and the object it was assigned. This parameter may have different algorithms to create a path between the two objects and a evaluation criterion to select the one with minimum crossing or minimum number of direction changes. Before finding a path between the objects, it is necessary to identify the connection points, origin (*Position Obj$_i$*), destination (*Position Obj$_j$*) and the obstacles to be avoided. Only after to know object destination, it will be possible to establish the dependence between them. This dependence is said to be dynamically ascertained. The obstacles in the path decision time is obtained in the parameter *Obstacles Path Obj$_i$*.

The derived parameter *Destination Obj$_i$* represents the object which Obj$_i$ was assigned, and the derived parameter *Group Obj$_i$* represents the objects assigned to the group of the Obj$_i$, case Obj$_i$ is type-composite.

SpADD's Object Oriented Class Model. In addition to the SpADD's canonical knowledge network model, the SpADD's framework also presents a SpADD's object oriented class model to support all SpADD's reasoning process, presented in Fig. 3. The main classes of the SpADD's object oriented class model are the primitive, derived and decided parameters classes. When a object is created, several instances of these classes are created according with the canonical model of the Fig. 2. These instances are related to form the parametric network of a specific problem

In Fig.3, thick lines represent inheritance between classes and thin lines the possibility of creating instances of the classes. The class *Parameter Manager* has methods to create instances of alternative values and of primitive, derived and decided parameters. The class *Evaluator* has methods responsible to calculate and evaluate the parameters' values. The class *Knowledge Base* is responsible to keep the problem's knowledge base. The class *Canonical Knowledge Base* has the knowledge about the SpADD problem to be solved, such as the parametric canonical network, and the methods to calculate each derived and decided parameter's value. This class is particular to each problem. The class *User Interface* has the methods for the user interface including a method to create a instance of the spatial problem.

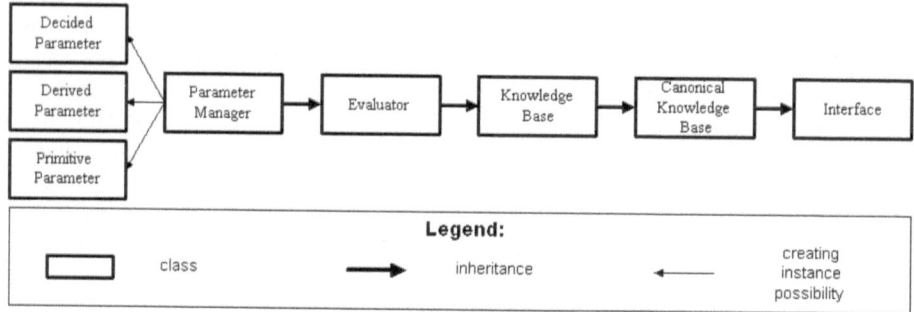

Fig. 3. SpADD's object oriented classes model.

4.2 SpADD's Reasoning

Reasoning in SpADD follows, except over cyclic dependencies, ADD's decision process, i.e., parameters can be evaluated only after their sub-parameters had been evaluated, in a depth-first search style. Decisions involve generating alternative values and evaluating them through a rational decision-making process. Alternative values in layout design domain are generated, instead of previously listed, using a diversity of generation algorithms, such as agglomerative nesting procedure [7] to generate objects' clustering.

SpADD uses an iterative resource-bounded procedure to treat the cyclic dependencies and generate alternative values. Each parameter that owns a cyclic dependence must have an initial hypothetical value. SpADD imposes an ordering on a cyclic parameter evaluation sequencing. First, all its acyclic parameters are calculated, like in ADD reasoning, considering the hypothetical value for the parameter. Afterwards, a new hypotheses is calculated to the cyclic parameter. If the difference between the new parameter value and the old one is significant, all cyclic parameters are recalculated. The evaluation loop continues until the difference between new and old hypotheses are less than an accepted value or after a certain number of cycles. This behavior guarantees search will end.

5   ADDSUB: A Working Prototype Applied to Assist Design and Documentation of Oil Pipeline Layout

Oil pipeline layout in deep water oil fields problem has been a good lab to test the feasibility of SpADD. We built a computational model, called ADDSUB, a working prototype of SpADD applied to assist design and documentation of oil pipeline lay out.

As described in introduction section, in the oil pipeline layout, the designers' tasks consists of identifying groups of oil target, positioning platforms to receive and treat the oil coming from a group, positioning wells in the target area to be as close as possible to the platform, and routing the oil pipeline to connect wells to platforms.

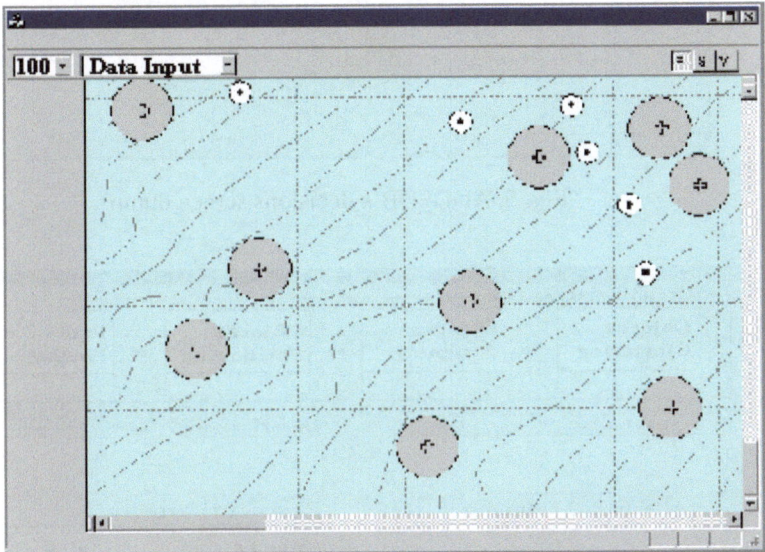

Fig. 4. ADDSUB's oil target areas as data input screen dump.

ADDSUB offers a design environment where the undersea topography and tex-ture, as well as, the existing objects are presented in a canvas area, as illustrated in Fig. 4. New oil target areas can be created and positioned by direct manipulation. Other input data are entered through wizards and dialog boxes.

Fig. 5 illustrates an oil pipeline layout design. Big circles represented the target oil areas, the small gray circles, the oil wells; the small rectangles, the platforms; the slim rectangles, the pipelines; the lines, the topography; and the rest are obstacles to the design.

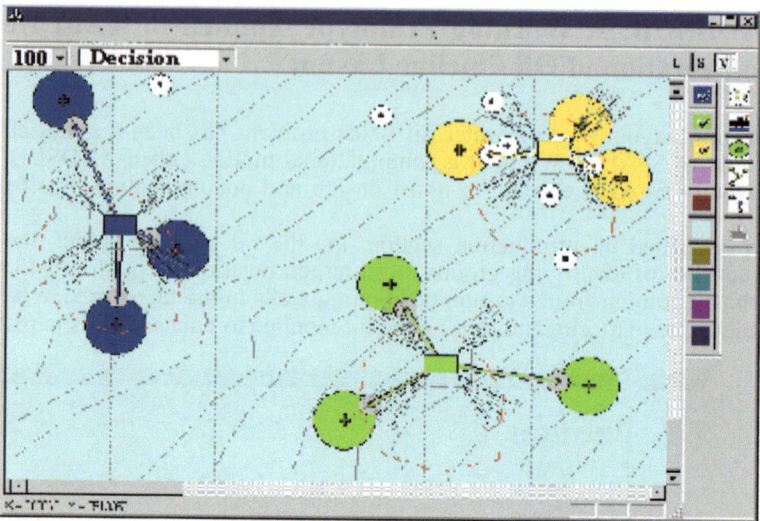

Fig. 5. ADDSUB's decisions screen dump.

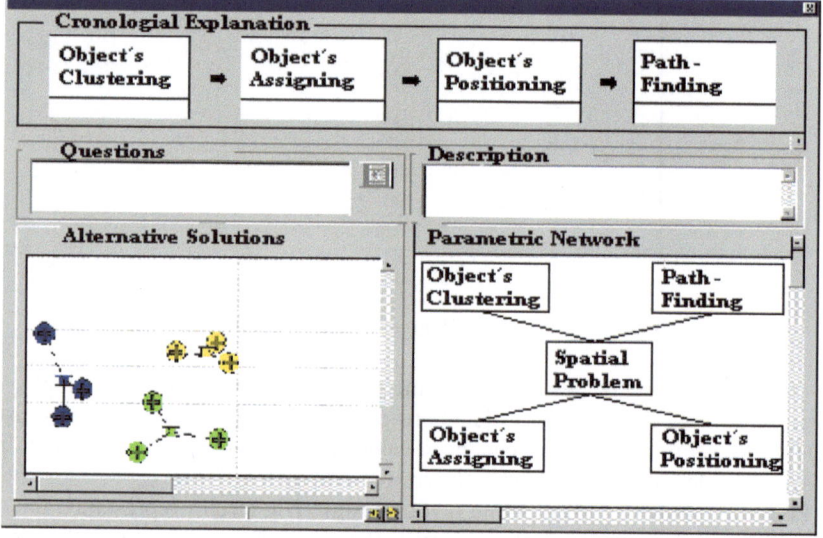

Fig. 6. ADDSUB's explanation screen dump.

ADDSUB operates in five different modes: *Data-Entry, Suggest, Verify, Knowledge Acquisition and Explanation* modes. In the *Data-Entry* mode, users input the data configuring the project to be developed. In the *Suggest* mode, users request suggestion from the system on the layout decisions. Fig. 5 illustrates a system output after an user requisition of the pipeline routing. In the *Verify* mode, users propose solutions and the system analyzes them. In this mode, partial solutions are considered, such as defining a subset of target areas that must be together. In the *Knowledge Ac-*

quisition mode, users may include or modify calculation methods, alternative solutions and design criteria. In the *Explanation* mode, users can obtain decision explanations. As shown in Fig. 6, the upper area presents the chronological order of the decisions, the lower right screen area presents the domain knowledge, the lower left screen are presents the considered alternative solutions, and the middle area presents the explanation.

Initial results demonstrated the success of the partnership designer and computa tional agent to find better solutions. Computational assistance was specially welcomed due to the threshold and horizon effects characteristics of the domain. Small changes in the object location turn almost optimum solution in unfeasible one. In addition, the platforms, pipeline and wells high cost made a small improvement in the layout leading to a great savings (in the order of thousands to million dollars savings).

6 Related Work

Improving design documentation and rationale for spatial layout design problems is a recent research topic in engineering, computer science and information systems. Many researchers in the area of spatial reasoning have studied each aspect of spatial layout design (clustering, assigning, positioning, route-finding and documentation).

Methods for each one of the spatial layout design decisions have been done. For example, over the last 3 decades, a wealth of algorithms and computer programs has been developed for cluster analysis [8] [7] [1]. In 1990, Kaufman introduced the main approaches to clustering and provided guidance to the choice between six methods [7]. In the path routing decision, we can use the Dijkstra's algorithm [4] for the computation of the shortest path between two given points on a network. In 1995, Beattie [2] presented her „tesseral" addressing, a alternative method for localization of points in space able to represent the domain in a uni-dimensional sequence. Finally, in 1992, Garcia presented her active design documentation model avoiding geometric reasoning [5]. These research efforts have treated specific aspects of spatial layout design in isolation from each other.

We have studied all this approaches and joined what they had of better to propose an approach to deal with SLDP, the SpADD approach.

7 Conclusions

In this paper we presented the SpADD framework, an extension of ADD design model applied to spatial layout design problems. Cyclic dependencies, unknown dependencies, independent decision ordering, multiple methods to alternative design generation, a canonical knowledge network and an object oriented class model were addressed by SpADD to be applied to spatial layout design problems.

An additional contribution of SpADD is its use as a tool for evaluating different methods of alternative design generation. For example, the clustering problems receives a great deal of attention from the optimization community ([8], [7], [1]). SpADD could be used as an evaluation tool contrasting the methods over a set of metrics.

A prototype system was developed for the domain of oil pipeline layout showing the feasibility of the approach.

We are currently working on clustering methods and on automatic explanation generation. We are studying the use of an auxiliary qualitative model to interpret quantitative decisions and generate understandable design decisions rationale to users.

References

1. Arabie, P; Hubert, L. J.; Soete, G. De (Eds.): Clustering and Classification. World Scientific Publ., River Edge, NJ, 1996.
2. Beattie, B.; Coenen, F. P.; Bench-Capon, T. J. M.; Diaz and Shave, M.J.R.: Spatial Reasoning for GIS using a Tesseral Data Representation. In Revell, N. and Tjoa, A.M. a(Eds), Database and Expert Systems Applications, (Proceedings DEXA'95), Lecture Notes in Computer Science 978, Springer Verlag, 1995.
3. Brown, David C.; Chandrasekaran, B.: Design Problem Solving: Knowledge Structures and Control Strategies. Morgan Kaufmann Publishers, Inc. 1986.
4. Dijkstra, E. W.: A note on two problems in connection with graphs, Numerische Mathematik, 1, 269-271. 1959.
5. Garcia, A. C. B.: Active Design Documents: A new approach for supporting documentation in preliminary routine design. A thesis submitted to the department of civil engineering and the committee on graduate studies of Stanford University in partial fulfillment of the degree of doctor of philosophy in civil engineering, August 1992.
6. Hernández, D.: Qualitative Representation of Spatial Knowledge, Volume 804 of Lecture Notes in Artificial Intelligence, Springer, Berlin, 1994.
7. Kaufman, Leonark; Rousseeuw, Peter J.: Finding Groups in Data. An Introduction to Cluster Analysis. Wiley series in probability and mathematical statistics. John Wiley & Sons, Inc. 1990.
8. Kovács, Z. L.: Redes Neurais Artificiais, Fundamentos e aplicações. Edição Acadêmica, São Paulo, 1996.
9. Sharma, J..: Integrated Spatial Reasoning in Geographic Information Systems: Combining Topology and Direction. A thesis submitted in partial Fulfillment of the Requirements of the Degree Doctor of Philosophy. The Graduate School University of Maine, May 1996.
10. Worboys, M. F.: Gis A Computing Perspective; Taylor & Francis, 1996.

A Systematic Approach for Building Ontologies

Ricardo de Almeida Falbo[1,2], Crediné Silva de Menezes[2], and
Ana Regina C. da Rocha[1]

[1] COPPE / UFRJ
Caixa Postal 68511, CEP 21945-970, Rio de Janeiro - RJ - Brazil
{rfalbo,darocha}@cos.ufrj.br
[2] Computer Science Department, UFES
Fernando Ferrari Avenue, CEP 29060-900, Vitória - ES - Brazil
{falbo,credine}@inf.ufes.br

Abstract. Currently, there is a considerable body of experience in building ontologies. Nevertheless, knowledge acquisition using ontologies is
still a research issue. The goal of this paper is to take a further step
towards a systematic approach for building ontologies. An approach for
engineering ontologies is presented with a case study. This approach incorporates the best features of the existing methods and proposes other
features, such as the use of a graphical language for expressing ontologies, an axiom classification and some guidelines for ontology capture,
formalization, evaluation and documentation. An ontology development
process model is also discussed, showing how to proceed in the development of ontologies.

1 Introduction

Traditionally, the development process of Knowledge-Based Systems (KBSs) was
viewed as a process of extracting knowledge from a human expert and transfer-
ring this knowledge into a KBS. This transferview, however, proved to be little
productive. Nowadays there is a consensus that the KBS development is indeed,
a modeling activity and many methods were proposed in this sense, most of
them emphasizing the task modeling, such as [1] and [2].

More recently, the domain knowledge modeling started to deserve more attention and ontologies have played an important role. In spite of ontologies are
being even more used, the engineering of ontologies is yet a research field. Several efforts have been made in order to define a systematic method for building
ontologies and some of them have yield worthy contributions, such as [3], [4]
and [5].

The goal of this work is to take a further step. Section 2 discusses the use
of ontologies in knowledge acquisition. Section 3 presents a graphical language
for expressing ontologies. Section 4 presents a systematic approach for building
ontologies. In section 5, a case study is presented. Section 6 discusses related
works. Finally, in section 7, the conclusions of this work are presented.

Helder Coelho (Ed.): IBERAMIA'98, LNAI 1484, pp. 349–360, 1998.
© Springer-Verlag Berlin Heidelberg 1998

2   Ontologies

It is impossible to represent the real world, or even some part of it, with all details. To represent some phenomenon or part of the world, that we call domain, it is necessary to focus on a limited number of concepts that are sufficient and relevant to create an abstraction of the phenomenon in hand. Thus, a central aspect of any modeling activity consists of developing a conceptualization: a set of informal rules that constrain the structure of a piece of reality, which an agent uses to isolate and organize relevant objects and relations [6].

An *ontology* is a specification of a conceptualization [5], that is, a description of concepts and relations that can exist for an agent or an agent community. Basically, an ontology consists of concepts and relations, and theirs definitions, properties and constraints expressed as axioms. An ontology should not be only an hierarchy of terms, but a framework talking about the domain.

One of the main benefits of the use of ontologies in the KBS development is the opportunity to adopt a more productive strategy to the Knowledge Acquisition (KA). In the traditional KA, for each new application to be built, a new conceptualization is developed. It reflects on how the KA is carried out: for each new KBS, an acquisition phase is accomplished, almost always from scratch, focusing all particularities of the system in hand. This approach however, is extremely expensive. As long as KA is the activity that requires the major efforts in the KBS development, it is important to share and reuse the captured knowledge.

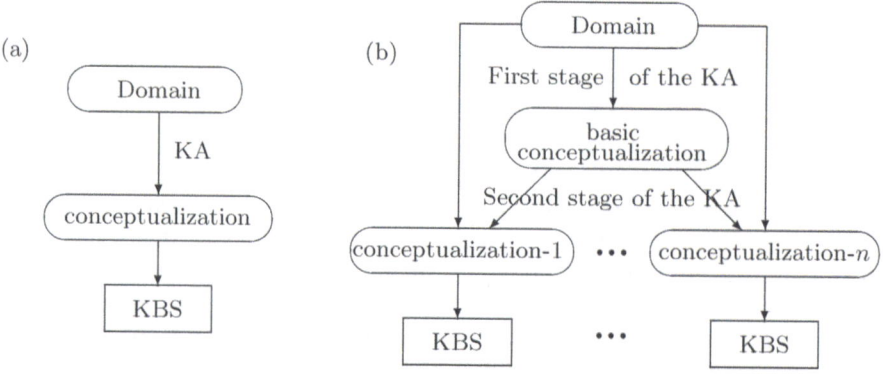

Fig. 1. (a) Traditional approach to KA and (b) Ontology-based approach to KA

In an ontology based approach, the KA can be accomplished in two stages. First, the general domain knowledge, relevant to several applications, should be elicited and specified as ontologies. These, in turn, are used to guide the second stage of the KA, when the particularities of a specific application are considered. In this way, the same ontology can be used to guide the development of several applications diluting the costs of the first stage of KA and allowing knowledge sharing and reuse. Fig. 1 shows these two approaches.

3   A Graphical Language for Expressing Ontologies

In the KA, the use of a graphical representation is essential in order to facilitate the communication between knowledge engineers and experts. In ontology building, such representation is basically a language representing a meta-ontology. So, this language must own basic primitives to represent a domain conceptualization and, in its simplest form, it should have notations to represent only concepts and relations.

Nevertheless, some types of associations have a strong semantics and, indeed, hide a generic ontology. For each one of these types, a specialized notation can be proposed. In fact, this is the striking feature of the Graphical Language for Expressing Ontologies (GLEO) presented here and what makes it different from other graphical representations: any notation, beyond the basic notations for concepts and relations, aims to incorporate a theory. In this way, axioms can be automatically generated.

In the current version, there are special notations for whole-part and sub-type associations. When we use a whole-part relation, we are incorporating a generic ontology of composition to the ontology in development. To represent this kind of relation, we used a filled line with a small circle close to the whole. When we develop a taxonomy of concepts, we are implicitly committing to a subsumption ontology. Since the sub-type association occurs between concepts and not between instances, we used a dotted line to represent this kind of relation, with an arrow pointing to the super-type. Fig. 2 summarizes the main notations of GLEO.

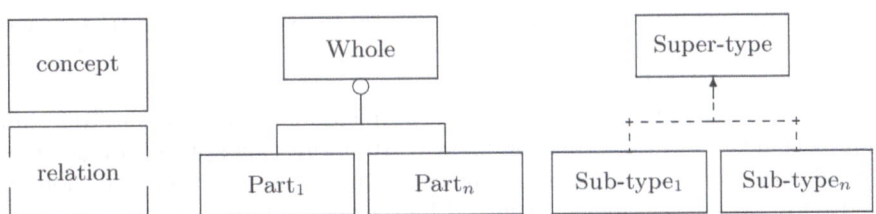

Fig. 2. Main notations of GLEO

The use of special notations to enhance different types of relations can be a direct way to integrate generic ontologies with domain ontologies. A tool for ontology development that adopt this philosophy embeds a powerful theory inclusion mechanism. Each type of relation specifying a generic theory can have its own notation and whenever it is used, ontologies would be automatically integrated. In this sense, GLEO should not be considered a static and finished representation: when a theory talking about some kind of association is identified, a specific notation can be included.

4   A Systematic Approach for Engineering Ontologies

Although there are in the literature some proposals for building ontologies, such as [3] and [4], this field is still object of several efforts. The goal of this section is to go one step ahead to transform the ontology development from art to engineering. The activities of the ontology development process are discussed and some guidelines about how to perform them are presented. Besides, a life cycle is proposed, showing the interactions between the activities.

Basically, the proposed method wrap the following activities: purpose identification and requirement specification, ontology capture and formalization, integrating existing ontologies, and ontology evaluation and documentation.

4.1   Purpose Identification and Requirement Specification

The first activity to be performed in the ontology development process is to clearly identify its purpose and its intended uses, that is, the competence of the ontology. The *competence* of a representation is concerned with the span of questions it can answer [4] or the tasks it can support. By establishing the competence, we reach an effective way to determine what is relevant to the ontology and what is not. We should also identify the scenarios that motivated the development of the ontology in hand.

Given the ontology purpose, we should specify its requirements. These should take into account the intended uses and can be stated as competency questions: the questions that the ontology should be able to answer [4]. By specifying a relationship between the competency questions and the motivating scenarios, we give an informal justification for the ontology and, what is better, we provide a way for its evaluation.

If the domain of interest is too much complex, we should use some decomposition mechanism to dilute this complexity. An interesting approach is to consider *leveled ontologies*: we start building core ontologies, basic for the domain in study; from these ontologies, others of high level are built, adding new elements and, thus, extending the ontologies of the lower level.

4.2   Ontology Capture

Doubtlessly, this is the most important step in the ontology development. The goal is to capture the domain conceptualization based on the ontology competence. The relevant concepts and relations should be identified and organized [3]. A model using a graphical language, with a dictionary of terms, should be used to facilitate the communication with the domain experts.

Primitive concepts - those that cannot be defined in terms of other concepts in the ontology - should be defined using natural language and examples. The choice of the terms to be used to make reference to the knowledge categories should be carefully made, avoiding terms with cloudy interpretation. Concepts that can be described using other concepts should clearly refer to them. We should also develop taxonomies, organizing domain knowledge classes and subclasses.

Concepts and relations are the basis of an ontology, but an essential feature is the definition of axioms. Simply proposing a taxonomy or a set of basic terms does not constitute an ontology. Axioms should be provided in order to fix the semantics of the terms. Axioms specify concept definitions and constraints over their interpretation. In this step, it is not necessary to write down formal axioms, rather these axioms should be written in natural language, considering only the domain constraints.

The axioms in an ontology can present two different forms and purposes: derivation axioms and consolidation axioms. *Derivation axioms* are those that allow new information to be derived from the previously existing knowledge. So, they are a way for deduction and represent logical consequences. *Consolidation axioms*, on the other hand, typically define constraints for establishing a relation or for defining an object as an instance of a concept.

The derivation axioms can have root in the meaning of the concepts and relations of the ontology or in the way these concepts and relations are structured. When axioms are defined to show constraints imposed by the way concepts are structured, we call them *epistemological axioms*. When they describe domain signification constraints, we call them *ontological axioms*.

This classification based on the nature of the axioms is a good guideline to drive the axiom definition. We should pay attention to capture axioms that consider the structuring of the concepts and relations (the epistemological axioms), their meanings and constraints (the ontological axioms) and the integrity laws that govern them (the consolidation axioms).

The process of defining axioms should be guided by the competency questions. The axioms in the ontology must be necessary and sufficient to express the competency questions and to characterize their solutions. Any solution to a competency question must be entailed by or consistent with the axioms in the ontology. If the proposed axioms are not enough for this purpose, then additional concepts, relations or axioms must be added to the ontology. In this sense, the ontology capture is an iterative process, strongly linked with the evaluation. There may be many different ways to axiomatize an ontology and the competency questions should be used to evaluate the completeness of the sets of axioms in a particular axiomatization [4].

Quality criteria for ontology design [5] should be observed, chiefly: clarity, concerning the meaning of the defined terms; coherence, mainly between the textual definitions and the examples; and minimal ontological commitment, to allow the parties committed to the ontology to be free to specialize and instantiate the ontology as needed. The last criterion is directly related to the axiom definition.

4.3   Ontology Formalization

The logical analysis of an universe of discourse is better performed when it is described using a formal language. In this language, in contrast to the natural language, we have signs that are unambiguous and formulations that are exact and, therefore, the clarity and correctness of a deduction can be tested with greater easiness and accuracy. A deduction in natural language often involves presuppositions which were not made explicitly, but which was taken for granted in the deduction process.

In the formalization, we should establish a formalism to represent the ontology knowledge categories. Once defined the representational formalism to be used, it is possible to fix the ontology terminology and, mainly, the semantics of its interpretation. It is important to stress that a formal ontology is not able to substitute the description of a conceptualization in natural language; rather it is to be used to support it or to be added to it, working as a device where some ideas are checked in relation to completeness and, perhaps, coherence.

In short, the claim is to explicitly represent the conceptualization captured in the previous step in a formal language, what involves the commitment with some meta-ontology, the choice of a representation language and the development of the formal ontology. When it is not necessary any special commitment with a specific meta-ontology that proves itself to be adequate to the ontology in development, the first order logic tends to be the most adequate formalism, since it is the formalism that embeds less ontological commitments.

To describe a first order formal language, it is necessary to specify the non logical symbols of its alphabet, that is, the *constants*, denoting specific individuals of the universe of the discourse, the *functional symbols*, denoting functions, and the *predicates*, denoting properties of and relations between the individuals. In fact, when the first order logic is the formalism adopted, this must be the first step in the formalization phase: to map the ontology elements in constants, functions and predicates. After that, it is possible to create statements about the individuals in the domain, the formal axioms.

4.4   Integrating Existing Ontologies

During the capture and/or formalization processes, it could be necessary to integrate the current ontology with existing ones [3], in order to seize previously established conceptualizations. Indeed, it is a good practice to develop general modular ontologies, more widely reusable, and to integrate them, when necessary, to obtain the desired result. If many details are necessary, the ontology must incorporate only the essential ontological commitments and the others should be described in a micro-theory [7] or in a high level ontology. Thus, we preserve the quality criterion of minimal ontological commitment.

4.5   Ontology Evaluation

Finally, the ontology must be evaluated to check whether it satisfies the specification requirements. Further, it should be evaluated in relation to some design quality criteria. The set of criteria proposed by Gruber [5] should be adopted both to guide the development and to evaluate the quality of the developed ontologies.

We should notice that this step can, and in fact should, be performed jointly with the capture and formalization steps, in an iterative process. The use of a graphical model is very important when evaluating an ontology with domain experts. Furthermore, the competency questions play an essential role in the evaluation of the completeness of the ontology, specially when considering its axioms. In a particular domain it is possible to write down a great number of axioms and, therefore, we have to pay attention not to write down more axioms than the necessary. In this context we ought to have in mind the principle of minimal ontological commitment and in hands the competency questions. The set of axioms must be necessary and sufficient to express the competency questions and to characterize their solutions and nothing else [4]. Redundant axioms or those that do not contribute to the competence of the ontology must be excluded.

4.6   Ontology Documentation

All the ontology development must be documented, including purposes, requirements and motivating scenarios, textual descriptions of the conceptualization, the formal ontology and the adopted design criteria. As the evaluation, the documentation is a step that has to occur in parallel with the others.

The terms captured in the domain conceptualization must be described in a Dictionary, considering two important principles: the auto-reference principle and the minimal vocabulary principle. The minimal vocabulary principle concerns the vocabulary used in the definition of the ontology terms. This vocabulary must be as small as possible and should not present any ambiguities. Any term without clear and unambiguous meaning must be defined as an entry in the Dictionary. The auto-reference principle says that the definition of terms in the Dictionary, when possible, should be done using terms that have already been described in it. Based in this principle, a potential approach to document an ontology is using a hypertext, allowing browsing along term definitions, examples and its formalization, including the axioms.

4.7   The Ontology Development Process

The ontology development process should be viewed as a strongly iterative process rather than sequential steps. The capture step can point new requirements. During the evaluation, we can notice that the identified terms are not enough to the intended purpose of the ontology, forcing backwards motion to the capture step. Similar situations can occur in the formalization step: inconsistency can be detected, causing a review of the specification and of the terms defined in the ontology. Finally, if integration of existing ontologies is necessary, it can have substantial impact in the definition and formalization of the terms. The steps of the ontology development process and their interdependencies are illustrated by Fig. 3.

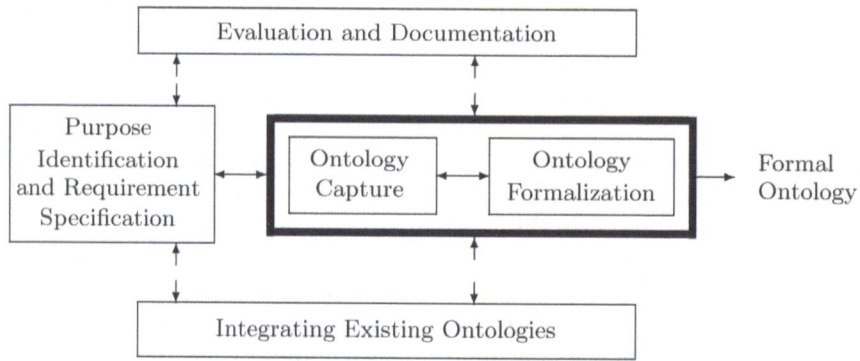

Fig. 3. Steps in the ontology development and their interdependencies.

The broken lines indicate that there is a constant interaction, albeit weaker, between the associated steps. The filled lines show the main work flow in the ontology building process. The box involving the capture and formalization steps enhances the strong interaction, and consequently iteration, between these steps.

Given the formal ontology, many times it is desired to make it operational. To do so, two other activities must be performed: design and coding. In the design step, concepts, relations and axioms of the formal ontology must be mapped to a format compatible with the chosen implementation language. In the coding step, the ontology is coded in the chosen language.

5   A Study Case: A Software Process Ontology

To illustrate the application of the proposed method, in this section we present part of the software process ontology developed to promote knowledge integration in the TABA Workstation [8], a software development meta-environment.

The TABA Project aims the construction of a configurable workstation for software development. Since the meta-environment and its instantiated environments need to handle knowledge about software development processes, this knowledge has to be shared along the Workstation as a whole. Thus, we used an ontology-based Knowledge Engineering approach to develop a modular knowledge base of software process to this environment.

The software process ontology aims to support the acquisition, organization, reuse and sharing of software process knowledge in the TABA Workstation, as shown in Fig. 4. Every knowledge based tool compromised with this ontology will share a common vocabulary, facilitating the communication between developers and, the most important, allowing the sharing and reuse of knowledge bases in the meta-environment as much as in the instantiated environments.

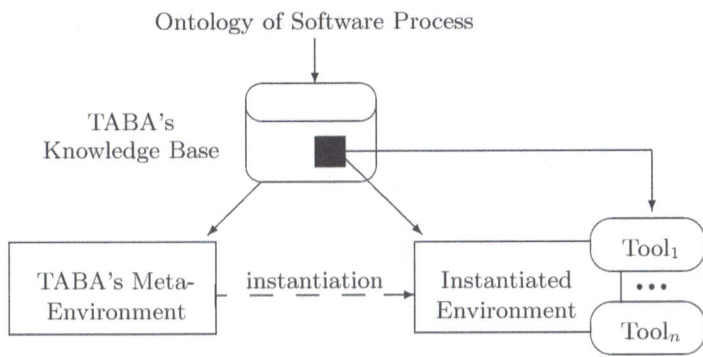

Fig. 4. Uses of the ontology in the TABA Workstation.

Given the complexity of this domain, we adopted a leveled approach for developing ontologies. The software process ontology was developed on the top of central domain ontologies, namely, ontologies of activity, procedure and resource. For each central ontology, the proposed method was recursively applied. In the formalization step, we used the first order logic and established a formal first order language about software processes.

Due to space limitations, it is not possible to present the entire ontology. Since the goal of this section is to show how to apply the proposed method, we decided to present only some aspects judged capable of illustrating its application. We presented parts of the activity ontology and of the software process ontology. The procedure and the resource ontologies are not presented. A more complete view of this ontology can be found in [9].

5.1   Activity Ontology

The concept of activity is in the core of any software process model. Activities can occur in several levels, from an elementary task to a development process phase. An activity is the basic transformational action primitive that uses input artifacts to produce output artifacts, supported by resources. Basically, an activity ontology must be able to answer the following competency questions:

1. Which is the nature of an activity?
2. In which sub-activities is an activity decomposed?
3. Which activities must antecede a given activity?
4. Which artifacts are input to, or produced by a given activity?

5. Which resources are required by an activity to be performed?
6. Which procedures can be adopted to perform an activity?

Fig. 5 shows a partial model of the activity ontology, but does not span all its terms. In fact, there are several other concepts in this ontology. For instance, to capture the dependence between activities, we defined concepts of pre-activity and post-activity. The terms used were defined in a Dictionary.

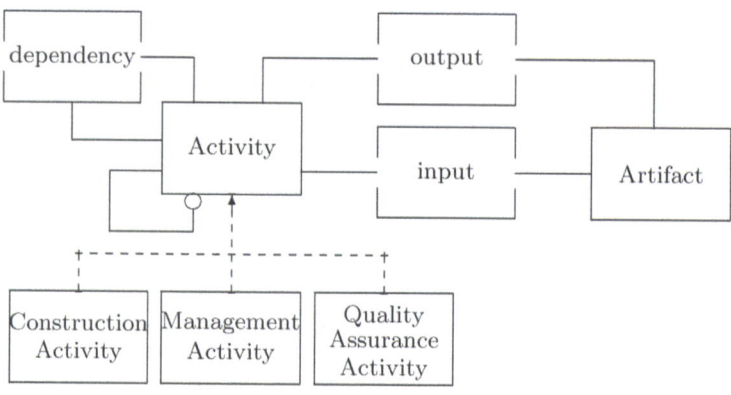

Fig. 5. Part of the activity ontology.

The axioms of the ontology were developed to provide a basic interpretation of the concepts in the ontology and to capture and write down the constraints imposed in the domain. The ontological axiom below, for instance, defines the concept of *pre-activity* from the input and output relations: an activity a_1 is a pre-activity of an activity a_2, if and only if, exists at least one artifact s that is an output of a_1 and an input to a_2.

$$(\forall a_1, a_2)(\text{preactivity}(a_1, a_2) \iff (\exists s)(\text{input}(s, a_2) \land \text{output}(s, a_1))) . \quad (1)$$

The predicate activity(a, t), denoting that the activity a is of the type t, was defined to formalize the existence of different types of activities. The parameter t can assume one of the following values: { *ConstructionAct, ManagementAct, QualityAct, CertificationAct, TestAct* }, representing each of the types identified in the taxonomy. Further, the following epistemological axioms hold:

$$(\forall a)(\text{activity}(a, \text{CertificationAct}) \lor \text{activity}(a, \text{TestAct}) \Rightarrow$$
$$\text{activity}(a, \text{QualityAct})) . \quad (2)$$

Since the first order logic is not a typed logic, it is necessary to define consolidation axioms establishing which types of objects can be used as an argument in a predicate. Thus, the following consolidation axiom, for instance, should be observed, where the asterisk (*) indicates that the value of this argument does not matter:

$$(\forall a_1, a_2)(\text{preactivity}(a_1, a_2) \Rightarrow \text{activity}(a_1, *) \wedge \text{activity}(a_2, *)) \,. \qquad (3)$$

5.2 Software Process Ontology

Given the basic ontologies, the software process ontology was built from them. Fig. 6 shows part of the final model of this ontology.

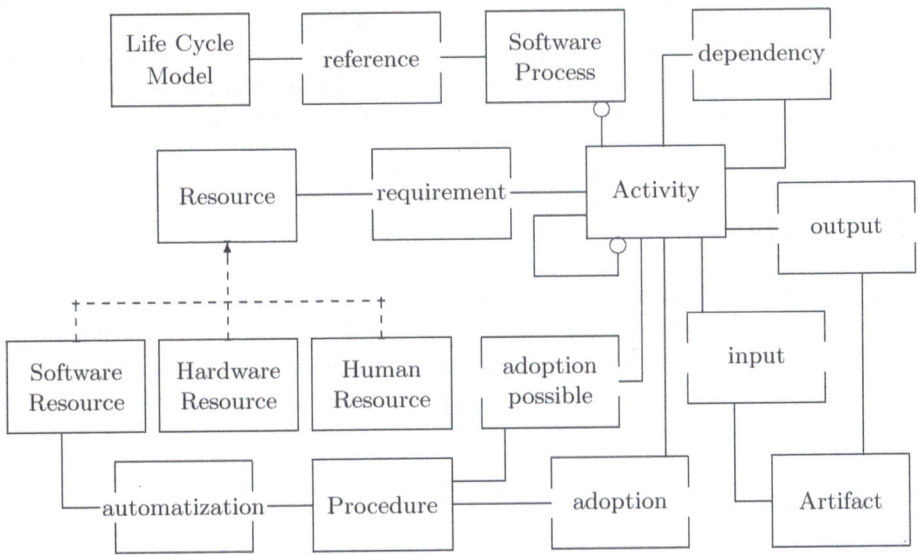

Fig. 6. Part of the software development process ontology.

Many other axioms were proposed. In the procedure ontology, for instance, the following consolidation axiom were defined in order to capture that the relation "adoption" is constrained by the relation "possible adoption".

$$(\forall p, a)(\text{adopotion}(p, a) \Rightarrow \text{possibleadoption}(p, a)) \,. \qquad (4)$$

6 Related Works

Uschold and King [3] proposed what they called "a skeletal methodology for building ontologies", defining a small number of stages that they believed would be required for any future comprehensive methodology. In this sense, the method here proposed followed some of their guidelines and stretched it towards a more systematic approach for building ontologies.

In the TOVE (*TOronto Virtual Enterprise*) Project, Gruninger and Fox [4] proposed a method for building ontologies that presents some features that are very proper to its context, the enterprise modeling. In fact, it can be considered an applied approach and not a general one. Nevertheless, many guidelines suggested by this method are interesting, such as the use of competency questions to guide the development, and were incorporated in the proposal presented here.

The leveled approach employed in this work can be viewed as an extension of the use of layered ontologies in CommonKADS [1]. In CommonKADS, ontologies are built in three layers, where each layer is formulated in terms of a lower-level, more widely applicable ontology. In the approach advocated here, there is not a pre-defined number of levels, nor rigid features for each level. The lowest level, as in CommonKADS, corresponds to the meta-ontology, but up to it, any number of ontology levels can be used. If generic ontologies are used, they must be placed in the lower levels. Core ontologies, basic for a wide domain, should be placed in the intermediate levels. In the higher levels, there must appear the application ontologies.

7   Conclusion

In order to develop KBSs with the desired quality and productivity, the knowledge acquisition must be conveyed *for* reuse. In this context, ontologies play an important role. In this paper we presented a method for building ontologies and parts of the software process ontology developed using the proposed method.

References

1. Breuker, J., Van de Velde, W.: CommonKADS Library for Expertise Modeling. IOS Press (1994)   349, 360
2. Steels L.: Components of Expertise. AI Magazine. Summer (1990)   349
3. Uschold, M., King, M.: Towards a Methodology for Building Ontologies. Workshop on Basic Ontological Issues in Knowledge Sharing, IJCAI'95 (1995)   349, 352, 354, 359
4. Gruninger, M., Fox, M.S.: Methodology for the Design and Evaluation of Ontologies. Technical Report, University of Toronto (1995)   349, 352, 353, 355, 360
5. Gruber, T.R.: Towards principles for the design of ontologies used for knowledge sharing. Int. J. Human-Computer Studies, 43(5/6) (1995)   349, 350, 353, 355
6. Guarino, N.: Understanding, building and using ontologies. Int. Journal Human-Computer Studies, 46(2/3) (1997)   350
7. Lenat, D.B., Guha, R.V., Pittman, K.: Cyc: toward programs with common sense. Communications of the ACM. August (1990)   354
8. Rocha, A.R.C., et al: TABA: a heuristic workstation for software development. COMPEURO'90, Israel (1990)   356
9. Falbo, R., Menezes, C., Rocha, A.R.: Using Ontologies to Improve Knowledge Integration in Software Engineering Environments. SCI'98/ISAS'98, USA (1998)   357

A Method to Diagnose the User's Level

Jean-Marc Nigro[1] and Patrick Ricaud[2]

[1] Université de Technologie de Troyes, 12 rue Marie Curie, BP 2060,
10010 Troyes Cedex (France)
jean-marc.nigro@univ-troyes.fr
[2] Laforia (tour 46-0), Université Pierre et Marie Curie, 4 place Jussieu,
75252 Paris Cedex 05 (France)
Patrick.Ricaud@poleia.lip6.fr

Abstract. This article proposes a method of automatic diagnosis of the level of knowledge reached by the user. The technique that will be used for that consists in comparing the choices made by the user with those made by an expert system under the same conditions. This comparison will enable us to know by who - the system or the user - the most efficient choices have been made. The data thus gathered are of the utmost importance for both explanatory and tutoring systems. Through the GénéCom and Bateleur systems, a method aimed at guessing and evaluating the user's intentions will be presented. This method will enable the system to define the level of the user and as a consequence to know what has to be explained to him. It will also enable the system to find out its own shortcomings and to know what it has to learn.

1   Introduction

This article proposes a method to evaluate the level of the user through the running of two rules-based systems: Bateleur and GénéCom. These two systems have been implemented and tested with successfully in LAFORIA (University of PARIS 6). Bateleur is able to simulate the decisions made by a user. Bateleur has been applied to the game of tarot. GénéCom is a system which generates comments. It is able to elaborate explanations of the choices made by the user. GénéCom uses Bateleur as a database of the domain of application. In order to give explanations, GénéCom needs to analyse the decisions of the user and it also needs to guess if the user is an expert or a beginner.

The problem of the representation of the user's knowledge is essential to produce a good diagnosis (and as a consequence: to produce good explanations [4] or comments). That is the reason why a good model of the user is primordial for the explanatory systems as well as for the tutoring systems [5]. Many researchers have taken an interest in this issue of user-modelling. Robert Kass [8] has made a list of the three types of modelling patterns concerning the knowledge of the learner in comparison with the knowledge of system:

Helder Coelho (Ed.): IBERAMIA'98, LNAI 1484, pp. 361-372, 1998.
© Springer-Verlag Berlin Heidelberg 1998

1. The *cover model* proposed by Carr and Goldtein [3] is the most simple among the three systems. It considers that the system has all the knowledge concerning the domain and that the learner has only a part of this knowledge. It has also been used by Clancey [6] in GUIDON and NEOMYCIN.

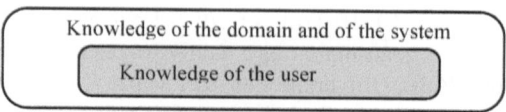

Fig. 1. Cover model.

2. The *differential model* proposed in the West system [2] suggests that the user has a part of the knowledge of the system and that the system has only a part of the knowledge of the domain.

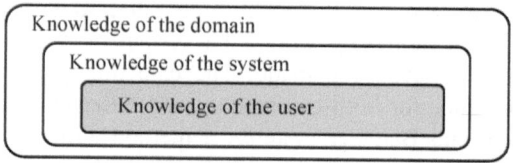

Fig. 2. Differential model.

3. The third *model* is called *disrupted*. It is based on the cover model, but "mal-rules" are added to the knowledge of the learner to model the mistakes of the user. This technique is used in systems such as Debuggy [1] and Proust [7].

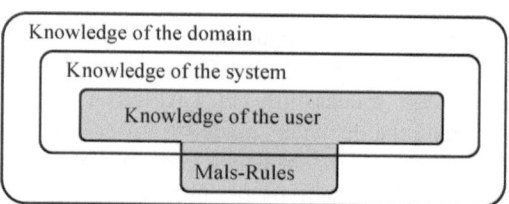

Fig. 3. Disrupted model.

The *complementary model*(see Fig. 4), proposed in our system, is a generalization of the cover model and of the differential system. Unlike previous models, we do not take for granted the superiority of the system on the user. We consider that the system may have to be run by various types of users, beginners as well as experts. The knowledge of the user may be more or less important than the knowledge of the system. Both the system and the user may also have their specific field of knowledge. In this case, they both have, besides their common knowledge, some part of knowledge that the other one does not have.

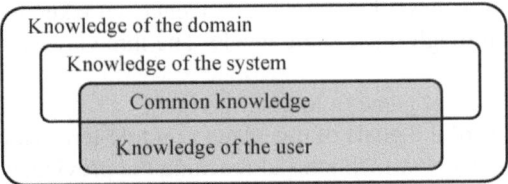

Fig. 4. Complementary model.

This type of modelling is interesting since it makes possible an adaptation of the behaviour of the system according to the level of the user:
- When the system finds out shortcomings in the knowledge of the user (see Fig. 5), it can generate explanations focused on the detected problem, in order to communicate its knowledge to the user.
- When the system realizes that the user has a better knowledge of a particular problem (see Fig. 6), it can start a mechanism of self-tutoring in order to improve its own knowledge.

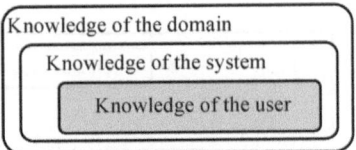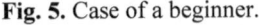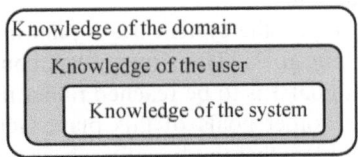

Fig. 5. Case of a beginner.   **Fig. 6.** Case of an expert-user.

The notion of "viewpoint" developed by Etienne Wenger [10] is also included in the functioning of GénéCom. Indeed, the system makes a pattern of the knowledge of the user, taking as a basis its own knowledge of the domain, which is stocked in Bateleur. Consequently, the behaviour of the user is analysed according to the point of view of GénéCom.

First, this article will present (in section 2) the three levels of decision-making used by Bateleur (the system which simulates the decisions of a user in the game of tarot). GénéCom takes for granted that these levels model the process of decision-making of the user. Then, section 3 will present the general functioning of Bateleur. The knowledge of Bateleur is used by GénéCom in order to define the level of the user. Section 4 will explain how GénéCom succeeds in guessing the intentions of the user by exploiting the information about a real game. Then, section 5 will present the mechanism used to evaluate the intentions of the user. Section 6 will propose a method aimed at making a diagnosis of the level of knowledge reached by the user.

2   The Different Levels of Decision-Making

We will limit ourselves to a reasoning process made of three levels of decision-making. Bateleur uses these three levels and GénéCom takes for granted that the user makes his choices through those same levels. The three levels of decision-making are the following ones:

1. The choice of a plan of game (a long-term view).
2. The choice of one of the goals of this plan (a middle-term view).
3. The choice of an action which aims at reaching the previously chosen goal (a short-term view).

The notion of strategy enables us to pass from the level of the *plan* to that of the *choice of the goal* ; while the notion of tactics expresses the transition from the level of the *choice of the goal* to that of the *choice of the action*.

2.1   Strategy: A Link between Plans and Goals

Strategy enables us to choose the goals to be reached according to the plan that has been set. For instance, each time that Bateleur [NIGRO 93] plays a card, it must choose among the goals of its plan of game the one which is best suited to the situation.

On Fig.7, the system has a plan made up of four goals. The strategy has concluded that goal 3 is to be reached rather than the three other goals of this plan. GénéCom considers that the list of goals are ordered by importance. The choice of the goal consists in deleting goals which can not be reached and to select the goal with the higher level of importance.

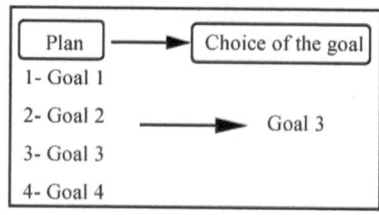

Fig. 7. Transition from the plan to the goal.

2.2   Tactics: A Link between Goals and Actions

Tactics consists in finding one action to be made in order to reach the previously selected goal. If several actions have been found, GénéCom takes one to chance.

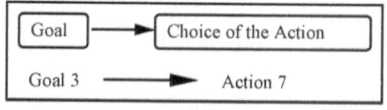

Fig. 8. Transition from the goal to the action.

3   The Functioning of Bateleur

With more than 400 rules in the game of tarot, Bateleur can be considered as a tarot-player of an average level. This system is based on rules of the first order, able to simulate the behaviour of one or several tarot-players. The simulation of a player's reasoning goes through the three levels of decision-making described in illustration 9.

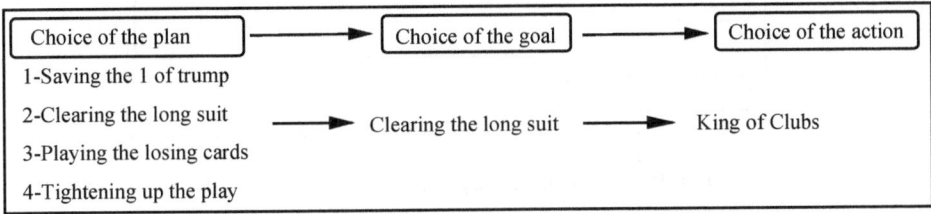

Fig. 9. Bateleur's different levels of decision-making.

In the example given in Fig.9, the plan selected by Bateleur is made up of four goals. For each trick, Bateleur chooses the goal which is the best suited to the situation (for instance "clearing the long suit"). Then the system selects the action which is the best suited to the chosen goal (for instance the "King of Clubs"). This structure presents a progressive refining in the decision of the choice of the action. Its advantage is that it gives us a sign of execution at various levels of abstraction ; thus making it easier to generate explanations and to adapt the tutoring process (see section 6).
We will note that Bateleur can change his plan during the session, but we will suppose in the article that only one plan can be considered for a better understanding.

4   The GénéCom System Guesses the User's Intentions

4.1   Search of the Possible Goals

This section will present the first stage reached by GénéCom. Considering the actions chosen by the user, GénéCom tries to guess the goals that the user wanted to reach. The system uses his meta-knowledge [9] to search in Bateleur's rule-database the different goals which may have triggered the rules that have activated the choice of the actions laid by the user.

For instance, in Fig.10, starting from the "Four of Spades" (fourth trick of the player), GénéCom searches in the goals used by Bateleur the goals triggering the rules concluding on the choice of this "Four of Spades": the player may have wanted to play his losing cards ; he may have wanted to bluff a long suit or he may have wanted to play his singletons.

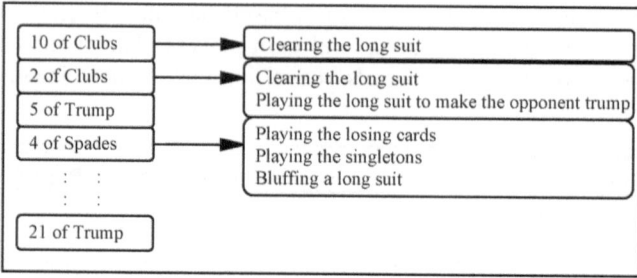

Fig. 10. Establishing the goals according to the cards.

4.2   Search of the User's Plan of Game

This section shows how GénéCom searches for the user's plan by taking as a basis the selected goals. This stage consists in finding one of the Bateleur plans which would explain the user's line of action. The system manages to do that by eliminating all the plans which do not contain at least one logical goal in each action.

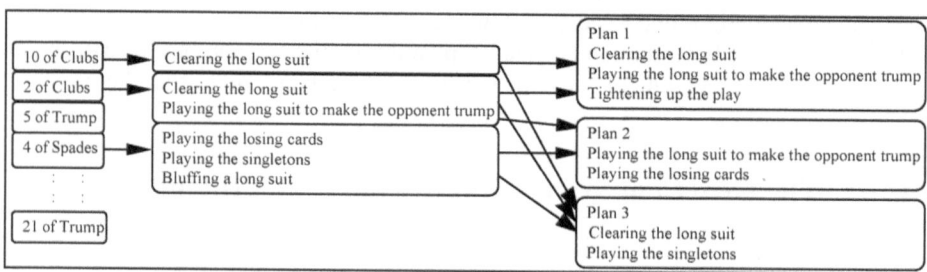

Fig. 11. Transition from the goals to the plans of the user.

In Fig.11, plans 1 and 2 have to be cancelled since they do not explain trick 4 (4 of Spades) and trick 1 (10 of Clubs). GénéCom assesses that plan 3 of Bateleur is the one corresponding to the user's strategy.

5   Evaluate the User's Intentions

This section will describe how GénéCom decides who - between the player and the Bateleur system - has made the best choice, whether at the level of the plan, of the choice of the goal or the level of the choice of an action. In order to separate the two possibilities, GénéCom uses Bateleur's database to simulate the consequences of both choices. In the case of tarot, it will simulate the actions of the four players until the end of the game.

Then GénéCom compares the assessments of both variants, which corresponds, in the case of tarot, to the difference in the number of points won by the two variants.

In the example given in Fig.12, the system is interested in the thirteenth trick of a game. Bateleur would have played the card **Cb** whereas the player put the card **Cj**. By simulating both possible ends of game, GénéCom finds out that the assessment made from the card chosen by Bateleur is better than the assessment made from the player's choice.

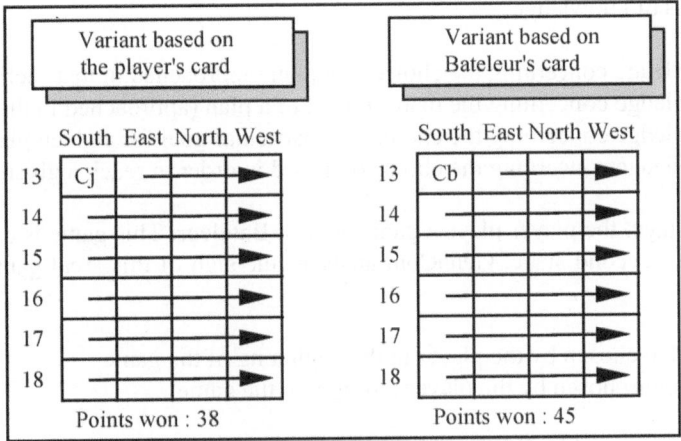

Fig. 12. The two variants based on two cards.

Actually, three cases can be observed:

1. Bateleur's proposal is the best one: the comment states that the user's choice is not interesting and that it would have been better to do as Bateleur did.

2. The user's proposal is the best one: the comment states that the user's choice is good and that it would have been wrong to think of doing like Bateleur. In that case, the self-tutoring programme enables GénéCom to learn the user's knowledge.

3. Both proposals are equal: the comment states that the user's choice is good but that it would have been possible to do like Bateleur. The self-tutoring programme can also be started.

6   A Method of Diagnosis Applied to the Game of Tarot

This section will present a method (applied to the game of Tarot) enabling us to set the level of knowledge of a user against the level of Bateleur for the choice of a plan and the management of this plan. The diagnosis at the level of the choice of a goal or an action follows the same principle.

In order to do that, it would be interesting to include the assessment of the real game in the analysis, instead of comparing the assessments of the two simulated variants (games played with the plan chosen by the player and with the plan chosen by Bateleur).

Thus, by comparing the assessments of the two variants and of the real game, the system can estimate the level of the player set against the level of Bateleur on four main fields of knowledge:

- Knowledge concerning the choice of a plan (approached in that section)
- Knowledge concerning the management of a plan (approached in that section)
- Knowledge concerning the choice of a particular goal for a given plan
- Knowledge concerning the choice of a card in order to reach a given goal.

In a first stage, the player plays a game against Bateleur. This game is called the "real game". In a second stage, GénéCom analyses the sign of this "real game" and establishes:

- The plan chosen by the player at the beginning of the game
- The goals chosen by the player throughout the game.

Taking as a basis the plan chosen by the player, GénéCom asks Bateleur to simulate the game without the player. The differences in results will be used to establish who - between the player and Bateleur - has managed this plan better. Then GénéCom asks Bateleur which plan it would have chosen with the same dealing of cards. If the plans are different, GénéCom gives a simulation with the plan chosen by Bateleur (Bateleur plays against itself).

The three games thus obtained lead to three assessments, which can be different in terms of points. These assessments are called:

- Real-Assessment for the "real game".
- Player-Assessment for the game simulated and based on the player's plan.
- Bateleur-Assessment for the game simulated and based on Bateleur's plan.

By comparing the assessments of the two simulated variants and of the real game, the system can diagnose the gaps in the levels reached by the player and Bateleur on the various fields of knowledge used in decision-making during the game (in our case, the choice and the management of the plan). The following diagram shows the three possible developments of the game.

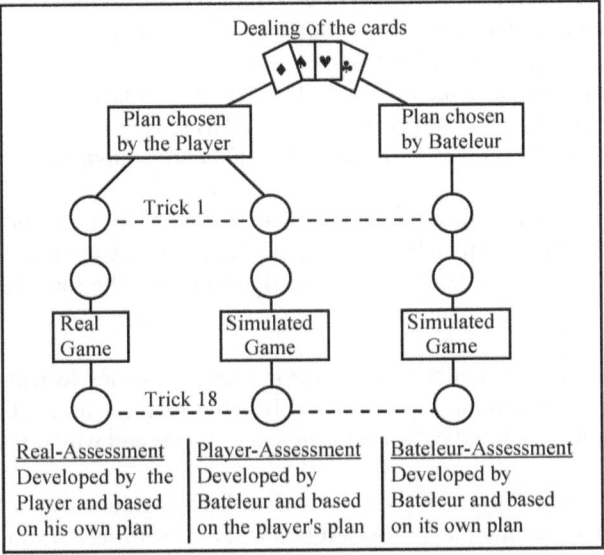

Fig. 13. Three possible developments of the game.

When the player's plan is different from the plan advised by Bateleur , GénéCom calculates the two variants. The first one is based on the player's plan. The second one on Bateleur's plan. The assessments of these three ends of game will enable us to diagnose the level of the player.

If we take the right to use comparisons of superiority and equality between the assessments, thirteen cases are possible which can be gathered in three categories:
- The three assessments are different.
- Two out of three assessments are equivalent.
- The three assessments are equivalent.

The analyse of these thirteen cases using the following notations:
- The sign ">" is used for " is better than".
- The sign "<" is used for " is worse than".
- The sign "=" is used for " is equivalent to".
- *Real-A* is used for "the assessment of the real game".
- *Player-A* is used for "the assessment of the variant calculated by Bateleur and based on the plan chosen by the player".
- *Bateleur-A* is used for "the assessment of the variant calculated by Bateleur and based on the plan chosen by Bateleur".

The comparison of these three assessments allows to extract many important information about choices and levels of the user in comparison with Bateleur:

- If (*Bateleur-A* > *Real-A*) or (*Bateleur-A* > *Player-A*)
  then the choice of Bateleur's plan is better than user's plan.
- If (*Bateleur-A* < *Real-A*) or (*Bateleur-A* < *Player-A*)
  then the choice of user's plan is better than Bateleur's plan.
- If (*Bateleur-A* = *Real-A*) and (*Bateleur-A* = *Player-A*)
  then the choice of Bateleur's plan and user's plan are equivalent.

- If (*Player-A* > *Real-A*) then the plan is better managed by Bateleur than the user.
- If (*Player-A* < *Real-A*) then the plan is better managed by the user than Bateleur.
- If (*Player-A* = *Real-A*) then the user and Bateleur have the same level to manage the plan.

When the user level is better than Bateleur, GénéCom tries to learn the user plan or the management. When the Bateleur level is better than the user's, GénéCom can generate a comment which indicates that Bateleur is better and why it is better.

For example, when *Player-A* > *Real-A* = *Bateleur-A*, Bateleur is a better manager of the player's plan that the player himself (*Bateleur-A* < *Player-A*) and the player's plan is better than Bateleur's plan (*Player-A* > *Bateleur-A*). GénéCom can learn that the player's plan is better than Bateleur's plan and it can explain that the player has chosen an excellent plan but has not been able to manage it. GénéCom presents Bateleur's management of this plan.

An other example: when *Player-A* < *Real-A* < *Bateleur-A*, the player manages his plan better than Bateleur (*Player-A* < *Real-A*) and Bateleur's plan is better than the player's plan (*Real-A* < *Bateleur-A*). GénéCom can learn to manage the player's plan and it can explain the reasons of the necessity to choose Bateleur's plan.

7   Limits

7.1   Taking Other Sessions Into Account

This method is based on the analysis of the consequences of a single session. The diagnosis established on the analysis of one session must be balanced by the diagnoses of many sessions by the same user.
Example: The choice of an excellent plan cannot by itself prefigure the good level of the user. It must be confirmed by a regularity in the choice of good plans and in the good management of these plans. Similarly, the excellent assessment of a session

based on an unexpected plan must not hide the bad management of a session on a particularly favourable conditions.

7.2   Pertinence of Solutions

The user's choices are judged and analysed in comparison with Bateleur knowledge (it is a relative reference). But, perhaps theses judgements and analyses are bad in the reality (with an absolute reference). The function of GénéCom is "like" an human: it judges, analyses, explains and learns in comparison with its own domain of knowledge (here Bateleur's knowledge).

7.3   Generalisation / Re-using

This method can be generalised to other domains under certain conditions:
• The domain of application must include a choice made by the user, liable to be criticised by the system.
• Then the user must manage this choice in order to reach a final state which can be evaluated.
• The domain must enable the system to develop a variant up to a terminal position, or at least up to a meaningful intermediary position liable to be compared to a position of the same order reached by the user.
• The domain must acknowledge that two "terminal" or "intermediary" positions can be unambiguously evaluated or compared.

Many domains can be quoted: strategic games, management actions portfolios, diagnostic of breakdown or dysfunction (when the user must test many parameters to locate the problem).

8   Conclusion

The method which is developed in this article can be applied to different levels of decision. The system will be able, for example, to consider that the user is very competent in a long-term planning but that he can not manage a short-term planning. The sixth section gives details on this method that enables us to make an automatic diagnosis of the level of knowledge of a human player as it is compared to that of Bateleur, which is taken as a reference. When the system considers itself better than the player on a particular field of knowledge, it will focus the comments it generates on this field of knowledge, in order to give the player, explanations targeted on his weaknesses. Taking the opposite method, when the system considers that the player is better than itself, this evaluation of self-diagnosis will give it the precise field of knowledge which must be improved. This diagnosis may possibly be used as a trigger to a tutoring mechanism aimed at modifying the evaluation which has proved to be in the wrong.

References

1.   Brown J. S. and Burton R. R., A paradigmatic example of an artificially intelligent instructional system. Int Jrnl of Man-Machine Studies, Vol 10, 1978.
2.   Burton and Brown, A tutoring and student modeling paradigm for gaming environments. Colman R. and Lorton P. (eds.), Computer Sciences and Education, ACM SIGCSE Bulletin (8), 1976.
3.   Carr and Goldstein, Wusor-II: a computer-aided instruction Program with student modeling capabilities, AI Lab Memo 417, MIT, Cambridge, 1977.
4.   Cawsey A., User modelling in interactive explanations. User Modelling and User Adapted interaction (3), 1993.
5.   Chin D. N., User modelling in UC, the UNIX consultant, In M. Mantei and P. Oberton (Eds.), Human Factors in Computing Systems - III, Amsterdam, 1993.
6.   Clancey W., From GUIDON to NEOMYCIN and HERCLES in twenty short lessons, AI Magazine, 7(3), 1986.
7.   Johnson W. L. and Soloway E. M., PROUST: knowledge-based program debugging. Proceeding of the seventh International Software Engeneering Conference, Orlando (Florida), 1984.
8.   Kass R., Student Modeling in Intelligent Tutoring Systems: Implications for User Modelling in Generation Mean, A. Kobsa and W. Wahlster (eds.), User Modelling in Dialog Systems, Berlin, 1989.
9.   Nigro J. M., GénéCom: a program which uses meta-concepts, IJCAI'95 Workshop - On Réflexion and Meta-Level Architecture and their Applications in AI, Montreal, 1995.
10.Wenger E., ARTIFICIAL INTELLIGENCE and TUTORING SYSTEMS Computational and Cognitive Approaches to the Communication of Knowledge, Morgan Kaufmann Publishers, inc, 1987.

Phonetic Classification in Spanish Using a Hierarchy of Specialized ANNs

Hernando Silva-Varela and Valentín Cardeñoso-Payo*

Departamento de informática (ETIT)
Universidad de Valladolid
47011 Valladolid, Spain
{hernando,valen}@infor.uva.es

Abstract. A neural net based methodology for phonetic classification with telephone speech in spanish is described. Because of the high computational requirements and error rates obtained by using a unique Multilayer Perceptron (MLP), a different approach is needed in order to improve the performance of the task.

In the proposed approach, the basic set of spanish phonemes is separated in groups according to articulation mode criteria and a Multilayer Perceptron (MLP) is trained for every phonetic group, along with a front-end MLP whose function is to distinguish between phonetic groups.

Experiments were made with speakers from the telephone speech OGI corpus in order to tune the parameters of the MLPs, as well as to evaluate the performance of the proposed methodology under different representations of the speech signal and modifying some parameters of the ANNs such as learning rate, topology and transfer functions.

Results of the experiments are summarized and some remarks are passed. Both, results and remarks, are based on the analysis of the confusion matrixes obtained when the trained MLPs are used to classify speech used for training as well as speech data that the MLPs haven't "seen".

1 Introduction

The computational science department of the University of Valladolid is engaged in the development of an Automatic Recognizer of Continuous and Spontaneous Speech (ARCSS) based in the connectionist approach Artificial Neural Networks - Hidden MArkov Models (ANNs-HMMs), whose theoretical foundations have been formally settled in [1]. The whole ARCSS system is outlined in figure 1, where the frame in dotted lines shows the work reported in this paper.

According to figure 1, the speech signal is transformed into a sequence of vectors of parameters in such a way that their representation is suitable for the whole task. These parameters are generally meaningful in the context of speech processing, as well as useful in reducing the amount of data.

---

* The authors wish to thank the Center for Spoken Language Understanding (CSLU) at the OGI for their kindness in providing the corpus for this worh.

Helder Coelho (Ed.): IBERAMIA'98, LNAI 1484, pp. 373–385, 1998.

The use of a MLP as a statistical estimator, instead of the conventional methods used in HMMs, has at least two advantages [2].

1 The conventional HMM method makes strong assumptions about the statistical features of the input such as parameterizing the input densities as mixtures of gaussian densities with no correlation between features, or as the product of discrete densities for different features considered statistically independent. These type of assumptions are not needed for a MLP estimator.
2 ANNs are a good match to discriminative objetive functions so that the probabilities are optimized to maximize discrimination between sound classes, rather than to closely match the distributions within each class.

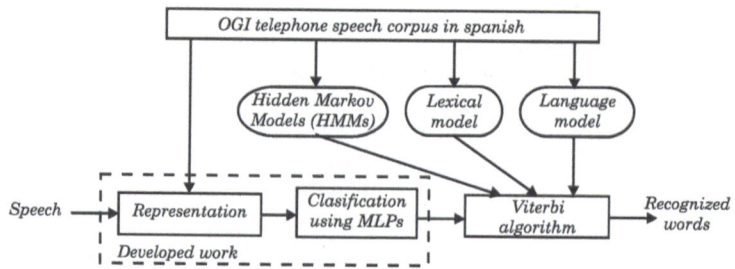

Fig. 1. Scheme of the whole ARCSS system in development

The hybrid HMM/MLP statistical estimator is represented in figure 2, where at every step n the acoustic vector x_n, as well as its context, are presented as inputs to the MLP. Local probabilities are generated by the ANN, which are used, after division by priors, as local scaled likelihoods in the Viterbi algorithm.

2   Motivation

Since the methodology outlined in section 1 has been used during the last years, we decided to use it as part of the ARCSS system in development. Therefore, an analysis of the spanish part of the telephone speech OGI corpus was made in order to set the feasibility of the above mentioned methodology.

The telephone speech OGI corpus is a multilanguage corpus recorded at the Oregon Graduate Institute of science and technology[3]; it is composed of recordings acquired through the telephone line with people speaking in 22 different languages. The main features of the spanish part of the corpus are:

1 108 hispanic speakers (74 men and 34 women).
2 Telephone speech recorded at 8000 samples per second with speakers from Mexico, Spain, Cuba, etc.; there are also many "chicano" speakers.
3 Contents per speaker:

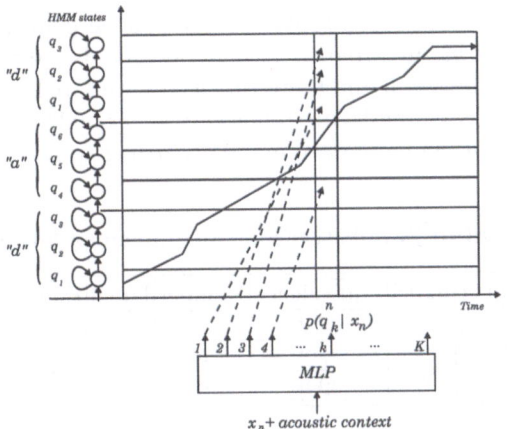

Fig. 2. Hybrid scheme for $p(x_n|q_k)$ estimation

a) Fixed words and phrases: 24 sec (3 sec, 3 sec, 8 sec and 10 sec).
b) Short descriptions: 42 sec (10 sec, 10 sec, 12 sec and 10 sec).
c) Samples of continuous elicited free speech: 50 sec.

Some parts of the spanish OGI corpus are labelled; in particular, the 50 seconds of continuous elicited free speech are labelled with a set of 204 labels taken from the Worldbet label set [3]. However, there are only a few dozens of basic labels in the corpus, which were expanded to 204 in order to account for especific features in some phonetic context of the speech; the expansion was made by adding diacritic information to the basic set of labels shown in table 1.

Table 1. Label set with diminished diacritics

NUMBER	LABEL	NUMBER	LABEL	NUMBER	LABEL	NUMBER	LABEL
1	a	16	E	31	w	46	.unk
2	e	17	.br	32	f	47	.ns
3	o	18	p	33	I	48	?
4	s	19	D	34	bc	49	.ln
5	.pau	20	pc	35	nj	50	aI
6	i	21	V	36	tS	51	.epi
7	n[	22	d[	37	?*	52	.nitl
8	t[	23	3	38	g	53	dZ
9	t[c	24	hs	39	L	54	?c
10	r(	25	d[c	40	tSc	55	U
11	m	26	.ls	41	.bn	56	S
12	l	27	b	42	j	57	T
13	k	28	x	43	&	58	h
14	kc	29	G	44	r	59	@
15	u	30	N	45	gc	60	0

Although table 1 contains 60 labels, they can be converted to 55 by using the equivalences shown in table 2. It can be seen by analyzing the table of substitutions that labels 4, 5 and 6 are replaced with labels already contained in table 1, whereas labels 1, 2 and 3 are replaced with a single new label not included in table 1. These replacements were made according to the documentation [3].

Table 2. Substitutions for undefined labels

Number	Label	Equivalence	Number	Label	Equivalence
1	?*	.glot	4	U	u
2	?	.glot	5	h	x
3	?c	.glot	6	0	o

Therefore, according to section 1, a single MLP was used as a phonetic classifier for the 55 phones listed in tables 1 and 2. Thereby, a speaker that was considered suitable for the experiments was chosen out from the corpus; several characteristics were taken into account during the selection of the speaker:

a) Their speech contains samples of all of the labels shown in tables 1 and 2.
b) Low level of background noise during recording.
c) Intelligibility.

Several experiments were made in order to tune the parameters of the MLP according to similar systems reported in the literature. The particular parameters applied as patterns to "feed" the MLP were the Perceptual Linear Predictive coefficients (PLP) [4], which have been widely used for speech processing.

It must be mentioned that in all of the experiments reported in this paper the speech parameterization was made at a rate of 10 miliseconds with frames spanning 25 miliseconds; namely, patterns for training and testing were fed to the MLP every 10 ms, with patterns representing 25 ms of a particular phone.

According to literature (v.g., [2]), a suitable topology for the MLP as phonetic classifier should contain between 500 and 4000 units in the hidden layer of a three layer system. Thereby, several experiments with MLPs whose hidden layers contained 1024 and 2048 neurons were carried out, as well as some others with smaller systems that did not work out at all.

All of the experiments reported in this article were made by supervised learning, where a desired output pattern was provided for each class so that the corresponding output neuron was settled to 1, and the rest of them to 0. Classification accuracy was measured by picking the MLP output with the highest value and making a comparison between the associated and the actual class.

Figure 3 shows the results obtained by classifying the same corpus used for training. Figure 3(a), in particular, shows the results obtained with a 12x1024x55 MLP, where the weights were updated every 100 iterations; the learning rate was settled to 0.01 and the inertia factor to 0.8. It can be seen that the correct percentage is barely 25 % and the correct curve has an irregular behaviour, since it rises and falls abruptly as training advances.

Figure 3(b) shows the results for an experiment developed under the same conditions above mentioned except for a change in the topology of the MLP to 12x2048x55. The only improvement observed is that the ANN learns faster compared to figure 3(a); however, the peak correct percentage is hardly 25 %.

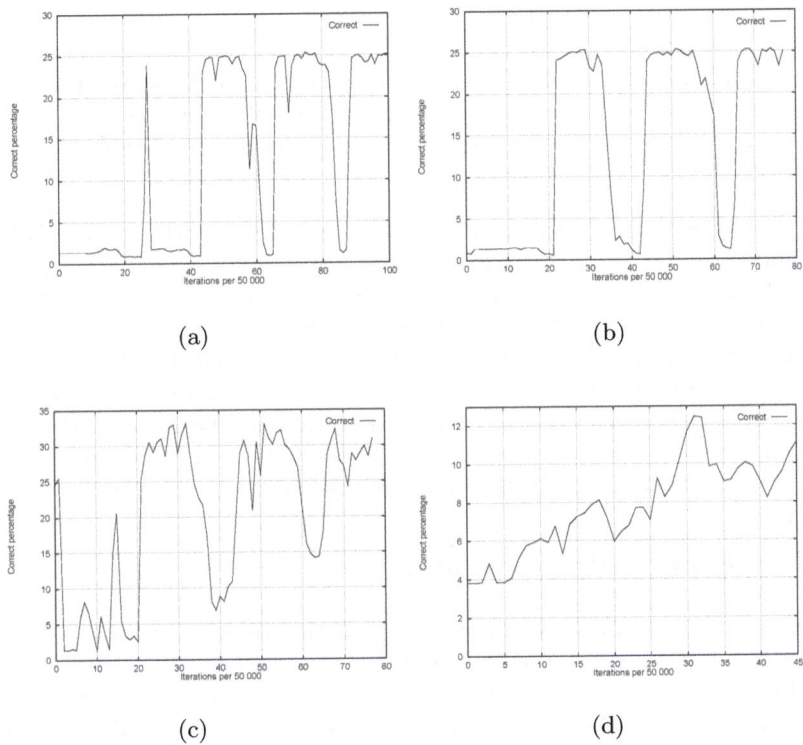

(a)   (b)

(c)   (d)

Fig. 3. Correct percentage in the classification of the corpus used for training

In figure 3(c) the same conditions of the experiment reported in figure 3(b), except for an increase in the learning rate to 0.1, were settled. Two improvements can be observed in this experiment: the MLP has learned slightly faster and the correct percentage increases up to almost 35 %.

Finally, in figure 3(d) the learning rate was settled to 0.01 and the topology was changed to 36x1024x55. At this time, we wanted to analyze the behaviour of the MLP by introducing context in the input patterns. Thereby, the ANN was fed with a contextual pattern spanning three single neighbour patterns.

It can be seen in this last figure that the correct percentage fairly increases as the training goes by. However, although the behaviour seems to be the expected, since the accuracy never falls abruptly, it is worse than in the rest of the experiments shown in figure 3, since the peak accuracy is only about 12 %. This experiment was interrupted due to computational expenses.

Several conclusions can be obtained from these experiments:

a) The correct percentages observed in all of the experiments are fairly low. Thereby, an approach to increase the classification efficiency is needed.
b) It seems necessary to use more than 2048 neurons in the hidden layer of the MLP in order to obtain better results than the ones observed.
c) Since the use of context has been reiteratively mentioned not only in the context of speech processing by ANNs, but also in another methodologies like Hidden Markov Models (HMMs) and Dynamic Time Warping (DTW), it must be considered in the design of the classification system.
d) A learning rate of 0.1 seems to work fine under the conditions of the experiments that we have carried out.

It should be noticed that conclusions b) and c) imply the use of MLPs with thousands of neurons and tens of thousands of weights, which are expensive to train. This fact can be verified in the scientific literature, where a mention is made that training of such ANNs is carried out in powerful parallel supercomputers [5].

On the other hand, we can not interpolate directly the results shown in the literature due to the fact that we are using a very different corpus (since we are interested in the spanish language), whereas the most of the reported experiments using MLPs as phonetic classifiers have been carried out in another languages (v.g., see [1] for german and english).

3   The Proposed Methodology

The main aim of the proposed methodology is that of designing a smaller system whose computational requirements are lower than those of the above mentioned. Therefore, we propose a hierarchically organized scheme for phonetic classification; such a system is shown in figure 4. In the proposed methodology, a front-end MLP classifies input patterns according to their articulation mode. It should be noticed that articulatory features are a very common mean of categorical classification and analysis in linguistics [6] [7].

Once the front-end MLP has been trained to distinguish between articulatory classes, input patterns are introduced for classification. As well as in the previous experiments, the class associated to the output with the highest value is chosen as the category that the input pattern belongs to.

Next, and once we "know" at some extent the category of the input pattern, the especialized MLP associated to the recognized category receives the input in order to accomplish the final classification. These especialized MLPs have been trained previously to discriminate between the phonemes inside each particular class provided by the front-end MLP. This scheme is closely related to Hierarchical Mixture of Experts (HME), a methodology that has been proposed recently as an approach to the principle divide-and-conquer [8].

It should be noticed that the scheme of figure 4 associates the input patterns labelled with one of the 55 non-diacritics labels of tables 1 and 2 to 26 phonetic classes. This reationship is shown in table 3 and is based mainly in the characterization described by Fuentes [7]. The label /ai/ is included as a phoneme for consistency with the documentation provided along with the corpus (v.g., [3]).

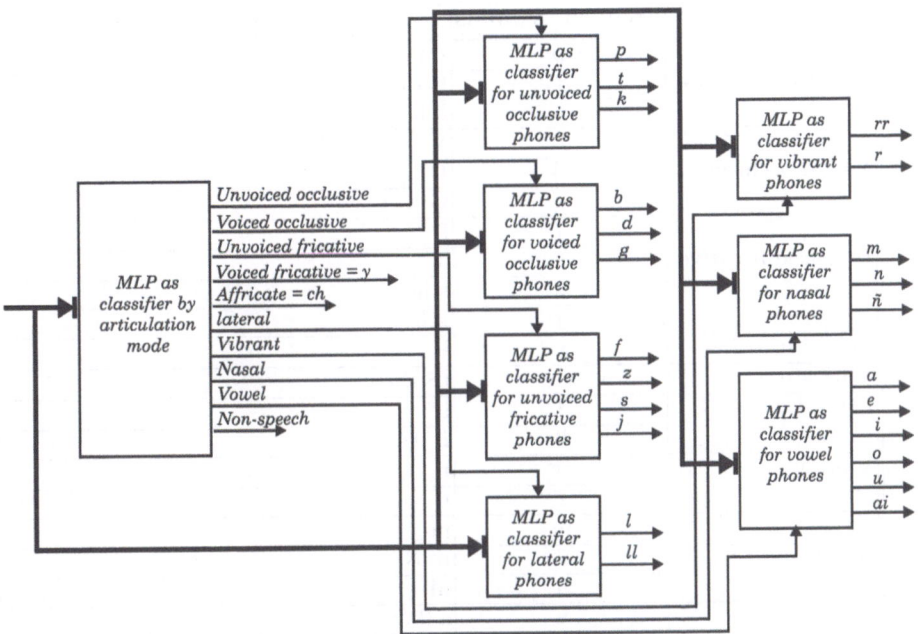

Fig. 4. Hierarchical scheme for phonetic classification

4   Experiments and Results

The experiments were carried out with several speakers of the OGI corpus by using four kinds of parameters as patterns: Linear Prediction Coefficents (LPC), *Cepstrum*, Perceptual Linear Prediction (PLP) coefficients and Mel *cepstrum*.

Furthermore, we experimented with the inclusion of parameters such as energy and Zero Crossing Rate (ZCR) at the frame level; both of them normalized to the range [0,1]. The use of contextual information was also observed during the development of the experiments.

4.1   The Front-End Classifier

The front-end classifier has a topology with 100 hidden units and 10 output classes; this arrangement was chosen after after several setup experiments. Learning rate and inertia were fixed to 0.2 and 0.8 respectively; the weights of the MLP were updated every 100 examples. Although the learning rate could seem high at a first sight, it was good enough to guarantee a fast learning as shown next.

Table 3. Worldbet to spanish symbol association

Category	Spanish symbols	Worldbet symbols
Unvoiced occlusive	p	p pc
	t	t[t[c
	k	k kc
Voiced occlusive	b	V b bc
	d	D d[d[c
	g	G g gc
Unvoiced fricative	f	f
	z	T
	s	s hs S
	j	x h
Voiced fricative	y	j
Affricate	ch	tS tSc
Lateral	l	l
	ll	L dZ
Vibrant	rr	r
	r	r(
Nasal	m	m
	n	n[N
	ñ	nj
Vowel	a	a 3 & @
	e	e E
	i	i I
	o	o 0
	u	u w U
	ai	aI
Non-speech		.pau .br .ls .glot .bn .unk .ns .ln .epi .nitl

Figure 5 shows some typical curves obtained by testing and monitoring the progress of the learning procedure in the front-end MLP. Figure 5(a), in particular, shows the correct percentage obtained when the training corpus is classified as function of the number of examples used for learning, whereas the error rate as function of the same parameter is shown in figure 5(b).

In order to provide a few parameters to evaluate the performance of the trained MLP, two measurements were obtained from the confusion matrixes: the average and the maximum correct percentage across training. These measurements were made with both training and test corpus for a particular speaker.

The results for all of the experiments accomplished during training and test of the front-end MLP for a particular speaker are shown in tables 4 and 5.

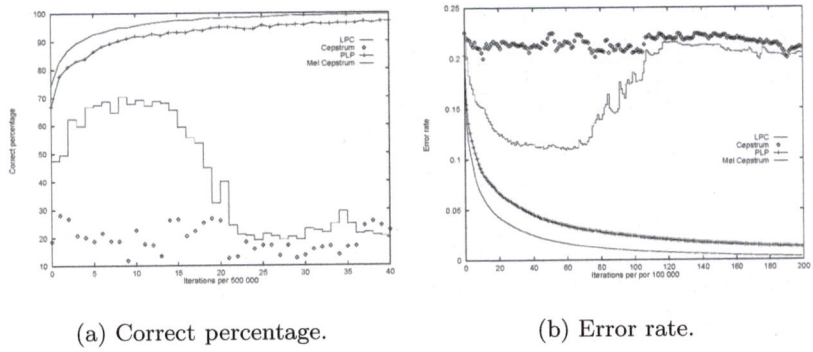

(a) Correct percentage.   (b) Error rate.

Fig. 5. Typical curves for a single MLP experimented

The correct classification percentages of tables 4 and 5 are shown for the four kinds of speech parameters used as input patterns. When size is settled to 14 it is refered as twelve basic parameters plus energy and ZCR; the rest of the rows include the results by using context of one, two and three neighbour frames.

It can be seen from table 4 that the results obtained are very irregular from one kind of speech parameters to another (v.g., from LPC to *cepstrum*). This situation is due to the great differences in dimensionality between one parameter and another, since energy at the frame level is closely related to either the *cepstrum* or the Mel *cepstrum*, whereas for LPC and PLP the parameter related to energy (v.g., the gain G of the predictor) is not included in the input pattern.

The experiments reported in table 5 were made in order to evaluate the performance of the classifier when the differences in the dimension of the input parameters are reduced. Thereby, the inputs to the MLP were normalized to the range [-1,1] prior to its application to the classifier for both training and test.

Furthermore, since it is well known that MLPs composed of traditional sigmoid functions with output range [0,1] in the hidden layer waste most of the early training in biasing its weights to the mean activation value, which is different from zero, we changed the transfer functions of this layer to the symmetric sigmoid with output range [-1,1] and mean value 0 [5].

4.2   The Intra-class Classifiers

A whole set of charts and tables like those shown in section 4.1 has been obtained for all but voiced fricative, affricate and non-speech classes at the output of the front-end MLP by training/testing the class-especific MLP for the final classification. However, on one hand, it is not necessary to use MLP for voiced

Table 4. Correct percentages for the front-end MLP whit no normalization

	TRAINING CORPUS							
SIZE	LPC		Cepstrum		PLP		Mel cepstrum	
	AVG	MAX	AVG	MAX	AVG	MAX	AVG	MAX
14	94.43 %	98.46 %	10.57 %	28.42 %	89.46 %	95.62 %	17.25 %	60.07 %
42	95.46 %	99.59 %	12.40 %	34.41 %	90.14 %	96.55 %	23.95 %	60.48 %
70	97.87 %	99.96 %	14.45 %	36.28 %	94.07 %	98.74 %	17.59 %	49.01 %
98	98.72 %	100.00 %	11.67 %	29.59 %	95.80 %	99.39 %	13.99 %	44.99 %
	TEST CORPUS							
SIZE	LPC		Cepstrum		PLP		Mel cepstrum	
	AVG	MAX	AVG	MAX	AVG	MAX	AVG	MAX
14	57.47 %	64.84 %	10.42 %	25.14 %	66.24 %	69.22 %	16.80 %	52.68 %
42	67.93 %	73.68 %	12.54 %	35.44 %	75.38 %	79.20 %	22.98 %	59.37 %
70	74.05 %	77.66 %	14.69 %	39.50 %	80.33 %	84.06 %	16.90 %	49.35 %
98	77.84 %	80.17 %	11.77 %	32.20 %	85.28 %	87.75 %	13.92 %	49.51 %

Table 5. Correct percentages for the front-end MLP whit normalization

	TRAINING CORPUS							
SIZE	LPC		Cepstrum		PLP		Mel cepstrum	
	AVG	MAX	AVG	MAX	AVG	MAX	AVG	MAX
14	87.10 %	94.33 %	89.18 %	95.50 %	88.91 %	96.03 %	87.95 %	95.78 %
42	97.04 %	99.80 %	97.85 %	99.96 %	97.45 %	99.92 %	97.07 %	99.76 %
70	98.59 %	100.00 %	99.03 %	100.00 %	99.03 %	100.00 %	98.82 %	100.00 %
98	99.17 %	100.00 %	99.48 %	100.00 %	99.45 %	100.00 %	99.30 %	100.00 %
	TEST CORPUS							
SIZE	LPC		Cepstrum		PLP		Mel cepstrum	
	AVG	MAX	AVG	MAX	AVG	MAX	AVG	MAX
14	60.17 %	63.42 %	54.46 %	62.45 %	68.12 %	73.48 %	63.86 %	66.95 %
42	66.95 %	72.51 %	63.64 %	68.09 %	70.19 %	75.34 %	70.86 %	74.41 %
70	71.58 %	76.28 %	71.03 %	75.43 %	76.93 %	81.06 %	76.37 %	78.79 %
98	76.95 %	80.37 %	76.33 %	80.21 %	83.39 %	85.16 %	76.48 %	82.20 %

fricative and affricate phones since there is only one item in each class so that no further classification is needed. On the other hand, we are not interested at this time in recognizing different classes of non-speech patterns.

Therefore, in order to summarize the results of the experiments, a single table containing the final results in phonetic classification for a particular speaker is included instead of a full set of charts and tables for every speaker. Table 6 shows the results for the best case of the PLP with three frames of context and no normalization (v.g., 98 inputs to the MLP).

It was found that in general the PLP parameters provide the best performance accross the whole set of experiments. However, there are especific cases where better results were obtained with another kind of parameters. The analysis and discusion of this cases is out of the scope of this paper.

Table 6. Results of the whole classification task for both the training and test corpus

CATEGORY	CLASS CORRECT		S	PHONEME CORRECT		NEAT ACCURACY	
	TRAIN	TEST		TRAIN	TEST	TRAIN	TEST
U. occlusive	99.18 %	92.51 %	p	100.00 %	71.43 %	99.18 %	66.08 %
			t	96.88 %	89.61 %	96.09 %	82.90 %
			k	95.65 %	84.42 %	94.87 %	78.10 %
V. occlusive	99.13 %	86.10 %	b	97.50 %	100.00 %	96.65 %	86.10 %
			d	100.00 %	97.44 %	99.13 %	83.90 %
			g	100.00 %	100.00 %	99.13 %	86.10 %
U. fricative	98.43 %	89.03 %	f	100.00 %	100.00 %	98.43 %	89.03 %
			z				
			s	100.00 %	98.51 %	98.43 %	87.70 %
			j	100.00 %	100.00 %	98.43 %	89.03 %
V. fricative	100.00 %	100.00 %	y	100.00 %	100.00 %	100.00 %	100.00 %
Affricate	100.00 %	100.00 %	ch	100.00 %	100.00 %	100.00 %	100.00 %
Lateral	98.43 %	90.36 %	l	100.00 %	100.00 %	98.43 %	90.36 %
			ll	100.00 %	100.00 %	98.43 %	90.36 %
Vibrant	100.00 %	70.49 %	rr				
			r			100.00 %	70.49 %
Nasal	98.00 %	89.84 %	m	100.00 %	98.41 %	98.00 %	88.41 %
			n	98.75 %	98.80 %	96.78 %	88.76 %
			ñ	100.00 %	97.62 %	98.00 %	87.70 %
Vowel	85.12 %	82.05 %	a	98.19 %	91.91 %	83.58 %	75.41 %
			e	94.37 %	85.47 %	80.33 %	70.13 %
			i	100.00 %	94.12 %	85.12 %	77.22 %
			o	98.70 %	90.36 %	84.01 %	74.14 %
			u	100.00 %	94.57 %	85.12 %	77.59 %
			ai				

It should be mentioned that a topology IxO^2xO was used for all of the experiments; I and O stand for the number of inputs and output classes respectively. Thereby, the number of hidden units was settled to the square of the output classes. Besides, since there were fewer training examples for the intra-class MLPs compared to the front MLP, the learning rate was changed to 0.1 and the weights were updated every 10 examples instead of 100 as done before.

There are some empty cells in table 6; when this situation occurs it should be understood that there were not examples of the particular phone to be used during the experiments. The last two columns of this table indicate the neat accuracy of the classification task for every particular phoneme; this is obtained by multiplying the percentages of accuracy for the earlier columns of training and test respectively.

5   Conclusions

A comprehensive methodology for the phonetic classification of speech signals in spanish has been described; such a methodology is based in the principle of divide-and-conquer by suggesting the the use of especialized MLPs as class and intra-class classifiers.

Although the use of several classifiers by phonetic categories is fairly more complex than a single phonetic classifier, it should be noticed that by summing up the number of hidden units of the especialized MLPs, and keeping the topology IxO^2xO above mentioned, no more than 200 hidden units are needed for the implementation of a hierarchical classifier for the set of phones of table 3, compared to the number of hidden units suggested for the single MLP [2].

On one hand, the use of the proposed methodology has the advantages of a faster training, due to the small number of neurons of the whole system, and, on the other hand, more control is gained on the experiments, since it is possible to set bounds for local observations in every single classifier.

It can be said, regarding the local observations, that small MLPs (v.g., two or three output classes) need very much less training than the bigger ones, and their performance is higher, as shown in table 6. On the contrary, large MLPs need very much training and their performance is lower than the smaller ones.

In some phonetic categories the PLP is not the best choice for representation, whereas with other ones the performance is insensitive or even slightly degraded by the use of context. These observations, that have not been analyzed here, could be useful in the design of a phonetic classifier with heterogeneous inputs (v.g., different representations of the input patterns at the speech frame level according to the classification made by the front-end MLP).

References

1. Bourlard, H. A. and Morgan N."Connectionist Speech Recognition: A Hybrid approach". Kluwer Academic Publishers, Norwell Massachusetts, USA, 1994, 312 p. 373, 378
2. Morgan, N. y Bourlard, H. (1995). "Continuous speech recognition". IEEE Signal Processing Magazine, May 1995, pp. 25-41. 374, 376, 384
3. Lander, T., (1996). "The CSLU Labeling Guide". Internal Report. Center for Spoken Language Understanding (CSLU) of the Oregon Graduate Institute of Science and Technology, Beaverton, Oregon, USA, 93 p. 374, 375, 376, 379
4. Hermansky, H., (1990). "Perceptual linear predictive (PLP) analysis of speech". Journal of the Acoustical Society of America, Vol. 87, No. 4, pp. 1738-1752. 376
5. Tebelskis, J. (1995). "Speech recognition using neural networks". Ph. D. thesis. School of computer science, Carnegie Mellon University. Pittsburgh, Pennsylvania, U.S.A. 180 p. 378, 381

6. Quilis, A. "Fonética acústica de la lengua española". Serie Biblioteca Románica Hispánica. Editorial Gredos. Madrid, España, 1988, 502 p. 378

7. Fuentes, J. L. "Gramática moderna de la lengua española" Serie biblioteca didáctica. Editorial Universitaria, Santiago de Chile, 1991, 520 p. 378, 379

8. Jordan, M. I. and Jacobs, R. A., (1993). "Hierarchical mixture of experts and the EM algorithm". Technical Report 9301, Department of Brain and Cognitive Sciences, Massachusetts Institute of Technology (MIT), U.S.A., 34 p. 378

A Generalisation Study on Neural Corner Detection

Aurora Pons[1], Reynaldo Gil[1], Roxana Danger[1], José M. Sanchiz[2] and José M. Iñesta[2]

[1]Departamento de Computación. Universidad de Oriente en Santiago de Cuba.
Patricio Lumumba s/n, 90500 Santiago de Cuba, Cuba.
[2]Departamento de Informática. Univ. Jaume I,
Campus Penyeta Roja, E-12071 Castellón, Spain.
e-mail: aurora@app.uo.edu.cu; {inesta,sanchiz}@inf.uji.es

Abstract: Dominant Point Detection (DPD) is one of the tasks in image analysis; it aims making polygonal approximations through the search of a set of points of relevance in a contour, reducing the amount of information. In this work, the ability of neural networks to learn the performance of several DPD algorithms is studied. For it a dynamic neural net that traverses the contour will be used, giving a relevance measurement for each point and detecting them through a simple post-processing phase. Different training sets and net configurations were used. The results of applying the neural algorithm to images of real objects show its validity, and also the ability of neural nets to learn previously unknown DPD algorithms.

1. Introduction

Polygonal approximations are often used as a data reduction procedure in digital curves. One of the main ways to perform this task is through Dominant Point Detection (DPD), that is the search for those points of highest significance in the curve, ideally preserving its morphology and reducing the amount of points in it. In [San96] the ability of artificial neural networks (ANNs) for learning the behaviour of a DPD algorithm [MO93] was proved. In that work was shown that a *Time Delay Neural Network* (TDNN) [Her91] was able to traverse a contour and detect dominant points with an 85% of coincidence with respect to the output of the algorithm, after a training session in which the net was informed about the points detected by the original algorithm.

It would be very interesting to show the ability of the nets to learn these kind of algorithms and to generalise this concept, in order to simulate the behaviour of other unknown algorithms. If this is possible any DPD algorithm that is suitable for a given task could be learnt by the net and executed in time no dependent of the complexity of the designed algorithm. Moreover, if the net is implemented in hardware, the important reduction of time would permit its inclusion in real-time image processing systems.

Helder Coelho (Ed.): IBERAMIA'98, LNAI 1484, pp. 385-396, 1998.
© Springer-Verlag Berlin Heidelberg 1998

This work tries to generalise our former results obtained with a single DPD algorithm and look for a network architecture able to provide the best results regardless of the algorithm considered. For it, we have selected five algorithms: Rosenfeld-Johnston (R-J) [RJ73], Rosenfeld-Weszka (R-W) [RW75], Freeman-Davis (F-D) [FD77], Teh-Chin (T-Ch) [TCh89], and Non-Colinear Dominant Points (NCDP) [Iñe98]. Those algorithms have been also extended to deal with open curves, in order to increase the cardinality of our training set, as explained below.

1.1 Dominant Point Detection in Open Curves

A number of algorithms (e.g. skeletonization) provide open curves from their output, so not only closed curves belonging to object contours are suitable to apply DPD algorithms on them. In order to use both open and closed contours for our training set, we have devised a way to apply the formerly cited algorithms (originally for being applied only in closed ones) to open curves, but keeping the nature of the algorithms invariant.

The algorithms studied need the determination of a support region for each point of the curve, in which the local discrete curvature is assessed. Sometimes a fixed number of points is considered, while for other algorithms it varies depending on the local features of each region. Among the former is the Freeman-Davis algorithm and the Teh-Chin and the NCDP for the latter. Rosenfeld-Johnston and Rosenfeld-Weszka, although also set variable support regions are set, they need a fixed number of points to be analysed before and after the point.

With open contours is impossible to satisfy the existence of the support region for the first and last points, at least. A possible solution for all those points in which the supporting region can not be determined is to artificially expand the curve keeping the smoothness in the first and last points. For this, a reflection of the curve with respect to extreme points is proposed with a number of points as needed by each algorithm. This way, the support region is always computable for all the points in the original contour, and the algorithms will work without any change in their procedure. Obviously, the first and last points are always labelled as dominant.

It is important to know whether both, the algorithms and the nets, are computing good approximations. As a measurement of the quality of the point selection, the Optimisation Error (E_0) [Iñe98] will be used. This number gives an integrated evaluation of the approximation to the quality of the curve and the information reduction rate. It is defined as $E_0 = E_{c_i} n_d / N^2$, where N is the length in points of the curve; n_d is the number of dominant points, and $E_{c_i} = \sum_{i=1}^{N} e_i^2$, is the mean squared error, being e_i the distance from the i-th contour point to the segment of the polygonal approximation that joins the dominant points before and after that point.

2. Neural Detection of Dominant Points

For DPD, an architecture based on dynamic neural nets of the kind TDNN [Her91, Ca96] was chosen. It can be shown that at each time t these nets behave like multilayer perceptrons, and therefore all the learning procedures for perceptrons are applicable for their weight adjustment [Sta92, Thi95, Loo96]. In this case, the dynamic aspect of the net is the traversing of the curve, and the temporal parameter is the position of the net on the curve as it is moving through it.

The support region is the zone of the curve used to calculate a local measurement of the discrete curvature. This measurement will be used to discriminate dominant points. For each contour point, those s-neighbours before and after it define a pattern in the training set. The multilayer net has a first layer of $2s+1$ neurons to input the values of the chain-codes for the support region of the point under study, a hidden layer with a number of neurons to be determined, and a single neuron in the output layer. The signal at the input neurons will be a modified Freeman chain-code representation of the support region, as it will be described in detail below, and the net will be trained to output a measure of the curvature at the central point of that region. A simple procedure will be applied to this value to determine whether the central point of the pattern can be considered as dominant.

Let a_i be the input value to the i-th input unit of the network. Since our curves are represented through 8-neighbour chain-codes (to the i-th point p_i arrives a segment whose direction is coded as f_i 0 $\{0,1, \dots ,7\}$), a change to this codification is needed to keep a_i in the interval $[0,1]$. To achieve a better generalisation of the curvature by the network, a codification independent of the contour orientation is desired. The new codification proposed for a_i, is computed as shown in Table 1.

Table 1. Freeman chain-code transformation.

$$\delta_i = f_{i+1} - f_i$$
$$\text{if } \delta_i > 4 \text{ then } \delta_i = 8 - \delta_i$$
$$\text{if } \delta_i < -4 \text{ then } \delta_i = 8 + \delta_i$$

δ_i	a_i
-4	0
-3	0.125
-2	0.25
-1	0.375
0	0.5
1	0.675
2	0.75
3	0.875
4	1

Target outputs have to be provided for training the network. For this, a PDP algorithm is applied to the curves to obtain the dominant points. Lets consider that we get M dominant points $\{dp_1,...,dp_M\}$, where $dp_j \in \{1,...,N\}$ ($j \in \{1,...,M\}$) indexes the order in the contour of the dominant point j, N being the size of the curve. As shown in [San96], the learning of the net is simplified if each dominant point is considered not just as a single point but as a "cloud" of influence, spreading itself to its vicinity.

For a point i, let $d_{min,i} = \min \{d_{i,dp1},..., d_{i,dpM}\}$ be the distance to the closest dominant point. Each distance $d_{i,dpj}$ can be computed as the norm of the vector that joins the co-ordinates (x,y) of the point i and the dominant dp_j; or to simplifying the calculations, computed as the difference between the positions of i and dp_j.

The spreading of the points can be done using a number of approximations; for example, through a triangular signal with a vertex at the dominant point:

$$t_i = \begin{cases} 1 - \dfrac{d_{min,i}}{v+1} & \textit{if } d_{min,i} \le v+1 \\ 0 & \textit{otherwise} \end{cases}$$; where t_i is the target output presented to the net during

the training process for the i-th point of the curve, and v is the maximum distance allowed in the analysis of the point. Other possibility is the use of a gaussian function centred at the dominant point, $t_i = e^{-\sigma d_{min,i}^2}$, where σ is a parameter whose value depends on the desired level of spreading. In the performed analysis, no significant difference has been noticed, so one can choose one or the other based on efficiency considerations.

Algorithm for preparing the training set:

For each point of the digital curves in the training set:

1. Apply the DPD algorithm to be learnt, finding the set of dominant points detected by it.
2. Compute the target output t_i in each curve point, according to the selected spreading function.
3. Apply the translation to the input code, obtaining signal A = $\{ a_1, ..., a_n \}$.
4. For each value, a_i, make a training pattern taking $\{a_{i\text{-}s},....,a_i, ...,a_{i+s} \}$ as input and t_i as output.

Once the training set is ready, the net is trained by the backpropagation algorithm [Tre95], using the error function $E = \dfrac{1}{2 N_p} \sum_{i=1}^{N_p} (t_i - O_i)^2$; where N_p is the number of patterns in the training set, t_i is the signal of the output neuron at the point p_i, and O_i is the actual signal of the output neuron when the net is centred at the point p_i.

The application of the DPD neural algorithm can be described as follows:

Algorithm of neural DPD:

1. Translate the Freeman chain-code of a curve F = $\{ f_1, f_2,..., f_N \}$ to the net input signal A = $\{ a_1, a_2, ... , a_N \}$ as explained above, being N the number of points in the curve.
2. Activate the net for each code segment of the chain $\{a_{i\text{-}s}, a_{i\text{-}s+1}, ..., a_i, ..., a_{i+s}\}$ getting the output signal B = $\{b_i, ..., b_n\}$ as an estimation of the local curvature at each point provided by the net.
3. Apply a curvature threshold κ_0 to the signal B obtaining a new signal C = $\{c_1, ...,c_n\}$ in the following manner:

IF $b_i < \kappa_0$ THEN $c_i = 0$ ELSE $c_i = b_i$

This signal is considered as formed by segments where $c_i > 0$ being separated by gaps where $c_i = 0$.

4. Calculate the centroid position c_j for each segment of the curve, and mark the closest point in the curve to that position as a dominant point. For segment j, *the centroid* is computed as $c_j = \sum_{i=ini_j}^{fin_j} i\, c_i \Big/ \sum_{i=ini_j}^{fin_j} c_i$;

where ini_j and end_j are the first and last positions of the segment.

The overall system performance is displayed in Fig. 1 in a schematic way. The three main parts: pre-processing, neural analysis, and post-processing can be identified. The items to be set are the net architecture and the threshold value. We aim to find a configuration able to learn any DPD algorithm based on the computation of local significance measures.

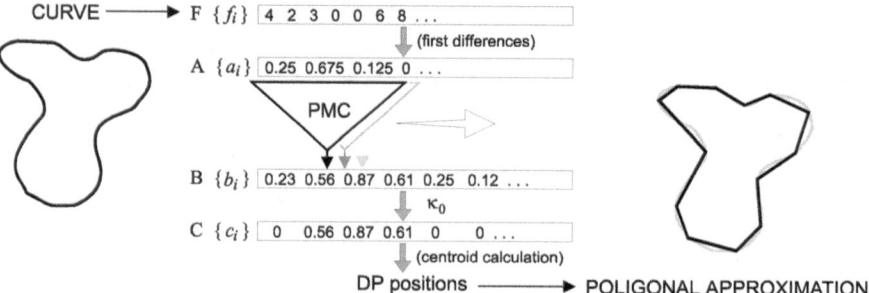

Fig. 1. Steps involved in the neural dominant point detection.

3. Results

3.1 Analysis of Open Curves

To test the efficiency of the proposed solution for detecting dominant points in open curves, closed contours of real objects were taken and 5 contiguous points were deleted, opening the curve. For each one, in closed and open version, every DPD algorithm considered was run. Then, the optimisation error was computed for each case, considering only the same portion in the closed contours that was used in the open ones, and including the extremes as dominant points in the latter. Results are shown in Table 2.

Table 2. Mean optimization errors for the open and closed contours, and the percentage of coincidence.

Algorithm	E_o (open)	E_o (closed)	% coincidence
R-J	0.1167	0.1337	91.5
R-W	0.1133	0.1259	93.5
F-D	0.1032	0.0822	95.5
T-Ch	0.0532	0.0603	97.1
NCDP	0.0532	0.0603	97.2

For all the algorithms tested, more than 90% of the dominant points found in the open curves matched the ones found in the corresponding closed ones, the optimisation error being similar for both cases, showing the validity of the approach solution.

3.2 Neural DPD

A set of 30 real images of natural objects, containing 490 contours and 39354 points was used. The set was divided into two groups: one for training and another for validation; in such a way that the first one contains roughly twice the number of curves than the second one. Finally, the training set had 315 contours and 26435 points, and the validation set had 175 contours and 12919 points.

In Fig. 2 the behavior of the net after learning one of the algorithms is shown. It can be seen how the net produces an output close to that of the algorithm. Different behaviors of other algorithms also cause different behaviors in the net output.

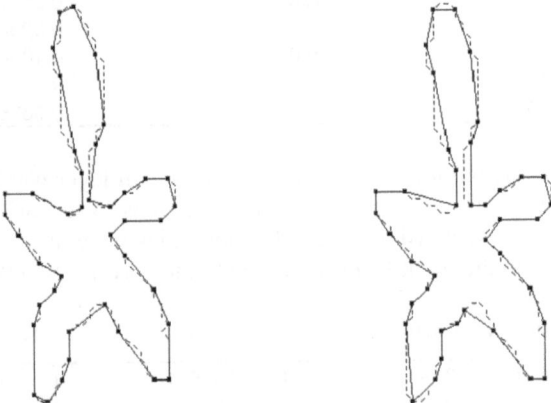

Fig. 2. Left: performance of the Teh-Chin DPD algorithm on a closed contour; Right: outcome of the net on the same contour after learning the behaviour of that algorithm.

The final aim is to study which net architecture behaves the best for the task of learning these algorithms. For each DPD algorithm a fixed network architecture will adopt a different set of weights. The generalisation experiment is not about the behaviour of a particular net, but on the parameters that are heuristically set in its architecture (number of neuron in the hidden layer, etc.).

Most of the DPD algorithms need some parameters to be conveniently adjusted; so, a study to select the best input parameters for each algorithm was made previously to the network training. The criterion to adjust these parameters was to obtain the minimum *mean optimisation error* for the training set. The following set of parameters was selected:

- Rosenfeld-Johnston: $m = n/10$
- Rosenfeld-Weszka: $m = n/10$
- Freeman-Davis: $m = 1$, $s = 5$
- Teh-Chin: using k-curvature (non parametric)
- NCDP: using k-curvature, $\kappa_u = 0.15$

The number of neurons in the input layer is usually set according to the nature of the problem. Here this number matches the size of the support region that depends on each algorithm. Thus, the number of input neurons will be also a parameter to be introduced in the study. To analyse the performance with different sizes of the support region, a study of all of the considered DPD algorithms was done varying their parameters and region sizes, and the suitable values obtained were between 5 and 13 input neurons. These results are shown in table 3.

Table 3. Widths of the support region for each considered algorithm.

Algorithm	Mean support region width	Optimisation error
R-J	10.2	0.2806
R-W	10.2	0.3034
F-D	5.0	0.1008
T-Ch	5.9	0.0611
NCDP	5.9	0.0625

The research on the number of neurons for the hidden layer was based on previous experiences [San96]. The number of hidden neurons was varied from 3 to 11. According to all of these considerations, 15 topologies were used, as shown in Table 4 (I: no. of neurons in the input layer; H: in the hidden layer; O: in the output layer):

Table 4. Configurations considered for the number of neurons for each layer.

I_H_O	13_11_1	13_9_1	13_7_1	13_5_1	13_3_1	11_9_1	11_7_1
11_5_1	11_3_1	9_7_1	9_5_1	9_3_1	7_5_1	7_3_1	5_3_1

With the 5 considered algorithms and the 15 configurations, 75 training sets were set up. Using the classic *Backpropagation* algorithm, with a learning factor of $\eta = 0.35$ and a momentum of $\mu = 0$, the nets converged in 75 epochs in average, with a mean square error between 0.01 and 0.06. To evaluate the generalisation capability of the nets, each one, trained with a different algorithm, was applied to the validation set, and the results were compared to the direct application of the corresponding algorithm on those curves.

3.3 Learning

One parameter that affects the error (E_o) obtained by the net is the curvature threshold, κ_0, chosen in step 3 of the neural DPD algorithm. Nine values of κ_0 were tested, (0.3,0.4,0.45,0.5,0.6,0.65,0.7,0.75,0.8), and different analyses were carried out.

In Fig. 3 the graphs for E_o for the validation set are displayed against κ_0. Each graph corresponds to a different algorithm, and their behaviour for the 5 topologies with minimum E_o is shown. As it can be observed, all the algorithms, but Freeman-Davis, reach the minimum E_o between 0.6 and 0.75. The best topology for each algorithm was different, as shown in Table 5, so a privileged architecture can not be considered a priori to face the second part of the study.

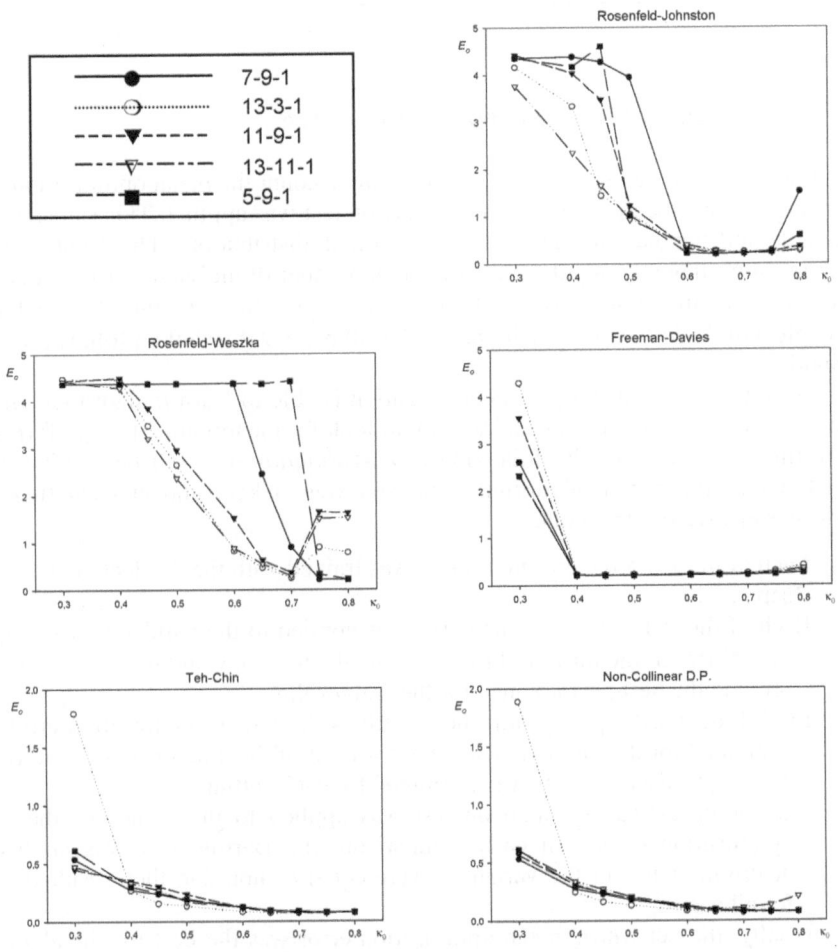

Fig. 3. Behaviour of the 5 studied algorithms for different configurations of the net when the output threshold is varied.

Table 5. Best resulting topologies from the study for each algorithm.

Algorithm	Topology	Threshold κ_0
R-J	5- 3- 1	0.60
R-W	9- 7- 1	0.75
F-D	7- 5- 1	0.45
T-Ch	11-3-1	0.70
NCDP	13-3-1	0.70

3.4 Looking for a Generalised Architecture

In order to select the best topology, taking into account the mean optimisation error for the algorithms, the multiple-mean comparison test was applied. This statistical test is suitable for populations that follow a normal distribution. The Central Limit Theorem shows that any population with a high number of individuals (more than 30) approaches that distribution [Her75], so we may assume that our 15 populations (topologies) of 45 *individuals* each one (5 algorithms × 9 thresholds) follow a normal distribution.

We want to show that if a given configuration is able to learn n algorithms, it will be able to learn one more $(n+1)$, and we aim to look for the topology that performs the best in this task. For this, the following *cross-validation* test will be applied. Each time, 4 out of the 5 five algorithms analysed were taken, and at each time, the following steps were carried out:

1. Each of the 15 topologies in Table 4 was trained with the 4 selected algorithms separately.
2. Each of those 15×4 neural networks was applied to the validation set, varying the values for the threshold to determine the topology and the value of κ_0 that provide the best performance for the 4 algorithms.
3. In each of those topology-threshold settings the global optimisation error was computed for the validation set, and for each of the 4 algorithms. Finally, the mean optimisation error was computed for each setting.
4. The multiple-mean comparison test was applied to the values of the mean optimisation errors. In each comparison, the Barttlet test was applied to determine whether the variances were equal or not, and they resulted equal for all cases.
5. Finally, the net whose mean optimisation error was the best for the algorithm left apart, was applied on the validation set using the best threshold.

The results obtained in the *cross-validation* test are shown in Table 6.

Table 6. Results for *cross-validation*.

Algorithms used for choose the best architecture	Best Topology ; Threshold	Algorithm for validation	E_o obtained using the validation algorithm	E_o for NN after learning the validation algorithm
R-J, R-W, F-D, T-Ch	9-7-1; 0.75	NCDP	0.06	0.07
R-W, F-D, T-Ch, NCDP	9-7-1; 0.75	R-J	0.31	0.27
F-D, T-Ch, NCDP, R-J	11-9-1; 0.70	R-W	0.30	0.36
T-Ch, NCDP, R-J, R-W	13-3-1; 0.75	F-D	0.17	0.25
NCDP, R-J, R-W, F-D	9-7-1; 0.75	T-Ch	0.06	0.08

In Table 6, the first column shows the algorithms that were selected for learning and the second one shows the topology and threshold that gave the best performance after learning those algorithms. Then, the algorithm left apart to test the learning capability of the selected net is indicated. As shown in the two rightmost columns, the values for the optimisation error obtained by the algorithm and by the net on the same set of curves, indicate that in all cases the net was able to learn that new algorithm, because the mean optimisation error obtained was similar by both methods.

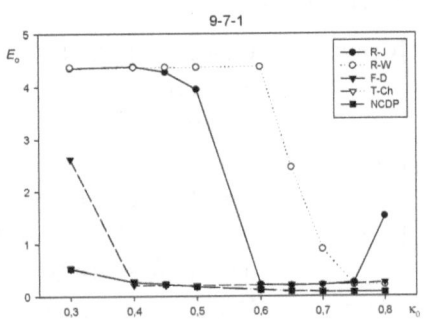

Fig. 4. Error curves for the best net configuration for every studied algorithm.

Finally, the multiple-mean comparison test was applied to find the setting topology - threshold able to learning the best the 5 studied algorithms, resulting topology 9-7-1 and threshold $\kappa_0 = 0.75$. The error curves obtained for algorithms with this net configuration are shown in Fig. 4.

4. Conclusions

In this work, a feasibility and generalisation study on the ability of multilayer artificial neural networks to learn the performance of dominant point algorithms has been presented. These algorithms are usually utilised as a way to build polygonal approximations of digital curves through the selection of local curvature maxima. A way to apply those algorithms to open curves has been also presented.

From the analysis of the results of the *cross-validation* experiment, it can be stated that a multilayer perceptron with the topology 9-7-1, followed by a threshold $\kappa_0 = 0.75$, is able to learn a vast variety of DPD algorithms, at least if they are based on a high curvature points. Thus, it can be concluded that the ANNs are able to perform this task successfully.

In the future other DPD algorithms and ANN paradigms will be incorporated to the study, seeking for more powerful architectures, or faster learning algorithms. The consecution of a reliable architecture to learn different algorithms will allow us to build polygonal approximations of digital curves in a time independent of the complexity of the algorithm simulated by the network. This fact also opens the door to the parallelisation of any DPD algorithm, regardless of its suitability for being parallelised, or to the hardware implementation of any detection procedure for real-time applications.

Acknowledgements

This work has been partially funded by Fundación Bancaja under project P1A96-18 and Generalitat Valenciana under project GV97-TI-05-26.

References

[Can96]   Cancelle, R. & R. Gemello. "Efficient training of Time Delay Neural Networks for sequential patterns". Neurocomputing, vol. **10**(1), pp. 33-42, 1996.

[FD77]   Freeman, H. & L.S. Davis. "A corner-finding algorithm for chain-coded curves". *IEEE Trans. Comput.*, vol. **C-26**, pp. 297-303, 1977.

[Her75]   Hernández, L.H. & A. Del Castillo. "*Probabilidades*", CUJAE, Ciudad de la Habana, 1975.

[Her91]   Hertz, J., A. Krog, & R.G. Palmer. "*Introduction to the Theory of Neural Computation*". Addison-Wesley, 1991.

[Iñe98]   Iñesta, J.M., Buendía, M. & Sart, M.A. "Reliable Polygonal Approximations of Imaged Real Objects Through Dominant Point Detection". *Pattern Recognition*, vol. **31**(6), pp. 685-699, 1998.

[Loo96]   Looney, G. "Stabilization and Speedup of Convergence in Training Feedforward Neural Networks". *Neurocomputing*. vol. **10**(1), pp. 7-31, 1996.

[MO93]   Melen T & T. Ozanian. "A fast algorithm for dominant point detection on chain-coded contours". *In Proc. of the 5th Int. Conf. on the Computer Analysis of Image and Patterns*. Budapest, Sept. 1993. Lecture Notes on Computer Science, Springer-Verlag.

[RJ73]   Rosenfeld A & E. Johnston. "Angle detection on digital curves", *IEEE Trans. Comput.*, vol. **C-22**: 875-878, 1993.

[RW75]   Rosenfeld A & J.S. Wezska. "An improved method of angle detection on digital curves". *IEEE Trans. Comput.*, vol. **C-24**: 940-941, 1975.

[San96]   Sánchiz, J.M.; J.M. Iñesta & F. Pla. "A Neural Network Algorithm to Detect Dominant Points from the Chain-code of a Closed Contour". *In*

| | *Proc. of 13th International Conference on Pattern Recognition; ICPR '96*. Vienna, Austria. IEEE Computer Society Press, vol. IV, pp. 325-329. 1996. |

Proc. of 13th International Conference on Pattern Recognition; ICPR '96. Vienna, Austria. IEEE Computer Society Press, vol. IV, pp. 325-329. 1996.

[Sta92]   Starita, A. & A. Sperduti. "Speedup Learning and Network Optimization with Extended Back Propagation". Technical Report. October 1992. Università Degli Studi Di Pisa. Dipartamento di Informatica.

[TCh89]   Teh, C. & R.T. Chin. "On the Detection of Dominant Points on Digital Curves". *IEEE Transactions on Pattern Analysis and Machine Intelligence*. vol. 2(8), pp. 859-872, 1989.

[Thi95]   Thimm, G. & E. Fiesler. "Neural Network Initialization". Proceedings of International Workshop on Artificial Neural Networks. Málaga-Torremolinos, Spain, June 1995. pp. 535-542.

[Tre95]   Trejo, L.A. & C. Sandoval. "Improving Back-Propagation: Epsilon-Back-Propagation". Proceedings of International Workshop on Artificial Neural Networks. Málaga-Torremolinos, Spain, June 1995. pp. 427-432.

Defeasible Constraint Solving over the Booleans

Pedro Barahona

Departamento de Informática, Universidade Nova de Lisboa
2825 Monte da Caparica, Portugal
email: pb@di.fct.unl.pt

Abstract. This paper extends a constraint solver over the booleans to make it defeasible, and embeddable in a general architecture for defeasible constraint solving. This complements previous work on defeasible solvers over finite domains and rational numbers. Similar to the latter, one approach uses witness variables to detect minimal conflict sets of constraints, but adds important overhead. Other approaches use data dependencies, as in finite domains, to detect conflict sets. Although these are not minimal, such approaches seem more promising due to their less complexity.

1. Introduction

Defeasible constraint solvers are suitable for over-constrained problems [JaFM96], namely model-based diagnostic applications, where defeasible constraints model faulty components, and planning/scheduling applications in which defeasible constraints represent preferences that may be left unsatisfied if necessary.

Defeating constraints is an important addition to a constraint solver in that a) upon being told a constraint which makes the constraint store inconsistent, it returns information on which constraints are effectively responsible for the inconsistency; and b) it enables the incremental defeat of a constraint, removing it from the constraint store and avoiding, as much as possible, to reset other constraints.

A general architecture to implement a Hierarchical Constraint Logic Programming instance ([BMMW89]) was presented in [HoMB96], with two main components, the Defeasible Constraint Solver and a Hierarchy Manager that tells and defeats constraints to the solver. The architecture is exemplified with linear constraints over the rationals, and extends work previously done with defeasible constraints on finite domains [MeBa93, MeBa95, MeBa96]. In this paper we complement such previous work with a study on defeasible boolean constraints.

Although boolean constraints are often more efficiently handled through finite domains techniques [CoDi94] in *one solution* applications, boolean solvers are still important (and offered by some systems, e.g. SICStus [SICS96]), namely when *all* solutions are sought, as in decision support systems, where a user may be interested in comparing the available solutions. By using incomplete reduction techniques, finite domain solvers rely on variable enumeration, and defeating a constraint eventually restart all such enumeration.

This paper studies the extension of a classical boolean solver to a defeasible setting and is organised as follows. In section 2 the original boolean solver is briefly discussed. Section 3 addresses extends the solver by adding witness variables. Section 4 presents an alternative approach, based on data dependencies, which is improved in section 5. Finally section 6 presents the main conclusions.

Helder Coelho (Ed.): IBERAMIA'98, LNAI 1484, pp. 397-408, 1998.
© Springer-Verlag Berlin Heidelberg 1998

2. Boolean Constraint Solving

Among other boolean constraint solvers [Benh93, Rauz93, MSSA93], the boolean unification algorithm developed in [BuSi87] is based on the theory of boolean rings, with operators + (exclusive disjunction) and • (conjunction). Function solve, below, produces, when possible, a most general unifier (m.g.u.) S of expressions B1 and B2, by *solving* B1+B2 (in this paper solving a constraint means unifying it with 0).

```
function solve(in C: constraint; out S: Substitution): boolean;
   case C=1: solve := false
   case C=0: solve := true; S := {}
   case C = A•v+B:                        % v is an arbitrary variable
      if solve ((1+A)•B, Sv) then
         V := apply(Sv,(1+A)•v'+B)       % v' is a fresh variable
         solve := true; S = Sv ∪ {v/V}
      else solve := false
      end if
   end case
end function
```

Solve succeeds if C is solvable, in which case it returns mgu S. The first two cases are obvious. In the third case, C is rewritten as A•v+B (where v is an arbitrary variable, not appearing in neither A nor B) and the rationale of the function is the following: since C cannot be solved iff A=0 and B=1, it must be imposed A=1 or B=0, i.e. (1+A)•B=0. This is done simply by solving an expression with one less variable, which justifies the recursive function call. Substitution v/(1+A)v'+B is the m.g.u. since if A=1 then it guarantees v = B (and A•v+B=0); if A=0 (and B=1), then v takes no role in solving the constraint, and is replaced by a new variable v'.

An m.g.u. is composed with previous substitutions in the usual way, and such composition implements a "constraint store". During program execution, boolean constraints are told to a constraint store (that maintains the composition of all the substitutions) and if the store is incompatible with a new constraint then its telling fails. Telling constraint C to a constraint store CSi can be defined as follows:

```
function tell(in C:constraint; CSi:Subst; out CSo:Subst):boolean;
   C1 := apply(CSi,C), tell:= solve(C1, S), compose(CSi, S,
CSout)
   end function
```

Example 1. Tell constraints {a+b, bcd, de+1} to an empty constraint store.

Telling the first constraint results in constraint store CS1={a/b}. Telling the second constraint to CS1 results in substitution {b/(1+c d)b'} which composed with CS1 becomes CS2={a/(1+c d)b', b/(1+c d)b'}. The third constraint yields {d/1, e/1} which composed with CS2 results in CS3 = {a/(1+c)b', b/(1+c)b', d/1, e/1}

Example 2. The set of constraints{a+b, b c d, d e+1, 1+a c} is unsatisfiable.

Applying the previous constraint store CS3 to constraint 1+ac results in 1+(1+c)b' c, which is simplified to 1, and fails trivially to be solved.

In CLP no effort is made to identify the constraints that caused the failure. Once a failure is detected, the usual backtracking mechanism is triggered to exploit alternatives [DHSA88, SICS96]. A defeasible system though, should identify the responsible constraints, and relax one of them with least computational effort.

Definition 1. A conflict set is a set of constraints that are not satisfiable.

Definition 2. A conflict set is minimal, if all its strict subsets are satisfiable.

In case of a failure, a Defeasible Constraint Solver ideally returns the set of all minimal conflict sets, so has to prevent the Hierarchy Manager from telling sets of constraints that include minimal conflict sets. However, this is not always practical.

For linear constraints over the rationals, the constraint solver keeps a solved form of the constraint store and it is easy to interpret the solved forms to identify minimal conflict sets [HoMB96, KoHo96]. In constraint solvers that use domain reduction techniques (e.g. for finite domains), conflict sets are identified by data dependency techniques [MeBa93, CoDR96], which do not ensure their minimality.

3. DCS through Witness Variables

This section introduces a defeasible constraint solver that relies on witness variables, thus resembling defeasible solvers for linear constraints over the rationals.

Definition 3. For any constraint C_i, there is an extended constraint $E_i=w_i \cdot C_i$, where w_i, the witness variable of the constraint, does not appear in any other constraints.

For example, constraint ab+bc+1 is extended to w_1(ab+bc+1). The purpose of such witness variables is threefold. Firstly, if a set of constraints is satisfiable then the extended constraints is satisfiable and no conditions are imposed on the witness variables. Secondly, when solving the extended set of constraints all minimal conflict sets are identified. Thirdly, a constraint is defeated by simply setting its witness variable to 0. These points are justified by the following theorem.

Theorem 1: A set of constraints $\{C_1, ..., C_n\}$ is satisfiable, iff the corresponding set of extended constraints $\{w_1 \cdot C_1,..., w_n \cdot C_n\}$ is solved by a substitution S that does not impose any constraint on the witness variables w_i.

Proof. => If the set of constraints is satisfiable then there is a substitution S, which does not include any of the witness variables and solves all the constraints C_i (i.e. equates them to 0). Since the extended constraints are the conjunction of a witness variable w_i and a constraint C_i, the same substitution S, with no constraints on the witness variables, also solves the set of extended constraints.

<= If the set of constraints is not satisfiable then the extended constraints may only be satisfied if (at least) one of the witness variables is set to 0. Hence, any substitution that solves the set of extended constraints includes one pair w_i/E_i .

3.1 Checking Consistency

This theorem suggests a change in the boolean unification algorithm that makes it defeasible. Instead of selecting arbitrarily a variable to be solved upon, the selection should only consider variables that are not witnesses. If this is impossible (only witness variables appear in the constraint to solve), then selecting a witness variables would force its substitution, which means, by Theorem 1, that the original set of constraints cannot be solved. This is done by the following adaptation of the previous function solve:

```
function solve_1(in C: const; out S: Subst, D: const): boolean;
    case  C=0: solve_1 := true; S := {}
    case  C = A•v+B:                           % where v ∉ {w1, w2,
..., wn}
          if solve_1 ((1+A)•B, Sv, D) then
              solve_1 := true,
              V := apply(Sv, (1+A)•v'+B),
              S = Sv ∪ {v/V}.
          else solve_1 := false,
          endif
      else                         % C only contains witness variables
          solve_1= false; D := C
    end case
end function
```

Telling an extended constraint is now done with the following function

```
function tell_1(in C:const;CSi:Subst;out CSo:Subst, D:const):
bool;
    C1 := apply(CSi,C),
    if solve_1(C1, S, D) then
        CSout := compose(CSi, S), tell_1 := true
    else  tell_1 := false
    endif
end function
```

Example 3. Tell constraints {ab+bc+1, ab+ac+1, a+b+c+1}to an empty CS.

In a non-defeasible setting, telling the first constraint to an empty substitution returns constraint store CS1 = {a/ c+1, b/1}. Telling the second constraint to CS1 results in constraint store CS2 = {a/1, b/1, c/0}. When telling the third constraint, CS2 is applied to the constraint that becomes 1 and can not be solved. In this defeasible setting, telling the first extended constraint $w_1(ab+bc+1)$ to the empty constraint store returns ECS1 = {a/ $\bar{w}_1a'+w_1e$, b/ $\bar{w}_1b'+w_1$} (for convenience, for any variable v, $\bar{v}$ denotes 1+v, i.e. logical ¬v). Telling the second extended constraint to ECS1 returns ECS2 = {a/$\bar{w}_1\bar{w}_2a'+w_1\bar{w}_2e'+w_2$, b/$\bar{w}_1b'+w_1$, c/$\bar{w}_2e'+w_1w_2\bar{b}'$}. Telling the third constraint fails returning expression D = $w_3(w_1+w_2 + w_1w_2)$.

3.2 Detecting Causes of Failure

This example shows that the expression on witness variables returned by function tell_1 identifies all minimal conflict sets in the original constraints. More formally,

Theorem 2: If a set of constraints C= {C_1, ..., C_{n-1}} is satisfiable but C'=C ∪{C_n} is unsatisfiable, then a) tell_1 succeeds for all the extended constraints $w_i•C_i$ where i<n; and b) tell_1 fails when the extended constraint $w_n•C_n$ is subsequently told, returning an expression D that encodes all the conflict sets in the set C'.

Proof. Since a) is a direct consequence of Theorem 1, only b) needs to be addressed. Theorem 1 guarantees that an expression D on the witness variables alone is obtained by solve_1 when constraint $w_n•C_n$ is told. Hence, satisfying the set of extended constraints requires that D is solved (i.e. equated to 0). Since the original set of constraints is unsatisfiable, satisfying the set of extended constraints requires that at least one of the witnesses is equated to 0. Hence, solving D identifies all the combinations of witnesses variables that must be set to 0, i.e. all the conflict sets.

Example 3b. Expression $D = w_3(w_1+w_2+w_1w_2)$ evaluates to 0 either when w_3 is set to 0 or when w_1 and w_2 are both set to 0. Therefore the minimal conflict sets in this example are $\{w_1,w_3\}$ and $\{w_2,w_3\}$. Since w_3 belongs to all (minimal) conflict sets, setting it to 0 solves all conflicts. Otherwise, both w_1 and w_2 must be set to zero.

For convenience, expression D should be converted in a form that allows easy identification of the minimal conflict sets. This form is identified in the following

Corollary. In the conditions of theorem 2, expression D returned upon telling constraint C_n is equivalent to $w_n(1+(1+w_{a1}...w_{a\alpha})(1+w_{b1}...w_{b\beta})...(1+w_{c1}...w_{c\gamma}))$, where $\{C_{a1}...C_{a\alpha},C_n\}$, $\{C_{b1}...C_{b\beta},C_n\}...\{C_{c1},...C_{c\gamma},C_n\}$ are the minimal conflict sets of C'.

Proof. This follows from the properties of boolean rings. Since C_n is a member of all conflict sets, setting w_n to 0 solves all conflicts. Moreover, no other constraint belongs to all conflict sets, otherwise the set $C = \{C_1 ...C_{n-1}\}$ would not be satisfiable. Thirdly, if w_n is 1, then expression D is evaluated to 0 iff one variable in each of the products $w_{i1}...w_{it}$ is set to 0. Finally, all the conflict sets in the expression are minimal, since for each non minimal conflict set $\{C_{a1}, ...C_{a\alpha},C_n,C_x\}$ represented by expression $(1+w_{a1}w_{a2}...w_{a\alpha}w_x)$ there is a minimal conflict set $\{C_{a1}...C_{a\alpha},C_n\}$ of the form $(1+ w_{a1}w_{a2}...w_{a\alpha})$ and $(1+x\ a)\ (1+a) = (1+a)$.

Example 3c. Expression $D = w_3(w_1+w_2+w_1w_2)$, from Example 3b, is equivalent to $w_3(1+(1+w_1)(1+w_2))$ that identifies all minimal conflict sets $\{w_1,w_3\}$ and $\{w_2,w_3\}$.

3.3 Defeating a Constraint

In this approach, defeating a constraint is trivial. All that is required is to set its witness variable to zero and make the appropriate simplifications.

Example 3d. Defeat constraint $w1(a\ b+bc+1)$ from ECS2 as defined in example 3.

Since $ECS2 = \{a/\overline{w_1}\overline{w_2}a'+w_1\overline{w_2}e'+w_2, b/\overline{w_1}b'+w_1, c/\overline{w_2}e'+w_1w_2b'\}$, composing it with $\{w_1/0\}$ returns the extended substitution $ECSx = \{a/\ \overline{w_2}a'+w_2\ ,\ b/\ b'\ ,\ c/\ \overline{w_2}e'+w_2b'\}$, which, after elimination of the renaming pair $b/\ b'$, is the substitution obtained by telling the second constraint $w_2(ab+ac+1)$ to an empty constraint store.

3.4 Discussion

Although the introduction of witness variables allows the detection of all minimal conflict sets, it does so by increasing the number of variables. This is of course a problem as checking satisfaction of boolean constraints is an NP-complete problem, whose complexity grows exponentially with the number of variables.

Efficient encoding (as those in [Brya86] used to speed up the boolean constraint solver of SICStus system) might improve the efficiency of a Defeasible Constraint Solver, but only a moderate number of witness variables can be used in practice. This limits the type of applications that can be addressed to those that naturally have a small number of defeasible constraints, or those in which the constraints can be organised in a small number of sets where either all or none are considered.

4. DCS through Data Dependencies

An alternative approach to adding witness variables is the use of data dependencies to identify conflict sets. This is the technique adopted in defeasible constraint solvers based on reduction techniques (e.g. finite domains), namely [MeBa93, CoDR96]. This section introduces a technique appropriate to the boolean domain.

4.1 Checking Consistency

Definition 4. For any constraint C, there is a labelled constraint L-C where L, the label of the constraint, is a unique identifier.

For convenience, positive integers are used as labels in this paper. In order to keep track of the data dependencies, labelled pairs are defined as follows:

Definition 5. For every pair v/V in a substitution, there is a labelled pair L-Z-v/V where L is the label of the constraint that originated the pair and Z is the set of labels of all the constraints (excluding L) that were used to obtain V.

Definition 6. A labelled substitution is a set of labelled pairs.

Function tell_2, below, tells a labelled constraint into a labelled substitution

```
function tell_2(in L-C: labelled_const; LCSi: labelled_subst;
              out LCSo: labelled_subst, X: setof labels): boolean;
    L1-Z1-C1 := apply_2(LCSi,L-C),
    if solve_2(C1, LCSi, S) then
        LS := add_label(L1-Z1, S),
        tell_2 := true, LCSo := compose_2(LCSi, LS),
    else    tell_2 := false, X := {L1}∪Z1
    endif
end function
```

Function apply_2 collects the labels of all the pairs used in the transformation of C into C1 (if v occurs in constraint C and LCSi contains the labelled pair Lv-Zv-v/V, then the set {Lv}∪Zv is a subset of {L1}∪Z1). Function solve_2 is similar to function solve of section 2 since the labels are ignored. Function add_label simply adds the label to all the pairs in the returned substitution S. Finally, compose_2 composes the two labelled substitutions avoiding repetitions on the labels. This can be illustrated with the constraints of Example 3.

Example 4. Tell labelled constraints {1 - ab+bc+1, 2 - ab+a c+1, 3 - a+b+c+1} to an empty labelled constraint store.
  Telling the first labelled constraint returns LCS1 = {1-{}-a/c+1, 1-{}- b/1}. Telling constraint 2-ab+ac+1 to LCS1 first applies LCS1 to the constraint, which results in 2-{1}-c, since variables a and b, whose pairs originated in constraint 1, are replaced in this constraint. Then, solving constraint c simply returns substitution c/0, to which the label 2-{1}is added resulting in {2-{1}-c/0}. Composing it with LCS1 results in the new constraint store LCS2 = {1-{2}-a/1, 1-{}- b/1, 2-{1}-c/0}. When constraint 3-a+b+c+1 is told to the constraint store, LCS2 is applied to the constraint, which becomes 3-{1,2}-1. This constraint cannot be solved and the set {1,2,3} = {3}∪{1,2} is returned by function tell_2.

4.2 Detecting Causes of Failure

Example 4 illustrates the role of the set of labels returned by function solve_2. If telling a constraint fails, it identifies the original constraints involved in the failure.

Proposition 1. The set of labels X returned by function solve_2 in case of failure, identifies a conflict set composed of the corresponding constraints.

Data dependencies do not guarantee that the identified conflict sets are minimal. As shown above, the minimal conflict sets for Examples 3 and 4 are {1,3} and {2,3}. In general, minimal conflict sets must be obtained by multiple interactions between the Defeasible Constraint Solver and the Hierarchy Manager. In the example above, if constraint 1 is defeated, the DCS would still return a conflict set {2,3}. Then the HM would still need to ascertain that constraint 3 is satisfiable (by defeating constraint 2) in order to guarantee that the conflict set {2,3} is minimal. A similar interaction would identify the other minimal conflict set {1,3}.

4.3. Defeating a Constraint

In contrast to the approach using witness variables, defeating a constraint L is not trivial. Not only the pairs originated by telling L must be removed from the store but also the consequences of this removal must be propagated to the other pairs as done by function defeat_2 below.

```
function defeat_2(in L: label; LCSi: labelled_): labelled_subst;
    LCS:= remove(LCSi, L),    RS := dependent(LCS, L),
    Reset := RS,
    while RS <> {} do
        RS := RS \ {R},            % R is an arbitrary element of RS
        LCS := remove(LCS, R),     RI := dependent(LCS, R),
        RS := RS \ {R} ∪ RI,       Reset := Reset ∪ RI,
    end while
    for L in Reset do
        C := constraint(L)         % original constraint with label L
        if tell_2(L-C, LCS, LCSx) then  LCS := LCSx
    end for
    LCS := LCSx
end function
```

Function defeat_2 firstly removes from the constraint store all the pairs originated by constraint L (i.e. of the form L-_- v/V). Then it removes from the remaining labelled pairs those depending on L. These pairs are removed recursively (while loop). Eventually a set of labels Reset is obtained representing all the constraints that are subsequently reset (i.e. re-told). As the initial constraint store is consistent, the reset is successful (for loop) and defeat_2 returns the new constraint store.

Example 4b. Defeat constraint 1- ab+bc+1 from LCS2 of Example 4.

Since LCS2 = {1-{2}-a/1, 1-{}-b/1, 2-{1}-c/0}, defeating constraint 1 begins by removing the first two elements of LCS2, resulting in LCS = {2-{1}-c/0}. Its only element, obtained from constraint 2, depends on constraint 1 and thus RS={2}. The first loop removes this element of LCS and makes Reset = {2}. Constraint 2 is then retold (c/0 cannot be obtained from constraint ab+ac+1, alone) and once this is done the labelled substitution { 2-{}-a/1, 2-{}- b/c+1} is returned.

4.4 Discussion

The technique presented keeps constraint stores much smaller than using witness variables, but does not provide minimal conflict sets. Although this is typical when using data dependency techniques, there is room for improvements. In the example above, the constraint store after telling constraint 1 is $\{1\text{-}\{\}\text{-}a/c+1, 1\text{-}\{\}\text{-}b/1\}$.

Applying this substitution to constraint $3\text{-}a+b+c+1$ results in $3\text{-}\{1\}\text{-}(c+1)+1+c+1$ which simplifies to $3\text{-}\{1\}\text{-}1$, unsolvable, yielding the minimal conflict set $\{1,3\}$. Clearly, the value of c is irrelevant to the conflict. But as constraint 2 originated pair $2\text{-}\{1\}\text{-}c/0$, and this is replaced in the unifier of a from constraint 1, LCS2 contains the labelled pair $1\text{-}\{2\}\text{-}a/1$. This introduces a data dependency of a on constraint 2, which is spurious with respect to the conflict set $\{1,3\}$.

Such spurious dependency could be avoided if $c/0$ were not composed with $a/c+1$. Usually this composition is done in non-defeasible settings, as the main goal is to detect failure efficiently. If the composition is not done at once it might have to be done several times as more constraints are told, to check consistency of all the constraints. However, in a defeasible setting, delaying the composition may pay off. On the one hand, the reported conflict sets are smaller. On the other hand, if less (and spurious) data dependencies are considered, the algorithm to defeat a constraint becomes more efficient, since less constraints are reset uselessly.

Another problem in detecting conflict sets is the sequence in which substitutions are applied to the constraint. For example, if constraint $3\text{-}ab+1$ is told to constraint store $\{1\text{-}\{\}\text{-}a/1, 2\text{-}\{\}\text{-}b/0\}$, replacing variable a followed by b results in $3\text{-}\{1,2\}\text{-}1$ that returns conflict set $\{1,2,3\}$. But if variable b is applied first, $3\text{-}\{2\}\text{-}1$ is obtained returning the (minimal) conflict set $\{2,3\}$. It thus pay off to simplify expressions after applying a substitution, and start by those with less dependencies. Such improvements are analysed more thoroughly in next section.

5. DCS through Improved Data Dependencies

5.1 Checking Consistency and Causes for Inconsistency

Spurious data dependencies may be avoided (to some extent) if new constraints are solved on fresh variables, i.e. those having no substitution in the constraint store. If one such variable exists, it should be selected (though carefully avoiding circular dependencies). This is the intended functionality of the pre_solve procedure below.

If it is possible to convert a constraint in a form $A\cdot v+B$ the procedure returns the substitution for v and a new constraint not including this variable, nor any variable previously defined in the constraint store LCS that depends on v. If needed, some pairs in LCS are applied to the constraint to eliminate such variables, in which case the label of the constraints on which these pairs depend are returned as set W.

```
procedure pre_solve(in C: constraint; LCS: labelled_substitution,
      out S0: Substitution, C0: constraint; W:set of Labels);
   if convert(C, LCS, A•v+B, W) then
      C0 := (1+A)B,  S0 := {v/(1+A)v'+B}
   else  C0 := C,    S0 := {}, W  := {}
   end if
end procedure
```

The second change, tell_2i, modifies tell_2 applying the substitutions incrementally, one variable at a time, and simplifying the result before replacing the next variable. The whole algorithm is presented in function tell_3.

```
function tell_3(in L-C: labelled_const; LCSi: labelled_subst;
               out LCSo: labelled_subst, Z: setof labels): boolean;
    pre_solve(C, LCSi, S0, C0, W)
    LS0 := add_label(L-W, S0), tell_3:= tell_2i(L-C0, LCSi, LCSx,
Z)
    LCSo := LCSx ∪ LS0,
    end function
```

Example 5. Tell labelled constraints {1-a+e, 2-ab+c+1, 3-ae, 4-c+bd, 5-a+d, 6-ab+cd+1} to an empty labelled constraint store.

This example of the new approach, is compared with the previous, by means of the evolution of the constraint store when constraints 1 to 4 are told.

		Tell_2			Tell_3		
Tell 1 - a+e		LCS1'	1- {}	-a/e	LCS1	1-{}	-a/e
Tell 2 - ab+c+1		LCS2'	1- {}	-a/e	LCS2	1-{}	-a/e
			2- {1}	-c/eb+1		2-{}	-c/ab+1
Tell 3 - ae		LCS3'	1- {3}	-a/0	LCS3	1-{}	-a/e
			2- {1,3}	-c/1		2-{}	-c/ab+1
			3- {1}	-e/0		3-{1}-e/0	
Tell 4 - c+bd		LCS4'	1- {3}	-a/0	LCS4	1-{}	-a/e
			2- {1,3}	-c/1		2-{}	-c/ab+1
			3- {1}	-e/0		3-{1}-e/0	
			4-{1,2,3}-b/1			4-{}	-d/(1+b)d'+c
			4-{1,2,3}-d/1			4-{2}-b/1	

When the fifth constraint is told no new variable exists, and tell_3 behaves similarly to tell_2. The evolution of the constraint and its dependencies is shown below

5- {} - a+d		
5- {4} - a+(1+b)d'+c	by replacing d	
5-{2,4}- a+c	by replacing b	
5-{2,4}- a+ab+1	by replacing c	
5-{2,4}- a+a+1	by replacing b	
5-{2,4}- 1	by simplification	

Hence tell_3 detects that the set of constraints {1,2,3,4,5} is unsatisfiable and further returns the conflict set {2,4,5}. This conflict set is a minimal conflict set, that could not be detected by tell_2. Even in its incremental version, based on the constraint store presented on the left column, the only conflict set that could be detected was {1,2,3,4,5} regardless of starting applying LCS4' on variables a or d.

5.2 Defeating Constraints

Defeating constraints in the new approach is similar to before, although the reset sets are usually smaller. This is illustrated in the following example.

Example 5b. Defeat labelled constraint 2 from the constraint store LCS4 of example 5, and then tell constraints {5-a+d, 6-ab+cd+1}.

Defeating constraint 2 imposes that constraint 4 is reset, before telling constraint 5 (in the previous approach, given the dependencies stored in LCS4', defeating the second constraint would reset not only constraint 4 but also constraints 1 and 3, i.e. all constraints would be reset!)

Defeat 2		LCS4a	1-{} -a/e
			3-{1}-e/0
Reset 4 -	c+bd	LCS4b	1-{} -a/e
			3-{1}-e/0
			4-{} -c/bd
Tell 5 -	a+d	LCS5	1-{} -a/e
			3-{1}-e/0
			4-{} -c/bd
			5-{} -d/a

Constraint $6-ab+cd+1$, has a single variable, b, not defined in LCS5. As c depends on b, c is first replaced to avoid circular dependencies. Applying tell_2i results in

$6- \{4\} - ab+bd+1$	by replacing c
$6-\{4,5\}- ab+ba+1$	by replacing d
$6-\{4,5\}- 1$	by simplification

which fails and returns the (minimal) conflict set $\{4,5,6\}$.

5.3 Comparing the Data Dependency Approaches

The previous examples informally provided some insight on the main features of the two data dependency approaches, as well as on their differences. This section addresses some formal characteristics of the approaches.

Proposition 2. Procedure tell_3 does not always detect minimal conflict sets (even in the best-case).

This property is inherent to the way in which constraints are maintained in the structure store. Some constraints have no reference to them free from data dependencies, in which case telling the opposite constraint may not return the minimal conflict set. For example if constraint $7-ae+1$ (opposed to constraint 3) is told to constraint set LCS4 of example 5, the minimal conflict set $\{3,7\}$ cannot be reported. Instead, conflict set $\{1,3,7\}$ is reported, since the labelled pair on variable e, originated in constraint 3, carries with it the data dependency on constraint 1.

Proposition 3. The constraint stores produced by tell_3 introduce no more data dependencies than those produced by tell_2.

This is due to the way they have been developed. In fact, as can be checked on example 5, they maintain the same information (given the same set of told and defeated constraints) but stored in different way. One may regard tell_2 as composing *eagerly* all the substitutions obtained in the process, whereas tell_3 composes these substitutions *lazily*. Nevertheless it can be shown that given the same sequence of told and defeated constraints, constraint store LCS_2 produced by tell_2 is the fixpoint of the composition of LCS_3, the constraint store produced by tell_3, with itself. The following proposition thus follows.

Proposition 4. All conflict sets returned by tell_3 are included in those of tell_2.

5.4 Redundant Constraints

In general it is important to detect redundant constraints, i.e. those entailed by others already told, as they increase the size of the constraint store (cf. the solver over linear rational constraints [HoMB96, KoHo96]). Once a constraint is entailed by others it may be ignored, *as long as those entailing it are not defeated*.

Similarly to conflict sets, entailing sets, with respect to a constraint C, could be defined as a set of constraints which entail C. A minimal entailing set w.r.t. constraint C is one whose strict subsets do not entail C.

Detecting redundancy, namely minimal entailing sets, is a difficult issue in systems using reduction techniques, and is based on the fact that telling a redundant constraint does not decrease the domains of its variables [MeBa93, CoDR96] and all the constraints that decreased the domain of these variables are potentially in the entailing set of the redundant constraint. In our boolean setting, that uses a solved form implementation of the constraint store, all that is required is to check whether telling the new constraint changes the constraint store.

Using function tell_2, a constraint L-C is redundant with respect to others if the result of the apply_2 function is L-Z-0, is which case Z is an entailing set of C.

Example 6. Tell constraint 8-ab+bd+1 to constraint stores of example 5.

Applying (apply_2) LCS4' to the constraint returns 8-{1,2,3,4}-0, so the constraint is entailed by the set of constraints {1,2,3,4}. Alternatively, applying (apply_3) LCS44 to the constraint returns 8-{2,4}.

In this case it is easy to see that the minimal entailing set is {2,4}, and that this is indeed the entailing set returned by telling (tell_3), but not by tell_2. The following propositions are justified with similar arguments used in the previous section.

Proposition 5. Procedure tell_3 does not always detect minimal entailing sets.

Proposition 6. All conflict sets returned by tell_3 are included in those of tell_2.

6 Conclusion

This paper discussed three alternative extensions to a classical constraint solver over the booleans in order to make it defeasible, and embeddable in a general architecture for defeasible constraint solving. This complements previous work on defeasible solvers over the finite domains and linear constraints over the rational numbers. The first approach uses witness variables and guarantees the detection of all minimal conflict sets of constraints, but introduces important complexity. The other approaches detect conflict sets by means data dependencies that are incrementally computed (either eagerly or lazily). Although fewer formal characteristics are derived, data dependency techniques seem more promising when dealing with moderate to high number of constraints.

The most promising approach (performing a lazy composition of substitutions) relies on selecting a variable from the constraint that is told, but may still be improved. The choice may prove wrong at the light of new told constraints and, in some cases, they can be changed "on the fly", without backtracking. Not neglecting the study of formal characteristics, we intend to test such improvements in problems with considerable size, to check the practical limitations of the methods.

References

[Benh93]   F. Benhamou, *Boolean Constraints in Prolog III*, in Constraint Logic Programming: Selected Research, F. Benhamou and A. Colmerauer (eds.), The MIT Press, 305-325, 1993.

[BMMW89] A. Borning, M. Maher, A. Martindale and M. Wilson, *Constraints Hierarchies and Logic Programming*, in Proceedings of the Sixth International Conference on Logic Programming, MIT Press, 149-164, 1989.

[Brya86]   R. Bryant, *Graph-Based Logarithms for Boolean Function Manipulation*, IEEE Trans. On Computers, August 1986.

[BuSi87]   W. Büttner and H. Simonis, *Embedding Boolean Expressions into Logic Programming*, Journal of Symbolic Computation, vol. 4, Academic Press, 191-205, 1987.

[CoDi94]   P. Codognet, D. Diaz, CLP(B): *Combining Simplicity and Efficiency in Boolean Constraint Solving*, in Programming Language Implementation and Logic Programming, M. Hermenegildo and J. Penjam (Eds.), Springer-Verlag, LNCS, vol. 844, 244-260, 1994.

[CoDR96]   P. Codognet, D. Diaz and F. Rossi, *Constraint Retraction in FD*, Foundations of Software Technology and Theoretical Computer Scienc, V. Chandru and V. Vinay (eds), Springer-Verlag, LNCS, Vol. 1180 , 168-179, 1996.

[DHSA88]   M. Dincbas, P. Van Hentenryck, H. Simonis, A. Aggoun, T. Graf and F. Berthier, *The Constraint Logic Programming Language CHIP*, in Proceedings of the International Conference on Fifth Generation Computer Systems, FGCS-88, 693-702, Tokio, Japan, December 1988.

[HoMB96]   C. Holzbaur, F. Menezes and P. Barahona, *Defeasibility in CLP(Q) through Generalised Slack Variables*, in Principles Practice of Constraint Programming, E.C. Freuder(Ed.), Springer-Verlag, LNCS vol. 1118, 209-223, 1996.

[JaFM96]   M. Jampel, E. Freuder and M. Maher (Eds.), *Over-Constrained Systems*, Springer-Verlag, LNCS vol. 1106, 1996.

[KoHo96]   A. Kotzamanidis and C. Hogger, *Intelligent Backtracking in a Logic Programming System with Linear Constraints over the Reals*, Proceedings of PACT'96, Practical Applications of Constraint Technology, London, UK, pp 427-444, April 1996.

[MeBa93]   F. Menezes and P. Barahona, *Preliminary Formalization of an Incremental Hierarchical Constraint Solver*, Proceedings of EPIA'93, 6th Portuguese Conference on AI, Springer-Verlag, LNAI Vol. 727, 281-296, 1993.

[MeBa95]   F. Menezes and P. Barahona, *An Incremental Hierarchical Constraint Solver*, in Principles and Practice of Constraint Programming, V. Saraswat and P. Van Hentenryck (Eds.), MIT Press, 291-316, 1994.

[MeBa96]   F. Menezes and P. Barahona, *Defeasible Constraint Solving*, LNCS vol. 1106, Springer-Verlag, 151-170, 1996.

[MSSA93]   S. Menju, K. Sakai, Y. Sato and A. Aiba, *A Study on Boolean Constraint Solvers*, in Constraint Logic Programming: Selected Research, F. Benhamou and A. Colmerauer (eds.), The MIT Press, 252-267, 1993.

[Rauz93]   A. Rauzy, *Using Enumerative methods for Boolean Unification*, in Constraint Logic Programming: Selected Research, F. Benhamou and A. Colmerauer (eds.), The MIT Press, 237-251, 1993.

[SICS96]   *SICStusProlog User's Manual*, Swedish Institute of Computer Science, 1996.

A Nonlinear Planner for Solving Sequential Control Problems in Manufacturing Systems⋆

Luis Castillo and Antonio González

Departamento de Ciencias de la Computación e Inteligencia Artificial
E.T.S. Ingeniería Informática. Universidad de Granada
18071 Granada, Spain
{L.Castillo,A.Gonzalez}@decsai.ugr.es

Abstract. The design of the sequential control program for a manufacturing system is a difficult task which is traditionally carried out by engineers. In this paper we present MACHINE, a nonlinear planner with an automata-based representation of operators, which is able to obtain control sequences for manufacturing systems. These control sequences are an abstract representation of a sequential control program which may be easily translated into real programs expressed as GRACFET charts or Petri nets.

1 Introduction

The design of sequential control programs for manufacturing systems is a difficult task which is traditionally carried out by engineers. Artificial intelligence planning techniques have proved to be very useful in the building process of such programs [5,7,9,10,14] obtaining error-free programs and saving engineering time, which makes it an area of increasing interest in the AI community. However, there are some features of manufacturing systems that are not considered or are not considered in enough detail. This work focuses on these features, perhaps the most important ones from a qualitative viewpoint, and in the building of a planning system able to deal with them. The reason for doing this is to show that the reasoning process about the actions that take place in a manufacturing system is slightly different from the process followed in most known artificial intelligence planners and that the results obtained could be more realistic if these features were considered.

In the next section, these features and their motivation are presented. The next sections are devoted to explaining how these features affect the model of action and how a general nonlinear planning scheme, like the one presented in POP [15], may be adapted to deal with these features configuring a planning scheme called MACHINE. The last section explains how some other interesting features should be included in this planning scheme.

⋆ This work has been supported by the CICYT under project TIC-0453.

Helder Coelho (Ed.): IBERAMIA'98, LNAI 1484, pp. 409–420, 1998.
© Springer-Verlag Berlin Heidelberg 1998

2   Description of the Problem

A manufacturing system is the set of processes, machines and factories where
raw products are transformed into higher value manufactured products. A very
simple manufacturing system, which will be used to introduce the problem is
shown in Figure 1.

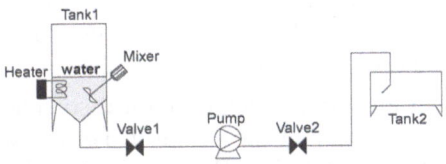

Fig. 1. An introductory manufacturing system

These transformations are made by the machines of the manufacturing system, called actuators. The operation of every actuator is defined by a finite state
automata where the states of the automata represent all the conditions in which
the actuator is intended to be, and every arc from one state to another represents an action of the actuator. For example, the automata which describes the
operation of Valve2 in Figure 1 would be the one shown in Figure 2.

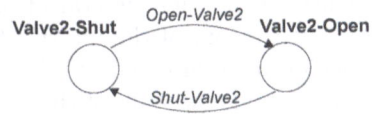

Fig. 2. The automata which describes the operation of Valve2

There are many representations for a control program for a manufacturing
system like, for example, GRAFCET charts, Ladder or Petri nets [6,11], but for
our purposes, the necessary level of detail to describe a control program is a
control sequence. A control sequence is *an ordered sequence of actions with all
of the actions of actuators needed to transform raw products into manufactured
ones.* The knowledge embeded in a control sequence is sufficient to reason about
the behavior of a control program, therefore, aforementioned representations may
be considered as lower level representations or extensions of a control sequence[1].
For example, a possible control sequence to heat and carry the water from *Tank1*
to *Tank2* could be like the one shown in Figure 3.

---

[1] In [2] we describe an methodology to translate these control sequences into
GRAFCET charts and Petri nets.

```
START→TurnOn-Mixer→TurnOn-Heater→TurnOff-Heater→TurnOff-Mixer→Open-Valve1
                                                                    ↓
END ← Shut-Valve1 ← Shut-Valve2 ← TurnOff-Pump ← TurnOn-Pump ←Open-Valve2
```

Fig. 3. A small control sequence

Apparently, a sequence of actions like this could have been generated by any of the state of the art planners, however it has some interesting features that makes it difficult to obtain mainly due to some inherent features of manufacturing domains which must be taken into account. Let us see these features.

The first one is that an action of an actuator is somehow *active* until the next change of state in the automata of the actuator. For example, let us consider the action Open-Valve1. It is executed in the sequence and the valve will be open, but it will be active until the execution of Shut-Valve1. Therefore, it seems reasonable to consider actions as intervals and that these intervals are defined by two points in the plan: the action itself and the next action of the same actuator which produces a change of state on it.

There are many approaches in the literature which consider actions as intervals like for example [1,3,12,13]. In some of them, the end of this interval is defined by the achievement of all of its effects and in the others the end of the interval has an implicit relation with the action itself (like for example a known duration). However, none of these conceptions adequately fit in this problem. Let us consider again the action of opening Valve1. It achieves its effects at some point before the starting of Pump and it continues *active* until the shutting of Valve1, later in the sequence, that is its interval of execution is [Open-Valve1, Shut-Valve1]. This shows that the end of the interval for the opening of Valve1 is neither defined by the achievement of its effects (it is later) nor depends solely on it (it depends on the next change of state of the actuator).

The second one, and very related to the former, is that, if actions are to be considered as intervals instead of as points then, in addition to classical preconditions, as conditions which must hold *before* the action, it is necessary to define of some kind of *simultaneous requirements* as conditions which must hold *during* the interval of the action. These requirements are a form of the *during* relation in [1]. For example, let us consider the action TurnOn-Pump. It requires the valves to be open before the pumping starts, but it also necessary for them to remain open until the end of pumping, that is, during the interval of execution defined as [TurnOn-Pump, TurnOff-Pump]. This kind of requirements is also present in the literature. They also appear in [13] and [7], but the difference here is that the interval which defines the protection for these *simultaneous requirements* doesn't end with the achievement of the effects of the action, but rather with the next action of the actuator that makes it change its state.

If actions are not considered as explained above, it is difficult to guarantee that valves should be open *during* the interval of execution of the pump, that is, in the interval [TurnOn-Pump, TurnOff-Pump], or that the water should be in agitation during the heating of the water or that `Valve1` should be closed during the agitation of the water.

And finally, if one thinks about the example from a causal viewpoint, then a strictly correct sequence would have also been the one shown in Figure 4 because there is nothing that tells the actuators to be off once the water is in *Tank2*.

```
START→TurnOn-Mixer→TurnOn-Heater
                         ↓
                   Open-Valve1
                         ↓
END←TurnOn-Pump ←Open-Valve2
```

Fig. 4. An alternative control sequence.

However, the truth is that there are *safe states* in the automata which describes the operation of actuators and that these states must be reached by every actuator before the end of the sequence, so the correct sequence is actually the one shown in Figure 3. One way to introduce this new feature in the process for the building of sequences could just be by including these safe states in the goal of the problem. Although this achieves a safe state for every actuator it seems too global, that is, it may be difficult to decide the point in the sequence in which the actuator reaches a safe state, or even if it would be necessary to use the same actuator later in the sequence and return it to a safe state. It seems that this decision is specific to each action that doesn't leave it in a safe state. Therefore, the need to leave the actuator in a safe state can be modeled as a later requirement of the actions, that is, as a condition that must hold *after* the action. In the example of the valve, the safe state is the one in which the valve remains shut, so the need to shut it as soon as possible could be modelled like a later requirement of the action which opens the valve.

These are the basic features which must be taken into account in order to enable a planning system to reason about the actions that take place in a manufacturing system. Since they do not fit adequately either into known models of action which consider actions as a point in a sequence, or in others which consider actions as intervals, the following model for actions and plans has been defined.

3   A Model for Actions and Plans

Every actuator in a manufacturing system is represented as an *agent* whose operation is described by a finite state automata. Thus, every agent has *a set of states* $\mathcal{E}$, which describe all the possible conditions in which it is intended to be, and *a set of actions* $\mathcal{A}$, each of whom describe a transformation as well as a change of state in the agent. Additionally, an agent has a *name* $\mathcal{N}$, which must be unique, *a set of variables* $\mathcal{V}$, which are used to represent the objects related to the operation of the agent (like for instance products, chemicals, interconnections points between agents or constants) and *a set of codesignation constraints* $\mathcal{C}$ defined on the set of variables, which define the set of valid values for every variable.

$$Agent = \langle \mathcal{N}, \mathcal{E}, \mathcal{V}, \mathcal{C}, \mathcal{A} \rangle$$

Every *action* of every agent is defined by a unique *name* $\mathcal{N}$, a set of effects, which is represented by means of an *addition list* $\mathcal{ADD}$, and a *deletion list* $\mathcal{DEL}$ of literals that represent the transformation made by the action, and a set of requirements, divided into a list of *previous requirements* $\mathcal{ANT}$, that must hold before the action, a list of *simultaneous requirements* $\mathcal{DUR}$ which must hold during the action and a list of *later requirements* $\mathcal{POST}$, that must hold after the action.

$$Action = \langle \mathcal{N}, \mathcal{ADD}, \mathcal{DEL}, \mathcal{ANT}, \mathcal{DUR}, \mathcal{POST} \rangle$$

Example 1 *This example roughly shows how* `Valve2` *seen previously could be described by this model (using a Lisp-based notation).*

```
(AGENT
   (N      Valve2)
   (E      OPEN SHUT)
   (V      ?SOURCE ?IN ?OUT ?CHEM)
   (C      (?SOURCE NIL)
           (?IN (PUMP))
           (?OUT (TANK2))
           (?CHEM NIL))
   (A
     (ACTION
       (N      Open-Valve1)
       (ADD    (STATE Valve2 OPEN)
               (OPEN-FLOW ?CHEM ?SOURCE ?OUT))
       (DEL    (STATE Valve2 SHUT))
       (ANT    (STATE Valve2 SHUT)
               (OPEN-FLOW ?CHEM ?SOURCE ?IN)
               (CONTAINS ?CHEM ?SOURCE))
       (DUR    (OPEN-FLOW ?CHEM ?SOURCE ?IN))
       (POST   (STATE Valve2 SHUT)))
     (ACTION
       (NAME Shut-Valve2)
       ...))
)
```

The description of the problems that appear in a manufacturing system consists of a set of transformations which must be made on raw products in order to obtain the manufactured ones. Although most of the manufacturing processes are quite complex, in this paper only simple transformations are considered; however, they are expressive enough to show the main difficulties during the building process of a control program. Thus, a problem $\mathcal{P} = \langle \mathcal{D}, \mathcal{I}, \mathcal{G} \rangle$ is defined by the following components.

Domain. A domain $\mathcal{D}$ is a knowledge-based model of the manufacturing system and it is divided into a set of agents, which represents the set of actuators, their operation and their interconnections described by this model of action, and a set of axioms, which describe facts which are always true.

Initial. The initial state $\mathcal{I}$ is a conjunction of literals which describe the initial state of both the manufacturing system, and the raw products.

Goal. A goal $\mathcal{G}$ is a conjunction of literals which describe the transformation needed to obtain manufactured products from raw ones.

The solution to these of problems consists in an ordered sequence of actions of the agents of the domain which achieves the goal starting from the specified initial state. This can be called a control program or an operation procedure [14], but in this paper it will be called a plan. This is only a structural description of what we consider a plan, the following explains in detail the semantics behind this conception of plan.

- The interval of every action is defined by two points. If the action is the last one carried out by an agent, then the interval is defined by itself and the dummy action END, otherwise, the interval is defined by itself and the next action of the same agent.
- Actions whose intervals overlap can be considered in parallel, that is, they are executed simultaneously.
- Although the examples seen so far show a total order of actions, plans can have a partial order structure. A partial order is used not only to represent a class of total order plans, but also to represent possible parallelism. For example let consider the manufacturing system shown in Figure 5.

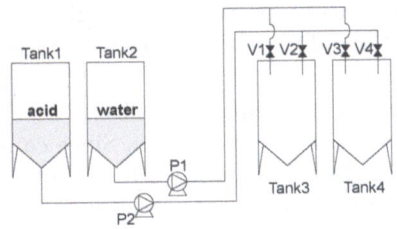

Fig. 5. A second manufacturing system

A plan to carry ACID from TANK1 to TANK3 and WATER from TANK2 to TANK4 could be the one shown in Figure 6. The fact that both branches of the sequence are unordered means that there is no commitment between them; therefore the intervals of actions in both branches could possibly overlap, that is, they could be possibly in parallel.

- An immediate consequence of considering actions in parallel is that if the intervals of two actions can possibly overlap, then both actions should not interfere, that is, they must not have any opposite effect.

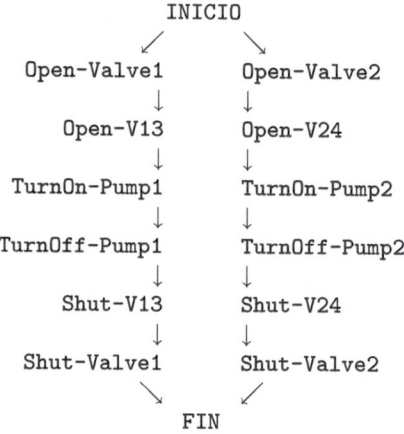

```
                         INICIO
                      ╱          ╲
            Open-Valve1            Open-Valve2
                 ↓                      ↓
              Open-V13              Open-V24
                 ↓                      ↓
            TurnOn-Pump1           TurnOn-Pump2
                 ↓                      ↓
            TurnOff-Pump1          TurnOff-Pump2
                 ↓                      ↓
              Shut-V13              Shut-V24
                 ↓                      ↓
            Shut-Valve1            Shut-Valve2
                      ╲          ╱
                         FIN
```

Fig. 6. A partially ordered plan

- Causal links are defined as intervals of protection for the literals that appear
  in the requirements lists. Since there are three lists of requirements of different nature, the interval which defines a causal link can differ depending on
  the type of requirement. The causal link associated with a previous requirement is defined from the producer of the literal until the consumer (in terms
  of [15]). When the requirement is a simultaneous one, then the causal link
  is defined from the producer until the end of the interval of the consumer.
  Later requirements have a different nature, they only need to be satisfied
  and they do not need to be protected throughout the plan like previous or
  simultaneous ones. Therefore, causal links with respect to later requirements
  are not considered.
- An action threatens a causal link if the literal associated to the causal link
  appears in the deletions list of the action. Since causal links represent intervals of protection for these literals, the interval of an action which threatens
  a causal link and the interval of the causal link must never overlap.
- Neither interferences nor threats are allowed in a valid plan and they must
  be avoided by the usual methods of promotion and demotion.
- The only notion of time in a plan like the ones in Figures 3 and 6 is the
  relative ordering between its actions, and this is only a qualitative notion like
  in [1] and [13]. The inclusion of a metric notion of time would be, of course,
  useful, however the main problem that appears in the building process of
  such a plan is the search for a correct interleaving of the actions and a
  qualitative notion of time is quite enough, although it is more conservative
  than a metric time, which would surely provide a more precise interleaving.

Bearing in mind these conceptions of actions, problems and plans, the following section describes a nonlinear planning scheme, called MACHINE, designed

by adapting the general ideas presented in POP [15], and is able to obtain the plans seen so far.

4   MACHINE: A Nonlinear Planning Scheme

MACHINE is a generative refinement planning scheme [15] whose algorithm is shown in Figure 7. The start point is a null plan with two dummy actions, START and END which encode the planning problem as in SNLP [8] and UCPOP [15]. Over this initial plan, a refinement process is applied which, at every step, solves a pending problem in the plan until there are no more pending problems or the problem cannot be solved. The different pending problems which may be found in a plan are pending subgoals (motivated by unsatisfied requirements) threats, interferences, and order inconsistency (motivated by a loop in the order structure, which must be a strict order). They all are included in an Agenda, which drives the refinement process. The search process to solve the tasks in the Agenda is a basic depth first engine over the set of choices to solve every task.

MACHINE(Domain, Agenda, Plan, Links)

1. When Agenda is EMPTY Return SUCCESS
2. Task ← **SelectTask**(Agenda)
3. Choices ← **HowToDoIt?**(Task, Domain, Plan)
4. Iterate over Choices until it is empty
   (a) How ← ExtractFirst(Choices)
   (b) **DoIt**(How, Domain, Agenda, Plan, Links)
   (c) When **MACHINE** (Domain, Agenda, Plan, Links) Return SUCCESS
5. Return FAIL

Fig. 7. The algorithm of MACHINE

MACHINE uses four data structures to store the information during the planning process: an Agenda, the Plan and its Links, and the Domain in consideration. The Domain is the knowledge-based model of the manufacturing system. The Plan is a partially ordered set of nodes, where every node may be an instantiated action from the Domain or a subgoal, together with its Links, that is, the set of the existing causal links, which describes the causal structure of the plan, the *plan rationale*. And the Agenda which is a set of tasks each of which describes a pending problem in the plan.

The three basic modules of MACHINE (shown in boldface) are described as follows.

SelectTask. This module selects the first task in Agenda in order to solve it. Tasks in Agenda are ordered using the following scheme: first, order inconsistency, then interferences, threats and subgoals. Order inconsistency is the first one because it has no solution and it always leads to backtracking. Subgoals are the last ones because they are delayed until all the interferences and threats are solved. In addition to this, subgoals are also ordered amongst them by their relative ordering in such a way that subgoals closest to START are solved before the furthest ones.

HowToDoIt?. This module builds a list with all the possible choices to solve a selected task from the Agenda. An inconsistent order has no solution, so the list will be empty. The choices to solve interferences and threats are the known methods of promotion or demotion, nondeterministically. Subgoals may be solved by either the axioms, an existing action in the plan or a new action from the domain. Since this process is based on a most general unifying algorithm, the codesignation constraints defined on the variables of the agents will play an important role by rejecting undesirable unifications.

DoIt. This module applies one of the existing choices in the list built by **HowToDoIt?** to solve a problem. Pending subgoals related to simultaneous and previous requirements are solved by producers which must be before the consumer action, and later requirements are solved by actions which must be after the consumer. The inclusion of a new action in Plan to solve a pending subgoal implies the following tasks. First, the inclusion of all of its requirements as pending subgoals in Agenda and the inclusion of the new causal link in Links (if an existing action were reused, the causal link were also included).

Second, when a new action is included in Plan, the end of its interval of execution is unknown, so, by default, it is assumed that its end is the dummy action END. However, the true end of all of the actions in the plan is continuously searched as shown in the previous sections. Since the end of the interval of an action implies a change of state in the agent which carries out the action, every time a requirement of change of state is solved by an action then the end of the interval of this action has been found, and it is updated in Plan and the causal links in Links related to this interval.

And third, if new interferences or threats have appeared, then include it in Agenda also as pending tasks. Interferences and threats are found when there is harmful overlapping between the intervals of execution of actions and the intervals defined by a causal link as explained in the previous section. Promotions and demotions to solve interferences and threats are not applied between actions but between their intervals of execution. When an action is promoted (or demoted) over another action, it is promoted over all its interval of execution, not only the action.

However MACHINE can delay the solution of some threats and interferences for a later moment in the resolution process. The reason is that, as mentioned before, not all of the intervals of the actions in Plan are known, some of them are known and some of them will be known as pending subgoals are solved. Therefore, if a threat or an interference is related to an undefined interval then it should be delayed until the end of the involved intervals are known. In order to do that, these kinds of threats and interferences are ordered in Agenda after pending subgoals giving them less priority. Later, if the solution of some of these subgoals finds the end of some of these problematic intervals, Plan will be updated and the threat of interference will be back at the begining of Agenda

418   Luis Castillo and Antonio González

and, so, solved appropriately. This is also a least commitment heuristic which could more or less say the following: *"I don't try to solve a problem if I don't know it exactly"*.

5   Experimental Results

MACHINE has been implemented in COMMON LISP and has been tested using the problems shown throughout this paper. It found the correct plan, i.e. control sequence, for all of them and its behavior is shown in Table 1. The final result of MACHINE is a control sequence, it is not exactly a control program but it has the necessary level of detail to be considered as such. Furthermore, in [2] we show in detail how these control sequences may be translated into GRAFCET charts [6] and Petri nets [11], as true representations for a control program, and very useful tools in the design and modelling of manufacturing systems.

Table 1. Some experimental results

Plan	Generated Nodes	Explored Nodes	Time
Figure 3	56	39	11 s
Figure 6	69	51	16 s
Figure 8	217	144	374 s

This table also includes the results of the real-size manufacturing problem shown in Figure 8 which gives an idea of the scalability of MACHINE in terms of complexity.

The problem consists in adding an ingredient (which is initially contained in ADDITIVE-1) to the milk initially contained in MILK-TANK and then proceed to bottle the mixture. The domain built for this manufacturing system has 4 axioms, 24 agents (valves, pumps, mixers, heaters, conveyor belts and a bottler) and 48 different actions. The final plan, which is not shown here due to space limitations, involves 40 actions.

6   Conclusions and Extensions

This work has been motivated by the need to apply artificial intelligence planning techniques to the design of control sequences for manufacturing systems. This need has shown that the domain of manufacturing system has some basic properties which must be taken into account in order to ensure a correct reasoning about the actions which take place in such a domain. The planning system presented in this paper, called MACHINE, deals with these features by

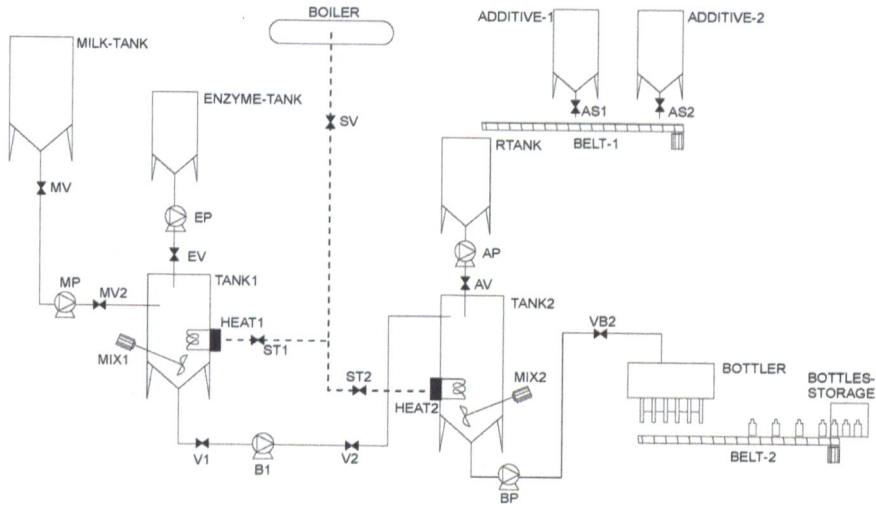

Fig. 8. A real world manufacturing system

using a nonlinear planning scheme based on POP and it is able to obtain control sequences for manufacturing systems.

Although MACHINE has been tested successfully on several problems it can only be considered as a step forward in the resolution of the problems which appear in manufacturing systems. The reason is that this is a very rich domain with many problems of different natures which should be taken into account by an autonomous problem solver, however, the truth is that the core of that problem solver is actually a planning system and that all of these problems may be built like folders or extensions over this planning core, configuring an integrated system. Some of these important problems, which will be dealt with in the near future, are the following:

 - Perhaps the most important problem is the inclusion of a metric time to quantify the intervals of actions, although in a flexible manner because even in real problems these intervals are not perfectly known. Time map managers [3,12] seem to be very promising in this task.
 - Manufactured products are really complex and a classic conjunctive goal is not enough to deal with complex goals. It is necessary to define behavioural goals as an *ordered* set of transformations on raw products, which is known as a *recipe*. At present, MACHINE does work with goals whose literals have a partial order structure, but it will be dealt with in a forthcoming paper.
 - In these domains, there are what could be called procedures: complex problems which can be decomposed into an ordered sequence of smaller subproblems. The planning system must know these procedures and it must also know how to work with them. This problem points directly to HTN techniques [4].

- The control programs seen in this paper are intended to work in an open loop manner, that is, with no feedback from the environment. Real control programs have feedback from sensors in the environment and the planning system must be able to include the information supplied by these sensors in the planning process. This seems the most challenging problem because it implies both:
  a) The ability of the planning system to adapt its behavior to the different ways in which sensors may appear. Case-based and analogical techniques seem very promising in this task because they also seem to be the techniques used by humans in the same role.
  b) And the ability to include some kind of conditional behavior in the plan because the information given by sensors is not always available at planning time.

References

1. J. F. Allen. An interval-based representation of temporal knowledge. In *IJCAI-81*, pages 221–226, 1981. 411, 415
2. L. Castillo, J. Fdez-Olivares, and A. González. An application of artificial intelligence techniques to the implementation and validation of control programs for manufacturing systems. Technical Report DECSAI-980111, University of Granada, 1998. 410, 418
3. T. Dean and D. McDermott. Temporal database management. *Artificial intelligence*, 32:1–55, 1987. 411, 419
4. K. Erol, J. Hendler, and D. S. Nau. HTN planning: complexity and expresivity. In *AAAI-94*, pages 1123–1128, 1994. 419
5. Y. Gil. A specification of manufacturing processes for planning. Technical Report CMU-CS-91-179, Carnegie Mellon University, 1991. 409
6. W. A. Gruver and J. C. Boudreaux. *Intelligent manufacturing: programming environments for CIM*. Springer-Verlag, London, 1993. 410, 418
7. I. Klein, P. Lindskog, and C. Backstrom. Automatic creation of sequential control schemes in polynomial time. Technical Report LiTH-ISY-I-1430, Linkoping University, 1993. 409, 411
8. D. McAllester and D. Rosenblitt. Systematic nonlinear planning. In *AAAI-91*, pages 634–639, 1991. 416
9. D. Nau et al. AI planning versus manufacturing-operation planning: A case study. In *IJCAI-95*, pages 1670–1676, 1995. 409
10. S. C. Park et al. Explanation-based learning for intelligent process planning. *IEEE Transactions on systems, man and cybernetics*, 23(6):1597–1616, 1993. 409
11. J. L. Peterson. *Petri nets theory and the modelling of systems*. Prentice-Hall, 1981. 410, 418
12. E. Rutten and J. Hertzberz. Temporal planner = nonlinear planner + time map manager. *Artificial intelligence communications*, 6:18–26, 1993. 411, 419
13. E. Sandewall and R. Ronnquist. A representation of action structures. In *AAAI-86*, pages 89–97, 1986. 411, 415
14. J. Soutter. *An integrated architecture for operating procedure synthesis*. PhD thesis, Loughborough University, 1996. 409, 414
15. D. Weld. An introduction to least commitment planning. *AI Magazine*, 15(4), 1994. 409, 415, 416

Author Index